FLORIDA STATE
UNIVERSITY LIBRARIES

JUN 1 3 2001

TALLAHASSEE, FLORIDA

National Accounting and Economic Policy

National Accounting and Economic Policy
The United States and UN Systems

Nancy D. Ruggles and Richard Ruggles

Foreword by Peter Hill

Edward Elgar
Cheltenham, UK • Northampton, MA, USA

© Nancy D. Ruggles and Richard Ruggles 1999

All rights reserved. No part of this publication may be reproduced, stored in a retrieval system or transmitted in any form or by any means, electronic, mechanical or photocopying, recording, or otherwise without the prior permission of the publisher.

Published by
Edward Elgar Publishing Limited
Glensanda House
Montpellier Parade
Cheltenham
Glos GL50 1UA
UK

Edward Elgar Publishing, Inc.
136 West Street
Suite 202
Northampton
Massachusetts 01060
USA

A catalogue record for this book
is available from the British Library

Library of Congress Cataloguing in Publication Data

Ruggles, Nancy D., 1922–1987
    National accounting and economic policy: the United States and
UN systems / Nancy D. Ruggles and Richard Ruggles.
    1. National income—United States—Accounting. 2. Finance,
Public—United States—Accounting. 3. United States—Economic
policy. 4. National income—Accounting. 5. Comparative economics.
I. Ruggles, Richard, 1916– . II. United Nations.
HC110.I5R84   1999
339.373—dc21   99–11538
                                                                              CIP

ISBN 1 85898 992 2

Printed and bound in Great Britain by Bookcraft (Bath) Ltd.

Contents

Foreword by Peter Hill   *vii*
Preface   *xiii*
Abstracts   *xix*
List of Tables and Figures   *xxv*

PART ONE   EVOLUTION AND CONCEPTS OF NATIONAL ACCOUNTING

1. National Income Accounting and its Relation to Economic Policy   3
   Richard Ruggles
2. Concepts of Real Capital Stocks and Services   39
   Richard Ruggles and Nancy D. Ruggles
3. The Evolution and Present State of National Economic Accounting   56
   Richard Ruggles and Nancy D. Ruggles
4. The Role of the National Accounts in the Statistical System   70
   Richard Ruggles
5. The Treatment of Pensions and Insurance in the National Accounts   91
   Nancy D. Ruggles and Richard Ruggles
6. National Income Accounting Concepts and Measurement: Economic Theory and Practice   129
   Richard Ruggles
7. The Value Added of National Accounting   162
   Richard Ruggles and Patricia Ruggles

PART TWO   UNITED STATES NATIONAL ACCOUNTS

8. The Evolution of National Accounts and the National Data Base   171
   Richard Ruggles and Nancy D. Ruggles
9. The United States National Income Accounts, 1947–77: Their Conceptual Basis and Evolution   185
   Richard Ruggles

10. Integrated Economic Accounts for the United States, 1947–80   243
Richard Ruggles and Nancy D. Ruggles
11. Integrated Economic Accounts: Reply   305
Richard Ruggles and Nancy D. Ruggles

PART THREE   UNITED NATIONS SYSTEM OF NATIONAL ACCOUNTS

12. The System of National Accounts: Review of Major Issues   345
Richard Ruggles
13. Financial Accounts and Balance Sheets: Issues for the Revision of the SNA   414
Nancy D. Ruggles
14. A Note on the Revision of the United Nations System of National Accounts   442
Richard Ruggles
15. Statistical Measurements for Economic Systems in Transition: Strategy for Implementing the UN System of National Accounts (SNA)   451
Richard Ruggles
16. Issues Relating to the UN System of National Accounts and Developing Countries   486
Richard Ruggles
17. The United Nations System of National Accounts (SNA) and the Integration of Macro- and Microdata   495
Richard Ruggles

Bibliography   *523*
Index   *537*

Foreword

Peter Hill

The papers in this volume span nearly half a century. Both the earliest and the latest papers appear in Part One of the volume, devoted to the evolution of national accounting. The earliest, by Richard Ruggles on 'National Income Accounting and its Relation to Economic Policy', was written in 1949, in Paris, for the Economic Cooperation Administration, or ECA, (the precursor of the OEEC and OECD). The two latest papers were written in 1993, one of which, 'National Income Accounting: Concepts and Measurement. Economic Theory and Practice', presented in 1993 at a conference in Siena, traces the origins of national accounting back over three centuries.

The first set of papers in this volume is mainly concerned with the evolution of national accounting in the present century, however, and particularly with the last 50 years.

The role of Richard Stone in the years following World War II is well known. His 1947 League of Nations report transformed national accounts from the compilation of a few macroeconomic aggregates into a complete system of interrelated economic accounts. However, other people were also active and made important contributions during this formative period for national accounts, not least Nancy and Richard Ruggles, who worked intermittently in Paris and Cambridge, England, between 1949 and 1953. The ECA needed comparable, analytically useful and policy, relevant information about the economic recovery of different countries which could also be used as the basis for allocating Marshall Plan aid. In other words, they needed a set of internationally comparable national accounts. In response to these policy needs, the Ruggles were instrumental in setting up, with ECA funding, a new National Accounts Research Unit in Cambridge under Stone's direction. The Ruggles also contributed to the work of the unit. The eventual output from this activity was the OEEC's *Simplified System of National Accounts* which was published in 1951. The United Nations *System of National Accounts*, or SNA, which was essentially the same system but with a few modifications, followed soon afterwards in 1953. Over the subsequent 40 years this system has evolved into the complex and sophisticated international system of accounts, the 1993 SNA, now used by almost all countries in the world, including the countries of the former Soviet Union. The 1993 SNA, the direct descendant of the 1951 OEEC and 1953 UN systems, which regrettably, but inevitably, is not quite so simple as they were, was produced and published jointly by five major international organizations, consisting of the IMF, World Bank, OECD and European Union in addition to the United Nations.

As in the postwar period, Nancy and Richard Ruggles continued to be among those who were most active in promoting the improvement and development of the SNA in the 40 years between 1953 and 1993. Nancy Ruggles worked for the UN on more than one occasion and, as Assistant Director of the UN Statistical Office, was in charge of the National Accounts Division from 1975 to 1980. Part Three of the present volume is devoted to papers on the subject of updating and revising the SNA. Two papers in particular, one by Richard Ruggles on 'The System of National Accounts: Review of Major Issues', completed in 1982, and one by Nancy Ruggles on 'Financial Accounts and Balance Sheets: Issues for the Revision of the SNA', published in 1984, significantly affected the direction which the planned revision of the SNA would take. Although signed individually, these papers reflected the views of both Nancy and Richard Ruggles, who may be presumed to have discussed these issues between themselves occasionally.

Although it may be appropriate to emphasize, especially for readers in the United States, the major and sustained contribution that Nancy and Richard Ruggles have made to the creation, elaboration and improvement of international standards in the field of national accounts, the major work in the present volume has to be their 1982 paper on 'Integrated Economic Accounts for the United States, 1947–80'. This paper, which has had to be shortened somewhat for the present volume, is a remarkable achievement. It presents the results of an ambitious research project which took some years to complete. Its purpose was to modify and extend the US national income and product accounts to achieve an accounting framework which could accommodate 'economic and social data at different levels of aggregation, from micro to macro, and embracing stocks as well as flows'. A second objective was 'to simplify and clarify the presentation of the transaction flows between the sectors and their relation to the major economic constructs'. Uniquely, an entire issue of the *Survey of Current Business* published by the Bureau of Economic Analysis (BEA) of the US Department of Commerce, that for May 1982, was devoted to the paper and its accompanying tables, together with comments from leading national accountants and economists in the United States and Canada. It is appropriate to quote from the Editor's Note (which is not reproduced in the present volume).

This issue . . . is devoted to the presentation and discussion of an integrated set of national income and product accounts and balance sheets for the United States.... These experimental accounts were developed by Richard Ruggles and Nancy D. Ruggles. Their qualifications for this undertaking are unique: familiarity with the intricacies of the U.S. national income and product accounts that may be unparalleled outside BEA; association with work in economic, social and demographic statistics at the United Nations; participation in the activities of the professional organizations in the field, especially the International Association for Research in Income and Wealth and its *Review of Income and Wealth*; and service as consultants on statistical programs in the United States and abroad. Their willingness to 'take the plunge' of putting together an integrated set of accounts, when — because of the size and nature of the task — it was clear that not all issues could be resolved, is another notable qualification.

Nancy and Richard Ruggles began by pointing out that national accounts should have three major functions. 'They serve as the coordinating and integrating framework for all economic statistics; they give timely and reliable key indicators on the performance of the economy; and they illuminate the relationships among the sectors of the economy that are fundamental to an understanding of its functioning'. The emphasis on the accounts providing an integrating framework, which is the core of the Ruggles' paper, was echoed ten years later in the opening sentences of the 1993 SNA which read: 'The System of National Accounts (SNA) consists of a coherent, consistent and integrated set of macroeconomic accounts, balance sheets and tables.... It provides a comprehensive accounting framework within which economic data can be compiled in a format that is designed for purposes of economic analysis, decision taking and policy making'. The integration is twofold. The same set of concepts, definitions and classifications used, based on economic theory, must be used throughout the entire system of accounts. Secondly, the data, which are typically derived from a wide range of quite different statistical sources, must be numerically reconciled with each other, this providing a powerful check on the reliability of the accounts and aggregates.

Another point stressed by Nancy and Richard Ruggles, which is also echoed in the 1993 SNA, is that the accounts can be compiled at any level of aggregation and not just for the economy as a whole: that is, for individual economic units such as households or enterprises; for groups of such units, i.e., sectors; or for all the units in the economy, i.e., national accounts. The term 'national' accounts has, by now, actually become an unfortunate anachronism because it perpetuates the myth that the main purpose of the accounts is to estimate one or two aggregates for the economy as a whole, such as GNP or national income, notwithstanding the fact that Stone was awarded a Nobel prize for his work half a century ago in developing a system of accounts which maps the flows taking place between different transactors, and groups of transactors, *within* the economy. The adjective 'national' was deliberately dropped from the title of the official accounts used within the European Union some time ago, the revised version of which (based on the 1993 SNA) is now described simply as the *European System of Accounts*, or *ESA 1995*. (The previous version, incidentally, was described as the *European System of Integrated Economic Accounts*.)

Given that economic accounts can be compiled at any level of aggregation, Nancy and Richard Ruggles went on to argue that: 'The ultimate objective should be an overall statistical system that would embrace economic, social, demographic and environmental data at all levels of aggregation.' This vision of an overall system integrating micro- and macrodata has dominated most of their later work. The 1982 paper points out that 'one of the most striking statistical developments over the last 20 years has been the increasing availability of microdata relating to individuals'. It also notes that 'the computer has changed the ways data are processed, stored and disseminated and has opened up administrative data sources not previously accessible'. This was written in the early 1980s when few, excepting the Ruggles, would have predicted the power of the computers routinely available on office desks today. Aligning micro- and macrodata is obviously desirable. The Ruggles repeatedly argued that it is also feasible.

They explain that 'the integration of the microdata with the sector accounts does not imply that the sector accounts should be aligned with or derived from any single microdata set. The macroaccounts, drawing upon many different sources, provide the control totals to which a variety of microdata sets can be aligned. Conceptual consistency between the sector accounts and the corresponding microunit information would make it possible to move back and forth among the different levels of aggregation and among related types of economic, social, and demographic data.' The advantages of such an overall system would be enormous. For example, economic growth at the level of GDP is no longer accepted as sufficient for judging the success or failure of economic policies as it is also necessary to know how the benefits, or losses, have been distributed among different socio-economic groups, how the environment has been affected, and so on.

The concern with micro- as well as macrodata led Nancy and Richard Ruggles to question certain concepts traditionally used in macroaccounting on the grounds that they may not accord with the perceptions of the individuals concerned and lead to data which are not useful for analytic purposes at a microlevel. For example, the Ruggles have criticized the conventional national accounting treatment of private pensions and insurance on these grounds. While there may be economic logic in the conventional treatments at a macrolevel, the results may sometimes be paradoxical at a microlevel. The Ruggles have repeatedly reminded national accountants that their conventions do not become justified merely because they are traditional and that some conventions remain rather more controversial than many national accountants would care to admit.

It has only been possible in a short foreword to touch on a small selection of topics from the large collection of papers assembled in this volume. The papers speak for themselves and demonstrate the magnitude of the contribution which Nancy and Richard Ruggles have made to the subject of economic accounting in the last half century. In contrast to many introverted and overly technical manuals and articles on national accounts, their papers are invariably clear, stimulating and readable. They show that economic accounting is an important and basic economic discipline, even if currently not very fashionable.

Preface

The topic of national accounts occupied a central role in the research and writings of both Nancy D. Ruggles and Richard Ruggles, but their introductions to the topic were quite different. In 1942 Richard Ruggles, prior to going to work for the Coordinator of Information (later known as the Office of Strategic Services), had became involved in the Kuznets world of national income measurement. For his Ph.D. thesis, *Price Structure and Distribution over the Cycle*, he worked in a neo-classical framework which, in line with Kuznets's definition of national income produced and national income paid, excluded government activity. In contrast Nancy D. Ruggles, after graduating from Pembroke College in 1943, went to work for the Tax Research Division of the US Treasury Department. At Treasury, she used the Keynesian national accounting framework for analyzing 'the inflationary gap' caused by World War II defense expenditures. In such a framework government played a central role.

After World War II, while at Harvard during the academic year of 1946–47, Nancy and Richard Ruggles collaborated in writing the chapters on national income accounting and income analysis for the Harvard Economics course, a syllabus that was used in the introductory course for more than a decade. During the summer of 1948, they went to Washington to consult with Milton Gilbert and George Jaszi at the National Income Division of the Department of Commerce in order to write the textbook, *An Introduction to National Income and Income Analysis*. A revised edition was published in 1956 under the title *National Income Accounting and Income Analysis*.

The essays in this volume are classified into three categories: (1) Evolution and Concepts of National Accounting, (2) United States National Accounts and (3) United Nations System of National Accounts.

PART ONE EVOLUTION AND CONCEPTS OF NATIONAL
                     ACCOUNTING

National Income Accounting and its Relation to Economic Policy was written in 1949, in Paris, for the Economic Cooperation Administration (ECA). Richard Ruggles had taken leave from Yale for the academic year of 1948–49 to work for the Office of the Special Representative of the ECA in Paris.

Nancy Ruggles had received a post-doctoral fellowship to study in Europe. The ECA was interested in using a national accounting framework for analyzing European economic recovery. In addition to publishing the booklet on national income accounting, Richard and Nancy Ruggles went to Cambridge, England to persuade Richard Stone to set up, with ECA funding, a special 'National Accounts Research Unit' (NARU). This unit served two functions: (1) it provided a center for training statisticians from national statistical offices in the compilation of national accounts and (2) it was given the function of developing a 'Simplified System of National Accounts (SSNA)' for use by the Statistical Office of the Organization for European Economic Cooperation (OEEC). In the summers of 1949 to 1953, Richard and Nancy Ruggles worked at the National Accounts Research Unit in Cambridge, England, and visited the Central Statistical Offices of the major OEEC countries. During the academic terms they commuted each week from New Haven to Washington to work at the Economic Cooperation Administration. With the help of Phyllis Leuchtenberg and Harrison Hemenway, they produced *National Accounts Data* books that compiled, for each of the OEEC countries, a simple five-account system of national accounts.

Concepts of Real Capital Stocks and Services focused on issues related to traditional national accounting and was presented at an Income and Wealth Conference on *Input, Output and Productivity Measurement*, in 1961. It was written at a time when increasing attention was being given to the problems involved in price and real output measurements of the national accounts. The paper questions the measurement of capital as output in the context of technological change, and the omission of intangible capital and research and development as capital formation. With respect to capital as a factor of production and the measurement of its productivity, the appropriate treatment of obsolescence of real tangible capital was discussed.

The Evolution and Present State of National Economic Accounting was written for a conference on national accounting held in 1968 by the Center for International Education and Research in Accounting at the University of Illinois. The objective of this paper was to provide for rather skeptical business accountants some background information on the development of national accounts and their possible integration with other economic and social data.

The Role of the National Accounts in the Statistical System is one of the four lectures presented by Nancy and Richard Ruggles at Statistics Canada in April and November 1984. The purpose of this lecture series was to provide statisticians at Statistics Canada working on demographic, social, and business statistics with a brief history of national income accounting since World War II and its relation to national statistical systems.

The Treatment of Pensions and Insurance in the National Accounts was originally presented at a National Accounts Experts Meeting of the

Organization for Economic Cooperation and Development (OECD) in Paris, May 1983. The comments of the participants were taken into account, and a revised version incorporating the comments of OECD participants was published in the *Review of Income and Wealth*.

National Income Accounting Concepts and Measurement: Economic Theory and Practice was written for a conference on *Accounting and Economics,* organized by Martin Shubik, and held in Siena, Italy in 1992. This conference focused on the relation between the accounting concepts and the concepts of economic theory.

The Value Added of National Accounting is a book review article that was written with Patricia Ruggles for the *Review of Income and Wealth,* 1995. The book commemorates 50 years of national accounts in the Netherlands, and contains articles relating to the history, development and future direction of national accounting in the Netherlands.

PART TWO UNITED STATES NATIONAL ACCOUNTS

The national accounts of the United States were of direct concern to Richard and Nancy Ruggles from their first contact with the subject in 1942–43 to their final effort to provide an integrated set of national accounts for the United States 40 years later in 1982. Their textbooks on national income accounting had as their major function the exposition of the US national income accounts. With the advent of the National Accounts Review Committee recommendations in 1957, Richard and Nancy Ruggles worked closely with George Jaszi, Director of the National Income Division of the Department of Commerce, in the shift from the 1947 system of US national income accounts to the five-account summary system that is still in use.

The Evolution of National Accounts and the National Data Base was written in 1971 for the 50th anniversary of the publication of the *Survey of Current Business.* This paper was not only intended to provide a chronicle of the origin and development of the United States national accounts, but its purpose was also to suggest improvements that could be made in the existing national accounts.

The United States National Income Accounts, 1947–77: Their Conceptual Basis and Evolution was written in the context of a National Science Foundation project on the 'Measurement of Economic and Social Performance'. It introduced the concept of transactors accounts for the household income accounts and balance sheets. At that time, the Bureau of Economic Analysis had not computerized the national accounts, so, for the project on the Measurement of Economic and Social Performance, the basic worksheets of the Bureau of Economic Analysis were keypunched at the National Bureau of Economic Research in New York under the direction of

Charlotte Boschan, and the necessary computer software was developed by Orin Hansen at Yale University. The computer at Cornell University was used to run the programs.

Integrated Economic Accounts for the United States, 1947–80, published in May 1982, was the culmination of more than a decade of research and development on the topic of United States national accounting. The final stages were carried out at the Institution for Social and Policy Studies of Yale University with the financial support of the Bureau of Economic Analysis of the Department of Commerce. The updating to take into account the comprehensive revision of the national income and product accounts completed in 1980 was carried out under the Retirement Security Project funded by the US Department of Health and Human Services. The Bureau of Economic Analysis and the Federal Reserve Board greatly contributed to the project. At Yale, Orin Hansen developed the software system NEAT (National Economic Accounting Tables) used to generate the integrated sector income accounts and balance sheets. These programs were modeled after the system developed by Steve Taylor for the Flow of Fund Accounts at the Federal Reserve Board, and the computerization was applied to the worksheets of the Bureau of Economic Analysis of the Department of Commerce. Catherine Viscoli at Yale implemented the documentation and statistical work. At the Bureau of Economic Analysis, John Musgrave, Jean Salter, Helen Tice, John Gorman and Edward Denison were very helpful in providing the necessary data and useful criticisms. The integrated accounts were greatly influenced by a number of previous research projects, in particular, (1) 'The Measurement of Economic and Social Performance' supported by the National Science Foundation, (2) research carried out for the United Nations on the *System of National Accounts (SNA)* and (3) various articles published in the *Review of Income and Wealth* all greatly influenced the final structure and content of the integrated system.

Integrated Economic Accounts: Reply, published in November 1982, was written in response to the eight extensive comments that had been published in the May 1982 issue of the *Survey of Current Business*, by Hans J. Adler and Preetom Sunga of Statistics Canada, Carol Carson, John Gorman, George Jaszi, Martin Marimont and Helen Tice of the Bureau of Economic Analysis of the US Department of Commerce, Stephen Taylor of the Federal Reserve Board, Edward Denison of Brookings, and James Tobin of Yale University. All of these individuals were either producers or users of national accounting data. As a consequence, the integrated system of accounts was primarily viewed from the 'macro' vantage point. The 'Reply', therefore, emphasized the importance of such things as microanalytic modeling, the usefulness of integrating social and demographic data with economic data, and the desirability of developing institutional and longitudinal microdata that could underlie the macroaccounts.

PART THREE UNITED NATIONS SYSTEM OF NATIONAL ACCOUNTS

The association of Richard and Nancy Ruggles with the United Nations System of National Accounts started prior to the first United Nations System of National Accounts (SNA) in 1952 and continued for more than 40 years. Richard and Nancy Ruggles were very much involved in the development of the OEEC 'Simplified System of National Accounts' (SSNA) at the National Accounts Research Unit in Cambridge, England. Subsequently, under Abraham Aidenoff at the United Nations, with Richard Stone as a consultant, the OEEC SNOW evolved into the initial version of the United Nations System of National Accounts (SNA). From 1957 to 1959, Nancy Ruggles was employed by the UN as an Economic Affairs Officer working with Jacob Mozak and Sidney Dell on the World Economic Survey. Starting in 1962, as Secretary of the International Association for Research in Income and Wealth (IARIW), Nancy Ruggles was very much involved in issues relating to the United Nations SNA through IARIW conferences and the journal *Review of Income and Wealth*. From 1975 to 1980, Nancy Ruggles served as Assistant Director of the United Nations Statistical Office and headed the National Accounts Division. After her resignation in 1980, she continued as a United Nations consultant and wrote numerous manuals for the UN SNA until her death in 1987.

The System of National Accounts: Review of Major Issues (1982), by Richard Ruggles, was commissioned by Svien Nordbatten, Director of the United Nations Statistical Office. It was presented to an Expert Group under the chairmanship of Claus Moser, Director of the United Kingdom Central Statistical Office. The writing of this paper took place when Richard and Nancy Ruggles were completing their work on the *Integrated Economic Accounts for the United States*. However, the United States system of national income accounts differed from the United Nations SNA, so that many of the issues to be examined were quite different.

Financial Accounts and Balance Sheets: Issues for the Revision of the SNA is an abridged version of a report with this same title by Nancy D. Ruggles, originally published in 1984 by the United Nations.

A Note on the Revision of the United Nations System of National Accounts was written by Richard Ruggles in 1990, and covers many of the same points as the previous writings, but updates them in a more summary and abbreviated form.

Statistical Measurements for Economic Systems in Transition: Strategy for Implementing the UN System of National Accounts (SNA) was presented at a Conference on *Economies in Transition: Statistical Measures Now and in the Future*, held in Sochi, USSR, October 1990. The paper indicates how, through the development of core transactor accounts for institutional sectors of the economy, it would be possible to move from the Material Product System (MPS) to the United Nations System of National Accounts (SNA).

Issues Relating to the UN System of National Accounts and Developing Countries was first presented at a Conference on *Databases for Development Analysis* held by the Yale Economic Growth Center in May 1992 and published in 1994. The paper examines the revision of the UN System of National Accounts in the light of specific problems in developing countries.

The United Nations System of National Accounts (SNA) and the Integration of Macro- and Microdata was written for the book *Socio Economic Accounts*, edited by John Kendrick and published by Kluwer in 1995. The essay argues that microdata bases are needed to address the economic and social problems of modern societies, and that the existence of administrative files, modern sampling methods and computer technology make the integration of macro- and microdata quite feasible now.

Richard Ruggles, May, 1998

Abstracts

PART ONE EVOLUTION AND CONCEPTS OF NATIONAL ACCOUNTING

1. National Income Accounting and its Relation to Economic Policy
   Richard Ruggles (1949)

   As national economies have grown in size and complexity, so has the need for accurate data by which to steer economic policy. The present national accounting uses five basic accounts (for producers, consumers, government, capital and foreign) and the paper presents the US national data for 1946–47. These accounts can be used to investigate the impact and effectiveness of policies designed to change the general level of production, the nature of this production across industries, how resources are allocated, and how the final product is distributed.

2. Concepts of Real Capital Stocks and Services
   Richard Ruggles and Nancy D. Ruggles (1961)

   The measurement of the stock of capital for the purpose of measuring the change in productivity raises many problems. Capital is both a component of output and, as capital stock, a factor of production. As part of current output, it involves the question as to whether capital that costs twice as much to produce is twice as much capital or whether economies of scale in the production of capital should be recognized. In measuring the stock of capital over time, how should technical changes in the design of capital be treated, and what should be the role of obsolescence that is itself a reflection of the improvement in capital?

3. The Evolution and Present State of National Economic Accounting
   Richard Ruggles and Nancy D. Ruggles (1968)

   The US system of national accounts has evolved over the years to meet specific objectives, but because of this it contains some vestigial features. The UN has proposed new accounts that give a chance to the US to rationalize its own national accounts. While the UN proposals have some deficiencies, they suggest numerous positive changes. The essay expands upon these proposals, and suggests integrating the national accounts with microdata on households and enterprises.

4. The Role of the National Accounts in the Statistical System
   Richard Ruggles (1984)

   The system of national accounts presently in place results from the top-down development of those accounts. When first developed, the data were so rudimentary that only the roughest aggregates could be presented, and as the data developed the income accounts were expanded by subtotaling by categories, industries and transactions. But this development is reaching its limits as the subcategories become more gothic and inflexible. With the development of the computer, microdata sets can be used more flexibly and easily. These show the transition between the micro- and macrodata to be uneven, rough, and sometimes misleading. The national accounts can contribute a consistent, coherent framework, while the microdata bring flexibility, but both need to be improved so as to provide a seamless transition from the accounts of the smallest economic actor to the national economy.

5. The Treatment of Pensions and Insurance in the National Accounts
   Nancy D. Ruggles and Richard Ruggles (1983)

   In the course of the nearly two decades since the United Nations System of National Accounts (SNA) was revised, the role of pensions and insurance in the developed western economies has been significantly altered. This paper investigates the impact on household income and saving of adopting a more consistent transactor/transaction approach for all pension and insurance transactions. Four main topics are covered: (1) social security, (2) private pensions, (3) life insurance and (4) casualty insurance. Each of these is considered in terms of the treatment of contributions, benefits, reserves and the income generated by them.

6. National Income Accounting Concepts and Measurement: Economic Theory and Practice
   Richard Ruggles (1993)

   National income accounting has been the result of evolutionary developments of economic theory and economic measurement. A historical overview of the United Nations System of National Accounts (SNA) and its current revision is provided. Specific attention is given to the sectoral accounting for saving and capital formation with special reference to the

US economy. Finally, the feasibility of integrating microdata with national accounts and the proposal for a core system of transactor/transaction based national accounting is discussed.

7. The Value Added of National Accounting
   Richard Ruggles and Patricia Ruggles (1995)

   This is a review article on a collection of articles celebrating 50 years of national income accounting in the Netherlands. Nineteen articles covering the history, current uses and future development of the Netherlands national accounts are presented. The discussion of the Dutch proposal for a system of 'core' accounts is particularly interesting and has significant implications for the potential integration of macro- and microdata.

PART TWO   UNITED STATES NATIONAL ACCOUNTS

8. The Evolution of National Accounts and the National Data Base
   Richard Ruggles and Nancy D. Ruggles (1971)

   The deep depression of the 1930s stimulated research into the measurement of national income in the United States and the first official estimates were published in the *Survey of Current Business* in 1934. With the mobilization for World War II, the more compressive measure of gross national product was developed, and in 1947 the national accounting aggregates were presented in a set of six articulated accounts. The simpler five-account system currently in use was adopted in 1954. A variety of proposed changes in the concept of capital, treatment of saving, and the form of the accounts are discussed. Finally, the relation of the national accounts to microdata is examined.

9. The United States National Income Accounts, 1947–77: Their Conceptual Basis and Evolution
   Richard Ruggles (1983)

   The paper consists of three major parts. First, the history of United States national income and product accounts is discussed, including the various reviews of them since 1947. Second, the various current proposals for the future development of the US national accounts are examined. Finally, an appendix is presented that demonstrates how a 'transactor' approach to the national accounts would alter the treatment of interest, insurance, and the role of financial institutions and their transactions in the national accounts.

10. Integrated Economic Accounts for the United States, 1947–80
    Richard Ruggles and Nancy D. Ruggles (1982)

    A set of transactor/transaction accounts for institutionally defined sectors of the economy (enterprises, households, government and rest of the world) are presented. These Integrated Economic Accounts (IEAs) combine the data contained in the United States Department of Commerce *National Income and Product Accounts* with the Federal Reserve Board's *Flow of Funds Accounts*. Specifically accounts are drawn up for production, income and outlays, capital transactions, revaluations and national wealth and balance sheets. Imputations are shown separately from the actual market transactions taking place, and special attention is devoted to the treatment of financial intermediaries. Considerable emphasis is placed on developing the national accounting framework so that it can serve as a framework for the microdata relating to enterprises and households. The final part of the paper deals with an analysis of 'Saving, Investment and Wealth' based on the data provided by the 'Integrated Economic Accounts for the United States, 1947–80'.

11. Integrated Economic Accounts: Reply
    Richard Ruggles and Nancy D. Ruggles (1982)

    Reply to comments published in the May 1982 issue of the *Survey of Current Business*, by Hans J. Adler and Pretom Sunga; Carol S. Carson and George Jaszi; Edward F. Denison; John A. Gorman; Martin L. Marimont; Stephen P. Taylor; Helen Stone Tice; and James Tobin.

PART THREE UNITED NATIONS SYSTEM OF NATIONAL ACCOUNTS

12. The System of National Accounts: Review of Major Issues
    Richard Ruggles (1982)

    This paper, commissioned by the United Nations Statistical Commission, examines the major issues relating to the United Nations System of National Accounts (SNA) since its last major revision in 1968. Four major areas are examined: (1) the measurement of market and non-market consumption by individuals, government and enterprises, (2) the measurement of income in terms of inflation, rent, intangible assets, pensions, insurance, capital transfers, financial leasing and the terms of trade, (3) the accounting structure and sectoring of the accounts and (4) extension of the accounts for quarterly data, regional accounts and for social and demographic statistics.

13. Financial Accounts and Balance Sheets: Issues for the Revision of the SNA
    Nancy D. Ruggles (1987)

    This paper is an abridged version of a report written for the United Nations Statistical Office as a part of the review of the System of National Accounts (SNA). Particular attention is paid to the problems of harmonization with the International Monetary Fund. Although the 1968 SNA did provide a place in the framework for financial transactions, it did not develop them in any detail. The changing nature of economic problems and policy concerns and the increasing focus on financial questions call into question some of the conventions that had been adopted. It is now apparent that some of the early decisions need reconsideration. This paper is not intended to propose solutions, but rather to reflect questions that have been raised and to present alternatives that have been proposed.

14. A Note on the Revision of the United Nations System of National Accounts
    Richard Ruggles (1990)

    This brief note raises a number of questions relating the current revision of the United Nations System of National Accounts (SNA). The proposed revisions treat inadequately: (1) the sectoring of the economy, (2) household capital formation and the valuation of owner-occupied housing, (3) pensions and insurance, (4) interest and (5) the structure of the accounts.

15. Statistical Measurements for Economic Systems in Transition: Strategy for Implementing the UN System of National Accounts (SNA)
    Richard Ruggles (1990)

    It is recognized that economies in transition will need to implement the United Nations System of National Accounts as soon as it is feasible to do so. When they do this, however, it is suggested that a set of basic core accounts should be developed that would provide a general framework for the statistical system. Such core accounts would be organized around institutional sectors and would record their actual transactions taking place within the economy. As such these core accounts would provide the basis for integrating macro- and microdata. Imputations and the rerouting of transactions required for the implementation of the United Nations SNA would be shown separately.

16. Issues Relating to the UN System of National Accounts and
    Developing Countries
    Richard Ruggles (1994)

    The recent revision of the United Nations System of National Accounts (SNA) represents improved harmonization of the international trade, balance of payments, government finance and monetary data collected by national and international statistical agencies. Although such harmonization is welcomed by the developing countries, a number of other major unresolved issues remain. Specifically, the SNA has not solved problems relating to: (1) delineation of the formal and informal sectors of an economy, (2) appropriate treatment of market and nonmarket economic activity, (3) satisfactory analysis of sector saving and capital formation and (4) harmonization of household sector macrodata with household survey microdata.

17. The United Nations System of National Accounts (SNA) and the
    Integration of Macro- and Microdata
    Richard Ruggles (1995)

    The United Nations System of National Accounts (SNA) was born in the world of macroeconomics, but it has its statistical roots in the data relating to the individual decision-making units of the economy. Since its inception, both the complexity of the economic system and the concerns with social problems have increased. Currently governments are faced with the need to evaluate both the macro- and microaspects of their policies relating to old age entitlements, health care, education, the environment and poverty. The national accounts alone are not sufficient for this task. Both the need and the technical feasibility of linking the macroframework with microdata have increased. The following discussion attempts to trace the evolution of the system with respect to the macro/micro linkage, and to indicate how the macroaccounts and microdata bases can be integrated.

List of Tables and Figures

TABLES

1.1	Simplified Income Statement for a Manufacturing Corporation for the period 1 January 19– to 31 December 19–	9
1.2	Production Statement for the Firm	11
1.3	Statement for the Value Added by the Firm	12
1.4	National Allocations and Expenditures Account for the United States in 1947	13
1.5	National Allocations and Expenditures for the United States in 1946 and 1947	14
1.6	Personal Income and Expenditure Account for the United States in 1946 and 1947	16
1.7	Government Receipts and Expenditures Account for the United States in 1946 and 1947	17
1.8	Rest-of-the-World Account for the United States in 1946 and 1947	18
1.9	Gross Savings and Investment Account for the United States in 1946 and 1947	19
1.10	National Accounts for the United States, 1939	22
1.11	Agricultural Account	24
1.12	National Income and Net National Product Account for the United States in 1946 and 1947	29
1.13	National Income Originating by Industry for the United States in 1946 and 1947	30
1.14	Number of Persons Engaged in Production by Industry for the United States in 1946 and 1947	32
5.1	Social Security, Pensions, Health and Life Insurance in the United States, 1965 and 1979	94
5.2	Comparison of Present SNA and Proposed Treatment of Social Security, United States, 1979	98
5.3	Comparison of Present SNA and Proposed Treatment of Funded Pensions, United States, 1979	104

5.4	Comparison of Present SNA and Proposed Treatment of Unfunded Benefits, United States, 1979	106
5.5	Comparison of Present SNA and Proposed Treatment of Life Insurance, United States, 1979	110
5.6	Comparison of Present SNA and Proposed Treatment of Health Insurance, United States, 1979	114
5.7	Comparison of Present SNA and Proposed Treatment of Group Life Insurance and Workmen's Compensation, United States, 1979	116
5.8	Adjustments to United States Data for 1979 as Shown in UN *Yearbook of National Accounts Statistics*	120
5.9	BEA, SNA and Proposed Treatment of Pension and Insurance Transactions in Household and Private Unincorporated Enterprise Income and Outlay Account, United States, 1979	123
5.10	BEA, SNA and Proposed Treatment of Pension and Insurance Transactions in Relation to GNP, United States, 1979	125
6.1	Household Saving, Capital Formation and Net Lending in the United States, 1947–90	146
6.2	Corporate Income Statements for the United States, 1983, Total All Industries and Industry Divisions	150
6.3	Household Current Income and Outlay Accounts, United States, 1980	157
6.4	Household Balance Sheets, Capital Transactions and Revaluations, United States, 1980	159
9.1	National Income and Product Account, 1939	189
9.2	Consolidated Business Income and Product Account, 1939	190
9.3	Consolidated Government Receipts and Expenditures Account, 1939	191
9.4	Rest-of-the-World Account, 1939	191
9.5	Personal Income and Expenditure Account, 1939	192
9.6	Gross Savings and Investment Account, 1939	192
9.7	National Income and Product Account, 1957	199
9.8	Personal Income and Outlay Account, 1957	200
9.9	Government Receipts and Expenditures Account, 1957	200
9.10	Foreign Transactions Account, 1957	201
9.11	Gross Saving and Investment Account, 1957	201
9.12	The United Nations SNA Matrix: A Symbolic Table	206
9.13	Comparison of the BEA Personal Income Account with the Household Sector Current Account for 1969	224
9.14	Household Sector Balance Sheets	231

List of Tables and Figures

10.1	Production Statement for a Nonfinancial Corporation	246
10.2	Gross National Product Account, 1978	261
10.3	Enterprise Gross National Account, 1978	270
10.4	Household Current Income and Outlay Account, 1978	272
10.5	Government Current Income and Outlay Account, 1978	273
10.6	Rest-of-the-World Current Account, 1978	277
10.7	Capital Accounts for the Nation, 1977–78	279
10.8	Sector Balance Sheets, 1978	284
10.9	Capital Accounts for Equipment Enterprises, 1977–78	286
11.1	Revised Estimates Resulting from Correcting Pension and Insurance Data	327
12.1	Summary of Comments on Proposed Changes in SNA Treatment of External Transactions	395
15.1	ENTCUR, Enterprise Current Receipts and Outlay Account	468
15.2	HHCUR, Household Current Market Income and Outlay Account	470
15.3	GOVCUR, Government Current Receipts and Outlay Account	471
15.4	ROWCUR, Rest-of-World Current Account	472
15.5	SICAP, Gross Saving and Capital Formation Account	473
15.6	FINACCT, Sector Financial Accounts, United States, 1980	474
15.7	IMPUTE, Imputation Model for United States, 1981	475
15.8	GNP–M, Gross National Income and Product Account: Market Transactions	477
15.9	GNP–T, Gross National Income and Product Account: Total Market and Nonmarket	479
15.10	NNP–T, Net National Income and Product: Total Market and Nonmarket	481

SAMPLE TABLES (all in Chapter 10)

1.1	Gross National Product Account	264
1.2	Relation of National Income, Net National Product and Gross National Product	266
1.10	Enterprise Gross Product Account	268
1.40	Household Current Income and Outlay Account	274
1.50	Government Current Income and Outlay Account	276
1.60	Rest-of-the-World Current Account	278
2.1	Capital Accounts for the Nation, 1977–78	282

FIGURES

10.1 Gross Capital Formation and Gross Saving, 1947–80   289
10.2 Cumulative Change in Household Net Worth and Net Saving, 1947–80   292
10.3 Components of Household Balance Sheets: Market Values and Cumulative Net Acquisitions, 1947–80   293
10.4 Components of Household Balance Sheets: Market Values and Cumulative Net Acquisitions in Constant Purchasing Power, 1947–80   295

PART ONE

EVOLUTION AND CONCEPTS
OF NATIONAL ACCOUNTING

1. National Income Accounting and its Relation to Economic Policy

Richard Ruggles
Yale University

National income accounting in recent years has passed the stage where it is of interest only to academicians, and has become an indispensable aid in the formulation of economic policy. This paper will discuss briefly: why national income accounting is necessary in current formulations of economic policy, what constitutes national income accounting as the term is generally used, and how national income accounting can be applied to specific problems in economic analysis.

1. NECESSITY FOR NATIONAL INCOME ACCOUNTING IN THE FORMULATION OF ECONOMIC POLICY

A full appreciation of the usefulness of national income accounting as it is applied to economic policy requires, first of all, some idea of the coverage of the term 'economic policy', both in past periods and in a modern industrial economy. The changing nature of economic policy has brought with it a need for a more comprehensive approach to economic analysis, an approach which is capable of presenting all of the pertinent information. It was because of this need that national income accounting has been developed, and the history of the development of national income accounting is in fact inseparable from the history of the economic problems posed by the Great Depression of the thirties, by the industrial mobilization for World War II, and by the postwar economic readjustments among nations. A brief account of this history will make clear what must be the more important characteristics of a system of national income accounting designed to be useful for problems of economic policy.

This chapter first appeared as a Report for the Office of the Special Representative in Europe, Economic Cooperation Administration, Paris, 1949.

Economic Development and Increasing Necessity for Economic Policy

The rapid industrial development of the western countries during the last 500 years has created a close mutual interdependence among the people of these countries, and it is from this interdependence that the problems of economic policy as we know them today have arisen. As long as small groups of individuals were relatively self-sufficient, the concept of private property and the feudal tradition together gave a determinate answer to the one major economic problem — who was to own or use the land. But as towns grew and some of the people ceased to be attached to the land, economic problems of a different nature arose. Since the manorial system permitted wages and most other payments to be made in kind, it had little need for money, but with the development of trade and specialization some sort of specie payment became necessary. It was soon evident that the general public had an interest in the creation of a satisfactory money system, since inefficient or dishonest control of the money system led to periods of inflation or deflation. Laws regulating banking practices and the control of the issuance of money were made in the public interest. In similar manner, specific policies in the areas of international trade and public finance became necessary. Tariffs were imposed on certain commodities and subsidies were granted to certain industries, on the ground of the general public interest. Taxation and government expenditures became increasingly important, both in periods of war as munitions were needed and in periods of peace as the domestic need for such things as streets, highways and general education increased.

It is important to realize that this increasing significance of economic policy results not from an increasing interest in or movement toward centralization and planning, but rather from the increasing complexity of economic activity itself, and from the emergence of specific problems to which solutions must be found. For example, the very existence of railroads and other public utilities poses a problem of policy about which a decision, conscious or unconscious, must be made. The variety of decisions that can be made is very great, ranging from complete government ownership and operation at the one extreme to allowing free entry into the utility field and complete freedom to the producers to charge any rates they might wish at the other extreme. But following either of these courses, or indeed any other course, would require an economic policy decision. The existence of problems necessitating economic policy decisions is quite independent of any particular solution that may be adopted. The adoption of economic policies does not imply the introduction of 'planning'; economic planning refers to one category of possible actions, but any other form of action or inaction taken to solve existing economic problems is fully as much an economic policy.

Problem of Obtaining Adequate Information for Economic Policy

With the realization that there are economic problems to which some sort of solution must be found it becomes obvious that, before any decisions are made, a careful consideration of all the relevant facts is of paramount importance. Facts by themselves rarely provide sufficient grounds for formulating a policy; in designing an adequate solution to any given problem attention must be given to the overall goals and aims of the society and it is, in this area, that different individuals and different political parties will have widely divergent views. Nevertheless, irrespective of the particular aims and goals adopted, it will be found that basic information about the economy is necessary in order to design policies that are capable of achieving their purposes. The obvious fact that a great many of the economic policies that are put into effect do not achieve their purposes can frequently be traced to a lack of information or to a misunderstanding of the relationships involved.

Unfortunately, the availability both of pertinent data and of adequate methods of analysis has lagged considerably behind the increase in the number and complexity of economic problems which must be faced. In the great majority of instances in which specific policies have in practice been found to be ineffective, unworkable, or definitely harmful, the technician has been at fault fully as much as the policy-maker.

At first glance, it may appear that the greatest contributing factor to the technical inadequacy of policy formulation is the lack of statistical information. Although this is often true, it is possible to overemphasize the importance of the lack of data with respect to the consideration of overall economic policies. In problems which require the consideration of the economy as a whole, it is rather the plethora of unorganized economic data which either engulfs the investigator or enables him to obscure the issues. Data on the whole economy in their complete detail are meaningless, but unless all of the data are presented the information will be one-sided. It is for this reason that it is often said that statistics will prove anything. By careful selection of certain data and omission or combination of the remainder, it is almost always possible to show only one facet of any situation. Different ways of combining, averaging, or aggregating data can give the individual investigator more than enough freedom to shape, consciously or unconsciously, almost any presentation into a form which supports his own views. It has, therefore, become imperative that some standard framework be erected which will enable the available economic information to be related objectively to the overall economic problems which have to be solved.

Historical Development of National Income Accounting

In its early stages, national income accounting was not designed as a method of presenting information relevant to general economic problems. For the most part, the first investigations on the subject of national income accounting were carried out by academic economists and institutions. Their primary concern was the building up of a series of aggregates for successive time-periods to show the total income of all individuals in a particular country. It was natural that these investigations should also concern themselves with production and with expenditures on goods and services, since when properly computed and adjusted these measures could be used to estimate the total amount of income payments indirectly. At this stage in the development of national income, however, there was no explicit attempt to construct a framework of data for the economy as a whole.

Considerable impetus was given to the work on national income by the Depression of the thirties. With the increase in unemployment, the lowering of wage rates, and the disappearance of profit, there was an obvious lowering of potential purchasing power, and for analytic purposes it was essential to be able to measure this change. The depression posed many economic problems which necessitated the formulation of specific economic policies. For example, with the fall in incomes, tax receipts fell, and the government was immediately faced with the choice of decreasing its expenditures accordingly, increasing the tax rates to try and raise more revenue, or borrowing to make up the difference between taxes and expenditures. In order to make intelligent decisions with respect to such problems, the government needed to know the type and magnitude of the effects which their tax collections and expenditures would have on the economy. In this connection information was required both on the total amount of income which was being received by individuals and on the total expenditures which were being made in the economy.

Recovery from the Depression brought with it interest in such things as the relative amount of investment expenditures and the accumulation of stocks by businesses. The central banks realized that it was only in relation to information of this nature that credit control could usefully be exercised with a view to keeping the economy on an even keel. The various individual components of national income and national expenditure, when placed within the framework of the other components, were gradually coming to be looked upon as useful information, important in and of themselves.

During World War II, a great many economic problems arose which required a general understanding of the economy. Nations were forced to undertake war production. Although many of the countries probably had no carefully thought-out economic policy, in some countries there was a concerted effort to achieve as great a degree of efficiency as possible. First and foremost, such an effort required a knowledge of how much would be available in the way of economic resources. All armament production plans had to be considered together in order to make sure that the supply of manpower and basic materials in the economy was sufficient to carry them all out. The total quantity of resources which were available obviously had a limit, and total overall production had to be designed to fit within this limit. To schedule a greater production would not only be unrealistic; it would cause serious bottlenecks in some areas and useless oversupply in others. To schedule less production than the available resources would permit, on the other hand, would be to operate at a level lower than full capacity. Accordingly, data on such things as the distribution of manpower among industries and the national income originating in the various industries became of extreme importance. For any realistic appreciation of the problem, furthermore, current consumption had to be taken into account. Not all production could be devoted to war purposes; the civilian population had to be supported if they were expected to turn out the war production. An examination of the minimum level of goods and services needed for consumption was therefore necessary, and national income accounting was again called upon to provide a framework showing the interrelationships among the end uses of production.

The task of deciding how the production plans were to be implemented, as well as the determination of the potential level of production, also required major economic policy decisions. The vast amount of war expenditure had to be financed, and the method of financing to be used was one of the most important questions which had to be faced. It was obvious that taxation should be increased, but how much could it be increased and how much additional tax revenue could be expected from the fact that the economy was working at a higher level of activity? And for that part of war expenditures which could not be financed out of taxation, how and from whom should the requisite funds be borrowed? What different repercussions on the economy would result from borrowing from banks as opposed to individuals, and what effect would such borrowing have upon the incomes of individuals and upon prices? In similar manner, how far could the price incentive be used to move resources such as labor from inessential to essential industries? Income payments would obviously be affected by any such use of the price incentive, and it was necessary to know the extent of the inflationary influence to be expected and whether means were available to offset it successfully. Finally, to what extent and by what means should civilian consumption be restricted to necessities? Relying on the price mechanism to provide the restriction again might result in a disastrous inflation, so that it was necessary to decide in what areas rationing and price control might be necessary. It is obvious that all of these problems are highly interrelated, and that they can only be solved satisfactorily if they are considered within one framework of data. Under the wartime pressures national income accounting was developed to provide such a framework. With this framework, it became possible to relate the amount of total available resources to the planned production for war and civilian consumption, and to examine the income payments and prices which would necessarily result from the adoption of any specific system of taxes, borrowing, incentive payments, price control and rationing. By the end of the war, national income accounting had thus emerged as an essential tool in the formulation of economic policy.

At the present time, most of the more advanced nations are using the national accounting approach to appraise their own current economic situations and to serve as a basis for designing realistic and consistent policies. The postwar period has brought with it a great many problems of readjustment. These readjustments, and the measures such as Marshall Plan aid designed to assist in them, can only have meaning in terms of the relevant economic magnitudes in the different countries. A suitable adjustment within any country must be defined in terms of full utilization of capacity, workable trade patterns, and a reasonable and maintainable allocation of production between investments and consumption. The information provided by national income accounts is essential for achieving such a balance. If nations are to avoid the evils of inflation and deflation they must carefully consider the repercussions of their tax policies, their debt management and other credit controls, and their general government expenditures; to disregard these repercussions is to invite disaster. The list of economic problems about which deliberate policy decisions are being made has in some countries been extended far beyond this minimum list. These countries are attempting to build up some industries in accordance with concepts of national defense and the requirements of international trade, and they are intentionally altering the income distribution and making certain services free to all individuals, according to some specified ideas of equity and of the general welfare. For all of these far-reaching changes in the economy, national income accounting is essential in order to ensure that what is attempted is within the bounds of possibility and is not inconsistent with itself. National income accounting obviously does not ensure the success of these or any other policies, but it can place them on a more reasonable and enlightened basis.

2. NATURE OF NATIONAL INCOME ACCOUNTING

The national income accounts are closely related to the individual current accounts which are commonly used to record receipts and expenditures. They provide a framework for portraying the current operation of the different sectors in the economy in much the same way that certain financial statements provide a framework for portraying the current operations of an individual enterprise. Basically, the national income accounts set up a system of classification that permits the making of a descriptive and factual record of what has happened in the economy. For many purposes, it is convenient to use a national accounting system composed of all five separate accounts, showing the economic activity of the producing, the consuming, and the government sectors, along with a record of the transactions with the rest of the world and a record of savings and investment.

An Account for the Producing Sector of the Economy

The account for the producing sector is built up from and summarizes the operations of individual enterprises. The basis of this account can best be demonstrated by showing how the records of economic activity for individual producers can be combined and consolidated to give a summary record for the whole economy. By tracing these steps through in some detail, the nature and meaning of national income accounts in general will be made evident.

The income statement and the activity of individual producers
In order to obtain a workable and systematic record of how his firm is operating, a producer ordinarily enters all of his business transactions in a set of accounts. With these basic accounts, summary statements can be drawn up which describe the activity of the firm in a comprehensive manner. The summary statement which refers to the current activity of a firm during any one given period is the income statement. A simplified example of such an income statement is given in Table 1.1 below.

Table 1.1 Simplified Income Statement for a Manufacturing Corporation for the period 1 January 19— to 31 December 19— ($000s)

Goods and materials purchased from other firms	$ 600	Sales to Company A	$ 700
Depreciation of plant and equipment	70	Sales to Company B	250
Taxes other than corporate profits taxes	40	Sales to Company C	375
Social insurance contributions	25	Sales to Company D	80
Wages and salaries	652	Other sales	110
Interest	15		
Provision for corporate profits taxes	37		
Dividends paid	50		
Undistributed profits	26		
Total allocations of current receipts	$1,515	Total current receipts	$1,515

The right-hand side of the income statement shows the sources from which the receipts of the firm were derived during the current time-period, in this case, sales to different purchasers totaling over a million and a half dollars. The left-hand side of the income statement shows how these receipts were allocated among the different kinds of costs incurred in producing the goods that were sold, how much was left over as profits, and how these profits were divided among income taxes, dividends paid to stockholders, and undistributed profits retained in the firm. The costs, in this example, total just under $1.4 million, leaving slightly over $100,000 as profits. The two sides of the income statement are, of course, always equal since on the one hand, they merely record where the receipts of the firm came from, and on the other hand, how these same receipts have been disposed of over the various items of costs and profits.

The income statement in this form refers to goods sold, not to goods produced. The individual firm is often interested primarily in sales, but for the purpose of deriving national income accounts, it is actual production which is important. The amount of goods sold by a firm in any period of time may be quite different from the amount of goods produced by that firm during the same period of time. Most firms have a stock or inventory of finished goods from which sales are made. The process of production adds goods to these inventories, and sales remove goods from these inventories. The amount of the net change in inventories reflects the difference between the sales and the production of the firm. The value of sales plus the net increase in inventories or minus the net decrease in inventories will equal the value of production. A statement of the production of a firm can thus be derived from the income statement by taking into account the change that has occurred in inventories, together with the costs and profits that would be related to that inventory change. The change in inventories will appear on the side of the production statement showing the sources of total current receipts; a net increase will be added to sales to obtain the value of production, and a net decrease will be subtracted. On the allocations side, the costs and profits will now refer to those goods which have been produced, rather than to those which have been sold; the only difference in the calculation is that a different bundle of goods is being examined. Table 1.2 shows how the income statement given in Table 1.1 might be revised to present a production statement for the firm.

A comparison of the production statement and the income statement shows exactly how the value of the inventory increase was distributed among the various kinds of costs and profits in the allocation of receipts. Since profits are by definition the difference between the total value of production and the total costs relating to that production, the two halves of the production statement will balance in the same way as in the income statement.

The production statement for the economy
The production statement for the individual producer shown in Table 1.2 provides the basis for developing a production statement for the whole economy. Much as the production statement for a firm is drawn up around the value of its output, a production statement for the economy can be drawn up around

Table 1.2 Production Statement for the Firm ($000s)

Allocations		Sources	
Goods and materials purchased from other firms	$640	Sales to Company A	$700
	70	Sales to Company B	250
Depreciation	40	Sales to Company C	375
Taxes other than corporate profits taxes	27	Sales to Company D	80
Social insurance contributions	695	Other sales	110
Wages and salaries	15	Inventory increases	100
Interest	49		
Provision for corporate profits taxes	50		
Dividends paid	29		
Undistributed profits			
Total allocations of value of production	$1,615	Total value of production	$1,615

the value of national output. The national output in terms of its market value, i.e., the total market value that has been created by the productive activity of the economy over the period of a year, is called the gross national product at market prices. It is this measurement on which the production statement for the economy will be centered.

This production statement will show who purchased the national output, and how the receipts from the sale of the national output were allocated among the different kinds of costs and profit in the economy. The economy will be treated as if it were a single firm, which produces and sells goods and pays the various factors of production within the firm. To accomplish this, all the production statements of individual firms will have to be consolidated and combined into one overall production statement that will add up to the value of the national output. A similar problem of consolidation often confronts a corporation that owns many interrelated plants. From the income statements of the individual plants alone it is very difficult to determine the results of the activity of the whole firm. A consolidated income statement is needed to present an overall view of the relation of this corporation's plants to the outside market. Such an overall view is obtained by omitting certain internal transactions. Although the accounting procedures involved in this process are in many cases complicated and lengthy, the principles upon which they are based are fairly simple. These same principles are utilized in drawing up a consolidated production account for the whole economy, as follows.

The total market value of the products turned out by a firm in a given period is not always a satisfactory measure of the productive contribution of that firm. The individual firm does not by its own activities and the activities of its employees create all of the market value of its products. Because goods and materials pass through many different firms in the process of their manufacture, the total value of production for the economy cannot be obtained by adding up the value of the goods produced by each firm. A product that had to pass through the hands of a number of firms in the process of its manufacture would increase the value of production of each of these firms by an amount equal to its total value, and adding up the value of production of all firms would count this same product a great many times instead of just once. A different measure is therefore needed, one that will count for each firm only the value it adds to the goods it processes.

The value added by a firm can be measured by the difference between the market value of the products that have been turned out by the firm and the cost of the materials and services it has purchased from other firms. This measure will exclude the contributions made by other firms to the total value of this firm's production, so that the remainder is equal to the market value created by this firm. It thus assesses the net contribution made by each firm to the total value of production, and by adding up all of these contributions it is possible to arrive at a total for the whole economy that will represent the market value of production. The derivation of the value added by an individual firm from the production statement is shown in Table 1.3.

Table 1.3 Statement for the Value Added by the Firm ($000s)

Allocations		Sources	
Depreciation	$70	Sales to Company A	$700
Taxes other than corporate profits taxes	40	Sales to Company B	250
Social insurance contributions	27	Sales to Company C	375
Wages and salaries	695	Sales to Company D	80
Interest	15	Other sales	110
Provision for corporate profits taxes	49	Inventory increase	100
Dividends paid	50	Total value of production	1,615
Undistributed profits	29	Minus: Goods and materials purchased from other firms	640
Total allocations of value added	$975	Total valued added	$975

The sources side of the production statement is adjusted by subtracting from the total value of production the cost of goods and materials purchased from other firms. The remainder represents the value added by the activity of this firm. On the allocations side the cost of goods and materials purchased from other firms is omitted; the remaining allocations absorb all of the value attributable to this firm.

An examination of the value added statement reveals that it is possible, in combining these statements for the economy as a whole, to consolidate the sources side of the account and so simplify it considerably. The sales to specific purchasers shown on the individual value added statement can conveniently be classified into four broad categories: sales to domestic producers, sales to domestic consumers, sales to the government, and sales abroad. For purposes of consolidation, it will be useful to divide sales to producers further into sales of capital equipment and sales of goods, materials and services for current use. But the purchases by producers of goods, materials and services for current use also appear on the sources side of the value added statement as a subtraction. These goods, materials and services purchased by producers must have been obtained either from other domestic producers or from abroad. That part purchased from other domestic producers is identical with the sales to producers of goods, materials and services separated out above, and can be subtracted directly from it. Both the sales and the purchases by domestic producers from each other will thus disappear from the consolidated value-added statement. The remaining part of the goods, materials and services purchased by domestic producers and obtained from abroad can be subtracted from their sales abroad, leaving net sales abroad. The sources side of the account thus reduces to the following items only: sales to consumers, sales to the government, sales to producers on capital account, net sales abroad and net change in inventories. The subtraction for goods, materials and services purchased from other producers found on the individual firm's value-added statement has thus entirely disappeared, having been subtracted from the appropriate categories of total sales.

The allocations side of the consolidated production statement for the economy follows directly from the allocations side of the value added statement for the individual firm, with some minor changes in terminology and the addition of several classifications that do not ordinarily appear on the income statement of a corporation, but do appear on other income statements in the economy. The consolidated production statement can be referred to as the national allocations and expenditure account. This account for the United States for the year 1947 is shown in Table 1.4.

Table 1.4 National Allocations and Expenditures Account for the United States in 1947 ($mn)

Allocations		Sources	
Depreciation	$13,299	Sales to consumers	$164,755
Taxes other than corporate profits taxes	18,488	Sales to government	27,952
Social insurance contributions	5,588	Net sales to abroad	8,898
Wages and salaries	121,913	Sales to producers on capital account	29,413
Income of unincorporated enterprises	45,997		
Net interest	4,293	Change in inventories	618
Dividends	6,880		
Corporate profits taxes	11,709		
Undistributed profits	11,195		
Adjustments to allocations	−7,726		
Total charges against GNP	$231,636	Total sources of GNP	$231,636

Source: US Department of Commerce, *Survey of Current Business*, July 1948, pp. 16–17.

A more detailed account for national allocations and expenditures in the United States for the years 1946 and 1947 is given in Table 1.5. This table uses the classifications and terminology that are in general use. 'Capital consumption allowances' includes for the economy virtually the same items that depreciation charges cover for the firm. 'Indirect taxes' are the same as 'Taxes other than corporate profits taxes' shown on all the previous accounts. The adjustments to allocations are of four kinds. They are: *business transfer payments*, which include primarily that part of the value of goods sold which producers do not receive because of consumers' bad debts, and also such

Table 1.5 National Allocations and Expenditures for the United States in 1946 and 1947 ($bn)

Allocations	1946	1947
Capital consumption allowances	$11.8	$13.3
Indirect taxes	17.5	18.5
Social insurance contributions	5.9	5.6
Wages and salaries	111.4	121.9
Income of unincorporated enterprises and rental income of persons	41.8	46.0
Net interest	3.4	4.3
Dividends	5.6	6.9
Corporate profits tax	9.0	11.7
Undistributed profits	7.2	11.2
Adjustments to allocations	−4.3	−7.8
Business transfer payments	(0.6)	(0.6)
Statistical discrepancy	(1.0)	(−3.4)
Current surplus and government enterprises minus subsidies	(−0.9)	(0.1)
Inventory valuation adjustment	(−5.0)	(−5.1)
GNP by Allocations	$209.3	$231.6

Expenditures	1946	1947
Consumers' expenditures	$147.3	$164.8
Durable goods	(16.2)	(21.0)
Non-durable goods	(87.5)	(96.5)
Services	(43.6)	(47.3)
Government expenditures on goods and services	30.8	27.9
Net foreign investment	4.7	8.9
Exports	(12.7)	(17.8)
Minus imports	(8.0)	(8.9)
Gross private domestic investment expenditures	26.5	30.0
New construction	(8.9)	(11.7)
Producers' durable goods	(12.8)	(17.7)
Net change in inventories	(4.8)	(0.6)
GNP by Expenditures	$209.3	$231.6

Source: US Department of Commerce, *Survey of Current Business*, July 1948, pp. 16–18, Tables 1, 2, 4 and 10.

allocations of total receipts as charitable contributions and prizes offered by producers to the public; *statistical discrepancy*, which results from the fact that the two sides of the account are estimated from different statistical data — theoretically there should be no difference between the two sides; *current surplus of government enterprises minus subsidies*, which is shown as a net item because it is not possible to obtain separate estimates of these two items from the United States statistics. Considered separately, the current surplus of government enterprises is the residual allocation item of government enterprises, in exactly the same manner that undistributed profits is the residual item for business enterprises. Subsidies are subtracted from the total allocations in the economy so that these total allocations will not add up to the total receipts of producers (i.e., market value plus subsidies), but rather only to the total market value of production (gross national product). And finally, there is the *inventory valuation adjustment*, which arises because, whenever prices change, an inventory profit or loss is automatically included in business accounts: inventories therefore are revalued so that the profit figures will not include this price change in inventories. On the other side of the account, the items which were shown as sales in Table 1.4 are termed expenditures in Table 1.5. The specific changes are self-explanatory.

The production statement for the economy is, thus, based upon a consolidation and combination of the production statements of individual firms. It shows the total market value of the national output. The sources side of the production statement for the economy shows the relation between the output produced and the output sold to the various purchasers in the economy. The allocations side of the national allocations and expenditures account show how the expenditures for the gross national product are split up among the various categories of allocations in the economy. The current transactions that have taken place over a given period of time have thus been so consolidated and combined as to reveal the pattern of productive activity in the economy.

An Account for the Consuming Sector of the Economy

The derivation of a summary account for the consuming sector of the economy does not involve the problems of adjustment and consolidation which are met in deriving the national allocations and expenditures account for the producing sector from the income statements of individual firms. The income and expenditure accounts for individuals can be combined directly to obtain the personal income and expenditure account for the consuming sector. Such an account for the United States in 1946 and 1947 is shown in Table 1.6.

Wages and salaries are by far the largest category of receipts of income. In addition to wages and salaries, income in the form of interest and dividends, and the income of unincorporated enterprises also arise from productive

Table 1.6 Personal Income and Expenditure Account for the United States in 1946 and 1947 ($bn)

Allocations	1946	1947
Consumers' expenditures	$147.3	$164.8
Durable goods	(16.2)	(21.0)
Non-durable goods	(87.5)	(96.5)
Services	(43.6)	(47.3)
Personal income taxes	18.9	21.6
Personal saving	11.8	8.8
Allocations of personal income	$178.0	$195.2

Sources	1946	1947
Wages and salaries	$111.4	$121.9
Income of unincorporated enterprises and rental income of persons	41.8	46.0
Net interest	3.4	4.3
Dividends	5.6	6.9
Net government interest (on the public debt)	4.4	4.4
Business transfer payments	0.6	0.6
Government transfer payments	10.8	11.1
Total personal income	$178.0	$195.2

Source: US Department of Commerce, *Survey of Current Business*, July 1948, pp. 16–18, Tables 2, 3, 7, and 9.

activity. Furthermore, both the government and the producing sector may make payments to individuals for reasons other than services rendered. The government may, for example, pay out relief or give bonuses to veterans, and producers may make contributions to charity, cancel bad debts or give out prizes for advertising purposes. All such payments are referred to as transfer payments.

On the allocations side of the personal income and expenditure account, it is useful to consider three basic categories: consumers' expenditures, taxes and other payments to the government, and saving. That portion of income which does not fall into either of the first two categories is automatically classified in the third category, saving. Thus the purchase of a house, using a part of current income to make this capital expenditure, would appear in the personal income account as personal saving; it would signify that the buyer had not *consumed* all the income that he was paid in this period. The purchase of a house is a change in the form of the buyer's assets from cash to property, but it is not a current consumption expenditure, and so does not affect his current account. The two sides of the personal income account again will always balance, because of the definition of personal savings as total personal income minus personal taxes and consumers' expenditures. For instance, the receipt by an individual of $1,000 of income would simultaneously increase his savings by the same amount. This additional saving can decrease only after the individual has had an opportunity to spend the money, thus increasing consumers' expenditures. Personal saving is the balancing item in the personal income account, in exactly the same way that profit is the balancing item in the income statement for a firm. The account for the consuming sector thus shows the economic activity of consumers in terms of the sources of their income and the pattern of their allocations.

An Account for the Government Sector of the Economy

The account for the government sector, like the account for the consuming sector, is merely a record of receipts and expenditures. The government sector includes all the agencies of the federal, state, and local governments, except the current accounts of government-owned productive enterprises. The latter are included in the producing sector in the statistics for the United States; purchases by such government enterprises on capital account are considered to be current expenditures of the government sector proper. Furthermore, under the system of government accounting used in the United States, all of the expenditures of the government itself are considered to be current expenditures and the government has no capital account. In most of the other countries that have national income accounts, a separation is made between the current and capital transactions of the government. In these cases, capital receipts and capital expenditures would be excluded from the current account of the government sector. The government receipts and expenditures account for the United States for the years 1946 and 1947 is given in Table 1.7.

Table 1.7 *Government Receipts and Expenditures Account for the United States in 1946 and 1947 ($bn)*

Allocations	1946	1947
Government expenditure on goods and services	$30.8	$27.9
Net government interest (on the public debt)	4.4	4.4
Government transfer payments	10.8	11.1
Government surplus	4.4	14.1
Total government expenditures and government surplus	$50.4	$57.5
Receipts	1946	1947
Indirect taxes	$17.5	$18.5
Social insurance contributions	5.9	5.6
Corporate profits taxes	9.0	11.7
Personal income taxes	18.9	21.6
Current surplus of government enterprises minus subsidies	–0.9	0.1
Total government receipts	$50.4	$57.5

Source: US Department of Commerce, *Survey of Current Business*, July 1948, pp. 17–18, Tables 8, 9 and 10.

The balancing item in the government sector account is the deficit or surplus of receipts over expenditures. Where total expenditures are smaller than total receipts, the surplus will be shown as a positive allocation item. A deficit will appear as a negative item on this side. The situation is directly comparable to personal saving on the personal income and expenditure account. Most of the other items are self-explanatory. The item 'Current surplus of government enterprises minus subsidies' appears as a receipt, since these current surpluses do constitute a receipt for the general government account. As was noted above, it is not statistically possible to separate out subsidies.

An Account for Transactions with the Rest of the World

No country in the world today is entirely self-sufficient and for this reason a complete record of economic activity will require some consideration of the transactions which take place between the domestic economy and the rest of the world. The rest-of-the-world account is a summary of the imports, the exports, the net capital movements and the changes in the gold stock which have taken place. This is shown in Table 1.8.

Table 1.8 Rest-of-the-World Account for the United States in 1946 and 1947 ($bn)

	1946	1947		1946	1947
Exports	$12.7	$17.8	Long-term net capital movement	$3.6	$7.7
Minus imports	8.0	8.9	Short-term net capital movement	0.9	0.0
			Change in gold stock	0.6	2.2
			Errors, omissions and adjustments	−0.4	−1.0
Net current exports	$4.7	$8.9	Net disinvestment in United States	$4.7	$8.9

Source: US Department of Commerce, *Survey of Current Business*, July 1948, p. 18, Table 11.

The balancing item on this account is that entitled 'Errors, omissions and adjustments'. Theoretically, the account should balance, but the nature of statistical estimates is such that exact balance cannot be expected. The rest of the world account as presented here is extremely condensed, and for any major consideration of balance of payments problems a much more elaborate and detailed presentation would be necessary, but the nature of the account would remain essentially unchanged.

An Account for Gross Savings and Investment

The gross savings and investment account presents no new information; it merely completes the accounting system. The meaning of this account in economic terms can best be understood if the type of transaction it contains is analyzed. The gross savings and investment account for the United States in 1946 and 1947 is shown in Table 1.9.

Table 1.9 *Gross Savings and Investment Account for the United States in 1946 and 1947 ($bn)*

	1946	1947		1946	1947
Gross private domestic investment	$26.5	$30.0	Capital consumption allowances	$11.8	$13.3
New construction	(8.9)	(11.7)	Undistributed profits	7.2	11.2
Producers' durable goods	(12.8)	(17.7)	Personal savings	11.8	8.8
Net change in inventories	(4.8)	(0.6)	Government surplus	4.4	14.1
Net foreign investment	4.7	8.9	Inventory valuation adjustment	−5.0	−5.1
Long-term net capital movement	(3.6)	(7.7)	Statistical discrepancy	1.0	−3.4
Short-term net capital movement	(0.9)	(0.0)			
Change in gold stock	(0.6)	(2.2)			
Errors, omissions and adjustments	(−0.4)	(−1.0)			
Total gross investment	$31.2	$38.9	Total gross savings	$31.2	$38.9

Source: US Department of Commerce, *Survey of Current Business*, July 1948, pp. 16–18, Tables 2, 5 and 11.

A careful examination of this account will reveal that every item in it has already appeared on the opposite side of one of the other accounts. The item 'gross private domestic investment', which appears on the left-hand side of the gross savings and investment account, can also be found on the right-hand side of the account for the producing sector, Table 1.5. 'Capital consumption allowances' appears on the right-hand side of Table 1.9, and it will be found on the left-hand side of the account for the producing sector. Each of the other items can similarly be matched with an identical item elsewhere in the system of accounts. In order to understand why specific items appear on this account, it will be necessary to consider the nature of the transactions involved.

Transactions can always be looked at from two points of view. Wherever there is a buyer, there must of necessity be a seller. If the buyer purchases a good for current use, the purchase will go down in his accounts as a current expenditure. Likewise, if the seller is selling his goods as a part of his regular economic activity, the sale is recorded on his books as a current receipt. Thus every transaction between sectors which is on current account for both the buyer and the seller will enter the national accounts twice. In one sector it will appear as an allocation of receipts, and in a second sector it will appear as a source of receipts. A review of the content of the system of national accounts described so far will verify that this is true for every transaction of this nature. But there are also other types of transactions. A producer may purchase from another producer capital goods which do not represent a *current allocation* for the buyer, but rather are of the nature of capital outlay. In such a circumstance, the transaction will not appear on the accounts of the buyer as a current allocation of funds. For the producer selling the capital goods, however, the receipt of income from this sale will be a current receipt. This transaction would appear as a source of receipts in the account for the producing sector, since it is included in the current sales of the seller, but it would not appear in the allocations of any other current account, since for the purchaser it is a transaction on capital account. The gross savings and investment account is designed to include transactions of this type. In similar manner, some current allocations of income do not result in the receipt of current income elsewhere in the economy. Personal savings, for instance, result from the failure to spend a portion of personal income received; since the essence of saving is not spending, this is an allocation of personal income which will not appear as a receipt on any other current account in the economy. Therefore it is entered on the gross savings and investment account. The gross savings and investment account thus shows all of those capital expenditures or capital allocations which, looked at from the opposite point of view, enter into the current accounts of any of the sectors of the economy.

The Major Characteristics of National Income Accounting

This presentation of a system of national accounts is intended to emphasize two major properties of such a system. First, it is possible to set up an account to show the current activity of any part of the economy and second, it is possible to show the interrelation of these various parts of the economy, by building a complete set of accounts in which every current transaction is shown both as an allocation and as a receipt. The division of the economy into three specific sectors and the use of a system of five accounts is in no way basic to the system. The illustrative accounts used above are merely one specific set of consolidated accounts based on the general principles of national income accounting. The form of the accounts might be quite different, and yet conform fully as much to the fundamental concepts of national income accounting. For many purposes it would be useful to divide the producing sector up into a number of separate industrial groups, each of which would have separate accounts, and it might also be preferable to show the purchases of producers from one another rather than consolidating them as is done in the national allocations and expenditures account. An example of such an expanded system of national income accounts for the United States in 1939 is shown in Table 1.10.

This table follows much the same general classification system as that which was used above for the five basic accounts, except that the business sector has been further broken down into individual industries. The column for an industry or sector shows how that industry or sector allocates its income, and thus corresponds to the left-hand side of its account; the row shows the sources from which it obtains its income, and corresponds to the right-hand side of the account. The total of each vertical column is equal to the total of the horizonal row having the same title. To demonstrate in more familiar form the nature of the table, the row and column for agriculture have been copied out side by side in Table 1.11; data from the column are on the left and data from the row are on the right.

This account shows the sources from which agricultural receipts were derived, and how these receipts were allocated among the different types of expenditures. In 1939, the total value of agricultural products (i.e., the total receipts from the sales of the agricultural industry) was $10.5 billion. Most of this production ($5.1 billion) went into the channels of wholesale and retail trade; some of it ($2.0 billion) went directly into manufacturing firms for further processing. Another $2.0 billion was purchased by the household sector directly, and $0.5 billion of agricultural products were exported to foreign countries. Contract construction used $0.4 billion of agricultural products, and agriculture itself used $0.3 billion of its own products.

On the allocations side, agriculture bought $3.8 billion of supplies from the business sector. Direct imports from foreign countries by agriculture amounted to only $0.1 billion. Taxes took another $0.5 billion of agricultural income and $1.1 billion was paid out in the form of wages and salaries. Interest charges amounted to $0.4 billion. After $1.0 billion was allotted for depreciation of farm equipment and buildings, $4.5 billion was left to farm proprietors as net income. The total allocations of farmers added up to more than the total value of farm production; the additional funds were supplied by the government subsidy to farmers of $0.9 billion. This subsidy is shown on the allocations side of the account as a negative item.

Accounts can be derived from the table for all other industries and sectors, just as the above account was derived for agriculture. Furthermore, any fully developed system of national accounts would allow the various industries and sectors to be broken down into much greater detail, in order to show their internal structure. Thus manufacturing is further subclassified into the following groups: food and kindred products, tobacco manufactures, textile mill products, apparel and other finished fabric products, lumber and timber products, paper and allied products, furniture and finished lumber products, printing and publishing, chemicals and allied products, products of petroleum and coal, rubber products, leather and leather products, iron and steel and their products, stone, clay and glass products, nonferrous metals and their products, machinery

Table 1.10 National Accounts for the United States, 1939 ($bn)

	Total business sector	Agri-culture	Mining	Contract con-struction	Mfg	Whole-sale and retail trade
Purchases from business sector	139.0	3.8	1.6	4.0	32.0	81.1
Agriculture	7.8	0.3	*	0.4	2.0	5.1
Mining	3.2	*	0.2	*	2.9	0.1
Contract construction	na	na	na	na	na	na
Manufacturing	51.4	0.3	0.2	0.9	17.2	31.4
Wholesale and retail trade	58.6	2.7	0.5	2.2	5.2	35.8
Finance, ins. and real estate	3.6	0.5	0.2	0.1	1.0	1.2
Transportation	6.0	*	0.2	0.4	2.0	3.1
Com. and pub utilities	4.6	*	0.3	*	1.5	1.8
Services	3.8	*	*	*	0.2	2.6
Purchases from rest of world sector	2.7	0.1	*	*	1.4	1.2
Payments to government sector	12.6	0.5	0.3	0.1	4.6	3.0
Indirect tax and nontax liability	9.4	0.5	0.2	*	3.1	2.4
Corporate profits tax liability	1.4	*	*	*	0.8	0.2
Social insurance contributions	1.8	*	0.1	0.1	0.7	0.4
Personal tax, nontax payments	na	na	na	na	na	na
Payments to individuals (household sector)	58.0	6.0	1.4	2.1	16.3	12.4
Wages and salaries	36.0	1.1	1.1	1.5	14.0	8.7
Net income of proprietors and rental income	14.5	4.5	0.1	0.6	0.4	2.9
Net interest	3.3	0.4	*	*	0.1	0.1
Net dividends	3.7	*	0.2	*	1.8	0.4
Transfer payments	0.5	*	*	*	*	0.3
Allocations to gross saving (capital sector)	8.4	0.1	0.4	0.1	2.9	1.2
Capital consumption allowances	7.9	1.0	0.4	0.1	2.2	0.6
Undistributed profits and statistical discrepancy	1.0	*	*	*	0.7	0.6
Current surplus of government and government enterprises, minus subsidies	–0.5	–0.9	*	*	*	*
Personal saving	na	na	na	na	na	na
Total allocations	220.7	10.5	3.7	6.3	57.2	98.9

*Less than $50 million.

(except electrical), electrical machinery, transportation equipment (except automobiles), and automobiles and automobile equipment.

Commodity classifications could be integrated into the national accounts approach by fitting them into broad industrial categories, as is done in the United Nations industrial classification system. For the capital sector, for example, 20 types of durable producers' goods are available in the United States system of national accounts. In similar ways, the imports and exports of the

Finance, ins. and real estate	Trans- portation	Com. and public utilities	Services	Rest of world sector	Govern- ment sector	House- hold sector	Capital sector	Total economy
2.9	1.9	2.1	9.6	3.8	5.2	63.7	9.0	220.7
*	*	*	*	0.5	0.2	2.0	na	10.5
*	*	*	*	0.5	*	*	na	3.7
na	na	na	na	na	2.3	na	4.0	6.3
*	0.4	0.2	0.8	1.1	0.8	0.8	3.1	57.2
2.0	1.2	1.5	7.5	1.5	1.2	35.7	1.9	98.9
0.3	*	0.1	0.2	*	0.2	11.0	na	14.8
*	*	*	0.3	0.1	0.1	1.2	na	7.4
0.2	0.3	0.2	0.3	*	0.3	2.0	na	6.9
0.4	*	0.1	0.5	0.1	0.1	11.0	na	15.0
*	*	*	*	*	*	0.4	0.9	4.0
1.9	1.0	0.9	0.3	*	0.3	2.4	na	15.3
1.7	0.7	0.6	0.2	na	na	na	na	9.4
0.1	0.1	0.2	*	*	na	*	na	1.4
0.1	0.2	0.1	0.1	*	0.3	*	na	2.1
na	na	na	na	na	na	2.4	na	2.4
8.1	4.3	2.7	4.7	0.2	11.2	3.2	na	72.6
2.3	3.4	1.5	2.4	*	7.5	2.2	na	45.7
3.8	0.1	*	2.1	na	na	0.2	na	14.7
1.6	0.6	0.4	0.1	0.1	1.2	0.8	na	5.4
0.3	0.2	0.7	0.1	0.1	na	na	na	3.8
0.1	*	0.1	*	*	2.5	*	na	3.0
1.9	0.2	1.2	0.4	na	−1.4	2.9	na	9.9
2.0	0.4	0.8	0.4	na	na	0.2	na	8.1
−0.1	−0.2	*	*	na	na	na	na	1.0
*	*	0.4	*	na	−1.4	na	na	−1.9
na	na	na	na	na	na	2.7	na	2.7
14.8	7.4	6.9	15.0	4.0	15.3	72.6	9.9	322.5

rest-of-the-world sector can be broken down by specific commodity. Even for the pattern of consumers' expenditures, specific commodity classifications will be found to be useful.

National income accounting thus provides a general framework into which the current activity of the economy can be fitted. Such a framework is essential to the formulation of general economic policy. Almost every economic policy of any importance whatsoever will affect the current economic activity of the

Table 1.11 Agricultural Account ($bn)

Allocations		
Purchases from the business sector		3.8
Agriculture	0.3	
Mining	*	
Contract construction	na	
Manufacturing	0.3	
Wholesale and retail trade	2.7	
Finance, insurance and real estate	0.5	
Transportation	*	
Communications and public utilities	*	
Services	*	
Purchases from the rest of the world sector		0.1
Payments to the government sector		0.5
Indirect tax and nontax liability	0.5	
Corporate profits tax liability	*	
Social insurance contributions	*	
Personal tax and nontax payments	na	
Payments to individuals (household sector)		6.0
Wages and salaries	1.1	
Net income of proprietors and rental income	4.5	
Net interest	0.4	
Net dividends	*	
Transfer payments	*	
Allocations to gross saving (capital sector)		0.1
Capital consumption allowances	1.0	
Undistributed profits and statistical discrepancy	*	
Current surplus of gvt and gvt enterprises, minus subsidies	0.9	
Personal saving	na	
Total allocations		10.5

Sources		
Total business sector		7.8
Agriculture	(0.3)	
Mining	*	
Contract construction	(0.4)	
Manufacturing	(2.0)	
Wholesale and retail trade	(5.1)	
Finance, insurance and real estate	*	
Transportation	*	
Communications and public utilities	*	
Services	*	
Rest of the world sector		0.5
Government sector		0.2
Household sector		2.0
Capital sector		–
Total economy		10.5

*Less than $50 million.

Sources: Sundry; see Richard Ruggles, *An Introduction to National Income and Income Analysis*, New York: McGraw-Hill, 1949, pp. 138–40, Tables 30 and 32.

different sectors of the economy, and at the same time will alter the relationships of the sectors to one another. It is only by understanding the changes which will result from putting specific economic policies into effect that policies themselves can be understood. The following section will show how national income accounts can be used in economic analysis, and how such analysis is useful as a basis for the formulation of general economic policy.

3. THE USE OF NATIONAL INCOME ACCOUNTING

National income accounting is useful primarily because it constitutes a systematic record of basic information about economic activity, presented in such a manner that it is usable for carrying out meaningful economic analysis. This, of course, does not mean that there are specific formulae which can be applied to the national income accounts to yield an adequate solution to all economic problems. The situation is more nearly analogous to that of the typical business firm. Accounts are necessary for any intelligent operation of a business firm; unless a manager knows about the costs, sales and financial condition of his firm, he is in no position to put well-designed policies into effect. But an adequate set of accounts does not by itself guarantee the success of the firm; there are no magic rules which the manager can apply to his accounts to solve all the problems he faces. For the policies of the firm to meet with success, they must be based on an intelligent appreciation of what has happened in the past, but they must also have behind them the creative ability and judgment of the policy-makers. In similar manner, the analysis of national accounts is necessary for the formulation of successful economic policies, but the accounts are not the only necessary ingredient. They do not and cannot provide a general panacea.

National Income Accounts and Economic Analysis

The term 'economic analysis' means many things to many men. To some, it brings to mind elaborate and detailed studies on a highly technical level. It is not in this sense that the term will be used in the following discussion; it will refer instead to the use of national accounts to obtain a general understanding of what is or what has been taking place in the economy. Four major areas of inquiry arise in an evaluation of what is taking place in the economy as a whole.

The *first* is a consideration of the general level of production in the economy. In most countries some measure of this nature serves as an overall barometer of the state of the economy. The *second* is an appreciation of how the nature of the production is changing. A general increase or decrease in total production never results from an equal change in all industries; some industries grow at the expense of other industries, and it is necessary to look beneath the general level of change to discover which industries are in the main responsible for the growth, the decline, or the altered nature of production. The *third*, closely related to the second, is the allocation of resources among industries. A limited quantity of resources is available in the economy, and the manner in which these resources are allocated among different productive uses is extremely important. The *final* area is the examination of the manner in which production is utilized in the economy. This field of inquiry is concerned with end uses: the changes which take place in consumption, investment, and government expenditures. The goals of economic activity are understandable only in terms of these end uses of production.

The general level of production
Gross national product at market prices has already been developed as a measure of national output. In deriving this measure, the total value of productive activity which has occurred in the economy was calculated by adding up the value added by each productive unit in the economy. The level of production for the whole economy can only be expressed in an aggregate of this general nature; the output of many unlike things can only be added together to obtain a total if there is some common basis for measurement. Expressing all production in terms of value provides such a common basis. But a statistical series showing gross national product at market prices in each year will not necessarily provide a satisfactory indicator of the level of production.

A change in gross national product may occur either because of a change in the level of production or because of changes in prices. In actual practice almost all changes in the gross national product are the result of both types of change. The most general method of dealing with this problem in the past has been to deflate each major category of expenditures in the gross national product by an appropriate index of its change in price. The figure so obtained is then considered to be a measure of the change in the physical volume of production in the economy. Because of the inadequacy of the price indexes which are used, however, such a procedure is not always satisfactory. More recently, attempts have been made to build up gross national product in terms of constant prices. This process involves obtaining for each of the goods and services which appear on the expenditures side of the national allocations and expenditures account an individual series on physical volume purchased.

These individual physical volume series are then combined into one total value series for the whole economy by valuing each commodity in terms of a fixed price rather than in terms of the changing prices applicable to each different year. The resulting change in the gross national product must be due to changes in physical output, since the commodities themselves are valued throughout the series of years in terms of the prices for one year alone (for example, constant prices). It would also be possible to compute an index of gross national product in constant prices by another method. If the production of each individual industry or economic activity could be reduced to a physical output series, it would then be possible to combine these series into a total for the whole economy by the use of value added weights. Constant value added weights could be used to combine a set of physical output series in exactly the same way that constant prices can be used to combine the set of series on physical volume of goods and services purchased.

There is a close relation between gross national product in constant prices and the more widely known indexes of industrial production. Both measures can be computed in exactly the same manner, and they may make use of the same basic data. The difference is one of coverage. Gross national product refers to *all* productive activity which takes place in the economy, whereas an index of industrial production ordinarily refers only to certain commodity-producing groups. Such economic activities as wholesale and retail trade, government services, finance and real estate, and all consumer service industries are omitted from most general indexes of industrial production. For the purpose of analyzing the economy as a whole, there is nothing to be gained by excluding these large areas of economic activity from consideration. For this reason, gross national product in constant prices is a more comprehensive measure of output in the economy than is an ordinary index of industrial production.

Gross national product at market prices is not the only national income accounting aggregate which can be used as an overall measure of the national output. No one measure is adequate for all purposes, since it can only present one point of view. Different measurements need not be contradictory; instead they may show different aspects of the same thing. Just as height and weight are different measures of size, so it is possible to set up different measures of production which consider output from different points of view. A number of different measurements of national output — all of them comprehensive in that they include all productive activity — can be developed by considering the allocations side of the national allocations and expenditures account. Two of these measures will be considered here.

Gross national product is produced at the expense of drawing down the previously existing stock of capital goods; the process of production uses up some of the value of the machines, equipment, inventories, etc., which were a part of the stock of capital goods at the beginning of the period. The gross national product therefore contains the contribution of past productive activity, as well as that of the present period. It is possible to derive another measure, 'net national product at market prices', which will exclude these contributions of past production, by deducting capital consumption allowances from the gross national product at market prices. Capital consumption allowances are an estimate of the capital goods used up by the economy during the period under consideration. Net national product excludes the contributions of past production (measured by capital consumption allowances), and is thus a measure of current production in the sense of production due to the activities of the current period alone, excluding the services of capital goods produced in the past. Both the gross and the net national product as described above are valued in terms of market prices, and so far there has been no mention of any alternative method of evaluating production. It would be quite possible, however, to value either an individual firm's output or the total national output at what it costs in terms of the factors of production used, rather than at what it brings on the market. Such a valuation in terms of factor cost would be more closely related to the utilization of resources in the economy.

An example may help to clarify this point. In 1947, the tobacco manufacturing industry produced tobacco products that it was able to sell on the market for about $3.0 billion. The goods, materials and services that it bought from other producers to make these tobacco products cost about $1.0 billion. Therefore, the manufacturers added about $2.0 billion of market value to the goods they purchased from other producers; this is the gross product of the industry, valued at market prices. But these tobacco products did not cost $2.0 billion to produce in terms of the factors of production that went into them. Tobacco products are heavily taxed, and the manufacturers paid over $1.5 billion in federal and state excise taxes alone. Of the amount remaining to the manufacturers after excise taxes (about $0.5 billion), a little less than $0.4 billion was available for allocation to the current factors of production, including profits. In other words the contribution of the tobacco industry was valued at about $2.0 billion on the market, yet, in terms of the cost of the current factors of production used, this contribution was worth less than $0.4 billion. The reason for the difference is of course that some of the allocations of the market value of output do not go to pay the factors of production. Indirect business tax and nontax liabilities to the government, such as excise and sales taxes, are legally required payments rather than costs incurred by the producer for employing specific factors of production. Social insurance contributions and taxes on the factors of production, however, are a part of the factor cost to the producer. He must pay them only if he hires the specific factor of production to which they relate; therefore they are a cost of using this factor of production. Such direct levies are quite different from indirect taxes. The indirect taxes do not fall on any specific factor of production and so cannot be considered part of the cost of hiring any specific factor.

Net national product at factor cost, since it is equal to the amount paid to the factors of production in return for their contributions to production, can also be considered as the factor income originating from production, or more briefly, for the nation as a whole, national income. Combining these two concepts, it is possible to draw up a national income and net national product account for the economy. Such an account for the United States for 1946 and 1947 is shown in Table 1.12.

The allocations side of this account contains only those allocations which can be considered 'factor' income. On the expenditure side, the gross national product at market prices has been reduced to represent the value of net product at factor cost by the subtraction of those allocation items which are not a part of factor cost. Like the previous accounts, the two halves of the national

Table 1.12 *National Income and Net National Product Account for the United States in 1946 and 1947 ($bn)*

Allocations	1946	1947
Social insurance contributions	$5.9	$5.6
Wages and salaries	111.4	121.9
Income of unincorporated enterprises and rental income of persons	41.8	46.0
Net interest	3.4	4.3
Dividends	5.6	6.9
Corporate profits tax	9.0	11.7
Undistributed profits	7.2	11.2
Inventory valuation adjustment	−5.0	−5.1
National income	$179.3	$202.5

Sources	1946	1947
Consumers' expenditures	$147.3	$164.8
Durable goods	(16.2)	(21.0)
Nondurable goods	(87.5)	(96.5)
Services	(43.6)	(47.3)
Government expenditures on goods and services	30.8	27.9
Net foreign investments	4.7	8.9
Exports	(12.7)	(17.8)
Minus: Imports	(8.0)	(8.9)
Gross private domestic investment expenditures	26.5	30.0
New construction	(8.9)	(11.7)
Producers' durable goods	(12.8)	(17.7)
Net change in inventories	(4.8)	(0.6)
Gross national product at market prices	209.3	231.6
Minus: Capital consumption allowances	11.8	13.3
Net national product at market prices	197.5	218.3
Minus: Indirect taxes	17.5	18.5
Business transfer payments	0.6	0.6
Current surplus of government enterprises minus subsidies	−0.9	0.1
Statistical discrepancy	1.0	−3.4
Net national product at factor cost	$179.3	$202.5

Source: US Department of Commerce, *Survey of Current Business*, July 1948, pp. 16–18, Tables 1, 2, 4 and 10.

income and net national product account will balance, since it has been derived from the gross national allocations and expenditures account by the subtraction of equal amounts from both sides.

Gross national product at market prices, net national product at market prices and net national product at factor cost (or national income) are thus all different ways of evaluating production in the economy. Not one of them is better for all purposes than the others; each is useful for some purposes. In making a choice between them, there is no question of which is the better measurement, but rather which measure is applicable to the specific problem being studied.

Sources of production in the economy

Once a measurement of total production has been obtained, it is useful to consider where in the economy this production originates. Logically any of the aggregates described in the last section could be broken down by the industry in which they originate, and there is considerable difference in the practices of different countries with regard to the particular measure which is used to show the relative importance of the different industries in the economy. In the United States, the measure chosen is the national income. Table 1.13 shows national income originating for the United States for 1946 and 1947.

The breakdown of this table by industry illustrates the manner in which national income accounting can be expanded for specific sectors of the economy which may be of special interest for particular problems. A more detailed treatment would be possible if desired: in the United States statistics, data are currently published on national income originating for over 70 industries. A comparison of the income originating in any one year in two different industries

Table 1.13 *National Income Originating by Industry for the United States in 1946 and 1947 ($mn)*

	1946	1947
Agriculture, forestry, and fishery	$17,972	$19,287
Mining	3,007	4,034
Contract construction	6,488	8,733
Manufacturing	48,125	61,715
Wholesale and retail trade	33,225	37,531
Finance, insurance and real estate	15,046	16,479
Transportation	10,318	11,382
Communications and public utilities	4,948	5,402
Services	17,184	18,831
Government and government enterprises	22,681	18,687
Rest of the world sector	295	419
Total national income	$179,289	$202,500

Source: US Department of Commerce, *Survey of Current Business*, July 1948, p. 19, Table 13.

will give a measure of the relative importance of these industries in terms of production valued at factor cost. In comparing different countries, also, the differences in the relative importance of industries will throw considerable light on the economic differences of these countries.

National product valued on the basis of income originating by industry could also be computed in terms of constant prices, in a manner similar to that employed in computing aggregate net national product at factor cost in constant prices. Such a procedure would in fact result in a set of physical output series for each industry, equivalent to industrial production indexes for these particular industries: they would show the change in the level of productive activity that had occurred in each of the separate industries.

A breakdown of the national income accounting aggregates by industry origin can thus reveal the structure of productive activity in the economy. The relative importance of production in the various industries can be obtained by a direct comparison of these data expressed in current prices. By using constant prices as the basis of valuation, the change in the level of production over a period of time can be shown separately for each industry.

The allocation of resources in the economy

Closely allied to the problem of where in the economy production originates is the question of where in the economy resources are allocated. For a complete study of resource allocation, there are considerable advantages to using a system of national accounts which includes the inter-industry transactions, such as that shown in Table 1.10. The use of industry accounts in which, through the process of consolidation, inter-industry transactions are omitted would in some cases give a distorted picture of resource allocation. In the first place, the definitions adopted for industries are usually legalistic or arbitrary, so that what is considered production within one industry and what is considered a separate industry sometimes bears little relation to economic processes. If all of the resources used (including goods and materials purchased from other firms) by each specific type of productive activity are not shown, a change in the definition of an industry or sector could make it appear that there had been a change in the patterns of resource use, even though no basic changes had taken place. In the second place, inter-industry transactions are in themselves of importance in the study of resource allocation, since substitution of one type of material for another, or of one factor of production for another, is often possible. For these reasons, any consideration of resource allocation by industry which omits the interrelationships among industries will of necessity be only a partial treatment. The expanded system of accounts shows all of the factors of production and all of the materials used in the productive activity of each industry, and makes it possible to trace the flow of resources through the economy. With such a system, a change in the definition of an industry, or a substitution in resources used — for instance, the purchase of materials for the direct employment of factors to produce the materials, would show up as shift in the distribution of the allocations of the industry involved, rather than an apparent change in the total amount of resources employed.

Although attempts are sometimes made to show the value of the resources employed in constant prices, in a manner similar to the calculation of output or expenditures in constant prices, such an operation not only is difficult but in addition is of extremely doubtful validity. Resources, because of their incomparable physical units, can only be measured in terms of the remuneration they receive. Different types of labor, for instance, are evaluated according to the pay they receive. But when an industry pays higher wages the increase may be due to either a higher wage rate for the same labor or the employment of a more efficient grade of labor; in other words, in the absence of specific information the change in the price of the resource cannot be distinguished from the change in the quantity or quality of the resource. The attempt to filter out price changes and show only quantity changes therefore has very little meaning. To provide a substitute approximation to the physical quantity of resources employed, many countries show the actual number of persons engaged in each industry, in addition to the monetary measure of the value of resources used. This breakdown of manpower for the United States for 1946 and 1947 is shown in Table 1.14.

For convenience, only the major industrial classifications are shown in the table, but the data do exist in the same detailed industrial breakdown as that for which national income originating is available. The need for manpower data

Table 1.14 *Number of Persons Engaged in Production by Industry for the United States in 1946 and 1947*

	1946	1947
Agriculture, forestry, and fishery	7,298	7,562
Mining	913	978
Contract construction	2,448	2,888
Manufacturing	14,691	15,484
Wholesale and retail trade	10,448	10,938
Finance, insurance and real estate	1,836	1,874
Transportation	3,070	3,066
Communications and public utilities	1,105	1,178
Services	6,724	7,051
Government and government enterprises	8,809	6,810
Rest of the world sector	3	2
All industries, total	57,345	57,831

Source: US Department of Commerce, *Survey of Current Business*, July 1948, p. 23, Table 28.

which fit into the national accounting system is so universally recognized that virtually all of the countries which have constructed national income accounts also make available similarly classified information on manpower.

The utilization of production
Economic activity is not an end in itself; it is undertaken in the hope of utilizing the goods and services which it yields in the satisfaction of wants. These end uses of gross national product appear on the expenditure side of the national allocations and expenditures account. This account shows the relative importance of those goods and services consumed by individuals, those purchased by the government, and those devoted to the formation of assets (inventories, plant, machinery, etc.) for use in future productive activity. It also shows whether a portion of current production has been devoted to net exports to foreign countries, or whether net imports from foreign countries have permitted the end uses to exceed production. A comparison of the relative proportions of the gross national product going into each end use in different time-periods or in different countries can also be useful in deriving an understanding of the structural differences in the economies.

As has been pointed out above, the end uses of gross national product can be valued in constant as well as current prices. For periods which are not far removed from each other, the calculation of the expenditures for gross national product in terms of constant prices will yield a measure of physical volume of the goods and services purchased by end-users. Consumers' expenditures in constant prices, for instance, will give some indication of the changes in the standard of living in terms of goods and services. Such a measure is far from entirely satisfactory as an indicator of how well off the individuals in a country are, but it probably serves this purpose better than any one other summary measure. In like manner, government expenditures and investment expenditures in constant prices can provide an index of the volume of goods going into these categories of end uses.

National Income Accounting and Formulation of Economic Policy

Although national income accounting is by itself in no sense a sufficient basis for formulating economic policy, it is of use in helping to answer certain questions about overall economic policies. These questions are of three types. Is the policy which is being considered capable of being achieved in terms of the availability of resources? How does the policy affect the operation of the economy in terms of prices, output and employment? What is the net effect of the policy in quantitative terms? Is it worth pursuing? Each of these questions will be examined in turn.

Economic policy and the availability of resources

Perhaps the majority of economic policies are partial, in the sense that they deal with only one sector or one industry in the economy, and implicitly assume that the rest of the economy will automatically adjust or be adjusted to fit in. Any adequate evaluation of the usefulness of such a policy, however, requires some idea of the extent of the adjustment that will have to be made in the rest of the economy. For this reason, one test of an economic policy which is partial in nature is the examination of how it fits into the framework of available resources. It might seem that almost any policy which advocates increased output somewhere in the economy is basically a good policy, since increased goods and services are a desirable goal. But, when the problem is considered in the context of the potentially usable resources in the economy, it is apparent that advocating an increase in one particular industry is tantamount to declaring that it will be more beneficial to use additional resources in this industry than in any other industry. In other words, such an economic policy, either consciously or unconsciously, involves a decision about which use of resources among all possible uses is preferable. For a valid defense of the policy, it would be necessary to show what additional resources would be needed to carry it out, from what part of the economy such resources could be obtained, and why this particular use would be more beneficial than alternative use of these same resources in other industries.

For all of these questions, the information available in the national income accounts is pertinent. The quantity of additional resources needed to carry out an economic policy cannot be computed without regard to inter-industry relationships. Should, for example, an increase in naval construction be proposed? It is not enough to consider the increased manpower required for actual construction. The manpower and facilities involved in the components industry, in the steel industry, in coal mining, and even in industries as far removed as chemicals and electric power, must also be considered. With a knowledge of the general requirements of the program, the national income accounts show the relative expansion in the output of these industries, or the contraction in the use of their products by other industries, which would be needed to carry the program forward. Alternatives to the proposed policy should also be considered in a similar manner — for instance, in this case it would be useful to study the cost, in terms of economic dislocation, of air fleets, relative to their possible substitutability for naval vessels. The usual comparison in money cost terms alone is not enough. Some parts of the economy cannot easily expand further, whereas other parts may actually be operating below capacity. To ensure the fullest possible utilization of resources such factors as these should be taken into account, and the final economic policy which is recommended should be based on the explicit belief that it is superior to all possible alternatives.

A second major group of economic policies are those which refer to the economy as a whole and are quite general in their coverage. An economic policy of this type is only meaningful if it fits within the limits of the existing resources of the economy, and if it is internally consistent. To try for output goals which far exceed the capabilities of the economy will result in an unbalanced economy, with serious shortages in some lines and supplies which cannot be used in others. Furthermore, the normal expansion of the economy is not brought about by an even overall rate of growth in all industries. The production of food, for example, will not increase at the same rate as the production of steel or even textiles. The rate at which different industries grow is governed by the manner in which the consumer spends his income, the kinds of goods and services which are purchased by the government, and the nature and level of the capital goods industries. Further differences in rates of growth are introduced by technological factors: the ability to utilize mass production permits some industries to operate at decreasing cost, whereas the limitation of available resources prevents expansion in others. Inventions and changes in technology also complicate the situation for almost all industries.

Because of these complexities met in analyzing overall economic growth, the governments of most countries in which national accounts are available use these accounts to make projections of the effects they believe their economic policies will have. These projections are frequently referred to as 'national budgets'; in effect they show the change that is to be expected in each part of the economy. Since these projections of the national accounts are usually presented in terms of constant prices, the separate accounts will only balance and tie in with each other if the net increase in output does not exceed the assumed change in available resources. The making of the projection therefore ensures that the projected changes will be within the expected potential limits of the resources. In this connection manpower budgets are usually also provided along with the national budgets. A comparison of the projected changes in output shown in the national budget and the projected changes in employment shown in the manpower budget will reveal the expected changes in productivity for each industry.

Using the national accounting system to integrate the effects of an overall economic policy with the economy as it exists and as it is expected to change in the future, it becomes possible to see whether the proposed economic policy is consistent with itself and whether it can be expected to produce a result superior to those of alternative general economic policies. Without explicitly making up some sort of projection of national accounts, it is almost impossible to draw up a general policy which is internally consistent and which is in accord with the expected future developments.

Economic policy and the operation of the economy
The foregoing discussion has been concerned with the capabilities and

consistency of economic policy in terms of resource allocation. There are many policies which would pass this type of examination, but which would still be harmful through their effects upon the operation of the economy. Badly designed economic policies can result in serious inflations or depressions, so that it is necessary to give careful consideration to the relation of any proposed policy to the actual functioning of the different sectors of the economy.

An example will demonstrate the use of national accounts for this purpose. Consider a proposal to reduce the public debt. This at first glance may seem to be an entirely laudable economic policy. It might well be demonstrable, in accordance with the foregoing section, that such an undertaking would certainly be within the capabilities of the economic system. Suppose that the actual mechanism proposed is increased taxation of individual incomes in order to obtain a government surplus to be used for debt repayment. Further let it be assumed, for the sake of concreteness, that most of the debt repayments would be to banks holding government bonds. Making use of the sector accounts, it is possible to trace through the effects of both the increase in taxation and the debt repayment. On the personal income and expenditures account, the amount of personal taxes paid would increase, and individuals would be forced to curtail either their personal savings or their consumers' expenditures. In practice it will be found that there is a tendency for both categories to absorb part of the decrease. Since every entry appearing on the account of one sector also appears on another account in the economy, it is necessary to look at the other accounts to see how they will adjust to the changes in consumers' expenditures. In the national allocations and expenditures account, consumers' expenditures must be reduced by the same amount that these expenditures were reduced in the personal income account. This of course means that the total for all expenditures (i.e., gross national product at market prices) must also be reduced, and it follows that if the account is to balance, the allocations will have to change simultaneously. In all probability, as a result of the decline in consumers' expenditures, producers will receive fewer orders and they will, therefore, cut back production, causing some unemployment. If producers do react in this way, the decrease in the gross national product will be largely absorbed by decrease in wages and salaries. This decrease in wages and salaries in turn must be entered on the personal income account, as a decline in personal income. Individuals will undoubtedly react to this decline in their incomes by cutting their expenditures again, and again producers will sell less and so be forced to dismiss more workers, increasing unemployment. In this manner a cumulative decline of output and employment in the economy can be started. Tracing through the effect of the debt repayment to the banks shows that it will not necessarily help the situation. The debt repayment represents a current payment by the government, but it does not represent a current payment of *income* to anyone in the economy. The debt repayment to the banks is from their point of view a capital rather than a current transaction. There is no reason to believe that producers will borrow to expand their investment expenditures merely because the banks now have cash instead of bonds: the level of gross domestic investment in the economy often depends on the current economic outlook — especially when it is unfavorable — more than upon the availability of bank credit. As a result, the more probable development is that with the initial declines in consumers' expenditures and in output and employment, producers will curtail their investment expenditures, so leading to an even sharper decline in gross national product, output and employment. The use of national income accounting thus reveals that this economic policy, designed in this particular way, on the surface apparently desirable, might actually have disastrous results.

Just as a badly designed economic policy can cause a depression, so it can also result in an inflation. Suppose for example that the government, although it desired to keep the budget balanced, decides to equalize incomes somewhat by removing some of the taxes from the lower income groups and placing equivalent taxes on the upper income groups. The immediate results of this action would appear on the personal income account as a rise in consumers' expenditures and a fall in personal saving. The lower income groups would be given larger incomes to dispose of by the tax reduction, and they would undoubtedly react by spending most of the additional money which became available to them. On the other hand, the people of the upper income groups who were now paying more taxes would have to reduce their savings in order to be able to meet the increased taxes and still maintain approximately the same standard of living. In terms of the national allocations and expenditures account, these reactions would appear as an increase in consumers' expenditures, and, if only a limited quantity of goods were available, the prices of consumers' goods would rise. Producers, because of the increase in consumers' expenditures, would have more money to allocate to the factors of production, and more would be available to meet labor's wage demands. Personal income would therefore increase, and consumers' expenditures would again rise, starting the spiral all over again. Producers' reactions to the higher level of activity in the economy would reinforce the spiral: they would increase their expenditures on capital goods and thus further increase the gross national product. Since only a limited amount of goods can be produced with existing resources, a point would be reached when all of the effect of increased expenditures would be felt in a rise in prices rather than in increased output. A badly designed economic policy can, thus, start either an inflationary spiral or a cumulative decline in output and employment.

The design of an adequate economic policy, therefore, demands a careful investigation of the effect the policy will have upon the operation of the economy in terms of prices, output and employment. If, in the examples considered above, it is decided that reducing the public debt and equalizing incomes are desirable ends in and of themselves, careful attention must be given to the design of the specific measures employed to accomplish these ends, in order that they shall not lead to economic disruption. Problems of this nature can only be analyzed adequately within the framework of the national income accounts. It is necessary to consider what will happen in each sector and how reactions to each change will affect the other sectors. Only a complete system of accounts is capable of making explicit the economic mechanisms involved.

Economic policy and its quantitative effect
The final question that must be considered is that of the actual results which an economic policy can be expected to achieve in terms of the goals of the society. National income accounting obviously can never give a complete answer to this question. The welfare of individuals cannot be measured in terms of a few summary measures. There are many nonquantitative ingredients — such things as working conditions, freedom of opportunity, and the moral and political temper of a country. But national income accounting can and does shed some light on what is happening to the end uses of production. The calculations of the expected expenditures on the national allocations and expenditures account in terms of constant prices will show the quantitative change which is expected to occur in the goods and services available for specific end uses. This information, even though it is by no means a complete basis for evaluating any policy, is very much needed.

A quantitative measurement of the net gain is necessary because a policy cannot be advocated solely on the grounds that its expected results would be beneficial. The expected benefits of the policy must be shown to be quantitatively great enough to make it worth while to undergo the risks involved. No action involving an estimate of the future is entirely without risk. Businessmen are constantly faced with the problem of choosing between those policies which have an excellent prospect of making a small gain and those policies involving greater risk but also a possibility of a correspondingly larger gain. Policies which have a large degree of risk attached to a small possible gain are naturally excluded from any reasonable consideration. In like manner, the expected results of an economic policy need to be estimated in quantitative terms in order that the possibility of gain may be weighed against the risks of failure. Many policies which in theory are beneficial may be found, when examined in quantitative terms, to make so little difference that they are not worth undertaking.

2. Concepts of Real Capital Stocks and Services

Richard Ruggles and Nancy D. Ruggles
Yale University

The measurement of productivity is one of the major purposes for which real capital stocks and services data are developed. The very concept of productivity implies that the contribution to output that a factor makes can differ for reasons other than differences in the quantity of that factor. The separation of such influences from quantity changes requires the development of indexes of factor inputs in quantity terms, which can be studied in relation to changes in output, also expressed in quantity terms. This paper will consider the concept of capital in this context.

But the requirements of other uses of concepts of capital stock and services must not be overlooked. In the first place, the measurement of output in real terms requires a determination of the quantity of capital produced. Capital formation not only provides for future input into the economic system; it is also a major component of gross national product and national income, and valid output indexes for the economy as a whole cannot be obtained without considering the method of measurement of the capital produced in different periods. Second, there are some purposes for which a measurement of real capital stocks and services is needed that is based upon the concept of capacity to produce. In the comparison of two different economies, for example, steel capacity may be a good indicator of the relative amount of real capital available in the two countries for the production of steel. For individual industries within countries, also, changes in capacity and in the utilization of capacity provide information relevant to questions of output, employment and investment decisions. And for the guidance of governments spending for social capital, a much wider concept of this sort is needed. Finally, the effort to obtain data in constant prices should not blind us to the large number of uses for which

This chapter first appeared in *Output, Input and Productivity Measurement*, Studies in Income and Wealth, Vol. 25, National Bureau of Economic Research, 1961.

constant price data are not relevant. In the analysis of the flow of funds, the financing of capital formation and decisions with respect to investment, the amortizations and revaluations engaged in by business are the realities of the situation. Deflation or other adjustments aimed at deriving 'real' data may obscure relationships which have an important bearing on decision-making in the economy.

1. THE QUANTITY OF CAPITAL AS A CONCEPT FOR PRODUCTIVITY MEASUREMENT

The concepts involved in measuring the efficiency of capital as a factor of production can be traced back to the basic notions underlying the theory of the production function. In the simplest case, the process is quite straightforward. For example, land, one form of capital, is considered to be one factor of production, labor another factor, and output the result of efficient combinations of varying quantities of these factors. Such a textbook presentation assumes a given state of technical knowledge, constant qualities of land and a constant quality of labor. No time-period is involved, and both factors can be measured in physical units. Land can be measured in acres and labor in man-hours. Such a production function can illustrate the principle of diminishing returns as one factor is increased and the other is held constant. It can also be used to determine whether there are constant returns to scale. There are no ambiguities in any of these concepts.

The introduction of differing qualities of a factor does not complicate the problem very much if quantity is measurable along with quality, and an unambiguous transformation of quality differences into quantity differences is possible. Thus if one piece of land is twice as good as another under all circumstances, the analyst can still study the relationship between land and output with varying amounts of labor. He has a choice of two procedures. Land can be expressed either on a straight acreage basis or in terms of its equivalent in acreage of a constant quality. In the first case, its varying quality will influence the capital–output ratios derived, but for many problems it is precisely this relationship which the analyst wants to study. The second case can also yield interesting results. It does not necessarily preclude productivity change, nor does it necessarily imply constant returns to scale, any more than the initial example cited.

Unfortunately, an unambiguous translation of quality into quantity is not always possible. It is more likely that, as differing intensities of labor are applied to two pieces of land of different quality, different ratios of relative output will emerge. In other words, the marginal rate of substitution of one kind of land for the other is different with different quantities of labor. This general point is raised by both Joan Robinson (1954, p. 95) and R.M. Solow (1956, p. 101) in their discussions of production functions and the measurement of capital. This presents the first so-called index-number problem in the measurement of capital. If we try to include quality differences in the measurement of the quantity of capital, we are saying that the quantity of a given item depends not only on the item itself but also on how much labor is used with it. Thus, the scale by which capital is measured shifts at different points on the production function.

But our problems have just begun. In this simple example no passage of time has been allowed, and thus no technical changes can take place. Also, we still have available a physical measure of the quantity of capital. Since the concept of a physical measure of capital simplifies the analysis so much, economists naturally try to extend it as far as possible. Thus, when they turn from the discussion of land to capital goods they tend to talk about identical machines which can be used in different quantities. Such a framework, however, cannot provide a satisfactory conceptual basis for capital measurement where physical measurement is not possible or where different kinds of capital are expressed in different physical units. The only recourse in these circumstances is to measure capital in some sort of comparable unit in the same way we measure output — in value terms.

Given this sort of measurement, and still staying within a single time-period, there are again two alternatives. First, we can measure capital in terms of input costs. This would mean that an item which costs twice as much to produce as another item is twice as much capital. In terms of the allocation of resources this might be satisfactory, but it leaves one incongruous result. It assumes that in the production of capital there are constant returns to scale, and in some cases this is at variance with common sense reasoning on the basis of physical units. For example, if two pipelines of a given diameter were laid together over a desert, the cost would be less than twice that of installing a single pipeline, due to the economies achieved by putting them in simultaneously. Thus, measured in cost terms the two pipelines are not twice as much capital as one pipeline, even though they function identically. The question here is whether economies in the production of capital goods should reduce the output of capital. Solely for the purpose of analyzing capital as an input, however, the cost basis of measurement would seem to be internally consistent. The second alternative would be to base the measurement of capital on its ability to produce, i.e., either on output or on capacity. But this method also involves problems. An index-number question arises if the marginal rates of substitution between different kinds of capital are different in the periods being compared. Furthermore — and this more seriously impairs the usefulness of this measure for the study of efficiency — since actual capacity or output is used as the measure of quantity, there can never be any change in the productivity of capital. Whereas the first of these alternatives attributes all increase in efficiency to the change in the productivity of capital itself, the second goes to the opposite extreme, attributing the increased efficiency to the greater economy with which capital can be produced.

By introducing time (i.e., technical changes and changes in prices), additional problems are raised. It is commonly held that technical change in the design of capital equipment should not be incorporated into the measurement of the quantity of capital, since this again would be attributing all quality change to changes in the efficiency of producing capital, leading to a productivity index in the use of capital always equal to unity. But it is extremely difficult and often unrealistic to abstract from technical change, unless one goes all the way in the other direction, as in the first of the two alternatives in the preceding paragraph. Although it may be possible to estimate what the capital stock of 1900 would cost in today's prices if the techniques, labor skills and materials of today were used to produce replicas of the buildings and machines of 1900, the reverse is not possible. The techniques, labor skills and materials of 1900 could not produce perfect replicas of today's plant and equipment, since the necessary technical knowledge and equipment would be missing. Thus, even though the problem can be stated in index-number terms, it cannot really be solved in these terms since comparisons can only be made in one direction. In order to get around this difficulty, it has been suggested that standard labor units expressed in terms of product be used to evaluate the cost of the capital stock in each period (Robinson, 1954, p. 86). But this leads to the anomaly that two identical plants would be assigned different capital values if they were produced at different times, although at one moment of time they would have the same cost and the same capabilities (Solow, 1956, p. 101).

There does not seem to be any satisfactory general solution to this problem. The basic fact is that capital in general has no physical units, and any arbitrary solution will predetermine the answers. It will, therefore, be useful to examine the measurements of real capital stock that are currently being made or proposed to see what assumptions they involve, and how these assumptions affect the analysis which is based upon these figures.

2. THE RATIONALE OF EXISTING MEASUREMENTS OF REAL CAPITAL STOCK

In a very stimulating paper presented at the 1953 Conference on Income and Wealth, Edward Denison (1953) set forth three possible methods of measuring capital. The first measures capital by cost. The second measures it by the capacity of the system as a whole to produce output. The third measures it by the contribution which the capital specifically makes to total production. Denison strongly favors the first method. He feels that the second, which makes the stock of capital proportional to total output, is essentially uninteresting, although it might be feasible statistically if certain arbitrary conventions were adopted. The third method, which involves evaluating the contribution to production of each kind of capital good, he believes to be completely beyond any hope of accurate independent measurement. Furthermore, as has already been suggested, method 3 would necessarily lead to an unchanging productivity of capital. Thus Denison settles on the first method, which corresponds fairly well to the current practice of the Department of Commerce in measuring gross capital formation in constant prices.

Even the valuation of capital at cost, however, is not simple and straightforward. If the price of producing capital goods did not change over a period of years, the gross addition to the capital stock in any year would be equal to the value of gross capital formation in that year. Unfortunately, however, the price of producing capital goods does change, so a price index for capital goods is needed to deflate the current price data. It is in arriving at appropriate price deflators that the most difficult conceptual problems of this method become apparent. The problem is somewhat similar to that which would be involved in determining changes in quantities of labor used, given only wage bills in current prices and no direct knowledge of wage rates, man-hours, or employment.

Although Denison wishes to exclude from his index of the output of capital those quality changes in capital goods arising from such things as improvements in design and serviceability, he does not wish to exclude changes in productivity in the production of capital goods. Thus, even though a machine can be produced in period 2 at half the price of the identical machine in period 1, the amount of capital represented by the machine should be the same in both periods. The price index for capital goods, therefore, should not be simply a weighted index of the prices of the inputs used to produce them. In practice this may be done in some areas (notably construction, where the price deflator is a weighted index of labor and materials costs), but Denison considers this an unfortunate defect since the deflated data obscure the productivity changes that occur within the construction industry.

The crucial problem is the separation of design improvements from changes in the cost of production, that is, increases in productivity of capital goods from increases in productivity in the production of capital goods. Design improvement in capital equipment often occurs through simplification. Welding may take the place of riveting, plastic parts may be substituted for metal, or stampings may be used instead of machined parts. Whether these are, in fact, identical machines (to be counted as the same amount of capital) or different machines (to be counted as more or less capital) can only be determined on the basis of function. If with such changes the machine serves the same function,

Denison would probably consider any associated cost changes to relate to the production of capital, i.e., the price index would change but the quantity of capital produced would not. On the other hand, if an increase in the cost of producing the machine were accompanied by improved functioning of the machine, Denison would allow these increased costs to be counted as increased capital because of changed technical specifications. In this case, the machine would be considered a different one, representing more capital, and the price index for producing capital might remain unchanged.

The most ambiguous problem arises in a situation where changes in the design of a machine both reduce its cost and improve its functioning. One is then faced with two alternatives: the cost of producing the machine has fallen, but the quantity of capital is unchanged, or the cost is unchanged but the machine is now a different one that represents less capital. Thus if there is any change in the functioning of the machine, we are forced to decide whether or not it is still the same machine. This decision, in turn, determines the behavior of the price index for capital, and this in turn determines the measure of the quantity of capital produced. Resort to important physical or performance specifications cannot avoid the consideration of function, since it is this that determines what specifications are important. In fact, since specification changes are basically changes in quality — which we wish to exclude from our measure of the quantity of capital — strictly speaking even the most minor changes should require that the machine be treated as a different machine. Pushed to its logical end, this argument leads to the measurement of price behavior by prices of input factors, rather than prices of units of capital output. In practice, this has happened in the construction industry, the problem of identifying units of output has proved so difficult that an output price index is recognized as unsatisfactory, and estimates of construction prices are based upon input prices instead.

Although it is possible to ask what it would cost to construct some standard structure, this would bias the price index in several ways. First, different indexes of change would be obtained for different standard structures: the cost of building an 1890 Victorian house would have changed differently from that of a simple colonial house. Second, as long as construction methods are different there will be differences in supposedly identical structures, and the importance of these differences can only be evaluated in terms of function. For instance, handmade trim for houses differs from machine-milled trim in significant detail. If one asks how much it would cost, given the technology of 1900, to produce trim with the same specifications as today's machine-milled trim, the cost of obtaining the same degree of regularity, in terms of man-hours, might be exorbitant. It would only be because regularity is not considered a very important aspect of the function of house trim that one could consider machine-milled trim and handmade trim the same thing. The use of chained indexes, etc., would perhaps diminish the statistical magnitude of this problem, but it could not eliminate it.

It should be noted that the index-number problem arising from cost-reducing technical change is different from the normal index-number problem: the latter would exist even in the absence of technical change in the cost of producing capital. The problem arises because, although we might now be able to reproduce exactly the products made in 1900, the reverse is not true. The valuation of the capital stock in 1958 as if it could have been produced in 1900 therefore necessarily involves the assumption that price indexes for the cost of capital based on those particular capital goods that are present in unchanged form in both 1900 and 1958 are representative for products which did change. (The use of chained indexes, etc., would perhaps diminish the statistical magnitude of this problem, but it could not eliminate it.) This assumption is, of course, quite likely to be invalid, because the newly introduced capital goods tend to be those for which the cost of production has fallen fastest. The price index based on 1900 would therefore be relatively too high, and the resulting quantity of capital too low. Similarly, taking 1958 as a base, goods which have disappeared since 1900 tend to be ones for which production costs did not fall as fast as for the new capital goods which supplanted them. Thus, while the index using 1958 as base year may be very different from that based on 1900, it too will minimize the increase in the efficiency of making capital goods.

A further consequence, as Denison points out, of adherence to the cost concept for measuring capital goods is that the principles of valuation that would be used for the output of capital goods are different from those commonly used for consumer goods. In measuring the volume of consumer goods we attempt, at least in theory, to include quality change as a part of output, where this measure of capital output tries to exclude it. Denison, however, is inclined to minimize the importance of this consideration. He suggests that quality change excluded from the measurement of capital goods will eventually show up as additional production of consumer goods, and that as long as changes in the quality of other factors of production cannot be taken into account, neglecting such changes in measuring the output of capital goods scarcely seems a critical weakening of the income estimates. For the purpose of the measurement of efficiency, there is a good deal of merit in this argument, but, as will be pointed out below, the qualification becomes more important when we consider other uses to which these estimates of capital stock are put.

A final problem in the interpretation arises in estimating the net value of the capital stock. The measurement of the capital stock not only requires valuation of newly produced capital goods; it also requires consideration of what has happened to the existing stock of capital. Denison would value capital consumption at base year cost for the particular types of capital goods used up. He argues that obsolescence should be charged at the time the capital good is discarded, and that it should be handled as a deduction from gross capital formation rather than as an addition to capital consumption. His rationale is that 'net capital formation' — the net improvement in the capital position of the economy — should be equal to the difference between the contribution to production by the new good (as measured by its cost of production) and the contribution which could have been made by the displaced capital good (as measured by the obsolescence charge).

On the other hand, a different treatment has been proposed by John Kendrick. He suggests (1956, p. 250):

> ... as nonpermanent assets age, their contribution to net output declines; this is the result of declining gross output capacity, increasing maintenance and repair costs, and creeping obsolescence. Obsolescence results in the reduction in the rate of return on old equipment, not only when the installation of new equipment leads to reduced product prices or higher factor prices, but also when the old equipment is utilized less intensively or in less productive activities. Empirical and theoretical considerations suggest that these effects may be assumed to occur gradually over the lifetime of groups of capital equipment.

It might be questioned, however, whether such considerations are relevant to the concept of capital discussed here. In view of the decision to exclude productivity improvement (i.e., increase in efficiency) from additions to the capital stock, it seems incongruous that decreases in the efficiency of existing capital due to ageing should be so carefully taken into account. Just as there is logic in saying that improved design of capital good is not more capital but an increase in its efficiency, so also it is perfectly reasonable to say that the efficiency of capital varies with its age, and that deductions from the quantity of capital to make the productivity of existing capital a constant over its life are not consistent with the desired concept.

Furthermore, as Kendrick implies by his inclusion of 'creeping obsolescence', the ordinary capital consumption allowance would considerably exceed the actual physical deterioration in a capital good over its useful life. Charging such obsolescence against existing capital is allowing for quality changes that have not occurred but are only expected to — those resulting from changes in the technical design of capital goods to be produced in the future. The same technical change that improves the quality of new capital will make the old obsolete. Kendrick's treatment of additions to the capital stock does not count the quality increase due to technical changes in new equipment, but it does take into account the reduction in the relative quality of the existing capital stock because of the increased technical efficiency of new capital equipment which could be constructed. Again, therefore, the treatment of new and old capital does not seem to be parallel.

A more consistent treatment would seem to require that if efficiency increases are to be eliminated from the measurement of the capital stock, efficiency decreases must also be eliminated. Capital should not be deducted from the total stock until its retirement, despite the fact that producers may, for financial reasons and in order to derive a meaningful profit figure, amortize it over its life. This procedure would carry Denison's method 1 a little farther, deriving net investment in each period as gross investment minus discards. Such a concept was used by Evsey Domar (1953) in discussing a model relating changes in capital to changes in capacity.

To summarize, conventional measures of real capital favor a concept based on the cost of production rather than on capacity, partly because of ease of measurement and partly because one of the major purposes of developing real capital data is the analysis of productivity changes. 'Cost', in these terms, is not simply the deflated value of the inputs; it is not intended that increased efficiency in the production of capital should reduce the amount of capital produced. This means that changes in the cost of producing capital must be analytically and statistically separated from changes in the efficiency of utilization of capital. Such a separation, however, requires a physically measurable unit of capital, and this in turn cannot be established without a consideration of the quality and function of capital equipment. Any attempt to separate quantity and quality without considering function is doomed to be arbitrary and subjective. It would perhaps be possible to derive a real capital measurement independently in terms of the quantity of input factors (labor, resources and savings), but this approach does not appear to have much support.

Time and technical change also create problems in the interpretation of the conventional measures of real capital stock. The thesis that real capital can be measured by what it would cost in the base year to produce the given year's stock is not meaningful if technical changes make the comparison an impossibility. If the most recent year is chosen as the base year, the comparison may be possible, but this may also produce a trivial and uninteresting measurement. Finally, in evaluating the net capital stock, one may question the practice of deducting a capital consumption allowance before a capital good is actually retired from service. Such an allowance is in fact an attempt to measure the decrease in the quality of the equipment, whether from physical deterioration or from potential technical obsolescence. Such changes in quality are intended to be excluded from this concept of the quantity of capital.

3. THE USE OF CAPITAL STOCK MEASUREMENTS

Despite these theoretical objections, one cannot help being impressed by the intrinsic interest of the real capital stock series that are obtained by the usual cost deflation procedures. For example, the capital–output ratios for manufacturing from 1880 to 1948 as given in Creamer's study (1954) are most illuminating and give rise to a number of hypotheses. One may reasonably ask why these results are so interesting if their theoretical structure is built on such shifting sands. In part the answer may be given by Creamer's effective demonstration that a number of variants of measures of capital and output yield the same general conclusion as to the pattern of change in capital–output ratios over the years. Creamer points out, for example, that the pattern of change of the capital–output ratios derived by measuring both capital and output in constant prices does not differ very significantly from that for capital and output expressed in the current prices of each period separately. This result would be expected if the price index used to deflate capital did not differ substantially from the price index used to deflate output. Relative to the other changes that occurred during the period, these differences in the price indexes were, in fact, rather small.

Some of the alternative measures discussed above might well yield quite different patterns of change. One cannot say how the ratio of capital to output would be affected in these instances. If the price deflator for capital had been based on the price indexes of input factors alone, not allowing for the change in efficiency in the production of capital, the price deflator would have been raised and, thus, gross capital formation over time lowered. On the other hand, deduction of retirements instead of an allowance for depreciation and obsolescence would probably increase the volume of the capital stock. If quality changes in consumer goods and perhaps capital goods were reflected more fully, output would have been larger throughout the period. The net effect on the pattern of change of the capital–output ratio is highly debatable. Capital–output ratios measured this way would not necessarily be more meaningful than Creamer's, but they might be less arbitrary and more internally consistent.

Furthermore, capital–output ratios based on current price data may also be quite meaningful, because they measure the capacity of the economy to produce in relation to its current efforts. An economy with a small capital–output ratio in this sense could turn out the equivalent of its capital stock in a brief space of time, whereas one with a high capital–output ratio would take many years to build up the capacity needed for the current level of output. By studying current relationships, the difficult problem of price deflation could be avoided. Most dynamic problems concerning capital and capital formation, furthermore, can more usefully be cast in current than in constant prices, since it is the actual flows of income and values in the various periods which are related in a time dimension.

Thus, before we attempt to solve the problem of measuring real capital, we should face the question of how to measure capital stock at a given moment in the prices of a single period. This is not nearly as perplexing as the measurement of capital over time, since many of the index-number problems are absent.

It is still true that a concept of capital that will be useful in the analysis of efficiency should probably not be measured in terms of capacity. Nevertheless, it would be useful to know what it would cost, given existing technology and capacity, to reproduce the *function* of the various capital goods existing in the economy. This does not require that products of another period be reproduced in their exact technological form, but rather brings into play the concepts of capacity, function and substitutability. In a normally competitive economy, this reproduction cost of capital goods (in terms of economic function) would approximate market value, so that we could also ask how a given increment in the volume of capital, valued at the cost of production, would affect annual rates of output. The relationship between the stock of capital, measured in current prices, and the current output or income of the economy in various periods would thus be somewhat similar to Creamer's measurements in current prices. Thus changes in capital–output ratios over time could be calculated without the use of indexes of the quantity of capital or of output.

4. THE MEASUREMENT OF THE REAL SERVICES OF CAPITAL

In the analysis of questions relating to the efficiency of capital, it is of course the services of the capital stock rather than the capital stock itself with which we are really concerned. Many analysts, however, use capital stock data, on the ground that, although the measurement of real capital stock is open to question, the measurement of the real services of capital is even more difficult. As Denison (1953) points out, in measuring real capital services, production cost is not available as a principle of valuation. One is forced to evaluate capital consumption in terms of the ability of capital goods to contribute to production in the future. For this reason it seems necessary here also, before evaluating real capital services, to consider how the services of capital can be valued in current prices.

When a producer purchases a capital good, he expects to use it over a given period. At the end of its useful life, he expects that it will have repaid in services at least its original purchase price. The apportionment of the cost over this useful life is a matter for philosophers and revenue agents. It may be argued, for instance, that the machine should be charged off in a manner which would equalize profit over the period, given no unexpected changes in prices, demand or costs. It is on this basis that peak load facilities of power plants and local transit systems are charged off against their period of use. Alternatively, it may be argued that the services of equipment are greater in its early life when it needs less repairs and maintenance and is utilized more fully. The essential consideration, in either case, is that expected returns be separated from unexpected returns in order to differentiate between operating income and capital gain or loss. If a plant burns down, this should be a capital loss and not a charge against the operating income of the plant in the year it happens. Similarly, unexpected obsolescence, or unexpected capital gain in monetary terms due to general price level rises, should be excluded from current services of capital and reflected instead as capital gain or loss. The services of capital should thus be valued (in current price terms) not in terms of original or historical cost but rather in terms of replacement cost, and the difference between historical cost and replacement cost should be considered capital gain or loss.

There is a problem in relation to gains arising from expected price level changes, but even here, it seems reasonable to distinguish operating income from the gain or loss arising from the producer's dealing in assets and liabilities. We follow this practice in national income statistics in adjusting the income concepts for inventory price changes, and it seems reasonable to make a similar adjustment with regard to capital consumption allowances (see, for example, *The National Economic Accounts of the United States*, Hearings before the Subcommittee on Economic Statistics of the Joint Economic Committee, 1957, esp. pp. 189–93, 153, Appendix tables A-1, A-11 and A-13).

The problem of converting capital services in current prices to capital services in constant prices is not simple. The same dilemma in the construction of a price index faces us here as in the measurement of real capital stock. To include all quality changes as changes in the quantity of capital is to make the resulting index meaningless for the measurement of productive efficiency. On the other hand, the attempt to eliminate those quality changes due to the technical design of capital and to retain those due to changes in the efficiency of production of capital and in its economic usefulness leads to serious difficulties. Of course, if the index for deflating capital services is about equal to the GNP deflator (as seems to be the case in the actual calculations) the relationship between capital services and output in constant prices will be the same as that in the current price data. The results of such a calculation, therefore, may not be meaningless, but what they will reflect will be the relationships in the current price data.

5. CAPITAL GOODS PRODUCTION AS A COMPONENT OF OUTPUT

In recent years the gross national product has steadily increased in favor as a measure of total output, and gross capital formation is a major component of GNP. In the valuation of capital formation as a component of output, certain problems arise in addition to those considered above.

Thus far in the discussion, we have considered only those forms of capital which have market value, and have been content to consider social capital in general as part of the setting within which self-liquidating capital is placed. It has long been argued, however, that certain government expenditures are of the nature of capital, and should be included in any general measure of capital formation. Such a procedure would result in shifting some items from current government expenditures to gross capital formation and including the services of government capital on the expenditure side as part of product and on the income side as an addition to capital consumption allowances.

It can be argued, alternatively, with respect to government enterprises but not to general government, that the services of government enterprise capital goods should not be added to the market value of output but, instead, the surplus of government enterprises should be reduced by the amount of capital consumption taking place.

In the most obvious case, where government enterprises sell their products on the market, such arguments are very persuasive: the form of industrial organization should make no difference in computing gross capital formation. In these cases the government has produced an asset which, like privately held assets, yields a stream of money income for future periods, and the parallel with the private producer is complete. The government may make a loss in the operation of the enterprise, but this situation is no different from the case where the government subsidizes a private industry. The extension of the argument to nonself-liquidating expenditures of the government on hard goods (i.e., goods made of wood, steel or concrete) is less clear, however. This procedure would include roads and other public works as gross capital formation. To the extent that such assets are in fact directly revenue producing (other than by taxes) and it can be determined whether or not they are paying for themselves, such a procedure is legitimate. Thus toll roads might well be considered part of gross capital formation. Government buildings also could be set up as a sort of government enterprise, charging each agency rent at appropriate market values for the space it occupies, thus treating government buildings much in the same way as owner-occupied housing. This has, in fact, often been suggested as a desirable budgetary reform.

On the other hand, the argument is much less clear for other government expenditures on durable goods. There seems little reason to treat nonself-liquidating roads and public works differently from government expenditures on research, education and public health, all of which also improve the amount of social capital available in the economy. The fact that an expenditure is embodied in physically durable materials is not really relevant, and there would be considerable disadvantage in trying to develop a concept of government capital formation which covered all improvements in social capital, since this is a question not of objective fact but of political philosophy.

Expenditures by business on research and development, unlike those by government, are treated in the national income statistics as intermediate products, and so do not add to final product. Such expenditures are becoming increasingly important in changing the setting within which the economy operates, and they are not fully reflected in the changing market value of assets which are counted in output. It would seem highly desirable, therefore, to include research and development in the list of final expenditures on goods and services, even if we exclude it from the concept of gross capital formation. It could, for instance, be carried as a separate item of current expenditure.

Another serious omission from the list of final expenditures is the amount which producers spend on current account for the repair and maintenance of existing capital stock. If these expenditures were constant or were proportional to output, this omission would not be serious, but in fact they vary considerably over time. When producers are making high profits they often take that opportunity to refurbish their plant and equipment. Conversely, in periods when they are having difficulty in paying dividends or even in meeting payrolls, they may postpone maintenance and repair expenditures. In the housing industry this cyclical fluctuation in repair and maintenance is well known. By omitting changes in repair and maintenance from our measure of gross production, we may be neglecting something that is just as important as changes in inventories. Overmaintenance unquestionably adds to the value of the capital stock, and undermaintenance reduces it.

In view of the importance of these two elements — research and development expenditures and repair and maintenance expenditures — serious consideration might be given to the development of a cruder concept of total output than we now have. This need not mean altering the present concept of GNP, but perhaps we could include information on research and development and repair and maintenance in a cruder concept of output which we might term 'gross national expenditure'.

In deriving indexes of real output of capital from the measure of output in current prices (however the latter is defined), many of the problems of deflation considered above are still relevant. If we adopt the solution proposed by Denison, changes in the quality of capital goods would be excluded from output. Output of capital goods would therefore be measured quite differently from that of consumer goods. If, in measuring output, we are trying to approach some sort of welfare index, it seems reasonable to argue that the well-being of a nation is related to its ability to sustain or raise its standard of living in the future, and that omitting the quality change in a nation's productive facilities drastically understates its real progress in this respect. Especially in the case of underdeveloped countries, where a great deal of effort is being put into developing productive capacity, a measure which grossly understates the change in this dimension does considerable violence to the basic purposes of the measurement.

As a final point in the discussion of capital as a component of output, consideration must be given to the derivation of net, as opposed to gross, product. The concept of net product is commonly assumed to be based upon the principle of keeping capital in some sense intact. But there are ambiguities in this concept too. In the first place, if real capital is measured by the cost method, the conventional concept of keeping capital intact is inapplicable. However, as Denison points out, from many points of view the concept of net product remains interesting and meaningful. Second, if, as suggested above, we extend the concept of gross investment to include repair and upkeep, it is necessary to consider the various levels of both maintenance and replacement required to maintain productive efficiency. But there is no unique level that will 'maintain capital intact'. Finally, a concept of real capital which includes reductions in the relative quality of existing capital (obsolescence) but does not include increases in the quality of additions to capital does not appear to be internally consistent. As Domar (1953) has pointed out, our concept of net capital formation as it has conventionally been handled assumes that depreciation equals replacement, and to the extent that this is not true, models based upon such a thesis may not be fully relevant to the questions they are designed to answer.

6. CAPITAL AND THE MEASUREMENT OF CAPACITY

Denison rejected his method 2 — measuring capital by capacity — not only because it made the concept of productivity of capital tautological but also because it posed serious problems of measurement. There are many circumstances, however, in which capacity is an extremely useful tool of analysis. Industry studies have long worried about capital coefficients, asking what amount of capital would be required, with existing technology, to obtain a given increase in capacity. Such studies are important for problems of economic development and for developing the capital portion of input–output matrixes. They are also useful in analyzing the effect of a change in demand for specific products on the capital goods industries. For growth models, also, capacity measurements are extremely important since such models involve an estimation of the impact of an increment of saving and investment on the future stream of income, saving and investment. Recently, capacity measurements have also been used in analyzing short-run fluctuations in income and employment. The underutilization of capacity for the economy as a whole has serious repercussions on the level of investment, which in turn affects the level of income and employment. Both private and government agencies are now engaged in making capacity estimates for various parts of the economy, and in view of the obvious usefulness of capacity as a basic concept in economics, it does not seem reasonable to suggest that efforts to obtain better capacity figures should be abandoned.

This does not, of course, mean that changes in capacity can be identified directly with what we have considered to be capital formation in this paper. Changes in capacity can also result from such things as research and development expenditures, government expenditures on education and health, and other expenditures which may carry with them a social product conducive to quality improvement.

7. FINANCIAL FLOWS AND INTEGRATED ECONOMIC ACCOUNTING

Before concluding this discussion, attention should be drawn once again to the desirability, in any measure of capital stocks and services, of maintaining consistency and comparability with other forms of economic accounting. In studying the financing of capital formation, for instance, it would be useful if capital formation were measured in such a way that it could be assigned directly to decision-making units and financing institutions, so that financial flows and real output could be related to one another empirically as well as theoretically. There are no serious conceptual problems standing in the way of such an integration. The measurement of the capital stock could very well be embodied in the national balance sheets developed for various institutional sectors of the economy. These balance sheets, in order to be useful in studying financial flows, must of necessity extend beyond the concept of national wealth (the capital stock), embracing in addition the financial assets and liabilities held by each sector, but this poses no special problems of integration. The objective of valuing capital in current prices set forth above could be met simultaneously with the maintenance of a record of actual historical financial flows, by carrying assets on each of the balance sheets at market value but showing in addition both realized and unrealized capital gains and losses.

REFERENCES

Creamer, Daniel (1954), *Capital and Output Trends in Manufacturing Industries, 1880–1948*, NBER, Occasional Paper No. 41.

Denison, Edward (1953), 'Theoretical aspects of quality change, capital consumption, and net capital formation', *Problems of Capital Formation, Studies in Income and Wealth*, **19**, 215–61.

Domar, Evsey (1953), 'Depreciation, replacement, and growth', *Economic Journal*, March, 1–32.

Joint Economic Committee (1957), *The National Economic Accounts of the United States*, Hearings before the Subcommittee on Economic Statistics of the Joint Economic Committee, 29 and 30 October.

Kendrick, John W. (1956), 'Productivity trends: Capital and labor', *Review of Economics and Statistics*, August, p. 250.

Robinson, Joan (1954), 'The production function and the theory of capital,' *Review of Economic Studies*, **55**, 95.

Solow, R.M. (1956), 'The production function and the theory of capital', *Review of Economic Studies*, **61**, 101.

3. The Evolution and Present State of National Economic Accounting

Richard Ruggles and Nancy D. Ruggles
Yale University and National Bureau of Economic Research

Economists used transactions information to summarize the behavior of the economic system as long as 300 years ago, when William Petty first prepared an estimate of the national income of England. Since then, a long list of scholars have estimated national income for almost every country in the world. Some investigators have viewed the national income as essentially the total of the income payments made to individuals or households in the nation. For some, the distribution of this income by size, occupation, or type of income was the real focus of interest. Others were more interested in the national income as the net product of the nation, and viewed it as the sum of the production in the various industries.

In order to develop economic constructs of this sort, economists were, of necessity, either implicitly or explicitly using accounting information. There were also other attempts to use transactions information, such as the development of a wholesale price index and a production index, but these efforts did not take a rigorous accounting approach and as a result their basic economic meaning has to this day remained vague and undefined.

In the United States, systematic work on national income was initiated at the National Bureau of Economic Research in the 1920s. In that period, Mitchell, King, Macaulay and Knauth made significant contributions to the measurement of national income in terms of both income payments and industrial distribution.

The depression of the 1930s, with its precipitous decline in income and employment, emphasized the need for more comprehensive information on the performance of the economic system, and concepts were developed and

---

This chapter first appeared in *International Journal of Accounting*, 4 (1), 1968.

sharpened in this period. The classic works written by Simon Kuznets in this field, dating from the late 1930s, provided the basis for future development. Largely because of the National Bureau's interest, the Conference on Research in Income and Wealth was established, and in the years since 1937 it has published over 30 volumes on this topic. In the late 1930s the Department of Commerce established a National Income Division, which started to prepare current estimates of national income on an official basis.

The 1930s also saw the major development of economic theory which was to convert the field of national income measurement into national income accounting. The Keynesian equation, $Y = C + I$, focused attention on the expenditures of consumers and investors, and emphasized the equality of savings and the accumulation of goods. The Keynesian theory also focused attention on the intersectoral relations in the economy. Consumers were differentiated from producers, and the existence of government and foreign trade transactions was recognized. Simultaneously in England, the Netherlands and Norway, a national accounting approach was utilized to show these intersectoral relations. In England, the construction of a national income accounting system was undertaken in 1940, when Richard Stone and J.E. Meade began working closely with Keynes in what later became the Central Statistical Office. In the Netherlands, the Central Bureau of Statistics in 1941 developed a system based on the national bookkeeping concepts of Ed van Kleef and in Norway, Ragnar Frisch published in 1940 a study entitled *National Accounting*. In the United States, the Office of Business Economics of the Department of Commerce, under Milton Gilbert and George Jaszi, was rapidly integrating the various sources of economic information into a unified set of national income statistics. At the same time Wassily Leontief's work on input–output was extending the scope of economic accounting to the analysis of inter-industry relationships.

With the outbreak of World War II, the work in England and the United States was rapidly accelerated to meet the pressures of wartime mobilization. The new national income accounting framework which distinguished different sectors of the economy was extremely useful for analyzing the impact of increased expenditures by the government on prices and output of the economy as a whole. In the Netherlands and Norway, work on national income accounts continued during the war despite the German occupation. Although there was no communication between the occupied countries and England and the United States, there was a remarkable similarity in the national income account developments.

Immediately after World War II, the design and development of national accounts was greatly accelerated. In 1946, Richard Stone prepared a monograph on social accounting for the League of Nations which was to become the cornerstone for the further development of the field. Many of the European countries undertook the compilation of national accounts at this time in order to help in planning economic recovery. The Organization for European Economic Cooperation fostered this development by using national income accounting as a basis for its planning. The OEEC set up a National Accounts Research Unit in Cambridge, England, which developed a standardized system of national accounts for the OEEC; this system with some modification later became the System of National Accounts adopted by the United Nations in 1952.

In the United States, the Office of Business Economics published the national income statistics in accounting form starting in 1947. The National Bureau of Economic Research also continued its research program in the area of economic accounting in the postwar period. The work by Morris Copeland on money flows, published in 1952, considerably expanded the horizon of national accounts in the direction of analyzing the sources and uses of funds by different sectors of the economy. The importance of this work was recognized by the Federal Reserve Board, which established as an integral part of its operation a Flow of Funds Division responsible for collecting and publishing current estimates in this area. The work of Raymond Goldsmith on national wealth and national balance sheets constituted another major innovation in the field of national accounts. In 1958, at the request of the Bureau of the Budget, the National Bureau set up a National Accounts Review Committee to evaluate the US national accounts. This committee worked closely with the Office of Business Economics, and a substantial revision was made in the form and extent of the US accounts.

In many of the other industrial countries, national accounts are now being used for economic planning and budgeting. In some countries, the government is required by law to present its budget in terms of the national economic accounting framework. In some, the national economic accounts contain financial transactions and input–output information. Countries initiating national accounts in the past few decades have had the benefit of the accumulated experience of others, and have not had to contend with the constraint of consistency with data for past periods.

In the less developed countries, national accounts are being used to an increasing extent as the framework for the planning of economic development. In some of these cases, the form of the national accounts differs considerably from that of the more developed countries, in view of the importance of the nonmarket sectors of the economy and the necessity of placing development expenditures in the context of the requirements for changes in economic structure.

The socialist countries have had yet another approach to economic accounting; since their concept of output is net material product, a somewhat different analytic framework has been required. In addition, the socialist countries have found it desirable to emphasize social and demographic data and their relation to the functioning of the economic system.

Finally, academic economists concerned with the analysis of economic growth, productivity and short-run economic models have elaborated and disaggregated the economic accounting framework substantially. The growing use of input–output analysis and the study of technological change have placed heavy emphasis on disaggregation of the production sector of the economy. Simultaneously, the construction of large many-variable models for the short-run projection of income and employment has resulted in detailed analysis of business, government and household behavior. The introduction of the computer has greatly facilitated the handling of data, and sample data are increasingly being used for the analysis of behavioral characteristics which can be applied in macromodels.

As a result of all these developments, the time has come to take a new look at national economic accounting systems to see to what extent the systems now in use meet current and anticipated future needs for economic information. The current effort by the United Nations to develop a new system of national economic accounting reflects this increased concern, and indicates that the present systems are not fully adequate for the tasks which they are required to perform.

1. THE PRESENT STATE OF US AND UN NATIONAL ECONOMIC ACCOUNTING

As has already been indicated, the present United States accounts are the result of a continual process of change. The system has continued to grow and provide additional detailed information so that at the present time the US national income accounts, together with input–output and flow of funds data, provide one of the most comprehensive sets of national accounting data to be found anywhere in the world. On the other hand, this process of evolution has resulted in a considerable number of anomalies. Vestiges of previous systems still remain, although their usefulness is no longer apparent and the adaptation to new kinds of information has been somewhat awkward and incomplete.

There are also major gaps still left in the system. Balance sheets and national wealth accounts do not yet exist on an official basis, and there is some question as to precisely how they should be fitted into the system. Little attention has been devoted in recent years to considering whether the economic constructs contained in the system are satisfactory. The United States is one of the few countries that does not provide a capital account for the government: all government transactions are considered to be current. Nor are households considered to engage in capital formation: all consumer durables are written off as current purchases. The concept of enterprise investment does not recognize research and development expenditures or other intangible capital outlays.

The present form of the account, furthermore, cannot readily encompass related social and demographic information. It is not possible, for example, to study problems of poverty or discrimination in the context of the data provided in the existing national accounts. Also, despite the technological revolution in the processing and handling of data caused by the computer, this factor is not reflected in the design or use of the economic accounting system.

The proposed UN system of national economic accounting is primarily aimed at expanding the comprehensiveness of the framework so that it can embrace all the related forms of economic transactions information. Although the proposed UN system does not yet include balance sheet information, its theoretical structure is such that this can be done. The UN system achieves the full integration of all forms of economic accounting through a matrix approach in which the different types of economic accounts and the various kinds of transactors and classification systems are interrelated. The system is quite complex and highly detailed. It starts with highly aggregated summary accounts for the economy as a whole, and by the process of deconsolidation, systematically moves to the more detailed information required for the various forms of economic accounts.

It is beyond the scope of this discussion to go into the details of either the present US system or the proposed UN system. It will be useful, however, to make some observations on specific aspects of the two systems.

2. THE STRUCTURE OF THE ACCOUNTS

One of the most basic considerations in the design of a system of national economic accounts is how the economy should be partitioned. The major sectoring of US and the proposed UN systems is somewhat similar, but there are significant differences. The US accounts provide a production account which embraces the productive activity of business, government, households and the rest of the world. Nonprofit institutions are included with households, and the business sector is implicit in the accounts, never being shown separately. The proposed UN system separates nonprofit institutions from households, and provides somewhat greater identification of an enterprise sector, although it is essentially defined residually as what remains after general government and nonprofit institutions have been taken out. Although the removal of nonprofit institutions from the household sector is an improvement, since it increases the homogeneity of the household sector so that all transactors in it are individuals acting in a household capacity, setting up a separate sector for nonprofit institutions does not seem justified. In the United States, nonprofit institutions account for only 2.5 percent of income originating in the economy, and it is probably true that nonprofit institutions are more important in the United States than they are elsewhere. In view of the enterprise-like nature of most nonprofit institutions, e.g., universities and hospitals, it does not seem unreasonable that these institutions should be classified as enterprises in much the same way as government enterprises are included in the enterprise sector.

On the other hand, both the US system and the proposed UN system include nonmarket activity as part of the activity taking place in the business or enterprise sector. Thus, food produced and consumed on farms and the services of owner-occupied housing are included as part of enterprise production despite the fact that these are nonmarket activities which actually take place in the household sector. There would be considerable advantage in defining the enterprise sector to cover actual market activities, thus separating the operations of the market system from imputed subsistence and nonmarket activities.

On balance, it seems most useful to set up a system of three major sectors: enterprise, general government and households. For these sectors, a basic eight-account system of national income accounts can be constructed, a consolidated national income and product account, income and outlay and capital formation accounts for each of the three sectors, and a consolidated external transactions account.

The national income and product account would show the production arising in each sector in terms of the use of the factors of production, and each sector's purchases of final goods, divided between consumption and capital formation. This would clearly distinguish between market and nonmarket activity, and would delineate the role of government and households in the economy.

The explicit income and outlay account for enterprises would show enterprise receipts of income and their allocations of it, including the use of some resources for consumption purposes. The enterprise sector, furthermore, lends itself to division into two different kinds of subsectors: industrial subsectoring, showing the classification of establishments by industries, and institutional subsectoring, showing the types of legal form into which enterprises are organized. For each of these kinds of subsectors, production, income and outlay, and capital formation accounts can be provided. In addition, it is useful to show for the industrial subsectors the stock of capital goods used in productive activity, and for institutional subsectors, financial transaction accounts and balance sheets.

The subsectoring of the government and of households would, generally, also be along institutional, social or demographic lines. For these subsectors, it should be possible to present accounts showing income and outlay, capital formation, financial transactions and balance sheets.

3. THE ECONOMIC CONSTRUCTS IN NATIONAL INCOME ACCOUNTS

Although this proposed structuring of the national income accounts is closely related to both the present US system and the proposed UN system, there are significant differences, and these differences have implications for the development of the major economic constructs. To some extent, the proposed changes in the structure of the accounts themselves alter the nature of the economic constructs, but in addition they also provide an opportunity for a systematic revision of economic constructs to make them more useful for economic analysis.

The explicit introduction of the enterprise sector makes it possible to obtain gross product originating in enterprises for the economy as a whole. As already pointed out, it is useful to distinguish the output generated by enterprises operating in the market sector from the outputs of general government and households which are never sold on the market. Thus economic activity of an imputed nature is separated from that involving actual transactions.

By providing the enterprise sector with an income and outlay account, it also becomes possible to introduce the concept of enterprise consumption. Since it is proposed to treat nonprofit institutions as enterprises operating in the market sector, it is necessary to report the consumption which they provide as enterprise consumption. The present US system includes such consumption with household consumption, and although it is not large it must be taken into account. If we admit the concept of enterprise consumption, however, it seems reasonable that a number of other expenditures of a consumption nature by business should be included in it. For example, in this country radio and television are supported by business advertising expenditures. In many other countries these activities are supported by tax revenues and are thus part of public consumption provided by government. It does not seem reasonable that the question of whether radio and television are to be considered part of final consumption should depend upon whether they are supported by taxes or advertising. But if radio and television are to be considered consumption goods provided by enterprise in the United States, a similar question should be raised with respect to certain other mass media such as newspapers and magazines, which are also supported by advertising revenues. There are also additional types of consumption goods which are paid for by enterprises directly, and are not included in the compensation of employees; for example, certain kinds of expense account living, or subsidized cafeterias and recreation facilities for employees. Although the magnitude of these is not now known, the expanded role of the enterprise in these spheres in recent years certainly makes this a question which should be investigated.

The capital formation activity of enterprises also needs further consideration. Current tax regulations permit businesses to write off many outlays which have their primary impact in the future rather than in the present. For example, research and development expenditures are becoming quite important, and should no longer be written off as part of current operating cost. Similarly, expenditures on the education and training of employees are sometimes very important. The concept of capital formation now used in both the US and UN accounts is restricted to producers' durable goods. It is interesting to note that the concept of capital used in the socialist countries is identical with this. The socialist countries use as their basic concept of output the net material product which equals the value of the physical commodities which are produced and excludes all services. For the United States, net material product would be approximately 20 percent lower than gross national product. Western economists have prided themselves on breaking free of such a materialistic concept of output, which is basically the original Adam Smith–David Ricardo view of production later adopted by Marx. But the western economists have not correspondingly altered their concept of capital, so that currently we use a material product concept of capital which is quite inconsistent with the measurement of output.

If we recognize research and development and enterprise education and training expenditures as capital formation, it will also be necessary to introduce the amortization of these expenditures over time. From a theoretical point of view, this is no different from the determination of depreciation and obsolescence for durable goods. In practical terms, it may require highly arbitrary assumptions, but no matter how arbitrary these assumptions are, they will be no more arbitrary than the present practice of writing off all such outlays as current cost.

Within the enterprise account, it would also be useful if more attention were directed toward the more uniform measurement of factor shares and profit. It is obvious that the changes suggested above with respect to research and development and education and training will have a major effect on the operating expenses, and thus on profit. In addition, however, the exact nature of profit from enterprise to enterprise in none too clear. In some enterprises, the capital which is used is borrowed, and interest is charged as an operating expense. In other enterprises, the capital is furnished by the enterprise itself, and profits therefore include a return to capital which is of an interest-like nature. George Stigler, in comparing profits between industries, excluded interest from operating expenses and added it to profits, so that he could use profits as a measure of the return to total capital used in the various industries. Although this procedure would be legitimate if profits consisted purely of the return to capital including risk, there is some question whether it is a meaningful procedure in a system where profit may be due to a large number of other factors. An alternative approach would be to impute a charge for the use of capital in the enterprise, and derive a net profit figure as a residual, excluding both actual and imputed interest. In other words, just as we now impute a charge for depreciation on capital goods, we would also charge an imputed interest rate for the use of capital. As in the case of depreciation charges for a given type of capital good, the imputed interest charge would be at a standard rate that would be the same for all enterprises. Instead of merely computing a depreciation charge to record the amount of capital consumed, a somewhat grosser charge would be computed to indicate the total capital charge. The imputed interest would appear as a separate factor share, which together with net profit would be equal to adjusted gross profit now shown. The value of this treatment becomes most apparent for the comparison of profits in industries where capital structures differ markedly.

For unincorporated enterprises where owners furnish a substantial portion of the labor, such as small retail shops or farms, an imputed labor compensation based on normal employee compensation in the industry or opportunity cost should be charged. In these instances, the residual return computed after this imputed labor charge would reflect the return in the enterprise over and above a proper allowance for the labor of the proprietor. In the case of some small businesses, this might well be negative, indicating that the proprietor was not earning as much as he would if he were employed otherwise.

For the household sector, the introduction of a capital formation account and a related balance sheet would be a substantial departure from the present US system and the proposed UN accounts. Neither the US nor the UN permits households to engage in capital formation on their own account. The purchase of owner-occupied housing is considered to be capital formation by fictitious enterprises in the owner-occupied housing industry, and all consumer durables are considered to be current expenditure. But in point of fact, however, households do own houses, and the services provided by owner-occupied housing represent a flow of services outside the market sector not unlike the subsistence activities of farmers. In fact, in many less developed countries, the provision of food and housing by the household is a significant part of total economic activity. The treatment of consumer durables as current expenditures also does some violence to the facts. The purchase of automobiles, for instance, is even more important in our economy than the purchase of houses, and automobiles represent a stock of durable goods which provides a flow of services over a significant period of years. This fact was dramatically revealed during World War II when the nation was forced to live off the stock of vehicles which it had accumulated in previous years. One of the hallmarks of modern economic development has been the rapid growth in the production of consumer durables. Such consumer durables as dishwashers, refrigerators, stoves and air conditioners are often included in the purchase price of the house to which they are attached, and they are often financed by the mortgage on the house. It does not seem reasonable to subtract from the value of the house the cost of the durable goods which are built into it, or to exclude them from capital formation on the ground that they have been purchased separately.

There is also another argument for considering expenditures on consumer durables as capital outlays. In the early years of a family's lifetime, expenditures on consumer durables (including such things as furniture) are likely to be particularly heavy. In contrast, retired persons spend relatively little in these categories. If the time distribution of the services of durables is not taken into account, the rates of consumption of families at different points in their life cycles will be distorted. It is true that the services of consumer durables do not constitute monetary income and retired people do need monetary income for some purposes (e.g., medicare), but the realities of the situation are that there are capital costs involved in setting up a household, and retired people are receiving a flow of services from the assets that they have accumulated during their lifetimes. In studying the development of the economy, furthermore, the accumulation of consumer durables over time by the household sector is, as has been shown by Juster in his National Bureau study of household capital formation and financing, an important dimension of economic growth and development. If this form of capital accumulation is not taken into consideration, an important set of information relating to economic activity and behavior will be omitted.

With respect to the government accounts, the suggested form of the accounts is in line with the proposed UN treatment, but it differs from the present US system. The present US system does not recognize capital formation by the government, and the introduction of a capital formation account and a balance sheet for the government would alter the present accounting system substantially. In effect the national accountant would be recommending the introduction of a capital budget — something which has been strongly opposed by many on the grounds that it would introduce irresponsibility in budgeting. Nevertheless, it is time that recognition was given to the fact that the government does make outlays which have their primary impact in future periods, and that these include not only the conventional durable-goods expenditures, but also outlays for development purposes such as education, health, urban redevelopment, etc. These are public capital formation in much the same way as research and development and education and training expenditures by business are private capital formation. This broader definition of capital formation would also differ from that of the United Nations, but in many developing countries expenditures on education and health may be more important for future economic development than expenditures on roads and public buildings.

Although the removal of capital formation outlays by the government from the current account does substantially increase the current surplus of the government, the figure which now appears as the surplus or deficit of the government sector is merely transferred to the capital formation account, and statistically and conceptually will be the same. Those who consider that the present measure of surplus or deficit has meaning, therefore, will continue to have the same concept available.

4. THE EFFECT OF CHANGING THE ECONOMIC CONSTRUCTS

The changes which have been recommended will have considerable impact on the measurement of gross national product and national income. Gross national product, which was reported by the Department of Commerce as $743 billion in the year 1966, would be raised by $160 billion to a level of $903 billion. The largest element in this increase is the gross flow of services provided by household capital, which is estimated at approximately $64 billion. The gross flow from the stock of government capital adds approximately $52 billion, and approximately $44 billion is added by taking into account enterprise research and development outlays ($26 billion) and consumption expenditures of at least $18 billion.

The increase in national income is somewhat less spectacular. National income as reported by the Department of Commerce was $617 billion in 1966, and it is estimated that this would increase by approximately $43 billion if the recommended changes were made. Most of this increase is due to the inclusion of the net flow of services yielded by the stock of capital used by households and government.

Perhaps even more important than the changes in the aggregate economic constructs, however, are the changes which would occur in intersectoral relationships. For example, household current saving would rise from $30 billion to $64 billion, and gross capital formation by households would total $100 billion. Approximately $58 billion would be provided by household capital consumption charges, leaving a net amount of $22 billion in financial assets acquired by households. These financial assets, of course, include the value of the real assets acquired by unincorporated enterprises owned by households. In contrast, enterprise capital formation was approximately $130 billion, of which approximately $105 billion was provided from internal sources. Further disaggregation of the enterprise sector by industry and the household sector by socio-economic groups would throw substantial light on the importance of various kinds of financing activity in the economic system.

5. THE INTEGRATION OF NATIONAL ECONOMIC ACCOUNTS

The desirability of integrating the different forms of national economic accounts with each other is generally recognized. The Department of Commerce now presents input–output information which can be directly related to the data contained in the national income and product account. The flow of funds tables are also directly tied in with the chief national income accounting aggregates. One of the major explicit objectives of the proposed revision of the UN system is the integration of the national economic accounting system to provide the information now contained in all the different kinds of existing national economic accounts.

The United States integration of national income accounts, input–output tables, and flow of funds accounts is, however, not complete. Different classifications of industries are used for input–output tables and the national income accounts, and it is difficult for the user to relate the information in one system to information in the other.

Similarly, the flow of funds and the national income accounts use somewhat different institutional sectoring, so that although the same economic constructs appear in the two systems, it is difficult to relate the information at a more highly disaggregated level. In contrast, the proposed UN system does present a single fully integrated system of economic accounting, employing consistent industrial and institutional classification systems. On the other hand, the proposed UN integration is so much concerned with providing the network of transactions that it gives inadequate attention both to the development of economic constructs and to the portrayal of the operation of the economic system. It has already been noted, for example, that a full set of sector accounts is provided for nonprofit institutions, despite the relative unimportance of this sector in most economic systems. Similarly, even in the most aggregated income and outlay account, minor flows such as net casualty insurance premiums and fines and penalties are treated on a par with such major flows as compensation of employees and final consumption expenditure. As a result, the UN system often presents the user with a considerable amount of unwanted information, on the one hand, and inadequate breakdown of major flows, on the other hand.

Although it is true that the proposed UN system does result in integrated economic accounts, it is also true that almost any simple system of sector accounts which provides for the systematic recording of production, income and outlay, capital formation, financial transactions and balance sheets can be used for this purpose. A deconsolidation of the national income and product account will result in input–output accounts such as are now contained in both the US and the UN systems. The financial transactions accounts and the balance sheets for the various institutional sectors of the economy provide the basis for the flow of funds accounts and national balance sheets.

In addition to the need for integration of the formal economic accounts, however, a method is also needed to introduce social and demographic information into the system. The formal economic accounts can provide some of this information, since they permit detailed breakdowns of data by socio-economic groupings. But such presentations are extremely limited since they depend upon the technique of cross classification. By their very nature such cross classifications present serious problems of aggregation, and they are often too unwieldy either to publish or to use.

Given the technology of the computer, there is another approach which can provide more meaningful integration of social and demographic information. If the economic accounts are organized so that the sectors and groupings can be directly represented by sample information, samples which in aggregated form directly correspond to the economic accounts can be used to achieve integration. For example, if the household sector is defined as consisting exclusively of households, it would be possible to construct a sizeable sample of households whose income, when properly weighted, would be equal to total personal income, and whose expenditures would correspond to total consumer expenditures as shown in the national income accounts. Although this has not been done as yet in the United States, a start in this direction has been made in the Census Bureau's 1-in-1,000 sample, which provides extensive data on each family in the sample. In this sample, information is provided on such things as age, education, employment, income, family composition, etc. — in all, some 40 characteristics are provided about the individuals in each household.

It is possible to use such a sample to study a variety of social and economic problems. Recently, James Schulz at Yale University used this 1-in-1,000 sample in a simulation of the aged population, intended to explore the problem of poverty among the aged 20 years hence. Using the 1-in-1,000 sample, he created an income statement and balance sheet for each household in the year 1960, taking into account information on income, occupation, pension rights, ownership of home, existing financial assets, rates of saving, and recent trends in wages, prices and social security payments. In order to get the changes from year to year, Schulz used a life process model which determined on a stochastic basis what happened to each individual in the sample each year. To determine whether an individual lived or died, for instance, mortality tables were consulted to obtain the probability of an individual of a given age and other characteristics dying within the year. A random number was then generated and compared with the probability limits. On this basis, a decision was made as to whether this individual lived or died. After simulating the behavior of each household over a 20-year period, Schulz took a census of his data for the year 1980 and determined the distribution of income and thus the extent of poverty as of that date. In the course of such a simulation it is possible, of course, to alter the assumptions or to change policy with respect to such factors as social security to see what impact such changes would have.

Other sets of microdata can be developed for other groups in the economy. Thus, for example, the Annual Survey of Manufactures of the Census Bureau consists of sample data for over 70,000 manufacturing establishments. Standard and Poor now provides the Compustat tape, containing quarterly information on the income statements and balance sheets of a large number of corporations. The Internal Revenue Service has samples of both individual and corporate income tax returns.

It is very important indeed that the national economic accounts be constructed so that they can take advantage of these microdata sets. In fact, it would be useful if national economic accountants systematically set about to provide sets of microdata to underlie the sets of aggregated data in the accounts, much as matrices of input–output data or financial transactions are now provided.

The time has come when we must recognize the existence of the computer and its capabilities of handling data. It is true that some detailed tabulations may be useful for reference purposes. The publication of detailed information by city and metropolitan area permits policy-makers in each city to use the tabulation to obtain the specific information of interest to them. But for the most part, massive detailed tabulations are not useful, since it is generally necessary to put the data back into machine-readable form before they can be used for analytic purposes. The national accountant in the future will be called upon to provide the detailed data in such machine-readable form. Although the systematic nature of the proposed UN system does lend itself to machine processing, it has not been developed in terms of the computer technology now available. It still conceives of national economic accounts as aggregated cross tabulations estimated on a cell-by-cell basis, rather than as the product of microdata sets.

In summary, the time has come to bridge the gap between micro- and macrodata. The macroeconomic accounts should serve to summarize the microdata, and economic constructs are needed to measure specific economic magnitudes. However, the macroeconomic accounts should go further than this. They should provide the framework and the context into which specific sets of microdata can be placed. The microdata in turn should be developed so that they form comprehensive sets of sample information for definable parts of the economic system. It should then be possible to tap the vast amount of data held by government and business organizations to provide more meaningful information about the operation of the economic system, and to relate it to the major social and economic problems of our time.

4. The Role of the National Accounts in the Statistical System

Richard Ruggles
Yale University

Last month the Nobel prize in Economics was awarded to Sir Richard Stone of Cambridge University for his major contributions to the field of national accounting. In announcing the award, Ragnar Bentzel, Secretary of the Nobel Committee, indicated that some younger economists might be surprised by Stone's designation for the prize since the national accounts are now taken for granted and few consider how they came into existence. Although Stone is indeed the legitimate father of national accounting, it could not have come into being without another parent, the statistical offices that have been actively engaged in developing and implementing the grand design which Stone envisaged. Without their years of development work, Stone's contributions would never have borne fruit. The topic I have been asked to discuss, namely the role of national accounts in the statistical system, is particularly appropriate for bringing out what Stone's contribution was, and how the work of national and international statistical organizations has built upon it.

It is useful to view national accounts and their role in the statistical system in a historical context, and I propose to do this by examining three sets of questions. First, how had national income estimation evolved before national accounts were developed, and what was the state of the statistical system at that time? Second, how did the national accounts develop from Stone's contributions and from the efforts of statistical offices, and in what way did the national accounts provide a framework for the statistical system? Finally, in view of the expanding needs for information and the changing technology of information processing, what should be the future direction of change in the form and content of national accounting and its relation to the statistical system?

This chapter first appeared as a Presentation to Statistics Canada, November 1984.

1. THE DEVELOPMENT OF NATIONAL INCOME: CONCEPTS AND MEASUREMENT

Early Measures of the Income of Nations

Contrary to what is perhaps common belief, national income measurement is not a recent development. Long before the establishment of economics as a formal discipline, tax administrators undertook to measure the income of nations in order to be able to carry out their administrative tasks better. In England, one of the first such studies was that of William Petty, a doctor and the tax administrator under Charles I. In 1676, he carried out a study called 'Political Arithmetik' which estimated the national income of England and Wales. Petty's method involved three steps. First, he estimated the population of England and Wales, concluding that it was six million persons. Second, he estimated the expenses per person for food, clothing, housing and other necessities. These he thought would come to 4½ pence per day or 7 pounds a year, making a total of 42 million pounds per year for the whole population. Third, in terms of the receipt of income Petty estimated that about half of the population was employed and that wages paid were 7 pence a day or 9 pounds per year, making a total wage payment of 27 million pounds a year; to this he added an estimate of 15 millions pounds a year for the income received from land rental, houses and other property, making the same total of 42 million pounds per year. On this basis, Petty concluded that this was the national income of England and Wales. He thought that a 10 percent tax rate was reasonable and that at this rate the government should be able to collect 4 million pounds — or if a war broke out he thought that taxes could be raised to 17.5 percent, which would yield 7 million pounds.

Shortly after the publication of Petty's estimates, Gregory King, a surveyor and map maker, prepared more extensive national income estimates for England and Wales. King had access to much better demographic data so that he was able to estimate the sources of income in terms of activity — that is agriculture, trade, etc. — and by social class. He related income to consumption expenditure broken down by type of good consumed and saving. He not only estimated income, but also developed balance sheets showing gold, jewels, furniture, clothing and inventories held. King's estimates for England and Wales were quite close to Petty's. They covered several years and included forward projections. He also made estimates for the national incomes of France and Holland — these international comparisons were made in order to appraise the potential of these countries for obtaining tax revenue needed for waging war and forecasting possible future developments.

In France, at about the same time, Marshal Vauban was making similar estimates, although in his case they were primarily based on the estimated value of agricultural production. Vauban's concern was with tax reform: he wished to estimate the yield of a universal gross income tax. Somewhat later, just before the French revolution, the French chemist Lavoisier, needing to raise funds for his scientific research, became a farmer general or tax collector, and developed estimates of gross national income, net national product and taxable national income in an effort to analyze potential tax revenues. In his case, however, the exercise had an unfortunate outcome. As a farmer general, he was executed during the revolution.

Almost all of these early efforts to measure national income arose from interest in discovering how much tax revenue could be obtained by the government under different tax arrangements. The approaches to estimation were all quite similar. The various investigators recognized the interrelation between production, income and expenditures, and made imaginative use of the available information. Given the primitive state of the basic information, it was indeed remarkable that the investigators were able to achieve any results whatsoever.

Early Concepts of Production

In general, these early measurements of national income focused on the income received by persons, rather than on the total national output. The concept of production as such did not come into consideration until the early economists became concerned with the theory of value. Early nation states had viewed gold and silver as the basis for successfully waging war, and Mercantilism had stressed the importance of trade, shipping and even privateering for the acquisition of gold and silver.

In contrast with this point of view, the Physiocrats, in the mid-1700s, developed a theory of value based on the premise that agriculture was the source of all production. They arrived at this conclusion from observing that in agriculture nature causes seed to multiply, but in other activities no such increase takes place — trade merely passes things around, and manufacturing merely changes the physical form of already existing products. This Physiocratic viewpoint was embodied in Quesnay's 'Tableau Economique', published in 1758. It showed how agricultural goods flowed into a variety of uses. This was one of the first demonstrations of the circular flow in the economic system and was a forerunner of what later was to become input–output analysis.

Adam Smith's *Wealth of Nations*, published in 1776, took issue with both the Mercantilist and Physiocratic positions. Smith thought that a nation's wealth should not be measured by its stock of gold and silver, but rather should be viewed in terms of its ability to produce a flow of goods. Furthermore, in contrast to the Physiocrats, Smith's theory of value did not limit production to agriculture. He considered that manufacturing was also productive, since the labor used increased the value of the basic materials entering into the manufacturing process. On the other hand, Smith argued that only the labor which was actually embodied in material products could be considered to be productive; labor used for such purposes as domestic services, for example, he considered to be unproductive.

Although Smith's concept of production was widely accepted and was adopted by Ricardo, Malthus and Mill as the foundation of classical economics, as time passed it drew major criticism. It was finally rejected by Marshall and other neo-classical economists at the end of the nineteenth century in favor of a more comprehensive concept, in which both material goods and non-material services were considered to be productive.

In a parallel development, however, Karl Marx was working out his labor theory of value, and he retained Adam Smith's distinction between productive and unproductive labor. The socialist countries have continued to use this distinction as a basis for their measurement of national income and product. Net material product in the Socialist System of Balances of the National Economy excludes services not directly embodied in material products from output on the ground that they are essentially non-productive. It is somewhat ironic that the only point of agreement between the capitalist countries and the socialist countries with respect to national income measurement is the definition of gross capital formation. Both include only material products in their measures — a position which is fully consistent with the socialist capital concepts of income and production, but is rather at odds with the western neo-classical concepts.

National Income and Product Measurements Prior to World War II

During the nineteenth and first part of the twentieth century a wide variety of national income estimates were produced for a number of countries. For the most part, however, these estimates did not reflect major organized research efforts, but rather were *ad hoc* and often back-of-the-envelope calculations made by individual investigators. In general, until the great depression of the 1930s government statistical offices were not involved in the estimation of national income. Canada, however, was one of the few exceptions. R.H. Coats had published unofficial estimates of Canadian national income as early as 1919, and these were followed in 1925 by official annual estimates prepared by the Dominion Bureau of Statistics.

In the United States, estimates of national income were made during the 1920s at the National Bureau of Economic Research under the direction of Wesley C. Mitchell. This work was taken over by Simon Kuznets in 1931, and in 1933, at the depths of the depression, Kuznets was called on to direct the preparation of national income estimates being undertaken by the Department of Commerce. His first report, *National Income 1929–32*, submitted in January 1934, assured the success of the undertaking. Interest in these estimates was very substantial. Until these data became available no one knew how far production and income in the United States had fallen from the peak in 1929. After the publication of this report, Kuznets continued to work at the National Bureau on such topics as the commodity flow method of estimating national income, for which he was later awarded a Nobel prize, but the Department of Commerce assumed the responsibility for producing the official national income estimates.

In many respects, the great depression of the 1930s provided a completely new thrust to economic measurement. Before the 1930s, economic statistics had been limited to time series of economic indicators such as freight-car loadings, pig-iron production, retail sales and the volume of bank deposits, together with some information on price movements. National income had the advantage that it provided both a comprehensive summary of the activity taking place in the economy, and breakdowns of the industrial composition of activity and the shares of income received by type of income payment.

Although the great depression had raised questions about the measurement of purchasing power and demand, consumption and other final uses were not adequately reflected in the national income measurements of the time. Emphasis upon the final use breakdown had to await Keynes's *General Theory of Employment, Interest and Money* which was not published until 1936 and thus did not have much influence upon national income measurement before World War II.

The State of Statistical Systems Prior to World War II

The statistical system in the United States in the 1930s underwent major expansion. After Hoover's initial spending cutbacks in 1931 and 1932 in an effort to balance the federal budget, Roosevelt created numerous programs aimed at economic recovery and reform such as the AAA, the Agricultural Adjustment Administration; the NRA, the National Recovery Administration; and the WPA, the Works Progress Administration. The administration of these new programs created an unprecedented demand for statistics. During this period, there was also a rapid increase in the ability to process and tabulate information. Rapid increases in the use of punchcards and tabulators provided a flood of new information. But the flood of new information was often overwhelming, much of it was fragmentary, there was no standard industrial classification system and there was little or no coordination among the statistical agencies. The early national income estimates were constructed by piecing together and reconciling data from many different sources, and thus they were viewed as a synthesis of existing data. They were not in any sense conceived of as providing a comprehensive framework for the statistical system — and indeed, there was little thought of the body of statistics that was collected as constituting a system. The situation in other countries at the end of the 1930s was no better.

2. THE DEVELOPMENT OF NATIONAL ACCOUNTS

Stone's World War II Contribution

Shortly after the outbreak of World War II, there was a major change in this state of affairs, brought about by the pressing needs of wartime planning and management. Richard Stone and James Meade, under the guidance of Keynes, developed for the UK Treasury an analysis of national income and expenditure for the United Kingdom which put into operational terms the concepts laid out in Keynes's *General Theory*. Stone had a background in accounting, and Meade, who was later also awarded a Nobel prize, was a convinced follower of Keynes. The results of their work, cast in the form of a national income and expenditure account, appeared first in a White Paper which came out in April 1941 as a part of the 1941 Budget.

The basic principle of casting national income and expenditure into the form of an account had already been suggested by economists working in other countries. Most notably in 1940, Ragnar Frisch in Norway had written about constructing national accounts for purposes of macroeconomic analysis, and at about the same time Jan Tinbergen in the Netherlands had used these concepts in his development of econometric models. Both Frisch and Tinbergen were later awarded Nobel prizes for their work in these areas.

It was clear that national accounting was an idea whose time had come. The ideas presented in the British White Papers were rapidly adopted in the United States by Milton Gilbert, who at that time was in charge of the national income work, and as early as 1942 a national income and expenditure account for the US economy was developed. Much use was made of this account in analyzing the inflationary gap which might be expected to result from the expansion of war expenditures.

Stone remained in charge of the UK national accounts work through the war. In 1944, a committee was set up with UK, Canadian and US representatives to develop a common national accounting concept, and Stone became chairman of this committee.

The League of Nations Study

In the fall of 1945, a Sub-Committee on National Income Statistics of the

League of Nations Committee of Statistical Experts was convened, again under Stone's chairmanship. This Sub-Committee issued a report on *Measurement of National Income and the Construction of Social Accounts*, which contained an appendix written by Stone laying out a complete system of national accounts. The conceptual basis of these accounts can best be described by quoting directly from this document, as follows:

> Instead of seeking to build up a single total, such as the national income, an investigation is first made of the classification of accounting entities, of the types of accounts that they keep and of the transactions into which they enter. In this way, all the transacting entities of an economic system are classified into broad sectors such as productive enterprises, financial intermediaries and final consumers, and a series of accounts for each of these categories is set up, in which the separate entries represent economically distinct categories of transaction. Economic activity is represented by money flows and related bookkeeping transactions, actual or imputed, between accounts. The national income and other similar aggregates are obtained from the system by selecting and combining the constituent entries in the accounts. In this way, a logical framework is presented into which the greater part of economic statistics can be fitted. This framework should prove useful in showing how far statistics actually available at any time fall short of a complete coverage of economic activity.

Although by now these basic principles of national accounting are well recognized, in 1945 they were major innovations which were not easily accepted. Kuznets, for example, viewed the national accounts as 'a dubious addition to the theoretical equipment by aid of which we define national income and reckon its distribution'.

In formulating this initial set of accounts, Stone followed generally accepted British commercial accounting practices of the time which in many respects were rather elaborate. For the sectors relating to business enterprises and financial intermediaries, he set up four accounts. First, an operating account was set up to show the receipts and outlays which were related to the operation of the business. Second, the surplus of receipts over outlays in this first account was then transferred to an appropriation account where non-operating receipts were added, and the disposition of the resulting total was shown in terms of dividends and withdrawals, direct taxes and transfers to capital and reserve accounts. Third, a capital account was set up in turn, to show the actual outlays for capital formation and inventory accumulation on the one hand, and on the other hand, the sources of funds for capital formation in terms of allowances for depreciation and transfers from the appropriation and reserve accounts. Finally, a fourth account, a reserve account, was set up to show the transfers to and from other accounts and the changes taking place in holdings of financial assets and liabilities.

The treatment of persons, public collective providers, social security and private pension funds was considerably simpler. Here, only two accounts were set up: a revenue account which was used to record current receipts and outlays, and a capital and reserve account which was used to reflect capital formation, capital transfers and changes in financial assets and liabilities.

The basic principles underlying these first accounts were indeed rather simple, but in practice they raised a number of perplexing questions as to how the economy should be sectored, what type of accounts are required, and how specific types of transaction such as interest, pensions and insurance should be treated.

The OEEC and the UN Systems of National Accounts

Nevertheless, immediately after World War II, the US Economic Cooperation Administration and the Organization for European Economic Cooperation decided that national income accounts should be used as a framework in planning European economic recovery, for evaluating the progress of individual countries, and as a basis for allocating Marshall Plan aid. Development of a system of national income accounts would make it possible to track the production, consumption and gross capital formation taking place in each country and to analyze the role which government policies, foreign trade and Marshall Plan aid were playing in the recovery process.

The main obstacle to adopting such a national income accounting approach was lack of appropriate information. Many participating countries did not have estimates of national income, much less national income accounts. Even where accounts did exist, there was no standard form which was comparable from country to country. Once again Stone was called upon. He was asked to set up a National Accounts Research Unit in Cambridge to bring together statisticians from the statistical offices of OEEC member countries to develop what became the OEEC 'Simplified System of National Accounts'. The resulting five-account system, which appeared in 1951, was far simpler than the system outlined in the 1947 League of Nations report: it consisted of consolidated current receipt and outlay accounts for enterprises, households and government, and consolidated accounts for gross capital formation and transactions with the rest of the world.

At this same time, Stone was also chairing an expert group which was appointed to draw up a System of National Accounts (SNA) for the United Nations. Understandably, the UN SNA bore a close resemblance to the OEEC system. The major differences were that a domestic product account and a national income account were substituted for the single consolidated enterprise account, and rudimentary capital reconciliation accounts were shown for households, government and the rest of the world. The latter were intended to show the impact of saving and investment on assets and liabilities, but they were at this stage very summary in nature. An additional feature of the first UN SNA was that standard tables were appended to the accounts which gave alternative or more detailed breakdowns of the data contained in the accounts and provided standardized classifications. With this first SNA as a basis, the United Nations Statistical Office developed a national accounts questionnaire which it sent out to countries to collect national accounting data, and in the late 1950s, it began publication of the *Yearbook of National Accounts Statistics*.

The 1968 Revision of the UN SNA

At the same time as the national income accounts were being developed, there were developments in related fields of economic accounting. Wassily Leontief, another Nobel prize recipient, had been working on input–output analysis since the 1930s. By analyzing inter-industry input requirements and the destination of industry outputs, Leontief was able to determine how the industrial structure of the economic system could be expected to change with changes in the final demand for goods and services. In the period after World War II many countries undertook construction of input–output tables, and in some countries, including Norway, Denmark and the Netherlands, attempts were made to integrate input–output tables with national income accounting.

During this period also, work was being done on flow of funds, national wealth and balance sheets. Morris Copeland at the National Bureau of Economic Research had developed sources and uses of funds accounts for recording money flows in an effort to obtain quantitative measures of the nature and volume of transactions taking place in the economy. The motivation for this work was Copeland's desire to estimate the component 'T' in Irving Fisher's quantity theory equation, $MV = PT$. Despite his main concern with deriving the aggregate value of all transactions, Copeland did for the first time direct attention to the creation of an accounting framework into which all transactions could be fitted. At this same time, Raymond Goldsmith was estimating national wealth and balance sheets. In order to do this, he developed the perpetual inventory method, which relies upon cumulating the capital formation data in the national income accounts over a long period to obtain an estimate of the stocks of tangible assets. These were combined with the financial transactions data in the flow of funds to obtain complete balance sheets.

It gradually became apparent that all of these economic accounting systems should be integrated into a single framework, and that the 1952 SNA was not sufficiently comprehensive in its scope to serve as such a framework. In the early 1960s, as a consequence, Stone was again called on to head an effort to create such an integrated system. Development of the revised SNA was a very large-scale undertaking, involving the cooperation of statisticians from many national statistical offices and the UN Statistical Office over a period of about five years.

The revised SNA appeared in 1968 and, as was intended, it provided a comprehensive and detailed framework for recording the stocks and flows of the economy. It brought together, into an articulated coherent system, data ranging in degree of aggregation from the consolidated accounts of the old SNA to detailed input–output and flow of funds tables. The production account of the old SNA was disaggregated into input–output accounts for industries and commodities, and the capital reconciliation accounts were dismembered into the transactions in financial assets and liabilities of the institutional sectors of the economy. The income and outlay and capital accounts of the nation were divided into corresponding accounts for institutional sectors and subsectors; and balance sheet and revaluation accounts for these categories of transactors and the nation were added. The revised system incorporated a classification of the activities of government so as to furnish more adequate data than the old SNA on the effect of government on the economy, in terms of the provision of social and community services and the redistribution of income. Constant price data on the supply and disposition of goods and services were also integrated into the structure of the system.

The revised SNA, like the old SNA, was designed to provide international guidance to national statistical offices wanting to improve, elaborate and extend their national accounts and their systems of basic statistics. By integrating and linking the definitions and classifications of all flows and stocks into a coherent structure, the revised SNA was meant to provide the basis for planning the gathering and compiling of the coordinated bodies of basic data required for economic and social analysis. It was recognized that many countries would not be able to compile all the data contained in the full system, but it was felt that the new system could establish goals for advancing national accounting and systems of basic statistics in the foreseeable future.

3. THE FUTURE DEVELOPMENT OF NATIONAL ACCOUNTS AND THE STATISTICAL SYSTEM

The Concerns of the 1970s and the National Accounts

It would be convenient at this juncture if one could say 'that is all there is to the story — the new SNA was a success and lived happily ever after — bringing sunshine and beauty into the lives of statisticians'. Unfortunately, or perhaps fortunately for the world, new concerns and new possibilities have altered our conception of both what economic and social information is needed and how it can be utilized.

In the late 1960s, almost before the ink was dry on the new SNA, the younger generation in particular started to question the values implicit in the traditional measures of economic progress. Specifically, it was argued that national income measures did not adequately reflect the deterioration of the environment, the using up of resources and the disamenities of modern society. Some viewed GNP as standing for gross national pollution, and urged that small was beautiful, and that happiness was learning to do without. Even those who did not take such extreme positions were forced to recognize that the data reported in the national accounts did not adequately measure the quality of life. Furthermore, there was an increasing concern with the distribution of well-being, as well as with the national totals contained in the accounts. It was argued that an increase in aggregate output might well be accompanied by a worsening in the distribution of that output.

In the United States, the government programs of the 'Great Society' were intended to address these concerns, and the statistical information required for their planning, administration and evaluation was very different from that envisaged by the SNA. What was needed was information about the demographic, social and economic characteristics of the population, so that programs could be designed to help those who needed help. Although the topic of income distribution was recognized in the revised SNA, serious attention was not given to establishing guidelines for income distribution statistics until almost a decade later, and relatively little attention was devoted to cost–benefit analysis or measurement of the effects of government programs on the distribution of income.

Perhaps the greatest blow to the use of national accounting as a basis for analyzing the behavior of the economy came from the stagflation which developed in the 1970s. Keynesian economists had held the view that inflation and recession could not occur simultaneously. With the Vietnam War and the subsequent energy crises, this view was largely discredited. Those advocating supply-side or monetarist economic policies felt that Keynesian income analysis was largely irrelevant. The supply-siders held that if taxes were reduced, this would create sufficient incentives so that the economy would operate in an optimal manner. The monetarists argued that the central policy problem was ensuring enough monetary restraint to prevent inflationary pressures, and that any other government policy actions would be ineffective since they would be fully discounted by business enterprises and consumers.

The inflationary process of the 1970s, of course, involved changes in relative prices and revaluations of assets and liabilities as prices rose and produced both capital gains and capital losses. Those who held tangible assets and owed fixed debt at low interest rates made large capital gains, whereas those to whom the fixed debt was owed suffered capital losses. Although the revised SNA did, in principle, make provision for balance sheets and even proposed revaluation accounts, these were not implemented in detail in the 1968 Blue Book, and as in the case of income distribution statistics guidelines for balance sheets and reconciliation accounts were not published until almost a decade later.

Finally, one of the more perplexing problems that bothered economists during the 1970s was the slowdown in productivity. Many different explanations were offered. Some economists attributed the decline to the failure of individual firms to invest sufficiently in new technology, others argued that the energy crisis had reduced the efficiency of the economy, and still others felt that the answer lay in the changing mix of goods and services produced in the economy. Whatever the true answer, it became apparent that although the national accounts were capable of demonstrating that a slowdown in productivity had taken place, they did not provide the highly disaggregated data needed to analyze precisely how and why the productivity decline occurred.

This failure of national accounts to accommodate the basic data required for explaining aggregate economic change in terms of the behavior and aggregation of individual economic units is a reflection of a deeper malaise. This is that macro- and microeconomics have developed as two separate and distinct bodies of doctrine — each having its own conceptual framework. The observed changes at the macrolevel are not purely the consequence of the behavior of representative microunits written large. The so-called aggregation problem is a reflection of systematic changes in the structure and composition of the microunits which constitute the economic system. Until ways can be found to integrate macro- and microeconomics, both theoretically and empirically, our understanding of the operation of the economic system will continue to be severely limited.

Attempts to Modify and Amplify the National Accounts

The concerns of the 1970s and the dissatisfaction with the existing national accounting framework led in a number of different directions. Some investigators undertook to adjust the existing national accounts aggregates in order to obtain better measurements of economic welfare.

Others sought to introduce additional imputations in order to increase the comprehensiveness of the national accounts and improve their usefulness for a wider range of economic analysis. Still others focused on social, demographic and other information which lay outside of the framework of the national accounts and sought ways in which to link this information with the accounts.

One of the most imaginative approaches involving the adjustment of national accounting aggregates was that taken by William Nordhaus and James Tobin in their 1970 National Bureau presentation 'Is Growth Obsolete?' In this paper, Nordhaus and Tobin attempted to develop a measure of economic welfare which excluded intermediate or instrumental expenditures, included the value of capital services of consumer durables and government capital and the value of leisure and nonmarket work, and made deductions for the disamenities of urbanization. They argued that consumer expenditures for commuting to work are instrumental rather than final consumption, and that many government purchases were either regrettables (such as national defense) or intermediate services (such as sanitation and police).

In terms of measurement, the question of how to value leisure and other nonmarket activity posed the greatest problem for Nordhaus and Tobin. If these were valued as the opportunity cost of wages foregone, growth was very much less than if they were valued in accordance with the price index for all goods and services. The calculation of disamenities of urbanization was particularly imaginative. Regressions were run between the population density of localities and average household income: since larger cities had higher income, the income differential was taken as the measure of urban disamenities. (Of course, if finer geographic divisions had been used, this method might have led to the conclusion that the wealthy suburbs of New York had more disamenities than Harlem.) In responding to the question, 'Is growth obsolete?' Nordhaus and Tobin concluded that 'Although GNP and other national income aggregates are imperfect measures of welfare, the broad picture of secular progress which they convey remains after correction of their most obvious deficiencies.'

In general, national accountants and statistical offices did not follow the Nordhaus–Tobin lead in the direction of making adjustments to the national accounting aggregates to reflect economic welfare. An exception was the study undertaken by the Net National Welfare Measurement Committee of the Economic Council of Japan. The same types of adjustments as those made by Nordhaus and Tobin were applied to Japanese GNP with remarkably similar results.

National accounting aggregates have always contained some imputations. Traditionally, imputations have been made for nonmarket agricultural production, the services of owne- occupied housing and services provided by financial intermediaries. Many economists have argued that the national accounts should be extended to embrace all other nonmarket activity, and that they should include intangible and human capital as well as tangible capital. John Kendrick and Robert Eisner developed estimates for such extended accounts for the United States.

Kendrick not only imputed the value of unpaid household work and the services provided by household and government capital, but he also made imputations for volunteer labor, school work, frictional unemployment and the investment (tangible and intangible) and consumption which business enterprises customarily write off as intermediate purchases of goods and services. In a related study, Kendrick also treated the cost of raising children and expenditures on education and health as part of the investment in human capital, which he valued by calculating the discounted sum of the stream of future earnings they could be expected to produce.

Although Eisner included most of these same imputations, he also made estimates of the net revaluations caused by relative changes in the value of tangible assets. The extended accounts drawn up by Kendrick and Eisner served to remind national accountants that the market transaction accounts with which they dealt were only a small part of the total picture of economic activity. In spite of this — or perhaps because of it — the general effect of these efforts was to make the profession even more conservative and cautious about modifying and extending the accounts.

For the most part, national statistical offices looked outside of national accounts for social indicators which could be used to monitor social conditions, formulate goals for social policy, and evaluate the social change taking place. In general, these social indicators consisted of time series data which were selected to describe the status and well-being of the population in such areas as health, public safety, education, employment, income, housing and leisure and recreation. During the 1970s the statistical offices of almost all of the major industrial countries issued publications containing 'social indicators'. In the United Kingdom, the publication was entitled *Social Trends*; in the US, *Social Indicators*; in France, *Donnees Sociales*; in Canada, *Perspectives Canada*.

It was in this context that Richard Stone, again working for the United Nations Statistical Office, formulated his System of Social and Demographic Statistics (SSDS). This system explicitly attempted to embed the social indicators into a larger framework of social, economic and demographic statistics which could be linked with the national economic accounts. Specifically, Stone set up social matrices in which opening states of the population evolved through life sequences into a closing state. Markov transition probabilities were used to move individuals through their life sequences. The life sequences and subsystems covered were: the size and structure of the population, family formation, social class, stratification and mobility, the distribution of income, consumption, accumulation and net worth, housing and the environment, allocation of time and leisure, social security and welfare services, learning activities and educational services, earning activities, employment and the inactive, health and health services and public order and safety, offenders and their victims.

In one sense Stone's SSDS was too ambitious, in that it undertook to develop a common method for analyzing and projecting all of the major life sequences — including some social phenomena not usually thought of as life sequences. In another sense, SSDS was too restrictive and simplistic: in order to avoid severe statistical difficulties Stone had to restrict the system to pairwise interactions. This also meant that SSDS, as a framework, was oriented solely to tabulations of data specifically designed for use in particular life sequences. Because of these limitations, SSDS has not been widely adopted as a basis for integrating social, economic and demographic data by national statistical offices.

For the purpose of development planning, the need to analyze the national accounts in conjunction with social and demographic information has led a number of investigators, including the World Bank, to construct social accounting matrices. These matrices, known as SAMs, follow the general approach which Stone developed in his use of matrices for the 1968 United Nations SNA. In that presentation Stone pointed out that new columns and rows can be introduced into a matrix of accounts to provide any additional breakdowns of information which users might desire. Although it has not been customary to standardize SAMs, the usual practice is to provide additional rows and columns to subsector the population by income, education, ethnic origin, or urban and rural and to subsector industry by traditional and modern. SAMs are not really a new departure in the integration of national economic accounts with social and demographic data; rather they show how subsectoring as envisaged by the SNA can provide for useful incorporation of social and demographic information within the framework of the existing accounts.

Finally, in France, the notion of 'satellite accounts' has been suggested as an information gathering framework which can be related to the national accounts. Satellite accounts can be drawn up either for economic activities such as agriculture, research, transportation, etc. or for social concerns such as health, education, alcoholism and the environment. Although satellite accounts are expected to bring together monetary and nonmonetary data and relate them to the national accounts, it is recognized that they will differ widely from field to field. The French experience with satellite accounts points up both the potentialities and the difficulties of the approach. On the positive side, it is apparent that much is gained by bringing together national accountants and statisticians who are specialists in various fields. On the less positive side, the approach is *ad hoc* in nature, and it is not always true that the resulting satellite accounts prove to be useful or have a lasting effect.

The Computerization of Data Processing

National accounting as it is known today is the product of the data processing systems which were in place during the periods in which it was designed and developed. As I said in discussing the state of statistical systems before World War II, data processing meant using punchcard technology to aggregate and tabulate raw data into summary tables. This was the only way the mass of detailed data could be reduced to manageable proportions and made meaningful. Raw data were considered to be merely intermediate steps in the process, and so they were usually discarded once the finished tabulations were produced. National accounts fitted well into this technology of data reduction by aggregation; indeed, they further reduced the large masses of tabulations produced by statistical offices into even more summary tabulations.

By the 1960s, however, the computer was changing the basic technology of data processing, and statistical agencies were beginning to realize that it was important to retain microdata in their disaggregated form, instead of the cross-tabulations which were generated from it. Ivan Fellegi in Canada, and Aukrust and Nordbotten in Norway were among the first ones in statistical offices to articulate this point of view.

In the United States, the maintenance of files of microdata by statistical agencies has had important analytic repercussions. One of the earliest of these followed from the release of a microdata file of individual tax returns by the Internal Revenue Service. Okner and Pechman at Brookings used this microdata file to analyze tax incidence and examine the impact of possible changes in the tax law. The success of this tax modeling has been such that it is now used by the Congress and the Treasury Department to analyze all legislation proposing changes in the tax law. Perhaps the most widely used microdata sets are the Public Use Samples based on the Census of Population. These have not only been produced as a part of the 1960, 1970 and 1980 censuses, but their success has been so great that the Bureau of the Census has gone back to the microfilm records of the 1940 and 1950 censuses and recreated Public Use Samples for these periods. Research workers have used these microdata sets for analyzing many problems involving social, economic and demographic data. For example, studies of the incidence of poverty, geographic mobility, environmental impact studies, labor force participation, the status of the aged and many more topics have been made. Other government agencies have also made microdata files available. Housing and Urban Development made its Annual Survey of Housing available. The Social Security Administration created a 1 percent sample of its Longitudinal Employer–Employee Data file. The Current Population Survey, which is the basis of US unemployment statistics, has been available for many years.

Initially microdata sets were viewed by statistical offices and administrative agencies as a byproduct of their activities. For statistical agencies, microdata represented merely a first stage in the statistical process of producing final tabulated reports. Administrative agencies viewed their microdata files as the administrative records to be used for program purposes, such as the determination of tax compliance, pension benefits or welfare payments. Consequently, the microdata sets supplied to users by both statistical and administrative agencies were often both unedited and undocumented. It was often the users who had to do much of the cleaning and correction needed to make the data usable for analytic purposes.

This situation is now changing: the concept of the data base is now widely accepted, and it is recognized that the creation of data bases is not a byproduct but an essential part of the statistical process, which may require even more care and effort than had gone into the development of final tabulations.

An example is the development of the US Census Bureau's LED file. Some 20 years ago, Shirley Kallek at the Bureau of the Census was involved in trying to create a longitudinal file of manufacturing establishment records. As a result of this effort she concluded that a number of procedures relating to the Annual Surveys of Manufactures and the Censuses of Manufactures needed to be changed. First, she found that the system of identification of establishments and their affiliation with companies was incomplete. In the basic information it was difficult to keep track of births, deaths and mergers of establishments. To correct this situation, permanent plant numbers were assigned to establishments, and a Standard Statistical Establishment List was developed that became a comprehensive register of all establishments and companies. Second, she found that many of the adjustments for undercount, missing values and errors in the data were corrected at the tabulation level rather than in the original microdata. Consequently, alternative tabulations run on the microdata would not agree with the officially published information. To correct this, she insisted that all corrections be carried back to the microdata, and documented through the use of flags. The resulting improvement of the basic microdata files has now made it possible to produce a Longitudinal Establishment Data file which covers all of the Annual Survey of Manufactures and Census of Manufactures data collected from 1972 to 1982, linking the records of individual establishments over time. In order to make this microdata base available to users, the Census Bureau has set up an Economic Studies Center which has the function of processing the LED file in accordance with users' requests, within appropriate confidentiality guidelines.

Recently, the Bureau of the Census has developed another new set of microdata files based on its Survey of Income and Program Participation (SIPP). SIPP is a nationally representative household survey providing detailed information on all sources of cash and non-cash income, eligibility and participation in various government transfer programs, disability, labor force status, assets and liabilities, taxes, pension coverage and many other items. The survey is quarterly, and each sampling unit and person carry the same identifiers from wave to wave so that records can be linked for longitudinal observation. Fully documented SIPP microdata files are scheduled to be released every four months. Just as the tax model released by the IRS more than 20 years ago has become indispensable in the design and administration of tax legislation, so SIPP promises to become a basic tool for the analysis and evaluation of government social policy.

The flood of microdata sets has changed the way in which empirical research is carried out. Simulation models and other analyses are often constructed at the microdata level, where it is possible to relate social, economic and demographic variables to one another.

All of these developments have taken place outside national accounting. While this is quite understandable, it has meant that the discipline which a more generalized national accounting approach could have contributed has not been realized. The strength of national accounting is that it constructs a comprehensive and consistent framework into which all economic data can be fitted. In contrast, many microdata sets, although they provide a wealth of detailed data, are found when compared with other sources to be biased or fragmentary. In household sample surveys, for example, it is usually found that the income which households report from government transfers and from interest and dividends is understated by 40–50 percent when compared with known payments by the government and known disbursements of interest and dividends. This means, of course, that the use of such household surveys for analyzing the distribution of income is quite inappropriate since both the low end and the high end of the distribution are understated. In many cases, the coverage of microdata sets may be partial, and research workers may be unaware of this if they do not have appropriate control totals against which they can match their data. Partly for these reasons, the large amount of microdata research now being carried out often comes up with conflicting and contradictory results.

Future Directions for National Accounting and the Statistical System

On the one hand, it is apparent that microdata files are here to stay: they provide the only way in which social, economic and demographic variables can be related to each other in analytically meaningful terms, and they provide the key to an understanding of the aggregation process. On the other hand, it is equally apparent that the overall framework provided by the national accounts is needed, both to establish the basic control totals and to relate the various parts of the economic system to one another. In considering future directions for national accounts and the statistical system, therefore, the two central questions which should be asked are: in what ways would national accounting need to be altered in order for it to be a more suitable framework for microdata, and in what ways would it be necessary to modify microdata sets to make them suitable for incorporation into a national accounting framework?

The SNA not only attempted to provide a framework for the statistical system, it also attempted to provide an aggregate data base of accounts and cross-tabulations which would give users all the information they might need to analyze the behavior of the economy. As a consequence, the SNA became complex, gothic in its structure, difficult to use, and even more difficult to implement. The transactor/transaction approach of the SNA, that is, dividing the transactors of the economy into sectors and recording their transactions in accounts, is a relatively simple principle which can provide the basis for integrating microdata with the national accounts. But some changes are needed to allow the simplicity to come through. Specifically, the sectors and subsectors in the national accounts need to be defined to be consistent with the reporting units used for microdata sets, and the transactions shown in the national accounts need to be consistent with those of the microdata.

The present dual sectoring system of the SNA recognizes that different reporting units provide different information, but it obscures rather than illuminates the important relationships which exist. By providing only production accounts for establishments and only income and outlay, financial and balance sheet accounts for enterprises, the important enterprise/establishment relationship is left in limbo. Similarly, although accounts are provided for households, no provision is made for social, economic and demographic information relating to the individuals composing the households. For government, the SNA provides only the most summary of sectoring, consolidating the activities of many different levels of government and budgetary units into a few accounts. Thus if the national accounts are to provide a framework for microdata, more attention will need to be given to the question of how sectors and subsectors in the economy should be defined in order to correspond more closely with the reporting units which provide the basic information.

With respect to the recording of transactions, a similar approach needs to be taken. Certain types of imputations and attributions now provided for in the SNA may turn out to be quite inappropriate when examined from the point of view of the individual transactor. For example, the treatment of owner-occupied housing in SNA imputes to the owner a rental payment equivalent to the space value of his house, and relegates the actual payments which a home owner makes for repair and upkeep, property taxes, mortgage interest and depreciation to a nominal industry of ownership. Although this fiction may be a useful one for measuring the aggregate value of home ownership, it creates a serious distortion in the presentation and analysis of the actual household outlays. Similar problems arise in the treatment of pension benefits, which are excluded from household income on the grounds that they reflect a drawing down of past accumulations in pension reserves.

It will also be necessary, of course, for statistical offices to undertake a number of reforms with respect to microdata in order to make them more suitable for integration with the national accounts. In particular, it is very important to develop registers and sampling frames to ensure that the universe of reporting units used for microdata corresponds to the sectoring and subsectoring specified for the national accounts. Administrative data may need to be augmented, in order to attain the more complete coverage required by the national accounts. Where a variety of different data sets containing related information exists, exact matching or statistical matching may be needed to provide more complete information. Editing and documentation are required before raw microdata can be considered as appropriate for analytic use. Both missing cases and missing values must be imputed, and inconsistent or impossible values corrected. Techniques need to be developed to correct or align biased responses with more valid data. Flags need to be provided to inform users about the nature of the edits and imputations performed. Where there are conflicting sources of information, new surveys or special investigations will need to be undertaken to resolve them.

Despite the obvious shortcomings of the SNA and the difficulties inherent in the development of microdata files, the accomplishments of the past 50 years should not be denigrated. In testifying before the Joint Economic Committee at the time of the revision of the United States national accounts in 1958, Martin Gainsbrugh, who was then President of the Industrial Conference Board, stated that 'The introduction and development of an integrated system of national accounts promises to rank in historic significance with some of the more heralded inventions of recent decades in the fields of the physical sciences. This growing family of income and product statistics is without question one of the major contributions — if not the greatest — of the economic fraternity thus far in the 20th Century.' When measured against the events since 1958, Gainsbrugh's comparisons with the physical sciences may overstate things a bit — after all the moon walk had not taken place, computers were not really developed, and color television had not reached its zenith. On the other hand, his statement is probably true even today with respect to economics — much of what was then regarded as achievement is now, rightly or wrongly, considered to be the wrong path. The role of national accounts in defining the economic system and bringing together and putting into order the masses of transactions information has not been questioned. Even the most avid monetarists and supply siders consider the national accounts indispensable for analysis of what is taking place in the economy.

Although the development of microdata has been less heralded than the national accounts, it is, coupled with advancing computer technology, the wave of the future. It is only through the use of microdata that the important relationships among social, economic and demographic information can be analyzed effectively. Already governments are recognizing that the implementation and evaluation of their policies depend on the development of appropriate microdata bases.

Looking back, in view of all that has gone before, one cannot say that this is just the beginning, and hopefully it's not the end. We are in the middle of what is an interesting and exciting development — let's carry on.

5. The Treatment of Pensions and Insurance in the National Accounts

Nancy D. Ruggles and Richard Ruggles
Yale University

1. INTRODUCTION

The approach of the United Nations System of National Accounts (SNA) to privately funded pensions and insurance is essentially a neo-classical one. Apart from the costs of operation, private pension contributions and life insurance premiums are considered to be a form of household saving, part of the accumulation of wealth by households that should appear as a category of assets on the household balance sheet. But publicly funded schemes — social security arrangements — are not treated in this way. Entitlements under public programs are not credited to households until such time as the benefits are actually received. In view of the increased importance of both the public and private components of social protection, a reexamination of the appropriateness of this difference in their treatment seems warranted.

A number of alternative proposals have been made for resolving the difference. On the one hand, it has been proposed that the value of social security entitlements should be included in household wealth, thus in effect treating public pensions like private ones. On the other hand, it has been argued that an increase in future pension and insurance entitlements is different in character from presently available household income, and that, in the household income and outlay account, it would be useful to show current benefit payments received instead of the accretion to future rights which may or may not be exercised. This would lead to treatment of private flows in a way more like the present treatment of public ones.

Questions have also arisen with respect to casualty insurance. Casualty insurance covers a wide variety of different kinds of risks, including sickness

---

This chapter first appeared in *Review of Income and Wealth*, **29** (4), 1983.

and accidents, unemployment and property damage such as fire and theft. SNA treats all of these risks in the same way — but a way that is quite different from the treatment of the risk protected against by life insurance. Country practices, for the most part, do not follow these SNA recommendations. In recent years, it has been suggested that the different kinds of casualty insurance should not all be treated alike. They are really very different in character, and each warrants separate consideration.

Despite the differences in the various forms of pension and insurance transactions, they should not be dealt with on an *ad hoc* basis; it is important that they all be fitted consistently into the basic transactor/transaction framework of SNA. As a basic principle, SNA constructs transactor accounts for recording the transactions in which transactors are involved. Although there are sometimes definitional problems in determining the specific transactions in which transactors are involved, as a general rule, the principle of 'benefit' is not considered to be relevant. Thus, if the government makes an expenditure on goods and services that are used to benefit households, on education for example, the expenditure remains a government outlay; it is not attributed to households even though they benefit from it. As a consequence of this focus on recording transactions, it follows of course that recorded household consumption expenditure does not measure total consumption of households. This treatment has the advantage, from an accounting point of view, that the national accountant is not called upon to make judgments about incidence: he only needs to know who pays, not who benefits or how much.

Although SNA is explicit about the treatment of transactions between government and households, it is less clear in applying the same principles to transactions between employers and households, perhaps because of a judgment that transactions between employers and third parties that were primarily for the benefit of employees were of little quantitative importance. With the increased importance of social security, pensions, insurance and health benefits, this question needs to be reexamined. In some instances, employers engage in transactions that, although of benefit to their employees, are and should be recognized as transactions between the employer and a pension fund, insurance company or health provider. In other instances, however, an employer may merely be serving as an agent for his employees, and it is the employee who should be considered to be engaged in the transaction. Thus, when an employer withholds income tax from an employee's wages and pays them to the government, it is appropriate to consider that the employer is acting purely as an agent, and to include the tax as part of wages paid to employees and also as taxes paid by households to government. Although it may sometimes be difficult to distinguish cases in which employers are directly involved in transactions with pension funds, insurance companies and health care providers from cases in which they are merely acting as agents for their employees, the distinction is analytically useful and is in accord with the broad transactor/ transaction approach of SNA.

To illustrate the magnitude of the shifts in the importance of pensions and insurance that have occurred, Table 5.1 presents comparative data for the United States for 1965 and 1979. Over this interval the contributions for and the benefits from public and private pension and health insurance plans increased six- to seven-fold. This rate of change was double the increase in personal income, and contrasts with purchases of life insurance and annuities, which increased more slowly than personal income. Table 5.1 also illustrates the variety of institutional arrangements which have been developed in connection with pensions and insurance. To the extent that the government and employers have assumed responsibility for social protection, the direct connection between contributions and benefits at the level of the individual household has been lessened.

2. SOCIAL SECURITY ARRANGEMENTS

The SNA Treatment

Consideration of SNA treatment of public social security arrangements is a useful point of departure, since this treatment is considerably simpler than that of private pension and insurance arrangements. In SNA, public social security arrangements may cover any of the risks that are covered by private pension funds and life insurance and many of those covered by private casualty insurance. The exact content depends upon each country's institutional arrangements but it often includes old age, disability, sickness and unemployment.

SNA distinguishes contributions for social security from taxes paid to government, but it effectively treats the contributions as if they were direct taxes on households. (The IMF *Government Finance Statistics Manual* goes so far as to call them taxes.) Both the employers' and the employees' shares of the contribution are included in the compensation of employees, so that they appear as an outlay on the production account of the employer and a receipt on the income and outlay account of households. Households, in turn, pay the whole contribution (both employers' and employees' shares) to the government. This is done even though, in most cases, the actual routing of the payment is from the employer to the government. Thus the treatment is the same as that of personal income taxes that are withheld from wages and salaries and paid by employers directly to the government.

Social security benefits appear as transfer payments from government to households in the income and outlay accounts of both. Their treatment does not differ from that of social assistance grants (which are defined, effectively,

Table 5.1 *Social Security, Pensions, Health and Life Insurance in the United States, 1965 and 1979 ($bn)*

	1965	1979	1979/1965
I. TOTAL CONTRIBUTIONS	68.8	377.4	5.5
A. Employers' contributions	34.2	233.4	6.4
1. Social security contributions	12.6	82.2	6.3
a. Old age and disability	8.9	51.9	5.8
b. Health and hospital	0.0	10.5	–
c. Unemployment	3.7	15.9	4.3
2. Pension funds and insurance	21.6	141.2	6.5
a. Pension plans	11.2	79.2	7.1
b. Group health insurance	5.9	41.6	7.1
c. Group life insurance	1.7	6.0	3.5
d. Workmen's compensation	2.8	14.4	5.1
B. Employees' contributions	14.0	88.8	6.3
1. Social security contributions	10.5	70.5	6.7
a. Old age and disability	10.5	57.3	5.5
b. Health and hospital	0.0	13.2	–
2. Pension funds and insurance	3.5	17.8	5.9
C. Personal contributions	20.6	65.2	3.2
1. Life insurance and annuities	16.6	51.0	3.1
2. Health insurance	4.0	14.2	3.5
II. INCOME EARNED ON RESERVES	8.2	36.0	4.4
1. Pension funds	4.8	26.3	5.5
2. Life insurance and annuities	3.4	9.7	2.6
III. TOTAL BENEFITS	64.0	346.7	5.4
A. Government transfers	26.6	172.8	6.4
1. Old age and disability benefits	18.1	102.6	5.7
2. Health and hospital benefits	0.0	29.2	–
3. Unemployment benefits	2.3	9.4	4.1
4. Workmen's compensation	0.6	2.5	4.2
5. Other welfare benefits	5.6	29.1	4.8
B. Employee benefits	27.6	149.5	5.4
1. Pension benefits	7.6	59.8	7.9
2. Health benefits	7.6	42.9	5.8
3. Group life insurance benefits	1.6	4.9	3.1
4. Workmen's compensation	1.5	7.9	5.3
5. Military and veterans' benefits	7.3	24.0	3.3
6. Other unfunded benefits	2.0	10.0	5.0
C. Personal benefits	9.8	24.4	2.5
1. Health insurance benefits	1.1	6.0	5.5
2. Life insurance and annuities	8.7	18.4	2.1
IV. PERSONAL INCOME	540.7	1,951.2	3.6

Source: US National Accounts, Flow of Funds, Life Insurance Fact Book.

as noncontributory welfare benefits). Benefits thus enter household income in the accounting period in which they are actually received; no attempt is made to show the build-up of entitlements to future benefits as an element of current household income.

The Treatment of Contributions

The identical treatment of employers' and employees' contributions for social security in SNA has the very great advantage of simplicity, and it was primarily on this ground that it was adopted. It may be questioned, however, on logical grounds.

The point at issue — which also arises in later sections of this paper — is whether certain transactions ought, logically, to be run through the household income and outlay account as transactions engaged in by households. It is of course true that when a flow is added to both household income and household outlay there is no change in household net saving. But interest in the household income and outlay account is not limited to the calculation of net saving. Total household income, its composition and its change are often the focus of analytic and policy interest.

The difference between the employers' and the employees' social security contributions is more than semantic, and their economic impact is not necessarily the same. In the United States, for instance, unemployment insurance is included in social insurance funds, and the employers' share therefore reflects the unemployment experience of different industries, changing differentially for different employers. If individual employers' contributions were raised to reflect increased unemployment in a given industry, the initial effect would be an increase in labor cost, and it is difficult to predict how much of this might be passed along to employees in the form of a decrease in wages. But if the employee contributions were increased, for example to provide more extended social benefits, the initial impact would be a reduction in after-tax income of households; whether (or how much) wages might rise to compensate is problematical. A preferential treatment might therefore be to treat only the employee contribution as an element of household income, since its impact on disposable income is direct whereas that of the employers' contribution is necessarily indirect.

The employers' contributions are, of course, still part of the employers' labor cost. With the proposed treatment, instead of being routed entirely through the household, the employers' labor cost is divided into two parts, one of which goes to households and the other directly to government. There is no theoretical reason why employers' labor cost need be identical to employees' labor income; indeed, even in the present SNA treatment the identity is not preserved in cases where indirect taxes are levied on labor employed.

The Treatment of Benefits

It has long been recognized that problems arise in drawing the line between social assistance grants, i.e., transfer payments to households, and direct government consumption expenditures. Much the same sort of problem occurs in connection with social security benefit payments.

The problem arises when the government pays for services rendered to households by third parties — in particular, by providers of health care. The payment sometimes takes the form of reimbursement of households by the government for health care expenditures the households have made, and is sometimes a direct payment by the government to the health care provider. SNA distinguishes transfer payments from consumption expenditures on the basis of the location of the decision-making power. When households are free to choose the service and its provider, the payment is considered to be a transfer payment from the government to the household. But when the government sets the terms and conditions for the supply of the service and designates the supplier, the payment is treated as a government intermediate consumption expenditure (which will ultimately pass into government final consumption through the medium of services produced by government for its own use).

Making this distinction has always caused difficulty, and recent studies of the European Community have proposed an alternative. They suggest that all third-party reimbursements should be considered government purchases, not transfer payments, and that transfer payments should be limited to cash payments to households for which no accounting is required. The EC studies further suggest that, when the government's role is purely financial and it contributes nothing to the actual production process, this expenditure should be treated as final, not intermediate, government consumption. This would introduce a new category of direct government final consumption expenditure, not now provided for in SNA.

The same considerations apply to social security benefits. The fact that the scheme which makes a payment for health care services is a contributory one does not alter the character of the payments. A plausible argument can be made, using the same criteria as for social assistance grants, that payments destined to third parties — i.e., health service providers — should be shown as direct payments to them, and not run through the household account.

The Balance Sheet

As the combination of ageing populations and world recession has led a number of social security schemes into temporary or permanent difficulties, the question has been raised as to whether the balance sheet of the social security fund should show an actuarial computation of the reserve required to meet already-incurred, or sometimes even anticipated, future obligations. This is a different question from that of whether the fund itself should be actuarially based. The method of financing social security that each country chooses for itself is a political decision. The question here is rather that of showing the possible consequences of the choices made. The proposal to show an actuarial computation of obligations incurred would parallel in many respects the treatment now recommended by SNA for unfunded private schemes.

Superficially, the proposal is attractive, but it does have some severe drawbacks. It would be a departure from the fundamental SNA principle of recording actual transactions, and would require a forecast of many elements that experience has demonstrated are very difficult to foresee. These include demographic factors — mortality, morbidity, disability, labor force participation — and such economic factors as interest rates, price movements and unemployment rates. Because of these difficulties, it seems preferable to keep such computations outside of the accounts, although they are of course of considerable analytic interest. As current controversies demonstrate, there is little likelihood that two researchers working on such estimates would arrive at the same figures.

Summary of Proposals

The effects of the changes relating to the treatment of social security that have been proposed in this section are shown in Table 5.2, which gives comparative T-accounts showing the present and proposed treatments. The figures entered in the accounts are drawn from Table 5.1, in order to put the questions into a somewhat realistic context.

No changes appear in the production account of employers, or in that of health care providers. It is necessary to separate employers' and employees' contributions for social security, but SNA now recommends showing this separation.

In the household income and outlay account, there is considerable simplification. Employers' social security contributions disappear from both sides of the account, and so do the items 'reimbursements for health care expenditures' and 'final expenditures for reimbursed health care services'. What remain are employees' social security contributions, as part of income and as a payment to government, and unrestricted cash social security benefit payments, as a part of income.

The government's income and outlay account, finally, is also unchanged. What has changed is the routing of certain receipts and outlays. Employers' social security contributions are received directly from employers, and payments for health care services are paid directly to health care providers.

Table 5.2 Comparison of Present SNA and Proposed Treatment of Social Security, United States, 1979 ($bn)

PRESENT SNA TREATMENT		PROPOSED TREATMENT	
Employers' Production Account		**Employers' Production Account**	
Employers' social security contributions	$82.2	Employers' social security contributions	$82.2
Employees' social security contributions	70.5	Employees' social security contributions	70.5
Health Care Providers' Production Account		**Health Care Providers' Production Account**	
Costs of providing health care services	$29.2	Costs of providing health care services	$29.2
		Final expenditures on health care services	$29.2
Household Income and Outlay Account		**Household Income and Outlay Account**	
Final expenditures for reimbursed health care services	$82.2	Employees' social security contributions	$70.5
Employers' social security contributions	70.5	Social security benefit payments other than health care	114.5
Employees' social security contributions	29.2		
Reimbursement for health care expenditures	70.5		
Social security benefit payments other than health care	114.5		
Government Income and Outlay Account		**Government Income and Outlay Account**	
Reimbursement for health care expenditures	$29.2	Final expenditures on health care services	$82.2
Employers' social security contributions	114.5	Social security benefit payments other than health care	70.5
Employees' social security contributions	70.5	Employers' social security contributions	$82.2
		Employees' social security contributions	70.5

3. PENSIONS

The SNA Treatment

Pension plans are arrangements through which employers provide for the payment of retirement incomes to their former employees or their dependents, usually in amounts related to the level of wages and length of service of the employee. Plans established by the government for its own employees are classed in SNA as pension plans, and not as social security. (This differs from US National Accounts practice, and explains some of the differences between Table 5.1 and the published US accounts. For additional detail on the adjustments required to the US National Accounts, see Table 5.8.) SNA treats pension plans in two different ways, depending upon whether or not they are funded. A plan is considered to be funded if the employer (and sometimes also the employee) makes regular contributions to a pension fund or insurance company, which in turn undertakes the responsibility for paying out pension benefits when the time comes for the employee to draw them. But it may also happen that an employer pays such benefits to his former employees and their families out of current revenues, without setting up a special fund for this purpose. Such an unfunded scheme may be voluntary, in that the employer is under no obligation to make the benefit payments, or it may be established as a part of the employment contract. A class of plans intermediate between the funded and unfunded is also found, in which the employer sets up a fund but retains full control of it himself, so that he has access to the fund's reserves and may be able to alter both the level of contributions and the level of benefits. SNA treats this last class as if it were unfunded.

Transactions relating to funded pension plans are treated in SNA as if they were discretionary household activities, similar to household purchases of other financial assets. Contributions to such funds (both employer and employee) are included as a part of the compensation of employees, and are thus included in household income. The costs of operating the funds are charged to household final consumption expenditure, and the remainder, which is equivalent to the net contribution, enters household saving. Interest earned on the funds' assets is imputed to households in their income and outlay account, and thus also enters into their saving. In the capital finance accounts of both households and pension funds, the excess of the net contribution and interest earned over pension benefits is shown as the net increase in household equity in pension fund reserves: an increase in assets for households and an increase in liabilities for pension funds. The value of this equity, which is in most cases equal to the total pension fund reserve, appears as an asset on the household balance sheet and a liability of the pension fund. The actual assets entering into its computation, of course, are shown in the pension fund balance sheet. Pension benefits, thus, are not considered to be household income in the period in which they are received; they enter the household accounts only as a component in computing the change in households' equity in pension funds — in other words, benefits are considered to represent only a change in the form of household assets.

For unfunded plans, SNA recommends that an imputed contribution should be calculated, of a magnitude that would be sufficient to support a fund from which future obligations could be met. This imputed contribution is included, along with actual contributions to funded plans, in compensation of employees and thus in household income. The imputed fund so created, however, is considered to remain under the control of the employer, not to constitute a household asset. It is therefore also necessary to show the imputed contribution as a transfer by households back to their employers, in the income and outlay accounts for both. Thus the entire transaction leaves the net saving and therefore, the balance sheets, of both households and employers unchanged from what they would have been without the imputation. It does, however, raise the level of household income, and it transfers the amount of the imputed contribution from the employer's production account to his income and outlay account. Benefits paid out under unfunded plans, unlike those paid out by funded plans, do enter into the current income of the recipient in the accounting period in which they are received. They cannot be regarded, like funded benefits, as a change in the form of household assets since there is no household asset to be drawn down.

The purpose of this treatment of unfunded pensions is, essentially, to correct the timing of the recording of costs. The obligation to pay future benefits is incurred at the time labor is employed and should be shown as a labor cost of that period, not the later period when benefits are actually paid, and this is what the imputation of the contribution accomplishes. SNA recognizes, however, that estimation of the amount of contribution required is likely to be very difficult. For all of the reasons noted above in connection with the estimation of social security entitlements, the margin of error involved is very large. As a practical procedure, SNA suggests two methods of estimation. One is to adopt the level of contributions required by a comparable funded plan. The second is to assume contributions equal to benefits paid. Most of the countries that have made these estimates have adopted the latter method.

The Treatment of Contributions

Funded plans
The same question may be raised in connection with employers' contributions to private pension plans as was raised above in connection with employers' contributions to social security. It relates to whether it is appropriate to run the

employers' contributions through the household income and outlay account. The employer often provides pension benefits by means of group plans or contracts, which are not individual arrangements made for each employee. In such a case, the employer is the purchaser of the pension arrangements for the benefit of his employees, rather than an intermediary between the individual employee and the pension fund.

To reflect this, it might be preferable to consider that the employer's contribution is paid into his own income and outlay account rather than to the household's income and outlay account. This change would mean that the employer, in his income and outlay account, was making a final expenditure on pension service charges for the benefit of his employees and providing a transfer to the pension fund equal to the net pension contribution. As in the case of social security contributions, however, it is probably useful to continue to run the employee's contribution through the household income and outlay account, both as income received and as an expenditure for pension service charges and a transfer paid to the pension fund. The receipts of pension funds would thus be shown explicitly as equal to the net contributions of employers and employees plus the interest received on pension fund reserves, and their net saving would be derived as the difference between total receipts and employee benefits paid out.

This explicit treatment of pension fund operations in the income and outlay account contrasts with the present SNA treatment, which shows only the net change, as an entry in the capital finance account. It would parallel the treatment of social security operations in the government income and outlay account.

It should be noted that this treatment splits the pension service charges between household final consumption expenditure and final consumption expenditure provided by the employer. This would necessitate setting up enterprise final consumption expenditure as a new category of final expenditures, directly parallel to nonprofit institution and government final consumption expenditures. Although the traditional SNA accountant may consider 'enterprise final consumption expenditures' an unacceptable innovation, it is logically required if employee benefits provided by employers are to be handled in a manner consistent with SNA treatment of all other benefits in kind. Indeed, the omission of enterprise final consumption expenditure is an anomaly resulting from SNA's implicit desire to identify the institutional category of 'enterprises' with the functional category of 'producers', which by definition can only be concerned with production activities.

Unfunded plans
Two questions may be raised with respect to the SNA treatment of imputed contributions to unfunded plans. The first is the same as that raised in the

preceding section about employers' contributions to funded plans. It may be questioned whether this contribution should be run through the household account in such a way that it increases household income. While it is legitimate to consider that it increases the employer's labor cost, a more appropriate treatment might show it as a payment from the employer's production account to his income and outlay account. But this is only true when it is possible to make an estimate of the contribution on some basis other than benefits paid. There does not seem to be much gained — beyond increasing employment opportunities for accountants — in entering the same figure on both sides of the income and outlay account as contributions received and benefits paid out. It does not accomplish the intended purpose of the imputation, which is to correct the timing, and it has no effect on enterprise net saving. A more straightforward procedure would simply treat the unfunded benefit payments as a part of current labor costs.

In this connection the results of the recent requirement of the US Securities and Exchange Commission that companies provide an estimate of their unfunded obligations are interesting. The range of variation in the estimates is very wide, even when the benefits provided are similar. The same is also true of company-controlled funds, where the most influential factor appears to be the company's profitability. The plans of profitable companies are overfunded, thus sheltering some income from tax, whereas the plans of unprofitable companies are underfunded.

The Treatment of Benefits

The SNA treatment of funded pension benefit receipts by households has aroused considerable concern. Omission of current benefit receipts from household income leads to a view of the distribution of income over the life cycle that might perhaps be consistent with a theoretical world of complete financial mobility and unlimited access to credit, but it is of little relevance to either the wage earner or the pensioner, both of whom must in most cases tailor their outlays to their current receipts. The wage earner does not have access to the sum represented by the pension contribution, and he normally cannot even borrow against it. The pensioner, on the other hand, does receive the benefit payment, and can spend it. For such kinds of analysis as the study of the determinants of consumption and alterations in consumption patterns, the present treatment introduces an unacceptable distortion. This point has been recognized in the SNA income distribution guidelines, where the use of an adjusted concept of household income that includes current pension benefit receipts is recommended. Inclusion of benefits in current income would also have the effect of placing recipients of funded and unfunded benefits on the same footing — a desirable result since it is unlikely that most pensioners recognize a difference. (There may in fact not be much difference, in cases where anticipated obligations exceed assets.) It would also place the recipients of private pensions on the same footing as recipients of social security benefits. It is of course true, in all of these cases, that the future entitlement does have value to its prospective recipient. But so do many other anticipated future events (such as the continued receipt of wages) that are not reflected in the accounts.

The Balance Sheet

The proposed changes in the treatment of pension contributions and benefits would entail corresponding changes in the balance sheets of households and pension funds. Households would no longer be credited with an equity equal to the value of the pension fund reserve; rather, this equity would remain with the pension fund.

Summary of Proposed Changes

Table 5.3 summarizes the impact of the proposed changes in the treatment of funded pension plans, in the form of T-accounts. The employer's pension contribution is routed to his income and outlay account, where it is split into two elements: pension service charges and net pension contribution. The pension service charge is final consumption provided to employees, and is reflected as a receipt in the pension fund production account. The net pension contribution is a transfer going to the pension fund income and outlay account. The employee's pension contribution is routed to the household income and outlay account, where the same two components, the service charge and net pension fund contributions, are shown as consumption expenditures and transfers respectively. The 'change in net equity of households in pension funds' item disappears from both the household and the pension fund capital finance accounts, and an equivalent amount appears instead as net saving of pension funds. Total saving remains the same: what in SNA is shown entirely as household saving is now split between households and pension funds.

Table 5.4 shows the impact of the proposed changes on the treatment of unfunded plans. The imputation of employers' contributions is omitted, and pension benefit payments are treated as part of labor cost rather than as a transfer, and flow directly from the employer's production account to the household income and outlay account without passing through the employer's income and outlay account.

Table 5.3 Comparison of Present SNA and Proposed Treatment of Funded Pensions, United States, 1979 ($bn)

PRESENT SNA TREATMENT		PROPOSED TREATMENT	
Employers' Production Account		**Employers' Production Account**	
Employers' pension contributions	$79.2	Employers' pension contributions	$79.2
Employees' pension contributions	17.8	Employees' pension contributions	17.8
Employers' Income and Outlay Account		**Employers' Income and Outlay Account**	
		Employees' pension service charges	$12.2
		Employers' net pension contributions	67.0
Pension Fund Production Account		**Pension Fund Production Account**	
Administrative costs of pension funds	$15.0	Pension service charges	$15.0
		Employers'	12.2
		Employees'	2.8
Pension Fund Income and Outlay Account		**Pension Fund Income and Outlay Account**	
Imputed interest to households	$26.3	Interest received on pension funds	$26.3
Net saving	0	Employers' net pension contributions	67.0
		Employees' net pension contributions	15.0

(cont.)

Table 5.3 (cont.)

Pension Fund Capital Finance Account					Pension Fund Capital Finance Account		
Net change in financial assets	$48.5	Net lending	$0		Net change in financial assets	$48.5	Net lending $48.5
Net contributions	82.0	Net change in equity of households in pension funds	48.5		Net contributions	82.0	
Interest received	26.3				Interest received	26.3	
Less: Pension benefits	59.8				Less: Pension benefits	59.8	

Household Income and Outlay Account					Household Income and Outlay Account		
Pension service charges	$15.0	Employees' pension contributions	$79.2		Employees' pension service charge	$2.8	Employees' pension contributions $17.8
Household saving	108.3	Employees' pension contributions	17.8		Employees' net pension contributions	15.0	Employees' pension benefits 59.8
		Imputed interest on pension funds	26.3		Household saving	59.8	

Household Capital Finance Account					Household Capital Finance Account		
Net charge in equity of households in pension funds	$48.5	Net lending	108.3				
		Net contributions to pension funds	82.0				
Net change in financial assets	59.8	Imputed interest on pension funds	26.3				
Pension benefits	59.8						

Table 5.4 Comparison of Present SNA and Proposed Treatment of Unfunded Benefits, United States, 1979 ($bn)

PRESENT SNA TREATMENT		PROPOSED TREATMENT	
Employers' Production Account		Employers' Production Account	
Employers' unfunded benefit contributions (to households)	$34.0	Employers' unfunded benefit contributions	$34.0
Private employees	10.0	Private employees	10.0
Military and veterans	24.0	Military and veterans	24.0
Employers' Income and Outlay Account		Employers' Income and Outlay Account	
Employees' unfunded benefit payments (to households)	$34.0		
Private employees	10.0		
Military and veterans	24.0		
Household Income and Outlay Account		Household Income and Outlay Account	
Employers' unfunded benefit contributions (to employers)	$34.0	Employees' unfunded benefits	$34.0
Private employees	10.0	Private employees	10.0
Military and veterans	24.0	Military and veterans	24.0
Employees' unfunded benefit payments (from employers)	34.0		
Private employees	10.0		
Military and veterans	24.0		

4. LIFE INSURANCE AND ANNUITIES

The SNA Treatment

The SNA treatment of life insurance and annuities is in most respects the same as its treatment of pensions. The chief difference lies in the method of computation of the service charge, i.e., the amount recorded as the output of the insurance company. For pension funds, this is equated to the fund's actual administrative costs, and pension fund reserves are derived residually. For insurance companies, however, it is the service charge that is derived residually, as the excess of gross premiums paid ($51.0 billion) and interest received ($9.7 billion) over the sum of claims paid ($18.4 billion) and net additions to actuarial reserves ($31.3 billion). This service charge ($11 billion) may, of course differ from the administrative costs actually recorded by the insurance companies and the difference constitutes their profit or loss.

SNA does not distinguish different kinds of life insurance. Thus ordinary life, group life, and term life are all included here. Nor is there a difference in the treatment of the different sorts of proceeds of life insurance policies. Annuities, death benefits, the maturing of endowment policies, and the withdrawal of cash surrender values all enter the accounts only through their impact on the capital finance account.

The Treatment of Contributions

Unlike pension funds, in the United States the greater part of life insurance and annuities is purchased by individuals for themselves, not by employers. Group life and industrial policies have been rising in importance relative to individual policies, but they are still a small part of the whole. Within the category of insurance purchased by households, however, there has been a shift away from conventional whole life and annuity policies, and toward term policies. These, like the group and industrial policies, do not really fit the SNA concept of life insurance. They do not embody any element of household saving, but rather are simply insurance against the risk of death. In SNA terms, they are much closer to casualty than to life insurance. In the subsequent discussion, therefore, term life insurance — both that purchased by households and that purchased by employers — will be considered in the section dealing with casualty insurance. This section will treat only whole life insurance and annuities, which can in fact be considered to embody a savings component.

Whole life insurance differs from pension fund accumulations in one very important respect. Normally, such insurance policies have a cash surrender or loan value, which is often close to the total amount of premiums paid in, plus the earnings thereon. This cash surrender value is in effect the savings component. In the United States, individuals often draw upon the life insurance they own to obtain funds to meet emergency needs or to provide down payments for major outlays such as automobiles and housing. Unlike pension fund reserves, therefore, it is quite appropriate to consider that households are the owners of life insurance and annuity reserves, at least up to the cash surrender value of their policies. Nevertheless, it still seems useful to show the transactions between households and insurance companies explicitly in their income and outlay accounts, rather than simply as net changes in the composition of assets and liabilities in the capital finance account. If this is done, the service charge will continue to appear, as it does in SNA, as an outlay on the household income and outlay account and a receipt on the life insurance company production account.

The net premium may then be divided into two components, one representing the increase in cash surrender value and the other the balance of the premium. The increase in cash surrender value is in SNA terminology the net increase in the equity of households in life insurance reserves, and household saving should be shown gross of this amount. The balance of the premium, after deduction of the increase in cash surrender value, should appear as an outlay on the household income and outlay account. In the income and outlay account of life insurance companies, the net premium appears as a receipt, and the increase in cash surrender value as the household's share of the excess of receipts over actual outlays. What enters the net saving of life insurance companies, therefore, is the balance of the net premium, after deduction of the increase in cash surrender value. The ultimate effect of the proposed change, thus, is to attribute a part of the net increase in the reserves of life insurance companies to their own net saving, rather than keeping all of it in the net saving of households.

It may be argued that cash surrender values are not easily obtained, or that they seriously understate the value of the life insurance owned by households. However, standard schedules exist for determining the cash surrender value of life insurance policies, and in the US these are usually printed in the policy itself. Although it is true that the cash surrender value is lower than the actuarial value of the entitlement, it is precisely this facet which the proposed treatment is trying to show. The excess of the actuarial value of the reserve over cash surrender value is not available to the policyholder, and is more appropriately treated, like the pension fund reserve, as an asset of the life insurance company rather than the policyholder.

The Treatment of Benefits

In SNA, all proceeds to households of life insurance transactions except for the interest on their equity in life insurance reserves is treated in the same way, as a change in the composition of their assets in the capital finance and balance sheet accounts. This appears to be an unwarranted oversimplification. There is a considerable difference, from the point of view of the recipient, between lump-sum transactions that really are of a capital character and the receipt of such regular income supplements as annuity benefits. Death benefits and other lump-sum payments such as cash surrender or maturing of endowment policies are properly treated in the household capital finance account in the way SNA treats them (although it would be useful to show more of the detail explicitly instead of only the net result). Annuities and other periodic payments, however, like pension benefits, should be shown in the household income and outlay account. Both lump-sum and periodic payments, under the treatment proposed here, would appear as outlays in the income and outlay account of life insurance companies.

The Balance Sheet

The changes proposed would alter some entries in the balance sheet and capital finance accounts. The net change in the equity of households in life insurance reserves would now refer only to cash surrender values of policies, in the accounts of both the companies and households. The net change in household financial assets would reflect directly only lump-sum payments like death benefits. Periodic payments like annuities would, of course, influence the capital finance account indirectly, through their impact upon household saving. Similarly, the impact of benefit payments upon the capital finance account of life insurance companies would be felt through its impact upon their net saving.

Summary of Proposals

Table 5.5 summarizes the proposed changes relating to whole life insurance. It may be noted that it was not possible, in the figures shown here, to separate whole life and term insurance purchased by households. Therefore, while group and industrial life insurance have been eliminated, the figures on net premiums and lump-sum benefits are too large by the amount of term insurance purchased by households included.

A note about data difficulties is in order here. It has been argued that the treatment proposed here is not feasible because the data are unavailable. This argument is, however, not very convincing, since it is apparent that insurance companies must have the information to meet their operating needs. What is lacking is an effective data collection program, and that should be entirely feasible to set up.

In the proposed treatment, the production and income and outlay accounts of the insurance providers and the income and outlay accounts of households

Table 5.5 Comparison of Present SNA and Proposed Treatment of Life Insurance, United States, 1979 ($bn)

PRESENT SNA TREATMENT		PROPOSED TREATMENT	
Life Insurance Production Account		**Life Insurance Production Account**	
Administrative costs and profits of insurance companies	$11.0	Administrative costs and profits of insurance companies	$11.0
Insurance service charges	$11.0	Insurance services charges	$11.0
Premium payments	51.0	Premium payments	51.0
Plus: Interest received	9.7	Plus: Interest received	9.7
Less: Benefits paid	−18.4	Less: Benefits paid	−18.4
Less: Change in actuarial reserves	−31.3	Less: Change in actuarial reserves	−31.3
Life Insurance Income and Outlay Account		**Life Insurance Income and Outlay Account**	
Imputed interest paid to households	$9.7	Interest received on insurance funds	$9.7
Interest received on insurance	$9.7	Net premiums received	40.0
		Death benefit payments	$11.8
		Annuity payments	6.6
		Increase in cash surrender value	12.6
		Net saving	18.7
Life Insurance Capital Finance Account		**Life Insurance Capital Finance Account**	
Net change in financial assets	$31.3	Net lending	$18.7
Net premiums received	40.0	Increase in cash surrender value	12.6
Interest on insurance funds	9.7		
Less: Benefits paid	−18.4		
Net change in household equity	$31.3		

(cont.)

Table 5.5 (cont.)

Household Income and Outlay Account				Household Income and Outlay Account		
Insurance service charge	$11.0	Annuity payments received	$6.6	Insurance service charge	$11.0	Imputed interest on insurance funds $9.7
Net premiums paid	40.0			Household saving	−1.3	
Less: increase in cash surrender value	−12.6					
Net saving	−31.8					

Household Capital Accumulation Account				Household Capital Accumulation Account		
Net lending	$−20.0	Net saving	$−31.8	Net lending	$−1.3	Net saving $−1.3
		Death benefits	11.8			

Household Capital Finance Account				Household Equity Capital Finance Account		
Net change in financial assets	$2.6	Net lending	$−20.0	Net change in household in insurance	$31.3	Net lending $−1.3
Death benefits received	11.8			Net change in financial assets	−32.6	
Annuity benefits received	6.6			Benefits received	18.4	
Less: Benefits paid	−51.1			Less: Premium payments	−51.0	
Increase in cash surrender value	12.6					

would show explicitly the breakdown of the gross premium into three components: the service charge, the increase in cash surrender value and the balance of the net premium. Benefit payments would be divided between periodic and lump sum, and the periodic benefits shown as household income. On the other hand, interest earned on the life insurance reserve fund but not actually paid out to households would no longer be imputed to them. Except for whatever impact it may have on cash surrender value, that interest serves to increase the net saving of life insurance companies. In the capital finance accounts, the net change in equity of households in life insurance reserves would be smaller and the net saving of life insurance companies larger, reflecting the attribution to households only of that part of life insurance reserves to which they have effective access through the cash surrender or loan value.

5. CASUALTY INSURANCE

The SNA Treatment

All types of casualty insurance are treated in SNA in the same way. Gross casualty insurance premiums are divided into two parts, the service charge and the net premium. The service charge is considered to be the measure of the gross output of the casualty insurance provider: it appears as a receipt on its production account. If the purchaser is a producer, the service charge appears as an element of intermediate cost in its production account; if the purchaser is a household, the service charge appears as a final consumption expenditure. The net premium, which is considered to be a payment for risk, is shown in the income and outlay accounts of both insurer and insured. In both cases, it appears as a separate entry; SNA considers that it is different in kind from all other types of transaction and cannot be combined with anything else. It is not, for instance, to be included in household consumption expenditure. Payments of casualty insurance claims also appear in the income and outlay accounts of both parties, again as separate entries.

By convention, the casualty insurance service charge for each type of casualty insurance is defined as being equal to gross premiums less claims paid. As in the case of life insurance, SNA recognizes that this may be quite different from actual service charges of insurance companies, as well as quite different from their actual costs of operation. It is considered, however, that the simplification thus introduced is warranted because of the difficulty of obtaining actual data. As a consequence of this convention, net casualty insurance premiums are, by definition, equal for each type of insurance and for the economy as a whole, to claims paid. Thus the casualty insurance entries consolidate out of the gross domestic product account. They do not consolidate out of the accounts for sectors and subsectors, however, because of the way SNA allocates the net premium. It is allocated among the purchasers of each type of insurance in proportion to the gross premium paid, so that for an individual purchaser it would be quite unlikely to continue to equal claims.

Casualty insurance covers a wide spectrum of different kinds of risks. They may be classified, broadly, into four groups: health and similar risks where the benefit takes the form of a payment to a third party, risk of loss of income, risk of death and risk of property damage. Different considerations seem important for these different categories, and the discussion that follows will employ this breakdown.

Health Insurance

In some countries, insurance against the need for paying out large sums to third parties is quite important. Health insurance is a typical, and in the US a fast-growing, example. Where health care services are not provided free of charge or as a part of social security by the government, private health insurance often fills the gap — either as a fringe benefit of employees or as a direct purchase by households. The problems which arise in this context have already been touched upon above.

One problem relates to health and similar kinds of insurance provided by employers to their employees as a part of their compensation. As in the case of employers' social security and pension fund contributions, it may be questioned whether the SNA approach of running the premiums paid by employers through the household income and outlay account is appropriate. If the premium payments are not routed through the household, it becomes necessary to find an alternative treatment for them. They are, of course, still a part of the employer's labor cost, and should appear as such in his production account. But instead of being routed to the household income and outlay account, it would be more appropriate to route them through the income and outlay account of the employer himself. This would mean that in the employers' income and outlay account, the employers' health insurance contributions will appear as a receipt and the employers' expenditure on health care insurance would be a form of enterprise final consumption provided as an employee benefit in the same way as it has been proposed that government health insurance expenditures should be treated as government final consumption provided for the benefit of households. In the household income and outlay account, only the premiums actually paid by the household would appear; but it would be the gross rather than the net premium that would appear as a final consumption expenditure.

The actual expenditures on health care, in turn, would under this proposal appear both as intermediate consumption of the insurance companies and

Table 5.6 Comparison of Present SNA and Proposed Treatment of Health Insurance, United States, 1979 ($bn)

PRESENT SNA TREATMENT		PROPOSED TREATMENT	
Employers' Production Account		**Employers' Production Account**	
Employers' health insurance contributions	$44.2	Employers' health insurance contributions	$44.2
Employers' Income and Outlay Account		**Employers' Income and Outlay Account**	
		Employers' expenditure on health care insurance	$44.2 Employers' health insurance contributions $44.2
Health Insurance Production Account		**Health Insurance Production Account**	
Administrative costs of health insurance companies	$9.5 Household expenditures for health insurance service charges	Purchases of health services Administrative costs of health insurance	$48.9 Employers' expenditures on health insurance $44.2 9.5 Household expenditures on health insurance 14.2
Health Insurance Income and Outlay Account		**Health Insurance Income and Outlay Account**	
Reimbursements for health care expenditures	$48.9 Net premiums received from households $48.9		
Health Care Providers' Production Account		**Health Care Providers' Production Account**	
Costs and profits of providing health care services	$48.9 Health care purchases (by households) $48.9	Costs of profits of providing health care services	$48.9 Health insurance purchases of health care services $48.9
Household Income and Outlay Account		**Household Income and Outlay Account**	
Net premiums paid by households $48.9 Employers' contribution 44.2 Personal contributions 14.2 Less: Health insurance service charges −9.5 Household expenditures for health insurance service charges 9.5 Health care expenditures 48.9	Employers' health insurance contributions $44.2 Reimbursement for health care expenditures 48.9	Household expenditures for health insurance	$14.2

receipts in the production account of health care providers. The value added — final output — of health insurance companies would be equal to their administrative costs, and the value added of health care providers would be equal to the costs involved in producing health care services.

These proposals with respect to the treatment of health insurance are summarized in Table 5.6.

Income Replacement

Income replacement insurance includes unemployment, disability, workmen's compensation and similar types of protection that provide benefits in the form of periodic payments over a relatively long term, rather than a single lump-sum settlement. They are most often found as fringe benefits of employment, and are paid for by the employer. The considerations noted in the previous sections about employers' contributions therefore also apply here. Running the employer's premium payment through the household income and outlay account is questionable.

There is also a second problem with this type of insurance. SNA's method of computing the service charge implies an annual balancing of premiums and claims; there is no provision for the establishment of a reserve that would allow for the spreading of risks over a longer time period (as is done with life insurance). Such an annual balancing, however, is scarcely likely in the case of unemployment insurance, where the whole objective is the spreading of the costs of unemployment evenly over the cycle instead of concentrating them in periods of recession. Unemployment insurance is the most obvious case, but even in others the assumption of annual balancing is often strained. It might, therefore, be preferable to set up explicit reserve funds for casualty as well as life insurance, and to adopt a more realistic measure of service charges.

Table 5.7 shows the impact of the proposed changes in the treatment of contributions, and incorporates a casualty insurance reserve. The figures shown should be regarded as illustrative only.

Term Life Insurance

In the discussion of life insurance above it was noted that term insurance does not share the characteristic established by SNA for life insurance — namely, incorporation of an element of saving — and therefore, that it might more appropriately be considered in the context of casualty insurance. Term life differs from the income replacement kinds of insurance discussed in the previous section principally in that it usually provides a single lump-sum payment rather than a continuing income. From the point of view of the recipient, this benefit is clearly a capital transaction. It is therefore appropriate to exclude

Table 5.7 *Comparison of Present SNA and Proposed Treatment of Group Life Insurance and Workmen's Compensation, United States, 1979 ($bn)*

PRESENT SNA TREATMENT		PROPOSED TREATMENT	
Employers' Production Account		**Employers' Production Account**	
Employers' group life insurance contributions	$6.0	Employers' group life insurance contributions	$6.0
Employers' workmen's compensation contributions	14.4	Employers' workmen's compensation contributions	14.4
Employers' Income and Outlay Account		**Employers' Income and Outlay Account**	
		Expenditure on group life insurance services	$1.0
		Expenditure on workmen's compensation services	4.0
		Net premiums on group life insurance	5.0
		Net premiums on workmen's compensation insurance	10.4
Insurance Companies' Production Account		**Insurance Companies' Production Account**	
Administrative costs and profits of insurance companies	$7.6	Administrative costs and profits of insurance companies	$5.0
Group life insurance service charges	$1.1	Group life insurance service charges	$1.0
Workmen's compensation service charges	6.5	Workmen's compensation service charges	4.0

(cont.)

Table 5.7 (cont.)

Insurance Companies' Income and Outlay Account			
Benefits paid on group life insurance	$4.9	Net premiums received for group life insurance	$4.9
Benefits paid on workmen's compensation	7.9	Net premiums received for workmen's compensation	7.9

Insurance Companies' Income and Outlay Account			
Benefits paid on group life insurance	$4.9	Net premiums received for group life insurance	$5.0
Benefits paid on workmen's compensation	7.9	Net premiums received for workmen's compensation	10.4
Change in reserves for group life insurance and workmen's compensation	2.6		

Household Income and Outlay Account			
Net premiums paid for group life insurance	$4.9	Employers' group life insurance contributions	$6.0
Net premiums paid for workmen's compensation	7.9	Employers' workmen's compensation contributions	14.4
Expenditure for group life insurance services	1.1	Benefits received from group life insurance	4.9
Expenditure for workmen's compensation services	6.5	Benefits received from workmen's compensation	7.9

Household Income and Outlay Account			
		Benefits received from workmen's compensation	$7.9

Household Capital Accumulation Account			

Household Capital Accumulation Account			
		Benefits received from group life insurance	$4.9

it from household income and outlay, and show it only as a change in household assets on the capital finance account. In other respects, its treatment should be similar to that of the income maintenance types of insurance. In particular, the employers' contribution should not be routed through household income and a method of computing the service charge that does not assume annual balancing should be adopted and an appropriate reserve set up. Table 5.7 also shows the impact of these proposals.

Property Damage

Property damage risks include fire, theft, and similar risks of damage to tangible property, as well as damage to intangible property such as copyright infringement. Loss of tangible assets through fire or theft is, clearly, a capital loss. SNA, however, treats both the net premium and the insurance reimbursements for such losses as transactions in the income and outlay account which for the economy as a whole are equal and offsetting. The rationale for this treatment of capital loss is that the charge for consumption of fixed capital that is included in the production account of producers includes an allowance for normally expected accidental damage to fixed capital. It is argued that, from the point of view of the economy as a whole, accidental damage is a regular, predictable, recurrent happening that should be shown in the current accounts, instead of being treated as a capital loss. SNA does allow, in the reconciliation account, for the treatment of accidental damage that differs from the expected amount as a capital loss (or gain, if less than expected), however. This argument is reminiscent of the use of retirement accounting in the railroad industry, where at one time the purchases of freight cars and locomotives were treated as current expenditures on the grounds that such purchases were made every year and so it was reasonable to treat them as outlays chargeable to current expenses. No self-respecting national accountant, however, would now accept such an argument for defining what should be included in gross capital formation. SNA's global view becomes less and less defensible as the accounts are disaggregated into sectors and subsectors, and it is of course completely inappropriate when considered from the point of view of the individual producer. It would, therefore, be more appropriate to treat major property damage as a capital loss, and the insurance reimbursement for it as a receipt in the capital finance account, not the income and outlay account. It would also then be appropriate to compute the capital consumption charge without an allowance for accidental damage, but to write off each year the capital losses that actually occur.

From the point of view of the purchaser of casualty insurance, furthermore, it may be questioned whether the administrative costs and profits of the insurance company constitute an appropriate measure of either final product or value added. Unlike a tax or compulsory transfer, the purchase of casualty insurance represents a voluntary expenditure for a service — namely, protection against loss — much in the same manner as an expenditure for a fire alarm system or security devices might be used to protect against the same kinds of loss. The fact that a loss does not occur does not mean that the purchaser has not received the protection he purchased. This suggests that it might be appropriate to consider the gross premium as an intermediate consumption expenditure (by producers) or final consumption expenditure (by households), and the net premium as part of the value added and operating surplus of the insurance companies from which transfers would be made to the capital finance accounts of those having casualty insurance claims.

Unfortunately information is not now readily available on casualty insurance premiums, claims and losses that can be used to analyze the differences which would result from alternative treatments. (Insurance companies, of course, do have this information, so that it would be feasible to collect it.) Furthermore, the questions which have been raised involve additional considerations relating to the treatment of capital consumption and the measurement of production which are beyond the scope of this paper.

6. SUMMARY OF THE EFFECTS OF THE PROPOSED TREATMENTS

The SNA Household Income and Outlay Account for the US, 1979

In order to analyze the cumulative effects of all of the proposed alternative treatments for different kinds of pensions and insurance on the SNA household income and outlay account, it will first be necessary to construct an SNA version of the US household income and outlay account for 1979. To some extent, this has been done in the 1981 UN *Yearbook of National Account Statistics*, but some further adjustments are needed to bring the account closer to SNA concepts and definitions and to make it consistent with the data shown in Table 5.1. The adjustments required are shown in Table 5.8. They are of four general types: exclusion of nonprofit institutions, reclassification of the pension contributions and benefits relating to government employees, inclusion of unfunded pension contributions and benefits and altered treatment of various categories of net casualty insurance premiums and claims.

In order to exclude nonprofit institutions from the household income and outlay account, it is necessary to exclude the property income which they receive and the final consumption expenditures they make. In addition, the transfers which households make to nonprofit institutions must be shown explicitly. These adjustments for nonprofit institutions are based on the

Table 5.8 Adjustments to United States Data for 1979 as Shown in UN Yearbook of National Accounts Statistics ($bn)

Household and Private Unincorporated Enterprise Income and Outlay Account	Table 5.1 data	UN data	Required adjustment	Total
RECEIPTS				
1. Compensation of employees		1471.6		
Plus: Unfunded employee benefits			+34.0	1505.6
2. Property and entrepreneurial income		386.3		
Minus: Property income received by nonprofit institutions			−5.7	380.6
3. Current transfers received				
a. Casualty insurance claims				
Medical vendor payments		19.4		
Net health claims	48.9			
Plus: Net difference			+29.5	
Plus: Net claims, group life insurance	4.9		+4.9	
Plus: Net claims, workmen's compensation ins.	7.9		+7.9	61.7
b. Social security benefits		176.2		
Minus: Pensions of government employees			−32.5	143.7
c. Social assistance grants		53.1		
Minus: Military and veterans' benefits	24.0		−24.0	29.1
d. Unfunded employee benefits				
Wage accruals less disbursements		0.2		
Unfunded employee benefits	34.0		+33.8	34.0
e. Other current transfers received		9.9		9.9
TOTAL Current Receipts		2116.7	+47.9	2164.6
DISBURSEMENTS				
4. Final consumption expenditures		1515.4		
Minus: Expenditures of nonprofit institutions			−43.8	1471.6
5. Property income paid		43.7		
Minus: Interest paid by nonprofit institutions			−1.7	42.0
6. Direct taxes, fees, fines and other payments n.e.c. to government				
a. Social security contributions		187.1		
Minus: Gvt contribution for employee pensions			−34.4	152.7
b. Income taxes		264.5		264.5
c. Other payments n.e.c.		10.0		10.0
7. Other transfers paid				
a. Net casualty insurance premiums		−		
Plus: Net health insurance premiums	48.9		+48.9	
Plus: Net group life insurance premiums	4.9		+4.9	
Plus: Net workmen's compensation ins. premiums	7.9		+7.9	
b. Transfers to private nonprofit institutions serving households		−	+36.5	36.5
c. Transfers to the rest of the world		2.2		2.2
d. Other current transfers except imputed		−		−
e. Imputed employee welfare contributions	34.0	−	34.0	34.0
Net Saving		93.8	−4.4	89.4
TOTAL Current Disbursements and Net Saving		2116.7	+47.9	2164.6

estimates contained in R. and N. Ruggles, 'Integrated economic accounts for the United States, 1947–80', *Survey of Current Business*, May 1982.

SNA takes the position that pension contributions and benefits relating to government employees are of the nature of private employer plans and should be so treated. In the UN *Yearbook* figures, however, social security contributions and benefits include government's contribution for employee pensions and pensions paid to government employees. Table 5.8 shows the adjustments needed for consistency with the related information for social security contributions and benefits in Table 5.1.

The adjustments for unfunded employee benefits consist of two elements. First, military retirement and veterans' benefits, which are unfunded in the US, must be added to government unfunded employee benefits and removed from transfer payments. This requires that they be added to the compensation of government employees, subtracted from social assistance grants, added to unfunded employee benefits received by households and added to transfers paid by households to employers. Second, no private unfunded employee benefits are listed in the accounts presented, and an arbitrary amount of $10 billion has been introduced in order to cover such unfunded employee benefits as tuition or education grants, thrift contributions, and other miscellaneous payments by employers. This amount has been added to the compensation of employees, added to unfunded employee benefits received and added to transfers paid by households to employers.

Finally, with respect to casualty insurance, the data provided in the UN *Yearbook* do not conform to SNA concepts. In SNA, net casualty insurance claims should equal net casualty insurance premiums for each type of casualty insurance. In the case of health, group life and workmen's compensation insurance, households are the only transactors involved in paying premiums and receiving benefits, so that for these types of insurance the net casualty insurance claims of households should be equal to net premiums paid by households. The adjustments made in Table 5.8 are those required to make the net casualty insurance claims and net casualty insurance premiums in the household income and outlay account consistent with the data in Table 5.1.

Despite the substantial number of these adjustments, the net change in total current receipts is rather modest, amounting to only $47.9 billion, an increase of about 2 percent. Net saving of households declined by $4.4 billion, a decrease of 5 percent. The adjusted estimates are required, however, so that the SNA treatment of pension and insurance transactions can be compared, in the next section, with the alternative treatments that have been proposed in Tables 5.2–5.7.

Effects of Proposals on Household Income and Outlay and GDP Expenditures

The differences between the SNA and proposed treatments of pension and insurance transactions in the household income and outlay account are shown in Table 5.9. The data shown for SNA in this table are the same as the adjusted data shown in Table 5.8, but somewhat greater detail is provided for pension and insurance transactions. This detail corresponds to the data shown in Tables 5.2–5.7. For comparative purposes, the unadjusted official data as published by the Bureau of Economic Analysis are shown in the first column.

The essential difference between SNA and the proposed alternative treatment of pension and insurance transactions that Table 5.9 emphasizes is that SNA attributes to the household transactions made on its behalf, whereas the alternative treatment omits from the household account transactions in which the household is not directly involved as a transactor. Thus, in the compensation of employees, SNA includes the contributions that employers make on behalf of employees for social security, private pension and welfare plans, and unfunded employee welfare benefits. The proposed alternative omits all of these contributions, and records as the compensation of employees received by households only that which is directly paid to them as wages and salaries. In property income, SNA imputes to households interest received by the pension and insurance sector. The proposed treatment leaves these imputations out of the property and entrepreneurial income received by households. The adjustments to transfers received by households are somewhat more complex. On the one hand, SNA does not include in household income the funded pension benefits and annuities which households receive, whereas the proposed alternative treatment does include them. On the other hand, SNA does include in household income reimbursements of health expenditures of households by government and/or private insurance, whereas the proposed alternative treatment excludes them.

On the disbursements side of the account, the reimbursed health care expenditures are included in final consumption expenditure by SNA, but are excluded in the proposed treatment. Social security contributions in SNA include the employers' contributions, but in the proposed treatment, since employers' contributions are not included in household receipts, they are excluded from household outlay. Similarly, employers' net private pension and welfare contributions are included by SNA, and excluded in the proposed alternative from both compensation of employees and household outlays. The proposed treatment does, however, record as current transfers paid by households both the employee contributions for pensions and insurance and premiums paid by households for life insurance and annuities in excess of the increase in cash accrual value. These differences between SNA and the proposed alternative treatment have a major impact on the measurement of net saving in the household income and outlay account. SNA net saving of households is $89.4 billion, whereas in the proposed alternative treatment net saving is only $8.0 billion. The difference between these two figures is accounted for by the saving shifted to the pension and insurance sector.

Table 5.9 BEA, SNA and Proposed Treatment of Pension and Insurance Transactions in Household and Private Unincorporated Enterprise Income and Outlay Account, United States, 1979 ($bn)

RECEIPTS	BEA	SNA	Proposed
1. Compensation of employees		1505.6	–
a. Wages and salaries	1237.6	1248.1	1248.1
b. Employers' contribution for social security	–	82.2	–
c. Employers' contribution for private pension and welfare plans	114.9	141.2	–
1. Funded pensions	50.5	79.2	–
2. Group health insurance	44.2	41.6	–
3. Group life insurance	5.8	6.0	–
4. Workmen's compensation	14.4	14.4	–
d. Unfunded contributions	–	34.0	–
1. Private employee benefits	–	10.0	–
2. Military and veterans' benefits	–	24.0	–
2. Property and entrepreneurial income	428.7	380.6	344.6
a. Imputed interest on pension reserves	26.3	26.3	–
b. Imputed interest on insurance reserves	9.7	9.7	–
c. Other property and entrepreneurial income	392.7	344.6	344.6
3. Transfers received	250.3	278.4	261.8
a. Casualty insurance claims	–	61.7	7.9
1. Health	–	48.9	–
2. Group life	–	4.9	–
3. Workmen's compensation	–	7.9	7.9
b. Social security benefits	151.4	143.7	114.5
1. Old age and disability	102.6	102.6	102.6
2. Health and hospital	29.2	29.2	–
3. Unemployment	9.8	9.4	9.4
4. Workmen's compensation	*	2.5	2.5
c. Social assistance grants	*	29.1	29.1
d. Unfunded employee benefits	*	34.0	34.0
1. Private	–	10.0	10.0
2. Military and veterans'	24.0	24.0	24.0
e. Other current transfers received	*	9.9	76.3
1. From rest of the world	–	1.3	1.3
2. Other	84.8	8.6	8.6
3. Funded pension benefits	–	–	59.8
4. Life insurance annuities	–	–	6.6
Less: Personal contributions to social insurance	–81.1	–	–
TOTAL Current Receipts	1951.2	2164.6	1854.5

*Entry included, but not specifically shown.

(cont.)

Table 5.9 (cont.)

DISBURSEMENTS	BEA	SNA	Proposed
1. Private final consumption expenditures	1507.2	1471.6	1378.4
a. Reimbursed health costs	*	72.1	–
1. Government reimbursement	*	29.2	–
2. Employers' reimbursement	*	42.9	–
b. Employer paid service charges	*	23.9	–
1. Pension service charges	*	12.2	–
2. Insurance service charges	*	8.9	–
c. Purchased insurance services and health care	*	28.0	28.0
1. Insurance service charges	*	22.0	22.0
2. Purchased health care	*	6.0	6.0
d. Other consumer expenditure	*	1350.4	1350.4
2. Interest paid	45.5	42.0	42.0
3. Social security contributions	–	152.7	70.5
a. Employers' contributions	–	82.2	–
b. Employees' contribution	–	70.5	70.5
4. Direct tax and other payments n.e.c. to government	301.0	274.5	274.5
5. Other current transfers paid	0.8	134.4	81.1
a. Net casualty insurance premiums	–	61.7	–
b. Transfers to nonprofit institutions	–	36.5	36.5
c. Transfers to rest of the world	–	2.2	2.2
d. Imputed employee welfare contributions	–	34.0	–
1. Private unfunded contributions	–	10.0	–
2. Military and veterans'	–	24.0	–
f. Life insurance and annuities paid	–	–	27.4
1. Net premiums paid	–	–	40.0
2. Less: Cash accrual value	–	–	–12.6
g. Employee net contributions to pensions and insurance	–	–	15.0
6. Net saving	96.7	89.4	80.0
TOTAL Current Disbursements and Net Saving	1951.2	2164.6	1854.5

*Entry included, but not specifically shown.

If the SNA and the proposed alternatives are compared with the US Personal Income Account published by BEA, a number of significant differences emerge, and these are also shown in Table 5.9. First, in compensation of employees, BEA omits employers' contributions for social security and treats military and veterans' benefits as transfer payments rather than a part of employee compensation. Second, in property and entrepreneurial income, BEA not only includes the imputed interest on pensions and insurance, but it also includes as imputed interest the services provided to individuals without charge by financial institutions. Third, transfer payments include government employee retirement benefits but exclude casualty insurance claims. Finally, personal contributions to social insurance are subtracted from income received to arrive at personal income (instead of being shown as a disbursement). On the disbursement side of the account, private consumption expenditure is larger than the SNA figure since it includes both nonprofit institution consumption

Table 5.10 BEA, SNA and Proposed Treatment of Pension and Insurance Transactions in Relation to GNP, United States, 1979 ($bn)

Expenditure on Gross Domestic Product	BEA	SNA	Proposed
1. Final consumption expenditure by government	474.4	437.9	467.1
a. Reimbursement of health costs	–	–	29.2
b. Unfunded military and veterans' benefits	–	24.0	24.0
c. Other final consumption expenditure by government	474.4	413.9	413.9
2. Final consumption expenditure by households	1507.2	1471.6	1378.4
a. Reimbursed health benefits	*	72.1	–
1. Government benefits	*	29.2	–
2. Employers' benefits	*	42.9	–
b. Employer paid service charges	*	21.1	–
1. Pension service charges	*	12.2	–
2. Insurance service charges	*	8.9	–
c. Insurance services and health care	*	28.0	28.0
1. Insurance service charges	*	22.0	22.0
2. Purchased health care	*	6.0	6.0
d. Other consumer expenditures	*	1350.4	1350.4
3. Final consumption expenditures by enterprises and nonprofit institutions	–	43.8	107.8
a. Reimbursement of health costs	–	–	42.9
b. Employer paid service charges	–	–	21.1
1. Pension service charges	–	–	12.2
2. Insurance service charges	–	–	8.9
c. Nonprofit institution final consumption	–	43.8	43.8
3. Gross capital formation	423.0	477.9	477.9
4. Exports of goods and services	215.0	215.0	215.0
5. Less: Imports of goods and services	245.1	245.1	245.1
Gross Domestic Product	2374.5	2401.2	2401.2

*Entry included but not specifically shown.

expenditure and the services provided free of charge by financial institutions to individuals. Transfers paid by households are very much smaller in the BEA accounts, since they are restricted to transfers paid to foreigners. All of these differences between SNA and BEA have relatively little impact on saving, however: personal saving in the BEA accounts is $96.7 billion, in comparison with the SNA net saving of $89.4 billion. Both of these figures are in marked contrast to the $8.0 billion of net saving resulting from the proposed treatment of pension and insurance transactions.

The effect of the proposed treatment on expenditures for gross domestic product is shown in Table 5.10. GDP as measured by SNA is not altered by the proposed treatment of pension and insurance transactions. Final consumption expenditures by households are reduced by eliminating benefits which are paid for by government or enterprises, and government final consumption expenditures and enterprise final consumption expenditures are increased correspondingly.

Analytic Significance of the Proposed Alternative Treatment

Any proposal for change requires justification. For the producers of national accounts, the costs of changing concepts, classifications and methods can be substantial. Consensus is usually difficult to achieve and is often so fragile that many prefer not to question practices sanctioned by time. For the users of the accounts, changes interrupt the continuity of time series, and require them to become accustomed to new forms of data.

Producers of statistics often take the view that their function is to produce the data that users need and want, and that it is up to the users to specify what these data should be. That, however, is not really a practical possibility. Users, at best, can do little more than state the nature of the problems they wish to address. They do not have — and cannot be expected to have — the necessary detailed familiarity with the data, and they usually do not have the comprehensive view of the statistical system that is the national accountant's hallmark. Most of the concepts employed by both economic theoreticians and econometric modelers are expressed at a level of generality that allows for a very wide range of interpretation, and few users have either the interest or the qualifications to examine the conceptual basis or statistical content of the data they use. It is the responsibility of the producers of the data — and especially of the national accountant — to ensure that the data measure what they purport to measure, and that what they purport to measure is relevant to the real world decisions about economic and social policy that must continually be made. Failure to accept that responsibility can have serious consequences, in terms of misunderstanding of the operation of the economic system and inappropriate policy decisions.

The objective of much economic theory is the derivation of generalizations stated in functional terms — i.e., devoid of institutional content. Thus, both macro- and microeconomic analysis deal with such abstractions as saving and investment, income and consumption, and wealth and the money supply, without considering the definitions of these concepts or their institutional setting: saving is considered to be the difference between income and consumption, neither of which is well defined; households are considered to be the ultimate recipients of all income and owners of all wealth, and the final decision-makers in the economy; and financial institutions are treated as mere intermediaries. Although the models devised by theorists are often complex and subtle, they generally achieve their rigor by using very simplistic concepts and assumptions that cannot easily accommodate the institutional characteristics of reality. But the tools with which the policy-maker must work always have empirical and institutional content. Household income and consumption expenditures need to be based on empirically observable transactions. A tax applies to specific taxpayers, it is a specific kind of tax, and it falls on a specific tax base. A monetary regulation applies to a specific type of financial institution, and new institutional forms may be devised purposely to avoid it.

National accounts have always reflected a somewhat uneasy compromise between these two approaches. The history of the growth and development of the accounts is the history of increasing institutional content. Sectors, industries, and types of transaction have increasingly moved toward reflecting the institutional diversity that actually exists. Thus the old SNA dealt with producers and consumers, whereas the present one deals with households and specific institutional types of enterprises. But at the same time, there are remnants of the functional approach. The urge to identify 'households' with 'consumers' and 'savers', on the one hand, and 'enterprises' with 'producers' and 'investors' on the other is very strong, and it is this attempt to have it both ways that accounts for many of the imputations now included in SNA. It is this attempt, also, that leads to a set of macroaccounts that are not congruent with the accounts of the reporting units, the transactors, of the system.

The consequence of this lack of congruence between the macro- and micro-accounts is that the macroaccounts cannot be used for analyzing questions which have institutional content, and which require disaggregation. Two major examples are analysis of the processes of financial intermediation and analysis of the distribution of income and household behavior. Both flow of funds data and distribution of income data are relative latecomers to the national accounts, and both reflect the movement toward increased institutional reality. The SNA guidelines on income distribution and balance sheets both recognize the need to adjust the concepts of the macroaccounts.

The proposals made in this paper reflect this point of view. Their objective is to bring the macroaccounts into closer conformity with the institutional world. For the most part, the direction of change is the same as that reflected in the more recent parts of SNA, the income distribution and balance sheet guidelines. The treatment of pensions and insurance is one of the chief areas where the present SNA follows a somewhat functional approach at the expense of institutional validity. (It is not the only one, of course — the treatment of owner-occupied housing and interest are prime examples of instances where the accounting conventions obscure rather than illuminate. But that is another paper.)

The issues at stake are not trivial, and they are not just accounting technicalities. They really determine our view of how the economic system operates. Moving saving from households to pension funds and life insurance companies, for instance, may focus the attention of policy-makers on the determinants of pension fund accumulation and the market behavior of the fund managers, rather than on measures affecting true household net saving, which turns out to be of very minor quantitative significance. The US household net saving rate of 4 percent shown in SNA is low, but that of less than half of 1 percent shown in the adjusted accounts is considerably smaller than the average statistical discrepancy, and rather obviously should not be used as the central variable for analyzing the determinants of the level of income and capital formation in the economy.

6. National Income Accounting Concepts and Measurement: Economic Theory and Practice

Richard Ruggles
Yale University

1. EVOLUTION OF THE CONCEPT OF NATIONAL INCOME

National income accounting is a development of the twentieth century, but the concept of national income on which it is based has undergone a slow evolutionary development going back more than 300 years. As economists have changed their view of the economic system, their concept of national income has also changed. The earliest economists did not distinguish between the concepts of national income and wealth. Gold was recognized as basic to a nation's strength and ability to wage war. Thus, in the sixteenth and seventeenth centuries, the Mercantilist school of economics viewed trade, shipping and even piracy as the basic productive activities in the economy since they were the main sources for acquiring the gold needed to support military ventures.

It was not until the eighteenth century that economists made a clear distinction between income and capital. France, at that time, was a rich agricultural nation with little manufacturing or trade. The physiocratic economists in France argued that income consisted of the consumable commodities produced by agriculture in the economy. They reasoned that only nature generates true surplus — i.e., seed multiplies into grain — whereas manufacturing merely alters the form of products and trade merely distributes already existing products. Quesnay (1760) developed a 'Tableau Economique' to demonstrate how the production generated in agriculture flowed into other parts of the economic system to be distributed to those in nonagricultural activities. The

---

This chapter first appeared in *Economic Notes*, **22** (2), 1993.

distinction between productive activity as exemplified by agriculture on the one hand, and sterile nonproductive activity on the other hand, as illustrated by manufacturing and trade, was central to the physiocratic concept of national income.

Adam Smith (1776) in England followed the physiocratic practice of distinguishing between productive and unproductive activity. However, England at that time was very much involved in manufacturing, commerce and shipping. Smith therefore expanded the physiocratic concept of 'productive' and argued that any activity relating to 'material goods production' was productive in nature — only those labor services not embodied in any material product were viewed as unproductive. The doctrine of material product was adopted by many economists, including Ricardo, Malthus, and Mill. It provided the basis for the later development of the Marxian material product system of accounts that was adopted by the Socialist countries.

There were, however, other economists during the eighteenth century who rejected the physiocratic doctrines and were not led astray by Adam Smith. As Studenski (1958) notes in his history of national income, the Italian economists. Galiani (1772), Verri (1771) and Palmieri (1787) all rejected the distinction between productive and unproductive labor. They maintained that all labor resulting in the production of useful and desired goods or services was productive and they identified the income of the nation as consisting of the value of such production. Unfortunately these views were never embodied in any attempts to measure the size or composition of the national income, and owing to the barrier of language their influence did not spread beyond Italy.

In terms of measuring income, there were also some estimators of national income in the seventeenth and eighteenth century who did adopt a broader concept of income. In particular, Petty (1676) and King (1696) in England and Boisguillebert (1697) and Vauban (1712) in France were concerned with measuring the total income accruing to the people in the nation. These concepts of national income did not stem from economic theory, but rather were concerned with measuring the income received by the population as a potential source of tax revenue for the king.

By the second half of the nineteenth century, however, economic theorists in general accepted a more comprehensive concept of national income. The neo-classical economists as exemplified by Marshall (1879) recognized the central role of utility in defining a more comprehensive concept of income. At the same time it was also recognized that the intermediate goods and services used in the process of production and the depreciation of plant and equipment needed to be excluded from national income.

On the other hand, it was not immediately clear how saving and capital formation should be treated. Fisher (1930) argued that the value of capital was determined by the discounted future stream of services it provided. He further concluded that income consisted solely of goods and services consumed — i.e., that saving and capital formation were not a part of the current income of the nation. This narrower concept did not receive full acceptance and a broader definition of national income came to be widely recognized. Economic theorists in general adopted the rather inadequate theoretical and empirical view, later articulated by Hicks, that income was the maximum amount that could be consumed during a given period while keeping capital intact (Reich, 1991). In this context, national income came to be defined as the sum of consumption and net capital formation in the economy.

2. THE MEASUREMENT OF NATIONAL INCOME PRIOR TO WORLD WAR II

Approaches to Measuring National Income

Although sporadic estimates of national income had been made by a number of investigators during the nineteenth century, it was not until the twentieth century that the systematic measurement of national income was undertaken. Prior to World War II, economic statisticians in the major industrial countries developed three different, but related, methods for measuring national income. These were termed the net product, net income and final sales methods. All three approaches were recognized as theoretically equivalent, but they were usually based on different sources of information and produced statistically different results.

The net product approach depended for the most part on data relating to production by industrial activity. Thus data on agricultural output, prices and costs were used to generate the net output produced by agriculture. Similarly, censuses of manufacturing were used to determine the value added in manufacturing industries. In many instances the more reliable and complete benchmark data provided by censuses had to be extrapolated by fragmentary and incomplete data. Regulatory data on public utilities provided the basis for estimating their net product. In service industries, it was often necessary to use estimates of gross margins and employment data to construct net product estimates.

The net income approach viewed the estimation process in terms of the distributive shares of income in the economy — i.e., wages and salaries, rental and entrepreneurial income, interest, dividends and income retained by corporations. In many instances the administrative data provided by government regulatory and taxing authorities were used. In other cases the income data were built up from the same sources as were used for the estimation of net product.

The final sales approach was largely dependent on the commodity flow method. This involved taking the sales of output by each industrial activity and splitting it up into intermediate sales to other industries, sales to government, sales abroad and sales to consumers. Transportation costs and wholesale and retail margins were added to arrive at the sales of goods and services to consumers. In some instances, data relating to actual government purchases and customs data relating to exports and imports of specific goods could be utilized.

Issues in the Measurement of National Income

In the context of such estimation procedures, a number of theoretical issues arose which in many cases have been settled more by statistical convenience or necessity than by the underlying logic. These issues involve the definition of capital formation and capital consumption, the treatment of government and intermediate costs, the production boundary and nonmarket activity and the role of interest.

The definition of capital formation and capital consumption

The concept of capital formation used in national income estimation has generally been restricted to a material product definition reminiscent of Adam Smith's material product concept and identical to the material product definition of capital in the socialist countries. Capital formation has for the most part been confined to the purchases of producers' durable goods, owner-occupied housing and inventory accumulation. With the exception of owner-occupied housing, the purchases of durable goods by households have been treated as consumption expenditures and, in the United States, government expenditures on durable goods or construction have also been treated as current expenditures rather than capital formation.

Intangible expenditures that provide services over an extended period of time have been excluded from capital formation and have been treated as either intermediate costs of producers or current consumption expenditures by households and government. Thus research and development have been considered as current production costs and expenditures for education and training have been classified as current consumption. In light of the broader neo-classical view of utility, this narrower material product concept of capital formation is difficult to defend. Indeed, many economists have urged a broader definition that would embrace human capital. But from the point of view of those estimating national income, the adoption of the capital formation criteria used by business enterprises offers a simple and operational solution to a problem that otherwise would be open to endless debate and controversy.

The estimates of capital consumption have been based on the estimated useful economic life of the different types of capital goods. This approach is quite appropriate in those instances where a capital good actually wears out or becomes useless due to changes in tastes. Generally speaking, the estimates of depreciation charged by producers are adjusted to take into account accelerated rates that may be allowed for tax purposes and changes in the replacement costs of capital goods.

In some circumstances, however, there may be a difference between the adjusted depreciation charge for an individual producer and what should be considered to be capital consumption from the point of view of national income estimation. For example, if there is a rapid pace of technical change in the efficiency of capital goods, individual producers must take this into account and replace their old equipment in order to remain competitive. New capital equipment will be purchased when its total cost is less than the marginal costs of operating with the old equipment. From the point of view of the economy, the faster obsolescence is not an additional cost, but is rather a reflection of the increase in the productivity of the new capital.

In still other circumstances where normal repair and upkeep maintain the usefulness of the capital, it may be inappropriate to charge any capital consumption. For example, if new road construction is treated as capital formation and the maintenance and repair of existing roads are considered current costs, a depreciation charge may not be appropriate. Similarly, some buildings that are fully maintained may last almost indefinitely.

It is difficult to arrive at accurate estimates of capital consumption since by their very nature these depend on subjective expectations about the future. The estimates of national income, however, are very sensitive to the estimates of capital consumption. As a consequence of this difficulty in measuring capital consumption in appropriate terms and the inability to distinguish net capital formation as such, national income estimators have gravitated towards providing estimates of gross income and product that are independent of capital consumption estimates.

Government and intermediate costs

Neo-classical economics viewed the economy as being composed of producers and consumers and gave little guidance to the treatment of government in the estimation of national income. Kuznets (1941) argued that indirect business taxes represented the purchase of government services by business and thus were intermediate products. As a consequence indirect taxes were omitted from the national income by distributive shares to provide the concept of national income at factor cost. At the same time national income based on final expenditures added up to the total including indirect taxes, and this variant was equal to national income at market prices.

With the growing importance of the government in the economy and the obvious lack of correspondence between indirect business taxes and the services provided to business by government, national income estimators have generally abandoned the concept of national income at factor cost and moved to the more comprehensive concept of market prices. Thus the compensation of government employees and government capital goods are viewed as contributing to gross income and government expenditures on goods and services are viewed as part of the final sales in the economy.

The production boundary and nonmarket activity
The question of what activities should be included in the production boundary of national income has been central to the construction of national income estimates. By and large national income estimators have viewed legal market production as constituting the central core of the system. There has been general agreement, however, that there are certain kinds of nonmarket activity that should be taken into account. In particular, the quantity of agricultural output directly consumed by farmers is estimated and an 'imputed' transaction valued at 'farm gate' prices is considered to have taken place. This imputed transaction is then added to both the estimates of production of the agricultural sector and the final consumption of households. In many of the more developed countries, the increasing commercialization of farms and the reduction in the size of the farm population has resulted in a significant decline in the importance of this imputation. For developing countries, however, the imputations for nonmarket agricultural activity constitute an important part of the national income estimation.

Imputations are also made for the services of owner-occupied housing. There has been a consensus that omission of the services of owner-occupied housing would seriously understate household consumption. For this imputation it is assumed that the home owner in effect pays an imputed rent to a fictional enterprise. The fictional enterprise, in turn, is assumed to pay the expenses related to the housing and to return any balance (positive or negative) to the actual owner as net rental income.

Many investigators have recommended additional imputations and have on occasion introduced these into their compilations. For example, housewife services, volunteer work, education, and even leisure have been imputed to provide more comprehensive estimates of production and consumption in the economy. Such extensions have been proposed by a wide variety of economists in the United States in recent years (Eisner, 1988; Jorgenson and Alvaro, 1983; Kendrick, 1979; Tobin and Nordhaus, 1972). Although such extensions demonstrate the importance of nonmarket activities and attributions for measuring economic welfare, they have not been incorporated into the official United States national income accounts.

In practice, those responsible for the official national income estimates in most countries have avoided including such imputations on the grounds that they are by nature highly arbitrary and would tend to swamp the harder data relating to the actual market transactions data in the economy.

The role of interest

The question of how interest receipts and payments should be treated has been one of the most controversial issues in the estimation of national income. It would be possible to treat interest payments as payments for the services of capital much in the same manner as rental payments are considered to be payments for the services of property (Sunga, 1988). On the other hand, it is also possible to view interest payments, like dividends, to be part of the distribution of the operating income of producers. Under this latter treatment, interest is considered to be a transfer payment, and does not constitute the sale of a service. Interest paid by consumers and government under this latter definition is, thus, excluded as a part of national income.

The treatment of interest as a transfer payment also raises problems in the measurement of output for financial intermediaries. In computing the net output or value added of financial intermediaries, interest receipts would have to be excluded as sales. As a consequence the costs incurred in providing financial services would greatly exceed the sales revenue. It is argued that, in reality, depositors receive 'imputed interest' on their deposits, and that in turn this income is used to purchase the financial services provided.

Although different countries use different methods to impute the services provided by financial institutions, there has been almost universal adoption of the principle that interest payments represent transfers of income rather than payments for the use of capital.

3. DEVELOPMENT OF NATIONAL INCOME ACCOUNTING

Initial National Income Accounts

It is generally recognized that Keynes's *General Theory of Employment, Interest and Money* (1935) set the stage for national income accounting. Although Keynes generally accepted the neo-classical functional view of the economy as consisting of production, consumption, saving and investment, his recognition of the equality of saving and investment provided the basis for an accounting approach.

Shortly after the outbreak of World War II, there was a major change in the measurement of national income brought about by the pressing needs of wartime planning and management. In a booklet, *How to Pay for the War*, Keynes (1940) outlined a system of five accounts: aggregate production, formation of income, private sector income and outlay, government sector income and outlay and aggregate capital formation. This system was fully articulated in that each accounting entry appeared twice — once on the debtor side and once on the creditor side. The concept of national income used in this framework was net national income at factor cost. The sectoring of the economy was still functional — i.e., production, private income and consumption, government and capital formation. Under the guidance of Keynes, Meade and Stone undertook a series of White Papers providing national income and expenditure accounts for the United Kingdom.

The basic principle of casting national income and expenditure into the form of an account had already been suggested by economists working in other countries. Most notably, in 1940, Ragnar Frisch in Norway had written about constructing national accounts for the purpose of macroeconomic analysis, and at about the same time, Jan Tinbergen in the Netherlands used these concepts in his development of econometric models.

It was clear that national income accounting was an idea whose time had come. The ideas contained in the British White Papers were also being developed in the United States by Milton Gilbert who at that time was in charge of national income estimation, and as early as 1942, the two sides of a national income and expenditure account for the US economy were developed. Considerable use was made of this account in analyzing the inflationary gap which might be expected to result from the expansion of war expenditures.

In 1947, a League of Nations report prepared by Stone on *The Measurement of National Income and the Construction of Social Accounts* was issued by the United Nations. The conceptual basis of these accounts can best be described by quoting directly from this document as follows:

> Instead of seeking to build up to a single total, such as the national income, an investigation is first made of the classification of accounting entities, of the type of accounts they keep and of the transactions into which they enter. In this way, all the transacting entities of an economic system are classified into broad sectors such as productive enterprises, financial intermediaries and final consumers, and a series of accounts for each of these categories is set up in which the separate categories represent economically distinct categories of transactions. Economic activity is represented by money flows and related bookkeeping transactions, actual or imputed, between accounts. The national income and other similar aggregates are obtained from this system by selecting and combining the constituent entries in the accounts. In this way, a logical framework is presented into which the greater part of economic statistics can be fitted. This framework should prove useful in showing how far statistics actually available at any time fall short of a complete coverage of economic activity.

Although by now these basic principles of national accounting are well recognized, in 1947 they represented a major innovation that was not easily accepted. Kuznets (1948), for example, viewed national accounting as 'a dubious addition to the theoretical equipment by aid of which we define national income and reckon its distribution'.

In formulating this initial set of accounts, Stone followed the generally accepted British commercial accounting practices of the time, which in many respects were rather elaborate. For the sectors relating to business enterprises and financial intermediaries he set up four accounts. First, an operating account showed the receipts and outlays which were related to the operation of the business. Second, the surplus of receipts over outlays in this first account was then transferred to an appropriation account where nonoperating receipts were added and this disposition of the resulting total was shown in terms of dividends and withdrawals, direct taxes and transfers to capital and reserve accounts. Third, a capital account showed the actual outlays for capital formation and inventory accumulation on the one hand, and on the other hand the sources of funds for capital formation in terms of depreciation and transfers from the appropriation and reserve accounts. Finally, a fourth account, a reserve account, was set up to show the transfers to and from other accounts and the changes taking place in holdings of financial assets and liabilities.

The treatment of persons, public collective providers, and social security and private pension funds was considerably simpler. Here only two accounts were set up: a revenue account, which was used to record current receipts and outlays, and a capital and reserve account, which was used to reflect capital formation, capital transfers and changes in financial assets and liabilities.

Conceptually, by focusing on transactors and their transactions, Stone's social accounting broke new ground. Rather than dividing the economy into functional sectors, he recognized different institutionally defined sectors in the economy. For each of these sectors, he set up accounts to record their actual and imputed transactions. From this accounting approach, he then built the economic constructs required for analysis of the behavior of the economic system.

Stone's 1947 system, however, did not provide the basis for the postwar development of national income accounting. The main obstacle to adopting such a national income accounting approach was the lack of appropriate information. Many of the participating countries did not have estimates of national income, much less national income accounts. A much simpler functional approach to national income accounting was, therefore, adopted by the Economic Cooperation Administration (EEA) and the Organization for European Economic Cooperation (OEEC) as the framework for post-World War II planning (R. Ruggles, 1949; R. and N.D. Ruggles, 1951; OEEC, 1952).

The initial OEEC system consisted of five summary accounts: national income and expenditure, government current receipts and outlays, household current receipts and outlays, transactions with the rest of the world and consolidated saving and capital formation account. This general form of national income accounting with minor modifications was adopted by the United Nations in 1952 as the basis for international reporting of national income accounts.

1968 United Nations System of National Accounts

At the same time as national income accounts were being developed, there were also developments in related fields of economic accounting. Wassily Leontief had been working on input–output analysis since the 1930. By analyzing inter-industry requirements and the destination of industry outputs, Leontief was able to show how the industrial structure of the economic system could be expected to change with changes in the final demand for goods and services. In the period after World War II, many countries undertook the construction of input–output tables, and in some countries, including Norway, Denmark and the Netherlands input–output tables were integrated with their national income accounts.

During this period, work was also being carried out on monetary and financial statistics. In the United States, Morris Copeland developed sources and uses of funds accounts for recording money flows in the economy in an effort to obtain quantitative measures of the nature and volume of transactions taking place in the economy. Despite his main concern with deriving the aggregate value of all transactions, Copeland did for the first time direct attention to the creation of an accounting framework into which all transactions could be fitted.

Estimates of national wealth and balance sheets were also being constructed by Raymond Goldsmith, using a perpetual inventory method. This involved cumulating the capital formation data in the national accounts together with information on the change in prices of assets to obtain estimates of the stock of tangible assets. These data were then combined with financial transactions data to obtain national balance sheets.

It gradually became apparent that all of these economic accounting systems should be integrated into a single framework and that the 1952 United Nations System of National Accounts was not sufficiently comprehensive in its scope to serve as such a framework. In the early 1950s, as a consequence, Stone was again called on to head an effort to create such an integrated system. As the architect of the SNA revision, he built it around the transactor/transaction principle that he had put forth in the 1947 League of Nations Study. But in reality the revised SNA was the product of committees; it was a large undertaking, involving the cooperation of statisticians from many statistical offices and the United Nations Statistical Office over a period of more than five years.

The revised SNA was completed in 1968, and as intended it provided a comprehensive framework for recording the stocks and flows in the economy.

A rather complex system of dual sectoring of the economy and specialized accounts was used. For production, consumption expenditures and capital formation, the economy was sectored into industries on the basis of establishments, governmental producers, nonprofit producers and households. For transactions relating to income and outlay and capital finance accounts, the economy was divided into institutional sectors, corporate enterprises, general government, nonprofit institutions and households.

The 1968 SNA was designed to provide international guidance to national statistical offices wanting to improve, elaborate and extend their national accounts and their systems of basic statistics. Paradoxically, although the well-known SNA Blue Book was recognized as the basic document describing the SNA, there was no agreement as to what actually constituted the SNA. The SNA theorists cited the Blue Book's extended accounting matrix as the embodiment of the SNA. But SNA practitioners were quick to point out that the extended matrix was merely used to illustrate the general nature of a complete accounting system and that it was never intended to be implemented. Instead, SNA practitioners argued that the heart of the SNA was contained in Chapter VIII of the Blue Book where examples of standard accounts and tables were presented.

But even the standard accounts and tables were of an illustrative nature and were never fully implemented by any country. Consequently, users of SNA national account statistics held the view that the SNA consisted of the data published in the United Nations *National Accounts Yearbook* which in turn was based on the United Nations National Accounts Questionnaire. Although the National Accounts Questionnaire was conceptually related to the standard accounts and tables contained in the Blue Book, it omitted many accounts and differed from others in important respects.

In 1979, there was a major revision and extension of the UN National Accounts Questionnaire that broke new ground and introduced new kinds of information not contemplated by the Blue Book. In particular it introduced a more complete system of accounts for the institutional sectors of the economy. The revised National Accounts Questionnaire consisted of 12 tables of summary data and 58 tables of more detailed data.

The elaboration of the UN SNA had relatively little effect on how aggregate national income was measured. The definition of capital formation was still restricted to reproducible tangible goods. Government purchases of goods and services were not treated as intermediate costs, but were classified as either capital formation or final consumption. Imputations, as previously, were primarily restricted to nonmarket agricultural production, owner-occupied housing, and services provided by financial institutions.

Although the SNA purported to record for the institutional sectors the actual transactions in which they were engaged, this principle was not always followed. For example, in the treatment of pension funds, the SNA attributes the employers' payment to pension funds as being paid directly to employees. Similarly the earnings of pension funds are also attributed to households as a receipt of income even when no such payment is made.

Conversely, the SNA in some instances removes some of the transactions that are actually made by a sector and attributes them to an 'artificial' transactor. This is true for household expenditures on the expenses of owner-occupied housing. In order to impute the value of owner-occupied housing, an artificial transactor is set up to receive the imputed housing payment made by home owners; the actual expenses of owner-occupied housing are then removed from household expenditure and are attributed to the artificial transactor.

In summary, the 1968 SNA, in principle, was based on a transactor/transaction approach to national accounting, but its sectoring and sets of accounts were complex and incomplete. The system did not record the actual transactions of the various transactors. In order to develop specific economic constructs, the SNA introduced imputations for nonmarket activity, and attributed actual transactions between two transactors to other transactors.

Proposed Revision of the UN System of National Accounts

Despite the apparent success of the 1968 revision of the SNA, within a decade there were calls for yet another revision. It was charged that although the presentation in the original Blue Book was sweeping and comprehensive, in many areas, such as sector financial accounts and balance sheets, the system was not adequately specified. It was also noted that in other areas, such as international transactions and government finance, the SNA presentation was in direct conflict with the data collected by other international statistical agencies. By 1980, therefore, the United Nations, together with other international statistical agencies embarked on a revision of the SNA that would 'clarify, harmonize and update' the 1968 Blue Book and its subsequent supporting manuals.

The new SNA revision is not expected to appear before 1993, but the proposed changes from the 1968 SNA are becoming apparent. The central framework retains input–output accounts as an integral part of the system for balancing supply and demand. Although the industrial classification of the economy is retained, the concept of 'dual sectoring' is abandoned. The total economy is divided into five main institutional sectors: nonfinancial corporate, financial corporate, general government, households and nonprofit institutions serving households.

Particular attention has been directed to introducing more comprehensive coverage of the financial sector and the identification and classification of financial instruments in light of the innovations in this field in recent years due to financial deregulation. The new system describes in considerable detail the links between the United Nations and the International Monetary Fund and related statistical systems on balance of payments, government finance statistics and money and banking statistics. Social accounting matrices are suggested as a way of providing demographic and social breakdowns of the household sector. Satellite accounts relating to such things as the environment or health systems are provided as a way of incorporating alternative measures or supplementary information.

The definition of gross capital formation, in the proposed SNA revision, has been expanded to include not only the production of tangible assets but also intangible assets such as mineral exploration, computer software and entertainment, literary and artistic originals. Research and development expenditures continue to be treated as intermediate consumption rather than as capital formation. Government expenditure on military facilities or equipment such as airfields, docks, roads, etc. are considered to be capital formations, but weapons-related equipment is excluded. Education is, whether paid for by government or households, considered to be current expenditure. Finally, there has been no change in the treatment of consumer durables as current expenditure, although it is suggested that the inventory of consumer durables should be presented as a memoranda item on household balance sheets.

In light of the increasing importance of pension systems in modern economies, the revised SNA is proposing a much more extended treatment of employer pension fund contributions, pension fund earnings and the payments of pension benefits. Valid delineation of these transactions is important for understanding the nature of saving in the economy and the distribution of income of the elderly population. As already noted, the existing SNA treats employers' pension contribution and the earnings of pension funds as household income, but excludes pension benefit payments from household income. Such treatment is in conflict with the definition of household income recommended in the UN guidelines on income distribution and with the existing practice of household sample surveys.

There has also been explicit recognition of the government reimbursement of household expenditures and transfers in kind to households. In making comparisons of the different levels of consumption over time or between different countries, it is necessary to take account not only the goods and services purchased by households but also consumption provided directly or indirectly to households by employers, government and nonprofit institutions. Previously the SNA treated these transfers as either as part of household income and household expenditures or as government current expenditures. However, in the interest of measuring the total consumption of households on the one hand and the expenditures made by the household out of their disposable income, on the other, it has become necessary to introduce these distinctions into the household account.

The most striking changes in the proposed revision of the SNA relate to the accounting structure of system that is being developed. In all, a set of 11 cascading accounts are proposed for recording transactions, imputations and rerouting of transactions taking place between sectors of the economy. The balancing item for each account appears as an entry in the following accounts:

1. Production
2. Generation of income
3. Allocation of primary income
4. Secondary distribution of income
5. Redistribution of income
6. Use of income
7. Acquisition of nonfinancial assets
8. Acquisition of financial assets
9. Other changes in the volume of assets
10. Revaluations
11. Balance sheet

The major function of these accounts is to set forth the actual, imputed and rerouted transactions for each sector in the economy in order to derive sets of specific macroeconomic constructs. Conceptually, however, these SNA accounts depart widely from the bookkeeping records that would be kept by the different groups of transactors.

4. EVALUATION AND CONCLUSIONS

Evolution of the National Accounts

The initial Keynesian national income accounting concepts developed during World War II viewed economic activity in neo-classical functional terms. The economic system was considered to consist of production, consumption, saving and investment. Production was measured in terms of net national income at factor cost, consumption was derived residually, saving included both household saving and the retained earnings of producers, and investment was defined as the net change in the stock of producers' durables and inventories. There was little attention given to the relation between the national income accounts and the accounts used by enterprises and households.

The system of social accounts outlined by Richard Stone (1947) in his League of Nations report put forth a system of transactor/transaction accounts for institutional sectors of the economy that was based on business accounting principles. In the post-World War II development of national income accounts; however, the 1947 system proposed by Stone was not pursued, and instead international statistical agencies and many national statistical offices adopted a rather simple five-account system built around production, private consumption, general government, external transactions and saving and investment. In terms of the macroeconomic aggregates contained within the national income accounts, however, the concepts of gross domestic product and gross capital formation were substituted for national income at factor cost and net investment.

It was not until the 1968 revision of the United Nations System of National Accounts (SNA) that institutional sectoring and transactor/transaction accounts became accepted principles of national accounting. However, the transactor/transaction approach of the 1968 SNA was in many instances violated in order to include imputations for nonmarket activity and to reroute actual transactions to different transactors. Furthermore, the institutional sectors were still identified with functional activities. Thus enterprises were not considered to engage in consumption, and households were not considered to engage in capital formation.

The current revision of the SNA represents a major expansion of the 1968 SNA in terms of the types of accounts, the rerouting of transactions and the number of macroeconomic constructs. The main objective of such accounts is to derive specific aggregates that will provide a macroeconomic view of the economic system. Conceptually, however, these SNA accounts depart widely from the bookkeeping and accounting records that are actually kept by different groups of transactors in the economy.

Accounting for Saving and Capital Formation in the Economy

In evaluating the usefulness of the national accounts for macroeconomic analysis, it is appropriate to examine how well they have performed in providing an understanding of the process of saving and capital formation in the economy. This has long been one of the major analytical questions confronting economists, and the national accounting framework has specifically been built around these economic constructs.

Keynesian analysis of saving and investment

The Keynesian analysis of saving and investment viewed the process as one in which the propensity to consume by consumers determined the amount of saving in the economy and the marginal efficiency of capital determined the amount of investment that producers were willing to undertake. One of most popular topics for Ph.D. dissertations in the late 1930s was the determination of the consumption function for the economy — typically these studies regressed consumption on some variant of national income or household income to determine the amount of saving that would be forthcoming under various conditions. Subsequently various theories of consumer behavior emerged to explain the saving taking place in the economy under various conditions.

Household saving and capital formation

The permanent income hypothesis postulates that consumers will choose a level of consumption that is consistent with their expected future incomes (i.e., long-run) and their desired equilibrium levels of saving. As a consequence, it is argued, that transitory changes in income will cause saving rather than consumption to fluctuate. In part, this explanation is supposed to account for the fact that saving and capital formation in the economy decline more than consumer expenditures during recessions.

The life cycle hypothesis of saving focuses on the distribution of saving over an individual's life cycle. It postulates that an individual will save for old age during productive years, and will draw on accumulated savings after retirement. The national saving rate would thus be strongly influenced by the age distribution of the population. In a population where the number of individuals in the working cohorts greatly exceeds the number in retirement, substantial net saving would be available to permit growth. Conversely, a population in which the retired cohorts were dominant would yield little or no net saving.

The emphasis of theorists on the role of consumer saving has been matched by the concern of economic policy with the level of personal saving. Personal saving is considered vital so that enterprises can undertake the capital formation required for increased productivity, international competitiveness and economic growth. National accountants have devoted considerable attention to the measurement of personal saving. Despite their efforts, the empirical measurement of personal saving has been quite unsatisfactory either for testing the various hypothesis about saving or for describing what is taking place in the economy.

To a major degree, the problems can be traced to the fact that the functional approach to the analysis of saving and investment deliberately abstracts from the institutional realities that shape both the saving and investment process and its measurement. The transactor units that exist in the economy are not, as the original Keynesian formulation suggested, consumers and producers, but households and enterprises. The transactor units differ from the functional ones in important ways. Households not only consume and save; they also invest, in houses and durable goods. Enterprises not only invest; they also save in the form of capital consumption allowances and retained earnings.

In the national income accounts, the item labeled 'saving' in the household sector account does not correspond to household gross saving, the net saving or the net lending of households for three reasons. Home ownership is treated as a fictional enterprise providing housing services to consumer–occupants; this fiction seriously distorts and obscures the actual transactions and saving of households. The accumulation of reserves in employer pension funds are treated as being paid out to individuals, and the actual payments of pensions to retired persons are omitted from household income. Finally, purchases by households of new owner-occupied housing and consumer durables are not recognized as household capital formation.

In order to include owner-occupied housing in the household sector, it is necessary to eliminate the imputed payment of space rental by home owners and to introduce the actual outlays made by home owners for such things as property taxes, repairs and upkeep, insurance costs and interest payments on mortgages. The capital consumption allowances for owner-occupied housing, however, are not an expense, but are reflected instead as part of the gross saving by households. When these adjustments are made in the United States National Accounts for the year 1989, the gross saving by households is increased by $89.2 billion over the official estimates of personal saving.

The national accounting treatment of pension contributions and benefits alters both the timing and magnitude of household income receipts. Employers' pension contributions are viewed as if they were paid directly to employees, and therefore they are included in personal income. Ownership of employers' pension fund reserves is attributed to households and their earnings are treated as being paid to households even though no such payments are made. It is somewhat inconsistent that retained corporate profits are not attributed to stockholders, but retained employer pension reserves are attributed to employees. Since employere' pension contributions and pension fund earnings are included as personal income, the national accounts exclude from personal income employee pensions actually paid to individuals in order to avoid double counting. Where the retired population receives substantial pension benefits, this treatment makes the analysis of the distribution of income somewhat meaningless.

Such national accounting treatment of private pension contributions and benefits is also in direct contrast to the household survey approach, which excludes employers' contributions to pension reserves from household income, but includes the payment of pension benefits. It is also in direct conflict with the national accounting treatment of social security contributions and benefit payments. In the United States National Accounts, both employer and employee social security payments are excluded from personal income, and social security benefit payments are included as income received by individuals. Reversing the treatment of employers' pension contributions and pension benefits would reduce the United States estimate of personal saving by $56.1 billion in 1989.

Table 6.1 Household Saving, Capital Formation and Net Lending in the United States, 1947–90

Line	Year	Household income and outlays			Household gross saving				Household gross capital formation			Household net capital formation		Household net lending + or borrowing –
		Gross income	Current outlays	Total	Capital consumption allowances		Net saving	Total	Housing	Durables	Total	Housing	Durables	
					Housing	Durables								
1	1947	205.0	178.6	26.4	2.8	11.0	12.6	29.9	9.5	20.4	16.1	6.7	9.4	–3.5
2	1948	225.9	191.5	34.4	3.3	12.6	18.5	35.2	12.3	22.9	19.3	9.0	10.3	–0.8
3	1949	227.1	194.4	32.7	3.5	14.2	15.0	36.4	11.4	25.0	18.7	7.9	10.8	–3.7
4	1950	254.1	210.8	43.3	3.8	15.8	23.7	47.3	16.5	30.8	27.7	12.7	15.0	–4.0
5	1951	286.0	239.7	46.3	4.4	18.5	23.4	44.8	14.9	29.9	21.9	10.5	11.4	1.5
6	1952	306.2	259.6	46.6	4.7	20.5	21.4	44.3	15.0	29.3	19.1	10.3	8.8	2.3
7	1953	326.2	275.3	50.9	5.0	22.4	23.5	48.2	15.5	32.7	20.8	10.5	10.3	2.7
8	1954	335.5	285.9	49.6	5.3	25.1	19.2	49.1	17.0	32.1	18.7	11.7	7.0	0.5
9	1955	358.4	303.9	54.5	5.7	26.2	22.6	59.2	20.3	38.9	27.3	14.6	12.7	–4.7
10	1956	383.3	324.7	58.6	6.2	29.4	23.0	53.8	15.6	38.2	18.2	9.4	8.8	4.8
11	1957	405.7	346.4	59.3	6.5	31.8	21.0	56.9	17.2	39.7	18.6	10.7	7.9	2.4
12	1958	424.2	360.2	64.0	6.9	33.5	23.6	55.2	18.0	37.2	14.8	11.1	3.7	8.8
13	1959	447.6	385.5	62.1	7.3	35.1	19.7	65.4	22.6	42.8	23.0	15.3	7.7	–3.3
14	1960	467.5	406.6	60.9	7.6	36.2	17.1	64.6	21.1	43.5	20.8	13.5	7.3	–3.7
15	1961	485.2	420.6	64.6	8.0	37.4	19.2	61.9	20.0	41.9	16.5	12.0	4.5	2.7
16	1962	511.2	443.5	67.7	8.3	38.4	21.0	68.2	21.2	47.0	21.5	12.9	8.6	–0.5
17	1963	539.3	469.0	70.3	8.6	39.9	21.8	74.9	23.1	51.8	26.4	14.5	11.9	–4.6
18	1964	571.5	489.4	82.1	9.0	41.7	31.4	80.1	23.3	56.8	29.4	14.3	15.1	2.0
19	1965	614.4	521.3	93.1	9.5	43.3	40.3	87.1	23.6	63.5	34.3	14.1	20.2	6.0
20	1966	665.6	567.4	98.2	10.1	45.4	42.7	90.5	22.0	68.5	35.0	11.9	23.1	7.7
21	1967	717.3	602.3	115.0	10.8	49.4	54.8	93.1	22.5	70.6	32.9	11.7	21.2	21.9
22	1968	781.3	658.5	122.8	11.7	54.1	57.0	105.6	24.6	81.0	39.8	12.9	26.9	17.2
23	1969	854.8	735.4	119.4	13.3	60.0	46.1	113.5	27.3	86.2	40.2	14.0	26.2	5.9
24	1970	920.5	785.9	134.6	14.3	65.8	54.5	112.8	27.1	85.7	32.7	12.8	19.9	21.8

25	1971	987.3	832.8	154.5	15.8	71.8	66.9	136.0	38.4	97.6	48.4	22.6	25.8	18.5
26	1972	1,072.4	913.1	159.3	18.2	76.4	64.7	158.6	47.4	111.2	64.0	29.2	34.8	0.7
27	1973	1,200.4	1,005.9	194.5	20.0	83.5	91.0	177.2	52.5	124.7	73.7	32.5	41.2	
28	1974	1,304.6	1,114.6	190.0	23.1	93.9	73.0	172.2	48.4	123.8	55.2	25.3	29.9	17.8
29	1975	1,426.6	1,204.2	222.4	25.7	107.0	89.7	184.2	48.8	135.4	51.5	23.1	28.4	38.2
30	1976	1,557.3	1,328.9	228.4	28.4	118.6	81.4	227.3	65.8	161.5	80.3	37.4	42.9	1.1
31	1977	1,712.4	1,469.1	243.3	32.7	131.2	79.4	271.9	87.4	184.5	108.0	54.7	53.3	-28.6
32	1978	1,915.0	1,650.7	264.3	37.9	146.8	79.6	307.7	101.6	205.6	122.5	63.7	58.8	-42.9
33	1979	2,160.5	1,881.1	279.4	43.9	165.0	70.5	311.7	92.7	219.0	102.8	48.8	54.0	-32.3
34	1980	2,426.0	2,121.1	304.9	49.2	186.2	69.5	298.8	79.5	219.3	63.4	30.3	33.1	6.1
35	1981	2,634.9	2,279.6	355.3	53.8	201.2	100.3	322.0	82.1	239.9	67.0	28.3	38.7	33.3
36	1982	2,786.1	2,426.0	360.1	56.8	214.1	89.2	323.6	70.9	252.7	52.7	14.1	38.6	36.5
37	1983	2,993.0	2,604.5	388.5	59.6	226.4	102.5	415.8	126.7	289.1	129.8	67.1	62.7	-27.3
38	1984	3,270.8	2,801.0	469.8	62.6	236.1	171.1	470.7	135.2	335.5	172.0	72.6	99.4	-0.9
39	1985	3,509.6	3,033.8	475.8	67.0	257.1	151.7	533.6	161.4	372.2	209.5	94.4	115.1	-57.8
40	1986	3,756.6	3,227.9	528.7	69.3	278.2	181.2	580.3	174.3	406.0	232.8	105.0	127.8	-51.6
41	1987	4,028.6	3,507.4	521.2	74.7	300.8	145.7	603.7	180.3	423.4	228.2	105.6	122.6	-82.5
42	1988	4,361.0	3,738.4	622.6	80.5	324.5	217.6	626.1	189.0	437.1	221.1	108.5	112.6	-3.5
43	1989	4,704.4	4,024.9	679.5	92.5	350.1	236.9	648.6	189.2	459.4	206.0	96.7	109.3	30.9
44	1990	4,994.1	4,348.6	645.5	93.5	379.2	172.8	643.1	178.8	464.3	170.4	85.3	85.1	2.4
45	1991	5,200.4	4,531.5	668.9	99.7	404.5	164.7	605.2	159.1	446.1	101.0	59.4	41.6	63.7
46	Total	69,315.8	59,701.5	9,614.3	1,281.5	5,160.3	3,172.5	9,595.8	2,771.1	6,824.7	3,154.0	1,489.6	1,664.4	18.5

Sources: IEA = 'Integrated Economic Accounts of the United States, 1947–1980', Richard and Nancy D. Ruggles, *Survey of Current Business*, May 1982. The IEA data have been revised and extended on the basis of more recent BEA and FOF data. The IEA adjustments that have been applied to the BEA personal income and outlay data are as follows: 1) Exclusion of nonprofit institutions income and expenditures from the household sector, 2) Inclusion of owner-occupied housing in household sector, 3) Exclusion of employer pension fund contributions and earnings from household income, 4) Inclusion of employer pension fund benefit payments as household income, and 5) Exclusion of consumer durable goods as current household expenditures.

BEA = Data published by the Bureau of Economic Analysis of the US Department of Commerce.

FOF = Data published by the Flow of Funds Division of the US Federal Reserve Board.

Finally, denying the possibility of household capital formation leads to some awkward problems of definitional inconsistency. Household appliances purchased as part of owner-occupied houses are included as part of the gross capital formation of the fictional enterprises set up to own owner-occupied houses. However, the same appliances purchased separately are treated as current consumption expenditures by households. Again, automobiles purchase by businesses are included in gross capital formation, whereas those purchased by households are considered to be current expenditures, even though the purchaser may borrow to acquire the automobile and view it as a capital purchase.

If these accounting modifications to the definition of household income and current expenditure are carried out for the United States national accounts, it has been determined that household gross saving did not significantly exceed household gross capital formation over the period from 1947 to 1991 (see Table 6.1). In other words, the household sector was not a net provider of funds to the other sectors of the economy. The year-to-year data showed that in periods of prosperity the gross capital formation of the household sector for owner-occupied housing and consumer durables often exceeded the gross saving supplied by households. In effect, this means that the current and capital outlays that households actually make during periods of prosperity tend to exceed the income they receive. Conversely, in periods of recession household gross capital formation has often grown more slowly or has declined more than gross saving. In these periods, the household sector has become a net provider of funds to the other sectors.

This behavior of household net borrowing and net lending is precisely the opposite of that implied by the permanent income hypothesis. The permanent income hypothesis overlooks two very important institutional aspects of household behavior. First, for many households, saving is contractual and cannot be changed easily in the short run; the prime examples are repayment of home mortgages and consumer debt. Second, the omission of household capital formation neglects the point that in the short run the capital outlays for owner-occupied housing and durables can be reduced without commensurately disturbing the household's basic standard of living. Therefore, household gross saving often tends to be relatively stable, and it is the capital outlays of households, not their saving, that reflect the fluctuations in income.

Aggregate household savings data cannot be used directly to test the life cycle hypothesis. Nevertheless, the importance of houses and consumer durables as elements of household spending and accumulation suggests a quite different scenario from that posited by the life cycle hypothesis. During the early years of the life cycle, households purchase houses and consumer durables and acquire mortgages and consumer debt. Gradually, with advancing age, mortgages and consumer debt are paid off. At the time of retirement households have considerable equity in houses and durables. Although there is a life cycle pattern, it is not the one suggested by the life cycle hypothesis. It is not accumulation for old age that drives the system. Rather, the dominant pattern relates to the acquisition of housing and durables by households in their formative years; in their middle and later years, they repay mortgages and consumer debt, thus increasing their saving and accumulating equity (Wolff, 1981).

Thus, the effect of this life cycle saving pattern on the supply of household saving available for nonhousehold capital formation is the reverse of that predicted by the life cycle hypothesis. A growing (and therefore young) population would not be a source of net lending, but rather would borrow from the other sectors to finance their purchases of houses and durables. Conversely, a declining population would include a large segment of households in the phase of their life cycle when they are paying off previously incurred debt, so that households as a group would be suppliers of funds to other sectors. With the prospect of an ageing population in the next few decades, therefore the household sector may be expected to contribute more rather than less to the financing of other sectors.

Enterprise saving and capital formation
The treatment of enterprise saving and capital formation in the national accounts raises other issues. The institutional sectoring of enterprises is primarily confined to distinguishing between nonfinancial and financial enterprises. Although the national accounts provide detailed production data relating to establishments classified by industrial activity for input–output analysis, these data do not yield information on enterprise saving and capital formation.

Data relating to enterprise saving and capital formation are contained only in the full set of operating, appropriation, financial accounts and balance sheets that are provided for broad institutional sectors (Postner, 1988). Although it is true that some conglomerate enterprises engage in many different kinds of economic activity, it is also apparent that there are major differences in the patterns of saving and capital formation for different kinds of economic activity. Thus enterprises in agriculture, mining, construction, manufacturing, public utilities, trade and services all operate under very different institutional and market constraints. It is to be expected, therefore, that the patterns of saving and capital formation of enterprises operating in these various activities may be quite different. For the US, special studies undertaken by the National Bureau of Economic Research during the 1950s (Kuznets, 1961) and more recent studies of Internal Revenue Corporate Tax Return data (see Table 6.2) indicate some of these differences in saving and capital formation behavior.

In agriculture, the pattern of saving and capital formation has been influenced by the changing value of farm land and the turnover of farms as farmers retire and new farmers purchase the land with new mortgages. This process has resulted in a situation where new farmers borrow extensively to provide the

Table 6.2 Corporate Income Statements for the United States, 1983, Total All Industries and Industry Divisions ($bn)

Line	Item	Total 1	10 Agriculture 2	20 Mining 3	30 Construction 4	40 Manufacturing 5	50 Transport and utilities 6	60 Wholesale and retail 7	70 Finance and insurance 8	80 Services 9
1	Number of returns	2,977,040	92,125	37,066	283,519	261,927	122,567	851,786	479,656	848,394
	Income statements									
2	Total receipts	7,092.0	58.7	131.2	290.0	2,544.0	654.2	2,116.1	882.7	415.1
3	Business receipts	6,330.6	55.1	122.5	280.9	2,418.3	627.8	2,071.3	362.6	392.1
4	Interest receipts	513.1	0.7	2.5	2.8	38.0	9.5	14.7	440.0	4.9
5	Dividend receipts	33.4	0.1	0.7	0.3	21.1	0.8	1.4	8.1	0.9
6	Rents and royalties received	83.3	0.6	1.6	1.5	34.4	4.9	8.3	24.4	7.6
7	Net gain on noncapital assets	26.1	0.3	0.8	1.7	3.8	1.8	1.6	14.9	1.2
8	Other receipts	105.5	1.9	3.1	2.8	28.4	9.4	18.8	32.7	8.4
9	Total outlays and retained earnings	7,092.0	58.7	131.2	290.0	2,544.0	654.2	2,116.1	882.7	415.1
10	Total operating costs	6,684.2	56.2	124.4	282.1	2,362.0	580.4	2,055.1	835.7	388.3
11	Costs of sales and operations	4,305.7	38.3	85.5	221.2	1,678.4	339.2	1,627.0	172.8	143.3
12	Compensation of officers	141.0	1.5	1.5	10.1	23.2	4.8	32.0	20.7	47.2
13	Repairs	74.5	1.0	0.8	1.4	28.1	28.3	7.4	3.8	3.7
14	Bad debts	30.6	0.1	0.6	0.6	6.8	3.1	4.8	12.9	1.7
15	Rent paid	104.8	1.4	1.4	2.3	26.4	14.0	31.0	12.1	16.2
16	Interest paid	475.2	2.9	6.8	4.9	74.0	36.8	27.6	310.4	11.8
17	Taxes paid (exc. fed. corp. tax)	173.4	1.3	4.0	6.2	73.3	28.3	29.3	17.2	13.8
18	Advertising	72.2	0.2	0.1	0.9	34.8	3.1	22.1	5.7	5.3
19	Pension, profit share stock, annuity	54.3	0.1	0.9	1.5	23.9	8.1	5.9	5.2	8.7
20	Employee benefit programs	58.9	0.2	0.8	1.6	31.4	7.5	8.0	5.0	4.4
21	Net loss, noncapital assets	7.5	0.1	0.3	0.1	1.2	1.0	0.5	3.9	0.4
22	Other deductions	1,186.1	9.1	21.7	31.7	360.5	106.2	259.5	266.0	131.8
23	Gross operating surplus	407.8	2.5	6.8	7.9	182.0	73.8	61.0	47.0	26.8

24	Depreciation	241.5	3.3	7.8	6.3	99.4	56.2	27.6	19.7	21.2
25	Amortization	4.1	0.0	0.1	0.0	1.5	0.6	0.4	0.8	0.7
26	Depletion	7.5	0.0	2.0	0.1	4.5	0.6	0.1	0.2	0.0
27	Net income	154.7	−0.8	−3.1	1.5	76.6	16.4	32.9	26.3	4.9
28	Dividends paid	128.1	0.2	2.7	0.8	43.3	24.5	12.6	41.6	2.4
29	Fed. corp. profit taxes paid	52.2	0.3	0.7	1.5	25.1	5.3	10.9	5.7	2.7
30	Contributions and gifts paid	3.3	0.0	0.1	0.1	1.8	0.4	0.3	0.4	0.2
31	Net income retained	−28.9	−1.3	−6.6	−0.9	6.4	−13.8	9.1	−21.4	−0.4
32	Net s-t capital gains less loss	4.9	0.0	0.1	0.0	0.3	0.1	0.1	4.2	0.1
33	Net l-t capital gains less loss	33.9	0.6	1.1	0.9	8.4	2.9	2.5	16.1	1.4
34	Net addition to surplus	9.9	−0.7	−5.4	0.0	15.1	−10.8	11.7	−1.1	1.1
35	Gross retained income	224.2	2.0	3.3	5.5	111.8	43.6	37.2	−0.7	21.5
36	Investment credit: cost of property	238.9	2.8	5.8	6.8	89.9	67.5	27.7	18.0	20.4

Balance sheets

37	Total assets	10,199.3	50.3	194.4	161.4	2,233.0	998.9	804.3	5,487.2	269.8
38	Financial assets	7,637.3	18.2	113.9	104.5	1,269.4	287.5	404.8	5,290.7	148.3
39	Cash	590.1	3.1	6.3	15.3	62.8	17.0	48.3	410.3	27.0
40	Notes and accounts receivable	2,676.9	4.4	23.1	40.3	493.9	93.0	199.5	1,779.1	43.6
41	Less: Allowance for bad debts	51.0	0.0	0.5	0.4	10.0	1.5	4.2	32.6	1.8
42	Other current assets	433.6	1.8	6.4	15.7	85.4	31.2	27.3	246.7	19.1
43	Mortgage and real estate loans	982.4	0.8	0.7	4.4	12.3	1.2	6.7	954.1	2.2
44	Government obligations	685.1	0.3	1.2	1.4	23.5	11.7	19.9	624.9	2.2
45	Other investments	1,798.1	4.0	63.8	13.8	435.6	102.1	74.8	1,069.6	34.4
46	Other financial assets	522.1	3.8	12.9	14.0	165.9	32.8	32.5	238.6	21.6
47	Nonfinancial assets	2,562.0	32.1	80.5	56.9	963.5	711.5	399.0	197.0	121.5
48	Intangible assets	87.6	0.1	4.0	0.9	48.9	7.8	7.2	11.8	6.9
49	Less: Accumulated amortization	25.0	0.1	1.2	0.2	15.0	2.0	2.1	1.7	2.7
50	Inventories	599.3	4.8	6.9	24.1	270.4	30.1	237.5	12.1	13.4
51	Depreciable assets	2,729.7	31.0	85.8	57.7	1,051.1	901.9	246.7	193.1	162.4
52	Less: Accumulated depreciation	1,024.3	16.5	34.5	32.0	466.7	239.0	108.4	59.4	67.8

(cont.)

Table 6.2, (cont.)

		10	20	30	40	50	60	70	80
	Total	Agriculture	Mining	Construction	Manufacturing	Transport and utilities	Wholesale and retail	Finance and insurance	Services
Line Item	1	2	3	4	5	6	7	8	9
53 Depletable assets	107.8	0.5	26.1	1.4	64.3	9.4	3.4	2.4	0.3
54 Less: Accumulated depletion	32.3	0.1	9.1	0.3	18.4	3.0	1.2	0.1	0.1
55 Land	119.2	12.4	2.5	5.3	28.9	6.3	15.9	38.8	9.1
56 Total liabilities and net worth	10,199.3	50.3	194.4	161.4	2,233.0	998.9	804.3	5,487.2	269.8
57 Total liabilities	7,554.7	36.8	108.7	119.9	1,279.9	604.6	539.3	4,670.4	195.1
58 Accounts payable	671.3	2.4	15.0	28.1	251.9	61.4	137.4	150.7	24.4
59 Bills and bonds under 1 year	759.4	9.8	12.3	21.2	164.5	43.7	141.8	334.8	31.3
60 Other current liabilities	3,513.3	1.9	10.0	22.1	206.6	89.0	83.8	3,070.3	29.6
61 Mtgs, notes & bonds over 1 year	1,323.0	16.4	49.4	31.0	378.5	306.4	119.8	343.4	78.1
62 Other liabilities	1,287.7	6.3	22.0	17.5	278.4	104.1	56.5	771.2	31.7
63 Total equities	2,644.6	13.5	85.7	41.5	953.1	394.3	265.0	816.8	74.7
64 Capital stock and paid in surplus	1,370.8	11.2	59.0	12.9	382.1	243.6	80.8	542.4	38.8
65 Accumulated surplus	1,273.8	2.3	26.7	28.6	571.0	150.7	184.2	274.4	35.9

Sources: Internal Revenue Service, Statistics of Income Source Book, 1983 Corporation Income Tax Returns.

capital gains of exiting farmers. From the point of view of farmers' current saving and capital formation, however, the gross saving represented by the capital consumption allowances charged by farmers has in recent years exceeded their actual gross capital formation.

The mining industry is very much affected by the tax laws. Capital expenses for drilling oil wells and for mine shafts have in the United States been treated as current costs for tax purposes. At the same time, depletion allowances have also been permitted. As a consequence, mining operations have often provided attractive tax shelters, where the owners can operate at a tax loss and take advantage of considerable cash flow. In some industries the profit to owners can be enhanced by borrowing to increase leverage.

The construction industry, aside from owner-occupied housing, generally operates on the basis of separate corporations or limited partnerships for individual projects. These are financed by mortgages, and in subsequent periods the existing stock of projects provides a flow of mortgage repayments. In periods of construction boom, the new mortgages are larger than the repayments taking place, but during recession the repayments exceed new mortgages. In other words, mortgage debt repayment by this industry is relatively stable and it is the new borrowing for construction that fluctuates widely over the cycle. The recent savings and loan crisis in the United States had its roots in loaning of funds for the overexpansion of certain types of construction activity in specific local areas.

According to the NBER financing studies, over the past 50 years manufacturing enterprises have generated gross saving that has been equal to or greater than its capital formation. In addition, the more detailed analysis based on corporate tax records suggests that the gross saving of individual industries within manufacturing is generally of the same magnitude as their gross capital formation. Examination of the balance sheets of manufacturing enterprises indicates that their holdings of financial assets are approximately equal to their liabilities.

Public utilities operate under regulatory controls with the result that there is little retention of earnings over and above capital consumption allowances. As a consequence, public utilities borrow funds for their expansion, and their balance sheets indicate that the liabilities they owe greatly exceed their financial assets.

Trade and services represent a variety of different situations. In the case of retail trade, gross saving generally exceeds gross capital formation other than inventory accumulation, but inventory fluctuations result in a corresponding fluctuation in borrowing. In the case of services, the situation is similar to the manufacturing industries, except in those cases where very small businesses are dominant. In these, gross saving is often less than the gross capital formation taking place.

Financial institutions are primarily engaged in borrowing and lending that obscures the actual gross saving and capital formation that may be taking place. However, it is apparent that pension funds retain large amounts of technical reserves that are set aside for future benefits. Since the increases in these reserves have been excluded from household income, they represent a source of gross saving in the financial sector. Similarly, reserves built up by casualty insurance such as automobile policies also create pools of gross saving which the financial sector has available for loaning to other sectors.

This brief overview of some of the factors relating to accounting for the gross saving and gross capital formation of different types of enterprises demonstrates the need for better institutional sectoring of enterprises in the national accounts. The present limited institutional sectoring of the national accounts in most countries and in the proposed revision of the United Nations System of National Accounts is completely inadequate for analyzing the process of saving and capital formation in the economy.

National accounts and microdata bases
Traditionally, there are two different needs for economic and social data. First, there is a need for highly aggregated macroeconomic data of the kind provided by the national accounts to provide an overview of the operation of the economy and to serve for general overall policy formulation. Second, there is also a need for much more detailed economic, social, demographic and regional data for the purposes of administration, regulation and detailed planning in such fields as health services, the environment and the elimination of poverty. In the current revision of the United Nations System of National Accounts, it is proposed that these needs be met by constructing satellite accounts, social accounting matrices or mesodata. Such supplementary data would address on an *ad hoc* basis the specific statistical requirements of various areas of concern and integrate them with the macrodata in the national accounts.

The basic methodology of national account estimation can best be described as 'cut and paste'. National accountants pride themselves on utilizing a wide variety of statistical sources and integrating them into a consistent set of macro-estimates. Specifically, they draw upon the aggregations of data generated by administrative and regulatory agencies and the cross-tabulations of censuses and sample surveys provided by statistical agencies. In view of the adjustments and reconciliations needed to produce a coherent and consistent set of macro-estimates, the amount of disaggregation possible is automatically restricted to the amount contained within the national accounting system. To the extent that satellite accounts or social accounting matrices are added to the system, the data for these also need to be handcrafted in order to be consistent with the macrodata in the national accounts.

In recent years, there have been two major developments that have altered the role of microdata in the statistical system. On the one hand, the development of sample survey methods has contributed greatly to the quality and quantity of the basic microdata that are available. On the other hand, the advance of computer technology has radically changed the way in which microdata are processed, stored and made available for analysis.

The development of sampling frames, registers and innovative collection techniques have made it possible to obtain reliable data more quickly and economically than previously. There has consequently been a considerable increase in the availability of microdata as policy-makers and other users are faced with questions that cannot be answered by traditional kinds of macrodata. This development has not been restricted to the more developed countries; it has been increasingly recognized that sample surveys may provide the best source of social, demographic and economic data in developing countries.

Advances in computer technology have revolutionized the approach to the processing, retrieval and analysis of data. Prior to the computer, the main objective of data processing was to reduce the large quantities of microdata to a manageable coherent form. This meant that the primary data were used to produce a set of prespecified tabulations. Editing and adjustments were generally carried out at the tabulated level. Once such tabulations were produced, the original data were usually considered to be of no further interest and were destroyed. The aggregate tabulations, however, by their very nature reduced the information content that could be obtained from the original data. With the increased ability of the computer to process, store and retrieve data, therefore, the focus of attention has shifted to the development of microdata bases containing the full information provided by the primary data. Improved methods of editing, cleaning and correcting are carried out at the microlevel of data and the microdata bases preserve the full information provided by the primary data.

The changing focus of policy, from an exclusive concern with macroeconomic policy to questions of distribution and social aspects of well being of the population, has increased the need for microdata bases integrated with the macroeconomic data in the national accounts. The increased policy importance of social programs has led to a demand for information on the interrelationships between government and households, on the size distribution of income, on the position of specific social and demographic groups and on distributions by region and by type of community. Such data for households are currently provided in the United States by regularly collected 'Surveys of Income and Program Participation'. Other microdata sets for households such as the IRS Tax Model containing individual tax returns are also in use.

Unfortunately, as yet, household microdata have not been integrated with the data contained in the Personal Income Account in the official National Accounts. The possibility of access to microdata has, however, led to a change in the perceived need for this kind of information. Where good quality and conveniently accessible microdata bases are available, planners and policy-makers do use them. The development of computer technology, furthermore, has made microanalytic modeling feasible, and this technique is increasingly being used by both researchers and policy-makers to simulate the distributional effects of changes in programs and to estimate their costs.

Proposal for a core system of transactor/transaction accounts
In principle the United Nations System of National Accounts records the transactions of institutional transactors, but significant exceptions are made in order to impute nonmarket activity, introduce artificial transactors and reroute actual transactions between two transactors to a third party. Although these exceptions have been introduced to improve the measurement of total output, consumption or welfare, they seriously impair the use of the accounts for analyzing the actual transaction flows in the economy and for integrating the macrodata in the national accounts with microdata bases.

An alternative proposal has been put forth (Van Bochove and Van Tuinen, 1986), suggesting that the accounting structure of the UN SNA should be organized in such a manner that it would provide flexibility. It was pointed out that major questions relating to the production boundary, the sectoring of the economy, and the valuation of transactions have a major effect on the national accounting system and that different researchers or politicians may have different requirements. It is argued that it is not the task of statisticians to make a choice between various options on behalf of users, but rather the system should be flexible to serve a variety of users.

The specific recommendation (Van Bochove and Bloem, 1986) is that a system of institutional core accounts and supplementary modules should be developed. The core accounts would be constructed according to three rules: the transactors of the system would be actual organizational units, the production boundary would be restricted to market transactions and transactions would be recorded for each transactor actually paying or receiving money.

The core system of accounts would thus consist of the market transactions relating to production, income and outlays and capital finance and accumulation of enterprises, government and households. The supplementary modules or 'building blocks' would contain imputations and rerouting of transactions that were found to be analytically useful. In the case of nonmarket activity, it would be possible to extend the production boundary further to include such things as housewife services, education, environmental changes, or even leisure without impairing the integrity and usefulness of the core data relating to market transactions. Similarly, attributions of income in kind provided by the government or employers to households and revaluations of assets and liabilities in the capital accounts could be shown without distorting the actual income and expenditures of households.

Furthermore, the use of core transaction accounts would make it possible to integrate the actual microdata provided by reporting units in different sectors of the economy with the macrodata contained in the national accounts. The key to such integration is consistency and standardization of definitions, concepts and classifications at both the micro- and macrolevels. An example of such a core account and related modules has been drawn up for the household sector current and capital accounts in the United States for the year 1980 (see Tables 6.3 and 6.4).

Despite the obvious shortcomings of the United Nations System of National Accounts and the difficulties inherent in the development of related microdata files, the accomplishments of the past 50 years should not be denigrated. The 1968 SNA provided a comprehensive national accounting system that

Table 6.3 *Household Current Income and Outlay Account, United States, 1980 ($bn)*

CURRENT CORE ACCOUNT		
Income	1 Wages, salaries and other labor income	1,352.8
	2 Proprietor and rental income	135.3
	3 Interest income	179.7
	4 Dividend income	54.1
	5 Transfer by enterprises	47.7
	6 Transfers by government	242.1
	7 Less: Withheld taxes (net)	−275.0
Outlays and saving	8 Total household monetary income	1,736.7
	9 Current consumption expenditures	1,240.8
	10 Transfers paid by households	40.9
	11 Tax payments	150.1
	12 Gross saving	304.9
	13 Total household monetary outlays and gross savings	1,736.7
IMPUTATION ACCOUNT		
Income	14 Owner-occupied housing gross imputed income	57.9
	15 Capital consumption	46.0
	16 Net return on equity	11.9
	17 Consumer durable gross imputed income	229.3
	18 Capital consumption	180.8
	19 Net return on equity	48.5
	20 Subsistence production imputed income	1.8
	21 Farm products consumed on farms	0.5
	22 Margins on owner-built homes	1.3
	23 Total gross imputed income	289.0
Outlays and saving	24 Consumption of imputed housing services	57.9
	25 Consumption of imputed consumer durable services	229.3
	26 Consumption of imputed farm products	0.5
	27 Saving from margins on owner-built houses	1.3
	28 Total imputed consumption and saving	289.0

Source: R. Ruggles and N.D. Ruggles (1986).

Table 6.3 (cont.)

ATTRIBUTION ACCOUNT			
Income	30	Benefits in kind provided by employers	55.5
	31	Health benefits	49.7
	32	Food and clothing	5.8
	33	Benefits in kind provided by nonprofits	58.5
	34	Nonprofits institution expenditures	48.8
	35	Nonprofits institution space rent	9.7
	36	Benefits in kind provided by government	288.7
	37	Education	141.0
	38	Health	105.5
	39	Welfare	14.5
	40	Housing and community services	12.9
	41	Recreation and other	14.8
	42	Total income from attributions	402.7
Outlays and saving	43	Consumption of in-kind education services	131.0
	44	Consumption of in-kind health services	155.2
	45	Consumption of in-kind housing services	12.9
	46	Consumption of other in-kind services	94.6
	47	Saving provided by in-kind services	0.0
	48	Total consumption and saving provided by attributions	402.7
EXTENDED HOUSEHOLD CURRENT ACCOUNT			
Income	49	Household nonmarket activity	1,264.9
	50	Unpaid household work	980.7
	51	Opportunity cost of students	284.2
	52	Entitlements	
	53	Net change employer's pension fund reserves	66.8
	54	Net change in social security entitlements	na
	55	Process benefits from time use and leisure	na
	56	Total extended income	na
Outlays and saving	57	Extended consumption	na
	58	Extended saving	na
	59	Total extended consumption and saving	na

articulated all of the transactions taking place in the economy. Although the stagflation of the 1970s and the subsequent disenchantment with Keynesian economic policy largely discredited macroeconomic analysis in academic circles, national accounts as such have continued to develop. The role of national accounts in defining the economic system and putting order into the masses of transactions information has not been questioned. Both national statistical offices and international statistical agencies now view the national accounts as the basic framework for the data relating to the economic system.

Although the development of microdata has been less heralded than the national accounts, coupled with advancing computer technology it is the wave of the future. It is only through the use of microdata that the important relationships among social, economic and demographic information can be analyzed effectively. As already noted, many governments are recognizing that

Table 6.4 *Household Balance Sheets, Capital Transactions and Revaluations, United States, 1980 ($bn)*

Line		Beginning balance	Capital transactions	Revaluations	End of year balance
1	Owner-occupied houses	1,771.0	39.2	156.3	1,966.5
2	Gross value	2,600.8	85.2	219.2	2,905.2
3	Less: Capital consumption	829.8	46.0	62.9	938.7
4	Consumer durables	874.4	33.9	89.7	998.0
5	Gross value	1,679.0	214.7	59.0	1,952.7
6	Less: Capital consumption	804.6	180.8	−30.7	954.7
7	Currency and deposits	1,451.6	174.9	–	1,626.5
8	Currency and checking accounts	250.3	15.3	–	265.6
9	Time deposits and money funds	1,201.3	159.6	–	1,360.9
10	Fixed claim assets	536.6	30.4	–	567.0
11	Government bonds	276.9	17.3	–	294.2
12	Corporate and foreign bonds	38.7	1.7	–	40.4
13	Mortgages	106.4	7.5	–	113.9
14	Other fixed claims	114.6	3.9	–	118.5
15	Equities held	3,159.5	−7.3	625.0	3,777.2
16	Corporate stock	745.9	−1.5	250.6	995.0
17	Noncorporate nonfarm equity	1,367.0	−3.8	252.6	1,615.8
18	Farm equity	616.9	−14.4	68.8	671.3
19	Pensions and insurance	199.9	12.4	2.5	214.8
20	Estates and trusts	229.8		50.5	280.3
21	Total assets	7,793.1	271.4	871.0	8,935.3
22	Fixed claim liabilities	1,336.2	109.2	–	1,445.4
23	Mortgages	856.5	83.8	–	940.3
24	Consumer credit	382.7	2.3	–	385.0
25	Other	97.0	23.1	–	120.1
26	Net worth	6,456.9	161.9	871.0	7,485.1
27	Tangibles	2,645.4	73.1	246.0	2,959.8
28	Net financial assets	3,811.5	88.8	625.0	4,525.3
29	Total liabilities and net worth	7,793.1	271.1	871.0	8,935.3

Source: R. Ruggles and N.D. Ruggles (1986).

the implementation and evaluation of their policies depend on the development of appropriate microdata bases.

Looking back, in view of all that has gone before, one cannot say that this is just the beginning, and hopefully it is not the end. We are in the middle of what is an interesting and exciting development that promises much for the future.

REFERENCES

Boisguillebert, Pierre le Pesant (1697), *Le Détail de la France*, Paris.
Copeland, Morris (1952), *A Study of Moneyflows in the United States*, New York.

Eisner, Robert (1988), 'Extended accounts for income and product', *Journal of Economic Literature*, December.

_____ (1989), *The Total System of Accounts*, Chicago.

Fisher, Irving (1930), *The Theory of Interest*, New York.

Frisch, Ragnar (1940), *Nationalregns Kapel*, New York.

Galiani, Ferdinando (1772), *Dialogues sur le Commerce de Blés*.

Goldsmith, Raymond (1962), *The National Wealth of the United States in the Postwar Period*, Princeton, NJ: Princeton University Press.

Gilbert, Milton and R. Bangs (1942), 'Preliminary estimates of gross national product, 1929–1941', *Survey of Current Business*, May.

Jorgenson, Dale and P. Alvaro (1983), 'The accumulation of human and non-human capital', in I. Moani and R. Hemming (eds), *The Determinants of National Saving and Wealth*, London.

Kendrick, John (1979), 'Expanding imputed values in the national income and product accounts', *Review of Income and Wealth*, December.

Keynes, John Maynard (1935), *The General Theory of Employment, Interest and Money*.

_____ (1940), *How to Pay for the War*, London: Macmillan.

King, Gregory (1696), *Natural and Political Observations and Conclusions Upon the State and Condition of England*, London: Macmillan.

Kuznets, Simon (1941), *National Income and its Composition, 1919–1938*, New York.

_____ (1948), 'National income: A new version', *Review of Economics and Statistics*, August.

_____ (1961), *Capital in the American Economy: Its Formation and Financing*, Princeton, NJ: Princeton University Press.

Leontief, Wassily (1941), *The Structure of the American Economy, 1919–1939: An Empirical Application of Equilibrium Analysis*, Oxford University Press.

Marshall, Alfred (1879), *Economics of Industry*, London: Macmillan.

OEEC (1952), *A Standardized System of National Accounts*, Paris.

Palmieri, Giuseppe (1787), *Pubblica Felicità*.

Petty, William (1676), *Political Arithmetick*.

Postner, Harry (1988), 'Linkages between macro and micro business accounts: implications for economic measurement', *Review of Income and Wealth*, September.

Quesnay, Francois (1760), *Tableau Economique*.

Reich, Utz-Peter (1991), 'Concept and definition of income in the national accounts', *Review of Income and Wealth*, September 1991.

Ruggles, Richard (1949), *National Income Accounting and Its Relation to Economic Policy*, Paris.

Ruggles, Richard and Nancy D. Ruggles (1951), *European National Accounts*, and *National Accounts Data Book*, Economic Cooperation Administration, Washington, DC.

_____ (1982), 'Integrated economic accounts for the United States', *Survey of Current Business*, May.

_____ (1986), 'The integration of macro and micro data for the household sector', *Review of Income and Wealth*, September.

Ruggles, Nancy D. and Richard (1992), 'Household and enterprise saving and capital formation in the united states: A market transactions view', *Review of Income and Wealth*, June.

Smith, Adam (1776), *Wealth of Nations*.

Stone, Richard (1947), 'Definition and measurement of the national income and related totals', Appendix in *Measurement of the National Income and the Construction of Social Accounts*, Studies and Reports on Statistical Method No. 7, UN, Geneva.

Studenski, Paul (1958), *The Income of Nations*, New York.

Sunga, Preetom S. (1988), 'Conceptual incongruity in the national accounts', *Review of Income and Wealth*, December.

Tobin, J. and W. Nordhaus (1972), 'Is growth obsolete?', *Economic Growth*, Colloquium V, New York.

United Nations (1953), *A System of National Accounts and Supporting Tables*, Series F, No. 2, New York.

_____ (1969), *A System of National Accounts*, Series F, No. 2, Rev. 3.

United Nations and OECD (1979), *Instructions and Definitions for the National Accounts Questionnaire*, revision.

Van Bochove, C.A. and A. Bloem (1986), 'The structure of the next SNA, review of basic options', *Statistical Journal of the United Nations*, ECE, December.

Van Bochove, C.A. and H.K. van Tuinen (1986), 'Flexibility in the next SNA: The case for an institutional core', *Review of Income and Wealth*, June.

Vanoli, Andre (1986), 'Sur la structure général du SCN à partir de l'expérience du systèm élargi de compatabilité national français', *Review of Income and Wealth*, June.

Vauban, Marshal (1712), *Dime Royale*.

Verri, Pietro (1771), *Economia Politica*.

Wolff, Edward (1981), 'The accumulation of household wealth over the life cycle: A microdata analysis', *Review of Income and Wealth*, June.

7. The Value Added of National Accounting

Richard Ruggles and Patricia Ruggles
Yale University and Joint Economic Committee

This collection of essays commemorating 50 years of national accounts in the Netherlands lives up to its title — it does add value to the field of national accounts. It successfully shows how the national accounts have evolved in the Netherlands over the last 50 years, and how macroeconomic modeling has interacted with the development of quantitative estimation of economic constructs. The book is not only useful for specialists in national accounting, but it also provides important insights for economists, statisticians and those concerned with public policy.

This work is the collaboration of 25 authors representing the Central Bureau of Statistics, other Dutch government institutions, Dutch universities, international organizations and economists from other countries. The representation of topics is equally broad, ranging from economic theory and policy to more technical topics such as input–output, time series analysis and environmental accounting.

All of this is an indication that, despite its age of 50 years, national accounting is alive and well — at least in the Netherlands. Indeed, this is in marked contrast with the situation in the United States, where the shock of stagflation in 1973 reduced national accounting to the role of providing economic indicators. It is no longer a topic in the subject listings of the *Journal of Economic Literature*, and it has been eliminated from the economics curriculum in most universities. Indeed, few economists in the United States outside of the Bureau of Economic Analysis are aware of the United Nations SNA. It is refreshing, therefore, to have a book that not only looks back to the origin and development of national accounts (Part I), and is very much concerned with current applications (Part II), but also looks forward to the future (Part III).

This chapter first appeared in *Review of Income and Wealth*, **41** (3), 1995.

One of the most distinctive contributions of this book has been its presentation of the evolution of the Dutch system of national accounts. J. Tinbergen, in Chapter 2 on 'Origin of National Accounts and Relation to Economic Theory', points out that national accounting is in essence the extension of accounting from an instrument used by individuals and enterprises to an instrument used by nations, and that economic theory related to national accounts consists of understanding the processes of production, trade and consumption. His vision of the future of national accounts encompasses not only historical research on the process of development and spatial analysis of economic activity, but also global analysis of environmental and sustainability problems.

G.P. den Bakker in Chapter 5 on the 'Origin and Development of Dutch National Accounts' provides a more detailed picture of the Dutch experience. The Tinbergen macroeconomic models gave the Netherlands a head start, and in 1941, van Kleef published his system of 'national book-keeping'. During World War II, the statistical work on national income estimation continued, and an input–output approach to national accounting was developed. Derksen and Oomens, who were in charge of national accounts during the war years and the period immediately following, were major influences, not only in the development of Dutch national accounting but also in the development of international standards.

In terms of the historical development of national income measurement, the essay by J.L. van Zanden in Chapter 13 on 'Historical National Accounts' shows how the development of historical national accounts has altered the analysis of economic growth. Prior to the development of reliable historical national accounts data, widely accepted theories on the stages of economic growth portrayed the industrial revolution as a decisive break with the past economic trend and a take-off primarily stimulated by an increase in the rate of investment. However, after the careful reconstruction of the national accounts for England in the eighteenth and nineteenth century by Phyllis Deane, it became apparent that the growth was more gradual and did not accelerate. The cotton industry, which some economic historians cited as the leading sector; was scarcely noticeable in the national figures. There was also no sudden rise in the investment rate. Dutch historians also debated the timing and nature of the industrial revolution in the Netherlands, and their work on Dutch national accounts has also led to a major revision of the analysis of economic growth and development in the Netherlands during the first half of the nineteenth century.

However, the more recent issues confronting Dutch national accounts are spelled out by H.K. Van Tuinen in Chapter 3, 'Issues in Dutch National Accounting, 1970–1985'. The specific issues examined are: the reliability of national accounts data, the informal economy, welfare and environment, inflation and the national accounting system as a whole. The issue of reliability is particularly difficult for national accountants. On the one hand, there is always considerable pressure to produce 'quick and dirty preliminary data' for purposes of economic policy, but at the same time significant revisions tend to be viewed as indications that the data are unreliable. Revisions that affect the continuity of time series are also felt to be disruptive. Under such conditions improving the reliability of national accounts has been difficult. Dealing with concerns about topics such as the informal economy, the measurement of welfare and the treatment of environment pollution has raised conceptual questions relating to the production boundary of national accounts and about the assignment of valuations. Dealing with the problem of inflation has not only involved the development of appropriate chain-weighted indexes, but has also raised important questions as to the meaning of inflation-adjusted income data.

The Dutch national accounts data are thus used in several very different contexts that require different concepts and specifications. As a consequence, Van Tuinen concludes that 'a fundamental problem with the national accounts is that many demands are made on the system and that responding to an increasing number of demands has made the system more and more complex'. The Dutch solution to this problem has been to propose a system of core accounts that records the actual transactions of the institutional sectors of the economy and provides supplementary modules around the core that would be more analytical and would reflect special purposes and specific theoretical views. It is regrettable that these principles were not adopted in the 1993 revision of the United Nations SNA, but they are not incompatible with it.

Part II of the book, 'Present Applications', is concerned with modeling, economic policy, input–output, time series and historical analysis. C.J. van Eijk in Chapter 8 on 'National Accounts and the Macroeconomic Revolutions of the Inter-war Period', demonstrated how statisticians, interacting with economists working on development of macroeconomic theory, improved the statistical information to be used for empirical research. In particular, the bilateral nature of the transaction framework enforced a discipline on both statistical measurements and the macroeconomic concepts. Improved information at the macroeconomic level helped to quantify economics. In Chapter 9, J.P. Verbruggen and G. Zalm, on 'National Accounts and Modelling at the Central Planning Bureau', indicate how, initially, there was a close relation between macroeconomic modeling and the development of the macroframework for the national accounts. But over the years, as the models of the Central Bureau of Statistics evolved due to changing economic conditions and policy issues, the national accounts and econometric models diverged. It is further argued, however, that such divergence may come to an end since both systems are gradually developing in the same direction — going from functional and macro-oriented systems to institutional and micro-oriented systems.

In terms of economic modeling, it is apparent that economists in the past have primarily been interested in defining macroeconomic concepts in terms of economic processes — i.e., production, consumption, investment and saving. The economic constructs of the national accounting system have been built around these concepts, and the institutional aspects of transactors and transactions were largely ignored. Indeed, early national accountants had difficulty in deciding how to treat government in the modeling of the economy. In keeping with the approach of neo-classical economic theory, many economists felt that, in order to be general, economic theory — and the data constructs on which it was based — should be institution free.

Many economists also believed that the major economic constructs should be comprehensive, and should not necessarily be limited by the actual transactions taking place in the economy. The production boundary, for example, should include some of the nonmarket activities that contribute to well-being so that the measurement of production and consumption would reflect the general level of welfare in the economy.

Finally, the commodity flow and input–output approach to the estimation of national accounts consisted of measuring the output of the economy in terms of industrial output of commodities, and then allocating these commodities after appropriate transport and trade margins to intermediate industrial use, exports, government purchases, capital formation and consumption. Under such procedures, the consumer sector in the economy was determined residually. As a consequence, the actual transactions of households were never incorporated as part of the national accounts.

The Dutch rationale for national accounts consisting of institutional sector transactor/transaction core accounts is based on changes in all of three of these underlying factors. First, as noted by Verbruggen and Zalm, econometric modeling is gradually developing from functional and macro-oriented systems toward more institutional and micro-oriented systems.

Second, as pointed out by Van Tuinen, the increasingly wide range of different demands on the national accounting system has made it more and more complex, and there is need for a simpler core system that can be augmented by the use of supplementary data.

Finally, the statistical resources available for the construction of national accounts have increased substantially. Administrative records, tax returns and sample surveys of enterprises and households provide a vast amount of data that can be drawn on to produce detailed transaction information for enterprises, governmental units and households. The national accounts are no longer solely dependent on the commodity flow approach, and it has now become feasible to construct transactor/transaction accounts for the institutional sectors of the economy.

In Part III, Chapter 14, A.M. Bloem describes the 'Present and Future of the National Accounts in the Netherlands'. It becomes apparent that the 1994 revision of the UN SNA as spelled out by C. Carson in Chapter 16, 'The New System of National Accounts: Its Role and Significance', and the statistical needs for the unification of Europe as indicated by both W.F. Duisenberg in Chapter 18, 'Monetary and Financial Statistics in a European Statistical System — A Central Banker's View' and by Y. Franchet in Chapter 19, 'Development of National Accounts and Related Statistics for the Unification of Europe', have all become driving forces in shaping the future development of the Netherlands system of national accounts. In addition, however, Bloem indicates that the Netherlands Central Bureau of Statistics has promoted the core-module approach discussed in Chapter 3 of this book. Specifically a number of different modules are being developed. A research and development module showing the costs and benefits of R&D is being developed in a national accounting context without disturbing the system. A time allocation module is being drawn from a Time Budget Survey and is expressed in physical units of time allocations. An environmental module that takes into account the deterioration of the environment is being constructed, and this is explained in greater detail by S.J. Keuning in Chapter 17, 'An Information System for Environmental Indicators in Relation to the National Accounts'. Finally, a tax module is being created by the tax authorities for forecasting tax receipts; the main element in this module is that some of the national income concepts are converted into fiscal concepts.

U.P. Reich points out in Chapter 15, 'The Dutch School of Thought in National Accounts', that flexibility is the main characteristic of the Dutch School of national accounts, but that what is flexible is their attitude towards the system of national accounts — not the accounts themselves. The rules of what is to be retained in the core are rather rigid. Flexibility applies to the supplementary modules, which may deviate between countries and not adhere to any international standards. In reality, however, this is diversity rather than flexibility.

The Dutch proposal that core accounts be developed for the institutional sectors of the economy is thus both theoretically desirable and statistically feasible. However, the proposal does not go far enough. The core macro-account for an institutional sector is, in reality, an aggregation and consolidation of the transaction accounts of the reporting units in that sector. The concepts for the core macroaccounts should be isomorphic with the concepts at the microlevel. From both a theoretical and statistical point of view, it would be highly desirable if core microdata sets could underlie the core macro-accounts.

The macroaccounts not only summarize, but they also suppress information. The aggregation problem presents serious difficulties in interpreting the behavior of time series or in analyzing the relationship among macroeconomic constructs. Macrorelationships are complex — they are not merely micro-relationships 'writ large' as is implied by many economic models. The existence of microdata and, in particular, longitudinal microdata, permits a fuller understanding of the behavior of macrodata. In this connection it is interesting to note that the microanalytic simulation approach developed by Guy Orcutt was stimulated by Tinbergen's econometric modeling.

From a statistical point of view, microdata sets that are fully aligned with the macrocore accounts are currently quite feasible. As already noted, there are large bodies of microdata in the form of administrative data and sample surveys. Registers exist to check the completeness of data sets, and computer technology is available to handle large bodies of data.

The macroeconomic accounts not only benefit from their integration with microdata bases, but, at the same time, the statistical system also benefits. By extending national accounting to microdata, it can serve as the vehicle for integrating economic, social, demographic and regional data. One of the major difficulties in using microdata in the past has been that different microdata sets purporting to cover similar reporting units come out with very different results. As a consequence, analyses of microdata have become suspect — it is felt that by selecting appropriate microdata sets, analysts can arrive at any conclusion they desire. By developing microdata bases that match the control totals in the macroaccounts, those using microdata will have greater assurance that the data they are using are representative, complete and unbiased.

What does the future hold for the national accounts? For the users of national accounts data, the existing computer technology is rapidly altering the way national accounts data are accessed. In the past, published national account tables have provided users with data in a fixed summary and understandable form. With the availability of 'World Wide Web' servers and user-friendly software, however, large data bases of disaggregated national accounts or microdata can be easily accessed by a wide variety of users and tailored to their specific analytic needs. Thus analysts concerned with the measurement of poverty, the incidence of the tax system, the analysis of economic growth or the allocation of government budgets will be able to specify the type of information and the level of aggregation that is desired. The 'what if' questions can be posed and the sensitivity of the analysis to different assumptions can be ascertained.

For the producers of national accounts data, computerization has also radically changed how national accounts are constructed. The computerization of the economic system means that new sources of data ranging from sample surveys, censuses, tax data, regulatory information and other administrative data can be utilized in their most detailed form to provide the basis for the national accounts. The existence of registers and sophisticated sample frames can enable the development of highly detailed data bases that are consistent with each other. In such a situation, it is the national accounts that will offer the framework for such integration. The Dutch proposal for a system of core accounts and supplementary modules carried out at the level of the individual reporting units can provide a logical approach to such a future.

The game has changed! The 1994 UN System of National Accounts already needs major reorientation in order to be adapted to the revolution that has taken place in information needs, availability and computer technology.

PART TWO

UNITED STATES NATIONAL ACCOUNTS

8. The Evolution of National Accounts and the National Data Base

Richard Ruggles and Nancy D. Ruggles
Yale University and National Bureau of Economic Research

During the last half-century, the *Survey of Current Business* has been the vehicle for the development of a comprehensive statistical reporting system on the operation of the US economy. Although economic and social developments over these 50 years have had a major influence in shaping the statistical reporting system, much of the progress which has been achieved can be directly attributed to the ingenuity and sheer hard work of those responsible for reporting on the state of the economy in the *Survey of Current Business*. During this period, the reporting system has moved from a collection of miscellaneous and largely unrelated time series of economic data to a highly articulated, comprehensive and integrated body of economic accounts. In part, this evolution reflects expansion in the quantity of data available, greater statistical refinement, and better adaptation of the reporting system to current needs. More important, however, the development of national accounts has both reflected and contributed to major changes in the nature of economic analysis. Most economists today can herald the development of the national economic accounts to describe and analyze the operation of the economic system as one of the greatest achievements of modern economics.

At this 50-year mark, it is appropriate that we take a backward glance to see just how these changes came about. From such an examination we can learn much about the forces that have shaped the development of the system and the kinds of changes that have been required to adapt it to meet the increasing demands of economic and social policy. Such a retrospective survey will also let us evaluate the responsiveness of the statistical reporting system to changed conditions and the extent to which it was itself a major force in the development of economic thought.

This chapter first appeared in *Survey of Current Business*, Part II, July 1971.

It will also be useful, at this half-century mark, to ask whether the present system fully meets the demands which are being placed upon it, and what changes should be made to ensure the long-run evolutionary development of the system. This is not a trivial task; since the pressure for widened economic and social action has brought with it information requirements which are different not only in quantity but also in kind from what is now available. The economic reporting system as now presented in the *Survey* can provide the basis for a more comprehensive framework of social and economic data. The question is mainly one of how to relate the national economic accounts more closely to the national data base.

Finally, it is also useful to speculate on the future evolution of economic and social statistical systems and on how the information they provide will affect the development of economic and social analysis. The computer is having a revolutionary impact on data processing, so that the social scientist now has available a completely new technology for solving economic and social problems. This technology has profound implications both for the development of reporting systems for economic and social data and for their use in economic and social analysis.

1. EVOLUTION OF THE REPORTING SYSTEM

The Great Depression

One of the effects of the 'Great Depression' of the thirties was a growing concern about the adequacy of the statistical reporting system. The miscellaneous series available at the beginning of the thirties were not comprehensive enough to give a valid report of the state of the economy, and they could not be added up to determine the overall effect of the events taking place. In 1932, the Division of Economic Research in the Department of Commerce, which then prepared the *Survey of Current Business*, undertook a study of national income, with the cooperation of the National Bureau of Economic Research. The results of this study were reported as Senate Document No. 124 of the 73rd Congress, 2nd session, entitled *National Income, 1929–32*. Beginning in February 1934, articles on national income were published at irregular intervals in the *Survey*. The initial estimates covered the national income paid out, by type of payment and by industrial division, and the national income produced. For the first time, it was possible to quantify the decline which had taken place in the US economy and to show how this decline affected different industries and different types of payments. A special Income Section — later National Income Section — was created in the Division of Economic Research and given the responsibility for providing annual estimates. By 1938, the pressure for a more current measure of the flow of income was such that the National Income Section initiated estimates of five monthly income payments in the US Examination of the *Survey* over these years shows a rapid development in the elaboration of detail and the sophistication of the national income data. As those who were part of the group at that time can testify, it was an exciting and stimulating period.

War Mobilization

The mobilization for World War II had a tremendous impact upon the development of the national income framework. In gathering the nation's resources for war, it was necessary to know not only the level of economic activity in various industries but also how the income generated by such activity was being used for the purchase of goods and services by consumers, business and government. Of course, by this time the Keynesian theory of income determination had been well absorbed, and the National Income Unit was well aware of the implications of this theory for the statistical framework. Furthermore, independent work had been done on specific components of final expenditures.

In March of 1942, it was all put together, and gross national product was born. Specifically, the gross national expenditure (or product) was shown in terms of government expenditures for goods and services, private gross capital expenditures, and consumer purchases. This added dimension assured the use of national income statistics as the primary tool of national economic policy. Resources were provided for the elaboration and development of such statistics. Ingenious methods were developed to tap a large number of statistical sources and to integrate them into a common framework. Data from the censuses of manufactures and business were used as the basis for commodity flow estimates. Income tax and social security data were used to provide information on income payments. War Production Board data yielded information on government defense expenditures. In short, World War II mobilized the statistical resources of the nation. The demands for national income information generated during the war resulted in the development of the system of national income accounts. In July 1947, a National Income Supplement to the *Survey* was published. For the first time, the system was set forth in terms of systematic, articulated accounts. Some 48 statistical tables were provided, all fitting into a set of six national income accounts. Sectors of the economy were explicitly recognized, with accounts for businesses, government, households and the rest of the world. The primary thrust of the national income accounting system, however, was still to show the net contribution of the different sectors to the aggregate national income and the income which each sector received as a result.

Consolidation and Extension, 1947–54

The period from 1947 to 1954 was one of consolidation and extension. The 1954 Supplement to the *Survey*, explaining the data and providing the basic tables, represented a substantial achievement; the sources and methods used in making the estimates were described in considerable detail. This Supplement represents a culmination of statistical effort which began with World War II.

Restructuring, 1954–65

Following the publication of the 1954 Supplement, there was a period of significant restructuring in both the form and the content of the national income accounts. In the 1958 Supplement to the *Survey*, now called *US Income and Output*, the data were recast into a simpler and cleaner set of national income accounts, which showed more clearly the operation of the different sectors of the economy. In particular, the activity of the government sector was shown in terms of its expenditures by function and object, giving a much clearer picture of the government's role in the economy. It is this version of the national income accounting system which continues to be used at present. Some refinements in definitions were introduced with the benchmark revisions described in the August 1965 *Survey*; the most important of these was the treatment of interest paid by consumers as a transfer rather than as a component of production.

Integrating Related Data, 1963–70

In recent years, the major change in the national income accounts has been their integration with other bodies of data. Input–output data have been integrated with the national income accounts, and input–output tables are now published by the Office of Business Economics. Considerable work has also been done in harmonizing the flow of funds data published by the Federal Reserve Board and the related national income data published in the *Survey of Current Business*.

2. A MODEL OF THE ECONOMY

Before the development of the national economic accounts, the national data base was largely unexploited for purposes of economic analysis. By its very nature it was highly fragmented and unintegrated. Although the population and economic censuses and the data collected by the Department of Agriculture and the Bureau of Labor Statistics did serve specific functions, they often remained isolated series which were not related to one another. Administrative statistics such as income tax data, social security data and government budgets were generally not utilized for economic analysis, despite their importance for reporting on the operation of major elements in the system. What the national economic accounts have achieved is the piecing together of the widely diverse fragments of the national data base into a coherent reporting system. To some degree, the data base has been responsive to this integrating influence, through the adoption of similar classification schemes and improvement in reporting techniques. The most striking change has been the growth of the data base itself, due to the increased collection of basic information and the expansion of government programs. Today, more than ever, an integrating framework is needed to provide the basis for putting order into the national data base itself.

De-emphasizing Welfare Measurement

Both the general public and economists have always wanted some overall measure of economic performance and welfare as a barometer which would tell how the economy is performing or how general welfare is changing. Thus the original impetus for the development of national income statistics by the federal government lay in the desire for some measure of the performance of the economy in the Depression of the 1930s. In seeking such a measure, economists have built from the network of transactions a variety of economic constructs: national income paid out, national income produced, gross national product, personal income, etc. The process of estimating these constructs required the generation of estimates of separate components of the totals. Initially, such components were merely steps on the way to the total, but inevitably they became of major interest in their own right. Thus such things as consumption expenditures, government expenditures, capital formation, saving, tax payments, and many other blocks of transactions became important parts of the economic accounting system. Despite the controversies as to whether government services were intermediate or final and the extent to which other costs were intermediate rather than final product, the evolution of the national accounts has been such that more and more economic activity has been covered, and less emphasis has been placed upon the welfare or barometric aspect of the major economic constructs.

Empirical Models of the Economy

The national accounts today provide a statistical replication of the economy, much as an engineer's scale model replicates a particular piece of equipment. In both cases, the object is to reflect accurately the features and characteristics of the thing which is being reproduced. In the case of national accounts statistics, the model is not an operating one but rather one which describes the economy at a point of time. To most economists the term 'model' implies a system of simultaneous equations, or at least behavioral characteristics, which determines changes over time. Such theoretical models, however, do not generally have the function of describing empirical relationships as they exist for a given point in time. In point of fact, empirical representational models such as national accounts are complementary to the behavioral models. It is indeed fortunate that the success of the national accounts need not be measured in terms of their ability to measure either welfare or performance. The increasing attention being given to problems such as pollution and the deterioration of the environment accents the deficiencies of a dollar valuation of output as a measure of welfare, nor are per capita income measures all that is needed to attack problems of racial discrimination, crime and inadequate housing. In terms of performance, technological change reflected in new products, better systems of communications and other benefits suggest the inadequacies of aggregate measures of real product. But the introduction of arbitrary value judgments to make adjustments or imputations for these factors may confuse fiction with fact and jeopardize the objectivity of the system of reporting. Those who wish to discard the whole national accounting system merely because its aggregate constructs do not provide good barometers misunderstand the function of the accounts. What they do show is how the government allocates its funds, what people spend their money on, which industries grow, how the money income is distributed, and many other things that are directly relevant to the way the economy works and what is taking place. Just as the businessman needs his accounts to understand the operation of his business, so a nation needs its accounts to understand its operation. Looking at the same set of accounts, different people will draw different conclusions, based upon their own value judgments and their own interpretation of the meaning of the information. To the extent that the national accounts leave out important information which is needed to understand the operation of the system, they are deficient, but to the extent that they record relevant information faithfully, they can be considered to be successful. Perhaps the most valid charge against the present national accounts is that there are serious omissions of important information which cannot be fitted into the framework of aggregated market transactions.

3. CHANGES IN THE PRESENT SYSTEM

The present system of national accounts in the US represents a substantial achievement. In completeness, detail, and reliability, the US accounts are second to none. They provide an excellent basis for understanding the operation of the economy. But this does not mean, of course, that we can or should expect the evolution which has been taking place to stop at this point. In the period since the last major revision of the accounts, important changes have taken place both in the demand for information and in the technology of data processing, and these developments suggest that the time has come to consider a number of innovations. Specifically, these innovations fall into three groups: revisions in the definition of major national accounting concepts, changes in the form of the national accounts and the development of microdata sets to provide for the integration of economic data with social and demographic information.

Revised Accounting Concepts

Intangible capital formation

One of the paradoxes of US national accounting concepts is that gross capital formation has been restricted to tangible capital, although output reflects both tangible and intangible goods and services. In this connection it is interesting to note that the socialist countries which follow the material product system of accounting use consistent definitions of output and capital formation, excluding intangibles from both. Thus the concept of capital formation used in western countries is identical with the socialist concept. For both modern industrial economies and less developed countries, however, the inappropriateness of a capital formation concept based solely on tangible capital is becoming increasingly apparent. In industrial economies, the role of research and development expenditures by both private enterprises and governments is increasing, and the use of resources for this purpose and their impact upon productivity are becoming more important. The present treatment of research and development expenditures consolidates them out of the accounts as an intermediate product which is embodied in the cost of producing current output. In less developed countries, expenditures in areas such as education, health and planning are written off as current outlays, whereas expenditures on roads, buildings, airports and other construction activities are considered to be capital formation. From the point of view of their impact upon future economic development, however, expenditures aimed at creating human and intellectual capital may be fully as important for future growth as expenditures on physical capital, and it may be perfectly legitimate to treat these expenditures as capital outlays and to amortize them over an appropriate period. Similarly, households may undertake to invest in intangible capital. Expenditures for educating children may make a significant contribution to the creation of human capital. For these reasons, it would seem appropriate to broaden the concept of capital formation to include intangible capital.

Government and consumer capital formation

In the US accounts it has also been a tradition to exclude even physical capital formation by either government or households. In most other countries and in the United Nations System of National Accounts government fixed capital formation is measured, but in the US such outlays are considered to be current outlays by the government. It would be useful to reflect government fixed capital formation in the US accounts. Similarly, expenditures on consumer durables, such as automobiles, household appliances, furniture, etc., are considered to be current consumption expenditures. Nevertheless, these durables last for a substantial period of time and provide a flow of services over time. It would, therefore, be useful to treat consumer durables as part of consumer capital formation and to include in current consumption the services of such assets as they accrue to the consumer.

Saving and investment account
These extensions of the concept of capital formation to include intangibles as well as tangibles and to recognize government and household capital formation would emphasize the desirability of separate saving and investment accounts for enterprises, government and households, instead of the present consolidated saving and investment account for the economy as a whole. Such a deconsolidation of the saving and investment account, furthermore, would make possible a closer integration of the national income accounts with the flow of funds, and the basis could be laid for the development of national wealth data and the creation of balance sheets for specific sectors of the economy, as has been recommended by various government committees.

Business consumption
The concept of consumption also needs attention. The present accounts include consumption by households and by government, but they make no provision for consumption goods and services provided by businesses. Yet businesses do provide consumption goods both to their employees and to the public. In some cases these take the form of fringe benefits or goods and services made available to employees. In other cases they are goods and services provided to the general public for advertising or other purposes. For employees, they may include medical benefits, subsidized cafeterias, entertainment, vacation facilities, travel expenses, etc. For the general public, they include support of mass media such as newspapers, radio and television, and direct provision of goods and services by enterprises as a part of their public relations effort. It is interesting to note that in countries where radio and television are operated by the government, their cost is included in total output as a part of government expenditures on goods and services, whereas in the US, radio and television are supported by advertising expenditures,however, they are treated as intermediate goods and services which are part of the cost of producing other goods. Although it would be possible to allocate this type of consumption to

individuals, a preferable treatment would be to recognize consumption goods provided by business as business consumption, much in the same way that goods and services provided by government are considered to be public consumption.

Changes in the Form of the Accounts

As has been indicated, the present form of the national income accounts has evolved in response to calls for information and out of the development of economics itself. The 1947 national income accounts constituted the first formal presentation of an accounting system for US national income data. The 1958 revision of this system was a major alteration: the accounting structure was cleaned up and the more important flows were shown more clearly. Since 1958 the structure has remained unchanged, although some of the classifications within the accounts have been altered to provide more relevant information. The time has now come to review the accounting structure again in the light of the changes which have taken place over the last decade and the tasks which the system is now be required to perform.

The government's need for detailed information on major economic and social problems has increased substantially over the past decade. The federal government has become involved in major social programs relating to education, health and welfare, and there is a pressing need for detailed information on the costs and benefits of specific programs in these areas. The present form of the national accounts does not easily lend itself to providing the kind of detailed data required for such problems. Therefore, *ad hoc* studies of a special nature are made, and the results are usually difficult to tie in with the overall accounts.

A second consideration is that the technology of data processing has changed significantly. Computers are now able to handle very large amounts of data and, as a result, it is possible to use information which has until now been buried in the files of administrative and statistical agencies. The present form of national accounts is not ideally suited to integrate such information. The technique of making aggregate estimates on the basis of tabulated data from a large variety of sources is still the basic methodology underlying national accounts estimation. Although this sort of technique is the only way to obtain consistency and comprehensiveness, the accounts should be drawn up so that they can take advantage of the bodies of data which are becoming available in computerized form.

Finally, the methodology of economic research has changed. Much of the earlier development of the national economic accounts went hand in hand with the development of macroeconometric models. These models are designed to explain the behavior of the economic system as a whole in terms of formal econometric relationships among aggregate economic variables. The size and complexity of these models has increased steadily, but often they are still inadequate for analyzing more detailed aspects of economic policy. To an increasing extent, economists are turning to the analysis of sample sets of microeconomic data.

Integrating Microdata

Each of these changes emphasizes the need to integrate microdata with macroaccounts. Large amounts of microdata now exist and are being used for purposes of economic analysis. The creation of a dual system of macroaccounts on the one hand and microdata on the other would indeed be unfortunate — as unfortunate as is the present division between the teaching of the macroeconomics of income determination on the one hand and the microtheory of the firm and the household on the other. What is required is a framework which will encompass both the micro- and the macrodata, providing us with both a unified system of information and a unified theoretical structure.

Sectoring principles
The key to this dilemma lies in the system of sectoring which is adopted at the macrolevel. The sectoring of the national accounts must correspond to identifiable sets of decision-making units, each of which may have an income statement and a balance sheet. The principle of disaggregation should ultimately be the separation of sets of reporting units, rather than the more detailed cross-classification of tabulated information. The use of samples of individual observations is considerably more efficient in reporting complex interrelationships among variables than cross-tabulations of aggregated data. As Richard Stone notes in his discussion of social and demographic accounting systems, a cross-classification of ten variables each of which has ten classifications would result in a matrix of 10^{10} cells, i.e., 10 billion (most of which, of course, would be empty). In contrast, ten pieces of information on every individual in the population of the US would contain only 2 billion elements, and the fineness of classification would be irrelevant, since the individual observations would be preserved. In most instances, of course, economists would prefer information on a sample of the population with a larger set of information on each reporting unit.

Household sector
The changes in sectoring which would be required in the national accounts to make them compatible with appropriate microdata sets are relatively minor. The most significant change would be in the definition of the household sector, since the personal income and outlay account at the present time includes the

transactions not only of individuals and households but also of nonprofit institutions. This classification was based on the contention that such organizations operated with motivations different from those of other enterprises, but the same could be said of government enterprises, and it is questionable whether a private university or hospital which is operated on a nonprofit basis is significantly different from similar institutions which are either government owned or of a private profit-making nature. If these nonprofit institutions were excluded from the household sector, it would be possible to consider the account for this sector as a consolidated income statement for all households. A sample of households should, therefore, provide much of the information for the macroaccount for all households. At the present time, the Office of Business Economics is engaged in constructing such a sample in order to obtain information on income distribution. Aligning the sample with the macromeasures of personal income can provide information on income distribution for different types of households and thus give social and demographic dimensions to income distribution data. Such an underlying sample of microdata would make it possible to subdivide the household sector into subsectors such as retired, unemployed, black, urban, or any other groups for which data are needed.

Enterprise sector
An enterprise sector should also be created. In some ways such an enterprise sector would resemble the business sector which appeared in the 1947 accounts. In that presentation, however, the major function of this sector was to derive the gross product originating in private business. The coverage of the enterprise sector which is suggested here would be somewhat broader than private business. It would comprehend all enterprises which operate in the market and have the equivalent of income statements and balance sheets. This would include corporations, unincorporated enterprises, government enterprises and nonprofit institutions. As with the household sector, it would, of course, be possible to group the various types of establishments in the enterprise sector as subsectors.

Government sector
The government sector would include the activities of federal, state and local governments and of those related agencies which do not operate as enterprises. The subsectoring here would depend upon the administrative and legal organization of the various government bodies. It would be useful for the sectoring to correspond to actual administrative procedures, so that the national accounts could be directly related to the fiduciary documents of the government.

4. DEVELOPMENT OF MICRODATA SETS

Matrix Presentation

The concept of microdata sets opens up the possibility of developing a comprehensive statistical system in which economic, social and demographic data can be fully integrated. In recent years, there has been considerable discussion of social accounts, conceptually similar to the national economic accounts but providing social and demographic rather than economic information. Unfortunately, however, there is nothing in the social sphere which corresponds to the network of transactions in the economic system. The social and demographic accounting matrices designed to show year-to-year changes proposed to the United Nations by Richard Stone become unwieldy and inflexible when used as a basis for analyzing even relatively simple problems. Such crosstabulations cannot serve as the basis for an integrated system of economic, social and demographic data. In contrast, macroeconomic accounts which are integrated with microdata sets can provide for integration of social and demographic data. Thus a sample of households can include data not only on income, assets and consumer expenditures but also on age, sex, race, education and occupation of the members of the household: they can even record how the individuals spend their time in different activities. For most social questions, such as discrimination, poverty, education and health, economic, as well as social, information is required. For analytic purposes, it would not be useful to develop a social information system separate from the economic information system. While it is important to develop overall social measures, they should not exist separately from the basic economic and social accounts. Rather, they should result from summarizing particular aspects of the economic and social accounts in a manner which reflects current social policy concerns. The best hope for useful social indicators, therefore, lies in the use of relevant microdata sets containing both economic and social information.

Reporting Units

The reporting units for which microdata sets are collected may, obviously, be units other than individuals, households, enterprises, firms or governmental budgetary units. Interest in the environment suggests that cities and regions may be appropriate reporting units. Such data, furthermore, can be directly related to the enterprises and individuals living in the region. Thus by systematically building microdata sets which can be linked at the level of the individual reporting unit, important bodies of information from different sources can be analytically related to one another.

Existing Microdata Sets

Microdata sets are not a project for the remote future; they are here. The Bureau of the Census pioneered in this area in the development of the 1-in-1,000 sample of the 1960 population census. The success of this microdata set for many kinds of economic and social research is attested by the present plan for development of 1-in-100 public use samples of the 1970 population census; six of these large samples, each containing 2 million cases, are projected. The Internal Revenue Service has also recognized the usefulness of microdata sets. It now uses samples of individual and corporate tax returns to evaluate the effect of alternative tax proposals, and to make revenue estimates. These same tax samples have been used by economists outside the IRS for studying a wide variety of important economic problems. The Social Security Administration has developed samples of its data covering individuals over a period of time. The Office of Economic Opportunity has collected samples designed to give special emphasis to low-income households. Currently, one of these surveys includes a program of re-interviewing over 5,000 households for a period of five years; this sample contains over 1,000 pieces of information on each household. Much of the government's current statistical reporting is also based upon sample collection. The Current Population Survey, which is the main source of data on unemployment, is a monthly sample of households. The Consumer Price Index, published by the Bureau of Labor Statistics, rests upon a consumer expenditure sample and monthly samples of prices.

New Synthetic Data Sets

The large number of well-defined samples which now exists provides a substantial portion of the national data base. Unfortunately, where these sets of data exist without being integrated into an overall framework, they are of limited usefulness. Thus, for example, the tax data do not cover individuals who do not file income tax returns, and such important information as the age of the individual and the composition of the household is not available from the tax sample. Other samples have other biases and data limitations. In order to create a microdata set which corresponds to a given sector or subsector of the economy, it is necessary to align the sample and to add information from a variety of sources. As the quality and comprehensiveness of different samples improve, this task will become easier. It is quite possible, however, that the national accountant will have to become involved in the task of combining information from different microdata sets so as to provide a new synthetic data set which contains more representative and comprehensive data. Thus, for example, samples on poverty groups can be used to supplement samples of income tax data. The 1-in-100 sample can provide social and demographic information. The fitting together of different samples to provide a common set of information could, in principle, be based either on an exact matching of individuals or a synthetic matching, imputing information for similar reporting units on a probability basis. Since most samples do not include the same individuals, the latter technique will have to be adopted in most instances. The resulting microdata set will therefore represent a synthetic sample, with the same statistical properties as the samples from which it was derived, but not containing information on any real individual. Such synthetic microdata sets, therefore, do not present the problem of confidentiality which many fear may result from the wide use of sample data.

The task of generating synthetic microdata sets which embody information from a variety of different sources is not unlike the task which the national accountant has faced in the past, that of piecing together bodies of information from a wide variety of sources to yield estimates for a particular transaction flow in the economy. Just as in the case of the national accounts, once the major outline of the system is established, the problem of filling in specific parts becomes much more manageable. What is in fact being proposed is that the model of the economic system which is spelled out by the national accounts be extended to include the detailed microdata sets which describe individuals, enterprises and government agencies. The development of microdata sets corresponding to the macroaccounts will, of course, be a gradual process. Their major function is to provide the detailed economic and social data needed to permit the use of simulation techniques and microanalytic models for the analysis of complex economic and social problems.

The New SNA

The new United Nations System of National Accounts (SNA) was developed specifically to provide for integration of the national economic accounts. It does represent a considerable achievement in this area but, at the same time, it is not ideally suited as a framework for microdata sets which contain economic, social and demographic data. The present US national income accounts are very much closer to what is in fact required, and it would seem highly appropriate that in the next decade they evolve into a full set of economic and social accounts embracing both macro- and microdata.

9. The United States National Income Accounts, 1947–77: Their Conceptual Basis and Evolution

Richard Ruggles
Yale University

1. INTRODUCTION

The national income accounts for the United States and their statistical implementation represent one of the major achievements in economics in the twentieth century. The design of the national income accounting system has been a cumulative development, which has been responsive both to the concepts embodied in modern economic theory and to the policy needs for information about the operation of the economic system. The implementation of the national income accounts in the form of a reliable and consistent set of statistical estimates represents an outstanding accomplishment on the part of those who have been engaged in this work over the last half-century.

The purpose of this paper is to examine the national income accounting system of the United States and to show how the system has evolved since it was first put in place in 1947. It is hoped that this examination will lead to a better understanding of how the present system came into being and why it has the characteristics it does. The examination will focus on the major conceptual issues that have arisen in connection with the establishment of the national income accounting system and its subsequent revisions, and it is in this context that questions will be raised about the problem areas that remain to be solved and the directions future developments may take.

The US national income accounting system has been characterized by relative stability and continuity. The process of change has been gradual and

---

This chapter first appeared in Murray Foss (ed.), *The U.S. National Income and Product Accounts, Selected Topics*, Studies in Income and Wealth, Vol. 47, University of Chicago Press for the National Bureau of Economic Research, 1983.

evolutionary, and when changes were made that seriously affected the comparability of data over time, the Bureau of Economic Analysis (BEA) has taken care to provide complete revisions which in all cases have covered the period since 1947 and have usually provided data back to 1929. Nevertheless, it is not feasible in a short paper to discuss chronologically all of the specific conceptual, methodological, classification and statistical changes that have been made, as they are far too numerous. Instead, the approach taken by this paper will be to review the accounts at the points when major revisions were made by BEA or its predecessor organizations. This will provide cross-sectional views of what the national income accounting system was like in certain benchmark periods.

Similarly, it is neither possible nor desirable to attempt to cover the whole body of national income accounting literature written in the last 30 years. Instead, this paper will focus only on work that is directly related to the US national income accounts and so can provide the basis for analyzing the central conceptual issues involved. Specifically, the documents that will be covered are: the 1951 and 1954 supplements to the *Survey of Current Business*, which presented in the fullest detail the sources and methods employed in preparing the US national income accounts; the proceedings of the 1955 Conference on Income and Wealth, published as *A Critique of the United States Income and Product Accounts* (Studies in Income and Wealth, 1958, Vol. 22); the Report of the National Accounts Review Committee, published in *Hearings before the Joint Economic Committee* in 1957; the proceedings of the 1969 Conference on Income and Wealth, published as *The Measurement of Economic and Social Performance* (Studies in Income and Wealth, 1973, Vol. 38); and the fiftieth anniversary issue of the *Survey of Current Business,* titled *The Economic Accounts of the United States, Retrospect and Prospect* (July 1971, Vol. 51, No. 7, Pt II).

In addition to examining the US national income accounts and discussions directly relating to them, it will also be useful to compare and contrast the US accounts with the United Nations System of National Accounts (SNA). The SNA currently serves as the basis for national income accounting in a considerable number of countries, and the differences between the UN system and that of the United States can illuminate some of the major conceptual issues involved in national income accounting.

Finally, it will be useful to examine the US national income accounts in the light of related statistical work currently under way in the BEA and other statistical agencies. This, together with the earlier discussions of conceptual issues, will lead to some conclusions as to the possible directions future developments might take.

2. THE MAJOR CONCEPTUAL ISSUES AND THE EVOLUTION OF THE US NATIONAL INCOME ACCOUNTS

The Pre-1947 Period

Although the first national income accounting system for the United States was published by the Department of Commerce in 1947, official estimates of the national income and its components had been made by the Department of Commerce since the mid-1930s. The process by which the national income estimates developed into a national income accounting system has been well described by Carol Carson. When the Department of Commerce, with the assistance of Simon Kuznets, first produced national income estimates in 1934, attention was focused on national income produced and national income paid out. National income produced referred to the net product of the national economy, and national income paid out referred to the compensation in money or kind paid for efforts in producing the net product. There was no sectoring of the economy, and emphasis was placed on the estimation of total national income, which was primarily used as an indicator or barometer of economic activity. What was also missing in these early measurements was the expenditure breakdown of national product. As Carson has noted, however, the origin of the expenditure breakdown in the United States predates the Keynesian model of income determination (i.e., $Y = C + I$). As early as 1932, Clark Warburton was working on the estimation of consumption and capital formation, and in 1934 he published a table on the composition and value of gross national product in which consumer goods and capital goods were shown. This was the first use of the concept of gross national product. Kuznets, in 1933, was also working on estimates of gross capital formation and consumers' outlay through a commodity flow approach. Finally, Lauchlin Currie at the Federal Reserve Board (FRB) was in 1934 working on the concept of pump-priming deficit and using this to analyze the net contribution of government to national buying power. At this time, however, there was still no consideration of sectors of the economy, and it is undoubtedly true that the subsequent development of the Keynesian framework had a considerable impact on the direction of the work during the latter part of the 1930s.

But, as Carson pointed out, it was the mobilization for World War II and the consequent demand for data relating to the economy as a whole that was primarily responsible for shaping the accounts. The central questions posed by the war were how much defense output could be produced and what impact defense production would have upon the economy as a whole. Answering such questions required analysis of total resource availabilities and of the income generated by the increasing production in relation to the availability of consumer goods. For example, the inflationary gap analysis of the Tax Research Division of the Treasury Department required information on how much income would be generated and how much of this income consumers could be expected to spend on available consumer goods. The emphasis thus shifted away from the earlier focus on national income aggregates to the estimation of how income was generated, received and spent by various sectors of the economy.

At the same time, during World War II, similar developments were taking place in England. Richard Stone was developing a national income accounting system for the United Kingdom, and the White Papers in which this work was reported were available in the United States. During 1944, meetings between US, British and Canadian experts were held to compare conceptual and statistical problems in national income estimation. In 1945, a group of experts on national income was convened by the League of Nations, and for this meeting Richard Stone drafted a national income accounting system which served as the basis for future international developments. By the end of the war, the stage was thus set for the emergence of a full-fledged set of US national accounts.

The 1947 National Income Accounts

The first US national income accounting system was published in the July 1947 Supplement to the *Survey of Current Business*. The presentation was designed to accomplish three objectives:

> (1) to complete the setting up of the whole body of national income statistics as an interrelated and consistent system of national economic accounts, (2) to improve the statistical procedures used in estimating all the series and to base them on the latest source data and (3) to incorporate a number of changes in the basic aggregates so as to achieve more generally useful and clear-cut definitions of national income and national product.

The system of accounts consisted of an overall account for the national economy, together with accounts for major sectors which would permit the tracing of various flows from one account to another. These accounts are shown below in Tables 9.1–9.6.

Table 9.1 is the summary income and product account for the nation. It is a summary account in that it brings together in a single account the current transactions recorded in the sector accounts of businesses, consumers and government. In drawing up the national income and product account, some difficult and controversial decisions had to be made regarding the activities that were to be considered economic production or income. Government interest, the services of housewives, and income from illegal activities were all excluded from national income and product. On the other hand, certain imputed items

Table 9.1 *National Income and Product Account, 1939 ($mn)*

Compensation of employees:		Personal consumption expenditures	$67,466
Wages and salaries	$45,745	Gross private domestic investment	9,004
Supplements	2,075	Net foreign investment	888
Income of unincorporated enterprises and inventory valuation adjustment	11,282	Government purchases of goods and services	13,068
Rental income of persons	3,465		
Corporate profits and inventory valuation adjustment:			
Corporate profits before tax:			
Corporate profits tax liability	1,462		
Corporate profits after tax:			
Dividends	3,796		
Undistributed profits	1,209		
Inventory valuation adjustment	−714		
Net interest	4,212		
National income	72,532		
Indirect business tax and nontax liability	9,365		
Business transfer payments	451		
Statistical discrepancy	462		
Less: Subsidies minus current surplus of government enterprises	485		
Charges against net national product	82,325		
Capital consumption allowances	8,101		
CHARGES AGAINST GNP	$90,426	GNP	$90,426

of income in kind were included, such as the rental value of owner-occupied housing and banking services rendered to persons without explicit payment.

Table 9.2 shows the income and product account for the business sector of the economy. In essence, this table is a consolidated profit and loss statement for current business operations. The business sector covers all firms, organizations and institutions that produce goods and services for sale at a price intended at least to approximate the cost of production. Mutual financial institutions, cooperatives, nonprofit organizations serving business, owner-occupied houses and government enterprises were all included in this sector.

Table 9.3 is a receipts and expenditures account for the government sector. It covers the consolidated general government operations of federal, state and local governments, including social insurance funds and the purchases of government enterprises on capital account, together with their net interest payments and operating surplus or deficit.

Table 9.4 presents the foreign account, which shows the transactions of the rest of the world with domestic businesses, persons and government, on a net basis.

Table 9.5, the personal income and expenditure account, includes not only

Table 9.2 Consolidated Business Income and Product Account, 1939 ($mn)

Compensation of employees:		Consolidated net sales:	
Wages and salaries:		To consumers	$63,816
Disbursements	$36,250	To government	5,375
Excess of accruals over disbursements	0	To business on capital account	8,563
		To abroad	1,123
Supplements:		Change in inventories	441
Employer contributions for social insurance	1,330		
Other labor income	431		
Income of unincorporated enterprises and inventory valuation adjustment	11,282		
Rental income of persons	3,465		
Corporate profits and inventory valuation adjustment:			
Corporate profits before tax:			
Corporate profits tax liability	1,462		
Corporate profits after tax:			
Dividends	3,659		
Undistributed profits	1,162		
Inventory valuation adjustment	−714		
Net interest	3,284		
Income originating	61,611		
Indirect business tax and nontax liability	9,365		
Business transfer payments	451		
Statistical discrepancy	462		
Less: Subsidies minus current surplus of government enterprises	485		
Charges against net national product	71,404		
Capital consumption allowances	7,914		
CHARGES AGAINST BUSINESS NATIONAL PRODUCT	$79,318	BUSINESS GROSS PRODUCT	$79,318

individuals in their capacity as income receivers but also the income and expenditures of nonprofit institutions serving households, and of private trust funds and private pension and welfare funds. It should be noted that transfers among these different groups, for example, between households and nonprofit institutions, pension funds, etc., all consolidate out.

Finally, Table 9.6 is a consolidated gross saving and investment account. It was pointed out that this account was presented on a consolidated basis because the data necessary for a complete accounting structure had not yet been developed. A logical and useful extension of the national accounting system, it was agreed, would be the construction of corresponding asset and liability accounts for each sector.

This system of six basic accounts not only showed how the different sectors were interrelated and fitted into the total economy, but it also provided a

Table 9.3 Consolidated Government Receipts and Expenditures Account, 1939 ($mn)

Purchases of goods and services:		Personal tax and nontax receipts	$2,440
Purchases of direct services:		Corporate profits tax accruals	1,462
Compensation of employees:		Indirect business tax and nontax accruals	9,365
Wages and salaries	$7,343		
Supplements:		Contributions for social insurance:	
Employer contributions for social insurance	199	Employee contribution	596
Other labor income	87	Employer contributions:	
Income originating and net and gross product	7,629	Business	1,330
		Government	199
Net purchases from business	5,375	Households and institutions	11
Net purchases from abroad	64	Deficit (+) or surplus (−) on income and product transactions	1,867
Transfer payments	2,512		
Net interest paid	1,205		
Subsidies minus current surplus of government subsidies	485		
GOVERNMENT EXPENDITURES	$17,270	GOVERNMENT RECEIPTS AND DEFICIT	$17,270

Table 9.4 Rest-of-the-World Account, 1939 ($mn)

Net payments of factor income to the United States:		Net disinvestment in the United States	$888
Wages and salaries	$2		
Interest	127		
Dividends	137		
Branch profits	47		
Income originating and net and gross profit	313		
Net purchases from the United States:			
From business	1,123		
From government	−64		
From persons	−484		
NET CURRENT PAYMENTS TO THE UNITED STATES	$888	NET DISINVESTMENT IN THE UNITED STATES	$888

framework for the extensive and detailed data generated by the Department of Commerce. By making relationships among the transaction flows explicit, and by providing control totals, the accounting system reduced the voluminous detail of the national income statistics to intelligible proportions. The 1947 Supplement contained 37 tables of annual data for the years 1929–46. Tables were given for each side of the six accounts, and often more detail was provided than was shown in the accounts themselves. For example, the tables relating to the rest of the world grossed up the net purchases from the United States to show both exports and imports. Some of the tables gave breakdowns

Table 9.5 Personal Income and Expenditure Account, 1939 ($mn)

Personal consumption expenditures:		Wage and salary receipts:	
Purchases of direct services:		Disbursements by:	
Compensation of employees:		Business	$36,250
Wages and salaries paid	$2,150	Government	7,343
Supplements paid:		Households and institutions	2,150
Employer contributions for social insurance	11	Rest of the world	2
Other labor income	17	Less: Employee contributions for social insurance	596
Interest paid	801	Other labor income:	
Income originating in and net product of households and institutions	2,979	Business	431
		Government	87
		Households and institutions	17
Institutional depreciation	187	Income of unincorporated enterprises and inventory valuation adjustment	11,282
Gross product of households and institutions	3,166		
Net purchases from business	68,816	Rental income of persons	3,465
Net purchases from abroad	484	Dividends	3,796
Personal tax and nontax payments	2,440	Personal interest income	5,417
Personal saving	2,701	Government transfer payments	2,512
		Business transfer payments	451
PERSONAL OUTLAY AND SAVING	$72,607	PERSONAL INCOME	$72,607

Table 9.6 Gross Savings and Investment Account, 1939 ($mn)

Business purchases on capital account	$8,563	Excess of wage accruals over disbursements	$0
Change in business inventories	441	Undistributed corporate profits (domestic)	1,162
Net disinvestment in the United States by the rest of world	888	Corporate inventory valuation adjustment	−714
Government deficit (+) or surplus (−) on income and product transactions	1,867	Statistical discrepancy	462
		Capital consumption allowances by private business	7,914
		Foreign branch profits (net)	47
		Institutional depreciation	187
		Personal saving	2,701
GROSS INVESTMENT AND GOVERNMENT DEFICIT	$11,759	GROSS PRIVATE SAVING	$11,759

of individual items in the accounts. Personal consumption expenditures were shown by type of product for 12 categories. Detail was provided on construction activity and producers' durable equipment by type. Information on the performance of different industries and their contribution to national output was provided through industrial breakdowns of specific components of national income originating and of employment, for major industry groups and for sub-industries at the 2-digit level.

Supplementary tables were also developed on a variety of topics. Among these were reconciliation accounts, which showed the relationship between the saving figures in the national accounts and the Securities and Exchange Commission data on liquid saving, and the relationship between corporate profits derived from corporate tax returns and the corporate profits concept in the national income accounts. Data were provided for monetary and imputed interest, showing the derivation of the net interest concept in the national accounts. A table was provided giving the major items of personal income and consumptive expenditures in kind.

In addition to the annual data, a set of eight tables gave quarterly data for the major national income aggregates and their components, including national income, gross national product and personal income, together with a table showing the relation among these concepts. Finally, monthly data were given for personal income by type of payment.

The 1951 and 1954 National Income Supplements to the *Survey of Current Business*

In both 1951 and 1954, the *Survey of Current Business* published National Income Supplements that contained a fuller explanation of the national income accounting system, a description of the sources and methods used in constructing the estimates and a full set of revised statistical data for all 48 tables contained in the 1947 accounts. There were no substantive revisions of the national accounting system in either 1951 or 1954; but in 1951, supplementary tables on gross national product in constant dollars together with the implicit price deflators for the years 1929–50 were added. This type of information was formally integrated into the standard tables of national income statistics in the 1954 edition.

Both the 1951 and 1954 Supplements were extremely important in providing the user public with a better understanding of the concepts involved in national income accounting and the methods of statistical estimation employed. In large part, the widespread acceptance which the national income accounts achieved during the 1950s can be attributed to the comprehensive and detailed work that went into these supplements.

In explaining the accounts, major emphasis was placed on what at the time was considered to be the fundamental concept of national income accounting, namely, the concept of factor cost. The concept of factor cost was considered basic to the definition of national income and product, since the output of the nation (national product) was the result of the services rendered by the agents of production (labor, capital, entrepreneurial ability, and natural resources used in the production process) that cooperated in the creation of that output. At the same time these services, valued in the market by their earnings, constituted national income. Furthermore, such a measure of the services rendered by productive agents was viewed as of central importance for studies of resource allocation. Thus, it would be important to know the incomes of various factors of production used in each industry in order to be able to compare the relative importance of different industries, or to provide information about the relative amounts of factors of production available for allocation to various uses, or to assess the relative importance of labor and property factors in the outputs of various industries.

It was recognized that the factors of production were not precisely defined in economic theory but to some extent had to be formulated with reference to the problem at hand. It was agreed, for example, that factor cost would not serve the intended purposes when factor returns were distorted by a temporary or permanent nontransferability of factors to other uses, or when they were affected by monopoly or by imperfect competition. It was further admitted that property income was only tenuously related to the measure of the contribution of property and enterprise needed for problems involving resource allocation, because it included a residual share (profits) which fluctuated widely over the business cycle. In spite of these difficulties and limitations, however, it was concluded that the idea of factor cost was of fundamental importance in economic analysis, and national income defined as the aggregate of factor earnings was the only general measure by which the idea could be quantified.

The factor cost concept had direct implications for the measurement of one of the central elements of property income, namely, interest, in the national accounts. Since interest could be both received and paid out by business, the Department of Commerce showed net interest paid as an element of factor cost. But this raised several problems. In the case of financial institutions, the amount of interest received generally exceeded the amount of interest paid out, so that net interest paid out by financial institutions was negative. In order to avoid showing negative output for financial institutions, it was considered that an imputation should be made to quantify the banking services that financial institutions were providing free to their depositors in exchange for the use of their funds. On the product side, the imputation would be recorded as a sale of banking services, and on the factor cost side it would be reported as imputed interest paid. It was recognized that the treatment of interest and the banking imputation might be criticized as 'unduly complex and more specifically as based on certain assumptions of doubtful validity'. In particular, the appropriate allocation of banking services was difficult, but it was thought that, all things considered, it was the most satisfactory procedure devised so far.

There were also other difficulties connected with the net interest component. Interest paid by the government, it was argued, should be excluded from the measure of output, since it was not considered to arise from current production. This meant that government interest payments, unlike wage payments to government employees, were not considered to be factor costs but rather were classed as transfers.

The treatment of life insurance and pensions also involved special considerations. In the case of life insurance, it was argued that the standard national income and product classifications broke down owing to its combined saving and insurance functions, and imputations were, therefore, required. In the treatment adopted, claims and premiums were disregarded, and the property income of life insurance companies that was withheld from policyholders was treated as if it had been actually disbursed in the current period. This item of property income became imputed interest in the net interest component of income. Finally, life insurance companies were regarded as implicitly charging policyholders for their services, and an imputation equal to their operating expenses was entered to make this charge explicit: in the business account, under sales to persons and in the personal income account, as a consumption expenditure. As a result of all these actions, life insurance companies were, in effect, treated as individuals rather than businesses. Claims and premiums were canceled out as though they were transfers among individuals, and the increase in life insurance reserves and retained income was treated as part of personal saving.

Private pensions were also integrated into the personal income account. Employers' contributions to private pension funds were included in the 'other labor income' of employees as if they had actually been received. Employee contributions to private pension funds were ignored, and neither the benefits paid out by private pension funds nor the reserves and income retained by such funds were explicitly shown in the accounts. Changes in private pension reserves and retained income would be reflected automatically as part of personal saving. The procedures followed for social security contributions were different, of course, since these were consolidated with the government sector. Any difference between social security contributions and benefits paid out was reflected in the government surplus or deficit rather than in personal saving.

The 1955 Critique of the US Income and Product Accounts

The 1955 Conference on Income and Wealth was devoted to an extensive and detailed examination of the US national income accounting system established in 1947. The participants in the conference had available to them not only the excellent statements on concepts, sources and methods in the National Income supplements to the *Survey of Current Business*, but also a major paper by George Jaszi, 'The Conceptual Basis of the Accounts'.

In his paper, Jaszi not only laid out the rationale of the US national income accounting concepts but he also raised questions that he felt had not been satisfactorily resolved. His discussion of accounting design in terms of sectoring and types of account was particularly illuminating. He pointed out that the principle of sectoring had not been clearly established and contained ambiguities. Although sectors are usually thought to reflect institutional groupings, functional considerations are generally also involved. Thus, although businesses, households and governments are different kinds of institutions, they also involve different functions, and there is a tendency to define institutions in terms of the functions in which they engage. The conflict between institutional and functional sectoring is particularly apparent in the case of unincorporated enterprises. The US national income accounts split the owner of an unincorporated enterprise into a business transactor with respect to his production, and a household transactor with respect to his income, expenditures and saving. This has suggested to some national accountants that it would be desirable to set up different types of accounts to show production, appropriation, and saving and investment for each sector.

Although Jaszi considered this possibility, he rejected it, since he concluded that introducing additional accounts and transferring subtotals from one account to another served only to make the accounting structure more complicated without increasing its information content.

Instead of increasing the complexity of the accounting structure, Jaszi proposed a revision of the 1947 six-account system into a simpler five-account system in which the business sector account would be consolidated with the national income and product account. The simpler version, he thought, would lose no useful information, and a number of inconsequential flows required to articulate the business sector with other sectors would be eliminated. Jaszi also thought it would be desirable to deconsolidate the saving and investment account to show separate accounts for nonfinancial corporations, financial intermediaries, persons, government and international transactors. He recognized the desirability of measuring government and consumer capital formation, estimating the stock of government and consumer durables, providing better estimates of replacement cost depreciation, and obtaining information on capital gains and losses. Thus it is apparent that, in 1955, Jaszi viewed the national income accounting system as the core of an extended and integrated system of economic accounts.

It was, however, the more traditional issues of national income accounting that occupied most of the attention of the conference and generated the most heated discussions. The issues that attracted the most attention were factor cost measurement, the controversy about intermediate output of government, and the treatment of interest, all of which centered on the correct measurement of output. Most of the participants were supportive of the concepts and procedures used by the Department of Commerce, but many were disturbed by the lack of symmetry between the treatment of consumer interest and government interest. No clear conclusions emerged on these topics, except the reaffirmation that the correct measurement of national income at factor cost was still considered to be of central importance.

The Report of the National Accounts Review Committee (1957)

In 1956, the Office of Statistical Standards of the Bureau of the Budget requested that the National Bureau of Economic Research form a National Accounts Review Committee to provide a review and evaluation of the national income and related accounts and devise a program for improving the accounts. To a major extent, this committee based its work on Jaszi's paper for the 1955 Conference on Income and Wealth, and expanded on his view of the national income accounts as the central core of a more general national economic accounting system. They endorsed Jaszi's proposal for the five-account system, and urged the development of a more comprehensive system of economic accounts in which input–output, flow of funds, balance of payments accounts and national balance sheets would be fully integrated with the national income accounts.

The committee also urged substantial expansion of the information on the government sector in the national income accounts. At the time, the accounts contained only one account for general government. Although this account contained separate information for federal and state and local governments, it did not link the federal receipts and expenditures with the federal budget or show federal expenditures by function and program. The committee urged that such information be provided. With respect to government interest payments, the report considered that the treatment of government interest as a transfer payment could be justified for interest on the war debt. Once the war was over, payments to holders of war bonds, like payments to war veterans, were made for a service in a period of the past, and there was no counterpart in the production during the years when the payments were actually made. But for debt used to finance tangible assets which contribute their services to production during the period when interest is paid, the committee thought that the case was different. Since most state and local debt is of this type, state and local government interest should be included in total output.

In connection with its report, the committee sent out questionnaires to business, labor and academic economists (but not to economists in the federal government) inquiring what they wanted in the national accounts. The responses to this questionnaire were very interesting. Highest priority was given to the development of quarterly estimates of GNP at constant prices. Additional items, listed in order of frequency of citation, were: (a) addition of information on the stock of consumer durables, (b) reconciliation of consolidated government receipts and expenditures of the federal government as shown in the national income and product accounts with the conventional and cash budget figures, (c) classification of government purchases of goods and services into current and capital expenditures, a distinction essential for the estimation of government saving and investment, (d) separation of nonprofit institutions and a few other groups now lumped together with households into the personal sector, (e) quarterly estimates of personal saving on a balance sheet basis, that is, as the result of independently estimated changes in the different types of assets and liabilities of households, (f) estimates of personal income in constant dollars and (g) estimation of gross national product and its principal components on a monthly basis. These results suggest that what users wanted were more frequent reporting of figures useful for monitoring and analyzing the state of the business cycle, and more detailed information on the government sector and consumer durables.

Between the 1955 Conference on Income and Wealth and the 1957 Report of the National Accounts Review Committee, there was a shift in emphasis in the discussions on national income. The 1955 conference concentrated on the question of the proper measurement of national income. The discussion in the National Accounts Review Committee was centered on questions of how the existing national income accounting system should be expanded and integrated with other kinds of economic data and how it could better serve the needs of users. The concern, in other words, was no longer with the definition of the aggregates but with the data system as a whole.

The 1958 and 1965 Revisions of the National Income Accounts

In 1958 the Department of Commerce published *US Income and Output*, a supplement to the *Survey of Current Business*, which for the first time since 1947 made significant changes in the national income accounting system and added very substantially to the information contained in the system. A new five-account system of summary accounts was adopted, which eliminated the business sector account in its entirety and dropped the subtotals showing income originating from the current accounts for government and households. The objective of removing this detail from the summary accounts was to display the broad measures and their interrelationships that had been found to be analytically most useful. The institutional structure of productive activity stressed in the 1947 accounts was no longer shown in the summary accounts, but it was felt that the gain in simplicity and in aptness for other principal uses more than outweighed this reduction in detail. The 1958 accounting system is shown in Tables 9.7–9.11.

Although the form of the summary accounts was altered, the basic accounting structure that lay behind the accounts remained essentially the same as before. But the new accounting system constituted a somewhat better

Table 9.7 National Income and Product Account, 1957* ($bn)

1. Compensation of employees:	$254.6	24. Personal consumption expenditures (II–2)	$284.4
2. Wages and salaries	238.1		
3. Disbursements (II–7)	238.1	25. Gross private domestic investment (V–1)	65.3
4. Excess of accruals over disbursements (V–11)	0.0	26. Net exports of goods and services	4.9
5. Supplements	16.5		26.0
6. Employer contributions for social insurance (III–18)	7.6	27. Exports (IV–1)	
7. Other labor income (II–11)	8.9	28. Imports (IV–2)	21.0
8. Proprietors' income (II–12)	43.0	29. Government purchases of goods and services (III–1)	85.7
9. Rental income of persons (II–15)	11.8		
10. Corporate profits and inventory valuation adjustment	41.9		
11. Profits before tax	43.4		
12. Tax liability (III–15)	21.6		
13. Profits after tax	21.8		
14. Dividends (II–16)	12.4		
15. Undistributed (V–12)	9.4		
16. Inventory valuation adjustment (V–13)	–1.5		
17. Net interest (II–18)	12.6		
18. National income	364.0		
19. Business transfer payments (II–21)	1.6		
20. Indirect business tax and nontax liability (III–16)	37.6		
21. Current surplus of government enterprises less subsidies (III–10)	–1.3		
22. Capital consumption allowances (V–14)	37.7		
23. Statistical discrepancy (V–16)	0.7		
GROSS NATIONAL PRODUCT	$440.3	GROSS NATIONAL INCOME	$440.3

*Numbers in parentheses indicate accounts and items of counter-entry in the accounts.

framework for fleshing out the accounts in greater detail and for presenting new kinds of information in a way that was fitted into the framework of the five-account system. A number of new kinds of information were introduced.

In the national income and product account, increased emphasis was placed on constant-dollar measurements. As had been suggested by the National Accounts Review Committee, quarterly estimates were provided of gross national product in constant dollars. The loss of information resulting from the omission of the business sector from the summary accounts was more than made up by increased information in the detailed tables on the legal forms of organization of producing entities.

The government sector provided a completely new breakdown of government expenditures by type and function for the federal and state and local governments. Furthermore, federal government receipts and expenditures were reconciled with the federal budget, so that the user of national accounts could trace the exact differences between the budget figures and the national accounts.

Table 9.8 Personal Income and Outlay Account, 1957* ($bn)

1. Personal tax and nontax payments (III–12)	$42.7	7. Wage and salary disbursements (I–3)	$238.1
2. Personal consumption expenditures (I–24)	284.4	8. Manufacturing	80.6
		9. Other private	117.4
3. Durable goods	39.9	10. Government	40.1
4. Nondurable goods	138.0	11. Other labor income (I–7)	8.9
5. Services	106.5	12. Proprietors' income (I–8)	43.0
6. Personal saving (V–10)	20.7	13. Business and professional	31.4
		14. Farm	11.6
		15. Rental income of persons (I–9)	11.8
		16. Dividends (I–14)	12.4
		17. Personal interest income	18.8
		18. Net interest (I–17)	12.6
		19. Net interest paid by government (III–9)	6.2
		20. Transfer payments	21.5
		21. Business (I–19)	1.6
		22. Government (III–7)	19.9
		23. Personal contributions for social insurance (III–19)	–6.6
PERSONAL OUTLAY AND SAVING	$347.9	PERSONAL INCOME	$347.9

*Numbers in parentheses indicate accounts and items of counter-entry in the accounts.

Table 9.9 Government Receipts and Expenditures Account, 1957* ($bn)

1. Purchases of goods and services (I–29)	$85.7	12. Personal tax and nontax receipts (II–1)	$42.7
2. Federal	49.4	13. Federal	37.4
3. National defense (less sales)	43.9	14. State and local	5.4
4. Other	5.5	15. Corporate profits tax accruals (I–12)	21.6
5. State and local	36.3		
6. Transfer payments	21.3	16. Indirect business tax and nontax accruals (I–20)	37.6
7. To persons (II–22)	19.9		
8. Foreign (IV–3)	1.5	17. Contributions for social insurance	14.2
9. Net interest paid (II–19)	6.2		
10. Subsidies less current surplus of government enterprises (I–21)	1.3	18. Employer (I–6)	7.6
		19. Personal (II–23)	6.6
11. Surplus or deficit (–) on income and product account (V–15)	1.7		
GOVERNMENT EXPENDITURES AND SURPLUS	$116.2	GOVERNMENT RECEIPTS	$116.2

*Numbers in parentheses indicate accounts and items of counter-entry in the accounts.

Table 9.10 Foreign Transactions Account, 1957* ($bn)

1. Exports of goods and services (I–27)	$26.0	2. Imports of goods and services (I–28)	$21.0
		3. Transfer payments from US government (III–8)	1.5
		4. Net foreign investment (V–9)	3.5
RECEIPTS FROM ABROAD	$26.0	PAYMENTS TO ABROAD	$26.0

*Numbers in parentheses indicate accounts and items of counter-entry in the accounts.

Table 9.11 Gross Saving and Investment Account, 1957* ($bn)

1. Gross private domestic investment (I–25)	$65.3	10. Personal saving (II–6)	$20.7
2. New construction	36.5	11. Excess of wage accruals over disbursements (I–4)	0.0
3. Residential nonfarm	17.0	12. Undistributed corporate profits (I–15)	9.4
4. Other	19.5		
5. Producers' durable equipment	27.9	13. Corporate inventory valuation adjustment (I–16)	–1.5
6. Change in business inventories	1.0		
7. Nonfarm	0.2	14. Capital consumption allowances (I–22)	37.7
8. Farm	0.8		
9. Net foreign investment (IV–4)	3.5	15. Government surplus (+) or deficit (–) on income and product account (III–11)	1.7
		16. Statistical discrepancy (I–23)	0.7
GROSS INVESTMENT	$68.8	GROSS SAVING AND STATISTICAL DISCREPANCY	$68.8

*Numbers in parentheses indicate accounts and items of counter-entry in the accounts.

The foreign sector transactions were expanded in detail and directly tied in with the balance of payments. A new table on US government net foreign assistance and balance of payments capital account was also provided.

With respect to personal income, data were provided on the distribution of income by size and by region. The size distribution was also broken down in terms of nonfarm families, farm families and unattached individuals. Monthly data on personal income by type of payment was also added. Finally, substantially more detail was given for consumer expenditures in constant dollars.

The savings and investment information was also expanded. A table showing expenditures on new plant and equipment by industry was provided, and the net stocks of structures and equipment and inventories for manufacturing, developed by the perpetual inventory method, were introduced. Finally, depreciation was given for corporate and noncorporate business by industry.

In brief, the 1958 revision represented a substantial increase in the amount of information contained in the national accounts, and this was accomplished in a systematic and orderly manner by fitting it into a simpler and more general framework. While to some degree this revision may have reflected the recommendations of the National Accounts Review Committee, in view of the timing of the publication in relation to the committee's report it is apparent that many of the changes contained in the 1958 revision must have been well under way before the committee finished its work.

Perhaps one of the more revealing sections in the report on the 1958 revision was that on directions of future research, which laid out in some detail the future plan of work of the National Income Division. It was stated that future development would be in the direction of deconsolidating the consolidated saving and investment account into sets of saving and investment accounts, or sources and uses of funds, for major economic groups. These proposed accounts would show transactions in financial assets and liabilities among domestic groups in relation to real changes in saving and investment. They would be drawn up for individuals, government, nonfinancial corporations and financial institutions. In discussing future plans, the specific problems involved in classification of both financial and tangible assets and the need to develop measures of capital consumption were recognized.

With respect to the personal sector of the economy, which still included nonprofit institutions and private pension and welfare funds, it was recognized that separate information on each of these entities would be desirable. In addition, it was suggested that it would be useful to split up the personal saving and investment account by major types of families, for example, farm proprietors, nonfarm entrepreneurs and wage and salary earners.

For the government sector, more work was planned on extending the functional breakdown of government expenditures, introducing more object-class details of expenditure and developing new information on the changes in financial assets and liabilities associated with the government surplus and deficit, this last bringing together information on inventories, public construction, realty holdings and purchases and stocks of durable equipment. Finally, more information was planned on the interrelationships among different governmental units.

Although some increase in regional work was planned, it was to be limited to states and standard metropolitan statistical areas (SMSAs). It was argued that disaggregation to the county level was beyond the resources of the Office of Business Economics (OBE).

One of the more interesting proposed extensions was the work planned in the field of income distribution. Here it was proposed that better information on the distribution of income could be obtained by the integration of data from federal individual income tax returns with data from census and other sample field surveys, with the results adjusted to control totals based on OBE measures of personal income. Although it is apparent that at that time this was conceived of primarily as bringing together various tabulations, it was pointed out that effective use of tax return data would require matching studies to relate the income of sample consumer units to the tax returns they filed, so that distributions of tax return income could be converted to a family income basis. It was also suggested that the Internal Revenue Service (IRS) audit studies could be used to correct underreporting of income to tax authorities. Further suggestions included using field surveys of consumer expenditures to provide information on taxes, consumption and saving by income group.

Finally, a program was laid out in the area of analyzing industry sales and purchases to determine direct industry sales in final markets and their interrelation with the network of other industry sales and purchases. In effect, what was being proposed was an approach to input–output.

After the 1958 revision, the next major revision occurred in 1965. The main purpose of this revision was statistical, and constituted comprehensive benchmark revisions centering on the incorporation of the 1958 economic censuses into the national income and product estimates. Since the 1958 revision, the OBE had taken over the work on input–output, and had produced for the year 1958 an input–output table that was integrated with the national income accounts. Aside from this major accomplishment, however, the 1965 revision indicated only modest progress on the ambitious program that had been laid out in 1958. Improved information was made available on the reconciliation of the government national income and product accounts to the consolidated budget. Better information was also provided on the nonmarket imputations contained in the accounts. Tables were added on gross corporate product and gross automobile product. Additional detail was provided on personal consumption expenditures in constant dollars. On the other hand, some of the tables that had previously been published were omitted, on the ground that new work in the areas concerned was in progress: these included the tables on expenditures on new plant and equipment, on sources and uses of corporate funds, on the size distribution of income, and on investment, depreciation, and capital stocks in manufacturing establishments.

In terms of conceptual changes, the 1965 revision was not very significant. The major change was the exclusion of interest paid by consumers from production. This was done in order to treat interest paid by consumers in the same way as interest paid by the government, and it was justified on the same grounds. It was noted that the treatment of both of these items was somewhat controversial, but on balance considerations seemed to favor the change that was made. The new procedure was one that was recommended by the United Nations and used by most countries, and reflected that UN view that payments of interest were not payments for services but distribution of income.

The United Nations System of National Accounts

After the 1947 League of Nations work by Richard Stone mentioned above, the Organization for European Economic Cooperation and later the United Nations both developed similar systems of national accounts which they proposed for international use. In July 1953 the United Nations published *A System of National Accounts and Supporting Tables* (Series F, No. 2, referred to hereafter as SNA). This first version of SNA bore a strong resemblance to the five-account system adopted by the United States in 1958. The most obvious difference was that in the SNA, instead of a single national income and product account, there were two accounts, one of which derived gross domestic product and the second national income. The US national income and product account was merely a consolidation of these two accounts. As with the US system, current income accounts were provided for households including nonprofit institutions and for general government. A rest-of-the-world account was also provided in both systems. One other difference between the US and UN systems was that the SNA made provision for rudimentary capital reconciliation accounts for each sector, whereas the US accounts employed only a consolidated gross saving and investment account for all sectors.

In the mid-1960s, however, a major revision of SNA was undertaken, and in 1968 a new *System of National Accounts* (Series F, No. 2, Rev. 3) was published. The new system was substantially and radically different from both the earlier United Nations system and the system being used by the United States. It was viewed by its originators as providing a comprehensive framework for all of economic accounting, and it stressed the integration of the national income accounts with input–output, financial transactions, capital stocks and balance sheets.

The revised SNA cast the accounting system into the form of a matrix, in which each row and column pair represented the two sides of an account. The theoretical scheme is shown in Table 9.12, together with a list of entries. It should be noted that the entries shown in this table do not represent single aggregate transaction flows; rather, they represent submatrices of transactions cross-classified by the categories indicated for the individual rows and columns. The matrix classifies entries into opening assets, production, consumption, accumulation, rest-of-the-world transactions (current and capital), revaluations and closing assets.

In addition to the matrix, the SNA also contained a proposed standard accounting structure and a large number of supporting and supplementary tables. The theoretical matrix was intended to be a quite general, flexible instrument from which many different specific applications could be drawn. The accounts shown in the 1968 SNA book represented one such specific application, but it was recognized that others were equally possible. The accounts were not, and were not intended to be, an isomorphic transformation of the matrix. The accounts were viewed as mainly of pedagogical use; the supporting and supplementary tables were meant to carry the burden of statistical presentation of data.

The basic structure of the new SNA introduced a number of new features. Some of the accounts were considered to be transaction accounts, since they brought together transactions of a given kind even when engaged in by different transactors. Other accounts were transactor accounts, since they brought together the transactions of specific economic units. In dealing with transactors, a further distinction was made. It was recognized that economic units could be grouped according to either the nature of their activities or their institutional form. For the activity (or industry) classification of transactors, which could be implemented most easily by using economic units defined on an establishment basis (plants, stores and the like), only production and capital formation accounts were provided. In contrast, the institutional classification required economic units classified by their legal form of organization and could be implemented most easily with enterprise-based data. For institutional transactors, only income and outlay, capital finance and balance sheet accounts were provided.

To establish links among the different principles of classification and sectoring employed, dummy transformation accounts were used extensively. Thus, for example, the link between commodities and industry activities for input–output purposes was accomplished through 'make-and-use' matrices, showing, respectively, commodities originating in different industries and commodities used by different industries. Similar dummy accounts were used to link the establishment-based production data (classified by industry) and the enterprise-based income and outlay data (classified by institutional form). The dummy transformation account technique was intended to avoid the necessity for certain cross-tabulations that were regarded as statistically difficult and conceptually questionable. But, by the same token, it resulted in the loss of some important kinds of information. Thus no information was given on the sources and uses of funds of industrial sectors, and conversely for institutional sectors no information was given on production activity. Capital formation by institutional sector was considered only in its financial aspects and was not given by type of asset.

Thus, although the matrix approach was quite general and did achieve the integration of all of the different forms of economic accounting into a single system, it did so at the cost of considerable complexity. The simple overview of the operation of the system was lost, and certain types of information, such as corporate profits by industry, or wages by legal form of organization, were eliminated from the system. The multiplicity of accounts, and the many minor flows given prominence in them, resulted in a system of gothic elaboration, in

Table 9.12 The United Nations SNA Matrix: A Symbolic Table

	1	2	3	4	5	6	7	8	9	10	11	12
OPENING ASSETS												
1. Financial assets												
2. Net tangible assets												
PRODUCTION												
Commodities												
3. Commodities, basic value					$T_{3.5}$	$T_{3.6}$	$T_{3.7}$	$T_{3.8}$				
4. Commodity taxes, net					$T_{4.5}$	$T_{4.6}$	$T_{4.7}$	$T_{4.8}$				
Activities												
5. Industries			$T_{5.3}$	$T_{5.4}$								
6. Producers of gvt services			$T_{6.3}$					$T_{6.8}$	$T_{6.9}$			
7. Private services: domestic service and producers of private n-p services			$T_{7.3}$					$T_{7.8}$		$T_{7.10}$		
CONSUMPTION												
Expenditures												
8. Household goods and svc												
9. Gvt purposes												
10. Purposes of private n-p bodies												
Income and outlay												
11. Value added			$T_{11.3}$	$T_{11.4}$	$T_{11.5}$	$T_{11.6}$	$T_{11.7}$					
12. Inst. sector of origin											$T_{12.11}$	
13. Form of income												$T_{13.12}$
14. Inst. sector of receipt											$T_{14.11}$	
ACCUMULATION												
Increase in stocks												
15. Industries												
16. Producers of gvt services												
Fixed capital formation												
17. Industries												
18. Producers of gvt services												
19. Producers of private n-p services to households												
Capital finance												
20. Industrial capital formation, land, etc.												
21. Capital transfers												
22. Financial assets												
23. Institutional sectors	$T_{23.1}$	$T_{23.2}$										
REST OF THE WORLD												
24. Current and capital transactions	$T_{24.1}$	$T_{24.2}$	$T_{24.3}$				$T_{24.6}$		$T_{24.8}$			
REVALUATIONS												
25. Financial assets												
26. Net tangible assets												
CLOSING ASSETS												
27. Financial assets												
28. Net tangible assets												

Note: The content summaries of the submatrices can be found on page 208.

13	14	15	16	17	18	19	20	21	22	23	24	25	26	27	28
										$T_{1,23}$ $T_{2,23}$	$T_{1,24}$				
		$T_{3,15}$ $T_{4,15}$	$T_{3,16}$	$T_{3,17}$ $T_{4,17}$	$T_{3,18}$ $T_{4,18}$	$T_{3,19}$ $T_{4,19}$				$T_{3,24}$ $T_{4,24}$					
	$T_{8,14}$ $T_{9,14}$ $T_{10,14}$										$T_{8,24}$				
										$T_{11,23}$					
	$T_{13,14}$										$T_{13,24}$				
$T_{14,13}$															
							$T_{15,20}$								
										$T_{16,23}$					
							$T_{17,20}$								
										$T_{18,23}$ $T_{19,23}$					
										$T_{20,23}$					
										$T_{22,23}$	$T_{22,24}$				
	$T_{23,14}$							$T_{23,21}$	$T_{23,22}$			$T_{23,25}$	$T_{23,26}$	$T_{23,27}$	$T_{23,28}$
	$T_{24,13}$							$T_{24,21}$	$T_{24,22}$		$T_{24,24}$	$T_{24,25}$	$T_{24,26}$	$T_{24,27}$	$T_{24,28}$
										$T_{25,23}$ $T_{26,23}$	$T_{25,24}$				
										$T_{27,23}$ $T_{28,23}$	$T_{27,24}$				

Table 9.12 (cont.)

Content summaries of the submatrices are as follows:

$T_{1.23}$ The holdings of financial assets by the institutional sectors at the beginning of the period of account.

$T_{1.24}$ The holdings of financial assets, issued by the country under study, by the rest of the world at the beginning of the period of account.

$T_{2.23}$ The holdings of net tangible assets by the institutional sectors at the beginning of the period of account. The resident economic agents from which the institutional sectors are built up hold between them all the tangible assets in the country in which they are resident; and, at the same time, the ownership of a tangible asset abroad is represented by the holding of a financial asset. As a consequence the rest of the world is not represented in the system as holding tangible assets.

$T_{3.5}$ The inputs of commodities, reckoned at basic values, into the productive activity of industries.

$T_{3.6}$ The inputs of commodities, reckoned at basic values, into the productivity activity of the producers of government services.

$T_{3.7}$ The inputs of commodities, reckoned at basic values, into the productive activity of producers of private nonprofit services to households. It is generally assumed that these inputs do not arise in the case of domestic services on an individual basis.

$T_{3.8}$ Commodities, reckoned at basic values, entering into the consumption expenditure in the domestic market of all households, whether resident or not.

$T_{3.15}$ Additions to the stocks of commodities, reckoned at basic values, held by industries.

$T_{3.16}$ Additions to the stocks of commodities, reckoned at basic values, held by the producers of government services

$T_{3.17}$ Commodities, reckoned at basic values, entering into the gross fixed capital formation of industries.

$T_{3.18}$ Commodities, reckoned at basic values, entering into the gross fixed capital formation of the producers of government services.

$T_{3.19}$ Commodities, reckoned at basic values, entering into the gross fixed capital formation of the producers of private nonprofit services to households.

$T_{3.24}$ Exports of commodities reckoned at basic values.

$T_{4.5}$ Commodity taxes, net, on the commodity inputs into the productive activity of industries. The sum $T_{3.5} + T_{4.5}$ represents these commodity inputs reckoned at producers' values.

$T_{4.6}$ Commodity taxes, net, on the commodity inputs into the productive activity of producers of government services.

$T_{4.7}$ Commodity taxes, net, on the commodity inputs of producers of private nonprofit services to households.

$T_{4.8}$ Commodity taxes, net, on commodities entering into household consumption expenditure in the domestic market.

$T_{4.15}$ Commodity taxes, net, on the commodities entering into the stocks of industries.

$T_{4.17}$ Commodity taxes, net, on commodities entering into the gross fixed capital formation of industries.

$T_{4.18}$ Commodity taxes, net, on the commodities entering into the capital formation of producers of government services.

$T_{4.19}$ Commodity taxes, net, on the commodities entering into the capital formation of producers of private nonprofit services to households.

$T_{4.24}$ Commodity taxes, net, on exports of commodities.

$T_{5.3}$ Commodity outputs, reckoned at basic values, of industries.

$T_{5.4}$ Commodity taxes, net, on the outputs of industries. The sum $T_{5.3} + T_{5.4}$ represents the commodity outputs of industries reckoned at producers' values.

$T_{6.3}$ Commodity outputs, reckoned at basic values, of the producers of government services.

$T_{6.8}$	Government services entering into household consumption expenditure in the domestic market.
$T_{6.9}$	Services produced for own use by government services.
$T_{7.3}$	Commodity outputs, reckoned at basic values, of producers of private nonprofit services to households.
$T_{7.8}$	Domestic services and private nonprofit services entering into household consumption expenditure in the domestic market.
$T_{7.10}$	Services produced for own use by private nonprofit services.
$T_{8.14}$	Final consumption expenditure on goods and services in the domestic market by resident households.
$T_{8.24}$	Final consumption expenditure on goods and services in the domestic market by nonresident households.
$T_{9.14}$	Final consumption expenditure by general government.
$T_{10.14}$	Final consumption expenditure by private nonprofit institutions.
$T_{11.3}$	Protective import duties.
$T_{11.4}$	Other import duties.
$T_{11.5}$	Values added, i.e., compensations of employees, operating surpluses, provisions for the consumption of fixed capital and indirect taxes, net, in the productive activity of industries.
$T_{11.6}$	Values added in the productive activity of the producers of government services.
$T_{11.7}$	Values added in the productive activity of domestic services and the producers of private nonprofit services to households.
$T_{11.23}$	The negative of charges for the consumption of fixed capital.
$T_{12.11}$	Compensation of employees and operating surpluses classified by institutional sectors of origin.
$T_{13.12}$	Compensations of employees and operating surpluses arising in institutional sectors classified by component forms of income. For example, compensation of employees is divided between wages and salaries on the one hand and employers' contributions to social security and private pension funds, etc., on the other.
$T_{13.14}$	Current income transfers, including transfers to property income, paid out by the institutional sectors (as sectors of receipt).
$T_{13.24}$	Current income transfers, including transfers of property income, paid out by the rest of the world.
$T_{14.11}$	Indirect taxes, net, paid to general government.
$T_{14.13}$	Gross receipts of income by the institutional sectors (as sectors of receipt).
$T_{15.20}$	Increases in stocks of industries.
$T_{16.23}$	The finance, provided by the capital finance account of general government, of the increase in stocks of producers of government services.
$T_{17.20}$	Total gross fixed capital formation of industries.
$T_{18.23}$	The finance, provided by the capital finance account of general government, of gross fixed capital formation undertaken by producers of government services.
$T_{19.23}$	The finance, provided by the capital finance account of private nonprofit institutions, of gross fixed capital formation undertaken by the producers of private nonprofit services to households.
$T_{20.23}$	The finance, provided by the capital finance accounts of the institutional sectors, of gross industrial capital formation (in stocks and fixed assets) and the net purchases, by these sectors of land and intangible assets other than financial assets.
$T_{22.23}$	Net acquisitions of financial assets by the institutional sectors.
$T_{22.24}$	Net acquisitions of financial assets, issued by the country under study, by the rest of the world.
$T_{23.1}$	The holdings of financial liabilities by the institutional sectors at the beginning of the period of account.
$T_{23.2}$	The net worth of the institutional sectors at the beginning of the period account.
$T_{23.14}$	The saving of the institutional sectors.
$T_{23.21}$	Net receipts of capital transfers by the institutional sectors.

Table 9.12 (cont.)

$T_{23.22}$	Net issues of financial liabilities by the institutional sectors.
$T_{23.25}$	Revaluations of financial liabilities held by the institutional sectors.
$T_{23.26}$	Revaluations of the net worth of the institutional sectors.
$T_{23.27}$	The holdings of financial liabilities by the institutional sectors at the end of the period of account.
$T_{23.28}$	The net worth of the institutional sectors at the end of the period of account.
$T_{24.1}$	Financial liabilities issued by the rest of the world and held by the institutional sectors at the beginning of the period of account.
$T_{24.2}$	The net worth of the rest of the world at the beginning of the period of account arising from its relationships with the country under study; that is to say, the negative of the rest of the world's net indebtedness to that country.
$T_{24/3}$	Imports of commodities reckoned at c.i.f. values.
$T_{24.6}$	Direct expenditure abroad on goods and services by the producers of government services.
$T_{24.8}$	Final consumption expenditure abroad by resident households.
$T_{24.13}$	Gross receipts of income (whether distributed factor income or other current transfers) by the rest of the world from the country under study.
$T_{24.21}$	Net receipts of capital transfers by the rest of the world.
$T_{24.22}$	Net issues of financial liabilities, taken up by the country under study, by the rest of the world.
$T_{24.24}$	The rest of the world's balance of payments on current account with the country under study.
$T_{24.25}$	Revaluations of financial liabilities issued by the rest of the world and held by the country under study.
$T_{24.26}$	Revaluation of the net worth of the rest of the world arising from its relationships with the country under study.
$T_{24.27}$	Financial liabilities issued by the rest of the world and held by the institutional sectors at the end of the period of account.
$T_{24.28}$	The net worth of the rest of the world at the end of the period arising from its relationships with the country under study.
$T_{25.23}$	Revaluations of financial assets held by the institutional sectors.
$T_{25.24}$	Revaluations of financial assets issued by the country under study and held by the rest of the world.
$T_{26.23}$	Revaluations of net tangible assets held by the institutional sectors.
$T_{27.23}$	The holdings of financial assets by the institutional sectors at the end of the period of account.
$T_{27.24}$	The holdings of financial assets, issued by the country under study, by the rest of the world at the end of the period of account.
$T_{28.23}$	The holdings of net tangible assets by the institutional sectors at the end of the period of account.

which the relation between the UN National Accounts Questionnaire and the basic SNA structure was not readily apparent to the user.

Since its introduction, the new SNA has been adopted in part by a great many countries but, in its entirety, by almost none. The main summary accounts on gross domestic product and national disposable income and the income and outlay accounts for government and households, which closely resemble both the old SNA and the US system, are widely implemented. For input–output analysis, make-and-use matrices are increasingly being adopted. Also, there is increasing interest among developed countries in the capital finance accounts, which show changes in financial assets and liabilities. On the other hand, the principle of dual sectoring with its accompanying dummy transformation accounts has not been widely followed. In general, countries seem to prefer a combination of institutional and industrial sectoring for both production and income and outlay information — not because the difficulties SNA sought to avoid are not recognized but because the information is useful and needed. For example, the European Community has developed the European System of Accounts, an adaptation of SNA that in essence provides full sets of accounts for both institutional sectors and industry branches.

Although the United States was initially represented on the Expert Group charged with drawing up the revised SNA, as the system developed it became evident that the direction in which it was going was quite different from that considered to be appropriate for the future development of the US system. In terms of the actual design of the US accounts, the revised SNA has to date had little impact. Like most countries, however, the US does provide information in SNA form in response to the UN National Accounts Questionnaire. The UN work has, furthermore, had more impact on concepts and definitions, as was noted above in connection with consumer interest.

The 1971 Conference on Income and Wealth

The 1971 Conference on Income and Wealth was concerned with the adequacy of the national income accounts for measuring economic and social performance. A number of participants at this conference expressed the view that the conference was in fact a continuation of the controversies and issues discussed at the 1955 conference. To some degree this was correct. The problem of distinguishing between intermediate and final product, for example, the question as to whether certain government expenditures were final product or merely intermediate goods, was raised and discussed at both conferences. There were, however, very marked differences even in the discussion of this topic. The 1955 conference had viewed national income almost entirely from the point of view of factor cost. But in the 1971 conference, factor cost was not even mentioned, and the discussion focused on the product side of the accounts.

More importantly, however, the major thrust of the 1971 conference was that a number of kinds of important and useful information were missing from the accounts and that these should be considered in the measurement of economic and social performance. It was argued that many nonmarket activities such as housewives' services, other household activity, and even leisure were extremely important for the evaluation of social performance and should be reflected in the national accounts. The need to establish capital accounts for consumers and government, and to impute the services of these assets, was pointed out. Intangible capital relating to research and development and to human capital provided by education, child rearing, and to skills obtained on the job was also emphasized. Direct consumption provided by business, such as television, expense account living and other amenities provided by employers to their employees or to the general public, needed to be considered. One of the problems leading to the most discussion was that of the environment. It was generally agreed that such environmental considerations as the quality of the air and water were important and that expenditures on improving the environment or preventing its further deterioration should not be ignored in the national accounts. There was no general agreement on whether these expenditures constituted intermediate or final products, but there was consensus that both environmental costs and environmental benefits should be reflected in the accounts.

There was also considerable discussion on the question of whether present methods of valuing goods at either market price or cost of production were appropriate in all uses. This question was raised particularly in connection with measuring government output, where those receiving the service might attach a value that was either more or less than cost. It was emphasized that the valuation in such cases might depend upon the distribution of the good or service, some recipients valuing it differently from others. Finally, the problem of quality change was recognized, and the value of hedonic measures in this connection was discussed.

What emerged very clearly from this conference was that many users considered that the present emphasis of the national income and product accounts on market transactions led to a perspective that was too narrow for the measurement of economic and social performance. It was cogently argued that additional information was required on nonmarket activity, on the services of consumer and government durables and intangible investment, and on environmental costs and benefits. It was also clear, however, that such extensions to the national income accounting framework involved imputations, the valuation of which was highly controversial and in many cases could only yield an order of magnitude. Those who used the national accounts for the analysis of economic activity in the short run, with a focus on inflation, the business cycle and fiscal policy, felt that the inclusion of such imputations would lessen the usefulness of the accounts. No satisfactory resolution of these conflicting objectives emerged.

The Economic Accounts of the United States: Retrospect and Prospect (1971)

At about the same time as the 1971 Conference on Income and Wealth, the Department of Commerce published a commemorative issue of the *Survey of Current Business* on its fiftieth anniversary, in which 43 contributors wrote individual articles about the national income accounts and offered suggestions for changes and additions.

In general, the contributors expressed their satisfaction with the present form of the national income accounts and the basic conceptual treatment of the flows. Although there was some reflection of the views expressed in the 1971 Conference on Income and Wealth, these were in general muted and more than balanced by those contributors who thought that the major function of the national income accounts should be to provide information for short-run analysis of the economy. In particular, some contributors did urge better information in the area of pollution costs and the environment, but many more were concerned with more timely and frequent publication of series that would be useful in forecasting or understanding current economic conditions. The view was expressed by some that the present accounts should not be tampered with, since they were currently performing a useful and important function. Aside from imputations, however, there were some concrete suggestions in specific areas. For example, a number of contributors were interested in seeing an expansion of the information on international transactions, citing the need for more detailed information on multinational corporations and on the bilateral dealings between the United States and specific countries and regions. In the area of input–output, it was suggested that it would be useful to adopt the SNA treatment, including make-and-use matrices. Probably the most frequent request for new information was for the extension of the national income accounting system into balance sheets containing information on capital stocks, not only for business but also for households and government.

As in the case of the 1955 Conference on Income and Wealth, George Jaszi closed the fiftieth anniversary volume with a review of all of the contributions. Although he noted resource constraints in a number of areas, he agreed that it would be desirable to construct balance sheets and to provide information on consumer and government durables. With respect to imputations, he noted that some were included in the accounts even in their present form and considered that some limited additions might be useful, but he warned that extensive imputation could destroy the value of the system and that restraint should be used in adding further imputations to the accounts. He specifically rejected the notion that welfare criteria should be allowed to alter the measure of gross national product. With respect to the design of the accounting structure and sectoring, Jaszi indicated general support for a system based upon recording the transactions of individual transactors in the accounts, with the objective of obtaining a meaningful summary picture of the economic process, and emphasized the importance of providing such an overview of the economy. He specifically rejected building the accounts on a dual sectoring principle (industries and institutions), and questioned the usefulness of elaborate matrix presentations of the accounts.

The 1975 Revision

The 1975 revision again was primarily statistical. The unusual size of the revisions was due in part to the length of the period — encompassing two economic censuses instead of one — which had elapsed since the last benchmark revision in 1965, and in part to the severe inflation and other economic changes which had made the task of estimating the national income accounts more difficult.

The only major conceptual change introduced in the 1975 revision was the shift of capital consumption measurement to an economic rather than a book value basis. The new measure of capital consumption involved two changes. First, the service lives of assets were changed from those permitted in the tax regulations to lives which more accurately reflect actual practice. Second, depreciation was valued at market rather than at historical cost. The difference between the book value of depreciation charged by enterprises and the replacement cost depreciation shown in the national accounts was shown as a capital consumption valuation adjustment which, like the inventory valuation adjustment, became an adjustment to the book value of enterprise profits. There were also other minor conceptual changes, among them the treatment of mobile homes and the purchase of consumer durables by landlords. Some new tables and series were provided. Greater detail was introduced in the constant-dollar data, and for a number of series constant-dollar figures were shown for the first time on a quarterly as well as on an annual basis.

Current Activities Related to National Income Accounting

There are several activities now under way that are not yet reflected in the most recent published form of the US national income accounts but are directly related and can be expected at some future time to be integrated with them. These are: the development of capital stock estimates for structures and durables of business, government and households; the estimation of the size distribution of income for families; and the development of measures of non-market activity within the framework of the accounts.

For more than a decade, BEA has been in the process of developing estimates of capital stock based on the perpetual inventory technique. The first report on such estimates was published in the December 1966 issue of the *Survey of Current Business* and since then, at irregular intervals, articles providing an increasing amount of information on the stocks of structures and durables in both current and constant prices have appeared. These estimates are directly related to the national income accounts, since they are based upon the data in the accounts relating to purchases of structures and durables and to capital consumption. But, because the national income accounts have not been extended to comprehend balance sheets, the capital stock data do not formally constitute a part of the national income accounting system. The Federal Reserve Board has more recently used the BEA estimates of capital stocks of structures and durables in conjunction with their own financial asset and liability data to produce balance sheets for enterprises and households.

With respect to the size distribution of income, the present methodology follows the lines suggested in the 1958 *US Income and Output* supplement, using data from IRS individual tax returns in conjunction with sample surveys collected by the Bureau of the Census. However, the current work involves matching and merging of computer files of microdata, using techniques of both exact and statistical matching of records that were not foreseen in 1958. An article on the size distribution of income for the years 1964, 1970 and 1971 was published in the *Survey of Current Business* in October 1974 and, at present, work is continuing on more recent size distribution estimates. Although the size distribution estimates are closely tied to and aligned with the national income estimates of personal income, major conceptual differences remain which prevent the size distribution work from fitting neatly within the national income accounts.

Finally, BEA has established a new program to develop measures of nonmarket activity within the framework of GNP accounts. In part, this work is a response to the emphasis put on this topic at the 1971 Conference on Income and Wealth, but it also reflects the strong interest in environmental studies within the Department of Commerce. The federal government's concern with the measurement of the costs of pollution control and environmental damage has stimulated work in this area. BEA's current program, however, includes not only environmental questions but also time spent in nonmarket work and leisure, the services of consumer durables and the services of government capital. The close relationship to the national income accounting system in this work is stressed, but as yet it has not been formally integrated.

3. DIRECTIONS FOR FUTURE DEVELOPMENT

National income estimation in the United States had its roots in the neoclassical concept of the factors of production, and initially it focused primarily on the measurement of net income and resource allocation. The policy needs arising from the Depression of the 1930s and World War II changed the focus to short-run macroeconomic analysis and resulted in a national income accounting system emphasizing the interrelationships among the sectors of the economy. It was in this context that the concept of gross national product came to dominate the earlier concept of national income, and the concern shifted from accurate measurement of specific aggregates to the analysis of market transactions and transfers among businesses, government and households.

Although more than 30 years have passed since the US national income accounting system was established, its basic structure has remained essentially unchanged. What has occurred instead is a continual improvement in the quantity and quality of the information provided. By and large, most users of the national income accounts are well satisfied with what the present system offers, and there are few who would wish to see radical changes made. This does not mean, however, that there is no room for further development in the US national income accounts. Rather, it suggests that desired changes can probably be accommodated within the existing framework.

In the review of the discussions of conceptual issues over the past 30 years, four general topics stand out as areas where further work is called for. These are: the sectoring, subsectoring and the structure of the accounts; the treatment of nonmarket activities and imputations; the basic accounting principles underlying the recording of transactions in the accounts; and the integration of financial transactions and balance sheets with the national income accounts. Each of these topics will be examined briefly in the following sections of this paper.

Sectoring and the Structure of the Accounts

Although this topic is central to national income accounting and has important implications for its future development, it has not engendered very much explicit discussion. The original 1947 six-account system recognized business, government, households and the rest of the world as the four primary sectors. In 1958, the system was reduced to five accounts, the business sector being consolidated with the national income and product account and not shown explicitly as a separate sector. This was done to reduce the number of minor and inconsequential flows in the accounts and to display the major flows in the economy more prominently and simply. The five-account system has continued unchanged to the present day and has served very well as the framework for the ever-expanding national income accounting statistics. It has successfully provided the kind of overview that was intended.

The dual sectoring of production accounts by industry, on the one hand, and income and outlay accounts by institutional sectors, on the other, employed in the United Nations SNA has been rejected by BEA on the grounds that it does not provide certain kinds of information now included in the US accounts, such as corporate profits by industry and compensation of employees by legal form of organization. Furthermore, the US statistics also provide a useful breakdown of industries within legal form of organization, a type of information that is automatically ruled out of the SNA.

However, some difficulties are encountered with the present system of sectoring. One set of problems concerns the personal income sector and raises specific questions as to the criteria on which sectoring should be based. As was noted in discussing the work on the size distribution of income, there is a lack of correspondence between the definition of the personal income sector, which includes nonprofit institutions, and the size distribution income concepts, which refer only to families and individuals. This problem has been recognized by BEA from time to time, when they have recommended subsectoring the personal income account so as to separate nonprofit institutions from households. The original argument for including nonprofit institutions in the personal sector rested on the fact that these institutions are final consumers, as well as on the pragmatic ground of ease of statistical estimation. While it is true, as Jaszi pointed out, that institutional groupings are often based upon such functional characteristics, it does not seem in this case that it is appropriate to combine nonprofit institutions and households in the same sectoral grouping. Behaviorally, the difference between an individual household and a nonprofit organization, such as a university or hospital employing a large staff, is very substantial indeed. For many purposes, it would be much more appropriate to group together nonprofit organizations and profit-making organizations in such fields as education and health.

Sectors should be drawn up on the basis of two criteria: the behavioral and decision-making processes underlying a sector's activity and the types and sources of information that are available relating to the transactors included in a sector. The accounts for a sector should be thought of as a consolidation or combination of the accounts of reporting units within the sector. For each sector, it should be possible to conceive of a microdata set of homogeneous units which, when aggregated, would yield the sector account. Thus, it should be conceptually and statistically possible to relate sample surveys of households to the aggregate data shown in the household sector account.

In terms of these criteria, it is evident that the personal income sector should be recast as a household sector, including all the families and individuals in the nation, but excluding enterprise-like organizations such as nonprofit institutions. This would not only permit better analysis of household behavior, it also would make it possible to use microdata for subsectoring the household sector into various social and demographic groupings. The benefits of the integration of microdata with national accounts do not, of course, all accrue to the national accounts. Microdata, based as they often are upon surveys, often contain substantial reporting biases which can only be discovered when they are matched against control totals obtained from other sources, such as are found in the national accounts.

In this connection, it is also necessary to consider the classifications of transactions employed in the accounts. It is unfortunate that at present the national accounts do not reflect in the detail of personal consumption expenditures the same classifications employed in the consumer expenditure surveys. If the national accounts and the consumer expenditure surveys were integrated around the same classification system, it would become possible to relate the expenditure pattern of different subsectors of the household sector to the total changes shown in the national accounts.

Shifting to a household sectoring, besides improving the integration of data, would also make possible a better integration of micro- and macroanalysis. In recent years there has been more and more interest in analyzing problems that require closely related micro- and macrodata. Thus, for example, the analysis of such questions as health delivery systems, social security and welfare reform requires examination of transactions information in the context of other non-transactions data in the household, such as household composition and the age, sex, race and employment status of its members. These problems are being analyzed increasingly through microanalytic simulation techniques using large microdata sets aligned with the national accounts. It is important that future efforts to construct important microdata sets, such as the Survey of Income and Program Participation currently in process, be conceptually and statistically integrated with the national income accounts; and, conversely, the national income accounts in the future will have to take these bodies of data into account, both in the sectoring of the economy and in the classification of transactions within sectors.

A second set of sectoring problems centers on the business or enterprise sector. Such a sector is of course still implicit in the US accounts even though it is not shown explicitly. In order to provide a more disaggregated view of output, prices, employment and productivity it would be useful to formalize the sectoring and subsectoring of enterprises. The precise subsectoring chosen should depend on behavioral homogeneity, the kinds of data available and analytic interest.

The same principles of sectoring noted above in connection with the household sector are applicable to the enterprise sector and its main subsectors. It should be possible to conceive of a microdata set of relatively homogeneous reporting units that would add up to the total for the sector or subsector. In many cases, microdata sets may be available from administrative, tax or regulatory records. For example, it may be possible to identify a utility subsector for which appropriate current accounts and balance sheets can be obtained for the individual reporting units. Although, in some cases, privacy restrictions may limit the use of individual records, in other cases much of the data is either of a public nature or can be provided in a form that would not involve disclosure.

In addition to accounts based on systematic and comprehensive sectoring and subsectoring of transactors, it may also be useful to develop special key sector or satellite accounts of either transactors or special groupings of transactions. For example, at the present time the US national income accounts contain an account for the gross output and income from housing, and it may be desirable to develop special accounts dealing with energy. Such supplementary or satellite accounts need not necessarily be fully articulated with other sector or subsector accounts, but they should, of course, be consistent with and fit logically into the national accounting system.

With respect to the structure of accounts for sectors and subsectors, US practice departs significantly, as was indicated above, from international recommendations, and it is appropriate to consider whether the international recommendations have merit. For the most part, the data do exist to construct the production accounts, appropriation accounts, capital accumulation accounts, capital finance accounts, reconciliation accounts and balance sheets that SNA calls for. But such an approach seems to have little to recommend it. The multiplicity of accounts seems designed only to derive subtotals, and it results in much duplication and loss of the comprehensive overview of the accounting system in a maze of detail. It seems more appropriate to move in the reverse direction, dividing the accounts for sectors into just two categories, current and capital. If this were done, the current accounts would show current receipts and outlays, and the capital accounts would show balance sheets and the related capital transactions and revaluations. As Jaszi has suggested, there is no need to enforce the same format on the accounts for different sectors. It is appropriate to organize the current account for business enterprises around the concept of gross product (or value added), whereas the current account for government can appropriately be centered on government revenue and that for households on household income.

Nonmarket Activity and Imputations

The topic of nonmarket activity and imputation is, of course, as old as the history of national income measurement. The paradox of the man who marries his housekeeper is an old, old problem. The 1947 US national accounts explicitly excluded such imputations as the services of housewives and illegal activities from the measure of national income, but a limited number of imputations considered to constitute a part of output were recognized. These were the imputed rental income of owner-occupied housing, the value of food and fuel consumed on farms, the value of food and clothing provided to the military, and banking services rendered without payment to depositors. In total, these imputations accounted, in 1947, for about 5 percent of GNP.

In the years since 1947, the topic of imputations has repeatedly been discussed. The 1955 Conference on Income and Wealth considered it in the context of the derivation of the national income aggregates. Much attention was given to the banking imputation, and general support was expressed for imputations relating to income in kind and owner-occupied housing. There were even some proposals that imputations should be made for the services of both consumer and government durables. But the possibility of imputations beyond the established production boundaries was not seriously considered. In contrast, the 1971 conference took a broader view of nonmarket activity and imputations in the context of measuring economic well-being and economic and social performance. Participants were no longer concerned only with imputations falling within the production boundary; they focused instead on the welfare of individuals. Questions discussed included human and other intangible capital and the flow of services it generated, the measurement of disamenities and environmental costs and benefits. Contributors to the fiftieth anniversary volume were generally more conventional in approach, but some support was expressed for extending imputations into such areas as pollution, the environment and nonmarket activity in the household. Despite this long discussion, however, the imputations in the national accounts still remain essentially as they were in 1947. At the present time, they constitute approximately 8 percent of GNP, the rise since 1946 being attributable mainly to the increased importance of the imputation for owner-occupied housing.

Furthermore, despite all the discussion about imputations, it has never clearly been established just what the term is meant to cover. Owner-occupied housing, payments in kind and the services of financial intermediaries are fairly self-evident — or, at any rate, users of the accounts are accustomed to them. But in the process of constructing national income accounts there are many instances of estimates which do not reflect market transactions and so involve some element of imputation. One of the most obvious of these arises in estimating capital consumption allowances. To the extent that capital consumption allowances are recorded as accounting entries in the books of enterprises, it can be argued that they do represent market transactions. But a number of adjustments are made to the recorded book values in order to convert them to economic depreciation and to include such elements as accidental damage to fixed capital. In a similar manner, an inventory valuation adjustment is introduced in order to exclude the effect of changes in the price of inventories from the current value of output. Most of these adjustments can be excluded from the category of imputations on the ground that they result from employing standard accounting rules to correct the accounts of enterprises, even when they involve introducing entries into the accounts where no such entries exist or are contemplated by the individual economic units. Thus capital consumption allowances are estimated for small businesses which may not actually charge any depreciation at all. Capital consumption allowances for owner-occupied housing depart further from recorded transactions. Such adjustments and corrections are useful and in some cases necessary. But care should be exercised to preserve to the fullest extent possible the information on the market realities, as they exist in the records of the transactors, separately from the adjustments. BEA has to date by and large followed this principle, explicitly showing the capital consumption and inventory valuation adjustments in the accounts.

But it is not such imputations to correct and adjust accounting flows that generally result in controversy. Rather, it is the imputations that range beyond the traditional limit of what is considered to be output that give rise to problems. The 1971 conference considered nonmarket extensions of the accounts for the study of long-term growth or changes, for the analysis of the structure of the economy at a given point in time and for policy purposes relating to important social and economic questions. For the study of economic growth over long periods of time, information was needed on the change in the amount of leisure, the change in nonmarket activities, the services of consumer and government durables, the incidence of regrettable necessities in the system and the amount of environmental disamenities. Quantitative estimates of the impact of all of these had been made and used by some researchers to adjust GNP. In order to analyze the structure of the economy at a given point in time, imputations taking into account the time-use patterns of households, the services of intangible capital and the benefits provided by employers to employees were considered important. For the formulation and evaluation of economic and social policy, another set of imputations was relevant, including imputations relating to pollution abatement costs and benefits, and imputations reflecting the distribution of health and welfare benefits and their relation to the distribution of income and tax payments. Such imputations, however, go far beyond the aggregate imputations contemplated for adjusting national income and gross national product. They involve attribution of the imputations to income groups or to specific individuals. Where imputations involve public goods, the attribution would be both conceptually and statistically difficult, if not impossible.

This discussion served mainly to emphasize that, unlike transactions data, there is no well-defined universe of nonmarket activities and imputations to be covered. The set of all possible imputations is unbounded. The only criterion that can be employed is whether the imputations are considered to be useful and necessary for the particular purpose at hand. In the fiftieth anniversary volume, Jaszi compared imputations to additions made to a house to adapt it to the needs of a particular family. He suggested that the additions may lack architectural unity, because they are shaped to the needs of the time and the resources available. This is indeed an apt comparison, especially when one reflects that in the case of the US accounts no additions have been made since the original building was set up in 1947. Jaszi foresaw, however, that some limited additional imputation might prove to be useful in the future.

Whatever decision is made with regard to extending the imputations in the national accounts, it is important that the imputations that are made be shown clearly and explicitly. BEA now provides a supplementary table showing all the imputations that are made in the national accounts, but in the main accounts the imputations are combined with market transactions. As long as imputations have been relatively minor, this has not been a matter of central concern. However, if imputations are extended into such areas as nonmarket household activity or even to the services of consumer and government durables, their magnitude could swamp the market transactions data in the accounts, and for many of these kinds of imputations, estimates for monthly, quarterly or, in some cases, even annual periods are not feasible or required.

Furthermore, for many of the imputations the problem of valuation is so serious that combining them with market transactions would introduce a factor of extreme arbitrariness. There are some cases where the valuation problem is relatively simple, as in the use of the rental value of equivalent space for owner-occupied housing. But in cases such as the value of leisure, the problem is not only difficult but essentially insoluble: one must decide whether the leisure of the wealthy is worth more than the leisure of the poor. For public goods, it is not at all clear whether the imputation should be based on the cost of providing the good or on the benefits to the recipient. For example, if the audience for public television doubles without any increase in the cost of providing the television service, has the output of public television services to households increased? Similarly, should food stamps be valued at their cost to the government, or at the value attached to them by the recipients? It is unfortunately true that no clear-cut principles have been established that will solve the valuation problems for all imputations.

For all of these reasons, an explicit separation of market transactions from imputations in the national accounts would seem highly desirable. One way of doing this would be to show market transactions separately from the imputations made in each sector account. It should be recognized, however, that imputations alone cannot meet the information needs for measuring economic and social performance. As some of the contributors to the fiftieth anniversary volume pointed out, no amount of imputation can convert a one-dimensional summary measure such as the GNP into an adequate or appropriate measure of social welfare. The problem is rather one of achieving an integration of macro- and microanalysis using economic accounting data in conjunction with social and demographic nontransactions data. As has already been emphasized, a rapidly emerging tool for accomplishing such integration is the construction of microdata sets, containing social, demographic and geographic data as well as economic data, to underlie the sector and subsector accounts.

The Recording of Transactions in the National Accounts

In the section of this paper on sectoring and the structure of the accounts, it was proposed that sectors and subsectors should be defined so that their accounts could be conceived of as the combination or consolidation of the accounts of a relatively homogeneous set of reporting units. This means that transactions recorded in the accounts for a sector or subsector should directly correspond to the transactions recorded for individual transactors. This principle was put forward to make the sector and subsector accounts more faithfully reflect the economic behavior and decision-making of the transactors, to ensure a direct correspondence between the aggregated data in the sector and subsector accounts and the data in the microdata sets of transactors and to permit a better integration of macro- and microanalysis, making use of social, demographic and other nontransactions data relating to transactor units in conjunction with transactions data.

Most users of the US national income accounts view the flows shown in the accounts as reflecting actual transactions. In many instances this is correct, but in a substantial number of cases there are significant differences between the treatment in the national accounts and that which would appear in the accounts of transactors. This is especially true with respect to transactions dealing with insurance, pensions and interest. It is not appropriate at this juncture to discuss in detail precisely how a 'transactor' approach to the recording of these transactions would differ from conventional national income accounting practices, but for those interested in this topic such a discussion is provided in the Appendix. For the present purpose, however, it is important to recognize that the aggregate view of transaction flows in the national income accounts should bear a direct and recognizable relation to the transactions as they are recorded in the accounts of individual transactors.

A Current Account for the Household Sector

The application of these principles for sectoring and recording transactions would result in a major reconfiguration of the national income accounts. Before going on to the discussion of the fourth topic listed above, therefore, it will be useful to summarize the impact of the principles discussed so far on the current transaction accounts.

An example of the current receipts and outlay account for a redefined household sector and its relation to the Personal Income Account of BEA is given in Table 9.13. This table shows explicitly the relation between the major income and expenditure flows as they now appear in the BEA Personal Income Account and similar flows in the redefined Household Current Income and Expenditure Account. A discussion of the differences between these flows will indicate the general nature of the changes that have been made.

The removal of nonprofit institutions from the personal income sector in order to restrict the sector to households will, of course, affect most of the

Table 9.13 Comparison of the BEA Personal Income Account with the Household Sector Current Account for 1969 ($bn current)

	BEA personal outlays and saving	Household current outlays and saving		BEA personal income	Household current income
Expenditures on durables	85.7		Wages and salaries	515.7	513.0
Expenditures on nondurables	247.8	238.5	Payments	513.0	513.0
Expenditures	244.8	244.8	Pay in kind	2.7	
Less: Increase in stocks	3.0	−6.3	Other labor income	28.5	
In-kind consumption			Fees and other pay	0.5	
Expenditures on services	248.2	147.8	Other benefits	27.9	
Household expenditures	147.8	147.8	Proprietor income	67.0	65.4
Nonprofit expenditures	15.5		Money income	65.4	65.4
Imputed banking services	9.8		Imputed income	1.6	
Imputed housing services	52.0		Rental income	19.6	8.5
Other benefits in kind	23.1		Paid to households	8.5	8.5
Interest payments	15.6	31.0	Imputed rent	11.1	
Consumer debt interest	15.6	15.6	Interest income	61.1	38.5
Mortgage interest		15.4	Paid to households	38.5	38.5
Tax payments	115.7	128.5	Paid to nonprofits	1.2	
Income taxes	101.5	101.5	Imputed interest	21.4	
Property taxes	0.8	13.6	Dividends	22.4	21.4
Other taxes and nontaxes	13.4	13.4	Paid to households	21.4	21.4
Personal contributions for social insurance		26.2	Paid to nonprofits	1.0	

Transfers paid	0.9	Business transfers	2.8
Gifts to nonprofits	14.2	Private pension payments	2.8
Transfers to abroad	13.3	Government transfers	11.9
Imputed outlays	0.9	Paid to households	54.4
Except owner-occupied housing	149.0	Paid to nonprofits	54.4
Owner-occupied housing	97.0	Benefits in kind	2.9
Gross household saving	52.0	Current market income	6.5
Capital consumption allowances	129.5	Imputed gross income	715.8
Consumer durables	59.4	Except owner-occupied	149.0
Owner-occupied housing	11.9	Owner-occupied gross income	97.0
Net household saving	58.2	Less: Employee social security	52.0
Personal saving (BEA)	40.6		26.2
Personal outlays and saving	754.7	Personal income (BEA)	754.7
TOTAL CURRENT OUTLAYS AND SAVING	864.9	TOTAL CURRENT RECEIPTS	864.9

income and expenditure flows. In the Personal Income Account, nonprofit institutions receive property income from enterprises and transfer payments from the government, and their expenditures are included in consumption expenditures. Furthermore, in the Personal Income Account the inclusion of nonprofit institutions with households means that the transfers between households and nonprofit institutions are consolidated out of the account. When nonprofit institutions are excluded from the household sector, it is necessary to show explicitly the contributions households make to charitable and religious organizations.

In the Personal Income Account, employees receive wages and salaries and other income paid by employers. Part of this income is paid in kind (food and clothing provided by the military) and part is withheld by employers for health and welfare contributions. Although the withheld health and welfare contributions are costs to employers, they do not represent actual receipts by households. Although imputing pay in kind is reasonable, imputing the value of health and welfare contributions or benefits to employees poses difficult conceptual and statistical problems. Even individual recipients themselves may be quite unaware of the actual magnitudes involved. While individuals may receive the benefits, the actual payments go to doctors and hospitals, and the specific individual may not know what the costs are.

Furthermore, what is being provided to employees by their employers is really the health insurance, which assures them of health care when and if they need it. To impute actual medical costs to individual patients would distort the distribution of income in a quite unrealistic way, since the very high cost of medical care of those who are seriously ill would immediately put them into a very high income bracket: the poor would never get sick. Health insurance and health care should represent final consumption output, but its direct allocation to specific individual households does not seem to be any more justified than the imputation to individual households of other public goods such as education, the use of highways and public libraries. For this reason it seems appropriate to treat employee health benefits as part of consumption provided by enterprises which, like government consumption, increases the welfare of households in general but cannot be allocated to specific individuals.

A different treatment is given to pension benefits, which are direct cash payments to individuals. Unlike the current practice in the Personal Income Account, these payments should not be netted with pension contributions but rather should be recorded as actual transfer payments by businesses or pension funds to individuals. It would also be appropriate, if information were available, to impute to individuals any change in the cash surrender value of pensions or life insurance resulting from employers' contributions. Other changes in life insurance and pension reserves, however, should not be treated as part of household income, on the grounds that households do not have access to this income and are in fact not even aware of its magnitude. Therefore, unlike the treatment in the Personal Income Account, these reserves would be excluded from the saving of households.

Rental income in the Personal Income Account, of course, includes an imputation for the rental income of owner-occupied housing. In the Household Sector Account, however, since market transactions are separated from imputations, rental income is reduced by this amount, and the rental income of owner-occupied housing appears as a nonmarket transaction.

Interest income in the Personal Income Account includes an imputation for the services of financial intermediaries. Since this is a nonmarket transaction, it has been excluded from interest income in the Household Sector Account, but it has not been included in imputed income received by households on the grounds that the allocation of banking services to individual households is both conceptually and statistically weak. To base the imputation solely on the size of bank deposits and to neglect banking services provided to borrowers is not readily defensible in a period when banks charge for their services, on the one hand, and pay interest on their depositors' accounts, on the other. Thus, like other unallocatable items, the services of financial intermediaries are considered to be part of consumption provided by enterprises.

With respect to transfers, it has already been noted that private pensions paid to households are included as part of household income, whereas in the Personal Income Account they are netted against pension contributions. In addition, the transfers recorded in the Personal Income Account as government transfers for hospital and supplementary medical insurance (medicare) have been removed, on the same grounds that private health benefits were removed. Such government programs do not result in increases in market income to individual households; rather they provide health services to the population just as education expenditures provide education services. Their allocation to individual households is no more justifiable than allocation of education or other services that are also provided to individuals.

In order to restrict the outlay side of the Household Sector Account to current transactions, it will be necessary to exclude expenditures on consumer durables and the change in household stocks of nondurables. Furthermore, the exclusion of the transactions of nonprofit institutions and of imputations from consumer expenditures means that in-kind consumption, expenditures of nonprofit institutions, imputed banking services, imputed housing services and other benefits in kind must also be excluded. On the other hand, adopting a 'transactor' approach means that the actual payments of mortgage interest and property taxes by owner-occupiers should be included. Finally, since nonprofit institutions are no longer consolidated with households, it is necessary to show explicitly the gifts which households make to these institutions.

In summary, what this redefined Household Sector Account is designed to do is trace transaction flows as they occur in the economy, carrying out only those imputations which can be directly allocated to individual households. Where goods and services are consumed by households as a group but the allocation to individual households is conceptually or statistically difficult, these items are treated in the accounts as public goods, whether made available by enterprises or government. The recognition of enterprise consumption as analogous to government consumption reflects the increase in the extent to which people's lives depend upon the fringe benefits provided by the society. One of the major characteristics of fringe benefits is that they are provided to specific groups as a matter of right, and the benefits accruing to any individual do not necessarily correspond to the contributions which are deducted from his earnings. Inasmuch as the individual has relatively little control over either the contribution which is deducted, on the one hand, or the nature and availability of the fringe benefits themselves, on the other, it seems reasonable to treat them in a way that is directly analogous to the treatment of taxes and government expenditures.

This does not mean that individual analysts should not study the distribution of the benefits of different kinds of public goods among different types of individuals or groups. Such research is needed, but it raises major theoretical problems of tracing incidence, and from the point of view of the national accountant it should be considered to be in the realm of analysis rather than statistical compilation.

The Integration of Financial Transactions and Balance Sheets with the National Income Accounts

When the US national income accounting system was first developed in 1947, it was noted that a gross saving and investment account was provided on a consolidated basis for the economy as a whole because the information necessary for a complete structure of saving and investment accounts had not as yet been developed. In Jaszi's discussion at the 1955 Conference on Income and Wealth, he proposed developing component saving and investment accounts for nonfinancial corporations, financial intermediaries, persons, including unincorporated enterprises, and government and international transactions. In the Report of the National Accounts Review Committee in 1957, the integration of the flow of funds financial transactions and sector balance sheets with the national income accounts was identified as being of highest priority. In 1958, OBE repeated its plans to implement a deconsolidation of the saving and investment accounts to show transactions in financial assets and liabilities for different sectors of the economy and to integrate information on tangible investment and durable goods stocks, including those of government and consumers. Again in 1971, both the Conference on Income and Wealth and the contributors to the fiftieth anniversary volume of the *Survey of Current Business* urged the integration of financial transactions and balance sheets with the national income accounts.

To some degree, work in this area has gone forward. BEA has been developing extensive information on the stocks of tangibles derived directly from the national income accounts by the perpetual inventory method. But no formal integration of this information with financial transactions or the national income accounts has emerged. Recently the Federal Reserve Board has produced balance sheets that include both BEA tangible stock estimates and FRB financial asset and liability estimates, integrated with the financial transactions in the flow of funds data. However, FRB does not provide balance sheets for the government sector, and since its major focus is on financial institutions the presentation does not provide for the nonfinancial sectors of the economy the kind of deconsolidated sector saving and investment accounts that were contemplated by BEA.

Certainly the idea of integrating financial transactions and balance sheets with the national income accounts is not just an idea whose time has come; history indicates that it came 30 years ago. What has prevented this development, that is universally recognized as desirable, from taking place? Primarily, as the original 1947 statement indicated, the problem has been one of obtaining the appropriate data. For most of the period under discussion, sufficient information was not available for either financial transactions or tangible investment. Over time, however, these data deficiencies have been remedied, and now it would be a practical undertaking to develop fully integrated capital transaction accounts and balance sheets through a marriage of the capital stock data produced by BEA and the financial transactions data produced by FRB.

In developing such integrated accounts, it is necessary to recognize that changes in balance sheet values occur not only as a result of actual transactions but also because of changes in the valuation of existing stocks. Thus, in using the perpetual inventory method for estimating the current value of the stock of a given tangible asset, account must be taken not only of the net purchases (i.e., purchases less sales) and capital consumption of the asset but also of the net revaluations of the existing stock due to price changes, capital losses and retirements. For financial assets, capital consumption does not enter as an element of change, and for many financial assets and liabilities revaluation is not required in order to obtain current market values. While sector balance sheets, like sector income accounts, reflect current market values, it is of course also possible to show at least the tangible portion of the balance sheet in terms of constant dollars, or if desired to present the whole of the balance sheet in terms of the purchasing power of some base period.

Balance Sheets for the Household Sector

An example of the household sector balance sheet, in terms of the stock of assets and liabilities, capital transactions and revaluations, is given in Table 9.14. In this table, the sector balance sheets appear both as opening balances at the beginning of the year and closing balances at the end of the year. This general approach is quite similar to that employed in the United Nations SNA. However, in this table the net current value of each tangible asset is explicitly derived from original book value, revaluations and capital consumption.

The first column shows the opening balance sheet. The gross stock at book value is obtained by adding up all net purchases for past periods, at the prices actually paid. To this gross stock at book value is added the cumulative revaluation needed to bring the past outlays to current market value. The book value of capital consumption as recorded in the accounting records, the capital consumption adjustment and the revaluations that are introduced to convert this book value to current value economic depreciation are all shown explicitly. The net current market value for any tangible asset is obtained by subtracting the cumulative current value of capital consumption from the current value of gross stock. For financial assets, the cumulative book value of purchases plus the cumulative revaluation equals current market value.

The second column shows current year capital transactions: the net acquisitions (purchases less sales) of assets during the period and the capital consumption chargeable against the asset during the period. Both capital consumption at book value and its adjustment to the concept of economic depreciation are given. The difference between the net acquisitions of a given type of asset and its economic depreciation during the period is equal to net capital formation. For financial assets and liabilities, the capital transactions reflect the amount of the asset or liability acquired during the current period.

The column showing revaluations during the current period reflects primarily the effect of price changes during the period upon existing capital stock. However, the value of the capital stock also must be adjusted downward (negative revaluation) to reflect retirements as well as any loss in value due to accidents, fire, or unforeseen deterioration.

The closing balance shown in the final column can be obtained by adding each of the rows across the table, producing new values for each element. The origin of the net worth of a sector can be traced to revaluations and net savings, and the disposition of net saving can be broken down between net acquisitions of tangible and financial assets.

This presentation thus does provide a deconsolidation of the saving and investment account such as Jaszi recommended as early as 1955. It is directly linked with the current accounts through expenditures on structures and durable goods by households, together with their gross saving, and it is derivable

Table 9.14 Household Sector Balance Sheets ($bn current)

	Closing/ opening balance (1968/69)	Capital transactions (1969)	Revaluations (1969)	Closing/ opening balance (1969/70)
Reproducible assets (net current value)	874.4	49.1	33.6	957.2
Residential structures (net current value)	482.9	16.5	26.9	526.3
Gross stock (book value)	450.5	28.4	−1.9	477.0
Plus: Revaluation	253.0		37.3	290.3
Equals: Gross stock (current value)	703.5	28.4	35.4	767.3
Less: Capital consumption (book value)	96.5	8.0	−1.1	103.4
Less: Capital consumption revaluation	124.1	3.9	9.7	137.6
Consumer durables (net current value)	310.5	26.3	3.3	340.1
Gross stock (book value)	540.3	85.7	−46.9	579.1
Plus: Revaluation	24.5		11.4	36.0
Equals: Gross stock (current value)	564.8	85.7	−35.4	615.1
Less: Capital consumption (book value)	241.9	56.9	−42.1	256.7
Less: Capital consumption revaluation	12.4	2.4	3.4	18.3
Inventories	81.0	6.3	3.5	90.7
Land	133.6		8.8	142.3
Fixed claim assets	671.5	44.2		715.7
Currency and deposits	480.9	5.3		486.2
Currency and demand deposits	109.7	−4.5		105.2
Time and savings accounts	371.2	9.8		381.0
Government securities	105.8	28.1		133.9
US Treasury issues	73.1	10.8		83.9
Agency issues	8.9	5.6		14.5
State + local obligations	23.8	11.7		35.5
Other fixed claim assets	84.8	10.7		95.5
Corporate + foreign bonds	3.5	3.2		6.7
Mortgages	44.6	2.1		46.7
Open market paper	10.1	5.3		15.4
Other financial assets	26.6	0.1		26.7
Equities	1,491.4	−6.6	−70.8	1,141.1
Corporate stock	731.3	−11.5	−92.9	626.9
Farm business equity	195.9	−1.5	8.8	203.2
Noncorporate nonfarm equity	317.6	1.5	19.1	338.2
Pension and insurance (cash value)	108.4	4.9	−0.3	113.0
Estates and trusts	138.2		−5.5	132.8
Total assets	3,170.9	86.7	−28.4	3,229.2
Liabilities	424.6	30.8		454.9
Mortgages	257.7	18.6		276.3
Consumer credit	126.9	10.8		137.7
Bank loans, n.e.c.	4.7	1.0		5.7
Other liabilities	35.2	0.0		35.2
Net worth (balance sheet)	2,746.4	56.3	−28.4	2,774.3
Net saving (current account)		58.2		
Capital gains + statistical discrepancy		−1.9		
TOTAL LIABILITIES + NET WORTH	3,170.9	86.7	−28.4	3,229.2

entirely from existing data. This same general framework could be used to present balance sheets and financial transactions for other sectors of the economy.

APPENDIX: FINANCIAL INTERMEDIARIES IN THE NATIONAL ACCOUNTS

The treatment of financial intermediaries is one of the most controversial issues in national income accounting. Generally, the measurement of output of financial intermediaries has been based on the concept of factor cost, viewed as the contribution of the factors of production; it has also been influenced by a concept of material output derived from the classical view of production in Smith, Ricardo and Marx. The approach has generally been of an aggregative nature, which either consolidates out of the system the financial transactions of the individual transactors or in some cases completely ignores them. In many cases, to the extent that the sales of financial intermediaries' services do not reflect factor costs, the market value of sales is not considered to be a correct measure of 'output'. The reconciliation of the receipts side of the account of financial intermediaries with the factor cost side is achieved by consolidating the receipts with claims or the transfers which financial intermediaries pay, and which in national income accounting terms are not considered to be part of output.

This national income accounting view is not fully consistent with the way transaction flows are viewed by individual transactors. If the macroeconomic accounting system is to correspond to the microeconomic accounting of individual transactors, it will be necessary, in a number of cases, to alter the treatment of financial transactions. This appendix examines, in some detail, the transactions relating to insurance, pensions and interest, comparing their present treatment in the national income accounts with the way they would be recorded in individual transactor accounts.

Fire and Casualty Insurance

Fire and casualty insurance is purchased by businesses and households as protection against the possibility of loss. Premiums are paid to insurance companies, which in turn use these funds to pay the claims of the insured suffering casualty losses and to cover the costs and profits of the insurance business.

Purchases by business

In the national accounts, the purchase of fire and casualty insurance by business is treated on a net basis (i.e., the claims paid to business are subtracted from the premiums paid by business). This net premium payment is, of course, by definition also equal to the costs and profits of the insurance companies. The fire and casualty losses are recorded in the national accounts as 'accidental damage to fixed capital', and this is added to capital consumption allowances. Thus, by understating the insurance premiums which business pays and equally overstating capital consumption, two wrongs come out with the correct profits.

In the actual accounts of businesses, these transactions would be recorded differently: insurance premiums paid by business would be considered to be an intermediate cost of goods and services purchased from other enterprises and would not be netted against claims, the claims received by business would be considered capital transactions offsetting the casualty losses, also considered capital in nature, and no addition would be made to capital consumption allowances for accidental damage to fixed capital.

It is apparent that the present national income accounting treatment of insurance transactions would be quite inappropriate for the accounts of the individual transactor. If this treatment were used, businesses suffering no loss would record the cost of insurance as the premiums actually paid, but for those having a loss the cost in insurance would equal 'net premiums', that is, premiums paid less claims received, and could be a sizeable negative flow; at the same time the fire or casualty loss would appear as a large increase in capital consumption allowances. These distortions are due in part to the failure of the national income accounts to achieve a proper separation of current transactions from capital transactions, and in part to a willingness to deal with consolidated accounts for all businesses as a group.

If the transactor's approach to the recording of fire and casualty insurance transactions of business were adopted for the national income accounts, it would not alter the measurement of total GNP. However, it would result in a decline in the product originating in enterprises buying insurance, since the cost of insurance would be considered to be total premiums rather than net premiums. This decline would be exactly offset by an increase in product originating in the insurance sector. Claims paid out would reflect that portion of the insurance sector's output that is paid over to claimants much in the same way that dividends represent payment of profits to stockholders. The transactor approach has the advantage of recognizing at the microlevel that total premiums paid by a firm are a current cost of operation and that casualty losses and reimbursements are adjustments to the capital account and not to current accounts.

Purchases by households
Household purchases of fire and casualty insurance are treated in the national accounts in a manner parallel to the treatment used for business. Households are considered to pay 'net premiums' (i.e., total premiums paid minus claims

received), which are by definition equal to the costs and profits of the insurance companies. However, from the transactor's point of view, it is the total premium that represents a consumer purchase, and again claims received are a capital transaction. The national income accounting approach, by combining a major capital receipt (claims received) with a relatively minor current outlay (premium paid), does violence to an individual household's account. It should be noted, however, that for the case of insurance purchased by households the adoption of the transactor approach would result in an increase in GNP, since now consumer purchases of goods and services will reflect total premiums rather than net premiums paid, and this increase will correspond to an increase in the measure of the output of the fire and casualty insurance companies serving households. From the point of view of opportunity cost and utility theory, such an increase is quite appropriate. What households are purchasing is protection against loss, and the cost of such protection for the individual transactor consists of the full premium payment and not the net premium.

Health Insurance

Health insurance premiums may be paid by employers as fringe benefits for their employees, or they may be paid by households directly. The benefits paid by health insurance companies may consist of either third-party payments to doctors and hospitals for the provision of health care to the beneficiaries, or they may be 'sick-pay' benefits paid directly to beneficiaries.

Purchases by business

In the case of health insurance provided by employers as a fringe benefit to their employees, the premiums paid by employers are considered to be 'other labor income' received by employees in the national income accounts. On the outlay side of the personal income account, employees are then considered to purchase: the services of health insurance companies as measured by their costs and profits, and medical care services as measured by the payments health insurance companies make to doctors and hospitals.

From the employee's point of view, this fringe benefit (health insurance) is not an actual payment of money income. It does not appear on the statement of income and withholding his employer gives him for tax purposes. In most cases employees are quite unaware of the amount of the premium the employer actually pays. Although this fringe benefit could be considered to be imputed income, for any specific employee its valuation poses serious problems: the proper value might bear little or no relation to the premiums paid by the employer. For example, families with more than one wage earner might have unnecessary double coverage. Presumably its value to a single person might be less than to a family. Young employees might value it less than older employees. There does not in fact seem to be more justification for making this imputation than for imputing a value for other fringe benefits, such as subsidized meals, parking, expense accounts, recreational facilities and even pleasant working conditions.

With respect to the administrative costs of health insurance and the costs of medical care provided by doctors and hospitals, the treatment in the national income accounts, if used as a basis for allocation to individual households, would involve gross distortions of income and expenditures. For individuals who were not sick, the cost would reflect only the operating costs of the health insurance companies, and it would appear, contrary to fact, that these individuals receive more 'other labor income' than they pay out in health insurance costs. For individuals who do receive medical care, it would appear that they spend more on medical care than they receive in other labor income. If transactor recording were adopted, employers would be recorded as purchasing health insurance for their employees. This would be reported as health services that enterprises provide their employees as a fringe benefit but would not appear in the employees' account as money income. The health insurance industry in turn would be considered as purchasing health services from doctors and hospitals. From the point of view of GNP and product originating by industry, this treatment would be identical to the current national income accounting treatment. From an aggregative point of view, the difference between the two treatments lies solely in whether employers' health insurance contributions are recorded as other labor income received by individuals, and whether the cost of health insurance and medical care is recorded as actual expenditures paid by individuals.

Sick-pay benefits
Payments of sick pay by health insurance and workmen's compensation are handled in the national income accounts by considering employers' contributions to be other labor income, and considering the costs of health insurance companies and the costs of medical care to be consumer expenditures. The difference between the health contributions included in other labor income and the costs included in consumer expenditures is equal to sick pay paid to individuals and the change in reserves of health insurers and workmen's compensation funds.

The national income accounting treatment contrasts with the transactor recording, which would treat sick pay as an actual payment of income to individuals and would exclude from household income and saving the changes in the reserves of health insurance and workmen's compensation funds. Again the transactor approach to the recording of these transactions would not alter GNP but would alter household income, household saving and changes in reserves held by business enterprises.

Purchases by households

When health insurance is purchased by individuals, the total premiums individuals actually pay are not recorded in the national accounts as consumer expenditures. Instead, the consumer expenditure for health insurance is considered to consist of the costs and profits of the health insurers; the cost of the medical care individuals receive is entered as a separate consumer expenditure. The difference between the premiums actually paid and these two categories of costs represents, as indicated above, the sick pay which is returned to individuals and the change in the reserves of the health insurers.

A transactor recording would require considering the full premium payment as a consumer expenditure of those paying it, and the receipt of sick pay as income of those receiving it. On this basis of recording, the change in the reserves of health insurance companies would be recorded as a change in 'income retained' by them rather than as saving by households.

As in the case of household purchases of fire and casualty insurance, this shift to a transactor basis of recording would result in an increase in GNP. The increase would be equal to the difference between the premiums paid by households and the costs and profits of health insurers and the costs of medical care; looked at in another way it would also be equal to sick pay and the change in the reserves of health insurers. Such an increase is justifiable, since the premiums paid by households represent a bona fide purchase of increased health security, which guarantees medical care and sick pay if and when required.

Life Insurance and Pensions

The treatment of life insurance and pensions in the national accounts follows the general approach described above for health insurance. If life insurance and pension contributions are made by an employer, these contributions are considered part of other labor income and are reflected in personal income. The costs and profits of life insurance companies are considered to measure the amount spent for life insurance and pensions, and the difference between the contributions included in other labor income and the costs of insurance included in consumer expenditures is equal to the life insurance benefits and pensions paid plus the change in the reserves of life insurance companies and pension funds.

Where an individual himself buys life insurance or contributes to pension funds, the premium he pays is not entered in the national accounts as an expenditure — only the costs and profits of the life insurance companies and pension funds are considered to be consumer expenditure. Thus, in this case also, the difference between the premiums actually paid and the costs charged as consumer expenditure equals the life insurance benefits and pensions paid and the change in the reserves of life insurance and pension funds.

In applying transactor criteria to the recording of life insurance and pension transactions, first it must be determined whether the transactions affect the balance sheet of the individual. In the case of term insurance or pension plans that are not vested, no cash surrender value or equity is built up for the individual. If an employer makes life insurance and pension contributions as part of other labor income, this is a fringe benefit. Those who do directly benefit in the current period are those who receive life insurance or pension payments. Life insurance benefits paid in a lump sum to heirs should be recorded in the capital accounts, together with other estate transfers. Life insurance annuities or pensions should be recorded as current income received by households. Individual purchases of term life insurance should be treated in the accounts like household purchases of other casualty insurance.

If life insurance and pension contributions result in an increase in the equity of individuals, this increase should be reflected in the balance sheets and current accounts of individual transactors. An increase in an individual's equity should be reflected in his balance sheet by an increase in the cash surrender value of his insurance and pension policies, but not by some pro rata share of the total reserves of life insurance and pension funds. Similarly, a portion of the premiums paid by individuals represents saving in the current income account of the individual, so that in fact the premium must be split into two elements, current insurance and saving. Aside from these considerations, the premiums paid for life insurance and pension funds and the benefits received should be recorded in transactor accounts as described for term life insurance.

In discussing pensions funds, the United Nations SNA proposes treating unfunded pension funds as if they were funded. This would involve imputing pension contributions for business and deducting them from profits. In effect, a dummy account for nonfunded pension funds would be set up showing the net cumulative imputed pension contributions and the unfunded pension liabilities and reserves. Although information on the liabilities of unfunded pensions is interesting and useful, it does not seem to be appropriate or realistic to treat such imputations as actual transactions.

Interest

There has been extensive and intensive discussion of the treatment of interest in the literature of national accounting, but at the present time there is surprisingly widespread consensus on how interest transactions should be handled in the measurement of the national income aggregates.

The 'net interest' approach

In the US national income accounts the concept of net interest was developed to handle interest transactions. Interest received by business is netted against the interest payments which business makes, yielding their 'net interest' payments. It is apparent that, if a business receives more interest than it pays out, this net interest flow will be negative. Several different rationales can be offered in support of this approach. It can be argued that interest is a payment for a factor of production, and net interest represents the net amount of this factor used by business. It can also be argued, however, that interest payments are not factor payments but, like dividend payments, represent a transfer of the income earned by a business to those having a claim on it. According to this view, interest received by an enterprise is like dividends received by an enterprise: both types of receipts represent income derived from the productive activity of other enterprises. On this basis, the interest any given enterprise receives should be excluded from the measurement of its output (income originating), and this can best be accomplished by omitting the interest received from the product side of the account and subtracting it on the income side from interest paid.

For financial institutions where interest receipts exceed interest payments by substantial amounts, the BEA procedure results in negative product. As a consequence, it has been found useful to recognize that financial institutions provide their depositors with banking services instead of paying interest, and these services, in effect, constitute imputed interest payments. Such imputed interest payments are valued at the cost of providing banking services to depositors. Once such imputations are introduced as part of interest paid by financial institutions, the net interest approach results in an income-originating measurement for financial institutions, which is equal to their costs and profits.

The United Nations approach

The United Nations SNA does not formally adopt a net interest approach, but because it separates production accounts from appropriation accounts the effect is the same. The production account for an enterprise shows on the product side the receipts from the sale of goods and services, and on the cost side the purchases of intermediate goods and services, capital consumption allowances, indirect taxes, compensation of employees and operating surplus. The operating surplus is, of course, a residual reflecting the difference between sales receipts and the costs of sales. It represents that part of factor income which is carried over to the appropriation account and is available for further distribution as income payments.

In the appropriation account of the SNA, other property income received, such as dividends and interest, is added to the operating surplus to show the total amount of income available. The disbursements side of the appropriation account shows the actual payments made. In the measurement of output, these procedures have the same effect as the net interest approach used in the US national income accounts, that is, interest received is excluded from the measurement of output.

Consumer interest payments
Despite the general consensus about the treatment of interest in the national accounts, present practices are at considerable variance with a transactor's approach to the recording of interest transactions in the accounts of households, enterprises and government. For the household account, the present net interest treatment excludes consumer interest as an element of consumer expenditure, and treats it as a transfer. From the point of view of the individual doing the borrowing, however, it is apparent that a useful service is being purchased. In many consumer expenditures, interest charges are implicit in the higher prices merchants charge where easy credit or charge privileges are granted. But, paradoxically, if a consumer discovers that he can buy at a lower price and borrows to finance the purchase, the explicit interest charge is, in the national accounts, excluded from consumer expenditures. The exclusion of consumer interest payments from the purchase of goods and services is usually based on one or more of the following reasons. First, it may be argued that no productive resources are involved in the loaning of money, and interest payments are merely a transfer paid by the borrower to the lender. This argument rests in large part on the proposition that income should be measured in terms of the costs of the factors of production, and interest represents only a redistribution of income and is not in itself a factor of production. Second, it may be argued, from a similar but slightly different point of view, that no real production has taken place and as a consequence there is no operating surplus out of which interest can be paid. Furthermore, since interest payments are considered transfers, payment of interest by consumers does not represent a purchase of goods and services. Finally, it is sometimes argued that the payment of consumer interest is 'unproductive', much in the same sense that Adam Smith argued that the services of domestic servants were unproductive. This view is unquestionably related to the medieval view that money-lenders are engaged in a form of usury that exploits the misery of debtors.

From the point of view of the individual consumers, however, the ability to borrow money, thus making it possible to acquire goods and services, does represent an increase in utility. If market valuations and opportunity cost are to be used to represent the value of goods and services, there is no logical reason from the individual transactor's point of view to exclude consumer interest as a legitimate purchase.

Enterprise interest payments
In the transactor accounts for enterprises, it is of course not customary to subtract interest received from interest paid. In computing operating surplus

an enterprise might exclude interest received, but this would be done to separate the normal business activity of the enterprise from its financial activities. For financial enterprises, where normal business activities are financial, it would be unreasonable to make such a separation. From a transactor point of view, it would be most logical for enterprises to treat their interest transactions as they treat rental receipts and payments. On the receipts side of the account, receipts from rentals are treated as the sale of goods and services; and on the outlay side, payments for rentals are an intermediate cost of goods and services purchased from other enterprises. As a consequence of this treatment of rental receipts and payments, it has been necessary to introduce into the national income accounts a supplementary 'rental income' industry to contain the rental payments made by enterprises to individuals or to enterprises not already classified in other industries. This rental industry does not, of course, include all rental payments, since many rent payments are made to enterprises in other industries. Nor does it reflect the actual use of buildings and equipment, since enterprises owning their own buildings and equipment do not make rental payments. For the rental industry, however, the gross rental payments received represent the value of their sales; after appropriate deductions are made for costs (including interest and taxes), the residual return appears in the national accounts as part of 'rental income of persons'.

This same treatment can also be applied to interest transactions. Interest received by enterprises would be considered to be a sale of goods and services and, like rental payments, all interest paid by enterprises would be considered an intermediate purchase from other enterprises. Under such a treatment it would be necessary to introduce a supplementary 'interest' industry which would be the recipient of interest payments made by enterprises to individuals or companies not already classified in other industries. The gross receipts or sales of this industry would be the interest payments they received, and any costs incurred in connection with the lending of such funds would be deducted before the payment of 'interest income to persons'.

It has been argued that one of the major reasons why interest should not be treated as a cost is that it would misrepresent the 'true' measure of value added or income originating in an industry. This same reasoning has also been applied to the treatment of rental payments — that these also represent part of the income generated within the enterprise. While from a production function point of view it may often be useful to take into account 'rented capital goods', as well as owned capital goods for analyzing capital coefficients, it does not follow that the national income accounts should be constructed solely with this criterion in mind. First, in operational terms it would be extremely difficult to reconstruct enterprise accounts so as to eliminate all rentals and/or purchases which represent the use of capital assets. If this were attempted, furthermore, it would of course be necessary to impute to the enterprises the cost of ownership, including such things as management, taxes, etc. In the case of rentals such as communications or computer services, which include highly sophisticated equipment together with software or other costs, the statistical estimation problems become unmanageable.

Furthermore, from the point of view of the enterprise as a profit-making institution, it is more reasonable to treat both interest and rental payments as intermediate costs of production rather than as part of income originating and/or profits. What gross product originating in an enterprise is supposed to represent is the value which is added to the contributions provided by other enterprises, and to deny that the provision of capital is a contribution is something that only a very conventional national accountant or a Marxist would dare to suggest.

The transactor approach to interest would alter the pattern of income originating in the national income accounts. It would reduce the gross product of the enterprises that borrow, and it would correspondingly increase the gross product of enterprises that lend. One of the major consequences of this change would be that the gross product of financial institutions, without any imputation for imputed interest, would be exactly equal to what is now computed using imputed interest. The reason for this is, of course, that this approach considers the interest received by financial intermediaries to be a sale of goods and services, and, on the cost side, interest paid is included as an intermediate cost. Such a treatment leaves compensation of employees, taxes, capital consumption and profits in gross product originating. This does not necessarily mean that the imputation for banking services should be abandoned; it does mean, however, that it is not required for measuring the gross product in financial institutions and should be justified on grounds similar to imputations for such things as television, radio and other media that are currently paid for largely by advertising expenditures but that do represent a useful product to consumers.

Government interest payments

The final problem with respect to interest transactions lies in the handling of government interest payments. The exclusion of government interest as payment for a productive service is an old and universal tradition in national income accounting. The original justifications were put forth in connection with the government war debt arising from World War I. It was felt that government debt incurred for a past war should not be considered output in later periods. The National Accounts Review Committee reviewed these arguments and generally supported them, but raised a question about the debts of state and local governments that have often been incurred for schools, sanitation systems, parks, roads and public buildings. With respect to the US national income accounts, it has also been argued that government durables are not considered to produce income and, therefore, since there are no real capital services that provide income, it would be inappropriate to count government interest.

Nevertheless, in a market economy it is appropriate to consider that services actually purchased represent output, even if they are in some sense wasted. Thus one does not ask whether a government employee is really worth what he is paid; the fact that he is paid for a service is taken as an indication that the service exists. The difference between a transfer payment and the purchase of services rests on whether some service is performed, not whether the service is used. Thus a pension paid to a soldier differs from current pay to a soldier in that no services are provided in the current period by the soldier receiving the pension whereas the current pay of the soldier represents services made available. Whether the services are in fact used is considered irrelevant.

From this point of view, the holders of government bonds are providing services fully as much as if they had purchased corporate bonds, and government interest payments should be recorded as the purchase of such services. Since government debt is fungible, furthermore, it is not appropriate to distinguish between debt incurred for war purposes, for fiscal policy purposes, or for the purchase of government durables. Those interested in measuring 'real production' or 'economic welfare' can impute any deduction they wish for what they consider to be the nonproductive use of government interest—or for that matter any other nonproductive use of resources.

REFERENCES

Juster, F. Thomas (1973), 'A framework for the measurement of economic and social performance', in Milton Moss (ed.), *The Measurement of Economic and Social Performance*, New York: Columbia University Press for the National Bureau of Economic Research.

Ruggles, Richard and Nancy D. Ruggles (1956), *National Income Accounts and National Income Analysis*, 2nd ed., New York: McGraw-Hill.

Ruggles, Nancy D. and Richard Ruggles (1970), *The Design of Economic Accounts*, New York: Columbia University Press for the National Bureau of Economic Research.

Ruggles, Richard and Nancy D. Ruggles (1973), 'A proposal for a system of economic and social accounts', in Milton Moss (ed.), *The Measurement of Economic and Social Performance*, New York: Columbia University Press for the National Bureau of Economic Research.

10. Integrated Economic Accounts for the United States, 1947–80

Richard Ruggles and Nancy D. Ruggles
Yale University

It is now generally recognized that national accounts have three major functions: they serve as the coordinating and integrating framework for all economic statistics; they give timely and reliable key indicators on the performance of the economy; and they illuminate the relationships among the sectors of the economy that are fundamental to an understanding of its functioning. During the past two decades, both the availability of data for national accounting systems and the uses of these systems have grown.

Two technological factors have altered the supply side. First, the rapid development of sampling theory and survey methodology has changed the way data are collected. Second, the computer has changed the way data are processed, stored and disseminated and has opened up administrative data sources not previously accessible.

At the same time, the increasing complexity of economic and social problems has led to more sophisticated types of analysis, involving both economic and social data. The emphasis of policy and analytic interest has changed from an exclusive focus on aggregate output to questions of distribution, and to social, as well as purely economic, concerns. This changing emphasis has significantly broadened the range of data for which the national accounts can serve as a framework, while the rapidly increasing volume and complexity of the data have intensified the need for a broader framework.

Thus, much has changed since the US national income and product accounts (NIPAs) were developed, and it is appropriate to consider how they can be extended to comprehend the new dimensions. A primary concern should be continuity: that which has already proved itself should be preserved. The aim should be evolution, not revolution; expanded accounts should retain at their

---

This chapter first appeared in *Survey of Current Business*, **62** (5), 1982.

core a set of NIPAs that look familiar and serve the same purposes as the existing accounts.

The purpose of the project on which this article reports was the modification and extension of the existing NIPAs to meet two primary objectives. The first was to improve the national accounting system as a framework for economic and social data at different levels of aggregation, from micro to macro, and embracing stocks as well as flows. The second was to simplify and clarify the presentation of the transaction flows between the sectors and their relation to the major economic constructs. Although, conceptually, such economic and social data are highly interrelated, statistically a number of different bodies of such data have been developed and are commonly used independently of one another. As the data available have grown in quantity and sophistication, gradual steps have been taken toward achieving both conceptual and statistical consistency among these bodies of data. This project is yet another step in that direction.

The report is divided into three sections. Section 1 outlines some of the conceptual issues that have been raised in connection with the BEA national income and product accounts and various possible extensions. Section 2 shows how an integrated economic accounting system can be implemented. Section 3 presents some of the empirical results that emerge from viewing the US economy in the context of the integrated system, directing particular attention to the analysis of saving, capital formation and revaluation. The Appendix discusses questions relating to financial intermediaries.

1. CONCEPTUAL ISSUES

Official work on the measurement of national income and its components was initiated in the Great Depression of the 1930s, and it crystallized into a formal accounting system in 1947 (Carson, 1975). In 1958, the accounting system was reorganized, and the five-account summary system introduced at that time has continued virtually unchanged to the present day. It has served very well as the framework for the ever-expanding body of NIPA statistics. It measures the nation's production, and summarizes the billions of explicit and implicit transactions that occur each year in a way that is comprehensible and useful for a wide range of economic analyses.

Why, then, should any changes in the present accounts be contemplated? As already suggested, the reasons lie in changes in the availability of data and in the analytic uses of the accounts. For instance, the 1958 system was not designed to accommodate data relating to either financial transactions or balance sheets. The flow of funds accounts developed by the Federal Reserve Board to record financial flows and the stock of financial assets and liabilities outstanding have been conceptually reconciled with the aggregates of the BEA national accounting system. However, the two systems remain separate and distinct. BEA has developed reproducible capital stock estimates that are directly related to the NIPAs, because they are based on estimates of purchases of structures and durables and of capital consumption using the perpetual inventory method (US Department of Commerce, 1982). The Federal Reserve has recently used these BEA estimates in conjunction with its own financial assets and liabilities data to produce balance sheets for enterprises and households (Board of Governors, 1980). However, balance sheets for the government sector have not been constructed, nor have the Federal Reserve balance sheets been integrated into the BEA framework. Until the sector income accounts and balance sheets are effectively integrated, the relation between current income measures and changes in balance sheets, and the role of revaluations, will remain murky.

A second area the 1958 system was not designed to accommodate was the size distribution of income: since 1958, both the availability of relevant data and the demand for analyses of income distribution information have increased by an order of magnitude. Until the recent budget stringency, BEA carried out work in this area that involved matching and merging of computer files of microdata, using both exact and statistical matching techniques that were not available in 1958. Although the resulting estimates were aligned with the aggregate estimates of personal income, major conceptual differences remained that prevented the size distribution work from fitting neatly into the NIPA system.

A third area the 1958 system was not designed to accommodate was nonmarket activity. BEA has had until recently a program to develop measures of nonmarket activity within the national accounting framework. The program included studies related to the measurement and valuation of time spent in nonmarket work and leisure, the services of consumer durables, and the services of government capital. The close relationship to the NIPAs has been stressed in this work, but it was not formally integrated.

A review of major conceptual issues involved in constructing a system of economic accounts follows. The issues are arranged in three groups: those relating to the measurement of production, the sectoring of the economy, and the integration of current and capital accounts.

Measurement of Production

The NIPAs are centrally concerned with the questions that are the essence of both macroeconomics and microeconomics: the determination of the level of output, the allocation of resources among competing uses, and the distribution of income to the factors engaged in economic activity. Measurement in all parts of such a vast and complex system as the US economy poses many conceptual and practical problems. BEA, of necessity, has had to resolve these problems. Before considering any extension or modification of the NIPAs, it will be useful to examine briefly the fundamental principles underlying BEA's measurements.

The general form of the national income and product account, which embodies the main measures of output, can be conceived of as a consolidation of the current accounts of nonfinancial enterprises. Complications arise, however, when the current receipts of an enterprise are derived from sources other than the sale of its products (i.e., from subsidies, dividends or interest), or when producers other than nonfinancial enterprises are considered (financial enterprises, government, nonprofit institutions, households and the rest of the world). The first section below presents the simple case. The following three subsections consider the treatment of nonproduction receipts and of types of producers other than nonfinancial enterprises, and problems that arise in defining the production boundary.

The national income and product account

The principles of measuring the output of a nonfinancial corporation that receives all of its income from the sale of its products can be demonstrated using a 'production statement' (Table 10.1). Such a statement resembles an income statement except that it shows the change in inventory, as well as sales, and the costs of production, rather than the costs of goods sold.

Table 10.1 Production Statement for a Nonfinancial Corporation ($000)

Current-account purchases	$120	Sales of products	$275
Depreciation allowances	20	Inventory change	25
Business transfers	5		
Indirect taxes	15		
Compensation of employees	100		
Interest paid	10		
Corporate profits	30		
Corporate profits taxes	*13*		
Dividends paid	*8*		
Undistributed profits	*9*		
Charges against value of production	$300	Value of production	$300

This enterprise's contribution to the nation's total output is the value it adds to the materials and supplies purchased from other producers. This *value added* is measured by subtracting its current-account purchases (i.e., goods and services purchased from other producers on current account) from the value of its production. For the corporation shown in Table 10.1, subtraction of its $120 of current-account purchases from the $300 that is the value of its production yields $180. This is its gross value added — or gross product. A measure of net product can be obtained by using the depreciation allowance as an estimate of the amount of capital consumed ($180 − $20 = $160). These measures, which are based on market price valuations, are not the same as the sum of payments to the factors of production if indirect taxes, such as sales or excise taxes, are levied on a product or if the corporation makes transfer payments, such as gifts to nonprofit institutions. For example, excise taxes on tobacco products and alcoholic beverages cause the sales price of these products to exceed, by a large margin, actual production costs. For the corporation in Table 10.1, subtracting indirect taxes and business transfers from net product at market prices yields net product at factor cost ($160 − $15 − $5 = $140). This same total can, of course, be derived by adding up the earnings of the suppliers of the factors of production — in Table 10.1, the sum of compensation of employees, interest paid and corporate profits ($100 + $10 + $30 = $140). (The production statement for an unincorporated enterprise would differ only in that proprietors' income would appear instead of corporate profits. It should be noted that the factor *cost* measure, which is often used in the analysis of resource allocation, is not actually the factor cost but rather the factor *return*. Factor cost and factor return would be the same only under conditions of perfect competition, perfect knowledge, perfect factor mobility and profit maximization. In practice, the profit share reflects many circumstances other than just the factor contributions of capital and entrepreneurship. Thus lower prices of farm products that are the result of an abundant harvest may well reduce the factor return in farming, although more factor resources may have been used.)

The general form of the national income and product account can be conceived of as a consolidation of the production accounts of individual nonfinancial enterprises like the one shown in Table 10.1. Gross product, net product and factor income at the enterprise level correspond to gross national product (GNP), net national product and national income around which the BEA accounts are constructed. At the national level, the sales of enterprises to one another on current account consolidate out, leaving final sales to consumers, to government and to enterprises on capital account, and net sales to abroad. These add up to GNP at market prices, shown on the right side of the national income and product account. The charges against GNP are shown on the left side in approximately the same categories as shown on the left side of the enterprise production statement.

Nonproduction receipts
Nonproduction receipts of enterprises introduce complexities into the national income and product account because they do not reflect output and, therefore, must be excluded from GNP. However, the exclusion must be done in a way

that does not distort the actual transactions flows. On the product (right) side of the national income and product account, exclusion is a simple matter — nonproduction receipts are simply omitted. On the cost (left) side, exclusion is not so simple — different types of nonproduction receipts are handled in different ways.

Subsidies are often given to enterprises by government so that enterprises can sell their products below cost and still continue to operate. BEA treats subsidies as a negative item on the cost side of the account, similar to indirect taxes (but in the opposite direction), and thus they are a part of the difference between national income at factor cost and GNP at market prices.

Dividends received by enterprises are not the recipient's output: to derive a measure of dividends paid from the enterprise's own output, dividends received are subtracted from dividends paid out.

Interest received by enterprises is treated like dividends received — as a subtraction from the payment — so that net interest paid out by enterprises as a group is shown in the national income and product account.

Other producers

Some problems arise in fitting producers other than nonfinancial enterprises into the same mold. In particular, the market value of production (i.e., sales receipts) cannot be used to measure the output of financial institutions, life insurance companies and pension funds, government, nonprofit institutions, households or the rest of the world. The essence of their treatment is the same in all cases: where output is not sold, and therefore, cannot be valued from the product side of the account, its value is taken to be equal to the costs of producing it.

For *financial institutions* such as banks and savings institutions, the net interest treatment described above eliminates most of their receipts from the product side of the account and creates a large negative net interest item on the cost side. This is not considered to be a valid picture of their actual output. Even though the exchange transaction is an implicit one, these institutions are considered to provide financial services to their depositors. The value of these services is imputed on the product (right) side of the account at an amount equal to the costs (including profits) of providing them. To bring the account into balance, an equivalent net interest paid item is imputed on the cost (left) side.

For *life insurance companies and pension funds*, premiums and contributions are not considered to measure the value of the service being provided, because they may include an element of saving. Here, also, the costs of life insurance companies are taken to measure the value of their services, and only that part of the premiums or contributions paid that is equal to these costs is treated as an expenditure on these services.

For *government*, the value of public goods is imputed, on the product side of the government production account, at an amount that equals the costs of providing the goods. Because the BEA accounts do not include capital formation for government and because the government does not pay taxes, depreciation allowances and indirect taxes are not included. Therefore, the only element of cost remaining after the deduction of purchases from enterprises is the compensation of government employees.

Nonprofit institutions obtain their receipts mainly from contributions, interest and dividends, and they often provide services without equivalent payment. In this case also, costs are used as a basis for measuring the value of the benefits provided. These costs consist of the nondurable goods and services the institutions purchase from enterprises, the compensation of their employees, and the imputed space rental value of the buildings they own for their own use, the last measured by interest and depreciation. Gross product originating (value added) excludes, of course, the goods and services purchased from business and is, therefore, equal to compensation of employees. The gross product arising from the ownership and use of buildings by nonprofit institutions is considered to originate in the real estate industry, in the same way as imputed gross product on owner-occupied housing.

Households employ factors of production, and thus create output, in only one special case: the employment of domestic service workers. Output is measured by the compensation paid to these workers, and this constitutes the gross product originating in households.

In the BEA accounts, the services of owner-occupied housing are not considered to be produced within the household. Rather, these services are treated as imputed purchases by households from fictitious unincorporated businesses. The imputed value of these services (space rent) is set equal to the rents on equivalent tenant-occupied housing. The imputed gross product of owner-occupied housing services is equal to this space rent less expenditures for repairs and maintenance. Gross product includes an imputed net rental income paid to households by the fictitious business; this income is the difference between space rent and the depreciation, repair and maintenance expenditures, property taxes, and mortgage interest incurred by the business.

Rest-of-the-world output is measured by the net factor payments received from abroad, including both the compensation of employees and property income.

Problems of the production boundary

BEA, in defining current-account purchases, closely follows the business accounting practices that are reflected in reports to the Internal Revenue Service, and these practices in turn determine the production boundary. Only a few adjustments are made. BEA reclassifies, as capital, certain outlays that are commonly charged by business to current expense. The depreciation allowances charged for tax purposes are revalued to reflect economic depreciation. Similarly, inventory changes are revalued so that they measure the change in the physical quantity of inventories valued at current prices.

Questions have, however, been raised about this production boundary. Some relate to the classification of market transactions. For example, when new environmental protection regulations were introduced, should the additional expense incurred have been considered an intermediate cost of production and, thus, an increase in the price of existing products, or should it have been treated as an additional output of the system? When government or households directly pay the costs of environmental protection activity, the resources devoted to it are reflected in government or household consumption expenditures, and so in GNP. To some, it does not seem logical that, merely because the society has sometimes succeeded in transferring the cost of pollution abatement and control to the polluter, the measure of output should be lowered. Like government expenditures, these services are provided to the public as a whole, rather than to specific categories of recipients. To count them as final output to be valued at the cost of providing them, environmental services provided by enterprises would have to be treated in a way that is parallel to the treatment of government services, and shown explicitly on the product side of the national income and product account.

The same sort of question has been raised about services provided to consumers without charge by business through advertising-supported media. Radio, television and newspapers are primarily supported by advertising, which is treated in the NIPAs (as in the tax law) as an intermediate product. Yet similar services provided by government or nonprofit institutions — for example, public television — are included in measures of output.

Questions have been raised also about business research and development expenditure, which is treated as a current cost. However, it may be argued that this expenditure represents a significant part of capital formation, and should be so treated.

In contrast to these arguments, which lead to extensions of the production boundary, others lead to its narrowing. It has been suggested that much of what is output in the present accounts is really part of the cost of operating the economic system. Thus many government activities, including police and fire protection, street cleaning, road maintenance and general administrative costs, may be considered to be intermediate. Even a substantial part of household expenditures, including commuting expenses and medical care, may be considered intermediate.

The controversy over what is intermediate and what is final product raises philosophical questions that are not easily resolved. But the national accounting system should provide enough information so that different measures can be constructed by users desiring them. This suggests that it would be useful to show separately in the accounts the categories of transactions about which questions have been raised, such as those relating to environmental cost, advertising and commuting.

Other questions about the production boundary extend beyond matters of reclassification of market transactions. In the view of some, it would be desirable to develop imputations for some kinds of nonmarket activity not now included in output. It is argued that housewives' services and do-it-yourself activities, for example, make a contribution to output that should be measured. Doing so, however, raises many problems. Accurate and valid measurements of the quantity of activity are difficult to obtain, and valuation poses serious conceptual problems. Should housewives' services be valued in terms of what they would cost if they were purchased, or in terms of what the opportunity cost is to the person carrying out the activity? What differentiates work from leisure, and how should leisure be valued, if at all?

The BEA accounts do include a number of nonmarket imputations, such as those for the value of food and fuel produced and consumed on farms and the rental value of owner-occupied housing and of buildings owned by nonprofit institutions. These imputations also raise problems of valuation, and it is not clear that the solutions chosen are always appropriate. In housing, for example, many owner-occupant costs reflect the purchase prices and mortgages of an earlier period. It is not obvious that the current market rental value is an appropriate shadow price in this case, any more than it would be appropriate to substitute shadow market rentals for the rents that are actually paid for rent-controlled apartments. The fictitious enterprise device used by BEA to remove owner-occupied housing from the household sector introduces a considerable element of arbitrary judgment. The household does not consider that it pays itself a rental-equivalent return as a part of its consumer expenditures, and contrary to what is indicated by the imputation, it does pay property taxes and mortgage interest. The tax preferences relating to property taxes and mortgage interest would certainly influence the valuation the owner places on the return to his home, and the valuations would be different for individuals in different income tax brackets.

In view of the inherent difficulties in imputing values to nonmarket activities, it would seem useful wherever imputations are made to recognize the imputed value as a different kind of statistical estimate by separating nonmarket activities from market transactions in the accounts.

Sectoring

It is the sector accounts in the five-account summary system — the accounts for persons, government, and the rest of the world in its transactions with the

United States plus the implicit account for business — that have provided the framework for integrating economic data from different sources and presenting the network of transactions flows in the economic system. As has already been noted, there have been major changes in both the supply and use of data since the sector accounts were developed, and it is important to consider the sectoring of the economy in the context of these changes.

Integration of economic and social data
By integrating data from a wide variety of sources — such as Census Bureau industrial censuses and business surveys, the Internal Revenue Service tabulations of tax returns, the Social Security Administration reports on wages and salaries, and the Bureau of Labor Statistics information on employment, wages and prices — into consistent estimates of transactions flows, BEA has managed to construct a comprehensive overview of the economy that cannot be obtained from any single source of basic data. At the same time, the sector accounts show how the different parts of the economy reported on in different sources are related to one another.

The present sector accounts do not, however, encompass all economic and social data; they are concerned only with current economic transactions viewed at a fairly aggregate level. It is increasingly recognized that the most promising approaches to the broader question of the integration of economic, social, and demographic data are those that take the NIPAs as the starting point for a wider data framework. Working outward and extending the framework of the national accounts to accommodate new kinds of data and different levels of aggregation seems to be an appropriate strategy. The ultimate objective should be an overall statistical system that would embrace economic, social, demographic and environmental data at all levels of aggregation. For the present discussion, it will be useful to focus on the appropriateness of the sector accounts as a framework for integrating the transactions flows in the NIPAs with economic, social and demographic microdata relating to individuals, governments and enterprises, and to consider how the sector definitions might be modified to serve this function better.

One of the most striking statistical developments over the last 20 years has been the increasing availability of microdata relating to individuals. These microdata sets have come from a wide variety of sources, including tax records, social security records, censuses of population and housing and specialized household surveys. In microunit form, these records often contain not only economic data, but also a wealth of demographic and social data, and they have been used for a broad range of studies relating to the tax system, social security, income distribution, employment behavior, etc.

Microdata sets for individuals and households often contain information on transactions that should conceptually be equivalent to similar transactions in the aggregate accounts. Yet, in practice, aggregations of microdata are often inconsistent with the corresponding national accounts estimates. Household surveys, for instance, seriously underestimate both the transfers that individuals receive from government and the dividends and interest that they receive from enterprises. For this reason, distributions of income using household survey microdata alone seriously underreport income in both the lowest and highest brackets of the income distribution relative to that shown for the middle brackets. Furthermore, it is difficult to make direct comparisons between microdata for individuals and households and the corresponding data in the aggregate accounts, because the personal sector is defined differently from the universes for the microdata sets. The BEA personal account contains not just households, but also nonprofit institutions serving individuals — churches, universities, hospitals and even insurance companies such as Blue Cross and Blue Shield. To align the macrodata and microdata, the NIPAs would need to show separately a household sector composed solely of units consistent with the household definition of the Census of Population.

For governmental units, microunit data are available for the various agencies of the federal government and the budgetary units of state and local governments. These data correspond closely to the BEA government sector when they are adjusted for such factors as differences between cash and accrual accounting and between fiscal and calendar years, and the treatment of capital transactions and intergovernmental transfers. These adjustments must be carried out at the microunit level rather than through the use of bridge tables at the macrodata level, so that the microdata can be used to generate statistics for intermediate levels of aggregation that are fully consistent with the macrodata sector accounts.

Enterprise microdata are also becoming increasingly available. Securities and Exchange Commission quarterly financial reports on corporations have been available for many years and are widely used. Now other government agencies also maintain microdata sets in computerized form relating to enterprises and their establishments, and these microdata sets could provide the basis for constructing more detailed subsector information for many parts of the enterprise sector.

The sectoring and subsectoring of the economy should take into consideration both the sources of data and the potential uses of the estimates. In some instances, established reporting systems, some of which already produce microdata sets, may provide an appropriate basis for defining subsectors that are useful for policy-relevant analysis. In other instances, however, it may be desirable to alter established reporting systems so that they can more adequately cover what would be logical and analytically useful subsectors of the economy.

It should be emphasized that the integration of microdata with the sector accounts does not imply that the sector accounts should be aligned with or derived from any single microdata set. The macrodata accounts, drawing upon many different sources, provide the control totals to which a variety of microdata sets can be aligned. Conceptual consistency between the sector accounts and the corresponding microunit information would make it possible to move back and forth among the different levels of aggregation and among related types of economic, social and demographic data.

The network of transactions flows

The sector accounts have been very successful in providing an overview of the transactions flows in the economy and summaries of the transactions data contained in the more detailed statistical tables. The amount of detail provided has been continually expanded. Nevertheless, some questions can still be raised about the treatment of specific categories of transactions.

In some instances, transactions that are important for particular sectors are consolidated out of the sector account entirely. For example, private pension benefits do not appear in the personal account, because private pension fund reserves are classified in the personal sector, with the result that transactions between households and pension funds consolidate out.

In other instances, imputations are made that the transactors of a sector would not recognize as transactions in which they were involved. For example, some of the fringe benefits provided to households by employers, the financial services provided by banks, and the interest earned on the reserves of pension funds are imputed as part of employee compensation or personal interest income, although the households to which they are attributed may be completely unaware of them. Similarly, some of the expenditures that employers make on behalf of their employees and the costs of providing financial services to depositors are recorded as consumer expenditures, although they would not be so considered by the consuming households. It has already been pointed out that for owner-occupied housing it is the imputed rental value that is included in consumer expenditure; the actual transactions relating to home maintenance, property taxes and mortgage interest are not.

It is essential to recognize that imputed transactions are different in nature from actual transactions and that, for many types of analysis, combining imputed flows with actual transactions flows in the sector accounts may impede analysis. While BEA does provide supplementary tables showing monetary and imputed interest flows and the imputations in the NIPAs, these tables are rather complex, somewhat bewildering, and difficult to relate to the transactions flows recorded in the sector accounts.

The question of whether a given transaction should be considered to be imputed does not always have an unambiguous answer. Some transactions that are not actually made by a given transactor would nevertheless be generally recognized as transactions in which he is engaged, albeit through an agent. For example, even though an employer acts as the taxpayer's agent in withholding income taxes from wages and paying them directly to the Internal Revenue Service, it is appropriate to consider taxes withheld as actually paid by the employee. Similarly, income reported on wage and tax (W-2) statements, which are used to report employee income for tax purposes, includes, in principle, some wages in kind (e.g., food, clothing and lodging furnished by the employer). It is appropriate to include their value in both wages and consumer expenditures. Yet, similar items may be provided in such a form (e.g., expense account meals, uniforms and hotel expenses) that the employee would clearly exclude them from both income and consumer expenditures. For some kinds of fringe benefits, furthermore, employees may be completely unaware of the costs involved, or consider them 'public goods'. Thus recreational facilities provided by an employer would not generally be considered by employees to enter either income or consumer expenditures.

The decision on classifying a transaction as actual or imputed will, in the last analysis, depend largely on how those involved view it. This view, in turn, will depend on such institutional factors as Internal Revenue Service rulings and withholding, as shown on payroll records, and on the general awareness of the actual costs and benefits by the transactors involved. Merely because it is occasionally difficult to draw a precise line does not mean, however, that such distinctions should not be made. For many kinds of analysis the distinction is important, and it should be shown in the sector accounts.

Integration of Current and Capital Accounts

The BEA five-account system includes a gross saving and investment account. Its gross capital formation consists of only two elements: gross private domestic investment, which appears as a final expenditure in the national income and product account, and net foreign investment, which appears in the foreign transactions account as the difference between payments to and receipts from foreigners. Its saving items are more numerous and somewhat more complex. They are the net saving carried out by each of the sectors, capital consumption allowances and additional items consisting of the difference between wage accruals and disbursements, capital grants received by the United States, and the statistical discrepancy.

The gross saving and investment account completes the double entry of transactions flows in the five-account system, showing all of the items that are not balanced by entries in the other four accounts. For example, gross private domestic investment is, in the national income and product account, a sale by the producers of capital goods; it is not balanced by a purchase in the current accounts, but by a purchase in the gross saving and investment account. The saving in each sector current account is the portion of current income not used for current outlays, and, accordingly, there is no balancing transaction in the current accounts; the balancing entry is in the gross saving and investment account.

Gross private domestic investment is defined in the BEA accounts as the sum of the fixed capital goods (structures and producers' durables) purchased by private domestic businesses plus the change in their inventories. Investment encompasses only what is embodied in the value of reproducible tangible assets. Thus an architect's fees embodied in the cost of a building are included, but research and development expenditures, which are not embodied in any particular physical asset, are not.

The BEA definition of gross capital formation is restricted to purchases by private domestic business, i.e., no capital formation is recognized for either government or households. Government purchases of structures and durable goods are treated as current expenditures. Household purchases of residential structures are considered to be purchases by fictitious unincorporated enterprises, and so appear in business capital formation. Household purchases of automobiles and other durables are treated as current expenditures.

The sector saving figures, which are derived as residual balancing items, have no transactions content. While the transactors in the sectors do engage in capital transactions, these are not shown in the BEA accounts.

Capital formation of government and households

The national accounting systems used by most international organizations, as well as those used by most countries, do provide for government capital formation. In all of these systems, the construction of buildings, the purchase of durable goods, and the accumulation of strategic inventories by the government are considered to be capital formation. (Defense goods, however, are generally considered to be current expenditures, whether durable or not.) BEA does identify federal as well as state and local government expenditures for structures and durable goods, and has generated, by the perpetual inventory method, estimates of the stock of these assets and the related capital consumption. Although these stock and capital consumption estimates have not as yet been incorporated in the BEA accounts, no major accounting problem prevents their incorporation.

For households, as was suggested above, much can be said for treating the purchase of owner-occupied houses as a capital transaction of households. Among the advantages is that owner-occupied houses could then be counted as an asset in the balance sheet of households. The necessary data exist in both macrodata and microdata form. For consumer durables also, the figures exist. BEA has computed the stock of these assets, the capital consumption allowances for them, and the value of the services they provide (Katz and Peskin, 1980). The stock and capital consumption data are in fact incorporated in the flow of funds table on capital transactions of the household sector, and it would be relatively simple to incorporate them into the BEA accounts.

From an analytical point of view, information on government and household capital formation and stocks is useful for many problems. Estimates of government capital formation are particularly important for international comparisons.

The nature of capital accounts

Capital accounts can be viewed as having three components: balance sheets, which record the stock of assets and liabilities; capital transactions accounts, which record transactions in assets and liabilities; and revaluation accounts, which record the change in the value of existing assets and liabilities due to price changes. Year-to-year changes in the balance sheet can be fully accounted for by changes recorded in the capital transactions accounts and in the revaluation accounts. Because the different components of the capital accounts are closely related, it is important that they have the same coverage, be based on a common system of classification, and employ consistent valuation principles.

The question of valuation is particularly difficult. A number of different valuations could be used: historical cost, current market, constant price, or discounted stream of future returns. Historical cost valuation has the advantage of reflecting the transaction values relevant to the decision to acquire an asset or liability. Its disadvantage is that the valuation on the balance sheet is dependent on when a particular asset or liability was acquired and how prices at the time of acquisition differ from present prices. Valuation in current market prices may, in some cases, be more difficult to estimate, but it is usually more meaningful. Market valuations are generated in two ways: by adjusting acquisition cost (and depreciation in the case of assets) to reflect the price changes that have occurred since the acquisition of the assets and liabilities, and by directly observing prices of particular assets and liabilities in the current period. Constant price valuation of certain balance sheet items is also useful for many types of analysis, for instance, analysis of changes in the quantity of tangibles owned by a sector.

Finally, economic theory suggests that assets and liabilities could be valued in terms of their discounted expected future returns. However, the stream of future returns would have to be estimated and appropriate discount rates would have to be selected. Because of the uncertainty attached to both of these, estimates of discounted expected future returns are difficult to make and to interpret. Because different individuals have different information available to them and value risk differently, the estimates of present value of expected future returns will vary. Furthermore, once discounted future returns are admitted as a basis for valuing tangible assets, it becomes logical to count as an asset anything that is expected to produce such a stream of future returns, so that the scope of what must be considered capital is greatly expanded. Human capital (in forms such as education and work experience) and rights to income (such as pensions and insurance, social security payments, and welfare and health benefits) would all need to be included, although as assets they may have no current market value and usually cannot be transferred. On the liabilities side of the account, future expected costs such as maintenance and even future expected illness would have to be allowed for. In light of these considerations, it is reasonable to suggest that, for intangible assets with no market value, it is illuminating to estimate value based on discounted future returns, but it must be recognized that these valuations are different from market valuations.

2. THE INTEGRATED ACCOUNTS

Relation of the Integrated Economic Accounts to the BEA System

The integrated economic accounts (IEAs) presented in this report do not constitute a new system; rather they are a further development of the BEA system. The changes that were made can be classed in five broad categories.

Modification of the sectoring

A few relatively minor modifications of the sectoring of the BEA system were made. The most important is redefinition of the personal sector to exclude nonprofit institutions. This redefinition leaves the personal income and outlay account with only the income and outlay of individuals and households. Defined in this way, it corresponds in principle to the group of transactors represented by a comprehensive microdata set of households.

Another sectoring modification sets up the enterprise sector and its subsectors explicitly. The enterprise sector is not shown separately in the BEA five-account system, although BEA provides national income by legal form of organization (BEA Table 1.14) and, in other tables, additional transactions detail by industry for both corporate and noncorporate enterprises. The sectoring and subsectoring used by the Federal Reserve in the flow of funds accounts corresponds closely to these BEA classifications by legal form of organization. By combining the BEA and Federal Reserve classifications, a consistent system of sectoring and subsectoring can be developed, as shown below.

    Enterprise sector
        Nonfinancial
            Corporate nonfarm

    Noncorporate nonfarm
    Farm
    Government enterprises
    Nonprofit institutions
  Financial
    Monetary authority
    Commercial banking
    Other banking
    Pensions and insurance
    Government financial agencies
    Other financial institutions
  Household sector
  Government sector
    Federal
    State
    Local
  Rest-of-the-world sector

Redefinition of capital formation
The definition of capital formation is broadened to recognize capital formation by households and government. This change does not pose either statistical or analytical difficulties. BEA now compiles stock and flow estimates of government and household outlays for structures, durables and inventories in a form that can be directly integrated with both the current accounts and the balance sheets.

Separation of nonmarket activity
Imputed valuations of nonmarket activity, e.g., the rental value of owner-occupied housing, are very different in nature from imputed valuations that reflect actual transactions, e.g., the cost of providing imputed financial services. As noted earlier, the valuation of nonmarket activity is speculative, and generally must be based on analogy with the market value of similar activity taking place elsewhere in the economy. Nonmarket imputations also pose two other types of problem. First, it is difficult to decide just where to draw the production boundary: there is increasing pressure to include such things as changes in environmental conditions and the nonmarket activity taking place within the household. Second, if imputed valuations for nonmarket activities are combined with actual transactions in the accounts, the accounts may be less useful for fiscal and monetary policy. An appropriate solution to these problems would be to show the nonmarket imputations that are included in the accounts separately from the actual transactions flows. In the IEAs, the following activities are shown separately as nonmarket imputations: nonprofit building

rent, owner-occupied housing, margins on owner-built homes, household durables consumed, farm income in kind and government durables consumed.

Reclassification of intersectoral transactions flows

Sector accounts generally record transactions in which the transactors of that sector are directly engaged. As has been noted, however, BEA has some imputations that show indirect involvement by a sector in the related market activities of other sectors. These imputations, while useful for some types of analysis, do obscure actual transactions flows. For many purposes, it is unrealistic to impute to individuals transactions about which they have little or no knowledge.

In light of these considerations, the IEAs record transactions in the sector accounts in a way that reflects the actual flows that occurred. First, for the holder of insurance and pension rights (both for private and government employees), the IEAs record the increase in cash value in his accounts, rather than the total increases in reserves accruing to the insurance companies and pension funds. Second, many fringe benefits provided by employers to employees are treated as a form of 'public good'; this treatment relegates the influence of these benefits to the same category as other situational variables like pleasant working conditions, rather than treating them as part of the employee's income or expenditure.

Third, transactions relating to owner-occupied housing (i.e., housing repairs, property taxes and mortgage interest payments) are recorded by the IEAs in the household current account rather than as activities of an unincorporated business enterprise. Finally, the assets and liabilities held by estates and trusts are considered to be held by financial institutions and only the net equity in such estates and trusts is reflected in the balance sheets of households.

Establishment of integrated current and capital accounts for sectors

To construct a consistent integrated system of accounts that includes stocks of structures, durables and inventories in the balance sheets of all sectors, expenditures for these assets must be designated as capital transactions in all sectors and excluded from sector consumption expenditures. The BEA system must be altered to show an explicit separation of the current and capital accounts of households and government.

By definition, capital transactions refer to changes in assets — financial and tangible — and liabilities. But capital transactions are not the only source of changes in balance sheets; revaluations are another source. For this reason, explicit sector revaluation accounts are useful. The revaluation accounts together with the capital transactions accounts show all of the changes in the value of assets and liabilities on the balance sheets.

Current Accounts

There are five current accounts in the IEAs and, with the exception of the account of the enterprise sector, each is similar in structure to its counterpart in the BEA summary five-account system. (In the BEA system, an account for the enterprise sector is not shown separately.) Some of the transactions flows differ, however, and these differences will be described in the following review of the transactions content of the major line items. For each account, its structure is brought out by explaining a 'basic' account, i.e., an account that presents transactions flows in highly aggregated form. Then there follows a description of the account in the full transactions detail that brings out the relation among the sector accounts.

The GNP account

The GNP account drawn up for the IEAs corresponds closely to the BEA national income and product account. Its role, however, is somewhat different. Because an explicit enterprise sector account has been introduced, the GNP account is no longer needed as part of the balancing system of sector accounts. Instead, it provides an overview of economic activity derived by consolidating the sector current accounts.

The basic account Table 10.2 is in three segments. In the first, the right side of the account shows the final uses of the gross domestic product: current consumption expenditures, gross capital formation, and net sales to the rest of the world. The left side shows the charges against gross domestic product. Two sources of gross product are given: enterprises (including government enterprises and nonprofit institutions) and government. Government product is shown net rather than gross because it does not include any allowance for the capital consumption of government structures and durables.

Table 10.2 Gross National Product Account, 1978 ($bn)

Charges against:			
Enterprise gross product	1,760.6	Current consumption expenditures	1,346.7
Government product	229.2	Gross capital formation	673.6
		Sales to rest of the world, net	−30.5
Charges against gross domestic product (market transactions)	**1,989.8**	**Gross domestic product (market transactions)**	**1,989.8**
Factor income from the rest of the world, net	29.2	Factor income from rest of the world, net	29.9
Charges against GNP (market transactions)	**2,019.8**	**GNP (market transactions)**	**2,019.8**
Charges against imputed nonmarket gross product	398.9	Imputed nonmarket outlays	398.9
Charges against GNP (market and nonmarket)	**2,418.7**	**GNP (market and nonmarket)**	**2,418.7**

Gross domestic product is defined as the output produced within the geographic boundaries of the United States. In addition, US enterprises and individuals may be paid factor income by the rest of the world or pay factor income to the rest of the world. These net factor incomes are shown on both sides of the account on the right, measuring output, and on the left, measuring income; they constitute the difference between gross domestic product and GNP, which is shown in the second segment. The third segment shows the imputed outlay and imputed income that arise from including nonmarket activity in output and income.

Table IEA 1.1, The gross national product account This table gives content to the broad aggregates shown in Table 10.2. The definitions of some of the flows in the GNP account of the IEAs are significantly different from those in the BEA national income and product account. Current consumption expenditures (IEA 1.1 line 1) and gross capital formation (line 12) are different from BEA's definitions of, respectively, personal consumption expenditures and gross private domestic investment.

For current consumption expenditures, it should be noted, first, that enterprise consumption expenditures (IEA 1.1 line 2) are explicitly recognized, and consist of: employee benefits in kind, nonprofit benefits in kind and financial services in kind. The IEAs treat employee benefits in kind (line 3) as expenditures made by employers on behalf of their employees. Nonprofit benefits in kind (line 4) are included by BEA as part of personal consumption expenditures because BEA's personal sector includes nonprofit institutions. When nonprofit institutions are removed from the household sector, the benefits they provide must be shown separately. Financial services in kind (line 5) in the BEA accounts are recorded as imputed interest paid to individuals and government and, consequently, as expenditures by them. In the IEAs, these imputations are excluded from both the income and the expenditures of households and government.

Second, the current consumption expenditures shown for households (IEA 1.1 line 6) and government (line 9) exclude these sectors' expenditures on capital formation. The items included in the BEA expenditures but excluded from current consumption expenditures in the IEAs are, for households, durable goods expenditures (line 19) and change in inventories (line 20) and, for government, expenditures on structures (line 22), expenditures on equipment (line 23), and change in inventories (line 24).

For capital formation, the IEA concept of gross capital formation (IEA 1.1 line 12) is, of course, very much larger than BEA gross private domestic investment, because it includes both household capital formation (lines 19 plus 20) and government capital formation (line 21). Enterprise capital formation (line 13), however, is somewhat smaller than BEA gross private domestic investment, because owner-occupied houses, which BEA considers to be business investment, have been reclassified to be part of household capital formation (line 18).

Net sales to the rest of the world (IEA 1.1 line 25) differs from BEA's net exports of goods and services in that it excludes net factor income from the rest of the world. Showing the latter (line 29) separately makes it possible to show both gross domestic product (line 28) and GNP (line 30). BEA shows gross domestic product only in the supporting tables.

Table IEA 1.1 shows imputations for nonmarket activity separately (line 31) from the measurements based on market transactions, to permit the expansion of nonmarket imputations without obscuring analysis of other transactions. In addition to the imputations made by BEA, imputations have been made for the services of consumer durables (line 37) and the capital consumption of structures and durables owned by government (line 40). Estimates of the value of these items are available in BEA's work on nonmarket activity and on stocks of tangible capital assets. The other imputations are as estimated by BEA for Table BEA 8.8. The services of owner-occupied housing (line 35), for example, is equal to BEA's imputed space rent of owner-occupied housing less the costs of its repair and maintenance. Household expenditures on repair and maintenance are excluded because they are already in market consumption expenditures. Similarly, the margin on owner-built houses (line 36) is shown as an imputed expenditure by households.

The charges against gross domestic product (IEA 1.1 line 56) are divided into those arising in enterprises (line 42) and government (line 54). The breakdown for enterprises shows how the product generated is allocated among compensation of employees, net interest, proprietors' income, rental income, net dividends, indirect taxes and nontaxes, corporate profits taxes, surplus of government enterprises and net transfers (lines 43–51). Enterprise gross saving (line 52) is determined residually, and shows the portion of enterprise product that is not paid out to other sectors. Receipts of enterprises not arising from their productive activity (i.e., interest, dividends and transfers) have been netted against the same category of payments made by enterprises, following the BEA practice. The BEA statistical discrepancy (line 53) has been allocated to the enterprise sector. Charges against government product consist entirely of employee compensation(line 55). This treatment accords with the BEA definition.

Net factor income from the rest of the world (IEA 1.1 line 57, equal to line 29) constitutes the difference between the charges against gross domestic product (line 56) and the charges against GNP (line 60). Similar charges against imputed nonmarket gross product (line 61) equal imputed nonmarket outlays (line 31) and represent the difference between the charges against GNP (market transactions) (line 60) and the charges against GNP (market and nonmarket transactions) (line 71).

Sample Table 1.1 Gross National Product Account ($bn)

	Line	1978		Line	1978
Current consumption expenditures	1	$1,346.7	Charges against enterprise gross product	42	$1,760.6
Enterprises	2	139.2	Compensation of employees	43	1,070.5
Employee benefits in kind	3	62.3	Net interest	44	20.6
Nonprofit benefits in kind	4	42.5	Proprietors' income	45	112.2
Financial services in kind	5	34.4	Rental income	46	17.5
Households	6	829.4	Net dividends	47	34.3
Nondurable goods	7	508.8	Indirect taxes and nontaxes	48	151.9
Services	8	320.6	Corporate profits taxes	49	83.0
Government	9	378.1	Surplus of government enterprises	50	5.9
Purchases	10	148.8	Net transfers	51	−30.6
Compensation of employees	11	229.2	Enterprise gross saving	52	289.0
Gross capital formation	12	673.6	Statistical discrepancy (BEA)	53	6.4
Enterprises	13	289.1	Charges against government product	54	229.2
Structures	14	111.6	Compensation of employees	55	229.2
Equipment	15	164.9			
Change in inventories	16	22.6			
Households	17	309.4			
Owner-occupied houses	18	94.5			
Durable goods	19	199.3			
Change in inventories	20	15.4			
Government	21	65.1			
Structures	22	27.8			
Equipment	23	31.0			
Change in inventories	24	6.2			
Sales to rest of the world, net	25	−30.5			
Sales to rest of the world	26	176.1			
Less: Purchases from rest of the world	27	206.6			

Gross domestic product (market transactions)	28	$1,989.8	Charges against gross domestic product (market transactions)	56	$1,989.8
Factor income from rest of the world, net	29	29.9	Factor income from rest of the world, net	57	29.9
			Factor income received	58	43.8
			Less: Factor income paid	59	13.8
GNP (market transactions)	**30**	**$2,019.8**	**Charges against GNP (market transactions)**	**60**	**$2,019.8**
Imputed nonmarket outlays	31	398.9	Charges against imputed nonmrkt gross product	61	398.9
Enterprises	32	7.1	Enterprises	62	7.1
Nonprofit building rent	33	7.1	Nonprofit building rent	63	7.1
Households	34	342.6	Households	64	342.6
Owner-occupied housing	35	126.9	Gross income on owner-occupied housing	65	126.9
Margins on owner-built houses	36	1.7	Margins on owner-built houses	66	1.7
Durables consumed	37	213.4	Gross income on durables	67	213.4
Farm income in kind	38	0.6	Farm income in kind	68	.6
Government	39	49.2	Government	69	49.2
Capital consumption of structures/durables	40	49.2	Capital consumption of structures/durables	70	49.2
GNP (market and nonmarket)	**41**	**$2,418.7**	**Charges against GNP (market and nonmarket)**	**71**	**$2,418.7**

Table IEA 1.2, Relation of national income, net national product, and gross national product This table gives the transactions flows that add up to national income and the adjustments needed to derive net national product and GNP. Because this table begins with the net aggregates at factor prices (in contrast to the gross aggregates at market prices of the preceding table), enterprise income originating (IEA 1.2 line 1) differs from charges against enterprise gross product in that indirect taxes, net transfers, current surplus of government enterprises, capital consumption allowances and the statistical discrepancy are excluded. It should be noted that retained enterprise income is equal to enterprise gross saving minus enterprise capital consumption; these concepts are explained below in connection with the enterprise current account.

Sample Table 1.2 Relation of National Income, Net National Product, and Gross National Product ($bn)

	Line	1978
Plus: Enterprise income originating	1	$1,416.7
Compensation of employees	2	1,070.5
Net interest	3	20.6
Proprietors' income	4	112.2
Rental income	5	17.5
Net dividends	6	34.3
Corporate profits taxes	7	83.0
Retained enterprise income	8	78.6
Plus: Government income originating	9	229.2
Compensation of employees	10	229.2
Plus: Rest-of-the-world originating, net	11	29.9
Factor income from rest of the world	12	43.8
Less: Factor income paid to rest of the world	13	13.8
Plus: Imputed nonmarket income originating	14	−139.9
Nonprofit building rent	15	1.5
Owner-occupied housing	16	65.8
Margins on owner-built houses	17	1.7
Consumer durables	18	70.3
Farm income in kind	19	.6
Equals: National income (at factor prices)	20	**$1,815.8**
Plus: Indirect taxes and nontaxes	21	178.1
Plus: Enterprise transfer payments	22	8.7
Plus: Net surplus of government enterprises	23	3.1
Less: Subsidies	24	−9.4
Plus: Statistical discrepancy	25	6.4
Equals: Net national product (at market prices)	26	**$1,996.4**
Plus: Capital consumption allowances	27	422.4
Enterprise capital consumption	28	180.6
Nonprofit-owned buildings	29	5.6
Owner-occupied housing	30	35.0
Consumer durables	31	143.1
Government structures and durables	32	58.2
Equals: GNP (market and nonmarket)	33	**$2,418.7**

Government income originating (line 9) and net factor income from the rest of the world (line 11) are the same as in Table IEA 1.1. Imputed income originating (net) in nonmarket activity (line 14) includes the items included in national income by BEA plus the net imputed value of the services of consumer durables (line 18). Consequently, national income (line 20) is larger than BEA's national income by the amount of these services.

Net national product at market prices (IEA 1.2 line 26) is obtained from national income by adding indirect taxes, enterprise transfer payments (net), net surplus of government enterprises, and the BEA statistical discrepancy, and subtracting subsidies (lines 21–25).

Finally, the difference between net national product at market prices and GNP (IEA 1.2 line 33) is capital consumption allowances (line 27). GNP as shown here exceeds BEA's GNP by the amount of gross income from consumer durables (lines 18 plus 31) and capital consumption of government structures and durables (line 32).

The enterprise current account

The current account for the enterprise sector represents a consolidation of the production accounts for all enterprises in the economy. 'Enterprises' include not only corporate and noncorporate private businesses, but also government enterprises and private nonprofit institutions.

The basic account In Table 10.3, the right side of the account shows enterprise gross product in terms of the net sales to different sectors of the economy. These sales represent the market value of output produced by the enterprise sector, and include capital purchases and changes in inventories as well as purchases for current consumption. The left side of the account, showing enterprise current outlays and gross saving, is identical to charges against enterprise gross product (IEA 1.1 line 42). On both sides of the account, market transactions and nonmarket imputations are shown separately. Nonmarket outlays, by definition, equal nonmarket sales.

Table IEA 1.10, Enterprises gross product account The elements of enterprise gross product (market and nonmarket) (IEA 1.10 line 30) have already been discussed in connection with Table IEA 1.1. The components of enterprise current outlays and gross saving (line 86), however, are given in considerably greater detail here so that they articulate with the transactions flows in the other sector accounts. Compensation of employees (line 31), for example, is broken down into five transactions flows (lines 32–37): wages and salaries (paid to households); social insurance contributions (paid to government); pension and other payments (paid to households); benefits in kind (provided to households); and compensation paid to the rest of the world.

Sample Table 1.10 Enterprise Gross Product Account ($bn)

	Line	1978		Line	1978
Sales to enterprises	1	$438.3	Compensation of employees	31	$1,070.5
Current purchases, net	2	139.2	Wages and salaries	32	908.2
Employee benefits in kind	3	62.3	Social insurance contributions	33	64.3
Nonprofit benefits in kind	4	42.5	Other labor income	34	97.6
Financial services in kind	5	34.4	Pension and other payments	35	35.3
Capital purchases	6	299.1	Benefits in kind	36	62.3
Structures	7	111.6	Compensation paid to rest of the world	37	0.5
Equipment	8	164.9	Net interest	38	20.6
Change in inventories	9	22.6	Interest paid	39	154.9
Sales to households	10	1,125.8	Households	40	109.7
Current purchases	11	816.3	Nonprofit institutions	41	2.7
Nondurable goods	12	507.1	Rest of the world	42	8.0
Services	13	309.2	Financial services in kind	43	34.4
Capital purchases	14	309.4	Less: Interest received	44	134.3
Owner-occupied houses	15	94.7	Households	45	90.4
Durable goods	16	199.3	Government, net	46	25.8
Change in inventories	17	15.4	Nonprofit institutions	47	1.5
Sales to government	18	213.8	Rest of the world	48	16.5
Current purchases, net	19	148.7	Proprietors' income	49	112.2
Capital purchases	20	65.1	Rental income	50	17.5
Structures	21	27.8	Net dividends	51	34.3
Equipment	22	31.0	Dividends paid	52	47.4
Change in inventories	23	6.2	Households	53	41.0
Sales to rest of the world, net	24	-17.3	Nonprofit institutions	54	2.1
Sales to rest of the world	25	167.4	Government	55	1.5
Less: Purchases from rest of the world	26	184.6	Rest of the world	56	2.7
			Less: Dividends from rest of the world	57	13.1
			Indirect taxes and nontaxes	58	151.9
			Corporate profits taxes	59	83.0

268

	60	Surplus of government enterprises	5.9
	61	Net transfers	-30.6
	62	Transfers paid	49.7
	63	Bad-debt allowances	7.1
	64	Nonprofit benefits in kind	42.5
	65	Less: Transfers received	80.3
	66	Household contributions to nonprofit institutions	32.8
	67	Government grants to nonprofit institutions	6.9
	68	Net interest and dividends received by nonprofit inst.	3.3
	69	Subsidies	9.4
	70	Government pension and insurance reserves	27.9
	71	Enterprise gross saving	289.0
	72	Retained corporate profits (adj.)	48.5
	73	Corporate profits (adj.)	165.8
	74	Corporate profits (book)	203.6
	75	Inventory valuation adjustment	-24.3
	76	Capital consumption adjustment	-13.5
	77	Less: Net corporate dividends	34.3
	78	Corporate profits taxes	83.0
	79	Capital consumption allowances (adj.)	180.6
	80	Nonprofit retained income	2.0
	81	Pension and insurance reserves	57.9
	82	Statistical discrepancy (BEA)	6.4
Enterprise gross product (mrkt transactions)	27	$1,760.6	83	Current outlays and gross saving (mrkt transactions)	$1,760.6
Imputed nonmarket enterprise sales	28	7.1	84	Imputed nonmarket enterprise outlays	7.1
Nonprofit building rent	29	7.1	85	Nonprofit building rent	7.1
Enterprise gross product (mrkt and nonmrkt)	30	$1,767.7	86	Current outlays and gross saving (mrkt and nonmrkt)	$1,767.7

Table 10.3 *Enterprise Gross Product Account, 1978 ($bn)*

Compensation of employees	$1,070.5	Sales to:	
Net interest	20.6	Enterprises, net	$438.3
Proprietors' income	112.2	Households	1,125.8
Rental income	17.5	Government	213.8
Net dividends	34.3	Sales to rest of the world, net	−17.3
Indirect taxes and nontaxes	151.9		
Corporate profits taxes	83.0		
Surplus of government enterprises	5.9		
Net transfers	−30.6		
Enterprise gross saving	289.0		
Statistical discrepancy	6.4		
Enterprise current outlays and gross saving (market transactions)	**$1,760.6**	**Enterprise gross product (market transactions)**	**$1,760.6**
Imputed nonmarket outlays	7.1	Imputed nonmarket sales	7.1
Enterprise current outlays and gross saving (market and nonmarket)	**$1,767.7**	**Enterprise gross product (market and nonmarket)**	**$1,767.7**

Net transfers (IEA 1.10 line 61) are somewhat more complex and include a number of quite different components. Transfers paid (line 62) consist of bad-debt allowances for uncollectable accounts receivable from households (line 63) and nonprofit benefits in kind (line 64). Transfers received (line 65) are funds received by enterprises that cannot be classed as sales of goods and services. These are: household contributions to nonprofit institutions, government grants to nonprofit institutions, interest and dividends received by nonprofit institutions and subsidies to enterprises (lines 66–69). Additions to government pension and retirement reserves (line 70) are considered to be transfers to enterprises because the pension and retirement schemes are usually operated as government or private nonprofit enterprises; consequently, government pension and life insurance reserves (line 81) are also included in the enterprise sector.

Enterprise gross saving (IEA 1.10 line 71) is residually determined, and consists of that part of enterprise gross product that is not paid out to others. The derivation of retained corporate profits (line 72) is shown explicitly. It equals the book value of corporate profits with adjustments for inventory valuation and for capital consumption, less payments of net corporate dividends and corporate profits taxes (lines 74–78). Capital consumption allowances (line 79) do not include capital consumption on buildings owned and occupied by nonprofit institutions. For this reason, the retained income of nonprofit institutions (line 80) is gross. Additions to pension and life insurance reserves (line 81) are shown as part of enterprise gross saving; this treatment contrasts with the BEA practice that puts these reserves partly into personal saving in the personal income and outlays account, and partly into government surplus in the government receipts and expenditures account. The remaining components of enterprise current outlays and gross saving have already been discussed in connection with Table IEA 1.1.

Subsectoring As part of the project, gross product accounts were prepared for the enterprise subsectors shown earlier. In preparing the estimates, unpublished detail in BEA worksheets was used; for some flows, enterprise sector flows were allocated on the basis of information in the Internal Revenue Service *Statistics of Income*. For the most part, the subsector transaction detail follows that shown for the enterprise sector as a whole, but in some cases, transactions flows were combined. For example, subsidies were netted against indirect tax and nontax payments, and bad-debt allowances and statistical discrepancies were combined with other adjustments.

The household current account
There are four major differences between the current account for the household sector in the IEAs and the BEA personal income and outlay account. First, the income and expenditures of nonprofit institutions are excluded. Second, expenditures on consumer durables and change in inventories are treated as capital, rather than current, and thus are excluded from the household current account. Third, as already noted, a number of transaction flows relating to fringe benefits provided by employers, pensions and insurance and owner-occupied housing have been reclassified. Fourth, a number of market and nonmarket imputations are excluded from both income and expenditures.

The basic account In Table 10.4, the right side shows the types of income that households receive, and the left side shows their gross current outlays and gross saving. Gross saving in this account is, of course, a residual; it shows the portion of the total income received by households used either to acquire assets (financial or tangible) or to discharge liabilities.

Table IEA 1.40, Household current income and outlay account Payments by enterprises to households and household payments to enterprises (including contributions to nonprofit institutions) have already been discussed in connection with the enterprise current account. The new transactions in this account are those between households and the government and between households and the rest of the world. The government pays wages and salaries (IEA 1.40 line 3) and makes transfer payments (line 13) to households, and receives from households tax payments (line 35) and personal contributions for social insurance (line 40). (Note: It could be aruged that some of the taxes that households pay are not 'current' outlays, and so should not be recorded in their current account. For example, from the viewpoint of householders, payment of estate taxes is a capital transaction in the capital account. To preserve

Table 10.4 Household Current Income and Outlay Account, 1978 ($bn)

Current consumption expenditures	$829.5	Wages and salaries received	$1,100.4
Interest payments	90.4	Interest income	109.7
Tax payments	285.0	Proprietors' income	112.2
Personal contributions for social insurance	69.6	Rental income	17.5
		Dividends received	41.0
Transfers paid	33.6	Transfers received	225.4
Gross saving	298.1		
Household current outlays and gross saving (mrkt transactions)	**$1,606.2**	**Household current income (mrkt transactions)**	**$1,606.2**
Imputed nonmarket gross outlays	342.6	Imputed nonmarket gross income	342.6
Household gross current outlays and gross saving (mrkt and nonmrkt)	**$1,948.8**	**Household gross current income (mrkt and nonmrkt)**	**$1,948.8**

comparability with the BEA accounts, however, this modification was not made here.)

The rest of the world pays wages and salaries to households (IEA 1.40 line 4), and receives current consumption expenditures (lines 30 plus 33) and transfers (line 43) from households. No interest and dividends are received directly by households from the rest of the world; rather, they are considered as being received by enterprises and in turn paid out by them to households. This procedure does not affect the amount of net interest paid by enterprises (the same amount is added and subtracted), but it avoids the somewhat difficult statistical problem of determining whether interest or dividend payments by the rest of the world are made to businesses or individuals.

Household gross saving (IEA 1.40 line 44) is quite different from BEA personal saving. The exclusion of imputed interest on pension funds and life insurance reserves and of employer contributions for pension funds and life insurance removes most of the increase in life insurance and pension fund reserves from gross household saving. Increases in the cash value of pensions and life insurance held by households, however, are included as part of household income, and thus a part of household saving. The altered treatment of owner-occupied housing also has a substantial impact. Imputed capital consumption allowances on owner-occupied housing, which BEA treats as part of business capital consumption, are included as a part of household gross saving. The elements of the imputed rental value of owner-occupied housing that reflect market outlays, such as repair and maintenance costs, mortgage interest and property taxes, are in household outlays. The net imputed rental income, however, is excluded from both household market income and market outlays. Finally, the exclusion of expenditures on consumer durables from current consumption expenditures leads to an estimate of household gross saving that is much larger than personal saving as measured by BEA. Gross saving is the residual in the account. Capital consumption allowances for owner-occupied houses (line 46) and durable goods (line 47) are identified within this total; the remainder is net saving (line 48).

In addition to the market transactions, imputed nonmarket gross income and outlays are shown for owner-occupied housing (IEA 1.40 lines 18 and 51), margins on owner-built houses (lines 21 and 52), household durables (lines 22 and 53), and farm income in kind (lines 25 and 54). It would be possible, of course, to extend the estimates of household nonmarket activity further, and provide imputations for, e.g., housewives' services and do-it-yourself activities.

Subsectoring Subsectoring of household current income and outlays has not been undertaken in the IEAs. However, because the household sector is now defined as coincident with the universe of households, microdata could be used to develop household subsectors defined in terms of socioeconomic groupings. In effect this subsectoring is being carried out in work on micromodeling the tax, health and welfare systems.

The government current account

The major difference between the current account for the government sector in the IEAs and the BEA government receipts and expenditures account is that expenditures for structures and durables are treated as capital, rather than current, outlays.

The basic account Table 10.5, the right side shows the receipts of the government, and the left side shows its current outlays and gross saving. Gross saving in this account, as in others, is a residual; it shows the portion of government total receipts that is not spent as current expenditures for goods and services, net interest or as transfers and subsidies. Imputed nonmarket income and outlays arise from the capital consumption of government structures and durables.

Table 10.5 Government Current Income and Outlay Account, 1978 ($bn)

Current purchases and compensation of employees	$368.4	Tax and nontax receipts	$527.3
Net interest	32.7	Social insurance contributions	161.8
Transfers and subsidies	230.9		
Gross saving	57.0		
Government current outlays and gross saving (market transactions)	**$689.0**	**Government current income (market transactions)**	**$689.0**
Imputed nonmarket gross outlays	49.2	Imputed nonmarket gross income	49.2
Government current outlays and gross saving (mrkt and nonmrkt)	**$738.2**	**Government gross current income (mrkt and nonmrktarket)**	**$738.2**

Sample Table 1.40 Household Current Income and Outlay Account ($bn)

	Line	1978		Line	1978
Wages and salaries received	1	$1,100.4	Current consumption expenditures	27	$829.4
Enterprises	2	908.2	Nondurable goods	28	508.8
Government	3	191.8	Enterprises	29	507.1
Rest of the world	4	0.4	Rest of the world	30	1.7
Interest income	5	109.7	Services	31	320.6
Proprietors' income	6	112.2	Enterprises	32	309.2
Rental income	7	17.5	Rest of the world	33	11.4
Dividends received	8	41.0	Interest payments	34	90.4
Transfers received	9	225.4	Tax payments	35	285.0
Enterprises	10	42.4	Income taxes	36	225.0
Pension and welfare payments	11	35.3	Estate and gift taxes	37	7.2
Bad-debt adjustment	12	7.1	Property taxes	38	27.2
Government	13	183.0	Other taxes and nontaxes	39	25.6
Social insurance payments	14	91.4	Personal contributions for social insurance	40	69.6
Other payments	15	91.6	Transfers paid	41	33.6
			Contributions to nonprofit institutions	42	32.8
			Transfers to rest of the world, net	43	0.8
			Gross saving	44	298.1
			Capital consumption allowances	45	178.1
			Owner-occupied houses	46	35.0
			Durable goods	47	143.1
			Net savings	48	120.1
Household current income (market transactions)	16	$1,606.2	Household current outlays and gross saving (market transactions)	49	$1,606.2

Household current income (market transactions)	16	$1,606.2	Household current outlays and gross saving (market transactions)	49	$1,606.2
Imputed nonmarket gross income	17	342.6	Imputed nonmarket gross outlays	50	342.6
Gross income on owner-occupied housing	18	126.9	Owner-occupied housing	51	126.9
Capital consumption	19	35.0	Margins on owner-build houses	52	1.7
Net imputed services	20	91.9	Durables consumed	53	213.4
Margins on owner-built houses	21	1.7	Farm income in kind	54	0.6
Gross income on durables	22	213.4			
Capital consumption	23	143.1			
Net imputed services	24	70.3			
Farm income in kind	25	0.6			
Household gross current income (market and nonmarket)	26	$1,948.8	Household gross current outlays and gross saving (market and nonmarket)	55	$1,948.8

Table IEA 1.50, Government current income and outlay account The only transactions that have not already been discussed are those between the government and rest of the world. These are the purchases from the rest of the world (IEA 1.50 line 23), sales to the rest of the world (line 24), interest paid

Sample Table 1.50 Government Current Income and Outlay Account ($bn)

	Line	1978		Line	1978
Tax and nontax receipts	1	$527.3	Current purchases	20	$148.8
Enterprises	2	242.2	Purchases from enterprises, net	21	148.7
Indirect taxes and nontaxes	3	151.9	Purchases from rest of the world, net	22	0.2
Corporate profits taxes	4	83.0			
Surplus of government enterprises	5	5.9	Purchases from rest of the world	23	8.9
Dividends received	6	1.5	Less: Sales to rest of the world	24	8.7
Households	7	285.0			
Income taxes	8	225.0	Compensation of employees	25	229.2
Estate and gift taxes	9	7.2	Wages and salaries	26	191.8
Property taxes	10	27.2	Social insurance contributions	27	27.9
Other taxes and nontaxes	11	25.6	Benefits in kind	28	9.6
Social insurance contributions	12	161.8	Less: Withheld employee compensation for benefits in kind	29	9.6
Enterprises	13	64.3			
Households	14	69.6	Net interest	30	32.7
Government	15	27.9	Interest paid	31	34.5
			Enterprises, net	32	25.8
			Rest of the world	33	8.7
			Less: Interest received from rest of the world	34	1.8
			Transfers and subsidies	35	230.9
			Enterprises	36	44.2
			Subsidies	37	9.4
			Nonprofit contributions	38	6.9
			Pension and insurance reserves	39	27.9
			Households	40	183.0
			Social insurance payments	41	91.4
			Other payments	42	91.6
			Rest of the world	43	3.8
			Gross saving	44	57.0
			Capital consumption allowances	45	58.2
			Net saving	46	-1.2
Government current income (mrkt transactions)	16	**$689.0**	**Government current outlays and gross saving (mrkt transactions)**	47	**$689.0**
Imputed nonmarket gross income	17	49.2	Imputed nonmarket gross outlays	48	49.2
Capital consumption of structures and durables	18	49.2	Capital consumption of structures and durables	49	49.2
Government gross current income (mrkt and nonmrkt)	19	**$783.2**	**Government gross current outlays and gross saving (mrkt and nonmrkt)**	50	**$738.2**

to the rest of the world (line 33), interest received from the rest of the world (line 34), and transfers paid to the rest of the world, net (line 43).

The gross saving of the government sector is larger than the government surplus shown in the BEA government sector account because purchases of structures and durables are excluded from current expenditures. Again, gross saving is a residual. It may be subdivided into capital consumption allowances and net saving.

Subsectoring Current income and outlay accounts were prepared for federal, state, and local governments. These accounts represent a deconsolidation in which the transfers between various levels of government are made explicit. Subsector accounts could also be constructed for specific states or for local governments in different regions, and, also, for some periods, by type or size of local government. The microdata in the Census of Governments provide the basic source for state and local governments. For the federal government, large amounts of detail are available by agency and by program from the Office of Management and Budget and the Treasury Department.

The rest-of-the-world current account
The current account of the rest of the world shows the transactions of enterprises, households and government with the rest of the world.

The basic account In Table 10.6, the right and left sides show, respectively, the payments to and receipts from the rest of the world. Except that factor payments are shown separately from the other imports and exports of goods and services, the categories are identical with those in the BEA foreign transactions account. As in the BEA account, net foreign investment is residually determined.

Table 10.6 Rest-of-the-World Current Account, 1978 ($bn)

Sales to the rest of the world	$176.1	Purchases from the rest of the world	$206.6
Factor income received	43.8	Factor income paid	13.8
Capital grants received by government, net	0.0	Transfer payments to the rest of the world, net	4.6
		Interest paid by government to rest of the world	8.7
		Net foreign investment	–13.8
Receipts from rest of the world	**$219.8**	**Payments to rest of the world**	**$219.8**

Table IEA 1.60, Rest-of-the-world current account Only net foreign investment (IEA 1.60 line 39) and capital grants received by government (line 16) are new transactions.

Sample Table 1.60 Rest-of-the-World Current Account ($bn)

	Line	1978		Line	1978
Exports of goods and services	1	$219.8	Imports of goods and services	18	$220.4
Sales to the rest of the world	2	176.1	Purchases from rest of the world	19	206.6
Enterprises	3	167.4	Enterprises	20	184.6
Merchandise	4	140.9	Merchandise	21	174.7
Other goods and services	5	26.5	Other goods and services	22	9.9
Government	6	8.7	Government	23	8.9
Military transactions	7	8.1	Military transactions	24	7.4
Other services	8	0.6	Other services	25	1.5
Factor income receive	9	43.8	Households	26	13.1
Interest income	10	18.4	Nondurable goods	27	1.7
Enterprises	11	16.5	Services	28	11.4
Government	12	1.8	Factor income paid	29	13.8
Dividends	13	13.1	Interest income	30	8.0
Retained corporate profits	14	11.9	Enterprises	31	8.0
Compensation of employees	15	0.4	Dividends	32	2.7
Capital grants received by the government, net	16	0.0	Retained corporate profits	33	2.6
			Compensation of employees	34	.5
			Transfer payments to rest of the world, net	35	4.6
			Households	36	0.8
			Government	37	3.8
			Interest paid by government to rest of the world, net	38	8.7
			Net foreign investment	39	−13.8
Receipts from rest of the world	17	$219.8	Payments to rest of the world	40	$219.8

Capital Accounts

Just as the GNP account shows how the output of the nation can be derived from current transactions, the capital accounts for the nation show how wealth — to be exact, changes in wealth — can be derived from capital transactions and revaluations. The structure of the capital accounts is brought out by explaining a set of 'basic' accounts for the nation.

Capital accounts for the nation

As noted earlier, capital accounts can be viewed as having three components: balance sheets, capital transactions accounts and revaluation accounts.

The basic capital accounts. Table 10.7 implements this view of capital accounts: it shows the end-of-year national balance sheets, for 1977 and for 1978 (cols 1 and 4), and the changes in balance sheet entries during the year 1978, in a capital transactions account (col. 2) and in a revaluation account (col. 3).

Table 10.7 Capital Accounts for the Nation, 1977–78 ($bn)

	1977	1978		1978
	End-of-year value (1)	Capital transaction account (2)	Revaluation account (3)	End-of-year value (4)
Reproducible assets	$6,108.4	251.2	642.2	$7,001.8
Land	1,715.4		284.5	1,999.9
Gold and foreign assets	14.3	−1.3	.2	13.2
Fixed-claim assets	5,496.6	772.4		6,269.0
Total assets	**$13,334.7**	**$1,022.4**	**$926.9**	**$15,284.0**
Fixed-claim liabilities	5,496.6	772.4		6,269.0
Net worth	7,838.1	249.9	926.9	9,015.0
Total liabilities and net worth	**$13,334.7**	**$1,022.4**	**$926.9**	**$15,284.0**

The balance sheets show the assets, liabilities and net worth of the nation. Four types of assets are distinguished: reproducible assets, including structures, durables and inventories; land; gold and foreign exchange holdings (including special drawing rights); and fixed-claim assets, such as currency and deposits, bonds, and mortgages. This last category of assets equals fixed-claim liabilities. In effect, the fixed-claim assets and liabilities show the fixed claims that transactors in the economy hold against each other, and, because the national balance sheet covers all sectors of the economy, the sum of these fixed claims when viewed as assets will be equal to the sum when viewed as liabilities. In practice, the statistical estimation of fixed-claim assets and liabilities utilize different sources, and therefore will usually result in different amounts being recorded as assets and liabilities. For this reason, a statistical discrepancy item has been included as a part of fixed-claim liabilities to bring the totals into balance.

Net worth represents the value of national wealth and is equal to total assets minus fixed-claim liabilities. Because fixed-claim liabilities by definition equal fixed-claim assets, national wealth equals the sum of reproducible assets, land, and gold and foreign exchange holdings. (As was noted in the discussion of the valuation of capital in Section 1, it would in principle be possible to impute a value for intangible capital — such as human capital — in the balance sheet. Such an imputation could be handled in the balance sheet in a manner parallel to that suggested for imputations for nonmarket activity in the current accounts.)

The transactions account records the net capital transactions that have taken place for each balance sheet category. For reproducible assets, they reflect the net capital formation of the economy. No net capital transactions are shown for land, because the amount of land purchased is equal to the amount of land sold; there is no change in the total amount of land owned by the economy as a whole. The holdings of gold and foreign exchange can change, however, and the net change in these holdings appears as the net capital transactions for this category. Similarly, holdings of fixed-claim assets and liabilities can change; thus, an increase in currency and deposits is an increase in the assets of those owning them, and an equal increase in the liabilities of the financial system. The net capital transactions recorded for fixed-claim assets and liabilities are those reported in the Federal Reserve flow of funds accounts. Finally, the change in net worth is the sum of the net accumulation of reproducible assets and of holdings of gold and foreign exchange, and net saving.

The revaluation account records the change in the value of assets and net worth due to price changes during the year. Because balance sheets are stated in current market values, revaluations can also be looked at as the difference between previous and current valuations. For land, all change in value is considered to be revaluation. When improvements increase the value of land, the improvements are considered part of capital formation and are included with reproducible assets. Fixed-claim assets and liabilities are considered by definition to be fixed in value, so that no revaluation is made. Nevertheless, the actual market values of some fixed-claim assets and liabilities do change. For example, the market value of bonds fluctuates with the rate of interest despite the fact that they represent a fixed capital sum. Because the sum is payable in the future, its present value depends on the rate of interest. For the accounts presented here, however, this type of revaluation has not been included.

Table IEA 2.1, Capital accounts for the nation Reproducible assets, land and net worth are shown classified by the sectors owning them, and financial assets and liabilities are listed by major type. The sector detail provided for net worth reflects not only the net worth that originates in a given sector, but also the transfers of equity to other sectors. For example, households own equities in many different kinds of businesses, in estates and trusts, and in pension and insurance funds (as well as directly in tangible assets or net fixed-claim assets). Enterprise sector net worth has been adjusted to reflect transfers of such equities to households, and government net worth has been adjusted to reflect the transfer of its pension and insurance reserves to the pension fund subsector of the enterprise sector.

Capital accounts for sectors

Sector balance sheets, like the balance sheet for the nation, show the four types of assets balanced by fixed-claim liabilities and net worth. In addition, however, each sector account shows, as a part of the assets of the sector, the equities it holds: in the national balance sheet, equities are shown as component elements of net worth. The sector deconsolidation for 1978 is shown in Table 10.8. Aside from the additional detail provided for equities, the total holdings of assets and liabilities for enterprises, households, government and the rest of the world add up to the same figures as appear in the balance sheet for the nation.

The deconsolidation of net capital formation is needed in order to reflect fully the actual capital transactions in which the sectors of the economy engage, and to permit the computation of balance sheet values for reproducible assets by the perpetual inventory method. An example of the accounting entries involved is given in Table 10.9, for equipment owned by enterprises. The book value of the gross stock, shown in column 1, line 2, is the starting point. It is the accumulated cost of equipment at time of purchase. To this is added revaluation of the stock (line 3), the difference between these book value figures and the value of equipment in 1977 prices. The result is the value of gross stock in 1977 prices, i.e., the gross stock at current value (line 4). Next, a deduction is made for accumulated capital consumption. The book value of this capital consumption is in line 5, and these figures are revalued to 1977 prices in line 6. The figure for the current value of the net stock of equipment in line 1, which is the end product of the computation, is the same as that for the end of 1977 in column 1, line 9, of capital accounts for the Nation (Table IEA 2.1).

Column 2 shows the capital transactions during 1978. Line 2 is gross capital formation, shown as the expenditures by enterprises on equipment in Table IEA 1.1. No revaluation is required for this current-year expenditure, so the same figure is repeated in line 4. Capital consumption and its revaluation

Sample Table 2.1. *Capital Accounts for the Nation, 1977–78 ($bn)*

	Line	End-of-year value 1977 (1)	Capital trans. account 1978 (2)	Revaluation account 1978 (3)	End-of-year value 1978 (4)
Reproducible assets (net current value)	1	6,108.4	251.2	642.2	7,001.8
Residential structures	2	1,715.7	62.4	270.4	2,048.5
Owner-occupied	3	1,320.6	59.7	205.4	1,585.7
Other	4	395.1	2.7	64.9	462.7
Nonresidential structures	5	1,921.5	36.0	211.1	2,168.7
Enterprises	6	1,171.1	33.0	128.7	1,332.7
Government	7	750.5	3.0	82.5	836.0
Durables	8	1,699.2	108.5	94.6	1,902.3
Enterprises	9	806.6	45.4	54.2	906.2
Households	10	702.3	56.3	28.8	787.4
Government	11	190.3	6.9	11.6	208.7
Inventories	12	771.9	44.3	66.1	882.4
Enterprises	13	527.8	22.6	58.8	609.2
Households	14	159.6	15.4	1.8	176.9
Government	15	84.5	6.3	5.5	96.3
Land	16	1,715.4		284.5	1,999.9
Enterprises	17	958.4		138.6	1,096.9
Households	18	358.8		79.9	438.7
Government	19	398.3		66.0	464.3
Gold and foreign exchange	20	14.3	−1.3	0.2	13.2
Fixed-claim assets	21	5,496.6	772.4		6,269.0
Treasury currency and special drawing rights cert.	22	12.6	0.6		13.1
Currency and deposits	23	1,467.0	159.9		1,626.9
Currency and demand deposits	24	349.9	33.4		383.3
Time and saving deposits	25	1,113.2	119.6		1,232.8
Money market fund shares	26	3.9	6.9		10.8
Federal funds and security repurchase agreements	27	28.2	11.5		39.7
Net interbank claims	28	32.2	14.9		47.1
Credit market instruments	29	3,288.8	469.7		3,758.4
US government securities	30	716.6	90.5		807.1
State and local obligations	31	261.4	26.1		287.5
Corporate and foreign bonds	32	400.7	31.8		432.5
Mortgages	33	1,021.1	148.3		1,169.4
Consumer credit	34	288.8	47.6		336.4
Bank loans, n.e.c.	35	301.4	57.4		358.8
Open-market paper	36	89.5	26.4		115.9
Other loans	37	209.2	41.6		250.7
Security credit	38	43.4	1.5		44.9
Trade credit	39	352.7	64.5		417.1
Other fixed claims	40	271.9	49.8		321.7
Total assets	41	**13,334.7**	**1,022.4**	**926.9**	**15,284.0**

	Line	End-of-year value 1977 (1)	Capital trans. account 1978 (2)	Revaluation account 1978 (3)	End-of-year value 1978 (4)
Fixed-claim liabilities	42	5,496.6	772.4		6,269.0
Treasury currency and special drawing rights cert.	43	10.2	0.5		10.7
Currency and deposits	44	1,498.8	159.1		1,657.9
Currency and demand deposits	45	381.7	32.6		414.3
Time and saving deposits	46	1,113.2	119.6		1,232.8
Money market future shares	47	3.9	6.9		10.8
Federal funds and security purchase agreements	48	53.3	22.4		75.6
Net interbank claims	49	22.8	15.7		38.5
Credit market instruments	50	3,288.8	469.7		3,758.4
US government securities	51	716.6	90.5		807.1
State and local obligations	52	261.4	26.1		287.5
Corporate and foreign bonds	53	400.7	31.8		432.5
Mortgages	54	1,021.1	148.3		1,169.4
Consumer credit	55	288.8	47.6		336.4
Bank loans, n.e.c.	56	301.4	57.4		358.8
Open-market paper	57	89.5	26.4		115.9
Other loans	58	209.2	41.6		250.7
Security debt	59	43.4	1.5		44.9
Trade debt	60	292.4	57.3		349.7
Other fixed claims	61	313.7	60.7		374.4
Statistical discrepancy and float	62	−26.7	−14.5		−41.2
Net worth	63	7,838.1	249.9	926.9	9,015.0
Enterprise net equity	64	1,471.9	95.3	178.7	1,745.9
Enterprise net worth	65	4,344.7	119.4	456.7	4,920.9
Less: Transfers of equity	66	2,872.8	24.2	278.0	3,175.0
Household equity	67	5,287.0	159.8	552.6	5,999.3
Corporate stock (market value)	68	590.8	1.1	26.4	618.3
Noncoporate nonfarm equity	69	731.8	2.7	122.9	857.4
Farm business equity	70	474.0	−11.5	80.5	543.1
Pensions and insurance (cash value)	71	174.3	12.2	0.2	186.7
Estate and trust equity	72	189.6		4.8	194.4
Other net worth	73	3,126.5	155.2	317.7	3,599.5
Tangible assets	74	2,541.3	129.7	317.7	2,988.6
Net fixed-claim assets	75	585.3	25.6		610.8
Government net equity	76	1,108.2	−14.4	198.1	1,291.8
Government enterprise equity	77	287.4	11.1	29.5	328.1
Other net worth	78	882.0	−18.3	168.5	1,032.3
Less: Pension and insurance reserves	79	61.3	7.2		68.5
Rest-of-the-world net equity	80	−55.6	−5.2	−2.4	−63.3
Less: Statistical discrepancy and float	81	−26.7	−14.5		−41.2
Total liabilities and net worth	82	**13,334.7**	**1,022.4**	**926.9**	**15,284.0**

Table 10.8 Sector Balance Sheets, 1978 ($bn)

	Line	Enter-prises	House-holds	Govern-ment	Rest of the world	Total
Reproducible assets (net current value)	1	3,294.7	2,550.0	1,157.2		7,001.8
Residential structures	2	446.5	1,585.7	16.2		2,048.5
Other structures	3	1,332.7		836.0		2,168.7
Durables	4	906.2	787.4	208.7		1,902.3
Inventories	5	609.2	176.9	96.3		882.4
Land	6	1,096.9	438.7	464.3		1,999.9
Gold and foreign exchange	7	11.7		1.6		13.2
Fixed-claim assets	8	3,914.6	1,777.5	350.7	226.2	6,269.0
Treasury currency and special drawing rights	9	13.1				13.1
Currency and deposits	10	171.9	1,317.9	95.9	41.2	1,626.9
Currency and demand deposits	11	107.0	227.5	29.7	19.0	383.3
Time and saving deposits	12	64.8	1,079.6	66.2	22.2	1,232.8
Money market fund shares	13		10.8			10.8
Federal funds and security repurchase agreements	14	29.7		10.0		39.7
Net interbank claims	15	54.4			−7.2	47.1
Credit market instruments	16	2,989.1	397.6	199.5	172.4	3,758.4
US government securities	17	431.5	183.4	54.4	137.8	807.1
State and local obligations	18	232.6	47.6	7.3		336.4
Corporate and foreign bonds	19	387.4	33.9		11.2	432.5
Mortgages	20	1,029.8	94.7	44.8		1,169.4
Consumer credit	21	336.4				336.4
Bank loans, n.e.c.	22	358.8				358.8
Open-market paper	23	54.6	38.0		23.3	115.9
Other loans	24	157.8		93.0		250.7
Security credit	25	36.9	7.9			44.9
Trade credit	26	391.6		8.9	16.6	417.1
Other fixed claims	27	227.9	54.1	36.4	3.3	321.7
Equities held	28	594.0	2,399.9	328.1	84.6	3,406.6
Corporate stock (market value)	29	373.8	618.3		42.1	1,034.1
Noncorporate nonfarm equity	30		857.4			857.4
Farm business equity	31		543.1			543.1
Pensions and insurance (cash value)	32		186.7			186.7
Government pension and insurance reserves	33	68.5				68.5
Estates and trusts	34		194.4			194.4
Foreign direct investment	35	151.8			42.5	194.3
Government enterprise	36			328.1		328.1
Total assets	37	8,911.9	7,166.0	2,301.9	310.8	18,690.6

	Line	Enterprises	Households	Government	Rest of the world	Total
Fixed-claim liabilities	38	3,991.0	1,166.6	941.5	211.0	6,269.0
Treasury currency and special drawing rights	39			10.7		10.7
Currency and deposits	40	1,657.9				1,657.9
Currency and demand deposits	41	414.3				414.3
Time and saving deposits	42	1,232.8				1,232.8
Money market fund shares	43	10.8				10.8
Federal funds and security repurchase agreements	44	75.6				75.6
Net interbank claims	45	38.5				38.5
Credit market instruments	46	1,557.2	1,136.5	902.6	162.2	3,758.4
US government securities	47	181.7		625.4		807.1
State and local obligations	48	17.6		269.9		287.5
Corporate and foreign bonds	49	389.4		0.8		432.5
Mortgages	50	428.0	740.6			1,169.4
Consumer credit	51		336.4			336.4
Bank loans, n.e.c.	52	292.5	19.9		46.4	358.8
Open-market paper	53	89.3	39.5	6.5	26.6	115.9
Other loans	54	158.7			46.0	250.7
Security credit	55	25.0	19.8	28.2		44.9
Trade credit	56	310.1			11.3	349.7
Other fixed claims	57	326.5	10.3			374.4
Statistical discrepancy and float	58					−41.2
Sector net worth	59	4,920.9	5,999.3	1,360.4	99.7	12,421.6
Transfers of equities	60	3,175.0		68.5	163.0	3,406.6
Corporate stock (market value)	61	1,022.9			11.2	1,034.1
Noncorporate nonfarm equity	62	857.4				857.4
Farm business equity	63	543.1				543.1
Pensions and insurance (cash value)	64	186.7				186.7
Government pension and insurance reserves	65			68.5		68.5
Estates and trusts	66	194.4				194.4
Foreign direct investment	67	42.5			151.8	194.5
Government enterprise	68			328.1		328.1
Net residual equity	69	1,745.9	5,999.3	1,291.8	−63.3	8,973.7
Less: Statistical discrepancy and float	70					−4,121.2
Total liabilities and net worth	71	8,911.9	7,166.0	2,301.9	310.8	18,690.7

Table 10.9 *Capital Accounts for Equipment Enterprises, 1977–78 ($bn)*

	1977	1978		1978
	End-of-year value (1)	Capital transaction account (2)	Revaluation account (3)	End-of-year value (4)
1. Equipment (net current value)	806.6	45.4	54.2	906.2
2. Gross stock (book value)	983.8	164.9	–49.1	1,099.5
3. Plus: Revaluation of stock	464.8		65.2	530.0
4. Equals: Gross stock (current value)	1,448.6	164.9	16.0	1,629.5
5. Less: Capital consumption (book value)	382.6	86.3	–47.6	421.3
6. Less: Revaluation of capitalconsumption	259.3	33.2	9.5	302.0

(lines 5 and 6) are components of the capital consumption and the capital consumption adjustment shown in Table IEA 1.10. The result is net capital formation (line 1).

Column 3 shows revaluations during 1978. The revaluations are composed of two elements. The first is the value of the capital stock that is retired or discarded (line 2) during 1978, and its associated accumulated capital consumption (line 5), both in book values. The second is an adjustment that is required to bring the gross capital stock and capital consumption valued at 1977 prices to the prices of 1978. For the gross stock, this 1977-to-1978 revaluation is shown in line 3, and for capital consumption in line 6. Line 1 is change in the prices of the net stock from 1977 to 1978.

Addition across the table — end-1977 values plus capital transactions plus the revaluations — yields end-1978 stocks at net current value, gross book value, and gross current value in lines 1, 2 and 4 of column 4.

Estimates in Constant Prices and in Constant Purchasing Power

The IEAs record transactions and corresponding balance sheets in the current prices of each period. However, some purposes, such as comparisons that involve the measurement of changes in output over time, require the use of constant-price estimates. The BEA implicit price deflators are used to obtain GNP in constant prices in the IEAs. In a somewhat similar manner, it is possible to make constant-price estimates of the stock of reproducible assets. The BEA implicit price deflators are used to obtain constant-price estimates for these assets in the IEAs.

The technique of using specific price indexes to derive constant-price estimates cannot be applied to all categories of flows and stocks. In many cases, meaningful price measures do not exist. Nevertheless, it is still useful to consider changes in the purchasing power of specific income flows or stocks of wealth over time. Although currency and bank deposits do not have prices, it is generally recognized that their purchasing power erodes with increases in the general level of prices. For assets such as corporate stock or land, where price information is available, it is reasonable to ask whether the increase in value has been greater or less than the change in purchasing power. Holders of assets that increase in price faster (more slowly) than the general level of prices can be considered to be making a real capital gain (loss).

In developing estimates in constant purchasing power, the GNP implicit price deflator was used as a measure of general purchasing power to deflate the assets and liabilities held by the various sectors.

3. SAVING, INVESTMENT AND WEALTH

The IEAs have introduced three modifications that can be viewed as extensions of BEA's five-account system. First, capital accounts have been integrated with the current accounts. It is now possible to see how current transactions generate gross saving, how gross saving is reflected in capital transactions, and how capital transactions, together with revaluations, account for changes in the balance sheet. Second, the IEAs have modified the sectoring and recording of transactions so that the national accounts can serve as a framework for both macrodata and microdata. As a result, the accounts facilitate a wide range of analyses: analysis requiring highly disaggregated data relating to specific groups or specific regions; analysis requiring the introduction of social and demographic information; and analysis requiring the linkage of micromodels to macromodels using simulation techniques. Third, nonmarket activity has been distinguished from market transactions. This separation allows the inclusion of new types of information without disrupting the present usefulness of the accounts.

Of the three extensions, only the introduction of capital accounts significantly changes the overview of the economy. This change comes about partly because of the establishment of capital accounts for households and government and partly because of the integration of new kinds of information that permit a better understanding of how saving, capital formation and revaluations are related to the process of wealth accumulation. This part will present a brief discussion of the resulting picture. The trends and cyclical behavior of capital formation and saving by sector are examined first. Then the focus narrows to the household sector for examination of the roles of saving and revaluation in the accumulation of wealth and of the changes in the components of the balance sheet.

Capital Formation and Saving

According to both neoclassical and Keynesian economics, producers hire factors of production, sell their output and purchase capital goods, and consumers receive income, purchase consumption goods and supply saving. The financial system is viewed as the instrument for translating the saving of consumers into the capital formation required by producers. Thus the theory is cast in functional terms. In practice, however, as interpreted by analysts and policy-makers, these functional activities acquire institutional characteristics: production and capital formation are identified with enterprises, consumption and saving with households, and financial intermediation with the financial system. Enterprises are not viewed as savers, and households are not considered to engage directly in capital formation.

The BEA NIPAs do not fully reflect this functional view of the economic system. The chief deviation from this view is that gross saving is recognized in the business sector, in the form of capital consumption and retained corporate earnings. On the other hand, household saving is considered to include the accumulation of pension funds even though households have neither control over nor access to these funds, and the payments of pension benefits consolidate out of the system altogether. Given these accounting practices, it is little wonder that the somewhat simplistic efforts by economists to analyze the determinants of aggregate saving and investment, and in particular the effect of the social security system upon them, have been unsuccessful.

The IEAs carry the institutional approach much further, keeping together all of the activities engaged in by particular transactors. The two principal changes — recognizing that households do directly engage in capital formation, and allocating saving to the sectors that actually do it — lead to a rather different view of the process of saving and investment.

Enterprise gross capital formation and gross saving on the IEA basis are shown in Figure 10.1 for 1947–80. For the period as a whole, the enterprise sector's gross saving was 95 percent of its gross capital formation. Despite considerable cyclical variation in the retained earnings of corporations, the steady growth of capital consumption allowances and of pension and life insurance reserves resulted in only moderate fluctuations in gross saving. In contrast, gross capital formation was considerably more sensitive to short-run economic conditions. Consequently, in the 1975 and 1980 recessions, gross capital formation was smaller than gross saving. In the sharp inflationary periods of 1950–51 and 1974, however, when retained earnings were severely reduced by inventory and capital consumption revaluations reflecting rising prices, gross capital formation exceeded gross saving by more than 20 percent. Thus both the cyclical variation of gross capital formation and the effect of inflation on adjusted retained earnings are major factors in explaining the differences between enterprise gross capital formation and saving.

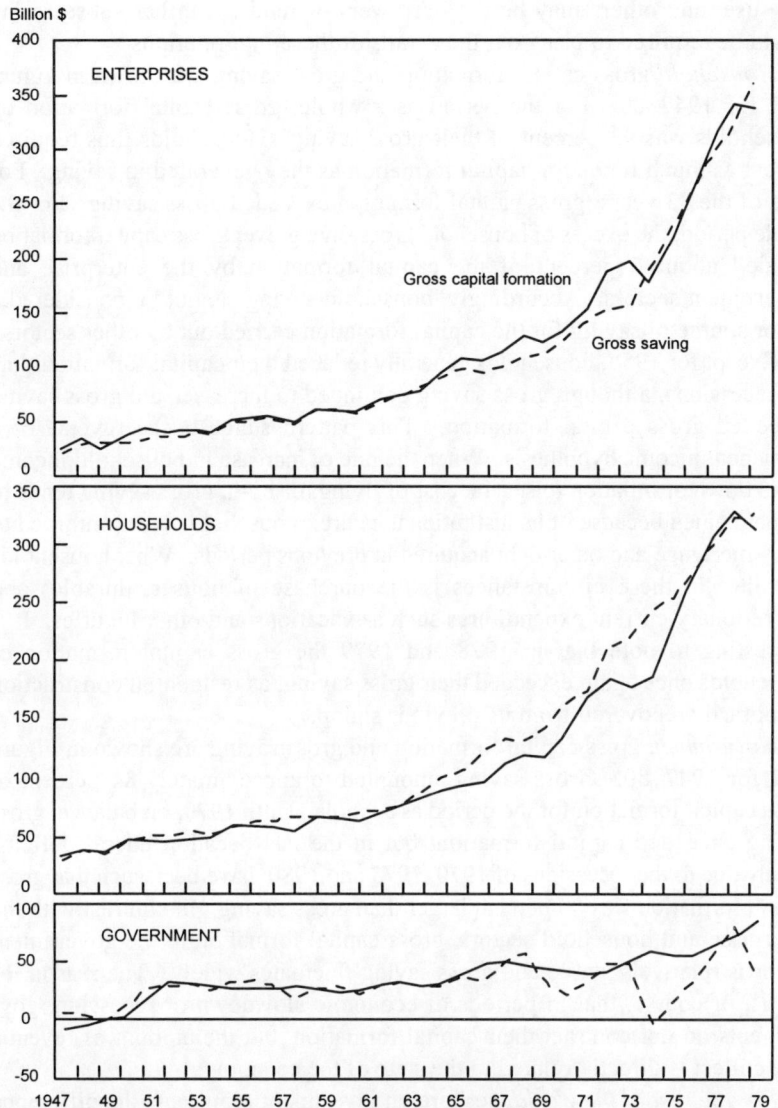

Source: US Department of Commerce, Bureau of Economic Analysis.

Figure 10.1 Gross Capital Formation and Gross Saving, 1947–80

Although, for enterprises in the aggregate, gross saving is almost equal to gross capital formation, it does not of course, follow that this near equality holds in each industry. Some industries may generate more gross saving than they use, and others may be net borrowers of funds. Further subsectoring would be required to bring out the details of these interrelations.

Household gross capital formation and gross saving are shown in Figure 10.1 for 1947–80. For the period as a whole, gross capital formation by households was 93 percent of their gross saving. Households thus required almost as much funds for capital formation as they generated in saving. For nine of the 33 years, gross capital formation exceeded gross saving. For the whole period, the excess of household gross saving over gross capital formation equaled about 6 percent of the capital formation by the enterprise and government sectors. Accordingly, household saving cannot be considered a major source of saving for the capital formation carried out by other sectors.

Except for 1954, households generally reduced their capital formation during recessions, although gross saving continued to increase, and gross saving exceeded gross capital formation. This pattern suggests the reverse of a permanent income hypothesis. When the rate of increase in household income slows down or inflation raises the cost of living, or both, gross saving tends to be maintained because of its institutional nature: households are committed to repay mortgage and other debt acquired in previous periods. What households can alter in these circumstances is the purchase of houses, durables and discretionary current expenditures such as vacations and other luxuries. It is interesting to note that in 1978 and 1979 the gross capital formation of households once again exceeded their gross saving, as residential construction temporarily recovered from its previous slump.

Government gross capital formation and gross saving are shown in Figure 10.1 for 1947–80. Gross saving amounted to approximately 84 percent of gross capital formation for the period as a whole. Until 1970, on balance, gross saving exceeded capital formation; but in the last decade, federal deficits, mainly due to the recessions of 1970, 1975 and 1980, have been such that gross capital formation was 50 percent larger than gross saving. In contrast with the enterprise and household sectors, gross capital formation in the government sector is relatively stable and gross saving fluctuates widely. The reason for this is, of course, that in periods of economic slowdown or recession, governments do not contract their capital formation, but the amount of revenue they collect is directly related to the state of the economy.

For the rest of the world, net foreign investment represents the difference between the sale of exports and factor income received from abroad and the purchase of imports and factor incomes, net transfers and government interest paid to abroad. In periods of domestic prosperity, imports rise faster than exports, reducing net foreign investment. Conversely, domestic recessions cause imports to fall faster than exports, increasing net foreign investment. Exogenous factors such as the oil crisis have also been important in affecting the amount of net foreign investment.

In summary, gross capital formation of enterprises and households rises faster than their saving in prosperity; conversely, in economic slowdowns or recessions, their gross capital formation tends to fall faster than their saving. In the government sector, gross capital formation is less affected by economic conditions, but gross saving fluctuates. In recession, it declines, and offsets the surplus saving of enterprises and households; in prosperity, it increases. This situation is due in large part to the automatic stabilizing effect of the tax system, which generates increased tax revenues in prosperity and decreased revenues in recession.

Household Net Worth and Saving

In neo-classical analysis, saving is considered to be the source of capital accumulation. Because the primary emphasis is upon productive activity, capital gains and losses are assumed either to consolidate out of the system (one man's loss being another man's gain) or to reflect only a change in the price level that does not correspond to any 'real' change in the economy. In the BEA NIPAs, capital gains are not considered to be relevant for measuring productive activity.

But if balance sheets valued in terms of current market prices are to be drawn up for the household sector, the role of revaluations cannot be ignored. Wealth-holders may belong to any sector, and they hold a variety of different assets and liabilities, so that capital gains and losses by sector and type of asset do not wash out even when adjusted for the change in the price level.

The cumulative change in household net worth and net saving for the period 1947–80 is shown in Figure 10.2. Throughout the period, net worth rose much more rapidly than net saving, reflecting the importance of revaluations in the increase in wealth. By 1980, the increase in household net worth over its 1947 level was approximately $7.1 trillion, of which $5.9 trillion was due to revaluations.

To a large extent, the revaluations reflect the decline in the value of the dollar. If this decline is taken into account, the increase in net worth more nearly corresponds to the increase in saving. Figure 10.2 shows both net worth and net saving in constant-purchasing-power dollars. The BEA GNP deflator was used to adjust the changes in net worth and net saving on a year-by-year basis. Removing price changes in this way emphasizes the fluctuations in net worth. In some periods, for example from 1962–68 and since 1975, net worth increased faster than net saving. But in some other periods, net worth contracted despite the continued growth of net saving. It is, thus, clear that

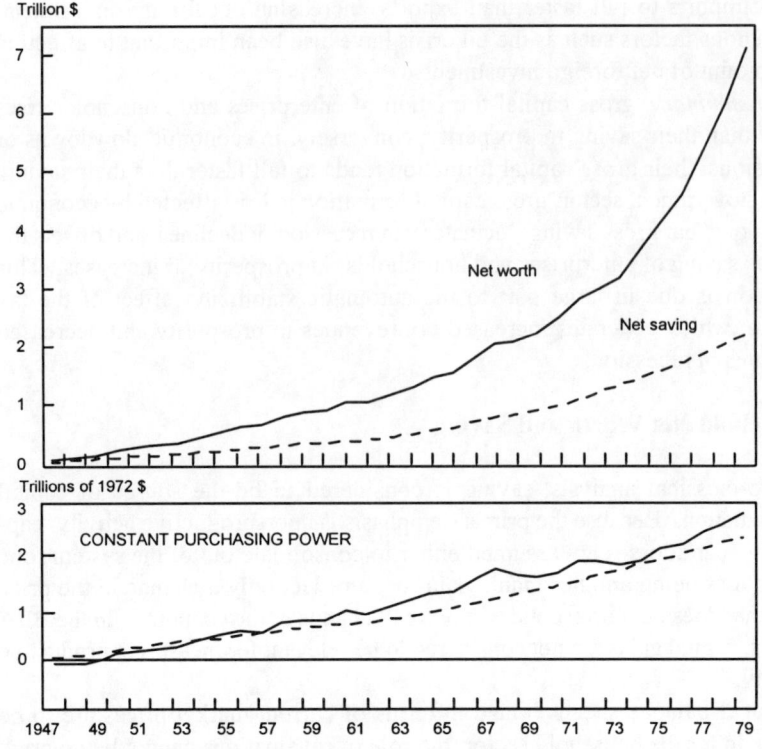

Source: US Department of Commerce, Bureau of Economic Analysis.

Figure 10.2 Cumulative Change in Household Net Worth and Net Saving, 1947–80

information on revaluations is important for understanding the change in both the current values and the real values of wealth.

Household Balance Sheets

In the balance sheets, the different components of assets and liabilities are differentially affected by capital transactions and by revaluations. To show this differential effect, household balance sheet components were classified into six broad categories: owner-occupied houses and land; corporate stock; fixed-claim assets; consumer durables and inventories; other equities; and fixed-claim liabilities. Figure 10.3 shows, for each of these categories, the market value, which includes revaluations, and the cumulative net acquisitions from 1947 to 1980.

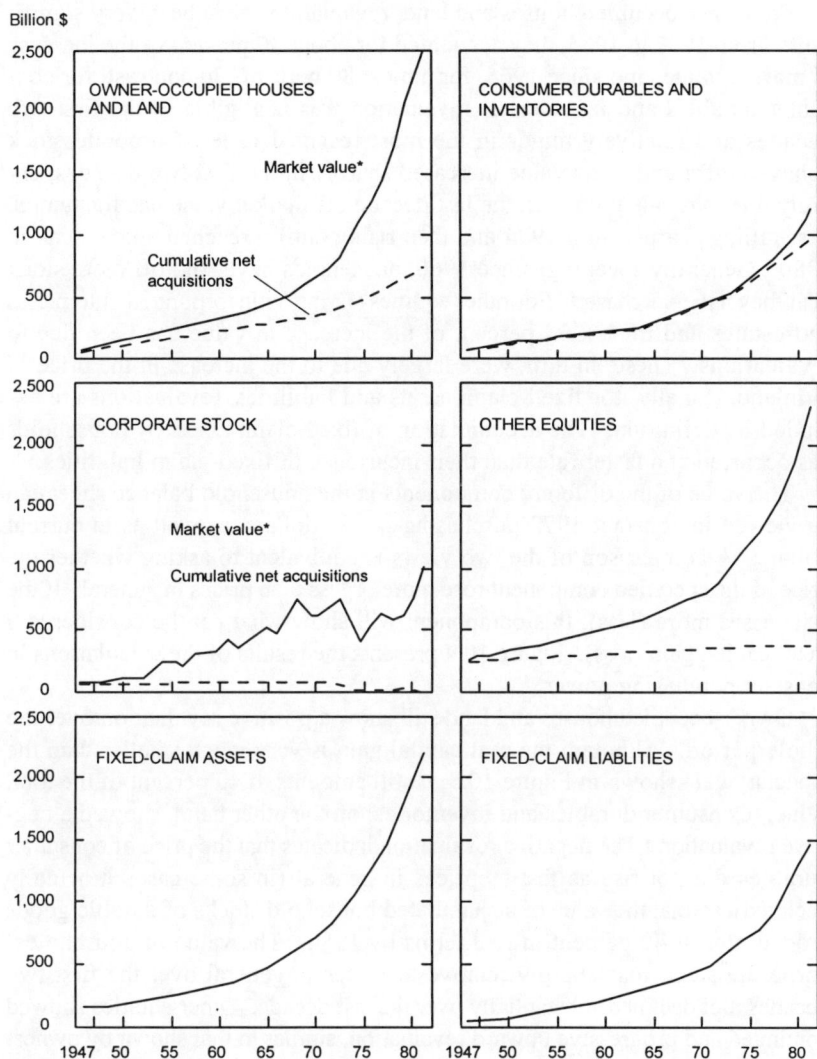

*For reproducible assets, net current value.

Source: US Department of Commerce, Bureau of Economic Analysis.

Figure 10.3 *Components of Household Balance Sheets: Market Values and Cumulative Net Acquisitions, 1947–80*

For owner-occupied houses and land, revaluations have been very significant. From 1947 to 1965, they accounted for about 30 percent of the increase in market value, and since 1965, for almost 80 percent. In contrast, for consumer durables and inventories, revaluation was negligible in the first two decades and relatively minor in the most recent decade. Corporate stock behaved differently. Its value increased sharply in the first two decades, entirely due to revaluations. In the last decade, its market value has fluctuated, first falling sharply until 1974 and then rising until it reached a new peak in 1980. Generally speaking, since 1960, households have sold off more stock than they have purchased. For other equities (farms, unincorporated enterprises and estates and trusts), 94 percent of the increase in value has been due to revaluations. These, in turn, were largely due to the increase in the price of farmland. Finally, for fixed-claim assets and liabilities, revaluations are excluded by definition. The accumulation of fixed-claim assets by households has occurred at a faster rate than their incurrence of fixed-claim liabilities.

The value of the different components in the household balance sheet can be viewed in constant 1972 purchasing-power dollars, as well as in current dollars. A comparison of the two views is equivalent to asking whether the price of the specified component rose more or less than prices in general. If the price rises more (less), this component will show what can be considered a 'real' capital gain (loss). Figure 10.4 presents the results of the calculations in constant purchasing power.

Owner-occupied houses and land still show a positive revaluation over the whole period. Although the real capital gain is very much smaller than the monetary gain shown in Figure 10.3, it still amounts to 40 percent of the total value. Consumer durables and inventories, on the other hand, showed a negative revaluation. The negative revaluation indicates that the price of consumer durables did not rise as fast as prices in general (in some cases it actually declined), so that the value of accumulated household stocks of durable goods eroded almost 40 percent in real terms by 1980. The value of households' corporate stock rose sharply relative to prices in general over the first two decades, but declined substantially over the last decade. Other equities showed continued and progressive upward revaluation, similar to that shown by owner-occupied houses and land, and for much the same reason. Finally, fixed-claim assets and liabilities showed the sharp erosion in the purchasing power of these assets and liabilities caused by the rise in prices. The holder of fixed-claim assets was losing in real terms, and, conversely, holding fixed-claim liabilities meant that the holder's debt burden was declining in real terms. However, these gains and losses cannot be fully evaluated without also taking into account the behavior of interest rates, which channeled some of the revaluation into current interest income and payments.

This summary examination of the differential behavior of the components

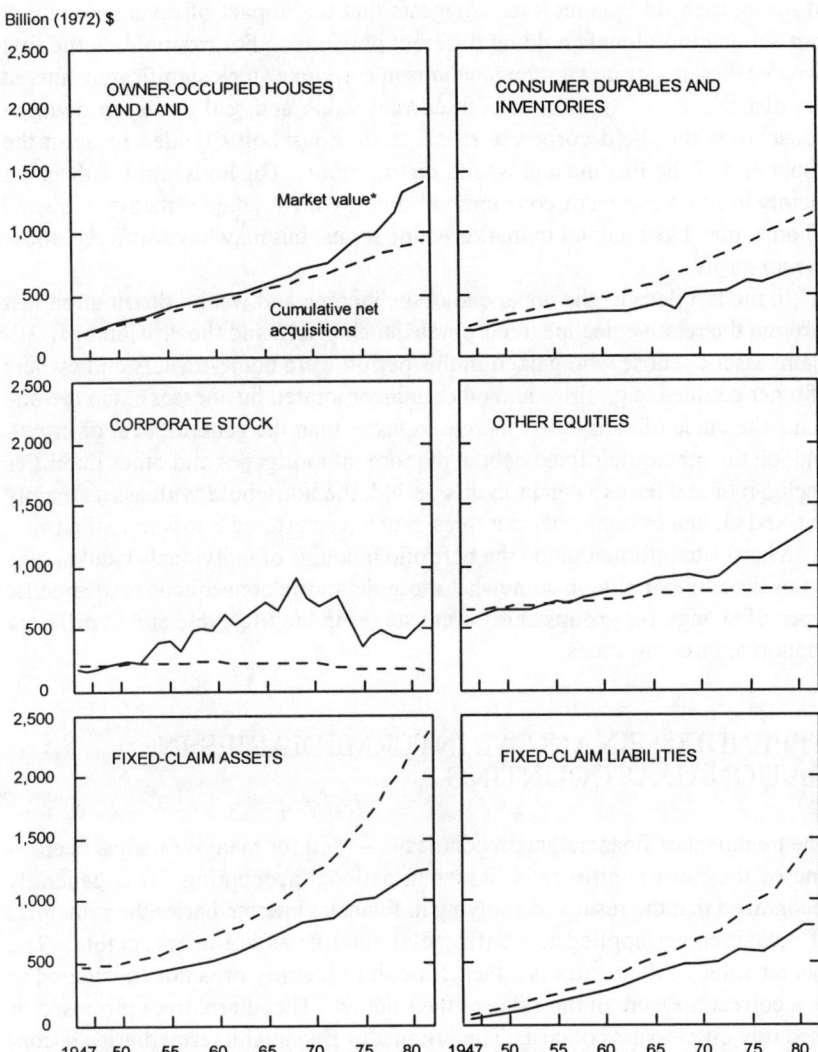

*For reproducible assets, net current value.

Source: US Department of Commerce, Bureau of Economic Analysis.

Figure 10.4 Components of Household Balance Sheets: Market Values and Cumulative Net Acquisitions in Constant Purchasing Power, 1947–80

of the household balance sheet suggests that the impact of revaluations will vary among individuals holding different portfolios. For example, in the first two decades, major upward revaluations in corporate stock significantly altered the distribution of wealth, in both current value and real terms, in favor of households that held corporate stock; these households tended to be at the upper end of the income and wealth distributions. The household with assets mainly in fixed claims or consumer durables, which rented rather than owned a home, may have gained in market-value terms, but may have suffered a loss in real terms.

In the last decade, the upper end of the income and wealth distribution lost through the relative decline in corporate stock prices and the erosion of fixed-claim assets. Those who gained in this period were home-owners and owners of other equities (e.g., firms and other unincorporated businesses). On the one hand, the value of their assets increased faster than the general level of prices, and, on the other, their fixed debt in the form of mortgages and other liabilities declined in real terms. Again in this period, the household with assets mainly in fixed claims or consumer durables may have suffered a loss in real terms.

Microdata information on the portfolio holdings of individuals would make it possible to examine in somewhat more detail the consequences of specific types of change for groups at different stages in the life cycle and in different economic circumstances.

APPENDIX: FINANCIAL INTERMEDIARIES IN NATIONAL ACCOUNTING

The treatment of financial intermediaries is — and for many years has been — one of the most controversial issues in national accounting. It is generally recognized that the results of applying to financial intermediaries the principles of measurement applied to nonfinancial enterprises are unacceptable. The market value of their sales is either difficult to identify or is not considered to be a correct measure of the value of their output. The alternatives proposed or used rely on measures of cost. The product of financial intermediaries is considered to be equal to the contribution of the factors of production they employ. This contribution, in turn, is usually measured on a net basis: receipts are deducted from the corresponding category of factor payments.

The resulting measures of production, however, are designed to derive a national aggregate, not to reflect the actions of individual transactors. From the viewpoint of the individual transactor, these measures often do not present a recognizable picture. If the macroeconomic accounting system is to function as an aggregation of microeconomic accounts, some reconsideration of the treatment of financial intermediaries is needed. This appendix compares the treatment by BEA with the treatment that would reflect the way the transactions would be recorded in individual transactor accounts.

Fire and Casualty Insurance

Fire and casualty insurance is purchased by businesses and households as protection against the possibility of loss. Premiums are paid to insurance companies which, in turn, use these funds to pay the claims of the insured suffering losses and to cover the costs and profits of the companies.

In the BEA accounts, the *purchase by business* of fire and casualty insurance is treated on a net basis, i.e., the claims paid to business are subtracted from the premiums paid by business. This net premium payment, of course, equals the pro rata share of the costs and profits of the insurance companies. Losses relating to fixed capital due to fire and casualty are recorded in the national income and product account as 'accidental damage to fixed capital' as part of capital consumption allowances. (Losses not relating to fixed capital are recorded in several other ways.) Thus, for businesses as a group, the understatement of the insurance premiums that business pays is offset by an equal overstatement of capital consumption, so that profits remain unaffected.

In the actual accounts of businesses, these transactions would be recorded differently. Insurance premiums paid would be a cost of goods and services purchased from other enterprises and would not be netted against claims, and the claims received, and also the losses they offset, would be recorded in the capital accounts. No entry would be made in capital consumption allowances for accidental damage to fixed capital.

The BEA treatment would be inappropriate for the accounts of individual transactors. Businesses suffering no damage to their fixed capital would record the premium actually paid. Businesses suffering damage, however, would record 'net premiums', i.e., premiums paid less claims received, which could be a sizeable negative flow, and the damage would appear as a large item in capital consumption allowances. These distortions are due partly to a questionable separation of current from capital transactions in BEA's accounts and partly to a willingness to deal exclusively with consolidated accounts for businesses as a group.

Recording these transactions as they are seen by individual transactors would not alter the measure of total GNP. However, it would result in a decline in the product originating in businesses buying insurance, because the cost of insurance would be measured by total premiums rather than net premiums. This decline would be exactly offset by an increase in product originating in the insurance sector, which would now measure output by total, rather than net, premiums. Claims paid out would reflect that portion of the insurance sector's output that is paid over to claimants, in much the same way that dividends represent payment of profits to stockholders. The transactor approach thus recognizes that, at the microdata level, total premiums paid by a business are a current cost of operation, and damage to fixed capital and claims paid with respect to it are adjustments to the capital account.

Purchases by households of fire and casualty insurance are treated in the BEA accounts in a manner parallel to the treatment used for business. Households pay 'net premiums', which equal their pro rata share of the costs and profits of the insurance companies. However, from the transactor's point of view, it is the total premium that represents a consumer purchase, and claims received are a capital transaction. The BEA treatment, by combining a major capital receipt (claim received) with a relatively minor current outlay (premium paid), distorts an individual household's account. Unlike the case of insurance purchased by business, however, the use of the transactor approach for households would result in an increase in total GNP, because consumer purchases would reflect total, rather than net, premiums paid, and this increase would, in turn, increase the output of the insurance companies without any offsetting decrease elsewhere. This outcome is quite consistent with opportunity cost and utility theory. What households purchase is protection against capital loss, and the cost of the protection for the individual transactor consists of the full premium payment.

Health Insurance

The discussion that follows is in terms of commercial health carriers and of medical care and hospitalization benefits. Nonprofit organizations, including workmen's compensation funds, are not discussed, nor are income loss benefits.

Health insurance premiums may be paid to health insurance carriers by employers as fringe benefits for their employees, or they may be paid by households directly. The benefits paid consist of direct payments to doctors, hospitals, and other providers of medical care and of direct payments to beneficiaries for reimbursement for out-of-pocket costs of medical care.

Premiums paid by employers for health insurance are, in the BEA accounts, 'other labor income' received by employees. On the outlay side of the personal account, employees purchase the services of health insurance carriers as measured by premiums less benefits and medical care services as measured by payments to providers of medical care.

From the employee's point of view, health insurance provided as a fringe benefit is not actual money income. It does not appear on his wage and tax (W-2) statement; in most cases, employees are quite unaware of the amount of the premium the employer pays. Although this fringe benefit could be considered imputed income, for any specific employee its valuation poses serious problems, and the proper value might bear little or no relation to the premiums paid by the employer. For example, the value of the insurance to a single person may well be less than to a family, and young employees might value it less than older employees. There does not seem to be more justification for this imputation than for imputations for subsidized meals, parking, use of expense accounts, recreational facilities, and even pleasant working conditions.

For the costs of services of the carriers and medical care services as measured by payments to providers, allocation of what is shown in the BEA accounts to individual households would give a grossly distorted picture of actual income and expenditures. For individuals who were not sick, an imputation of the 'average cost' as income and expenditure would be an overstatement — they did in fact have no health expenditures. For individuals who did receive medical care, their imputed income and expenditures would be understated by use of an 'average cost'.

To replicate the accounts of individual transactors, employers should be recorded as purchasing health insurance as a fringe benefit for their employees; this transaction should not appear in the employees' accounts. The health insurance industry, in turn, should purchase medical care from providers of such services. This treatment would yield the same estimates of GNP and product originating by industry as the BEA treatment.

Premiums paid by individuals for health insurance are not recorded in the BEA accounts as consumer expenditures. Instead, the consumer expenditure for health insurance is the costs and profits of the carriers; the cost of the medical care individuals receive is a separate consumer expenditure.

To replicate the accounts of individual transactors, the full premium should be recorded as the purchaser's expenditure. As in the case of household purchases of fire and casualty insurance, this shift to a transactor basis would result in an increase in GNP. The increase would be equal to the difference between the premiums paid and the costs and profits of health insurers and the costs of medical care. Such an increase in GNP is justifiable because the premiums paid by households represent a purchase of health security that guarantees medical care.

Life Insurance

The discussion that follows is generally applicable to insured pension funds. Life insurance premiums, like health insurance premiums, may be paid either by an employer for their employees or by a household directly. For the former, BEA treats premiums as other labor income.

When an individual pays the premium, it is not entered in the BEA accounts as a consumer expenditure; only the expenses of the life insurance companies are considered consumer expenditure. In both cases, in terms of standard life insurance accounts, the difference between the premiums actually paid less expenses charged as consumer expenditure equals benefits paid plus profits of the life insurance companies plus the change in their reserves less investment income earned.

In order to record premiums as they appear to individual transactors, it must first be determined whether the transactions affect the individual's balance sheet. For term insurance, no cash surrender value or equity is built up, and from the individual's point of view the treatment should be the same as for casualty insurance. If an employer pays the premium, the payment is a fringe benefit and should not enter the employee's income. Those who do directly benefit in the current period are those who are paid the claims. Claims paid in a lump sum should be recorded in the capital accounts, together with other estate transfers. Annuities should be recorded as current income received by households. Individual purchases of term life insurance should be treated in the accounts like household purchases of other casualty insurance.

If life insurance premiums result in an increase in the equity of individuals, this increase should be reflected in their balance sheets and current accounts. The appropriate measure of the increase in an individual's equity, however, is the increase in the cash surrender value of his policies, not a pro rata share of the total reserves of life insurance companies. Further, a portion of the premiums paid by individuals represents saving in the current account, and this amount, too, is best measured by what actually accrues to him — the change in his cash surrender value. Aside from these considerations, the premiums paid for whole life insurance and the claims paid should be recorded in transactor accounts in the same way as described for term life insurance.

Interest

The BEA accounts employ the concept of 'net interest'. Interest received by enterprises is netted against the interest they pay. At least two rationales for this treatment can be offered. It can be argued that interest is a payment for a factor of production, and net interest represents the net amounts of this factor used by enterprises. Alternatively, it can be argued that interest payments are not factor payments but, like dividend payments, represent a transfer of the income earned by an enterprise to those having a claim on it. According to either rationale, interest received is derived from the productivity of other enterprises, and should be excluded from the measurement of the output (income originating) of the receiving enterprise. This exclusion can best be accomplished by omitting the interest received from the product side of the account and subtracting it on the income side from interest paid.

For financial institutions whose interest receipts exceed interest payments by substantial amounts, this procedure results in negative product. As a consequence, it has been found useful to recognize that depository institutions provide services, instead of paying interest, to their depositors, and these services, in effect, constitute imputed interest payments. Such imputed payments are valued at the cost of providing the services. Once the imputations are introduced, the net interest approach results in an income-originating measure for these financial institutions that equals their costs and profits.

The United Nations system does not formally adopt a net interest approach, but, because it separates production accounts from appropriation accounts, the effect is the same. In the production account for an enterprise, the operating surplus is a residual reflecting the difference between sales receipts and the costs of sales. It represents that part of factor income that is carried over to the appropriation account where dividends and interest are added to derive the total amount of income available for distribution. The disbursements side of the appropriation account shows the payments made. Because interest transactions are not recorded in the production account, they do not enter the measurement of output.

Enterprise interest

In the accounts of individual enterprises, net interest received is not customarily netted against interest paid. In computing operating surplus, an enterprise might exclude interest received, but the purpose would be to separate normal business activity from financial activities.

From the point of view of an individual enterprise, it would be more logical to treat interest transactions like rental receipts and payments. On the receipts side of the account, rents are treated as the sale of services, and on the outlay side, rents are an intermediate purchase of services from other enterprises. This procedure results in a correct measure of product originating in rental transactions in the enterprise sector. The excess of rents paid by the enterprise sector over rents received by it is rents received by households. To convert these rents into a measure of product originating, the rental expenses are deducted from gross receipts. This residual item is called 'rental income of persons'.

Under a treatment similar to that used for rental transactions, interest received by enterprises would be considered a sale of services, and interest paid by enterprises to other enterprises would be considered an intermediate purchase. The excess of interest paid by the enterprise sector over interest received by it is interest received by households. To convert these interest transactions into a measure of product originating, any costs incurred in connection with the lending would be deducted before the payment of 'interest income to persons'.

It has been argued that interest should not be treated as an intermediate purchase, because this would misrepresent the 'true' measure of value added, or income originating, in an industry. This reasoning has also been applied to rental payments. For example, production function analysis may require a measure of capital goods used, irrespective of whether owned or rented. However, it does not follow that the NIPAs should be constructed solely with such analysis in mind; what an enterprise's gross product originating should represent is the value that is added to contributions of other enterprises. In addition, it would be extremely difficult to reconstruct enterprise accounts to treat rented and owned capital goods symmetrically. To do so, it would be necessary to impute the costs of ownership, including such items as management costs and taxes, to the using enterprise.

The transactor approach to interest would alter the pattern of gross product originating. It would reduce the gross product of the enterprises that borrow, and correspondingly increase the gross product of the enterprises that lend. One of the major consequences would be that gross product of depository institutions, without imputed interest, would be exactly equal to what is now computed including imputed interest. The reason is, of course, that the interest received by depository institutions would be a sale of goods and services, and on the cost side, interest paid would be an intermediate purchase, leaving in gross product originating exactly what is now in the BEA accounts. This approach does not require the abandonment of the imputation for depository services; it does require, however, that the imputation be justified on grounds similar to those that might justify imputations for television, radio and the media, which are paid for largely by advertising expenditures.

Consumer interest payments
In the BEA personal account, the interest treatment excludes consumer interest from consumer expenditure; it is treated as a transfer. However, for the individual borrower, the extension of credit is a useful service, and it is purchased like any other consumer service. In many cases, interest charges are implicit in higher prices where credit or charge privileges are granted. Paradoxically, if a consumer buys at a lower price for cash and borrows to finance the purchase, the interest charge is, in the national accounts, excluded from consumer expenditures. If market valuations and opportunity cost are to be used to represent the value of goods and services, there is no reason from the individual transactor's point of view to exclude consumer interest as a purchase of credit services.

The exclusion of consumer interest payments from consumer expenditures is usually based on one or more of the following arguments, which are variants of the same theme. First, it may be argued that no productive resources are involved in the loaning of money. Interest represents only a redistribution of income, and is not in itself a factor of production. Second, it may be argued that no production has taken place, and, as a consequence, there is no operating surplus out of which interest can be paid. In both cases, interest payments are considered transfers rather than purchases of services. Finally, it is sometimes argued that consumer interest is 'unproductive', in much the same sense that Adam Smith argued that the services of domestic servants were unproductive.

Government interest payments

The BEA accounts also exclude government interest from purchases of services. The exclusion is an old and universal (if not honorable) tradition in national accounting. The original justification was made for World War I debt. It was argued that interest on government debt incurred for a past war should not give rise to output in later periods. The National Accounts Review Committee in 1958 generally supported this argument, but raised a question about the debt of state and local governments, which has often financed capital assets, such as schools, providing current services. With respect to the BEA accounts (as opposed to those of most other countries), it has also been argued that, because government durables are not capitalized and are not considered to produce income, no real capital services are performed, and it would, therefore, be inappropriate to include a measure of these services.

BEA's treatment of government interest is at variance with the general principles underlying its system. In a market economy, services purchased are considered to represent output, even if they are in some sense wasted, as in waging wars. Thus one does not ask whether a government employee performs a service; the fact that he is paid is taken as an indication that the service exists. A similar argument can be made that if interest is paid, then credit services exist.

The difference between a transfer payment and the purchase of a service rests on the question of whether a service is performed in the current period, not on whether the service is used. Thus a pension paid to a veteran differs from the pay of a soldier in that no services are provided in the current period by the veteran, whereas the pay of the soldier represents services made available. Whether the services are used is considered irrelevant.

Based on these principles, the holders of government bonds are providing services fully as much as if they had purchased corporate bonds, and government interest payments should be recorded as the purchase of services. Furthermore, because government debt is fungible, it is not appropriate to distinguish between debt incurred for war purposes, for countercyclical measures or the purchase of government durables. Those interested in measuring 'economic welfare' can impute any deduction they wish for what they consider to be the nonproductive use of government credit — or for that matter any other nonproductive use of resources, like the 'regrettable necessities' some analysts have tried to identify. But this is analysis, not accounting period, not on whether the service is used.

REFERENCES

Board of Governors of the Federal Reserve System (1980), *Balance Sheets for the US Economy*, June.

Carson, Carol S. (1975), 'The history of the national income and product accounts: The development of an analytical tool', *Review of Income and Wealth*, **21**.

Katz, Arnold J. and Janice Peskin (1980), 'The value of services provided by the stock of consumer durables, 1947–77: An opportunity cost measure', *Survey of Current Business*, **60**.

US Department of Commerce, Bureau of Economic Analysis (1982), *Fixed Reproducible Tangible Wealth in the United States, 1925–79*, Washington, DC: US GPO.

11. Integrated Economic Accounts: Reply

Richard Ruggles and Nancy D. Ruggles
Yale University

1. INTRODUCTION

In the May 1982 issue of the *Survey of Current Business*, a set of national income and product accounts and balance sheets was presented by the authors under the title 'Integrated Economic Accounts for the United States, 1947–80'. These experimental accounts were followed by eight comments by reviewers who had had substantial experience in the construction and/or use of the national accounts. (The reviewers were Hans J. Adler and Preetom S. Sunga, Statistics Canada; Carol S. Carson and George Jaszi, BEA; Edward F. Denison, formerly at BEA; John A. Gorman, BEA; Martin L. Marimont, formerly at BEA; Stephen Taylor, Board of Governors of the Federal Reserve System; Helen Stone Tice, BEA; and James Tobin, Yale University.) This article responds to the issues raised by the reviewers, clarifies or amends some of the arguments advanced in the original presentation, and in general continues the dialogue on this topic.

The discussion is divided into three sections. The first section is concerned with the issue of integration of economic accounts: the role of the national accounts, the implications of integration for the sectoring of the accounts, and how microdata can be related to the macroaccounts. The second section deals with more detailed questions relating to the definition and use of the transactor approach, the treatment of specific transactions, and the form of presentation of the accounts. A concluding section summarizes the views of the reviewers with respect to the proposed modifications and extensions and evaluates the role of the national accounts in the future development of the US statistical system.

This chapter first appeared in *Survey of Current Business*, **62** (11), 1982.

2. INTEGRATION OF THE ECONOMIC ACCOUNTS

The Role of the National Accounts in Integration

The nature of integration

Carson and Jaszi indicated in their comments that, although integration has long been recognized as a desirable objective, the presentation of the integrated economic accounts (IEAs) did not clearly specify what it meant by the term, either with respect to coverage or with respect to the kinds of linkages an integrated system's parts must exhibit. The point is very relevant — integration may be as respected as motherhood, but it is much more difficult to define. In one sense, the present national income and product accounts (NIPAs) and their supplementary tables constitute an integrated system of core accounts and related data. As Denison observed, the great strength of the NIPAs lies in their use of a few simple formal accounts that are supplemented by many supporting tables tied to these accounts. The supporting tables disaggregate the summary accounts in various ways and provide details of their composition.

In another sense, however, there is a broader role for the national accounts that suggests that they, because of their comprehensive nature, can and should provide a coordinating and integrating framework for all economic statistics. In this broader sense, the economic statistics of the United States cannot be considered to be integrated, and the NIPAs do not play a large part. Integration in this broader sense would require using common definitions and classification systems consistent with the national accounts for related data from different sources, and establishing the major economic constructs of the national accounts as control totals to which various parts of the statistical system must be related. The United Nations System of National Accounts (SNA) envisages such a role for the national accounts in the integration of all economic statistics, and many other countries do use their national accounts to serve this purpose. But the NIPAs do not function this way in the US statistical system. Rather, BEA considers its task to be primarily one of drawing upon a large number of fragmentary, diverse and uncoordinated sources obtained from different government agencies, in order to piece together a set of core national accounts and supporting tables. Feedback, in terms of influence upon the basic data, is limited and in many instances nonexistent.

In both of these senses, integration is a matter of degree. There is, of course, no one point at which a statistical system becomes 'integrated'. Integration in the first sense can be increased by extending the comprehensiveness of the core system of accounts. In the second sense, it can be increased by utilizing the national accounts more fully as the framework for the wider statistical system. The IEAs attempted to move in both of these directions, by expanding the NIPA core accounts to include financial transactions and stocks and redesigning the accounts to serve more adequately as a coordinating framework for economic and social data at different levels of aggregation.

Enlarging the national accounts

With respect to the first of these directions, that of expanding the scope of the NIPA core accounts, the reviewers did not disagree with the objective. It was noted by Tobin that the very essence of an accounting system — for a household, an enterprise, or a nation — is a consistent joint evaluation of stocks and flows; the national accounting system should show how changes in balance sheets from one date to another arise from incomes, outgoings, and reevaluations in the intervening period. The United Nations SNA calls for such an arrangement, as was pointed out by Adler and Sunga, but no country (including Canada) has ever previously published a full set of such integrated accounts. As Taylor observed, the flow of funds (FOF) accounts of the Federal Reserve Board are at an aggregate level both statistically and conceptually integrated with the NIPAs of BEA as a logical deconsolidation of the NIPA gross saving and investment account. However, most users do consider that NIPA and the FOF accounts are separate and distinct, rather than integral parts of the same system. This perception is reinforced by the differences in sectoring and classifications used in the two systems. The IEA presentation combined the two sets of data into a common framework with a single system of sectoring, and provided the capital accounts and balance sheets for the government sector as well as for the sectors covered by the FOF accounts.

National accounts as a statistical framework

With respect to the second objective, that of redesigning the national accounts so that they can serve as a framework for a system of economic and social data at different levels of aggregation, a number of reviewers expressed substantial dissent. The dissent took two forms: some felt that the objective was mistaken and others that it was impractical of achievement.

Both Marimont and Denison felt that this objective imposed features that were irrelevant or harmful to the analytic usefulness of the accounts. Marimont did not specify what these features were. Denison felt that the GNP account in the IEAs is not appropriate for the measurement of production, because it employs gross rather than net concepts. Although it is true that the IEAs are centered around the concept of GNP rather than that of national income, this feature of the system is based on the belief that GNP is analytically a more useful concept for many purposes than national income; it is, of course, unrelated to the use of the national accounts as a framework for microdata. The rationale underlying the design of the IEAs was that the analysis of macro-accounts requires an understanding of microeconomic behavior, and as a consequence it is important to use the same concepts at both the macrodata and microdata levels. It would have been equally possible to build both the national income and product account and the enterprise sector accounts around net concepts, which in turn could be related to microaccounts also constructed on a net basis.

Carson and Jaszi did not so much question the objective as express skepticism about the possibility of achieving it. They doubted, for instance, that it would be possible — or could seriously be proposed — to develop the accounts in such a way that they would embrace the broad spectrum of data included in the Census Bureau's Social Indicators. Whether such data could in practice be integrated into the IEA framework depends upon whether microdata sets exist that contain the basic information and can be adjusted to fit (both conceptually and statistically) the major economic constructs of the IEAs. It is our belief that such microdata sets do exist, and that they can be integrated with the macroaccounts. It seems worth examining this question more closely.

Appendix A to *Social Indicators III* describes in some detail the 27 major sources of data that were used in compiling this volume (Bureau of the Census, 1980). Approximately 14 of the sources relate to households or individuals and contain microdata that could in principle be fitted into the household sector of the national accounts. These include, for example, the Census of Population and Housing, the Current Population Survey, the Health Interview Survey, the National Crime Survey, Statistics of Income, the Survey of Income and Education, Social Security Benefit Data and the National Travel Survey. Indeed, many of these sources have already provided microdata for 'exact matched' or 'statistically matched' files used in conjunction with the existing national accounts. Another seven of the sources of data listed were reports containing microdata from governmental units (e.g., Annual Surveys of State and Local Governments) and surveys of health and educational institutions; it should be possible to relate all of these to the government sector and its subsectors in the national accounts. In some instances the device of satellite accounts suggested by Adler and Sunga might prove to be useful for breaking out the more detailed information (e.g., data relating to the health subsector or to institutions of higher learning). As might be expected in a volume on social indicators, relatively few (four only) of the listed sources referred to enterprises, but these, including the Current Business Survey, the Consumer Price Index, and the Producer Price Index, could all usefully be developed as microdata sets integrated with the national accounts. In the case of both the consumer and producer price data, this would require using classification systems for the price data that are consistent with the classifications used in the national accounts — something that, somewhat incredibly, is not now done.

Of all the sources of data for *Social Indicators* listed in Appendix A, only one — the Uniform Crime Reporting Program — appears to be inappropriate for integration with the national accounts. The reporting units in this case are law enforcement agencies in various localities and the data reported are various types of crime committed. There are a few more sources of this type among the less important sources not listed in Appendix A, which reported automobile accidents, deaths by fire and atmospheric pollution; the microdata in these sources also consist of reports by specific localities. These location-specific types of information suggest the desirability of including locational attributes in the microdata for households, enterprises and governments. Localities could then be treated as reporting units providing data on crime, accidents, and environmental conditions occurring within them. Such linkages to the national accounts would be extremely useful for examining the costs and benefits of programs carried out by different levels of government or for evaluating the welfare of individuals living in a given area.

National accounts as a measure of welfare

Adler and Sunga asked why the rationale for both the established and new treatments of national accounts were not viewed with some welfare consideration in mind. We would argue that the IEAs were specifically designed to take several important aspects of welfare measurement into account. The literature on welfare economics has made it clear that the presently existing macroeconomic constructs of the national accounts, which are primarily composed of transactions data, cannot provide an adequate basis for the measurement of welfare. In the first place, welfare is not merely a function of the total amount of income and wealth in a nation; it is obviously related to the distribution of that income and wealth. In the second place, the boundary established by transactions omits many elements that are directly relevant to welfare, such as nonmarket activities, environmental conditions and other factors affecting the quality of life. The IEAs attempted to be responsive to both of these dimensions of welfare measurement in their effort to establish linkages between the aggregates of the macroaccounts and the economic and social microdata for households and individuals, in order to permit the analysis of distributions of income and wealth, and to separate market transactions data from nonmarket information, in order to allow for the expansion of nonmarket imputations without impairing the usefulness of the accounts for analyzing the behavior of the market economy.

The establishment–firm dichotomy

Adler and Sunga and also Carson and Jaszi expressed disappointment that the problems of integrating input–output into the accounts were not considered. In particular, they were concerned with the lack of comparability between the establishment-based industry classifications used for input–output analysis and the firm-based industry classifications used for saving, financial transactions and balance sheets.

Both the NIPAs and the United Nations SNA view input-output as a deconsolidation of the production account for the Nation, and IEAs adopt this same approach. Although there are problems of execution, these problems were felt to be too technical, too detailed and too well recognized to merit specific consideration in the discussion of the IEAs.

We would argue, furthermore, that the specific establishment–firm problem raised by the reviewers is not properly a question of integration in the sense that this term has been used in the discussion to this point. It does not arise from lack of statistical coordination, but from the inherent situation. A single firm may own establishments in different industries, and it is not, therefore possible to choose a single industry classification for the firm that is the same as the industry classification of its establishments. The fact of the matter is that it is really inappropriate to classify a firm's activity in a single industry if it is actually engaged in several industries. The firm can be, and in the NIPAs is, classified as the industry accounting for the largest share of its output, but this cannot be expected to lead to the same distribution as a classification of establishments. Indeed, the 'establishment–firm dichotomy', as it was raised by Carson and Jaszi, has a direct parallel in the 'individual–household dichotomy' in the household sector. As is true in the case of the firm, the household may cover a number of subunits (individuals) who have diverse characteristics (e.g., age, sex, education, occupation). Although it is possible to classify the household subunits into groups based on these characteristics, it is not possible to classify households in these terms. Nevertheless, such classifications of households are often made. For instance, all households whose head owns a business may be classified as entrepreneurial even if other household members are wage earners. The concern for establishment–firm classification problems and the neglect of individual–household classification problems are, of course, direct reflections of the production focus of the NIPAs.

As Adler and Sunga suggest, the establishment–firm classification problem can only be resolved by utilizing information at a more disaggregated level, where data are available for production and capital formation at the level of the individual establishments owned by the firm and financial transactions and balance sheets at the level of the firm itself. Such microdata sets can, in fact, be constructed, and we are at the present time developing, in conjunction with the Bureau of the Census, a longitudinal file for manufacturing establishments and firms at the microunit level for the period 1972–80. One of the immediate questions for which this microdata set is being used is the one raised by Carson and Jaszi — i.e., analysis of how the activities of the individual establishments contribute to savings of firms and how in turn these savings are related to capital formation at the establishment level. This sort of question obviously cannot be answered satisfactorily by the highly aggregated data in the macroaccounts, and requires the use of microdata. But in order to use the microdata on firms and their establishments to explain the behavior of aggregates in the macroaccounts, the same concepts of saving and capital formation must be used at the microdata and macrodata levels, and the microdata, when combined, must aggregate to the same constructs in the macroaccounts.

Sectoring of the Economy and Integration

NIPA sectoring and IEA modifications

The NIPA sectoring of the economy grew out of the measurement of income originating in the different parts of the economy. The sector accounts in the original 1947 version of the NIPAs were drawn up to show the derivation of national income originating in business, households and nonprofit institutions, government and the rest of the world. Nonprofit institutions were grouped with households not only because on a conceptual level they were, like households, considered to be final consumers of goods and services, but also because on a statistical level final consumption was estimated by the commodity flow method, which resulted in a total that could not be broken down between households and nonprofit institutions.

The five-account system introduced in 1958 dropped the account for the business sector, and reorganized the other sector accounts to display all of their income and outlays, rather than focusing on the derivation of the national income originating in each sector. Nevertheless, the present NIPAs retain the 1947 sector definitions. They continue to provide information on gross product, net product, and income originating in the business sector (BEA Tables 1.5, 1.6, 1.9, 1.10 and 1.12), even though they do not include an explicit business sector account. In the industrial breakdowns of product, income and employment (BEA Tables 6.1–6.26), the concept of 'private domestic industries' is also introduced; this is broader than the concept of 'business sector' in that it includes nonprofit institutions and domestic service workers but it is narrower in that it excludes government enterprises. Neither of these NIPA concepts is fully satisfactory, and the differences between them can result in confusion. On the one hand, the BEA business sector does not in fact represent production units motivated by profit, because it includes government enterprises and the imputed services of owner-occupied housing. On the other hand, the exclusion of government enterprises from the BEA industrial breakdowns of product, income and employment (despite the fact that these units are included in the BEA business sector) results in underreporting of those industries where government enterprises are important, and the industrial composition of government enterprises remains a mystery. With respect to the household sector, the inclusion of nonprofit institutions reduces the usefulness of the household sector account for those concerned with analyzing household income, consumer expenditure and saving. It is especially difficult to relate the household account to more disaggregated data, such as the size of distribution of income and the socio-economic composition of the household sector. For these reasons, the IEAs made the following modifications in the NIPA sectoring:

	IEA Concepts	**NIPA Concepts**
	Enterprise Sector	= Business Sector
		+ Nonprofit institutions
		+ Domestic service workers
		− Owner-occupied housing
or alternatively:		
	Enterprise Sector	= Private Domestic Industries
		+ Government enterprises
		− Owner-occupied housing
and:		
	Housing Sector	= Households and Institutions
		− Nonprofit institutions
		− Domestic service workers
		+ Owner-occupied housing

These sectoring modifications met with considerable opposition from the reviewers. Only Tobin unqualifiedly stated that moving nonprofit institutions out of the household sector was an improvement. Taylor approved, in general, of the modification of the household sector account, but questioned whether charities and foundations should not be treated as financial rather than nonfinancial enterprises. Adler and Sunga agreed that removing nonprofit institutions would improve the household sector, but feared that placing them in the enterprise sector would blur the character of the enterprise sector as being composed of production units motivated primarily by profit. Tice agreed that the changes in sectoring improve the homogeneity of the household sector, but felt that this is at great expense to the usefulness of the enterprise sector. Carson and Jaszi indicated that putting nonprofit institutions in the enterprise sector would increase the heterogeneity of that sector and would have a high cost in terms of the number of additional items required to implement the move. Denison felt that nonprofit institutions are consuming units akin to both households and governments, and, furthermore, that combining them with the producing units in the business sector whose output is normally sold to other sectors and can, therefore, be independently measured, would be unsatisfactory for the measurement of productivity.

The majority of the objections to the IEA sectoring modifications centered on their impact on the enterprise sector. The sections below discuss first this general question, and then take up some of the specific points.

Heterogeneity of the enterprise sector

Although one can understand the almost universal desire to define the enterprise sector as a homogeneous grouping of production units motivated primarily by profit, the reviewers' comments seem somewhat incongruous in the context of present BEA practices. In view of the concern for the business sector expressed by many of the reviewers, one would have expected to find that it played an important role in NIPAs. As already noted, however, the NIPAs do not contain an account for the business sector and restrict its role to the presentation of a few summary aggregates. Even there, the NIPA business sector, despite protestations of Denison and of Adler and Sunga, is not restricted to producers selling to other sectors or profit-making producers because it includes both government enterprises and the imputed rental value of owner-occupied housing. In all the tables that present breakdowns by industry, BEA abandons the concept of the business sector and uses instead the concept of private domestic industries, which does include both nonprofit institutions and domestic service workers. Thus neither of the concepts that are now used in the NIPAs meets the criterion of 'purity' set forth by the reviewers. Furthermore, both NIPA categories are already very heterogeneous, covering a wide variety of nonfinancial and financial enterprises organized as cooperatives, mutuals, public authorities or public corporations. Such organizations may operate primarily for the mutual benefit of the groups they represent by providing goods and services at lower cost, rather than by maximizing profit. To limit the enterprise sector to a homogeneous group of private profit-motivated organizations would reduce its coverage well below that of either of the present NIPA concepts, and the problem of the treatment of the excluded enterprises would remain.

Nonprofit institutions

Although Carson and Jaszi are quite correct in indicating that additional entries are needed to move nonprofit institutions from the household to the enterprise sector, the information provided by these entries would be useful and is long overdue. It is not merely clutter in the accounts. More information needs to be provided about the operation of the nonprofit subsector of the economy, especially if, with the reduction of the government sector, it is expected to take on expanded functions. Even by BEA's own measure, the gross product originating in nonprofit institutions is equal to or larger than that of the farm subsector, and for the farm subsector, BEA goes to the length of publishing a complete table on farm output, gross product and income.

The view put forth by Denison that nonprofit institutions are consuming units like households seems to be inappropriate for many nonproft organizations, such as Blue Cross and Blue Shield, major private universities, and nonprofit private hospitals. These organizations receive their funds from a variety of sources, including the sale of their services. In their manner of operation, they are much closer to other private organizations in the same industry than to individual households. Perhaps, as Taylor suggests, some of the nonprofit organizations such as foundations might more appropriately be classified as financial rather than nonfinancial enterprises, but they are clearly enterprises and not households.

Owner-occupied housing

The transfer of owner-occupied housing from the business sector to the household sector caused relatively little comment. Both Taylor and Tice approve of the treatment of owner-occupied housing as a household activity rather than an activity of the business sector — a treatment that, as they point out, is incorporated in the FOF accounts. Taylor commends it as being more in accord with institutional realities. Adler and Sunga were somewhat concerned that the transfer would blur the traditional concept of the household as a consumption unit. This is indeed true, and intentional; the IEAs explicitly recognize that nonmarket production does take place in the household sector.

Carson and Jaszi question whether this change in classification results in saving and investment patterns for the household and enterprise sectors that are more meaningful than those in the NIPAs. From a theoretical point of view, we would argue that the explicit IEA treatment is more informative, because it records the household's costs of home owning (repair and upkeep, property taxes and mortgage interest) as household outlays, where they can be analyzed in the context of household behavior. In addition, the IEA treatment is consistent with a balance sheet for the household sector that shows the value of the house as an asset and the mortgage as a liability; to exclude these items from the household balance sheet — as the present BEA treatment requires — is surely unrealistic.

Denison opposes treating owner-occupied housing differently from tenant-occupied housing; he is primarily concerned with the situation where dwelling units are sometimes occupied by their owners and sometimes rented, with the consequence that each time an owner-occupied house is rented it would, strictly speaking, have to be shifted to the enterprise sector. We agree with Denison that frequent shifting would be undesirable, and in such cases of temporary or seasonal rental we would suggest that the house be retained as a household asset. This treatment would mean that only those housing units whose rental is undertaken primarily as a business activity would be recorded in the enterprise sector.

Domestic service workers

The treatment of domestic service workers in the NIPAs is both a triviality and an anomaly. Domestic service, measured by the compensation of domestic service workers, is in the NIPAs the only production taking place in the household. This figure does not, however, reflect all the purchases of domestic services by households. If house cleaners, gardeners, carpenters trash removers or babysitters are hired on a fee-for-service basis, these transactions are treated as purchases of goods and services, and those involved in providing the services are considered to be self-employed; it is only when their compensation is considered to be 'wages' that they are treated as household employees. The proposal in the IEAs was to treat all such providers of domestic service households as self-employed. Although Denison considers this to be unnecessary and artificial, it seems to us to represent a tidying up of messy detail that has long been overdue. There would be no significant change in the household account; the compensation paid to domestic service workers would still be recorded as a purchase of domestic services by households. In the enterprise account, domestic service workers would be included together with other self-employed persons providing household services.

The need for subsectoring
The logical conclusion to be drawn from the discussion of sectoring is that, in view of the heterogeneous nature of productive activity, subsectoring the enterprise sector is needed. Such subsectoring was carried out in the fuller version of the IEAs, although space limitations precluded printing data for the subsectors in the *Survey* article, and these data are available on computer tape from BEA. The subsectors of the enterprise sector presented are as follows:

Enterprise sector
   Nonfinancial enterprises
      Corporate nonfarm
      Noncorporate nonfarm
      Farm
      Government enterprises
      Nonprofit institutions
   Financial enterprises
      Monetary authority
      Commercial banking
      Other banking
      Pension and insurance funds
      Government financial agencies
      Other financial institutions

Microdata and their Integration with the Accounts

In the IEA presentation, considerable emphasis was placed on the desirability of using the national accounts not only as a conceptual framework for economic data in general, but specifically as a statistical framework for microdata sets related to the sectors and subsectors of the accounts. Only a few of the reviewers commented on this feature of the IEAs. Those who did, raised questions concerning the difficulties of developing appropriate microdata sets, and expressed considerable skepticism as to its practicality. At the same time, one comment noted that this is a 'growth industry', and another concluded that this is intuitively the way to go, in spite of its difficulties.

Microdata for the household sector
Denison states that the IEAs not only fail to meet the objective of providing a framework for household microdata, but the objective itself is a chimera. This view is based on two arguments. First, there will be differences among microdata sets in the definition of the reporting unit — households, families, dwelling units, individuals, taxpayers, etc. — so that there is no general concept they can follow. At best, the household account can be consistent with only one microdata set, and for all others a bridge table would be needed; therefore, why not use a bridge table for all sets? Second, Denison points out that bridge tables will also be needed because aggregates of microdata treat on a combined or gross basis items that are netted or consolidated in the national accounts.

We would argue that this view reflects a fundamental misunderstanding of our objective. Just as the aggregate national accounts do not conform to any specific raw tabulation, there is no expectation that the microdata sets underlying them should conform to any specific single survey or other source. Rather, the principle is that the macroaccounts should be viewed conceptually as the aggregation (including consolidation or netting where appropriate) of a theoretical set of microaccounts. Given appropriate data sources, the national accountant or others should be able to construct, by appropriate adjustment of the available microdata from many different sources, microdata sets approximating the theory that would underlie each sector of the national accounts. A relatively modest household microdata set that is integrated with (i.e., consolidates to) the household sector of the national accounts could yield useful disaggregations of the major items of income and expenditure, and provide related social and demographic information. The fact that there exists a variety of other unadjusted microdata sets is aside from the issue, just as is the existence of unadjusted aggregate data.

In terms of reporting unit, the important issue is that the microdata set that is to underlie the household sector have the same coverage as the household sector of the national accounts. Some of the reporting units mentioned by Denison, such as taxpayers, would clearly be inappropriate as the basis for constructing a microdata set to represent the household sector, because they cover only part of the population included in the household sector of the national accounts. A comprehensive microdata set for the household sector containing data relating to all individuals in the population, in which the attributes of the individuals are specified, would permit the extraction of data on the basis of any reporting unit for which information exists (e.g., taxpayers, wage earners, school children), and users would be able to analyze the relation of various reporting units to each other. As previously noted, the problem here is directly analogous to the establishment–firm relation for enterprises. One of the functions of the microdata set is to clarify the relations among all of the attributes of the microunits involved.

Carson and Jaszi, and also Denison, raised questions about institutional populations such as soldiers and residents of prisons and sanitariums. These people do not really cause any conceptual problems: to the extent that such groups receive income and purchase goods and services, their income is included in household income and their purchases are included in household expenditures. They should, therefore, be included as identifiable units in the household microdata. The goods and services provided to them free of charge should, of course, be recorded as part of the expenditures of the governments or nonprofit institutions providing them.

Bridge tables are useful and appropriate in many circumstances. Thus, for example, BEA Table 3.18B, showing the relation of federal government receipts and expenditures in the NIPAs to the Unified Budget, establishes important linkages between these two kinds of information. Where there are different uses of data calling for different tabulations, such bridge tables showing the relation between the aggregate tabulations are often useful. But this is quite different from using bridge tables to adjust raw tabulations of microdata at the aggregate level. As is noted below in connection with establishment microdata for the Census of Manufactures, adjustments made to tabulations of microdata at the aggregate level are not as satisfactory as incorporating such adjustments into the microdata themselves. The reason for this is that different aggregations of the microdata will add up to the correct control totals only if the adjustments are made at the microdata level; if the adjustments are not carried back to the microunits they will have to be done over again whenever a new tabulation is made.

With respect to Denison's second point, bridge tables would in general not be required in those instances where the aggregated data are shown on a consolidated or net basis and the microdata provide gross data. The present government sector in the NIPAs is on a consolidated basis, whereas the subsector accounts for the federal government and for state and local governments show the transfers between these levels of government on a combined basis, and no bridge table is provided or required. It is easy to move from a more to a less gross basis as data are aggregated. What is not possible is to go the other way:

if flows are shown combined or gross at the aggregate level, it is necessary that they also be available on this basis at the microdata level.

The enterprise sector and statistical consistency

Adler and Sunga cite the difficulties even in a fully integrated statistical agency like Statistics Canada of linking microdata originating from differently defined units of collection (i.e., establishments and firms), and suggest that the resource costs are more than can be faced with equanimity. They note that even such seemingly simple steps as ensuring that establishments or firms in sets of data originating from different surveys are always classified in the same industry and location are often frustrating and always time and resource consuming.

These problems, however, are not problems that are restricted to the development of microdata sets. Although the problems become glaringly obvious in the microdata context, they are equally important, and equally present, in the context of the aggregate accounts. Thus, for instance, if one source is used to make estimates of output by industry and another source is used for employment and hours, inconsistency in the industrial classification of establishments or firms will result in errors in the measurement of productivity by industry. It is not true, as the observations of Adler and Sunga might imply, that merely because the errors caused by inconsistent classification of industry and location in different sources are not obvious in macrodata, such errors can be swept under the rug. Nor can it be assumed that they will somehow average out. What is required for coordinating different sources of data is, of course, a complete industrial register that lists all firms, their establishments, and the location and industrial classification of each establishment. Most countries have come to recognize that such a register is a prerequisite not only for providing adequate sample frames, but also for coordinating statistics from different sources. The US Census Bureau has begun to develop such a register, but confidentiality restrictions have so far prevented its use by other statistical agencies. The development of proper statistical procedures may be frustrating and even costly, but the confusion that results from the lack of coordination is even more frustrating and far more costly to users as well as producers of statistics.

The availability of microdata

Consistent with their skepticism concerning the possible integration of the data in *Social Indicators* with the national accounts, Carson and Jaszi do not believe that the quantity of usable microdata is as large as we suggested and, given the substantive difficulties and costliness, they are less optimistic about the prospects for integrating microdata and macrodata. While conceding that the possibility may exist for households, they state that if the prospects and problems of the use of microdata for the enterprise and government sectors had been examined more thoroughly (e.g., the previously noted establishment–firm dichotomy and also differences in business accounting practices), the provision framework for microdata might have been given a smaller weight in the redesign.

With respect to the general question of the quantity of usable microdata available, it is true, of course, that all national accounting estimates are in large degree based on tabulations of microdata, and these basic sources are prime candidates for the construction of microdata sets that are integrated with the national accounts. In some cases, these may be administrative data provided by the Internal Revenue Service, the Social Security Administration, or other regulatory or statistical agencies. The raw tabulations are not usually incorporated directly into the national accounts estimates, because adjustments for conceptual differences, underreporting, or incomplete coverage are generally needed. It is, of course, necessary that the same adjustments also be introduced into the microdata if they are to be coordinated with the accounts, but the experience of the statistical collection agencies has indicated that such procedures are both feasible and highly useful for the data collection process itself. Thus, in connection with the Census of Manufactures, it is now customary to introduce into the records of the individual establishments the necessary edit corrections, imputations for missing data and other adjustments so that the final computer tabulation will be exactly consistent with what is published (Waite, 1982).

With respect to the specific question of microdata for establishments, because of the relatively small number of large enterprises and establishments that account for most of the production taking place in the United States, it is both feasible and desirable to build comprehensive microdata sets by using exact matching. As already noted in the discussion of the establishment–firm classification problem, a longitudinal microdata file for firms and establishments has been developed for the manufacturing sector for the period 1972–80. This file utilized exact matching and contains data for approximately half a million manufacturing establishments for the census years 1972 and 1977, and about 80,000 establishments for the other years covered by the Annual Survey of Manufactures (R. Ruggles and N.D. Ruggles, 1982). A microdata base being developed by the Small Business Administration covers all firms and establishments in the economy (including nonprofit organizations and family businesses). A number of publicly available sources, such as the Dun and Bradstreet Market Identifier File (credit listings) and the Market Data Retrieval File (yellow pages listings), have been merged and matched to produce a Master Establishment List of approximately 8 million establishments. Further research has been done to develop an Establishment and Enterprise Microdata File (about 4.7 million establishments), which provides information on the relation between enterprises and establishments (Small Business Data

Base and Other Sources of Business Information, 1982). The file is being validated by making comparisons, within the proper confidentiality safeguards, with government administrative files relating to corporate and noncorporate tax returns and employer social security and unemployment insurance files. Finally, more detailed financial data (income accounts and balance sheets) are being merged into the file on an exact match basis for all those businesses for which such data are available (about 800,000 cases). All publicly traded companies (approximately 10,000) are, of course, included. The objective of this research is the development of a totally integrated and weighted sample of 200,000 to 300,000 enterprises that will provide employment, sales and financial data on a longitudinal basis.

With respect to the government sector, the feasibility of the development of microdata has also been demonstrated. John Quigley and James Trask at Yale University, with National Service Foundation support (and BEA assistance), undertook to develop microdata sets for government units that were fully integrated with the government sector of the NIPAs. The basic source for the microdata set was the data tape from the Census of Governments for 1972, which provided individual accounts for 75,000 budgetary units; these units included not only federal, state and local governments, but also other public bodies such as public authorities, regional agencies, and school and water districts. The microaccounts covered the sources of revenue by type and the outlays by function, and also provided capital accounts for: the federal government, by states and the District of Columbia (51); State governments (50); county aggregates of local governments (3,118); standard metropolitan statistical areas (100 largest); and separate accounts for central cities, suburban rings and regional governments (for the largest 100 standard metropolitan statistical areas) (Quigley, 1977; Quigley, Trask and Trask, 1977). This project established the feasibility in terms of cost and validity of using the Census of Governments data to develop a microdata set of government units that is integrated with the national accounts.

With respect to household microdata, the view of Carson and Jaszi that the development is substantively difficult and costly stems, no doubt, from BEAs experiences in the development of the estimates of the size distribution of personal income using both exact and statistically matched microdata. This experience underscored the need for a household sector in the national accounts that is conceptually compatible with microunit information. Much of the difficulty BEA encountered arose, first, because it was necessary to develop, within the personal income concept, another concept of family income, which could be distributed by size. Second, it should be borne in mind that the microdata effort in which BEA engaged was pioneering research, and much was learned in the process; certainly those who were directly involved in that research have a much more positive view of the level of success achieved and the future potentiality of integrating household microdata and the national accounts. Finally, the question of cost should be kept in perspective. In absolute terms, the microdata work in BEA was quite modest, and relative to the total of all BEA activities it was almost imperceptible.

3. THE RECORDING OF TRANSACTIONS

The Transactor Approach

The IEAs view the national accounts as being composed of sets of sector accounts, which in turn represent aggregations or consolidations of sets of microaccounts for individual transactors. At the sector level of aggregation, the transactors are classified into enterprises, households, government and the rest of the world. The accounts for both the individual transactors and for the sectors of the economy relate to productive activity, current income and outlays, capital transactions, revaluations of balance sheet items, and balance sheets. This is the basic framework used for the recording of transactions in the IEAs.

This view of the accounting system is strongly opposed by Marimont, who argues that the national accounting structure should be designed in accordance with what is needed for a comprehensive understanding of how the economy operates. After the total system is designed, Marimont suggests, the national accountant can then develop methods for adapting the data for individual transactors. Marimont does not, however, suggest how a system developed in the way he suggests would differ from one conceptually based on individual transactor accounts, nor does he indicate what criteria he would use. The history of the development of the BEA accounts suggests that he may have had in mind constructing the system around the derivation of a few aggregates such as national income, and saving and investment. This was the original basis of the 1947 NIPAs, and still plays a large role. The transactor approach of the IEAs subscribes to Marimont's principle that the accounting system should be designed in terms of what is needed for a comprehensive understanding of how the economy operates, but it suggests that this can best be accomplished by providing organized and systematic information on the transactions and balance sheets of different groups of transactors. As Tobin points out, the existing NIPAs do not in fact provide a satisfactory conceptual framework for the tracking and consistent evaluation of stocks and flows needed for understanding economic behavior.

In implementing the transactor approach, the IEAs made a sharp distinction between actual market transactions and imputations for nonmarket activity. Many of the reviewers raised questions about the definition of imputations, as well as about the usefulness of this separation. In the discussion of financial intermediaries, Annex 1 of the IEA presentation leaned heavily upon how the transactors themselves viewed the transactions. Carson and Jaszi, Denison and Marimont all questioned this 'transactor approach'. Denison pointed out that different transactors may view the same or similar transactions quite differently, and Carson and Jaszi and also Marimont commented that the IEAs did not consistently embody this principle.

In view of the questions that have been raised about the definitions and principles that underlie the transactor approach, a reexamination of the treatment of specific imputations and transactions is in order. It was certainly not our intention, in introducing the transactor approach, to record the same or similar transactions differently based on how individual transactors view them.

Imputations

Carson and Jaszi, Denison, and Marimont raised many objections to the IEA treatment of imputations. Carson and Jaszi felt that there are conceptual problems in determining what should be considered to be an imputation. Denison objected to assigning the market transactions aggregate a central role because he felt that there is no simple and noncontroversial concept of money income and expenditure. Marimont found the treatment of imputations troublesome and indicated that there is a need to define more precisely what kinds of transactions are to be classified as imputations. Finally, all of these reviewers agreed that the separation of nonmarket imputations resulted in more complex accounts, which were less convenient and informative than the NIPA presentation.

In the IEAs, *nonmarket* imputations relate to activity that is not measured by actual market transactions; a clear example of a nonmarket imputation is the services of owner-occupied housing, which BEA values at its equivalent space rental value. This IEA definition of nonmarket imputation contrasts with the more comprehensive BEA definition of imputation which includes, in addition, some activities (e.g., financial services) measured in terms of the (market) costs of providing them.

Carson and Jaszi suggest that the separation of market transactions from nonmarket imputations in the IEAs was primarily motivated by the belief that, compared to actual market transactions, the estimates for nonmarket imputations were relatively speculative. This is a very considerable oversimplification of our position. We recognize that there are actual transactions in the accounts that are speculative because reliable data are not available for estimating them, but we would not favor classifying these transactions as nonmarket imputations. We also recognize the controversial nature of the treatment of certain actual transactions, such as the cost of financial services, but again this is no reason to group such transactions with nonmarket activity. We agree that the concepts of economic depreciation and household capital consumption are conceptually somewhat shaky, quite apart from the question of the availability of data; in this case we feel that these are nonmarket imputations for which there is no transactions counterpart, and they should be embodied in the accounts in a way that does not impinge upon market transactions measurements. We do not feel, however, that food and fuel produced and consumed on farms should be classed as market and included in farm market production and consumption expenditures by households, merely because it is considered to be a 'hard' estimate. Finally, we would argue that the separation of nonmarket imputations is not particularly complex and that it is analytically useful.

The accounts as a framework for market transactions
The primary function of the national income and product accounts has been to provide a framework for displaying the interactions of different sectors of the economy with one another in terms of the market transactions in which they engage. For analyzing the behavior of prices, output and employment, it is this network of market transactions that is the prime focus of attention. There are, of course, a great many transactions for which it is difficult to obtain sound statistical data. In such instances, the national accountant attempts to make the best estimate possible, recognizing that omission of a legitimate entry in a full set of market transactions would result in a greater error than including an inaccurate estimate. Thus BEA does include estimates of such items as tips paid to waiters and waitresses and the payments made to babysitters. It was not the intention of the IEAs, and we agree that it would be quite inappropriate, to classify transactions as market or nonmarket on the basis of reliability.

Market imputations in the accounts
Market imputations are defined in the IEAs as activities that are valued in terms of their costs of production rather than in terms of the market value of their sale. Examples of market imputations are the measurement of the value of financial services provided by banks, the change in inventories and final consumption expenditures of the government.

With respect to the treatment of financial services, the problem is more one of where to draw the boundary between intermediate and final product than of market versus nonmarket activity. The decisions may be controversial, but the measurements involved are all market-determined. In the United Nations SNA, all financial services are treated as an intermediate product, whereas BEA treats part of them as final product. Financial services are not the only example of this sort of problem. As was suggested in the discussion of the IEAs, there are other kinds of expenditures that BEA currently treats as intermediate that might be considered final expenditures; these include research and development, radio and television, and other consumption provided by enterprises. Conversely, as Tobin suggests, some of the current expenditure of government might be considered to be intermediate rather than final. Such shifts in the production boundary may well occur within the framework of a system of accounts drawn up in terms of market transactions, without involving any nonmarket imputation.

Denison does not consider inventory change to be based on market transactions, and he states that including it in income results in abandoning the market transactions concept. From the point of view of the IEAs, however, inventory change is based on market transactions, because it is the difference between costs of production and sales, both measured by market transactions. Even the inventory valuation adjustment is merely a correction in the application of accounting methods — presumably there are accounting records, and there are market transactions on which the correction is based.

Carson and Jaszi and also Denison took the position that government consumption expenditures should not be considered an imputation, but rather should be viewed as final purchases. This seems very reasonable, and IEAs do not preclude such a treatment because government expenditures are considered to be market transactions. The United Nations SNA does set up a production account for government, in which its purchases from business and the compensation of government employees are considered to be inputs that, in turn, are used to produce government outputs. United Nations SNA, thus, treats the purchases from business as intermediate goods, and government final consumption is treated as an imputed purchase by the government of the output it has itself produced. While technically correct, this United Nations SNA approach is awkward and for most government final consumption unnecessary, and the alternative BEA explanation is simpler. The BEA interpretation is not, however, in conflict with IEA.

Economic depreciation

The IEAs do not consider that economic depreciation is a market transaction, and recognizes this by building the national income and product account and the sector current accounts around gross market transactions. Thus gross saving in each sector account is the balancing item, representing the difference between total current market receipts and total current market outlays. As a balancing item, it is independent of the estimate for economic depreciation. This does not mean, as Marimont suggests, that capital consumption is treated as a market transaction in the household account; rather, in this context, capital consumption and net saving are essentially memorandum items attached to total gross saving in each account, showing its possible division into these two components.

Food and fuel produced and consumed on farms

Carson and Jaszi indicate that the estimate of food and fuel produced and consumed on farms is not so speculative that it requires a different kind of statistical estimate. The IEAs classed it as a nonmarket imputation for two reasons. First, it is production and consumption that does not go through the market, and it is not at all clear either conceptually or statistically just what is or should be included under this rubric. For example, should kitchen gardens and poultry raised by farmers be included? If not, on what grounds should they be excluded if other food and fuel is included? If they are included, why should not the kitchen gardens and poultry raised by nonfarmers also be covered? (The latter figure really would be speculative!) Should the processing of the food, i.e., the slaughtering and curing of meat and canning of fruits and vegetables, also be included? If farm wives' canning activity is covered, should that of other housewives not also be included? Second, it is not clear what value should be placed on such home-consumed production — the opportunity cost that could be obtained by selling the product, the input costs, the price the farmer would have to pay for the product if he bought it, and the value which the farmer would himself assign to the output as a consumption good all are possibilities. Although farm income in kind is less than 1 percent of farm gross output (under $1 billion in 1980) and its estimation may seem to be a trivial matter, these questions of valuation are precisely the same as those that arise in connection with the valuation of owner-occupied housing, and that estimate is not trivial in size.

The separation of nonmarket imputations

It is true that separating market transactions and nonmarket activity increases the complexity of the accounts and makes them more difficult for those who are accustomed to the NIPAs. But this increase in complexity can easily be exaggerated, and it is the market transactions accounts that represent the core of the system; these accounts record all transactions between different transactors. The imputations for nonmarket activity are estimates of the production and consumption activity that is internal to a sector and does not go through the market. The NIPAs can neglect the distinction between market and nonmarket activity because they postulate a single correct specification of the production boundary — one that includes exactly the correct amount of nonmarket activity. Many proposals are now being made, however, to extend the conventional production boundary to include such things as the services of government and consumer durables and the nonmarket activity of the household. If consideration is given to any of these, it will become increasingly important to preserve intact the core set of transactions relating to market activity. It is better, perhaps, to build in the possibility of some flexibility, rather than to be forced to cling to an outmoded definition of the production boundary beyond its useful life.

Benefits in Kind

Certain benefits in kind provided by business are treated in the NIPAs as income received by the beneficiaries, and correspondingly, as expenditures by them. Thus, some of the financial services provided by banking institutions are considered to be income in kind received by households and government and also expenditures by them for these services. Similarly, fringe benefits in kind that employers provide to their employees are included both in other labor income and in expenditures and personal saving of households. In the IEA system, however, benefits in kind are treated as final expenditures of the provider of the benefit, and no attributions of income and expenditure are made to the accounts of those who theoretically benefit. Both financial services provided by banking institutions and the fringe benefits in kind provided by private employers are treated in the IEAs as enterprise final consumption expenditures.

Part of the rationale for this treatment is that the recipients might not recognize these benefits in kind as income. In light of the comments of the reviewers, this rationale requires reexamination. Carson and Jaszi argue that the significance of many fringe benefits in collective bargaining is prima facie evidence that employees not only recognize them, but also attach considerable importance to them. It is apparent, however, that workers may recognize and attach value to many other improvements in working conditions, such as safety, working environments and hours, and yet BEA does not treat these amenities as part of personal income. Nor does BEA treat benefits in kind provided by government, such as education, public health and community services, as part of personal income and personal consumption expenditures, although again individuals receiving them may recognize them as benefits. In view of this murkiness, there is much to be said for considering all benefits in kind to be final expenditure of those making the expenditures, irrespective of whether individuals recognize or attach importance to their receipt. The analyst can then make further attributions to the groups he considers to be the beneficiaries, if he wishes. The United Nations SNA, for instance, includes a supplementary concept called 'total consumption of the population', in which all of these attributions are made. But this is provided in addition to, not instead of, household consumption expenditure.

Pensions and Insurance

In the IEAs, the assets of pension funds and life insurance companies are attributed to their prospective beneficiaries only to the extent that they have a cash surrender or loan value. Otherwise, households are not credited with 'wealth' representing the capital value of future pension benefits. Although

Taylor and Tobin find this general treatment useful and satisfactory, Denison and Gorman take issue with it.

Revised estimates

Since the publication of the 'Integrated Economic Accounts', Gorman has correctly pointed out that, in transferring fringe benefits in kind from household to enterprise consumption, the IEAs should have deducted from household consumption expenditures only the cost of services provided by pension and insurance funds. What the IEAs did deduct was not only these services but also the net addition to pension and insurance reserves. These corrections affect enterprise consumption, household consumption, and household gross and net saving. The published and the revised estimates are given in Table 11.1.

Table 11.1 Revised Estimates Resulting from Correcting Pension and Insurance Data ($bn)

	Enterprise consumption expenditures		Household consumption expenditures		Household gross saving		Household net saving	
	Published	Revised	Published	Revised	Published	Revised	Published	Revised
1969	39.8	34.9	386.3	391.2	129.5	124.6	58.2	53.3
1970	46.0	40.9	418.0	423.1	143.2	138.1	65.1	60.0
1971	52.0	46.2	443.6	449.4	164.1	158.3	79.3	73.5
1972	59.7	52.6	477.5	484.6	173.1	166.0	80.3	73.2
1973	67.0	58.2	521.4	512.6	212.5	203.7	111.6	102.8
1974	79.2	69.0	576.2	586.4	218.2	208.0	104.3	94.1
1975	92.6	80.1	628.5	641.0	240.8	228.3	111.9	99.4
1976	101.1	86.2	688.4	703.3	251.6	236.7	109.0	94.1
1977	120.8	103.7	749.2	766.3	271.2	254.1	112.6	95.5
1978	139.2	120.2	829.4	848.4	298.1	279.1	120.1	101.1
1979	154.9	135.3	935.3	954.9	319.4	299.8	118.6	99.0
1980	174.8	154.1	1,052.7	1,073.4	324.5	303.8	97.9	77.2

BEA does not prepare estimates of pension fund operating expenses, because they are not needed for the NIPAs. Preparation of reliable estimates at the present time is not possible because insured pension fund operating expenses are buried in the data for life insurance carriers and there is evidence of a massive shortfall in the existing Securities and Exchange Commission data on noninsured pension plans. Under these circumstances, the estimates of pension fund operating expenses for the IEAs were based on a simple-minded extrapolation of the 1977 ratio of pension fund operating expenses to employer contributions; data for the ratio are from an Internal Revenue Service tabulation of Form 5500 published in the *Statistics of Income Bulletin* (1982).

These revisions do not affect the balance sheet estimates for either enterprises or households, because the balance sheets were based on FOF data.

They do, of course, affect the residual discrepancy between net saving as derived from the balance sheet and as derived from the current account, which was given as part of the addenda to the household balance sheet.

Pensions and life insurance

Denison considers that all private pension and life insurance reserves (as well as the saving of nonprofit institutions) belong in the household sector, because they are all of value to households as prospective beneficiaries. Even term policies or invested pension plans with no cash surrender value, he feels, may be currently valuable to the holder because they may make it possible to obtain further insurance without examination or at lower cost. The IEA view, in contrast, is that households do not in fact own or control the noncashable portion of private pension and insurance reserves, and therefore this part of the reserves should be excluded from their balance sheets. Although the households may be beneficiaries of pensions or insurance in the future, the IEAs do not record this as household income until such time as it is actually received. As for the view that term insurance and invested pension plans may be currently valuable to the owner from the point of view of buying insurance, so is being a veteran, young or female, and these factors are not reflected in the accounts.

Gorman opposes the proposed change on the grounds that life insurance carrier saving, and therefore corporate profits, would be increased by the excess of the increase in aggregate reserves over the increase in cash surrender values, and that he is not aware of any aggregate data on cash surrender value. With respect to the first point, there is no necessity for increasing corporate profits by the excess in aggregate reserves; if indeed the excess aggregate reserves are actuarially or legally required, they represent a legitimate earmarked reserve that would not be available for distribution as profits to the stockholders, although they would still constitute part of gross saving. With respect to the second point, although there may be no readily available aggregate data on cash surrender value, insurance companies do provide their policyholders with this information, and this can be used to develop the necessary aggregate estimates.

Denison questioned the transfer of government pension reserves from the government to the enterprise sector. These reserves largely pertain to state and local government employees, and the transfer reflected the fact that the employee pension funds of state and local governments are generally held by government financial enterprises. It is debatable whether these pension funds should be classified with other pension funds or with other government financial institutions, but they should clearly be a part of the enterprise sector rather than of government. The IEAs did not intend to alter the federal government's retirement system through the pension and insurance sector, and Taylor's point in this case is well taken.

Taylor raised a question about the possibility of estimating unfunded liabilities of retirement systems, i.e., the difference between the present value of future payments due from retirement systems and the capital value of the assets of the systems. He recognized the asymmetrical nature of such estimates: they have important implications for employer groups supporting such systems but may have little meaning for workers covered by the plans because they are illiquid and are fairly abstract concepts. For this reason, he suggested including such estimates as peripheral or memorandum information without incorporating them fully into the accounts. Furthermore, he felt that social security plays a role for individuals parallel to that of retirement systems, and its capitalized liabilities might be included in the memo table even though social security wealth is not capitalized in the household account. At first glance, such an approach seems both reasonable and attractive, but the highly speculative nature of the estimates becomes evident when one recognizes the extent to which assumed future changes in the price level and the interest rate dominate the results. In the case of social security liabilities, it would also be necessary to forecast the ages at which people will retire in the future, the effect of other related government programs and private pension plans, and probable changes in entitlements. Furthermore, it would not be appropriate to capitalize social security liabilities without at the same time capitalizing the future stream of social security revenues, and this would involve forecasting social security tax rates, wage rates and employment. One needs only to refer to past estimates relating to the future of the social security system to see that such estimates are different in kind from the reporting of past events with which the accounts are concerned.

Fire and casualty insurance

IEA Annex 1 considered the treatment of fire and casualty insurance in the accounts. The IEAs agree with the NIPAs that the value added of fire and casualty insurance companies is correctly measured by net premiums (gross premiums minus claims paid). Annex 1 raises the question, however, as to whether this is also the correct measure for computing value added of a firm purchasing fire and casualty insurance, or whether this cost should be measured by the gross premium. Gorman emphasizes that all accidental damage to fixed capital, whether insured or not, is included in the BEA accounts in capital consumption allowances. This means, in fact, that what are capital losses to individual firms are written off at the aggregate level as capital consumption. If there were no insurance at all in the economy, this practice would be equivalent to including in each firm's capital consumption allowance a charge equivalent to self-insurance against accidental damage, which for the economy as a whole would equal the accidental damage actually occurring. In an economy where all firms were fully insured, BEA's allowance for accidental damage plus net premiums paid would be equal to gross premiums paid. The net premiums paid by firms to insurance companies would then appropriately represent the cost of the services of the insurance industry for spreading these risks. The question that remains, however, is whether the BEA treatment, which was designed for consolidated aggregate income and product accounts, is also appropriate for the IEA system, which is based upon production accounts and balance sheets drawn up at the firm and establishment levels. From this point of view, it would seem more suitable that the actual gross premiums paid by a firm be treated like any other item of current cost, and that the losses due to accidental damage and the reimbursement for such losses paid by insurance companies be treated as adjustments to the balance sheets rather than to the production account.

Health insurance

With respect to health insurance, Gorman indicates that the BEA procedure is based on the principle that medical consumption should be shown in the personal income and outlay account when the consuming individual decides which doctor or hospital shall provide the service. For this reason, BEA includes medical expenditures financed by the government under the Medicare program in the personal income and outlay account. The IEAs, in contrast, take the position that when the government sets the standards, circumstances or conditions under which expenditures are to be made and requires accounting for reimbursement, the reimbursements should be considered to be government expenditures and treated as the provision of benefits in kind. In the IEAs, transfer payments from government to households are restricted to cash payments that do not require evidence of expenditure for reimbursement. On this basis, the medical expenditures financed under the Medicare program were considered to be government expenditures. In the case of medical care paid for by an insurance policy purchased by a household, only the premium is considered in the IEAs to be a household expenditure. Similarly, the premium paid by employers for health insurance for their employees is treated as a benefit in kind included in enterprise consumption expenditures. Gorman suggested that this would lead to double counting of final consumption, but it does not. The sum paid to the medical provider by the insurance company would be an intermediate product.

Interest

Although the IEAs retained the BEA net interest approach, in Annex 1 on financial intermediaries we raised a question as to whether that approach is really appropriate for the measurement of output and in the treatment of interest payments by households and government. We suggested that consideration be given, instead, to treatment of interest as the purchase and/or sale of a service, similar to BEA's treatment of rent. Adler and Sunga indicate that they would not be averse to seeing the logic of such a treatment followed to its conclusion.

Denison does have some misgivings about the BEA treatment of consumer interest, but he does not believe that its inclusion in personal consumption expenditures and output would help; in particular he raised a question about deflation, wondering how in a constant-dollar series the inclusion of consumer interest would resolve the trouble introduced by prices that are raised to cover implicit credit costs. As Denison implies, the implicit credit costs 'are already included in the price indexes'. The price a consumer pays for a product covers a variety of conditions of sale, including credit arrangements, delivery, and refund policy. Under these conditions it does seem appropriate also to take explicit interest costs into account.

Gorman notes that the treatment of interest as a cost of production would have the consequence that the measure of a firm's output would be a function of the distribution between borrowed funds and equity capital. A firm that borrowed part of its capital would, other things being equal, have a lower value added than a firm that operated entirely on equity funds. Gorman does not believe that such a measure of value added would be interesting. Yet the question of borrowing versus the use of equity capital is directly analogous to that of producers who rent the buildings and equipment they use instead of owning them; those who rent will have a relatively smaller value added than those who own their buildings and equipment. The distinction, in both cases, seems entirely proper.

Gorman also, like Denison, has difficulty with the concept of deflation of interest as a service. If interest were treated as a cost, a rise in the interest rate would, *ceteris paribus*, reduce current-dollar value added, but the constant-dollar value added would be unchanged. Consequently, the implicit price deflator of value added would fall. Gorman says that he does not understand what such a decline in the implicit deflator would mean. This is, however, not really an anomaly. When interest is treated as a cost of production, a change in its price would have the same effect on deflation as a change in the price of any other element of cost. For example, if the price of raw materials rose, other things being equal, valued added would decline but constant-dollar value added would remain the same, leading to a decline in the implicit deflator of value added. This outcome is the result of using double deflation methods and is to be expected.

Perhaps for most users the most questionable aspect of treating interest as a payment for a service related to government interest. Government deficits that require borrowing — and therefore the payment of interest — may result from a decline in revenues due to recession, and may have no observable counterpart in the physical output of goods and services. In such a situation, however, payments of interest may be more in the nature of a government expenditure not dissimilar to a public works program, designed to stimulate the economy. When government borrowing is an element of fiscal policy, such as borrowing funds from producers and consumers in wartime in order to reduce the volume of their expenditures in the economy, it can be argued that those lending the money are indeed performing a service by refraining from spending some of the income they have received. If governments borrow for the purpose of capital formation, they are operating in the same manner as business firms, and those providing the necessary funds to permit the capital formation can be viewed as contributing a service for which interest represents a legitimate payment.

Gross Capital Formation and Saving

The IEAs expanded the NIPA concept of gross capital formation by including government purchases of structures and durable goods, personal consumption expenditures for durable goods, and the nondurables goods that are added to household and government inventories. Surprisingly, the inclusion of government capital formation elicited relatively little comment. Tice pointed out that the United Nations SNA recognizes government capital formation, and that it might be useful for the NIPAs to do so. Tobin went further and stated that crediting governments for the value of their physical assets is an accounting reform long overdue in this country.

The IEA treatment of household purchases of durable goods as capital formation is in accord with the FOF treatment, and is generally approved of by Taylor and Tice. Marimont, in commenting that the IEAs did not consistently embody the transactor approach, remarked that the IEA treatment of household durables leads to household saving that few households are likely to recognize and that even fewer lending institutions would give much weight to in evaluating the credit-worthiness of a householder applying for a loan. But the purchase of durable goods such as an automobile or house furnishings is often recognized as a capital expenditure by householders. The saving for such a purchase may occur in advance as the householder accumulates the required funds, or the purchase may be financed by a loan. When there is a loan, the lending institution does indeed recognize that it is for a capital expenditure, and it is shown in the household accounts as saving when it is paid off. As has been pointed out above, however, the recording of transactions in the accounts should not depend solely on how individuals view the transactions, but rather on what is appropriate for the analytical usefulness of the accounts. The primary reason for treating household durable goods as capital assets on the balance sheets of households and depreciating them over the period of their economic life is that they last for more than one accounting period.

Whether an estimate of net imputed income should be included for consumer durables, as it is for owner-occupied housing, is a somewhat more debatable issue. Denison questions such an imputation on the ground, among other reasons, that it differs from the treatment of government durables. There is much to be said for this position — but this same argument also applies to the net imputed income estimate for owner-occupied housing. Elimination of both of these imputations would make the treatment of owner-occupied housing and consumer durables consistent with the imputation used for government structures and equipment in the accounts.

With respect to saving, Denison feels that the IEA expanded net saving is much less interesting for the analysis of economic growth and fluctuations than NIPA net saving. The IEAs net saving shows what each sector contributes toward financing all capital formation, whereas NIPA net saving shows what each sector contributes toward financing private business sector investment (including owner-occupied housing). Which of these is the more interesting figure is a function of one's model of economic behavior. It may be noted, however, that much of the difference between IEA and NIPA sector net saving does not arise from the expansion of the gross capital formation concept but from the IEA modifications of NIPA sectoring, the largest contributing factors being owner-occupied housing, nonprofit institutions and pension and insurance reserves. Without these changes, NIPA household and government sector net saving could be derived from IEA net sector saving for these sectors by simply subtracting their respective net capital formation.

The Form of the Accounts

In her comments, Tice points out that, by and large, what the IEAs have done is move existing pieces into a new configuration, and she therefore considers it legitimate to ask whether all this rearrangement makes us any better off: are the IEAs more precisely estimated and more illuminating than the existing NIPAs and FOF accounts? By definition, of course, the IEAs are exactly as precisely estimated as the NIPAs and FOF accounts, because they are merely a reorganization of the data provided by the two systems. This has some drawbacks. As Tice noted, reliance on the FOF accounts resulted in two major deficiencies in the IEAs: the omission of revaluations for fixed-claim assets and the placing of all changes in land value in the revaluation accounts.

Those with the most extensive comments on the form of presentation were Tice and Tobin. Denison's comment was limited to the point that a gross saving and investment account such as BEA provides is very useful and its absence from the IEAs makes it much more difficult to obtain an overview. All the information that would be shown in such an account is already included in each sector's capital transaction account, but nevertheless, we agree with

Denison that a combined gross saving and investment account would be useful and should be presented.

IEAs and the FOF accounts

Tice finds the IEA presentation difficult, unclear, and confusing for the user of the FOF accounts, for three reasons. First, she feels that it is unfortunate that the IEA current accounts stress gross saving and investment while the capital accounts for the nation use net concepts; as a result, she considers it difficult to relate the current and capital accounts conceptually or empirically. At the same time, she considers that too much information is provided in the sector capital accounts, where net concepts of capital stock are derived from gross investment flows. Second, she cites the lack of enterprise sector discrepancies between net saving as measured in the current and capital accounts as a severe limitation of the IEA system. Finally, she feels that, in terms of presentation, the IEAs are not as convenient for the analysis of financial markets as the FOF system because, in that system, time series are typically given for each of the component accounts separately — capital transactions, revaluations and balance sheets. Her conclusion is that clearly the specialist user of the FOF system probably will not find the IEAs to his liking and not really appropriate for his purposes, but for the NIPA user the IEAs are a useful introduction to this financial information. But even here she finds problems, considering that the asset detail that is retained may be overwhelming for the NIPA user at the same time that it is insufficient for the FOF specialist.

On the gross/net question, the IEA income and product accounts — like those in the NIPAs — are centered on gross capital formation and gross product, but the IEA balance sheets are based on current market values, which, of course, reflect net values. The only way to use the same concepts in both forms of accounts would be to adopt net capital formation and net product as the basis for the current accounts. While some might feel that this would be desirable, a majority of users, as indicated by the practices of most countries, have shown a preference for gross concepts in the current accounts. This does not, of course, preclude relating the current and capital accounts, because full details are given in the sector capital accounts on gross capital formation and capital consumption.

With respect to Tice's desire to have the discrepancies of net saving in the enterprise sector shown as an addendum item, this is simply done and the more recent versions of the IEAs do incorporate this item. As Tobin observed, the unexplained discrepancies are disturbingly large and a concerted effort is needed to diagnose and remedy these inconsistencies.

With respect to the form of the IEAs, it is true that their design is not based on the FOF system, and FOF specialists may ask the reason for this. Although the FOF system presents detailed data on financial transactions, it contains only very rudimentary information on other aspects of the national accounts, and it could not very well serve as the basis for a comprehensive framework. It was considered more appropriate for the IEAs to extend the NIPAs along the lines suggested by the United Nations SNA to comprehend capital transactions, revaluations and balance sheets.

Tice observes that the IEA method of consolidating net worth for the enterprise and household sectors is different from the FOF consolidation. The IEAs subtract the equity owned by households (including the market value of corporate stock held by households) from enterprise net worth, whereas the FOF presentation leaves enterprise net worth intact and reduces household net worth correspondingly. Tice points out that the FOF treatment suggests a more important role in wealth owning for enterprises and may lead to useful insights about the control and likely use of this wealth. Tobin, however, notes that the IEA consolidation results in a consistent way of handling deviations of 'q' from 1. Such a measure is, of course, not available in the FOF treatment, and it is not readily apparent what theoretical meaning or analytic use can be attributed to the FOF measure of household net worth reduced by enterprise net worth. Furthermore, because the unconsolidated enterprise net worth is also explicitly given in the IEA sector account, it can be used when this concept is analytically appropriate.

Taylor objected to the sharp division in the IEAs between the current and capital accounts. He felt that this tends to obscure profoundly the definitional connections between these two accounting forms in ways that are not helpful to the inexpert user and that can easily lead to error. The same sharp division is, however, also found in the Summary of Flow of Funds Accounts table presented in the May 1982 *Survey*. Indeed, the capital transactions account of IEAs contains essentially the same transaction flows as are shown in that table. Even in the more detailed sector statements of saving and investment published by the Federal Reserve Board only summary totals are provided for current income outlays.

The sharp division between current and capital transactions could be avoided by listing all transactions together in terms of sources and uses funds — as the FOF accounts once did. The sources and uses approach is quite appropriate where the focus of interest lies in the analysis of a limited number of transactions over a period of time. The distinction between current and capital is really quite arbitrary, and for different purposes different classifications may be desired. However, this approach becomes more awkward as increased detail is given, and it does not solve the problem of relating capital transactions to the revaluation and balance sheet items. The FOF presentation avoids these problems by limiting the income and expenditure flows to a few summary measures, and providing completely separate revaluation and balance sheet information.

Adler and Sunga made a similar point in suggesting that, as is done in Canada, the capital finance account might directly follow each sector's income and outlay account. This is appropriate in Canada, however, primarily because Canada does not have either revaluation accounts or balance sheets, and so does not need to find a place for them.

A matrix presentation

Tobin suggests that the IEAs could be displayed somewhat more informatively if a matrix presentation were used. For balance sheets, there would be a matrix for each date with a row for each asset and debt category and a column for each sector. Each cell (ij) would display the net position (positive, negative, or zero) of the sector (i) in the asset (j). When information permits, the gross positions, positive and negative, could be shown in the cell with the net holding equaling their difference. The same matrix format can, of course, record the changes in sector holdings of assets from one date to another. Within each cell there would be, as in the IEA tables, two entries, one for the sector's net purchases or sales of the assets at the prices of the period, and one for revaluation of assets previously acquired. For any sector, the sum of all these entries is the change in the net worth, similarly split between the value of net acquisitions (which is the net saving of the sector) and revaluation of existing holdings. Finally, a second flow matrix can be constructed that will also lead to the same estimates of sectoral net saving. In this matrix, the columns are the same, but the rows represent transactions other than the purchase or sale of assets. The row categories are types of transactions like taxes, transfers, income payments, consumption outlays and labor compensation. If the list is exhaustive, their net sums will be the saving figures. Tobin indicates that the format he is advocating is like that used in the European System of Accounts of the European Economic Community (its Table T2) except that he would like to consolidate the rows for assets and liabilities of the same type.

Such a matrix approach does have the advantage that it provides an overview of the structure of the economy at a given point of time and of its changes from one date to another. As Tobin observes, it can be carried out at different levels of aggregation. At more detailed levels of aggregation where many sectors and subsectors are shown and assets, financial instruments and current transactions are classified in some detail, the matrices would become quite large, however. Like large input–output tables, they would then be difficult to present or use in table form.

The need for alternative forms

The matrix approach to the presentation of data is diametrically opposite to the time series approach recommended by Tice for financial analysis, and, like the IEA system, it maintains the sharp difference between current and capital transactions to which Taylor has raised objections. It is thus apparent that different uses may call for different forms of presentations.

Whatever the form of presentation, the summary accounts should have the function of providing an overview of the economy and defining the framework of the economic accounting system, much in the same way that BEA's five-account system provides an overview of production, distribution and use of the nation's output and a formal accounting framework for more detailed supporting tables. As the system of economic accounts is extended, however, the task of interrelating all of its component elements becomes more complex. It may, therefore, be useful to display a number of alternative (but, of course, consistent) presentations at a fairly summary level, including time series, matrices, and related accounts, so that users can choose the forms that suit them best. The FOF presentation has adopted this sort of approach in providing accounts not only for transactors, but also for specific transactions.

For the more detailed data, it is apparent that for the research analyst this is best made available in machine-readable form so that it can be processed and analyzed by computer. The IEA tables published in the May 1982 *Survey* represented only the tip of the iceberg — data were presented only for the period 1969–80, and only for the four major sectors of the economy. Data for these sectors are available for the full period 1947–80, and data for 14 subsectors are available for the period 1958–75, all on computer tape obtainable, as noted earlier, from BEA.

4. SUMMARY AND CONCLUSIONS

IEA Objectives and the Reviewers' Responses

The modifications and extensions proposed by the IEAs

The IEAs proposed both to modify the existing NIPAs and to extend their scope. The modifications were based on the principle that the aggregate accounts for the nation and the sector accounts should be viewed conceptually as combinations and consolidations of the accounts of individual transactors. This principle led to three specific types of modification. First, the NIPA sectoring of the economy was altered, removing nonprofit institutions from the household sector and setting up an enterprise sector. Second, some modifications were introduced in the treatment of specific flows in the NIPAs, including such items as owner-occupied housing, government and consumer durables and pensions. Finally, market transactions and imputations for nonmarket activity were separated so that additional imputations could be introduced without impairing the usefulness of the system for the analysis of the market economy.

Two types of extension of the NIPAs were envisioned. First, the IEAs introduced accounts for stocks — balance sheets — and integrated them with the flow accounts within its modified framework of aggregate national accounts and sector accounts. This entailed construction of the revaluation accounts needed to show how balances at the end of a period are derived from those at the beginning of the period. Second, the IEAs proposed extending the national accounting framework to embrace microdata as well as macrodata. It is our view that it is now feasible, statistically as well as conceptually, to construct composite microdata sets for households, enterprises and government units that would consolidate to the sector accounts of the nation. Such microdata sets can accommodate a wide variety of economic, social, demographic and locational information relating to individual microunits.

The BEA response

The IEA proposals for modification and extension of the national accounts encountered substantial opposition from those who had been intimately involved in the original design or more recent implementation of the NIPAs. The proposed sectoring changes were rejected, on the grounds that the objective of establishing sectors compatible with the accounts of individual transactors is a chimera, and that the removal of nonprofit institutions from the household sector would complicate the accounts and increase the heterogeneity of the enterprise sector. The IEA modifications in the recording of transactions were opposed on the grounds that the principles on which these changes were made were neither consistent nor valid. Specifically, strong support was voiced for retaining the BEA treatment of owner-occupied housing, consumer durables and pensions. One comment did, however, recognize that the question of consumer and government capital formation has long been a controversial topic and that the proposed IEA treatment seemed sensible. The proposed separation into market transactions and nonmarket imputations was rejected both because it was considered to increase the complexity of the accounts and because the imputations contained in the NIPAs were not considered to be more speculative or different in kind from market transactions.

The extension of the NIPAs to embrace balance sheets was discussed by only one BEA staff member. A detailed examination of the IEA capital accounts was provided, and the question was posed as to whether the IEAs were more illuminating than the existing accounts. The general conclusion was that the IEA presentation was clearly not as convenient for the analysis of financial markets as FOF accounts, and the specialist user of that system would not find it to his liking. For the NIPA user, however, the IEAs were considered to be a useful introduction to this financial information. The proposed IEA extension involving the development of microdata underlying the accounts was generally regarded by all the BEA staff who commented as both impractical and too costly.

The response of outside reviews

The outside reviewers were, on the whole, more receptive to the modifications and extensions proposed by the IEAs, although the viewpoints they represent are quite varied. In the comments relating to the modifications of sectoring, there was considerable support for removing nonprofit institutions from the household sector, but one comment expressed concern for the effect this would have in blurring the profit-motivated character of the enterprise sector. With respect to modifications in the recording of transactions, strong approval was given to the alteration in the treatment of owner-occupied housing, government and consumer durables and pensions, although in relation to owner-occupied housing and consumer durables one comment noted that the proposed treatment would alter the traditional concept of the household as a consumption unit. There was some support for, and no opposition to, the separation of nonmarket imputations from market transactions; it was felt that this would permit the future expansion of estimates, if desired, into other nonmarket areas.

With respect to the extension of the NIPAs to embrace balance sheets, all of the outside reviewers were strongly in favor of such a development, but they differed in their views on the form of presentation of this information. There was agreement that capital accounts showing stocks of durables should be developed for the government sector, and that owner-occupied housing and consumer durables should be included in the balance sheets of households. There was relatively little discussion of the incorporation of microdata. One comment noted, however, that although the development of microdata was both difficult and costly, the micro–macro data methodology intuitively points in the right direction.

The National Accounts as a Framework for the Statistical System

One of our major purposes in developing the IEAs was to demonstrate that, with some modifications and extensions, the NIPAs could be used as a comprehensive framework for the US statistical system. Although our presentation of the IEAs strongly emphasized this objective, this topic was not commented upon by either the BEA staff or the outside reviewers. Nevertheless, we would argue that it is this aspect of an integrated and expanded system of accounts that is most fundamental and important for the future development of both the national accounts and the US statistical system.

The Bonnen Report on 'Improving the Federal Statistical System' (*Statistical Reporter*, 1980) pointed out that there were over 100 federal agencies with statistical programs, and the statistics that are produced in smaller statistical units or as a byproduct of administrative and regulatory data are often unreliable and poorly designed for their purposes. Restrictions on interagency sharing of data for statistical purposes result in lack of comparability of data produced by different agencies as well as failure fully to exploit data bases developed at substantial costs. There is not enough interaction between data producers and data users, including policy analysts and policy-makers, largely because they are in different agencies. As a result, producers are insufficiently informed about the utility of the data they provide, and analysts are often unaware of important limitations of the data they use. As these conclusions of the Bonnen Report clearly imply, the term 'statistical system' as applied to the United States is indeed a misnomer. The statistical resources that exist in the United States are highly fragmented and uncoordinated.

Prior to the 1970s, the Office of Statistical Standards of the Bureau of the Budget and its predecessor organizations made an effort to improve the quality of statistics through forms review and review of the budgets of the statistical agencies, and by establishing outside review committees. Although such efforts were useful and in some degree successful, they were quite inadequate to deal with the highly decentralized statistical system. Since that time, however, the situation has steadily deteriorated. In 1971, the function of statistical coordination was assigned to the Statistical Policy Division of the Office of Management and Budget. By 1977, the staff had been reduced to 29, from the level of 69 its predecessor had had in 1947. In 1978, the Statistical Policy Division was abolished and the coordination function was moved to the Office of Federal Statistical Policy and Standards in the Department of Commerce, with further reduction of staff. That office has now been abolished, and at the present time the only statistical coordination function that remains in the federal government is in the Office of Information and Regulatory Affairs of the Office of Management and Budget — which is primarily concerned with meeting the mandates of the Paperwork Reduction Act, not with improving statistics.

In the context of the fragmentation and decentralization of statistical activities, coupled with the abandonment of serious efforts to achieve substantive coordination, the attempt to develop a comprehensive framework for the statistical system may seem to be an exercise in futility. Certainly BEA itself is in no position, in terms of either authority or budget, to bring about an integrated statistical system, and the Office of Management and Budget has neither the required staff nor the inclination to be concerned with this topic.

Nevertheless, some things can still be accomplished. Perhaps the most obvious and immediate step that could be undertaken would be a joint effort by BEA and the Federal Reserve Board to develop a system of accounts that would embrace the NIPAs, FOF accounts and balance sheets, using common classifications of transactions and of sectors and subsectors. In such a common system, it would, of course, be reasonable that BEA would produce more detailed and expanded information relating to the current accounts and reproducible capital stocks, and the Federal Reserve Board would specialize in producing the financial information. The two agencies might indeed present different levels of detail in their respective publications, but it would be most useful if both sets of information were recognizable as parts of the same system of accounts.

There are also other areas where inter-agency cooperation would be desirable. There would, for example, be considerable advantage in having common classifications for the price information collected by the Bureau of Labor Statistics and for the industry and final product information in the national accounts. The fact that these systems differ reflects in large part the periods in which they originated, not present needs. Similarly, much would be gained by allowing all agencies providing data classified by industry to use the Standard Statistical Establishment List as the basis for assigning industrial classifications to their reporting units.

These partial and *ad hoc* measurements cannot, however, be expected to achieve the type of integrated statistical system here being proposed. To achieve this, it would be necessary to formulate in some detail an overall accounting system that is capable, not only of integrating all economic data, but also as serving as a framework for social, demographic, environmental and regional information. Such a system would need to provide for the interrelation of macro- and microdata.

The required system cannot be expected to emerge without consideration of many of the important specific issues involved. The National Accounts Review Committee, which was convened by the Office of Statistical Standards a quarter of a century ago, was a useful device in setting forth the major issues of national accounting as viewed at that time. Similarly, in the development of the revised United Nations SNA, major issues were reviewed by those concerned with national accounting from many different countries, who met regularly over a period of years. The time may now be appropriate to assemble a new group of producers and users of statistics embracing not only those concerned with the national economic accounts, but also those involved in a wider spectrum of other types of information. In this connection, consideration should be given to the experiences of other countries in the development of their statistical systems, and to the emerging international statistical standards. Even if no immediate action is contemplated, such an effort to design an integrated set of national accounts and related data would be extremely important in helping to determine the future architecture of the statistical system. Without some overall plan to follow, the US statistical system will remain fragmented and uncoordinated.

REFERENCES

Quigley, John (1977), 'The spatial distribution of public sector activity: A preliminary report', *Proceedings of the 1976 General Conference of the Society of Government Economists*, Washington, DC.

_____ with Gail Trask and James Trask (1977), 'Income and product accounts for the local public sector', Institution for Social and Policy Studies, Working Paper 795, Yale University.

Ruggles, Richard and Nancy D. Ruggles (1982), 'The development and use of longitudinal establishment data', Report on workshop held in Reston, VA, 14–15 January 14–15.

The Small Business Data Base and Other Sources of Business Information: Recent Progress (1982), *The State of Small Business: A Report of the President*, Appendix B.

Waite, Preston J. (1982), 'Imputation methodology, economic censuses and surveys', prepared for the Census Advisory Committee Meeting, 8 October.

PART THREE

UNITED NATIONS SYSTEM OF
NATIONAL ACCOUNTS

12. The System of National Accounts: Review of Major Issues

Richard Ruggles
United Nations Statistical Office

1. INTRODUCTION

The Statistical Commission (UN, 1981) at its twenty-first session:

1. endorsed the report of the Expert Group Meeting on Future Directions for Work on the United Nations System of National Accounts (E/CN.3/ AC.9/5), with general approval of the priorities stated therein;
2. emphasized the role of SNA as a framework for the statistical system and as a point of reference in establishing standards for related statistics, and urged therefore that increased emphasis be placed upon the coordination function of the Statistical Office, which should continue to take a leadership role in that activity;
3. considered that SNA, by reason of its comprehensiveness, should rank ahead of standards developed for particular fields of economic statistics; when such other standards are under review, the organizations responsible for them should endeavor to achieve consistency with SNA and, where differences remain, explain the reasons for them and provide a full reconciliation with SNA;
4. urged that specific proposals be developed with regard to needed short-term clarification and updating of SNA, if possible for submission to the Commission at its twenty-second session, with the assistance of *ad hoc* expert groups on external transactions and possibly other topics;
5. recognized the need, within the limits of available resources, to initiate research studies with a longer time horizon, in order to meet demands for new kinds of information;
6. endorsed the use of the *Handbook of National Accounting* series as a vehicle for disseminating the results of future work on national accounts, including expanded and updated manuals on sources and methods and longer-term

This chapter first appeared as an Expert Paper for the United Nations Statistical Office, ESA/STAT/AC.15.2, April 1982.

research studies and, in particular, requested the inclusion in the series of the draft manual on external transactions;
7. welcomed the proposed cooperation of international agencies, individual countries and groups of countries in the work of further conceptual development of SNA, and endorsed the need for formalization of such cooperative and consultative arrangements in order to avoid conflicting and duplicative work (UN, 1981).

This report takes these actions by the Statistical Commission as the point of departure for: developing general proposals for organizing and scheduling future work on the system of national accounts; reviewing the major issues relating to updating, clarification and harmonization of SNA; and formulating limited specific proposals with respect to short-term action on SNA. As directed by the Commission, emphasis is placed upon SNA as a framework for the statistical system and upon the function of the Statistical Office in establishing and coordinating standards for related statistics, following the general priorities established in the report of the Expert Group on Future Directions for Work on SNA of May 1980 (UN, 1980b).

Section 2 of the report examines the development of SNA and its current status, the types of future work required, the methods of implementing such work, and proposals for organizing and scheduling it. Section 3 is concerned with cataloging and examining the various problem areas relating to updating, clarification and harmonization of SNA. Finally, Section 4 contains specific proposals that might be implemented in the short term.

2. GENERAL PROPOSALS FOR ORGANIZING AND SCHEDULING FUTURE WORK ON THE SNA

Historical Background and the 1968 SNA

Background

On an international level, work on national accounts dates from the 1947 report of a League of Nations subcommittee on national income statistics under the chairmanship of Richard Stone, entitled *Measurement of National Income and the Construction of Social Accounts* (UN, 1947). That report formalized work that had been going on in a number of countries since the mid-1930s. It reflected both theoretical concerns with the role of saving, investment, and aggregate demand in the determination of national income, and practical experience of countries during World War II with the role of the government in the mobilization of a war economy. Along the same path, in the immediate postwar period the Organization for European Economic Co-operation (OEEC) (1950) developed a Standardized System of National Accounts (SSNA) that was used to monitor and analyze the economic recovery programmes in member countries.

The first United Nations Expert Group on National Accounts was also chaired by Richard Stone; on the basis of its work, the initial United Nations System of National Accounts was published in 1952. The 1952 SNA established the national accounts as the primary body of economic data that countries should develop as the basis for reporting on the growth and development of their economic systems, and as a major tool for the formulation of economic policy. Publication of the *Yearbook of National Accounts Statistics* by the UN Statistical Office further stimulated countries to develop national accounts data in a form consistent with SNA.

The basic structure of the 1952 SNA closely resembled OEEC's SSNA. There were some differences, however. A major one was that SNA provided summary capital reconciliation accounts, which were intended to provide more information on the financial flows underlying the process of saving and investment. As it turned out, however, this initial effort was not fully successful: on the one hand, the accounts were too rudimentary and consolidated to be analytically useful, and on the other, few countries were able at that time to provide the required information.

The 1968 system of national accounts

There were a number of developments during the 1950s and early 1960s that created a need for a basic revision of the 1952 version of SNA. The most dominant was, perhaps, the increasing amount of economic data that was becoming available. In particular, input–output and flow of funds data were being developed in many countries and it was apparent both to the producers of the statistics and to their users that these types of information were directly related to the national accounts. There was therefore a strong push towards integrating all forms of economic accounting data within a common framework. There was also a perception that, particularly for developing countries, more data were needed on the structure and growth of production, so that specific programmes and policies aimed at faster rates of economic growth could be designed in the context of the total economy.

The revised SNA published in 1968 (Studies in Methods, Series F, No. 2, Rev. 3, hereafter referred to as the Blue Book) responded to these developments (UN, 1968a). First, it provided a comprehensive framework that integrated production accounts with input–output data and integrated income and outlay data with capital finance accounts and balance sheets. Second, it placed increased emphasis on detailed production accounts. A dual sectoring system was introduced, providing a kind-of-activity classification for production-related information and an institutional sectoring classification for income and outlay and financial and balance sheet information.

It is apparent that, as conceived in the matrix presentation in Chapter 2 of the Blue Book, SNA is a system of great generality adaptable to almost any form a compiler may require. Perhaps unavoidably, this very generality has led to some confusion. Chapter 2 of the Blue Book, in effect, requires the compiler to do more than adapt — he must really design his own system. It is perhaps for this reason that those looking for more definite recommendations have tended to concentrate on other aspects of SNA.

Many producers of data consider that the definitions and classifications presented in Chapters 5–7 of the Blue Book are the heart of SNA. These definitions and classifications have been much used by countries newly embarking on national accounts, and in this use they have proved to be very valuable. They are concrete and specific, and they leave relatively little for the compiler to decide for himself.

An accounting formulation of the system is presented in Chapter 8 of the Blue Book. The accounts are divided into three classes, and within each class there are several types of account. Class I accounts are the consolidated accounts for the nation as a whole. Class II accounts, called 'Production, consumption expenditure, and capital formation accounts', are deconsolidated by kind of activity. Class III accounts, called 'Income and outlay and capital finance accounts', are deconsolidated by institutional sectors.

The accounts shown are described in the Blue Book as a selection of the material contained in the total system. The selection from the total system presented in the standard accounts differs somewhat from the selection contained in the illustrative matrix in Chapter 2 (SNA, Table 2.1); the standard accounts are in some respects more consolidated than the matrix and in some respects less consolidated, and some parts of the information shown in the matrix are omitted from the accounts. The standard accounts are not presented as recommendations for countries to adopt in the form shown, but rather simply as examples. However, the accounts play a very important role in that it is largely the accounts that determine the flow definitions. When data are compiled in accordance with these flow definitions, this accounting structure is implicit in it.

In addition to the standard accounts, Chapter 8 also presents a set of 26 supporting and supplementary tables. The coverage of the tables is not exhaustive: they do not include all the information required to complete the accounting structure (or to construct the matrix). Thus countries basing their data compilation efforts on the table forms will not obtain a set of national accounts; rather, they will have selected national income statistics. This approach, while simpler in some respects, does lose one of the major advantages of the accounting approach, namely the automatic consistency requirements imposed by the need to balance accounts and to articulate them.

From the beginning of work on the revision of SNA in the early 1960s, the development of a questionnaire to be used for international reporting of national accounts information was seen to be a very important part of the whole endeavor. The Statistical Commission emphasized that while simplification and selection were necessary it was also important for the questionnaire to retain the skeleton of the accounting framework. However, the questionnaire that was developed in the early 1970s was not based on either the matrix or the accounts, but rather was drawn mainly from the supporting tables. Like the tables from which it was drawn, it was neither complete nor systematic; rather, it was intended to display the most readily available and important series.

Developments since 1968

Implementation of SNA

The programme laid out in the Blue Book envisaged a number of supplementary publications to fill out parts of the system not covered there, or covered in only a rudimentary way. In the interval since then, much of this program has been implemented. Guidelines on balance sheets and reconciliation accounts (UN, 1977c), income distribution (UN, 1977d), input–output tables (UN, 1973), price and quantity statistics (UN, 1977b), tangible capital assets (UN, 1979g), national accounts in constant prices (UN, 1979b), producers' price indexes (UN, 1979c), and prices in external trade have been published, as has a study of the feasibility of welfare-oriented measures to supplement the national accounts and balances (UN, 1977e), and a revised and expanded classification of the functions of government (UN, 1980g). Recommendations concerning industrial and agricultural statistics have been elaborated within the SNA framework.

In about 1975, the United Nations Statistical Office began a review of countries' experiences in implementing SNA. An Interregional Seminar on the Revised System of National Accounts was held in Caracas in December 1975 (UN, 1977a). Regional meetings held in Africa in 1975 and 1979, in Western Asia in 1978, and in Europe in 1978 (UN, 1979h) and 1980 (UN, 1980a) also contributed substantially to the review. A preliminary report (UN, 1978b) on the findings of the review was presented to the Statistical Commission at its twentieth session in 1979, and the Commission concluded that an Expert Group should be convened to consider the status of work on SNA, and to discuss the directions of future work. Such an Expert Group was convened in April 1980 (UN, 1980b).

The Expert Group expressed general satisfaction with the basic structure of SNA, and stressed its importance as a point of reference for the integration of basic statistics, in both developing and developed countries. The importance of continuity was emphasized, both for compilers and for users of the statistics. There was, however, considered to be a *prima facie* case in favor of an increase in consistency among the international statistical systems, and unanimous agreement that some updating and clarification of SNA was required. There was general support for the concept of SNA as an open-ended, flexible system adaptable to countries' needs. Participants noted that the national accounts should be conceived of as a framework for micro- as well as macrodata. There was general approval of the concept that new and experimental kinds of information should be presented in a way that preserves the core of the accounts on an internationally comparable and stable basis. With regard to priorities for further work on SNA, the group considered that, while the Statistical Office should continue its work on the clarification of concepts and classifications where problems have arisen in the application of SNA, it was equally important that resources be devoted to work on the further extension and development of the system. The group felt that so many important topics were included in this category that it was unlikely that they would receive the attention they deserve unless additional resources were provided.

A report (UN, 1980c) summarizing the work on reviewing SNA and suggesting future directions for work on national accounts was considered by the Statistical Commission at its twenty-first session in 1981. That report incorporated the views of the Expert Group, as well as of the regional meetings and the Caracas Interregional Seminar. Discussion of that report led the Commission to the recommendations outlined at the beginning of this report. The present Expert Group has been convened in accordance with the Commission's recommendation.

The Handbook of National Accounting series

During the course of the review of SNA, the need for a continuing vehicle to accommodate all of the technical studies in national accounting undertaken by the Statistical Office became apparent. Such technical studies should, in the first place, include better explanatory materials. Because SNA itself is complex, it is essential to describe and explain it in a way that is not complex, and that can readily be followed by interested practitioners. Second, there is a great need for pedagogical materials describing the simpler kinds of uses of national accounts and national accounting data. Third, documentation is needed on sources and methods. Finally, a vehicle is needed for the studies arising from work on the further extension and development of the system.

To meet these needs, a publication series with the overall title of *The Handbook of National Accounting* has been established. Present plans call for six volumes of the *Handbook* in the near future; an additional three or four are projected, and others may be undertaken as the need and possibility arise. At the time of writing, two volumes are undergoing final review, one is in process, and preliminary drafts of the remaining three of the first group exist. These six volumes, and their present status, are as follows.

Vol. 1. Introduction to National Accounting: A first draft of this volume is now in preparation. It is designed to provide an introduction to national accounting for those without any previous acquaintance with the topic. It will briefly describe the purpose and uses of national accounting data, present the basic structure of SNA, and introduce the necessary concepts and classifications. It will, to the extent appropriate in the context, embody the points of clarification, updating and modification agreed upon up to the time of its completion. To some extent, it will serve as a more easily accessible version of the Blue Book, as updated. For a more detailed treatment of particular topics, however, it will be necessary to consult the more specialized volumes of the series.

Vol. 2. Gross Domestic Product: A draft of this volume is now undergoing final review. The volume discusses sources and methods for compiling gross domestic product by kind of activity and by final use. It is intended to be helpful to national accounts compilers, primarily in countries newly embarking on the compilation of national accounts or extending their work on them. The volume is divided into two parts. The first, organized by kind of activity, discusses gross output, intermediate consumption, value added and the cost components of value added. The second discusses final expenditures on GDP, by type of expenditure.

Vol. 3. Income and Outlay and Capital Finance Accounts: A preliminary draft of this volume has been prepared. It discusses sources and methods for compiling SNA's Class III accounts, on income and outlay and capital finance. A revised draft will embody agreed-upon updates and modifications, as well as clarifications.

Vol. 4. Public Sector Statistics (PSS): As noted below, this volume has been the focus of much attention over the past five years, and it is now at the final review stage. It covers the content and use of public sector statistics, as well as sources and methods of compiling them. Considerable effort has been devoted to harmonization of this volume with the IMF's *Government Finance Statistics (GFS)*, and the two volumes should be considered to a large extent as complementary; PSS does not repeat material that can be found in GFS. Rather, it discusses the extensions and modifications of the GFS cash accounts needed to obtain the broader coverage of SNA. A detailed reconciliation of data contained in the GFS tables with those required for the National Accounts Questionnaire is included. PSS also includes the revised and extended Classification of the Functions of Government (also available in a separate publication, Series M, No. 70) (UN, 1980g).

Vol. 5. Financial Flows: A preliminary draft of this volume has been prepared. This draft is an explanation of sources and methods of compiling Table 24 of the Blue Book. It is anticipated that a revised version will embody a somewhat broader coverage of the topic, including balance sheets and reconciliation accounts. It should also provide a reconciliation with IMF statistics in related areas; to this end the cooperation of IMF is necessary.

Vol. 6. External Transactions: A draft of this volume is before this Expert Group, and it is discussed in more detail below. The draft has been circulated both to experts on the topic and to national statistical offices and international organizations. Completion of a final version awaits decisions on the matters raised in Part 2 of the consultant's report. The final version will include a reconciliation with the IMF's (1977) *Balance of Payments Manual.*

Projected future volumes of the *Handbook* for which a need is now apparent include income distribution statistics, input–output tables, and possibly regional and quarterly statistics. In addition, there is widespread demand for a volume on the uses of national accounts.

The National Accounts Questionnaire

For the 1980 round of data collection, a revised National Accounts Questionnaire was introduced (UN and OECD, 1980). The revised questionnaire reflects the experience gained since 1968 by countries in implementing SNA, as well as the problems encountered in the international reporting of comparable data. In revising the questionnaire, great care was taken to preserve the continuity of established time series. A major objective of the new questionnaire, however, was to make the data more accessible to those who are not experts on SNA. To that end, several steps were taken:

1. The questionnaire was designed to help the user find the particular information that is wanted. Summary but comprehensive data are presented first, followed by more detailed breakdowns and elaborations. The detailed tables are grouped by topic, and they are related to the summary data.
2. Many of the relationships among the flows that are implicit in the structure of SNA but might not be apparent to the non-expert have been shown explicitly. This will facilitate both compilation and interpretation of the data, and it will help users relate the data in international publications to national data systems with which they may be more familiar.
3. Terminology that is used in SNA in special senses is explained, usually by showing the composition of the items involved.
4. The level of detail called for has to some extent been adapted to what experience suggests countries can supply. Where the detail serves to clarify the content, however, it has in general been retained in the detailed sections of the questionnaire, even though it is not generally supplied.

A second aim of the new questionnaire looks forward to the future. Some tables have been included in which much interest has been expressed but for which few countries can yet supply data, as for instance the tables on capital finance and capital stocks. Also, the questionnaire employs some concepts that were not emphasized in the Blue Book (although provided for), but for which there now appears to be widespread demand. Among the most significant of these are the separate identification of marketed and nonmarketed output and of public and private activity in a number of tables, and the provision of production accounts for institutional as well as kind-of-activity sectors.

The questionnaire is divided into four parts. Part 1 contains summary but comprehensive information, in current and, where appropriate, constant prices. In addition to the basic gross domestic product account, this part includes summary information on government receipts and disbursements, enterprise and household income and outlay, and external transactions; a summary capital transactions account; information on gross product by institutional sector of origin and kind of activity; and finally a table showing the relations among the aggregate concepts. Seven of the tables in this part form a simple, closed and balancing set of flow accounts, drawn from the much more complex and elaborate standard accounts of SNA; these tables can, therefore, be used not only to provide an overview of the operation of the economic system but also as a guide to the more detailed data that follow and as a framework to enforce conceptual and statistical consistency. The tables that are not part of the balancing system are reconciled to the same totals, so that their relationships are clearly indicated.

Part 2 contains detailed breakdowns of the final expenditure components of gross domestic product (consumption, capital formation, exports and imports) in current and constant prices, together with supporting tables giving additional information on government outlays and capital stock. Part 3 contains detailed institutional sector accounts, based upon those in Chapter 8 of the Blue Book and in the *Provisional International Guidelines on the National and Sectoral Balance-Sheet and Reconciliation Accounts of the System of National Accounts* (Series M, No. 60) (UN, 1977c). Part 4 contains kind-of-activity breakdowns.

New instructions and definitions for the questionnaire, with blank table forms, were issued jointly by the United Nations Statistical Office and the Organization for Economic Cooperation and Development in 1980. It is anticipated that the questionnaire and the instructions will be updated periodically to incorporate agreed modifications, where this can be done without breaking the continuity of existing time series.

Future Work and its Implementation

The nature of required future work

The development of national accounting represents one of the major achievements of the twentieth century in the fields of economic analysis and economic statistics. From the point of view of economic analysis, the national accounts have given empirical content to the economic concepts needed for measuring economic performance and for modeling the operation of the economic system. From the point of view of economic statistics, the national accounts have provided a comprehensive framework that can be used to integrate many different kinds of economic information in such a way that they form a unified system of data. The need for such a unifying framework has increased as the volume and variety of economic data and their analytic uses have both increased.

SNA has played a central role in this development. From the beginning, it was shaped to measuring economic performance and demonstrating the interrelationships among the various parts of the economic system. As an international system, it embodied the national accounting experiences of many different countries. The 1968 revision of SNA went further, however, and broke new ground: it laid out a comprehensive national accounting system that could be used as a framework for basic statistics and as a point of reference in establishing standards for related statistics. In the period since 1968 subsequent publications have fleshed out the SNA, and as time has passed it has gained wide acceptance.

As the Statistical Commission's recommendations indicate, there is now a general consensus that in the immediate future work should focus on clarifying and updating SNA in order to remove ambiguities, ensure consistency and adapt to new uses of data and harmonization of SNA with the statistical standards used by other international organizations.

Clarification and updating of SNA are necessary to take changing conditions into account and to develop those parts of the system that have not as yet been fully implemented; not all parts of SNA are sufficiently spelled out so that they are unambiguous and operational. In a system as large as SNA, conflicts or inconsistencies may also arise that need to be resolved. Principles adopted for operational convenience in one part of the system may be found to be analytically unacceptable as the system is extended to comprehend new kinds of information. As has been noted, both the 1952 and 1968 versions of SNA reflected the economic events and policy concerns of the periods in which they were developed. Since 1968, there have been further developments and new requirements for information.

Harmonization, in the view of the Statistical Commission, should rest upon a recognition that SNA, by reason of its comprehensiveness, should rank ahead of standards developed for particular fields of economic statistics, and that it is the responsibility of the sponsors of such specialized standards to achieve consistency with SNA, to explain the reasons for any remaining differences, and to provide a full reconciliation. Such an insistence upon the primacy of SNA is reasonable if the different parts of the statistical system represented by specialized sets of data are to be successfully integrated, and if international comparability is to be achieved. But if SNA concepts and classifications are to serve as standards for all uses, it becomes the responsibility of SNA to ensure that these concepts and classifications adequately meet the needs of all users. SNA should be capable of accommodating the relevant specialized data needed by other organizations.

In the 1968 design of SNA, many parts of the system were not fully implemented, and the concepts and classifications adopted were those convenient for the immediate use. Organizations working in specialized areas are, of course, each able to devote much more attention to their own area, and they may have found that certain other definitions and classifications are more useful or more operational than those of SNA. In such cases, harmonization may involve a reexamination of the concepts and classifications used by SNA to determine whether additional detail or some other modification can be introduced that will simultaneously meet both the overall requirements of SNA and the specialized requirements of particular fields. As has repeatedly been emphasized, the proliferation of standards causes difficulties for both users and producers of statistics, and the coordination function at the international level should be a high priority concern of UNSO. This effort can only succeed, however, where a willingness exists to adapt *both* SNA and the related systems of statistics.

Implementation of future work
It is not anticipated that the work on updating, clarification and harmonization will be embodied in a new Blue Book in the near term, for two reasons. On the one hand, the general principles underlying SNA as described in the 1968 Blue Book will continue to be useful and valid. On the other hand, since 1968, the expansion and development of SNA has been such that it would no longer easily fit within a single volume. As the discussion above of the *Handbook of National Accounting* series indicated, a number of separate volumes on specific aspects of SNA is needed. This is important both for harmonizing SNA with specialized areas of statistics and for providing specialized users with information on a sufficiently detailed level without burdening them with similar details on other parts of SNA. Inasmuch as the *Handbook* volumes provide the basic and most detailed guides to SNA, it is not only appropriate but essential that they embody the results of the work on updating, clarification and harmonization of SNA. As new work reaches fruition, new volumes may be added, and existing volumes will need to be revised at periodic intervals.

It will also be necessary from time to time to incorporate these results in the National Accounts Questionnaire. In so doing, care should, of course, be exercised to maintain the integrity of time series in so far as possible. Both the form of the tables and the instructions for filling them out, including the discussion of concepts and classifications, should reflect the work on updating and harmonization. Conversely, as has been true in the past, country experience in filling out the questionnaire is an important input to future work.

Proposals for organizing and scheduling future work

The Statistical Commission played an important role both in establishing the initial SNA and in its revision in 1968. In doing so it drew heavily on *ad hoc* Expert Groups, and was assisted by regional advisory groups on national accounts, in particular the Working Group on National Accounts of the Conference of European Statisticians. But conditions have changed, and for the work ahead there are a number of reasons why the existing arrangements are inadequate.

Under present circumstances, the time that the Statistical Commission can devote to the topic of national accounts and balances is severely limited: it generally consists of less than one half-day every two years, and is not sufficient to provide detailed oversight of the many important issues involved. The increasing recognition of SNA as a framework for the statistical system and as the basis for establishing standards for related statistics has meant that the scope of future work has been increased by a major order of magnitude. Although the Statistical Office should take an active role in the coordination of standards, it has neither the resources required to develop such standards in all of the areas related to SNA nor the authority to see that they are implemented. This has become increasingly evident in recent years, as the budget of the Statistical Office has declined in real terms and the shortage of qualified staff has become more severe. New arrangements are needed for the organization and scheduling of future work.

With respect to the harmonization of standards, it is apparent that those international organizations and specialized agencies that are directly involved in the development of systems and standards need to be brought together on a cooperative basis. The burden of work can then be shared, and conflicting or duplicative efforts can be avoided. In terms of implementing a common set of standards, furthermore, representation of those directly involved is essential.

In addition to international organizations and specialized agencies, the participation of experts from different countries is needed. On many topics, countries can draw upon their own experts to appraise the usefulness of proposed changes and to assess the feasibility of their implementation, and the support and agreement of country experts is essential to the acceptance of proposed standards by individual countries.

Finally, an important requirement is continuity of participation, so that work can go forward on a systematic and continuing basis. Although *ad hoc* Expert Groups are useful for focusing on specific problems from time to time, they cannot provide the kind of continuous supervision that is essential to a long-term organized effort.

There are precedents for the establishment of such a continuing cooperative effort. At the nineteenth session of the Statistical Commission in 1976, it was agreed that a long-term effort was required for revision of the International Standard Industrial Classification (ISIC) (UN, 1968b). To this end, a cooperative arrangement was sought with other international organizations and experts from individual countries, and a continuing Joint Working Party on World Level Classifications was established under the sponsorship of EUROSTAT and UNSO, with the active participation of CMEA and OECD. This working group has met on a regular basis since 1977. They have completed an intermediate-level classification of transportable goods and are now working on services, with a view to a complete revision by 1985.

It is proposed that a somewhat similar cooperative and continuing working group be established on SNA. As already indicated, in addition to UNSO the group should include the major international organizations concerned with systems and standards (OECD, EEC, CMEA) and representatives from the specialized agencies (IMF, ILO, FAO, World Bank, UNESCO, UNRISD) and the regional commissions. Finally, experts drawn from different countries should be included. As in the case of the ISIC group, a commitment to continuing participation of the same individuals should be sought. The group would be expected to meet on a regular basis (at least once or twice a year), and would be responsible for scheduling the work and assigning tasks to individual organizations and countries, reviewing working papers and proposing recommendations for Statistical Commission approval. The costs of operating this continuing working group should be shared jointly by those participating in it.

The detailed scheduling of future work should be left to this continuing working group. But it is appropriate for the present *ad hoc* group to consider the broad terms of reference of the work. One result of the present discussions, therefore, should be a time frame. The Statistical Commission has asked for proposals relating to possible immediate modifications of SNA, and this is the topic of Section 4. But these are, of necessity, minor points. The broader questions cannot be dealt with in this fashion. Specifically, should the work of the continuing working group be aimed at a major revision of SNA (comparable to that of 1968) at some foreseeable date, and if so how distant? Or should it look upon the task as one of more or less continuing adjustment, without envisaging a major break, at least for the next decade or so?

3. REVIEW OF MAJOR ISSUES IN THE UPDATING AND HARMONIZATION OF SNA

Since the publication of the revised SNA in 1968, numerous questions about it have been raised in interregional and regional seminars on national accounts, Expert Group meetings held by the United Nations, and meetings held by other international organizations, as well as by national statistical offices. Not all of the points, of course, are of equal importance. Some issues are fundamental and relate to basic concepts, whereas others are relatively insignificant and, no matter how resolved, do not seriously affect the form or content of the system. With respect to reviewing issues relating to the updating and clarification of SNA, the primary focus should be on the more significant questions. For the harmonization of different statistical systems, however, even the minor differences among different systems must be resolved, in order to simplify the work and eliminate duplication and confusion among statistical systems.

SNA is a comprehensive system. It is neither feasible nor desirable to deal with its individual elements on an *ad hoc* basis. In many instances considerations relating to the treatment of a specific flow or transaction raise broader issues of consistent treatment elsewhere in the system. For this reason, therefore, it will be useful to group the issues relating to updating and classification in the context of broad issues, rather than in terms of the lists of individual items that have emerged from the many working papers and meetings on these topics. Most of the topics listed can be grouped under the following general headings: problems relating to the measurement of consumption, problems relating to the measurement of income, problems relating to the accounting structure and sectoring, and further extensions of SNA. With respect to harmonization, another five categories can be distinguished: external transactions, public sector statistics, monetary statistics and flow of funds, income distribution statistics, and input–output and activity classifications.

The discussion of these issues in this section is presented, not with a view to their immediate resolution, but rather to ensure that the catalog of major issues is complete, and to elicit the views of the Expert Group members on their appropriate formulation, relative priority, and procedures for resolution.

Updating and Clarification

Measurement of consumption

Individual consumption paid for by government As has been pointed out by Jean Petre (1981), over the past 30 years there has been a marked increase in the extent to which governments supply goods and services to individuals free or virtually free. One of the most rapidly growing areas of such activity is health services. The exact procedures employed for this purpose differ from country to country and change over time. Institutional arrangements both for delivering health care and for paying for it are highly varied, and the same ultimate end may be achieved in ways that look quite different. Petre argues that the treatment of these expenditures in the international systems of national accounts is not entirely satisfactory from either a theoretical or a practical point of view. For some purposes, the analyst is interested in actual expenditure flows, and for other purposes in final consumption. Questions arise both in distinguishing between these two concepts and in measuring each of them.

SNA, in line with its transactor/transaction approach, purports to record the actual transaction flows that occur in terms of which transactor is making the expenditure, not in terms of which is receiving the ultimate benefit. But it is still sometimes difficult to determine what should be counted as government expenditure and what as household expenditure. In the case of a national health scheme in which individuals are reimbursed for their health care expenses, but are free to choose both the practitioner from whom they receive care and the terms on which treatment is furnished, SNA considers that the individuals are the purchasers of the service furnished, and that the financing by the government is a transfer payment. On the other hand, in circumstances where the government arranges for and specifies in detail the terms and standards of furnishing the good or service, SNA considers the government to be the purchaser, and the expenditures are included in government intermediate consumption (SNA, para. 6.74). This is the SNA solution even in those cases where the government's role is limited to providing reimbursement for the costs involved.

In practice, the SNA 'free choice' criterion is often difficult to apply. For instance, reimbursement may be limited to specific kinds of expenditures made under specific conditions; this is a limit on free choice, but it is not clear to what extent SNA intended to consider it so. Furthermore, even if conceptual distinctions can be made between different institutional situations, it may not be possible to identify them statistically.

As a consequence of these difficulties, Petre suggests that criteria be developed to distinguish more clearly between 'cash benefits' and 'benefits in kind'. He proposes that cash benefits be limited to benefits that households receive without having to produce evidence of actual expenditure, and that only these cash benefits be treated as actual transfer payments. Goods and services provided by the government either directly or through reimbursement of expenditures for which supporting evidence is required would all be classed as benefits in kind, and would be recorded as a government expenditure on goods and services.

A further question is raised in the Petre paper regarding the nature of government expenditures on goods and services. SNA considers that all such expenditures are intermediate consumption, no matter what use the government makes of the goods and services in question. But there are occasions when the government's role is purely financial. In some cases, it may not itself take delivery of the goods and services, and on other occasions, it may merely distribute without alteration goods which it has purchased. In both of these situations, Petre proposes that the goods and services that are provided to individuals should be regarded as final rather than intermediate consumption expenditure by the government.

Conclusion. The SNA treatment of individual consumption paid for by government needs to be clarified so that it is more consistent with the transactor/transaction principle of recording flows. In particular, situations where the government partially or fully reimburses households for their expenditures should be treated in a way that is more consistent with other situations in which the government provides goods and services to households.

Total consumption of the population Despite the focus in SNA on the allocation of expenditure, the usefulness of a consumption concept that covers not only the expenditures households make out of their incomes but also outlays made by enterprises, government and nonprofit institutions that benefit households directly has been recognized for some time. The term 'total consumption of the population' has been applied to this wider consumption concept. This concept overcomes to some degree the apparent differences in consumption levels arising out of differences in institutional arrangements.

A variety of concepts of this general type have been proposed in different contexts. The Material Product System (MPS) of the Soviet Union (UN, 1971) embodies a concept of total consumption of the population. The UN (1977d) *Provisional Guidelines on Statistics of the Distribution of Income, Consumption and Accumulation of Households* introduces a concept of total consumption of the population that differs somewhat from that of MPS. The concept has also been considered in connection with the development of social and demographic statistics and in the discussion of welfare-oriented measures to supplement the national accounts and balances (UN, 1977e), where it was pointed out that although total consumption of the population is a useful measure, there are considerable statistical difficulties in estimating the items of expenditure of enterprises, government and nonprofit institutions that should be regarded as direct additions to household consumption expenditures. Finally, a similar concept is used in the International Comparison Project (ICP) (Kravis et al., 1975), where expenditures by government for education, health, recreation and housing are added to final consumption expenditure of households to arrive at what is there called 'final consumption expenditures of the population'. A report (UN, 1978c) summarizing the work on this concept was presented to the Statistical Commission at its twentieth session in 1979.

Total consumption of the population is defined in MPS as the sum of household consumption financed from personal income and that financed from other sources; consumption financed from other sources includes services provided free or at reduced charges to the population by the 'social consumption funds' of enterprises, government and other institutions. Thus total consumption of the population includes all services in the fields of housing, education, culture, arts, health, sports, social welfare and recreation, regardless of whether they are purchased from enterprises or financed from the government budget or the resources of cooperatives, enterprises, or other institutions.

The income distribution guidelines (SNA, para 5.7) state that:

> The concept of total consumption of the population is designed to include the value of those goods and services that government, nonprofit institutions and enterprises furnish free or at reduced charges and that are clearly and primarily of benefit to the households as consumers. Only those benefits in kind that are not part of wages and salaries should be covered. In selecting the goods and services to be included in total consumption, it is necessary to take account of the difficulties of allocating their value among the various groups of households for which information is wanted.

Both of these usages take roughly the same view of what should properly be included in total consumption of the population as an addition to personal consumption expenditure, namely those elements of public or enterprise expenditure, the benefits of which may be assigned to individuals rather than to the population as a whole. However, as the discussion in the ICP volume makes clear, without further specification this is not an operational definition, and in practice MPS and the income distribution guidelines include quite different baskets. There are some elements of government expenditure, according to the criterion of assignability to individuals, that clearly belong in total consumption, such as health services delivered directly to individuals. There are other elements that clearly should be excluded, such as defense and public administration. But in between there is a rather wide range of expenditures that are much more difficult to classify. They include sports and recreational facilities, parks and other community amenities, education, a variety of welfare services, housing facilities and the like which clearly benefit individuals but the costs of which cannot generally be assigned to specific persons or households. It may be questioned, furthermore, whether assignability should be the desired criterion if the objective is to measure all of the items of consumption that contribute to the welfare of the population. Many elements of collective consumption paid for by the government (such as parks) do contribute to welfare, and conversely, many elements of private consumption that are actually paid for out of personal income are in fact enjoyed collectively (such as theater performances and sporting events). This element of ambiguity, and the essentially arbitrary character of the decisions made, has been recognized from the inception of work in this area.

The Petre papers (1981, 1982) consider the possibility of integrating such a concept of total consumption into the standard accounting framework, and come to the conclusion that it would be useful to explore a dual classification:

	Expenditure of:			
	General Government	Private nonprofit	Households	Total
Individual consumption				
Collective consumption				
Total				Total consumption of population

Adding across the rows would then yield total individual consumption and total collective consumption, and adding down the columns would yield total final consumption expenditures of, respectively, general government, private non-profit institutions, households, and the whole economy. Some of the cells, in particular collective consumption of households, might be empty. As the MPS and income distribution guidelines suggest, in addition to the columns shown in Petre's table, an additional column showing the contribution of enterprise expenditures to consumption would also be useful; this is further discussed below.

Before such a dual classification could be implemented, however, it would be necessary to arrive at a consensus on the definitions of the various categories, a consensus that does not as yet exist. Petre's paper makes some proposals with respect to the definition of 'individual' and 'collective'; alternative proposals are made in several of the other discussions of this question mentioned above.

Conclusion. SNA does not now distinguish sufficiently between consumption expenditure and consumption, and it is not possible to obtain total consumption of the population directly from the accounts. Clearer distinctions need to be established so that it will be possible to derive both final consumption expenditures by sector making the expenditure and total consumption of the population by type of consumption.

Treatment of subsidies to consumption In measuring consumption, it has also been pointed out by Petre that certain types of subsidies may represent a method by which the government shares the costs of certain consumption items. Such a consideration underlay the recognition in the UN income distribution guidelines that total consumption of the population should include housing and pharmaceutical subsidies. Where, as a tool of public policy linked to social price discrimination, the government subsidy is intended as a partial payment for goods and services consumed by an individual, Petre outlines three possible treatments.

The first is continuation of the present SNA treatment, which records the payment as a subsidy to the producer, and records the value of the sale by the producer as the actual expenditure made by individuals. No government expenditure on goods and services would arise from this transaction. This approach accurately reflects actual market transactions, but does not measure the true cost of goods and services consumed.

A second approach, currently employed by several countries, would impute a transfer payment to households equal to the amount of the subsidy, and impute an additional expenditure by households for the purchase of the subsidized good at its full cost. This solution correctly reflects the cost of goods and services consumed, but it violates the principle of recording actual transaction flows.

The third solution would treat the subsidy as a purchase by the government from producers, recorded in the accounts as part of the final consumption of government. This solution both adheres to the recorded transaction flows and at the same time shows final consumption in terms of its cost, shared between households and government.

Conclusion. SNA treats all subsidies as transfers that add to the income of producers, and are excluded from expenditures for consumption. In measuring total consumption of the population, however, it is recognized that some subsidies (such as housing and pharmaceuticals) should be considered to add to consumption. This conflicting treatment of subsidies should be clarified and made consistent.

Enterprise consumption expenditures Unlike the government, enterprises in SNA are not considered to make final consumption expenditures. All current purchases of goods and services are classified as either intermediate consumption of goods and services or benefits in kind paid to employees as a part of their compensation. Two questions may be raised about this treatment. First, is the present treatment of benefits in kind consistent with the transactor/transaction principles discussed above in relation to individual consumption paid for by the government, and second, is a concept of enterprise final consumption expenditures needed in order to derive total consumption expenditures of the population?

When an enterprise provides health care for its employees, SNA considers the cost of such health care to be part of wages, and it is imputed both as wages to the employees and as a consumption expenditure by them. This contrasts with the SNA treatment described above, where health care is provided by the government to individuals; then it is recorded as government expenditure. But enterprises, like general government, may make expenditures that are clearly of benefit to individuals without the individuals concerned having free choice; furthermore, when the benefits take the form of facilities of which an individual may make use without charge, the individual will have no sense of their cost. It may be questioned, therefore, whether it is appropriate to treat such benefits in kind as expenditures that households make out of their disposable income.

An alternative treatment would be to consider that the employer, by providing benefits in kind to his employees, is making final consumption expenditures similar in nature to the expenditures made by general government on behalf of individuals. These enterprise final consumption expenditures would be recorded as a part of employee compensation (benefits in kind), but not as part of wages actually paid out to employees. Enterprise final consumption expenditures would appear, along with household and government final consumption expenditure, in the final uses of GDP. This would not alter the total of final consumption expenditures, of course, since household consumption expenditures would be reduced by an amount equivalent to the increase recorded for enterprise final consumption expenditures.

Such a treatment would also move SNA closer to the practice followed in the System of Balance of the National Economy (MPS), where a final use category entitled 'outlays on recreational, cultural, etc. facilities for employees by enterprises' is recognized. In some respects the MPS treatment goes beyond a mere reclassification of final consumption expenditures, and involves some expenditures that SNA would treat as intermediate consumption. Any reclassification of enterprise expenditures from intermediate to final would, of course, change the magnitude of GDP.

There have been suggestions in recent years that some such reclassifications might be appropriate in SNA. It is argued that enterprises do provide goods and services of a final consumption nature over and above the products they sell and the benefits in kind they provide to their employees. Some of the expenditures that enterprises are required by government to make are intended to reduce pollution, improve safety, or serve the public welfare in such ways as providing for the handicapped. These mandated expenditures are an alternative to government expenditures of the same type. Thus pollution abatement expenditures by an enterprise may be a direct substitute for taxes and government expenditures on pollution abatement. If the government made the expenditure, it would be considered final output. Should the fact that the society succeeds in shifting the cost of pollution control to the producer alter its character as final output?

Questions have also been raised about another category of intermediate consumption expenditures of enterprises, namely advertising expenditures devoted to the support of radio and television, newspapers and magazines. It has been suggested that international comparability among countries with different institutional arrangements would be improved if such activities were included in final output, as they are in countries where they are financed either out of the government budget or by a direct license fee.

A final question relating to the boundary between intermediate and final consumption concerns the services provided by banks and other financial institutions. The 1952 version of SNA had allocated imputed banking services to specific users, and the banking services allocated to households and government were classed as final consumption. The 1968 version of SNA, in the interest of ease of compilation, adopted various simplifying assumptions relating to bank service charges. It recognizes an imputation for service charges for which no explicit payment is made, but imputes all banking services as an intermediate consumption item for domestic producers as a group. Where the activities of the financial intermediaries in question are small relative to the GDP, simplifications at the macrolevel may not matter. But where financial intermediation is an important share of total activity, and especially where countries have significant international financial activity, the simplification gives misleading results. It may be preferable both to separate the imputed from the actual payments and to recognize some portion of the banking services as enterprise final consumption expenditures. The recognition of banking services as output sold to the rest of the world is especially important for small countries that are important financial centers, like Luxembourg, Switzerland and Singapore, where the present treatment leads to a substantial understatement of GDP. It would also facilitate reconciliation of national accounts data with balance of payments data.

Conclusion. SNA does not provide for a category of enterprise final consumption expenditure. There are a number of instances, however, where enterprises provide goods and services in kind to their employees or to the public, and if the transactor/transaction principle is followed consistently such transaction flows should be recorded as enterprise final consumption expenditures. This problem should be reviewed to consider whether the concept of enterprise final consumption expenditures should be introduced into SNA.

Nonmarket imputations Nonmarket imputations have always been recognized as a necessary component of the national accounts. The chief nonmarket elements now included in SNA are subsistence agricultural activities in developing countries and space rental of owner-occupied housing in developed countries. In many developing countries a large proportion of the population is engaged in agricultural activity, the output of which they consume directly instead of selling on the market. The national accounts have always attempted to capture this nonmarket activity, and to show how the total of market and nonmarket production changes over time in the process of economic development. In developed countries, it has generally been recognized that owner-occupied housing provides housing services that should be counted as a part of total consumption.

The Blue Book was quite specific regarding the scope and definition of the nonmarket activities to be included in output. Its decisions primarily reflected two criteria: what was directly comparable to production taking place in the market and what it was considered feasible to measure, given existing statistical resources. Thus SNA excluded from output those activities taking place within the household whose products were seldom or never marketed. Since the 1968 revision, however, there has been substantial demand for the development of more comprehensive measures of consumption. Furthermore, the household sample survey has come to occupy a much more important place in the tool-kit of developing as well as developed countries, and such surveys greatly expand the realm of what it is possible to collect data for. As the United Nations National Household Survey Capability Programme begins to bear fruit in the next few years, the number of countries able to make use of household surveys will increase significantly. Explicit consideration therefore needs to be given to what kinds of nonmarket imputations it would really be useful to include.

With respect to subsistence production and consumption, the discussion paper prepared for the 1980 Expert Group meeting proposed certain modifications in the Blue Book rules. The Expert Group voiced no objections to the proposed changes, but considered that a much more intensive study of actual country practices was needed. In brief, the proposed modification would broaden the Blue Book's rule to include any activity that is found empirically, either as a consequence of a household survey or by any other means, to be significant in any given country. In many cases, this means that activities not on the SNA list will be included. SNA, for instance, includes the production of manufactured products like shoes, clothing and small metalware only when they are produced by persons who sell some of their output. There seems to be no good reason, apart perhaps from data availability, for this restriction, and for some countries it may result in the omission of significant amounts of output.

There is increasing interest, furthermore, in the nonmarket household activity now excluded from the scope of output. Exclusion of household nonmarket activity can lead to distorted conclusions when comparisons are made either between countries or over time. In a number of countries, the increasing participation of women in the market labor force has made the investigation of the changing nature of their activity within the household particularly important. In some countries a majority of adult women are now in paid employment. In other countries, or in the same country 20 years ago, the proportion would be much smaller. It is important to know what the impact of this increased labor force participation has been upon the household activities that have traditionally been women's work. There are a number of possibilities. Paid workers may be hired to replace the formerly unpaid services of housewives. Other family members may take on an increased share of the work within the household. The new labor force participants may simply be working longer and harder, doing both the household work and their paid employment. Or the quantity of household work done may be reduced. Time use studies suggest that what is in fact happening is a combination of all of these. A measure of either output or well-being that does not take this phenomenon into account is clearly missing an important dimension. To a considerable degree, the Blue Book's borderline between subsistence output, to be included in production and consumption, and household activity, to be excluded, reflects a sexist view that is gradually changing. Subsistence activities, for the most part, are male activities; household activities are female ones. Thus, winemaking is included, cooking is not; caring for animals is, caring for children is not; and communal volunteer projects like road building and similar kinds of activities are, but those of women's groups running volunteer community service programs like libraries, health services and school services are not. This disparity in treatment should be remedied.

In considering the impact of nonmarket activity, the method of valuation used is of central importance. SNA recommends that nonmarket imputations be valued at producers' prices of similar marketed goods and services; this is in line with its focus on production activities, and it is appropriate for the measurement of the total output of particular goods (such as agricultural products), whether produced for own consumption or for sale. Valuation at producers' prices will also, under certain circumstances, measure producers' opportunity costs when they consume their output instead of selling it on the market. The problems of valuation are more difficult, however, for the kinds of nonmarket activity not now included in SNA. In order to value household activity, for instance, it is necessary to decide whether to use the opportunity cost of the housewife in the labor market or the cost of hiring comparable household services on the market. For analyzing resource allocation an opportunity cost valuation might be appropriate, but for measuring consumption of household services, a market valuation might be better.

In developed countries, the largest existing imputation is usually that for the services of owner-occupied housing, and in this case SNA departs quite far from its own transactor/transaction principles. It may be questioned whether this departure is necessary or appropriate. In imputing the services of owner-occupied housing SNA treats owners of dwellings as proprietors of fictitious unincorporated enterprises engaged in the business of renting their houses to themselves. An imputed space rental value is included in household consumption expenditure and in the receipts of the fictitious enterprise. The fictitious enterprise, in turn, pays for the repair and upkeep and the property taxes and charges for consumption of fixed capital. Its operating surplus is then returned to the household as imputed entrepreneurial income.

One of the consequences of this procedure is that in an inflationary period when rents are rising similar increases in housing costs (and corresponding increases in imputed income) are attributed to home owners, even in those cases when the costs associated with owning may not have changed appreciably. The home owner's actual situation may be more analogous to that of a renter in a rent-controlled dwelling. In the case of rent control, the accounts record the actual rent, not its shadow market price.

It would similarly seem reasonable that the accounts should show explicitly the actual transactions involved in owning, in such a manner that the actual consumption expenditure attributed to households is not distorted. What is really being imputed is consumption of fixed capital and entrepreneurial income; showing these imputations separately would make it possible to analyze the total consumption of housing services as well as the expenditures for it. It may be doubted whether most owner-occupiers consider that their housing cost includes capital consumption, or even more certainly, a return to themselves as owners. Their behavior is much more likely to be influenced by what they actually must spend. For studies of demand, market analyses and the like, it is this actual expenditure that is relevant. Also, it is important to know, for the determination of taxation and fiscal policy, what part of indirect taxation is actually paid by households in the form of property taxes, and what part of interest paid by unincorporated enterprises is actually mortgage interest on owner-occupied dwellings.

Problems also arise in connection with consumer durables. SNA does not recommend that imputations be included in the accounts for the services of consumer durables, including automobiles, that households own. But when the institutional setting changes slightly so that household appliances are included as part of the cost of housing (owner-occupied or rented), or automobiles are rented or provided as benefits in kind to employees, their services are included in the measurement of both output and household consumption expenditure; indeed, it would be difficult statistically to exclude them. In view of the growing importance of consumer durables in many countries, it is increasingly difficult to justify the differing treatment of durables and houses.

A final question regarding nonmarket imputations relates to the services provided by government infrastructure and durables. SNA does include an imputation for the services of government buildings, but it is argued that other parts of the infrastructure have an indefinite life if properly maintained, and that the maintenance expenditure measures the value of the service provided. With fluctuations of government budgets, however, it is evident that there may be periods when the infrastructure is undermaintained, and others when basic improvements are introduced which should be counted as additions to the capital stock. An argument can, therefore, be made that all government capital stock, and not only its buildings, should be assigned a finite lifetime and depreciated.

Despite this pressure to open up the boundaries of what is defined as consumption to include additional kinds of nonmarket activity and the services of durables, however, there has also been strong resistance to losing sight of the transactions-oriented base of the national accounts. This reluctance stems not only from the belief that the basis for valuation of market transactions is more apparent and the data are likely to be relatively much firmer, but also from the perception that market transactions are often the vehicle for implementing economic and social policy. There is serious concern that the pursuit of comprehensive measures of well-being should not be allowed to destroy the usefulness of the system for analysis of fiscal and monetary policy. A solution that would respond to both sets of concerns might articulate the sector accounts in terms of the actual market transactions taking place, and display nonmarket transactions separately in such a way that new kinds of information on nonmarket activity will be available within the accounting framework, without impairing the more traditional uses of the system.

Conclusion. SNA introduces imputations into the accounts to cover nonmarket activity. There are, however, both boundary and valuation problems that need to be clarified, relating in particular to subsistence, household activities, owner-occupied housing, consumer durables and the government infrastructure. The question also needs to be considered whether the distinction between actual market transactions and nonmarket imputations should be made more explicit in the accounts.

Measurement of income

Effects of inflation on the measurement of income The inflation in the major industrial countries during the past decade has raised questions about the measurement of income in the national accounts. Much of the discussion has centered around the recording of interest receipts as an income flow, at a time when it has generally been recognized that the high nominal interest rates were in part compensation for the erosion in the purchasing power of the fixed-claim asset to which the interest related. The question was posed whether some sort of adjustment should be introduced to separate the interest payments into 'real' interest and capital repayment flows.

SNA does, in fact, introduce 'price-corrected' information into the accounts in connection with two items: the consumption of fixed capital and the change in stocks. With respect to the consumption of fixed capital, true depreciation valued at replacement cost is substituted for the actual depreciation charged on the books of businesses. Business accounting practices for tax purposes in many countries permit the application of accelerated depreciation rates to the book value of fixed capital. In periods of stable prices this results in a depreciation charge that exceeds replacement cost depreciation, but in periods of high inflation the depreciation charged, if based on book value, may be less than replacement cost depreciation. With respect to the change in stocks, business accounts often show the change in the money value of stocks. In order to measure output correctly, however, what is required is the value of the change in the physical volume of stocks, and that is what SNA calls for.

Since these adjustments are included in SNA, it is reasonable to consider whether further adjustments in the accounts might be appropriate in order to show the effects of changing price levels on specific components of income. In a study prepared for OECD and EUROSTAT, Jack Hibbert (1982) examined these issues, and came to the following conclusions:

(i) The existing SNA and ESA concepts of income and saving should be retained.
(ii) In order to interpret the statistics satisfactorily, particularly during periods of relatively high inflation, data on the levels of assets and liabilities held by each of the main institutional sectors in the economy need to be made available within a framework integrated with the main accounts relating to transactions.
(iii) Although further work is needed to explore in detail the implications of using different numeraires as the basis for estimates in terms of current and constant purchasing power, the long-term inflationary losses on assets and liabilities subject to relatively small or negligible money holding gains or losses probably fall within a fairly narrow range, whatever numeraire is chosen.
(iv) Even a relatively unsophisticated method of estimating these inflationary losses, within a systematic framework of the kind envisaged at (ii) above, would be of considerable value to users of the statistics.
(v) Much of the information needed is already available in the major industrialized countries, but if the database is to be developed in such a way as to provide internationally compatible results, a lead is needed from the international agencies.

These conclusions were based on a recognition that it was not logical to make adjustments for the loss in the purchasing power of interest-bearing financial claims while neglecting to take into account losses or gains relating to noninterest-bearing assets. Hibbert concluded that in order to deal fully with this problem what was required was a complete integration of the sector current income and outlay and capital finance accounts of SNA with revaluation accounts and balance sheets so that estimates of gains and losses could be made in terms of both current and constant purchasing power.

SNA clearly envisages such a complete and integrated set of accounts, but the guidelines developed in 1977 (UN, 1977c) were considered provisional, since few countries at that time had successfully compiled reconciliation accounts and balance sheets that were integrated with the current flow accounts. Hibbert, therefore, recommends that the UN Statistical Office, OECD and EUROSTAT, as a part of the review of SNA, organize further discussion of the technical statistical issues involved with the objective of reaching international agreement on a definitive integrated system of reconciliation accounts and balance sheets. He further urges that member countries should be strongly encouraged to develop work on sector balance sheets, concentrating initially on data for the household sector where the need appears to be the greatest from the point of view of users and to provide, on a regular basis, estimates of sectoral gains and losses on holdings of assets and liabilities in purchasing power terms.

The Hibbert study thus recasts the original issues relating to 'inflation accounting' into the broader context of an integration of current accounts and balance sheets. This reformulation is fully consistent with the basic principles of SNA, and demonstrates the relevance of the system for analyzing the impact of the inflationary process upon the different sectors of the economy. The issues of inflation accounting have thus been converted into questions of how best to implement the objective of a fully integrated system of current accounts and balance sheets.

Conclusion. The SNA income and outlay accounts do not adjust transaction flows such as interest and other property income for the effects of inflation upon the purchasing power of assets. Rather than attempting to introduce such adjustments into the income and outlay accounts, however, it seems more appropriate to measure the capital gains or losses involved by developing an integrated set of income and outlay, capital finance, reconciliation and balance sheet accounts in both current and constant purchasing power prices. Such a development is fully consistent with the basic principles of SNA, and would require only further development of the existing accounts.

Treatment of land and subsoil and intangible assets A number of special problems arise in accounting for the increase in value and/or the using up of assets that are not created in the ordinary way by capital formation. This class includes subsoil assets like petroleum and mineral ores, of course, but it is not limited to them. Agricultural land, stands of timber and, in some institutional and climatic settings, water rights all pose very similar problems. Intangible nonfinancial assets like patents and copyrights also fall into this group.

SNA now includes a formal accounting for such assets and their use. Their capital value in principle enters into the national and sector balance sheets, valued, in so far as possible, at current market value as reflected in recent sales of similar assets. New finds, natural growth, and the creation of intangible assets, however, are not considered capital formation; rather, they enter the balance sheet through the capital reconciliation accounts. The costs of development of such assets enter the accounts in several ways. For resources that are in principle renewable, like agricultural land, orchards, plantations and tree farms, development costs are included in gross fixed capital formation. For nonrenewable resources like subsoil assets, however, a distinction is made between costs of exploration and costs of development. Only the costs of developing proven reserves are capitalized; exploration costs are written off as current costs.

A number of questions have arisen about this treatment. One deals with the scope of what is included in development costs that are to be capitalized. Exploration and development, it is suggested, are no longer separate activities but rather one continuous process; new finds are no longer a gift of nature attributable largely to chance but rather the result of systematic development requiring large expenditures, all of which should be capitalized. This view recognizes that a certain percentage of exploratory work will not produce usable results, but this is considered to be a predictable cost, similar in a way to accidental damage to fixed capital.

A second question concerns depletion. It is argued that many resources are not inexhaustible (as the present treatment implicitly assumes), but rather that using them depletes a finite resource. As a consequence, it is contended that depletion should be counted as a current cost. The resource base is of course not static, and depletion may be offset by new finds. It is therefore suggested that the net change in reserves — new finds less depletion — should appear in the production accounts as a part of current output. But 'reserves' are very difficult to define, and even more difficult to value. It is generally agreed that what should enter into the balance sheet is 'proven' reserves. The definition of proven reserves stipulates that they must be economically exploitable at current costs and prices. In a world of increasing scarcity and rising relative prices of all subsoil assets, what is economically exploitable is not fixed. Increases in the quantity of proven reserves are just as likely to come from an increase in relative prices as from new finds.

The 1980 Expert Group expressed general support for a calculation of the change in the value of proven reserves that would explicitly include allowances for both new finds and depletion, as well as for the effects of price changes. It was considered, however, that this should properly be reflected in the balance sheet and reconciliation accounts and not in the current flow accounts. The conceptual difficulties of this measurement were emphasized; it was pointed out that it was really an attempt to estimate the replacement value of what was, in fact, irreplaceable. With respect to the appropriate treatment of exploration costs, differing views emerged but a majority of the group favored retention of the present treatment, noting that exploration costs were intrinsically no different from other research costs and, if the one were capitalized, the other ought to be as well.

There are some other problems relating to this class of assets that need further clarification. One concerns land and its rent. SNA considers net land rent to be property income. Rents of buildings, equipment, etc. are, however, considered to be payments for the purchase of services, and they enter into the production accounts of both the purchaser (as intermediate consumption) and the seller (as sales). Net rents of buildings and equipment thus enter into the determination of operating surplus, like receipts from any other kind of productive activity. In the case of land, however, rents are treated differently. The net rental receipts, after deduction of associated costs like maintenance expenditures and real estate taxes, do not enter operating surplus but are shown as a separate source of income in the income and outlay account. Net land rentals paid are not part of the cost of production (even of farmers operating on rented land) but rather a redistribution of income. Countries for the most part do not make these distinctions between land rents and building rents, citing both statistical and conceptual difficulties. The statistical problem of separating land rent from rent of the building occupying it is particularly acute, but questions have been raised about the conceptual propriety of treating even agricultural land rent differently from other costs.

A final problem of clarification concerns intangible nonfinancial assets. SNA requires that purchases of such intangible assets as copyrights and patents should be shown in the capital finance account, where they are treated like net purchases of land. This category does not, however, include the sale of leases, exploitation rights, etc., where the eventual title reverts to the original owner; these are treated like land rent. None of the countries responding to the SNA questionnaires provides such separate data on purchases and sales of intangible assets. No distinction is made between payments for the purchase of intangible assets and those made for the use of such assets: the total amount is presumably included in property income as a component of rents and royalties. It is not clear whether countries encounter statistical difficulties in making the separation, or whether they reject it on theoretical grounds. The right to use subsoil resources is usually given for a set period of time. If at the end of this period the resources are exhausted, it is difficult to decide if the payments were made for the use of the right or if the right was transferred altogether. A similar difficulty of distinguishing between an outright transfer and use arises for copyrights and trademarks.

Conclusion. SNA includes land and subsoil assets as part of balance sheets, and their change in value as part of the reconciliation account. Questions have been raised with respect to the treatment of exploration costs and depletion in the case of subsoil assets, the treatment of rent in the case of land, and the treatment of royalties, licenses and fees in the case of intangible assets. Many of these issues involve problems of statistical implementation as well as conceptual clarification.

Pensions, insurance and capital transfers The SNA treatment of life insurance and pension contributions and benefits is the conventional national accounting one. Both are considered to have been earned (or purchased) when the pension contribution or premium payment was made, and both are attributed to the households who will be the eventual beneficiaries. Contributions to pension funds and life insurance premiums paid by employers are shown as part of compensation of employees. Households' equity in life insurance and pension funds is shown as a household asset and a liability of financial institutions, and the change in this equity is shown in the household capital finance account. The change in equity, in turn, reflects net premiums less benefits and annuities paid. Only the service charge portion of the premium payments or contributions appears in household consumption expenditures. Receipts of pension benefits and life insurance annuities, however, are considered to represent only a change in the form of household assets, and not a current income flow. Thus what appears in the accounts of households is the change in their net equity in these funds, not their actual cash receipts.

This treatment was originally devised during the 1930s, when these forms of deferred compensation were less common, and for the most part, were restricted to the upper end of the income distribution where a calculation of income based on the net change in asset position might not be unrealistic. It was perhaps still defensible in 1968. In 1982, it is highly questionable. In some countries pensions and annuities have come to play a very important role, and constitute the major source of income for a growing segment of the population. What counts, to the pensioner, is his monthly check, not the reserves of the pension fund or insurance company that pays it. His claim to a share of the fund's assets is purely hypothetical; he has no control over it and no access to it. For such uses as studies of consumer behavior or analyses of levels of living or income distribution, household income should reflect what the households themselves consider their income to be.

A treatment that would come closer to reflecting the factors actually influencing economic behavior would leave the reserves of pension funds and insurance companies with the companies involved, attributing to households only the cash redemption value of their holdings. This would, of course, not alter GDP, but it would show the distribution of income flows more realistically. It would also bring the handling of private pensions much closer to that of public social security contributions and benefits. The whole of social security contributions is treated as, essentially, a direct tax on households, and the whole of the benefit as a contribution to household income. Rights to future social security benefits are not capitalized and they are not considered to be a household asset.

Some employers provide their employees, or former employees, with welfare benefits such as pensions and medical care, but do not make any regular contributions into a fund to cover the cost of the benefits provided. The various benefits are paid out of current revenue as the need arises. From the employee's point of view, receipt of these benefits is clearly of value, and from the employer's point of view the payment of these benefits is clearly a cost of employing labor. For these reasons, SNA recommends that compensation of employees should include an imputation for such 'unfunded' welfare contributions, and that household consumption expenditures should include an imputed payment for them (SNA, paras 7.17–7.18). SNA recommends that the imputation be based upon what it would cost the employer to provide the benefits on a funded basis, i.e., on the amount of regular contributions that would have to be paid into a fund sufficient to generate an investment income to cover the costs of benefits actually paid out. It is evident that such an estimate would be a highly subjective one since it depends on forecasting over a future period such factors as interest rates, pension and benefit adjustments, and the number of those eligible for benefits. An alternative suggested by SNA is to compute the contributions for each year as equal to the benefits actually paid. This method has the advantage of simplicity and appears to be used by the majority of countries that make estimates of unfunded welfare contributions. It should be noted, however, that this second method really begs the question: it substitutes current cost outlays for an accrued obligation. Rather than employ this device, it might be preferable to show only the actual transactions that occur. In effect the SNA imputation of unfunded pension and welfare contributions violates its transactor/transaction criterion. The employer does not actually make a contribution, and his current outlays are in fact coincident with the cost of the benefits provided in the current period.

A somewhat different problem arises in the treatment of casualty insurance claims. Unlike life insurance annuities and pensions, all such claims paid out by insurance companies are considered in SNA to be current income of the recipients. They include, however, a number of quite different kinds of claim, and it is not clear that all of them should be treated in the same way. One large subset is concerned with income replacement; this includes unemployment insurance, part of accident insurance, and similar payments where the intent is to provide a replacement for current income lost because of some insured casualty. But there is another large category where what is being replaced is not current income but a capital loss. Fire, theft and all kinds of damage insurance fall into this category. These payments are not current income, but rather are offsets to capital losses. It may be questioned, therefore, whether it would not be more appropriate to enter them, together with the capital losses, as changes in the balance sheet. The income-replacement kinds of insurance claims are very much like pensions, and should probably be treated in the same way, but the capital-replacement claims are quite different.

Two objections have been raised to the treatment of casualty insurance benefits as a capital item. First, it is pointed out that SNA includes accidental damage to fixed capital in the consumption of fixed capital that is charged on the current account. The argument in support of this position is that a more or less predictable amount of accidental damage occurs each year in the economy as a whole, and for that reason it is a part of the current cost of doing business. Such an aggregate view of production, however, violates the transactor/ transaction principle. Similar reasoning, for instance, would lead even capital formation to be considered a current outlay, since a more or less predictable amount occurs each year. Certainly from the point of view of those individual establishments incurring accidental damage such as fires, the losses are obviously capital losses, and should be treated as such in the accounts.

Secondly, it is pointed out that SNA requires that any transfer that is considered to be capital by one party to it must be treated as capital for both; thus treating the insurance benefit as a capital receipt would require that it also be treated as a capital outlay by the insurance company — a clearly undesirable result. This requirement in SNA was intended to preserve the identity of saving and investment in the accounts, without having to introduce capital transfers paid or received into the equation. But it is obvious that as in the case of expenditures for capital goods, it is theoretically possible for a transfer to be considered capital by one transactor and current by the other. The true identity is to be found *after* capital transfers. As more interest focuses on the integration of current accounts, capital transaction accounts and balance sheets, the artificial restriction relating to capital transfers becomes more and more awkward.

Conclusion. SNA treats pension and insurance contributions and benefits in terms of the net accumulation of equity by households. When the reserves accumulate in pension and insurance companies and are not fully reflected in increases in actual household net worth (i.e., cash redemption value), this may not be consistent with the transactor/transaction principles of SNA. Somewhat related questions can be raised concerning the treatment of casualty insurance premiums and benefits that involve capital transfers. These issues should be examined with respect to the need for further clarification to introduce consistency of treatment.

Financial leasing Considerable interest has arisen in both EUROSTAT and OECD in the topic of financial leasing (SOEC, 1981b). The use of financial leasing as a method of financing the acquisition of equipment has increased significantly in recent years (owing in part to favorable tax treatment), and it is considered that the SNA treatment of leasing in general is no longer adequate.

A financial lease is a long-term contract between the owner of a good (the lessor) and the user of the good (the lessee), whereby the lessee has possession and use of the good against payment of specified rentals over a well-defined period during which the agreement cannot be terminated. The rental is sufficient to cover the capital outlay and all subsidiary and financing costs. The costs of maintenance and repair, and all risks connected with the subject of the lease, are borne by the lessee, and it is the lessee who selects the asset and deals with the supplier. The role of the lessor is purely financial; the lease is an alternative to other financing methods (loan or hire-purchase).

An operating lease, in contrast, is regarded by both parties as a market service. The lessor, in general, cannot expect to recover his full capital outlay in one leasing, which will generally be short term. The lessor is prepared to take back the asset between leasings for repair and overhaul. In order to maintain a flexible supply of leasing services, the lessor must generally maintain a stock of the assets in question. Thus the lessor's services are not confined to financial intermediation.

The proposed new treatment of financial leasing under consideration by EUROSTAT and OECD is as follows.

1. At the time the primary lease is signed the lessee should be treated as purchasing the capital asset out of a loan provided by the lessor for that specific purpose. The transactions would be recorded in the balance sheet of the lessee and in the capital finance accounts of both the lessor and lessee.
2. The rental payments should not be treated as intermediate consumption by the lessee, but as a charge against gross operating surplus. The rental payments would not appear at all in the production account of either lessor or lessee. The amount deducted from gross operating surplus for consumption of fixed capital would be retained by the lessee, and not paid over to the lessor.
3. The rental payment should be split into two components representing repayment of the loan and interest on the loan outstanding. That part representing interest would appear as a payment of actual interest from the lessee to the lessor in the income and outlay accounts of both. That part representing repayment of loan capital would appear in the capital finance accounts of both.
4. The full equivalent of the market value of the leased good should be recorded in the balance sheet, and an offsetting entry should appear in the financial accounts as a liability; the latter should include the value of any option to purchase at the end of the lease period.

These proposals have been discussed and approved in principle by the member countries of both the European Community and OECD. Some details remain to be cleared up; EUROSTAT is engaged on that task.

Conclusion. SNA makes no distinction between operating leasing and financial leasing. However, it is generally recognized that financial leasing is really a method of financing the purchase of assets, not a true rental. It seems appropriate therefore to treat financing leasing differently from operating leasing. This would require altering the SNA definition of leasing.

Terms of trade The 1980 Expert Group proposed that a study of methods of separating relative price changes from inflationary (or general) price changes would be useful. Terms of trade measurement is a special case of this problem: measures of real GDP may differ significantly depending on whether terms of trade changes are included or not. It was noted that although the price and quantity statistics guidelines recommend exclusion of terms-of-trade effects, the International Comparison Project includes them in its measures of purchasing power parities. Because of recent swings in commodity prices, furthermore, gains and losses from changes in the terms of trade can be important in short-term forecasting. However, there is no consensus on methods of measuring terms-of-trade effects, and a number of different procedures are currently being used.

In the earlier discussions of this topic during the 1960s, it was sometimes concluded that the effects were relatively small and import and export price indexes of such poor quality that the effort to measure terms-of-trade effects might not be worthwhile. This situation has now changed; the problem is much more important, and the quality of the statistics is somewhat improved. The Expert Group thought that a new attempt to measure these effects might, therefore, be useful.

Conclusion. SNA, in developing price and quantity comparisons of exports and imports, deflates them by domestic prices. Interest in the terms of trade suggests, however, that methods should be explored for incorporating a separation of relative and general price changes into the general framework of the accounts.

The accounting structure and sectoring

The accounting structure The accounting structure of SNA is based upon a dual classification of transactors. One set of accounts is given for establishment-type units classified by kind of economic activity (industry), and a different set of accounts is given for enterprise-type units classified into institutional sectors based on financial role and behavior. For kinds of activity, the accounts relate to production, consumption expenditure, and capital formation (Class II). For institutional sectors, income and outlay, capital finance, reconciliation and balance sheet accounts are provided (Classes III and VII). It is only in the consolidated accounts for the nation (Class I) that the relation between the production and expenditure accounts and the income and appropriation accounts is given.

The limitation of accounts for kinds of activity to production and related activities derives from the lack of financial independence of establishment-type units; if they are part of a larger enterprise, they usually are not centers of financial decision-making. It may not be possible to separate their assets and liabilities from those of other establishments of the same parent enterprise. It therefore may not be possible to construct a complete set of accounts for establishments classified by kind of activity.

No such limitation applies to enterprises classified by institutional sector, however. A complete set of accounts embracing production, income and outlay, capital finance, reconciliation and balance sheets is both conceptually valid and statistically feasible. For many purposes, such a full set of accounts is analytically very useful. Thus, for instance, it is not possible to determine compensation of employees paid by the different institutional sectors unless production accounts are provided for them.

ESA does provide production accounts for both branches (kinds of activity) and institutional sectors. The recent revision of the UN/OECD National Accounts Questionnaire also introduced production accounts for institutional sectors. There remain, however, some differences between the ESA accounts and those employed in the UN questionnaire. Some of these are more matters of presentation than substance, and it would be useful in the interest of both producers and users if these could be resolved. Proposals have been made from time to time that the joint UN/OECD National Accounts Questionnaire should be extended to serve EUROSTAT's needs as well. To date, however, this has not been found to be feasible.

In addition to the provision of production accounts for institutional sectors, there is another feature of the European accounting structure which might be considered in the SNA context. That is the structuring of the production account so that it yields gross value added as the balancing item, rather than net operating surplus. Value added is intrinsically a much more useful and interesting figure than operating surplus, and one that is basic to the kind of activity breakdown. Part 4 of the UN National Accounts Questionnaire does implicitly contain such a production account, in Tables 4.1 and 4.5. But it is not part of the standard (Class II) framework.

Conclusion. SNA does not specify production accounts for institutional sectors, but such accounts are included in ESA. The ESA production accounts provide somewhat different information from the SNA production accounts. It would be useful to examine the feasibility of bringing the SNA and ESA accounting structures into closer alignment with each other.

The sectoring of enterprises and households In an attempt to accommodate widely differing institutional arrangements in different countries, the 1968 SNA introduced a new kind of enterprise concept, midway between corporation and unincorporated enterprise, called quasi-corporation. This concept was intended to recognize that there are some enterprises which, without being formally incorporated, behave in most respects like corporations.

SNA gives directives on which enterprises are to be considered quasi-corporations. In order to be so classed, the incomes and outlays of the enterprise and all the tangible and financial assets and liabilities connected with the business should be controlled and managed independently and separate, complete records should be available for all of these items. Unfortunately, however, it has not turned out in practice that countries have found this rule easy to use. Country practices are quite varied. A number of countries include only public quasi-corporations in the corporate and quasi-corporate sector, relegating all others to the household sector. Some make no attempt at all to identify quasi-corporations, putting all public unincorporated enterprises into the general government sector and all private ones into the household sector. A few move the other way, putting all unincorporated enterprises into the quasi-corporate category, thus in effect retaining the enterprise concept of the 1952 SNA. The problem SNA was trying to address is nevertheless a real one, and a solution is needed.

SNA leaves unincorporated enterprises that are not considered to qualify as quasi-corporations in the household sector, if private, or the general government sector, if public. The principal reason advanced for this treatment is that it is not possible to separate the unincorporated enterprises out. But this argument is not very persuasive. Public unincorporated enterprises are discussed in the next section. With respect to private unincorporated enterprises, the separation between households and private unincorporated enterprises in the production account is clear: SNA does not consider that any production apart from domestic services takes place in the household, so that any other production taking place in the combined household and unincorporated enterprise sector is by definition attributable to the unincorporated enterprises. This is recognized in the activity classification, where no problem is encountered in including the production of small unincorporated enterprises with that of other enterprises in the appropriate industry. In the income and outlay account, the question is similarly moot, since in SNA unincorporated enterprises are not considered to have income and outlay transactions, apart from the inclusion of their operating surplus in the income of households. As a consequence, apart from domestic servants, a combined household/unincorporated enterprise sector would have the same production account as a pure unincorporated enterprise sector, and the same income and outlay account as a pure household sector. This is *de facto* the solution adopted in ESA for these accounts.

Where the sector definition does make a difference, however, is in the capital finance and balance sheet accounts. SNA takes the position that the proprietor of a small unincorporated enterprise will 'frequently mingle and manage together the financial transactions and holdings of the business and his other activities' (SNA, para. 5.72). Although this argument is at first glance reasonable, in practice different financial instruments are used for the household and the small business (e.g., consumer debt and trade debt), so that for the purpose of analyzing financial flows a useful separation can be made — much in the way that institutional arrangements make it possible to separate the productive activities attributable to the small business from the consumption activities attributable to the household. Indeed, those who are concerned with the development of financial statistics and balance sheets and their integration with the national accounts argue that what is really not feasible is to separate the financial activities of small business from those of large business (e.g., separation of trade debt by size of enterprise) — a separation that is required if small business is to be kept in the household sector. In terms of the household balance sheet, furthermore, what should appear is the net equity of the proprietor carried as an asset, and derived from the balance sheet of the small business much in the same way that the operating surplus is derived for a small business from its production account. The development of a separate balance sheet for unincorporated business would result in the same 'net worth' on the household balance sheet, but it seems inappropriate to include as assets in the household balance sheet the agricultural land, store fixtures, and stock in trade that may be used in a small business, or to include its trade debt as a household liability.

ESA uses a size criterion for separating private quasi-corporations from unincorporated enterprises. Their rule specifies that to be considered a quasi-corporation, an agricultural enterprise must have at least 20 employees, an industrial enterprise at least 100 and a service enterprise at least 50. This rule, of course, has the effect of limiting private quasi-corporations to quite exceptional circumstances; in most countries there would be relatively few unincorporated firms large enough to qualify as quasi-corporations. Though it is definite, problems have arisen in its application since the required data often are not available broken down both by size and legal form of organization.

Taking data sources into account, in fact, in financial statistics it is easier to distinguish the types of financial instruments that are related to businesses on the one hand and households on the other than to attempt to obtain information, for any given instrument, on the legal form of organization and the size distribution of borrowers or holders. Again with respect to microdata sources, including household surveys and tax information relating to enterprises, sector definitions that separate households and businesses are much easier to handle than those that require a breakdown of businesses by size and legal form.

Conclusion. SNA defines a nonfinancial enterprise sector that includes corporate and quasi-corporate enterprises and a household sector that includes nonfinancial unincorporated enterprises. The criteria for distinguishing between quasi-corporate and unincorporated enterprises are not entirely satisfactory, and the inclusion of unincorporated enterprises with households raises some problems with respect to financial statistics. These issues need to be examined to determine whether a more appropriate sectoring for enterprises and households can be developed.

The public sector In its main text, SNA does not identify a public sector. Such a sector is discussed in Chapter 9, the supplement intended for developing countries. But it is, of course, not only in developing countries that information on the public sector is of great importance. In most countries the public authorities at all levels now play a large part in both economic and social affairs. One of the consequences of this fact of modern life is that new methods have had to be found for analyzing the effects of public sector activities on the rest of the economy and society, and for providing information about them to those responsible for deciding how best the government should act in the general interest of the community. The national accounts are, of course, concerned only with describing public bodies as transactors. It is well to recognize that this is only part of the total picture of their effects on the nation, since it leaves out activities of a regulatory nature.

It was because of the demands of users of the statistics that work was first started in the Statistical Office on the production of a manual of public sector statistics to supplement the Blue Book discussion of this topic. That work has brought to light a number of problems. An important one concerns the scope of the public sector and how its component parts fit together.

The public sector, as defined in Volume 4 of the *Handbook*, is composed of general government and public enterprises. General government, in turn, consists of producers of government services and departmental enterprises. Although departmental enterprises are not explicitly recognized in the Blue Book they are implicit in it since they constitute the difference between general government (the institutional sector) and producers of government services (the kind-of-activity sector).

SNA's intent, in distinguishing general government and producers of government services, was to ensure that producers of government services did not include government departments, establishments and similar units that sell to the public or furnish to the government itself goods and services of a kind 'which are often provided by business establishments' (SNA, paras 5.10–12). It was considered that such units should be treated like business establishments, especially for purposes of valuation of their output and its classification by kind of activity. Two subclasses of these types of government activities were identified: those whose output was delivered to other units of government (called ancillary agencies) and those selling their output to the public — those same unincorporated public enterprises excluded from public quasi-corporations on the ground of small size and/or incomplete accounts. Typical examples of the first subclass are repair shops, printing establishments and munitions factories. An example of the second, which will normally be small in size, might be a cafeteria in a public building.

As the complexity of both government operations and private business operations has increased, however, it has become increasingly difficult to decide what ancillary activities are of a type 'often provided by business establishments'. In addition to the agricultural, manufacturing and construction activities specifically mentioned in SNA, large parts of the administrative, legal, personnel management, computing, property management, protection, refuse collection, and similar services engaged in by government are similar in virtually all respects to activities carried on by business establishments. An attempt to remove all of the activities of government that could fall into any other kind-of-activity class is likely to be counterproductive, since it would leave little but defense, and even that could be questioned.

Where the output of ancillary agencies is delivered to other governmental units, furthermore, questions may be raised as to whether the prices charged reflect true market prices, since both the buyer and seller are under the same control. Where prices do not reflect market prices, they should not be used in valuing the output of these units. The principal reasons for distinguishing such units from producers of government services thus often disappear.

It seems reasonable, therefore, that ancillary agencies should be limited to units that not only produce outputs of a type often produced by business enterprises, but also price them competitively. Where the prices differ from market, or where information on market prices is lacking, it will be less misleading to include these units with producers of government services.

Problems also arise with respect to departmental enterprises selling to the general public. Such units must be distinguished, on the one hand, from public quasi-corporations, and on the other from producers of government services, mainly on the basis of the way they operate. Where such units are large in size and keep complete accounts separate from those of their parent agencies, it is the clear intent of SNA that they should be considered public quasi-corporations and excluded from departmental enterprises (and from general government). This is true even if the unit is required to turn over all of its profits to its parent organization, or if its capital needs are met by grants from that agency. (In such cases, the entities in question are likely to have complete production accounts, but their income and outlay and capital finance accounts may be limited to trade credit and accounts receivable and payable, SNA, Table 5.1, item l(b).) It is also true even though the unit may as a matter of public policy adopt pricing policies that do not cover its full costs so that subsidies are needed (SNA, para. 5.10). But there must, of course, be some limit to the size of the subsidy, and for the purposes of the *Public Sector Statistics* manual the convention is adopted that when the sales price covers less than half the cost the product is effectively being given away and the unit is operating like a producer of government services.

In SNA, only 'large' unincorporated enterprises that behave in most respects like corporations are intended to be designated quasi-corporations. 'Small' public units are to be left with the general government sector. But circumstances differ so greatly among countries, especially among countries at different stages of development, that it is not possible to give an exact specification of what is large and what is small. Thus, the operative criterion is likely to be the existence of adequate separate accounts. Small scale operations that are incidental to the activities of their parent organizations will seldom have such accounts, and it will seldom be worth the statistician's time and effort to try to estimate them. Without accounts, they cannot be treated as quasi-corporations.

Distinguishing the small-scale selling activities that should be treated as departmental enterprises from those that should be treated as incidental activities of producers of government services is even more difficult, and it is here especially that country experience suggests that the effort may not be worthwhile. The SNA criterion is the possibility of compiling complete production accounts, so that an operating surplus can be derived. That, apart from size, is effectively the same as the criterion used to identify public quasi-corporations, and units for which such accounts are readily available should probably be considered to be quasi-corporations. Where accounts are not available, the activity will of necessity have to be treated as a producer of government services. In practice, therefore, this subclass of departmental enterprise ought to be small or nonexistent. Country experience confirms that this is the case.

For both analytical and statistical reasons, there is thus much to be said for abandoning the concept of departmental enterprise, and classifying the units involved as either public enterprises or producers of government services. If the sales involved are substantial and intended to cover cost, and represent an arms-length relationship between buyer and seller, it would be appropriate to consider even ancillary agencies selling primarily to government to be quasi-corporate public enterprises. But if the sales are incidental or are not intended to cover costs, the activity should be considered to be that of a producer of government services. Producers of government services in the activity accounts would then coincide with general government in the institutional sector accounts. There might then be no reason to retain the two different terms: both might be called general government, or simply 'government'.

The institutional sector 'general government' is also subdivided into subsectors that relate to social security funds and the various levels of government. The social security funds subsector consists of government bodies that administer funded social security schemes. These are schemes imposed by governments and controlled by them for purposes of providing social security benefits for the community or for large sections of the community, including, for example, old age, disability and survivors' benefits, reimbursements for medical expenses and in some cases the provision of medical services. Social security funds exclude, however, schemes for government employees formulated by an organ of government solely in its role as an employer, and similar schemes provided by private businesses for their employees.

Boundary problems arise in distinguishing social security funds that should be treated as government from those that should be classed as either public or private financial institutions. The decision in SNA rests primarily upon the criterion of control. In practice, institutional arrangements are found that range all the way from total financing and control by the government to complete independence from public control and no public financing. Where a fund is considered to exist but the fixing of levels of contributions and benefits is a government function not at the discretion of the fund, the fund should clearly be included in government, but as would be the case for other earmarked funds controlled by the government, there seems no valid reason for considering it to be a separate subsector. Where the fund managers not only have discretionary authority to engage in capital market operations but the contributions and/or benefits are determined by the outcome of these operations, a case can be made for treating the fund as a financial institution — public or private depending upon how the fund managers are chosen. SNA does not recommend this treatment (SNA, paras 5.27, 5.57). However, institutional practices have changed somewhat in the interval since 1968, and some exceptions may now be warranted. Mandatory schemes shade imperceptibly into private pension and insurance schemes. Where the extent of public control is limited to a requirement that private insurance be carried, even if there is some regulation of charges and benefits, it seems reasonable that the scheme should be excluded entirely from the public sector. Where there is an independent public financial institution in charge of social security, it seems reasonable to exclude it from the general government sector, although it should be included in the public sector. Thus it appears that there may in fact be no circumstances under which a social security subsector of general government would be justified. The question as to whether there is a social security fund subsector is, of course, a separate question from that of distinguishing social security contributions as sources of revenue and social security benefits as types of outlay; these are shown explicitly in the SNA general government income and outlay account.

Despite the considerable attention devoted to distinguishing producers of government services from general government and the attempt to define a social security subsector, the Blue Book classifications of both government revenue and government outlays still left much to be desired from the point of view of analytic usefulness. There is, effectively, no classification of revenues in the Blue Book. The Public Sector Manual has adopted the IMF classification of revenue, although as noted in the discussion of harmonization of public sector statistics this does raise some problems of consistency. *A Revised Classification of the Functions of Government* (COFOG) was published in 1980 (UN, 1980g), and a new table on government outlays by function and type has been included in the revised UN/OECD questionnaire (UN and OECD, 1980).

Conclusion. SNA defines a kind-of-activity classification called 'producers of government services' and an institutional sector called 'general government'. The difference between these categories has been difficult to define conceptually, to measure statistically, or to justify analytically. At the same time, SNA fails to provide some needed classifications, such as one of revenues, and some of its classifications, such as that by type of outlay, need further clarification. Consideration also needs to be given to whether the distinctions provided in SNA are valid, operational, or useful. The subsector for social security funds also needs further clarification as to the circumstances under which such a sector should be considered to exist.

Other sectoring considerations SNA's institutional breakdown of the economy includes five major domestic sectors and nine subsectors, as shown below:

1. Nonfinancial enterprises, corporate and quasi-corporate
    a. Private
    b. Public
2. Financial institutions
    a. The central bank
    b. Other monetary institutions
    c. Insurance companies and pension funds
    d. Other financial institutions
3. General government
    a. Central government
    b. State and local government
    c. Social security funds
4. Private nonprofit institutions serving households
5. Households including private nonfinancial unincorporated enterprises

Some of the issues relating to this sector classification have been discussed above. But there are two additional respects in which the SNA treatment of sectoring is not entirely satisfactory: nonprofit institutions are treated as a main sector, on the same level as households and general government, and there is no overall enterprise sector that brings together information on all enterprise activities.

Treating nonprofit institutions as a major sector presents difficulties for many countries since data relating to nonprofit institutions are generally unavailable. As a consequence strict adherence to the SNA sectoring system would mean that sectoral breakdowns of the major transaction flows could not be obtained. Furthermore, given the relative size of the nonprofit sector, most countries do not consider it worthwhile to invest the statistical resources needed to obtain the required data, and nonprofit institutions are by default included in some other sector. In many cases, it is not clear just where they are included, since this largely depends on the nature of the statistical sources used. The outlays of nonprofit institutions on construction or rental of buildings, hiring employees, and purchasing intermediate goods and services will tend to be included in the same statistical sources that report such data for enterprises. On the other hand, to the extent that nonprofit institutions purchase the same goods and services as households and estimates of household expenditures are determined residually in the accounts, these household expenditures will also include similar nonprofit institution expenditures.

The SNA treatment of nonprofit institutions as a major sector, requiring the introduction of unwanted and usually unavailable detail into the main accounts, is thus symptomatic of a more general problem of the SNA sectoring system, namely the lack of satisfactory summary information for major sectors of the economy. Specifically, an overall enterprise sector bringing together the activities of corporate and quasi-corporate nonfinancial enterprises, financial institutions, and the unincorporated businesses currently included in the household and general government sectors would be very useful. Were this done, it would be appropriate to include nonprofit institutions as an additional subsector of this enterprise sector. Many nonprofit organizations such as universities, hospitals and research organizations operate in ways that are very similar to public or private enterprises, and their income and expenditures are very different from those of households. Although it would be possible to include them with general government, to do so would reduce the usefulness of the general government accounts for analyzing the behavior of the government. The aggregate enterprise sector, furthermore, is not really composed of a homogeneous group of private profit-making entrepreneurs operating on the textbook competitive model, but rather embraces a wide spectrum of activities such as nonfinancial public enterprises, central banks and pension funds, which are often operated by administrators motivated by considerations other than profit maximization. Including nonprofit institutions as an additional subsector would not increase the heterogeneity involved. A sectoring system modified as suggested in the preceding sections and including a combined enterprise sector might look like the following:

1. Enterprise sector
   a. Nonfinancial
      Private enterprises
      Public enterprises
      Nonprofit institutions serving households
   b. Financial

　　　　The central bank
　　　　Other monetary institutions
　　　　Insurance and pension funds
　　　　Other financial institutions
2. General government
　　a. Central government
　　b. State and local government
3. Households

Conclusion. SNA does not provide for a general enterprise sector, but splits enterprises up among three major sectors. Furthermore, nonprofit institutions, serving households, are treated as a major sector, despite their relatively small size in most countries and the difficulty of obtaining adequate information about them. Consideration should be given to whether some modification in the sectoring would clarify their interrelationships and provide a more useful overview of the economic system.

Extensions of the accounts

Quarterly accounts Quarterly national accounts represent an important policy tool for monitoring the short-term functioning of the economy in many countries. Although monthly time series on such things as unemployment, prices and retail sales do exist, generally the shortest period for which comprehensive national accounting information is provided is the calendar quarter.

The Blue Book suggests that the four Class I accounts provide a summary national accounting system that can be made available on a quarterly basis (SNA, para. 1.76). However, the Class I accounts are too consolidated to be effective for most short-term monitoring and forecasting purposes. Thus, for example, the Class I accounts do not show complete sectoral interrelationships involving the government and household sectors; the composition of saving, in terms of retained profits of business, household saving and government surplus or deficit, is not provided; direct tax payments by businesses and households are not given, nor are government transfer payments to households. Yet quarterly data often exist for both government revenue and government expenditure, so that the basic elements of the government income and outlay account can be constructed. Similarly, many countries develop quarterly estimates of wage and salary payments and other household income from administrative data and/or household or employer surveys. Quarterly changes in consumer expenditures can often be based on retail sales surveys, so that complete quarterly household income and outlay accounts can be constructed. Foreign trade data and balance of payments information are also usually available quarterly. For short-term monitoring purposes, therefore, it is possible to construct quarterly national accounts that are analytically substantially more useful than the SNA Class I accounts.

On the other hand, it is also apparent that the detailed data called for in the SNA Class II and Class III accounts cannot usually be obtained on a quarterly basis. Thus, data for the detailed production accounts by industry, and the income and outlay and capital finance accounts for the institutional sectors other than households and general government, are not generally available on a quarterly basis. For these reasons, the Blue Book recognizes that countries may wish to develop intermediate consolidations for their own internal uses (SNA paras 1.76–1.82). But the Blue Book itself provides little guidance on the nature of such a quarterly system of national accounts.

In the design of quarterly accounts, two criteria need to be considered. First, what are the analytic needs of users, in terms of the kinds of information and the level of detail required? Second, what is the availability of data for making quarterly estimates and how does it affect the shape of the accounts? Country experience indicates that these criteria often conflict, with the result that the information in the quarterly accounts falls short of what analysts would really like to have. To some extent the statistical system may respond to this demand by establishing new surveys or by processing new kinds of administrative information in order to generate the desired data. Thus quarterly accounts that have been developed in different countries are the result of an evolutionary process that reflects the interaction of the need for short-term data and the development of the sources and methods used for estimating them.

Despite differences in country practices, quarterly national accounting systems do have a number of features in common. First, the accounting aggregates employed are comprehensive, in that they are intended to cover the whole economy and not merely some aspects of it. Second, the accounting framework is designed to provide a consistent and integrated set of information that shows how the different parts of the economy are related to one another and to the economy as a whole. Finally, the quarterly accounts cumulate to the annual national accounts, even though they contain less detail. It follows therefore that SNA quarterly accounts should be a subset of the SNA system.

Thus quarterly accounts lying between the Class I accounts and the Classes II and III accounts are needed to provide a basis for short-term analysis, as well as for a more satisfactory overview of the economic system. Although Part 1 of the revised UN/OECD National Accounts Questionnaire does provide a summary set of accounts for annual data, it was not designed to consider the kinds of information that might be available on a quarterly basis, or for meeting the needs of short-term analysis. These questions can only be resolved in terms of the experiences of the countries that have developed quarterly accounts.

Conclusion. SNA does not provide a set of summary accounts that are suitable as a basis for quarterly accounts. Country experience in the compilation and use of such accounts would be very helpful in developing appropriate guidelines, and it would be useful if a joint study on this topic could be undertaken.

Regional accounts The Blue Book suggested that any system of national accounts could be subdivided by region, and that although it would be helpful in due course to add a regional dimension to SNA, in view of the many other problems on which work was needed such an extension of the system did not have a high priority (SNA, para. 1.90). In Chapter 9, which deals with the adaptation of the full system to developing countries, the Class IV accounts in essence break the Class II and III accounts down by regions (or urban/rural), deconsolidating the transactions among regions. At the same time, it is pointed out (SNA, para. 1.78) that regional accounting was not discussed in the main text primarily because it was felt that more practical experience and discussion was desirable before an attempt to set standards was made.

In developing regional information, like quarterly information, both the need for information and the availability of data have to be considered. Some types of regional information are very much needed for the implementation of government economic and social policies. This is particularly true in countries where programs are developed either to assist in economic development of poorer regions, or to redistribute income among regions.

In terms of data availability, some sources of data can automatically provide regional information as a byproduct. Thus complete censuses or large bodies of administrative data such as tax returns and social security reports can provide regional breakdowns as a part of normal processing of the basic data. On the other hand, where national estimates are based on sample surveys it may be very costly to enlarge the sample enough to yield reliable regional breakdowns. Any system of regional data will, therefore, have to balance the cost of developing regional breakdowns against its usefulness. Some kinds of data that would be needed to construct complete regional accounts, furthermore, require more than a simple breakdown of national aggregates. This is true wherever interregional flows are involved. The most usual approach to regional data, therefore, starts with the more readily available information, not with complete accounts. Again, it will be most helpful if countries can share their experiences in the design and generation of regional information.

Conclusion. Although SNA recognizes the desirability of regional accounts, it offers no practical discussion of the problems. As in the case of quarterly accounts, it would be useful if the experience of countries could be brought to bear on this topic.

Social and demographic statistics The 1980 Expert Group on national accounts noted in its report that progress in development of the framework for social and demographic statistics (FSDS) had been slower than initially hoped, and that one of the most promising approaches now appeared to be starting from the national accounts. In this context, the national accounts are conceived of as a frame not only for macrodata but for microdata as well. The ultimate objective is an overall statistical system embracing economic, social and demographic data. In approaching such a system, the group suggested that working outward from the national accounts is appropriate, since the national accounts are in a much more advanced state of development. In order to serve this purpose, some adjustments and accommodations may be needed in the national accounts. Some of these are discussed above in connection with the measurement of consumption and income and with reference to the more consistent application of the transactor/transaction principles of SNA: many of the adjustments are needed not only for the integration of social and economic data but also to improve the usefulness of the accounts for purely economic analysis.

The integration of economic, social and demographic data which is envisaged will need to accommodate data on all levels of aggregation. Macro- and microdata should not be thought of as alternatives, but as complements. Each provides necessary support and supplementation of the other: together they are a much more powerful tool than either separately.

Microunit-level data provide support for the aggregate-level data in a number of ways. First, a microdata base is an efficient way to store the data required to obtain more detailed disaggregations of the macrodata. The distribution of income, for example, can more easily be obtained by aggregation of an appropriate microdata base that is aligned with the relevant aggregates than by more traditional methods of disaggregation.

Second, microdata provide a simple means of separating the changes observed in the macrodata into structural and behavioral components. A change in the aggregate level of income, for example, may arise either from widespread changes in the incomes of all or most households, or from a change in the distribution of households between high- and low-income groups. A special but important case of the latter is rural to urban migration. Where an observed increase in aggregate income comes about solely because of the increased income of urban in-migrants, with little change in the incomes of either those remaining in rural areas or those who were already in the cities, the policy response called for might be quite different from that which would be appropriate if the increase in income affected all groups in the society more or less equally.

Third, underlaying the macrodata with appropriate microdata provides a convenient way to link the data observed at the macrolevel to characteristics or attributes that are not easily aggregated, or for which the numeraires employed in the aggregate data (monetary units, people, etc.) may be inappropriate. One may wish, for example, to know the relation of household income to family composition, location, or socio-economic categories. These are easily handled as attributes of individual households.

Conversely, the macrolevel framework is equally necessary as a support for microlevel data. In the first place, it provides the framework within which the microdata fit, and makes it possible to obtain an overview of the whole picture, to place a particular microanalysis into appropriate perspective. It is helpful for policy-makers dealing with a particular client group, for instance, to know how important that group is in the population as a whole and in various segments of it. What proportion of the total number of households is below the poverty level? What proportion of the households below the poverty level have no gainfully employed member, and what proportion of the gainfully employed are in poverty? The approach to poverty will be quite different if poverty households are 80 percent or 20 percent of the total; if they are mainly unemployable, mainly economically active but unemployed, or mainly employed but at jobs that do not yield a living wage.

Secondly, macrodata can provide convenient summaries of important aspects of the microdata at intermediate levels of aggregation. The satellite accounts of the national economic accounts serve this function. Such an intermediate-level aggregation may be used, for instance, to examine in more detail than the aggregate systems commonly have room for such questions as the financing of the health care system. The subsectoring of the household sector introduced into the World Bank's social accounting matrices (SAMs) also falls into this class: subgroups of the population such as farm households, the aged, or households below the poverty level can be examined in this way.

Third, the macrodata provide constructs that may themselves be important elements in the microanalysis. The consumer price index, for example, or aggregate measures of the change in productivity or the change in the birth rate may have an impact upon the circumstances and behavior of individual microunits, either through such legally mandated links as escalation clauses in wage contracts or indexation of social security benefits, or through policy responses to macrostatistical triggers. In this connection, macrolevel social indicators are an important statistical output.

From the point of view of the development of an integrated information framework, it is necessary to specify and design both the macrosystems and the microsystems, in such a way that they form an integrated and articulated whole. Unfortunately, many of those concerned with the development of macrosystems have failed to consider the nature of the microdata systems that underlie them, and upon which they much conceptually rely. Conversely, those concerned both with household surveys and with the collection of data from firms and governmental units have often not considered the macrodata systems into which the microdata must fit. The importance of developing a fusion of macro- and microanalysis is increasingly being recognized; for this to be possible a prerequisite is integration of the data.

The required integration of macro- and microlevel data is in practice gradually coming about, less by design than by necessity. The greatest progress is being made where the data are needed for specific policy purposes, mostly concerned with measuring the benefits and costs of specific government programs. Statistical offices have not been the moving force in these developments, which have often been undertaken by policy users rather than producers of the statistics. The time has come when the further development of the structure should be considered explicitly by the producers of statistics, in order to insure that its growth is rational and directed, and not left to chance and the accidents of funding.

Conclusion. SNA has been very successful in developing a framework for macroeconomic data. The same general principles that underlie SNA can be applied to microdata, and the use of the same conceptual framework for macro- and microdata will not only promote their integration but can also bring with it integration of economic, social and demographic data. Microdata derived from administrative sources and from sample surveys are becoming increasingly important both as the basis for national accounts estimates and as independent bodies of data used for policy analysis. Those who are concerned with the design and development of the national accounts should give special attention to methods of bringing about their integration with microdata.

Harmonization

External transactions

As was reported to the Statistical Commission at its last session (UN, 1980d), the United Nations Statistical Office has for some time been engaged in an attempt to clarify the content of the external transactions components of the national accounts, develop the methodology required for their preparation, and improve their comparability with the balance of payments statistics collected by the IMF. The Bureau of Statistics of the IMF has cooperated actively in the latter endeavor. In pursuit of these objectives, a two-part report was prepared by a consultant to UNSO, Mr P.N. Atcherley of the Australian Bureau of Statistics (UN, 1980h). The first part of the report is a draft volume of the *Handbook of National Accounting* series, discussing sources and methods. The second part discusses problems that arise in harmonizing the national accounts and the balance of payments, identifying the sources of difference, and presenting a number of alternatives for achieving a closer treatment.

In the course of preparing the report, discussions were held with a number of national statistical offices and international organizations, and a questionnaire was circulated to an additional group of national offices. A number of experts also provided comments. The report was considered briefly by the Expert Group on national accounts that met in April 1980, and by the Statistical Commission at its last session. The Commission recommended that an Expert Group consider the questions raised. In preparation for such a discussion, the report has been circulated to national statistical offices and international organizations for comment, and the staffs of UNSO and the IMF have prepared analyses of the questions at issue.

The consultant's report received much commendation from those who offered comments. It was considered to be an excellent document and extremely useful and important in identifying the differences between SNA and the *Balance of Payments Manual* (BPM) and proposing changes and clarifications to SNA. In general, the comments voice support for the approach of the report, which states: 'Consistency with the conceptual framework was regarded as the prime objective but some weight also had to be given to analytic usefulness, data availability, and the desirability of consistency with the BPM and other international standards.' The comments stress, however, that harmonization of SNA and BPM is very important, and should be sought in all cases where differences are unnecessary. Compatibility in international guidelines would simplify compilation of statistics and minimize competing demands on source material.

The discussion that follows deals primarily with questions of harmonization between SNA and BPM, and summarizes the responses received. A detailed discussion of the responses is available in background document ESA/STAT/AC.15/4 (UN, 1982).

In the case of approximately a quarter of the sources of difference between SNA and BPM identified in the Atcherley report, there appears to be a fairly widespread agreement that adoption of the BPM treatment or a close modification of it would be desirable, either for theoretical or data availability reasons or because the differences are trivial. These items are listed in the top panel of Table 12.1. Most of them would have no effect upon the format of the Questionnaire tables, although some of the reconciliation items in Questionnaire Table 2.17 would become unnecessary. (It may be noted that these reconciliation items are almost never supplied in country questionnaire responses.) Quantitatively, the most important of these changes are likely to be those concerning the treatment of reinvested earnings of direct investment companies and the treatment of financial leasing. In both of these cases, adoption of the BPM criteria would require additional specification and explanation, beyond that contained in BPM. For financial leasing, as indicated above, the SNA treatment in general has raised problems. The data problems involved, however, may be somewhat less in the case of transactions between residents and nonresidents, and the advantages of adopting the BPM treatment are

Table 12.1 *Summary of Comments on Proposed Changes in SNA Treatment of External Transactions*

	Responses		
	Agreeing	Disagreeing	Other
A. Majority favors adoption of BPM or modified BPM criteria			
Timing: Change of ownership	6*+	4	1
Financial leasing: Impute ownership change	9	–	3
Goods on consignment: Ownership change	7*	3	–
Arbitrage profits: Realized capital gain	6+	2	1
Reinvested earnings: Gross	10*+	1	1
Gold: Monetary/nonmonetary	5	2	2
Definition of domestic territory	7	–	–
Illegal transactions: Include	8*+	–	1
B. Majority favors retaining SNA or modified SNA criteria			
Scope: Transactions only	8+	1	–
Transfers between affiliated enterprises	9+	–	–
Compensation of employees: Factor income	9	–	–
Airport taxes: Transfer	6	2+	–
Compulsory fees: Transfer	6	2+	–
Classification of financial assets: Retain	6	1+	3
Degree of netness: Retain	8	1	–
Revaluation of official reserves: Exclude	10+	1	–
Reimbursable travel expenses: Retain	8	–	–
Bunkers: Transport	3+	7	1
C. Majority favors new proposal			
Merchanting transactions: Record net	7+	1	1
Nonfinancial intangible assets: Combine	8+	1	1
Withholding taxes: Treat gross	6+	2	–
D. No consensus			
Current and capital transfers: Combine	5+	7	2
Imports f.o.b.	4	6	–
Immovable tangible assets: Like other assets	5	4	1
Long-term/short-term loans: Abandon	4	7	–
SDRs: Exclude	4	4	2
Insurance: Like BPM	4	4	–
Stock dividends: Exclude from transactions	2	3	3
Bad debts: Current transfer	4	4+	3
Goods for processing: Ownership change	7+	4*	–
Mobile equipment	5	2	2

Notes:
* Indicates position taken by 1980 Expert Group.
+ Indicates position taken by majority of expert commentators.

significant. This treatment is broadly similar to that proposed by OECD and EUROSTAT in their study of this question.

In approximately a further third of the cases, there is substantial agreement among respondents that the SNA treatment should be retained. These are for the most part cases that are considered to involve fundamental principles of SNA, though their quantitative importance is generally small and data problems may be considerable. The second panel of Table 12.1 lists this group. In two of these cases SNA excludes from the current account revaluations that BPM includes. In several other cases, BPM includes in transportation items that SNA would class as taxes, fees, or intermediate consumption. Two cases relate to the classification of assets and liabilities and to the consequent netness with which data are to be reported; here it is considered that consistency with the type-of-claim classification used throughout SNA should be paramount.

In three cases, shown in the third panel of Table 12.1, the Atcherley report proposes changes, which are favored by the majority of respondents, that do not arise primarily from differences between SNA and BPM. One relates to the treatment of nonfinancial intangible assets (patents, leases, etc.). This is a general question, not limited to external transactions, and it is discussed above on page 372. SNA requires the separation of transactions involving outright sales of these assets from those merely reflecting their use; revenues from the latter are to be treated as property income in the income and outlay account, but the former appear only in the capital finance account. In practice, the line between the two types of transaction is both conceptually and statistically difficult to draw, and countries, in general, do not attempt it. The proposal of the report, concurred in by all but two of the comments, is that the distinction be abandoned. The two countries favoring retention of the distinction on theoretical grounds agree that it is likely to be statistically impossible, and indeed, to date no country has provided this information in a questionnaire response, either for domestic or international transactions.

A second of these questions concerns withholding taxes on property income. This is not discussed explicitly in either BPM or SNA. Gross or net treatments are possible; the report favors gross treatment, and a majority of respondents concur on the grounds of consistency with the treatment of similar domestic transactions. Those opposing this treatment cite data problems. It is desirable that, whatever conclusion is arrived at in this case, the same treatment be adopted for the balance of payments.

A third question concerns merchanting transactions — i.e., purchases of goods in a second country for sale in a third country. Most respondents agreed with the report's proposal to record such transactions net (amounts receivable less those payable), as the provision of a merchanting service, though questions were raised as to whether this is, in fact, different from either SNA or BPM and as to exactly how it would be implemented. In any case, clarification of the guideline is needed.

On the remaining questions raised in the Atcherley report, no clear consensus has emerged. In some cases, the questions raised apply to domestic as well as foreign transactions, and they need consideration in that context. This is true, for instance, of the problems of distinguishing current and capital transfers, of distinguishing short- and long-term loans, and of the treatment of insurance. In some cases, the report's proposal to move to the BPM treatment for the sake of harmonization, even though this would clearly be in violation of general SNA principles, meets with some approval but more opposition: this is the case with the proposal to treat imports f.o.b. The remaining three questions deal with immovable tangible assets, stock dividends, and IMF Special Drawing Rights; on all of these further work is needed before any decision can be taken.

Public sector statistics
The need for harmonization of guidelines on public sector statistics issued by different international organizations has repeatedly been stressed by the Statistical Commission. Work has been under way for a number of years on the attempt to bring the UNSO *Handbook of National Accounting* volume on *Public Sector Statistics* (Vol. 4) into closer harmony with the IMF's *Government Finance Statistics* manual (1974), while still recognizing the differing needs served by the two. The Expert Group that met in April 1980 was unanimous in its desire for a single set of guidelines. It recognized that different users have different needs and that one set of guidelines need not mean a single set of data. But it considered that the differing needs should be set out much more concretely, and that there should be a presumption against differences unless a pressing need for them could be demonstrated.

During the interval that has elapsed since then, considerable progress has been made in the harmonization of these two sets of standards. Revised versions of both manuals have been prepared, and differences between them in matters of definition, classification, etc., have been significantly reduced. Where differences remain, they have been pointed out and the basis for them explained. There remain broad differences in approach reflecting the different uses intended — for instance, SNA includes imputed items and uses accrual accounting, whereas GFS relates only to cash transactions — but the *Handbook* volume views the cash accounts as a starting point and discusses how they can be adjusted to obtain the more comprehensive accounts required for SNA. The *Handbook* volume, furthermore, includes a discussion of public financial institutions, whereas GFS is limited to general government and nonfinancial public enterprises. The *Handbook* also covers constant price statistics, not covered in GFS. For the core items of the accounts that do appear in both GFS and SNA, however, the *Handbook* relies heavily upon the discussion of sources and methods that appears in GFS, and suggests that the two manuals should be regarded as complementary.

One area where a difference of classification does remain is in the treatment of capital transfers. As was noted above in the discussion of external transactions, SNA's treatment of capital transfers leads to problems of coordination with other types of statistics, since the convention that what is a capital transfer for one party to a transaction must be a capital transfer for both is difficult to apply to specialized bodies of data. In the public sector field, specifically, it causes problems in the classification of estate and inheritance taxes (which are capital transfers in SNA, and current revenues in GFS). This general topic is mentioned above on page 376.

A second difference in classification relates to the monetary authority, which GFS identifies but PSS does not. GFS removes certain monetary functions that may be performed by the Ministry of Finance or the Treasury from general government in the interest of functional homogeneity; PSS leaves these functions in general government in the interest of institutional fidelity.

There also remain various differences in terminology. GFS includes social security contributions in tax revenues, whereas they are separately specified in SNA. The definition of what a social security contribution is remains the same in the two systems, however. Similarly, much of what SNA calls capital transfers paid by government are called grants in GFS.

Finally, some problems remain in the interpretation and application of the concept of departmental enterprise. In GFS, the category is used broadly as a device to allow IMF to reclassify elements of national statistics to meet its own view of what belongs in government. The *Handbook*, however, is intended as a guide for countries' own use, and it therefore takes a more restricted view. This question is discussed in Section 3 above.

The *Handbook* volume on *Public Sector Statistics* is now (February 1982) in final review; it is expected that it will be issued before the next session of the Statistical Commission. Completion of the revision of GFS is anticipated in the spring of 1982, and its publication should follow shortly thereafter. The staffs of both organizations have been mindful of the frequently reiterated desire, particularly on the part of users concerned with the national accounts, for a single set of guidelines covering both financial and national accounting statistics. It is considered that the present versions of *Public Sector Statistics* and *Government Finance Statistics* represent major progress toward achieving that goal. Before attempting to produce a single volume, however, it seems desirable that some years of experience with the new versions of PSS and GFS should be allowed to accumulate, in order to indicate where there may be remaining difficulties, a need for further clarification, or an expansion of the discussion.

Monetary statistics and flow of funds
In the field of flow of funds and monetary statistics, less progress on coordination and harmonization has been made than had been hoped for in the report to the last session of the Statistical Commission. As noted above,

Volume 5 of the *Handbook of National Accounting* will cover capital finance, flow of funds, changes in assets and liabilities, balance sheets and related areas. A preliminary draft dealing with sources and methods for compiling SNA, Table 24, has been prepared; it is intended that its coverage will be broadened in the next draft.

The International Monetary Fund is also working on guidelines covering the monetary statistics which they publish in *International Financial Statistics*. A draft of those guidelines has been completed. It had been expected that co-ordination would be possible during the preparation of that draft, but in the event this did not happen. It is to be hoped that UNSO will be given access to the IMF draft manual before it is finalized. An effort will then be made to identify differences and eliminate them where possible.

Income distribution statistics
Distribution statistics were a part of the programme of further development laid out in the Blue Book in 1968. Following a series of working party and Expert Group meetings and consideration by the Statistical Commission, *Provisional Guidelines on the Statistics of Distribution of Income, Consumption, and Accumulation of Households* (Series M, No. 61) was published in 1977.

In a parallel development, work was undertaken on the development of the UN's Framework for Social and Demographic Statistics (FSDS), reflecting the changing emphasis of policy to include social as well as purely economic aspects of the distribution of the well-being of the population. A number of publications dealing with the conceptual aspects of these questions have been prepared (UN, 1975b, 1977e, 1978a, 1979d). The increasing policy importance of social programs leads to a demand for information not only on the size distribution of income, but on the interrelationships between government and households, on the position of specific demographic groups and on distributions by region and type of community. Policy-makers need to know both what the distribution of welfare and income is and how it is affected by specific government programs. Early approaches to this problem took the route of trying to specify in advance a limited list of time series that might be expected to meet most needs. This approach ran into difficulties, however, because it proved to be impossible to establish criteria for selection of series to be included. A framework constructed in this way runs the risk of early fossilization: it may be preserved as a relic, but it will not often be used since most analytic questions are likely to require data that are not included. It has become increasingly clear that what is needed is a framework that will accommodate whatever data exist, on any level of aggregation; in particular, it must be able to accommodate both aggregate systems like SNA and the increasingly available sets of microdata which are the basis of distributional analyses. Recent UNSO conceptual work has been aimed in this direction (UN, 1979a,c, 1980h).

Since about 1980, the Development Research Center of the World Bank has been engaged in an ambitious Living Standards Measurement Study (LSMS) (Grootaert, 1981). LSMS is set up as a four-year study in three phases, covering: conceptual work and analysis of existing data, new field work, both experimental and of a substantive nature and the writing of six topic studies regarding policy issues relevant for developing countries. The first year and a half of the project was devoted largely to conceptual issues, and three Expert Group meetings have been held. Issues considered have included the construction of equivalence scales, the links between employment and welfare measurement, the extraction of short-run fluctuations from income measures, and the use of housing characteristics as a dimension of socio-economic groupings. LSMS was established in part to guide the data collection process toward producing data that could attempt to answer questions of interest to policy makers. Such questions were considered to center about which groups in society are getting better or worse off in terms of the locally relevant welfare criterion, and in which dimensions they especially do so. Ultimately, the study is striving to come up with the simplest possible survey instrument, set of tabulations and analytical tools to help answer questions regarding the changing levels of living between groups as a result of development policy.

Unfortunately, however, there is an enormous gap between these efforts at conceptual development and what is actually undertaken in terms of data collection. The International Labor Office has been in the forefront of international data collection. A recent paper by Wouter van Ginneken (1981) surveys the latter. Data collection efforts from the early 1970s, when Felix Paukert collected distribution data for 56 countries using primary income as the income concept and the household or family as the income unit. In 1975, the World Bank published a compilation of data prepared by Shail Jain for 83 countries; that collection contains distributions with varying income concepts, income units and geographical coverage. An OECD-sponsored study by Malcolm Sawyer was published in 1976, containing comparable pre- and post-tax income distribution data on a per household and a per capita basis for about 12 OECD countries. P. Visaria, in a paper for the World Bank, reviewed Asian income distribution data, and Oscar Altimir produced comparable data for seven Latin American countries. An attempt was made in the late 1970s by the member countries of the CES to produce a set of comparable data for the ECE region, but in the end it proved unsuccessful. The UN Statistical Office in 1980 published a survey of income distribution statistics in 60 countries, without attempting to achieve comparability among them. ILO, in connection with the World Bank's LSMS project, is now engaged in generating new distributions for about 30 countries.

What emerges clearly from all of these studies are the practical difficulties of obtaining conceptually valid distribution statistics even for money income.

To date, very few attempts have been made to go beyond that; even the LSMS questionnaire, despite the effort put into conceptual development, will not really do so. Before much headway can be made, there are many practical questions that need to be resolved. Some of these are noted briefly here.

The first set of questions has to do with what it is that is being distributed. What is the universe covered? What is the reporting unit, and what is the unit (or units) of analysis? What is the concept of income or other welfare measure used?

The UN income distribution guidelines emphasize the importance of conceptual consistency with the national accounting and demographic aggregates, but even when this is the intent statistical consistency with the aggregates is seldom achieved. There are many reasons for this, and some are inherent in the available statistical tools. Sample surveys will consistently underestimate some categories of income: property and entrepreneurial income in virtually all countries, and transfer payments in most. Wages and salaries, on the other hand, are usually more completely reported. Property income affects mainly the upper income groups; transfers mainly the lowest. Thus differential underreporting of different types of income will distort the resulting distributions. Ways need to be found to repair these deficiencies.

Distribution data based on household surveys customarily employ the household as the reporting unit, though definitions of household vary. But distributions derived from administrative data may often use other units, such as taxpayers or wage earners.

Units of analysis also vary widely. It is increasingly recognized that analytic units need not be the same as the reporting unit, and distributions of households are giving way to per capita, per earner, per adult, and a variety of equivalence unit distributions. The implications of all of these need further study, and work is needed on the concepts and definitions required.

A major problem relates to the income concept. For practical reasons, it is usually limited to primary income or, at best, total money income. The current ILO project will attempt to approximate a broader concept, namely total available income as defined in the UN guidelines. It includes wages and salaries in cash and in kind (excluding social security and private insurance contributions), net income from self-employment (including consumption of own produce), income from personal property and investment (including imputed rent of owner-occupied housing), social security and private insurance transfers, minus personal income and property taxes. Such a broader concept will, in all likelihood, give different results from those obtained with the narrower concepts commonly employed. It still, however, does not encompass many of the other nonmonetary components of well-being identified in LSMS and FSDS. Nor does it encompass the elements of government consumption expenditure for the benefit of individuals discussed above in connection with total consumption of the population. A few researchers have constructed distributions of the latter sort for single countries (US, UK), but these are still in the experimental stage.

The problems discussed above in connection with the measurement of consumption also, of course, arise in measuring its distribution, often in even more untractable form. With respect to benefits in kind, it is often the case that from the point of view of the recipient cost is a poor measure of value; the recipient may not be aware of cost, and he may place quite a different value (or no value) on the benefit. In the case of entitlements, potential recipients may use them in varying degrees: some may use the sports ground often, others never. Future entitlements — social security benefits, job tenure — are even more difficult. Work on these questions is at a very early stage. Some studies have been made of the way recipients value some benefits in kind (food stamps, for example). Some work has also been done on evaluating future entitlements. As yet, however, no consensus has emerged.

Apart from these questions of definition and coverage, there are also statistical problems that need study. One is the impact of using grouped data in the construction of distributions; some studies have shown that this has an important impact, whereas others seem to indicate that it is not significant. A final question relates to summary measures: there is little consensus on appropriate ways of displaying distribution information.

Each of the agencies engaged in work on distribution is now working more or less independently. If consistent standards are to be developed, some means will have to be found to promote communication among them.

Activity classifications and input–output

In the area of activity classifications and input–output statistics, the chief questions of harmonization among international organizations arise between the United Nations and EUROSTAT. The UN's activity and commodity classifications, ISIC and ICGS, differ significantly from those developed by EUROSTAT for the use of the European Community, NACE and CLIO, both in detail and in basic organizing principles. This has long been a source of frustration to both compilers and users of the data.

At its nineteenth session the Statistical Commission approved a general long-term program of work on harmonization of economic classifications, leading to the eventual production of a combined trade/production commodity classification. One of the first steps in this direction was considered to be a revision of the International Standard Industrial Classification of All Goods and Services, ISIC. The Commission recommended the establishment of a consultative panel to provide advice and guidance over the time span covered by the work program. Accordingly, a Joint UN/EUROSTAT Working Group on World Level Classifications was formed (with generous financial support by EUROSTAT). It first met in November 1977, and has been meeting at approximately biennial intervals since then. In addition to UNSO and EUROSTAT, the group includes representatives of other international organizations (including OECD and CMEA), regional commissions (ECE and ESCAP), and about 10 countries. Considerable emphasis has been placed on continuity of participation by the same individuals.

At its first meeting the group concluded that in the design of the various activity and commodity classifications, the Harmonized System (HS) then under construction by the Customs Cooperation Council was central, in that it could provide the necessary building blocks. The Statistical Commission concurred in this view, and urged a strengthening of UNSO participation in the work on HS. Limitations of resources, however, prevented this work from receiving as much attention as would have been desirable.

One of the chief problems in reconciling ISIC and NACE concerns energy. The present version of ISIC is production-function oriented; thus it separates the various levels of extraction and processing of energy materials and the production of energy, whereas in NACE these are combined in an energy branch. The initial proposal made by UNSO for the revision of ISIC would have created a new major division for fuel and energy production, embracing all levels. This proposal was discussed at length by the Joint Working Group, but was ultimately rejected on the grounds that such a change would not be in accord with ISIC basic principles of classification, and that the concept suggested for energy, if extended to other broad categories, would change the nature of the classification.

Accordingly, early in its endeavors, the Working Group concluded that the most promising avenue toward harmonization of ISIC and NACE lay in the construction of an intermediate-level classification at about the ISIC 3-digit level, to which both ISIC and NACE (the General Industrial Classification of Economic Activities within the European Communities), and also the corresponding CMEA classification, SCEB (Classification of the Branches of National Economy of the CMEA Member Countries), could be reconciled.

At its second meeting, the Working Group focused on those parts of the classifications in which the activity results chiefly in the production of transportable goods. Those parts of the classifications covering construction, trade, finance, government and other services were left for consideration at later sessions. The objective was to produce an identical, or virtually identical, intermediate-level classification made up of standard categories of activities so that data collected according to one of the three classifications involved (ISIC, NACE and SCEB) would be equivalent to data obtained through use of the other two classifications, at the intermediate level. The intermediate-level categories would not necessarily be arranged in each of the classifications so that simple aggregation would produce the same higher-level groups. Convenient as this might be from an international point of view, discussion at the first session of the Working Group had shown that such an outcome would be difficult to achieve.

The proposed intermediate-level classification contains 57 categories. The 3-digit level of ISIC contains 40 major groups in the part covering industries producing transportable goods and energy. It is anticipated that, when the revision of ISIC is completed, it will not contain many more categories at either the 3-digit or the 4-digit level than the 1968 ISIC.

The Working Group has now passed on to consideration of nontransportable goods and services. Similar intermediate-level categories have been established in this area.

The Group has also considered problems of harmonizing classifications of activities and products, on the basis of studies of individual industries undertaken by EUROSTAT. An immediate result of this work has been the formulation of proposals for somewhat modifying HS so as to take more careful account of the industrial origin criterion in its dissections. Another result should be a better understanding of the relationship between ISIC and the Standard International Trade Classification (SITC) (UN, 1975a), leading to closer coordination between the two classifications after 1985, by which time it is expected that the major revisions of the Customs Cooperation Council Nomenclature brought about by the coming into force of HS will have been completed. The closer relationship between a revised ISIC and a post-1985 SITC should, in the first instance, draw together the activities of the intermediate-level categories discussed above and the 2-digit and 3-digit levels of SITC. Construction of the combined trade/production commodity classification remains the ultimate objective of the UNSO program. Reduced resources, however, have forced a stretching out of the timetable.

It is also chiefly with EUROSTAT that problems of coordination of standards relating to input–output statistics arise. At base, these problems derive from differences in procedures for defining establishments and classifying them by activities in SNA and ESA. SNA has a broader definition of establishment, which recognizes that establishments may produce products that are not typical of their main kind of activity, but which cannot, for statistical and accounting reasons, be separated into separate establishments. ESA, on the other hand, insists that an establishment be limited to homogeneous output, allowing only for byproducts as untypical output. Consequently, ESA has no need for the make-and-use matrices employed by SNA (Blue Book supporting Tables 2 and 3). SNA recognizes that for analytic use it will often be necessary to convert the make-and-use matrices into a single square matrix, but it considers that the two matrices are more convenient and realistic for data collection purposes.

4. PROPOSALS FOR SHORT-TERM ACTION

In reviewing the major issues relating to the updating and harmonization of SNA in Section 3, it was concluded that in most instances further study and discussion of alternative solutions was needed. Even in those cases where it might appear that a relatively simple and straightforward solution could be adopted, questions of principle arise that may have important repercussions on other parts of SNA. Furthermore, as was noted in Section 2 of this report, the usefulness of any proposed changes and the feasibility of their implementation needs to be examined by a continuing working group, composed of experts from both international organizations and individual countries, who can accept a long-term responsibility for the further development of SNA. It is only with the support and agreement of such a group that any major revisions in SNA can be contemplated.

In light of these considerations, only very specific and limited proposals can be made for implementation in the short term. Those discussed in this section are of two types: proposals on external transactions made in the Atcherley report for which it has been found that there is wide support, and limited proposals concerning other minor questions of definition and classification that have been discussed by the 1980 Expert Group and other meetings and have received general approval.

Proposals Relating to the External Sector

As was noted above, there appears to be a reasonable degree of consensus among both the experts consulted and the country commentators on a certain number of the proposals relating to the treatment of external sector transactions made in the Atcherley report. Eight of these involve retention of the present SNA treatment, and thus involve no change (at least in SNA). In a further eight cases, however, a change to the BPM treatment or a modification of it is proposed, and in four cases other changes are proposed. These proposals are presented individually below. For a detailed discussion of the considerations involved, the reader is referred to Part B of the Atcherley report, and to the analysis of country responses (ESA/STAT/AC.15/4).

Timing of recording of exports and imports
It is proposed that change of ownership be adopted as the time of recording of exports and imports, recognizing that complete adjustment to this basis may not be statistically feasible. In addition, while not part of the BPM recommendation, it would be useful to specify, in a supplementary table, the reconciliation between the value of merchandise exports and imports as recorded in

international trade statistics and as recorded in the national accounts. (Modified BPM)

Financial leasing
It is proposed that change of ownership be imputed to goods shipped on financial lease. An offsetting financial claim would need to be imputed to record the credit extended to the lessee, together with imputations for repayment of, and property income on, the loan. However, the BPM definition of financial leasing should be replaced by the OECD/ EUROSTAT definition. (Modified BPM)

Goods shipped on consignment without change of ownership
It is proposed that goods shipped on consignment without change of ownership should not be included in exports and imports until change of ownership occurs. (BPM)

Profits or losses on arbitrage transactions
It is proposed that any profit or loss on arbitrage transactions in foreign exchange with nonresidents should be treated as the realization of a capital gain or loss resulting from two changes of ownership, and hence that it should be included in the capital account item that refers to the asset concerned. (BPM)

Reinvested earnings of direct investment enterprises
It is proposed that reinvested earnings of 'direct investment enterprises' (i.e., their net saving) should be included in property and entrepreneurial income in the External Transactions Account, and an equivalent amount should be shown as net incurrence of foreign assets/liabilities (classified according to the appropriate types of financial claims). This approach thus involves an imputed income outflow and an imputed capital inflow (vice versa for foreign direct investment enterprises of resident direct investors). Definitions would be required for 'direct investment enterprises', 'direct investors' and 'direct investment capital'. These could be as specified in BPM, with the addition of a more specific rule on the proportions of equity ownership that constitute a direct investment relationship; 25 percent might be specified as a minimum. (Modified BPM)

Gold
It is proposed that gold be divided into monetary gold (owned or under the control of the monetary authorities as a financial asset) and nonmonetary gold (all other), as in BPM. Unlike BPM, however, it is proposed that gold monetization/demonetization and valuation changes be recorded in the reconciliation account. (Modified BPM)

Definition of domestic territory

It is proposed that the domestic territory of a country be defined so as to allow the option of either including or excluding overseas territories and possessions, with a preference expressed for exclusion unless such territories and possessions are economically integrated and the compilation of separate accounts is impractical. In addition, it is proposed that references to mobile equipment be removed from the definition of domestic territory. (Modified BPM)

Illegal transactions

It is proposed that illegal activities in which the receipts are obtained with the unenforced consent of the payer should be included within the production boundary. In particular, smuggling should be included in imports and exports. (BPM)

Scope of the external transactions account

It is proposed that the scope of the external transactions account should be confined to transactions; reclassification of gold from a commodity to a financial asset should be shown in the reconciliation account. This differs from SNA only in the treatment of gold reclassification. (Modified SNA)

Transfers of goods between affiliated enterprises

It is proposed that transfers of goods between related legal entities, except branches, be treated the same as transfers between unrelated entities (as in SNA). It is proposed that transfers between branches and parents be treated as changes of ownership (as in SNA) except in certain specified cases such as operational lease arrangements. The precise exceptions would need to be specified; the list given in BPM could be used as a starting point. (Modified SNA)

Withholding taxes on property income

Withholding taxes on property income should be recorded in terms of the gross flows. (Not covered)

Merchanting transactions

It is proposed that merchanting transactions be recorded on a net basis (i.e., amounts receivable less those payable) as the provision of a merchanting service. No entries would be required in merchandise exports or imports. (Differs from both BPM and SNA)

Other Proposals

The proposals enumerated in this section are all ones that have been discussed in earlier meetings, including the 1980 Expert Group and various regional meetings. They met with general approval in those discussions. Most are matters of definition of flows; a few relate to classification.

Military expenditures

SNA treats all expenditure by governments on goods for military purposes as current, i.e., as general government intermediate consumption, with the exception of the construction and improvement of family-type dwellings. It is generally considered that the exception of family dwellings only is too restrictive, and it is proposed that other goods that may frequently be used for civilian as well as military purposes such as schools, hospitals, airfields and motor vehicles should also be included in capital formation. This would avoid erratic fluctuations when such goods are formally transferred to civilian use. It would also conform to what seems to be the most frequent country practice.

A second question relates to the definition of 'military'. When the government itself produces the goods in question, it is proposed that only the final output be considered military, not the purchase of capital equipment to be used in military production.

These two proposals taken together would substantially limit the extent of military expenditure of a capital nature classed as current intermediate consumption. It would largely consist of items with no civilian use, mainly armaments and military installations of a nonconvertible type.

Uncompleted construction

In both SNA and MPS work put in place on heavy machinery and equipment, ships and aircraft is included in change in stocks. For construction, however, the treatment differs. In MPS uncompleted construction is also included in the change in stocks, but in SNA such partially completed construction is included in gross capital formation. The European System of Accounts adopts still a third treatment, in which progress on construction is recorded as change in stocks until a buyer is found. In the *Guidelines on Statistics of Tangible Assets*, which are intended for use in connection with both SNA and MPS, it is recommended that uncompleted construction should be shown as a separate category, and not included in either gross capital formation or change in stocks. It is not proposed to go that far in the SNA accounts, but it is proposed that expenditures on construction should be divided into completed and uncompleted construction.

Own account capital formation

While there is general agreement that own account capital formation should be valued, for purposes of measuring output, at its cost of production, questions have arisen on what is to be included in such costs. It is proposed that the cost of production of own account capital formation be defined to include direct costs actually incurred plus a pro rata share of overhead or indirect costs, but without any allowance for a profit margin.

The definition of dwellings
SNA now lacks an explicit definition of 'dwelling', and in view of the considerable importance of dwelling construction in total fixed capital formation, such a definition is needed. The definition should be consistent with that recommended for housing censuses. It should include summer houses, chalets and similar premises purchased for use during holidays and weekends. It should also include outlays on mobile homes which are used as the sole or principal residence of a household. However, trailers or caravans purchased by the household sector for recreational purposes should be treated as consumer durable goods. The precise line between these last two types of unit should be determined by countries in accordance with national circumstances.

Livestock
SNA requires that livestock be separated into two categories. Animals raised for breeding stock, wool, milk, etc., should be considered to be capital assets. Those raised for slaughter, however, should be counted as inventories. To determine whether an increase in the size of a herd should be treated as fixed capital formation or as a change in stocks, it is first necessary to determine what the animals are to be used for. In some countries there is a clear distinction between the two types of livestock: dairy cattle would never be confused with beef cattle. But in most developing countries the distinction is much less clearcut. Most animals, whatever their initial use, are eventually slaughtered for food. Furthermore, many countries find it statistically impossible to make the split, even when it is considered that there is a conceptual difference. It is therefore proposed as an alternative criterion to apply to livestock the same rule that is applied to other assets. Livestock that will be harvested in less than a year should be classed as inventory; that with a longer life should be classed as a capital good. Countries with well-defined stock-raising or poultry industries, where the animals are raised only for slaughter, might continue to use the original criterion.

Value added tax
At the time SNA was last revised, the value added tax was not in widespread use and it is not specifically discussed in the Blue Book. With the adoption of the value added tax by the member countries of the European Community, however, an explicit treatment has become essential. ESA has employed two methods of handling VAT. At first, before all of its member countries had implemented the VAT, gross registration was recommended: both the gross tax levied and the deductible amounts were shown explicitly for each

kind of activity. As implementation of the tax was completed, ESA shifted to net registration, which shows only the amount of tax actually paid — the gross amount levied less the deductible. Compatibility with ESA would seem to be an overriding criterion here, and it is proposed to adopt the ESA treatment.

Profits and losses of public enterprises

SNA proposes a number of different treatments of profits and losses of public enterprises, depending on the circumstances. For incorporated public enterprises, all payments to cover losses are considered to be subsidies, whereas profits are divided into normal and above-normal components. The above-normal component is considered to be an indirect tax. For quasi-corporate public enterprises, however, losses are considered to be subsidies if intended to compensate for a deliberate policy of maintaining price below cost, but otherwise, they are negative entrepreneurial withdrawals. Above-normal profits of quasi-corporate monopolies are again considered to be indirect taxes. For unincorporated government enterprises not considered quasi-corporations, losses are always treated as negative operating surplus, but above-normal profits are indirect taxes. These rules are generally ignored by countries. No country is known to make a distinction between normal and above-normal profits. Profits of fiscal monopolies are in some countries treated as indirect taxes. Losses, however, are seldom classified into those related to price policy and others. The procedure that might best preserve the freedom of the user to adapt the data to his own needs would be to show profits and losses of public enterprises that are transferred to general government as a separate item in the general government income and outlay account, and it is proposed that this be done.

REFERENCES

Adler, Hans (1981), 'Selected problems of welfare and production in the national accounts', Paper prepared for the 17th General Conference of the International Association for Research in Income and Wealth, August.

Aukrust, Odd and Svein Nordbotten (1973), 'Files of individual data and their potentials for social research', *Review of Income and Wealth*, **19** (2).

Blades, Derek W. (1980), 'Survey of country practices in compiling balance-sheet statistics', *Review of Income and Wealth*, **26** (3).

Choudhury, Uma Roy (1981), 'The UN system of national accounts: Indian experience', Paper prepared for the 17th General Conference of the International Association for Research in Income and Wealth, August.

Council for Mutual Economic Assistance, Standing Commission on Statistics (1972), *Basic Methodological Regulations*.

Ferran, Bernardo (1981), 'Notes on national accounts and developing countries', Paper prepared for the 17th General Conference of the International Association for Research in Income and Wealth, August.

Foulon, A. (1982), 'Proposals for a homogeneous treatment of health expenditures in the national accounts', *Review of Income and Wealth*, **28** (1).

Grootaert, Christiaan (1981), 'The conceptual basis of measures of household welfare and their implied survey data requirements', Paper prepared for the 17th General Conference of the International Association for Research in Income and Wealth, August.

Gutmann, Pierre (1981), 'The measurement of terms of trade effects', *Review of Income and Wealth*, **27** (4).

Hibbert, Jack (1982), 'Report on the effects of inflation on the measurement of income and saving', prepared for EUROSTAT and OECD (Preliminary draft).

Hill, T. P. (1975), *Price and Volume Measures for Non-Market Services*, Statistical Office of the European Communities, Doc OS/5/75, April.

_____ (1979), 'Do-it-yourself and GDP', *Review of Income and Wealth*, **25** (1).

International Monetary Fund (1974), *A Manual on Government Finance Statistics: Draft.*

_____ (1977), *Balance of Payments Manual*, 4th edition.

Kravis, Irving B., Zoltan Kenessey, Alan Heston and Robert Summers (1975), *A System of International Comparisons of Gross Product and Purchasing Power*, Johns Hopkins University Press.

Organisation for European Economic Cooperation (1958), *A Standardized System of National Accounts, 1958. Revision and extension of A Simplified System of National Accounts.*

Pathirane, Leila, and Derek W. Blades (1981), 'Defining and measuring the public sector: Some international comparisons', Paper prepared for the 17th General Conference of the International Association for Research in Income and Wealth, August.

Petre, Jean (1981), 'The treatment in the national accounts of goods and services for individual consumption produced, distributed or paid for by government', Paper prepared for 17th General Conference of the International Association for Research in Income and Wealth, August.

_____ (1982), 'Le concept de la consommation totale de la population et ses incidences sur les valeurs, les volumes et les prix', Paper prepared for meeting on the International Comparison Project, Luxembourg, 11–15 January.

Saunders, Christopher (1980), 'Measures of total household consumption', *Review of Income and Wealth*, **26** (4).

Statistical Office of the European Communities (1981a), *European System of Integrated Economic Accounts (ESA)*, EUROSTAT/CA-28-79-415-EN-C.

_____ (1981b), 'Treatment of financial leasing in national accounts, 21 May 1981', EUROSTAT/Al/CN/8-e.

_____ (1981c), 'Minutes of the meeting of the working party on national accounts, 20 and 21 May 1981', EUROSTAT/Al/CN/12-e.

_____ (1981d), 'Proposals for incorporating a dual breakdown of final consumption (By sector affecting the expenditure and by type of consumption) into the ESA and the SNA, 13–14 October 1981', EUROSTAT/A1/C1/13.

United Nations (1947), *Measurement of National Income and the Construction of Social Accounts*, Report of the Subcommittee on National Accounts of the League of Nations Committee of Statistical Experts, Studies and Reports on Statistical Methods No. 7.

_____ (1952), *A System of National Accounts and Supporting Tables*, Series F, No. 2.

_____ (1968a), *A System of National Accounts*, Series F, No. 2, Rev. 3.

_____ (1968b), *International Standard Industrial Classification of All Economic Activities (ISIC)*, Rev. 3.

_____ (1971), *Basic Principles of the System of Balances of the National Economy*, Series F, No. 17.

_____ (1973), *Input–Output Tables and Analysis*, Series F, No. 14, Rev. 1.

_____ (1975a), *Standard International Trade Classification*, Rev. 2.

_____ (1975b), *Towards a System of Social and Demographic Statistics*, Series F, No. 18.

_____ (1975c), 'Draft international standard classification of all goods and services (ICGS)', E/CN.3/493

_____ (1977a), *Report of the Interregional Seminar on the Revised System of National Accounts*, DP/UN/INT-72-104

_____ (1977b), *Comparisons of the System of National Accounts and the System of Balances of the National Economy. Part One: Conceptual Relationships*, Series F, No. 20.

_____ (1977b), *Guidelines on Principles of a System of Price and Quantity Statistics*, Series M, No. 59.

_____ (1977c), *Provisional International Guidelines on the National and Sectoral Balance-Sheet and Reconciliation Accounts of the System of National Accounts*, Series M, No. 60.

_____ (1977d), *Provisional Guidelines on Statistics of the Distribution of Income, Consumption and Accumulation of Households*, Series M, No. 61.

_____ (1977e), *The Feasibility of Welfare-Oriented Measures to Supplement the National Accounts and Balances: Technical Report*, Series F, No. 22.

_____ (1978a), *Social Indicators: Preliminary Guidelines and Illustrative Series*, Series M, No. 63.

_____ (1978b), 'Review of countries' experiences in implementing the revised system of national accounts', E/CN.3/507.

_____ (1978c), 'Total consumption of the population: technical report', E/CN.3/512.

_____ (1978d). *Progress Report on Harmonization of Economic Classifications*, E/CN.3/514.

_____ (1979a), *Studies in the Integration of Social Statistics: Technical Report*, Series F, No. 24.

_____ (1979b), *Manual on National Accounts at Constant Prices*, Series M, No. 64.

_____ (1979c), *Manual on Producer Price Indices for Industrial Goods*, Series M, No. 66.

_____ (1979d), *Improving Social Statistics in Developing Countries: Conceptual Framework and Methods*, Series F, No. 25.

_____ (1979e), *The Development of Integrated Data Bases for Social, Economic and Demographic Statistics*, Series F, No. 27.

_____ (1979f), *National Accounting Practices in Seventy Countries*, 3 vols, Series F, No. 26.
_____ (1979g), *Guidelines on Statistics of Tangible Assets*, Series M, No. 68.
_____ (1979h), Conference of European Statisticians, Working Party on National Accounts and Balances, Report of the Ninth Session Held in Geneva 13–17 February, CES/WP.22/55.
_____ (1980a), Report of the Tenth Session Held in Geneva 25–28 February, CES/WP.22/63.
_____ (1980b), Report of the Expert Group on Future Directions for Work on the United Nations System of National Accounts, 27 May, E/CN.3/AC.9/5.
_____ (1980c), Future Directions for Work on the System of National Accounts (SNA), E/CN.3/541.
_____ (1980d), Relationship of the Revised System of National Accounts to the International Monetary Fund's Balance of Payments Manual, E/CN.3/542.
_____ (1980e), Progress Report on the Harmonization of Economic Classifications, E/CN.3/545.
_____ (1980f), The Role of Macro and Micro Data Structures in the Integration of Demographic, Social and Economic Statistics, E/CN.3/552.
_____ (1980g), *Classification of the Functions of Government (COFOG)*, Series M, No. 70.
_____ (1980h), Draft Report on the Review of the External Transactions in the United Nations System of National Accounts, ST/ESA/STAT.103.
_____ (1981), Economic and Social Council. Official Records. Supplement No. 2. E/CN.3/564.
_____ (1982), A Review of Proposed Changes to SNA in Respect of External Transactions (Country Replies and UN Position), ESA/STAT/AC.15/4.
United Nations and Organisation for Economic Cooperation and Development (1980), *Instructions and Definitions for the National Accounts Questionnaire*.
van Ginneken, Wouter (1981), 'Generating internationally comparable income distribution data: evidence from the Federal Republic of Germany (1974), Mexico (1968) and the United Kingdom (1979)', Paper prepared for the 17th General Conference of the International Association for Research in Income and Wealth, August. Contains a review of international work on income distribution.
Van Tongeren, Jan W. (1979), 'A review of selected aspects of the United Nations system of national accounts in the light of countries' experiences', *Review of Income and Wealth*, **25** (2).
Vanoli, André (1978), 'Les notions de consommation élargie', *Economie et Statistique*, No. 100.

13. Financial Accounts and Balance Sheets: Issues for the Revision of the SNA

Nancy D. Ruggles
Yale University

This paper is an abridged version of a report with the same title originally written for the United Nations Statistical Office, as a part of the ongoing review of the System of National Accounts. Its purpose is to identify the issues in the financial statistics area that need to be considered in the course of the review. Particular attention is paid to problems of harmonization of SNA with related standards of the International Monetary Fund. The 1968 SNA provided a place in the framework for financial accounts and balance sheets, but did not develop them in any detail. In the 19 years since the revised SNA was published, policy and analytic interest in financial questions has greatly increased, and much work has been done on conceptual development and statistical compilation of financial statistics, both within and outside of the SNA framework. It is now apparent that some of the early decisions taken when financial considerations were not the focus of attention need reconsideration, some of the makeshift solutions that have grown up over time are no longer adequate, and some issues that have not been dealt with at all need to be addressed. This paper is not intended to propose solutions, but rather to reflect questions that have been raised, and to present alternatives that have been proposed.

1. FINANCIAL ACCOUNTS IN THE SNA FRAMEWORK

One of the new features of the 1968 SNA (UN, 1968; specific definitions and classifications and standard accounts were later provided in UN, 1977a, 1979) (hereafter referred to as the Blue Book) was the introduction of much expanded financial information. This expanded financial information is fully integrated

---

This chapter first appeared in *Review of Income and Wealth*, 33 (1), 1987.

into the accounting framework, as a further elaboration of the saving and net lending figures derived in the current accounts. The framework now provides a complete accounting of the process by which the economy moves from its position at the beginning of the period (the opening balance sheet) to its position at the close of the period (the closing balance sheet). This paper is concerned with the capital finance account, the reconciliation account, and the balance sheet. These parts of SNA have been much less thoroughly developed than the accounts dealing with production and income flows, and a number of problems need consideration in the review of SNA. This discussion draws upon UNSO's Draft Manual on Financial Statistics (prepared with the assistance of Jacques Mayer), as well as the International Monetary Fund's *International Financial Statistics* (IFS), *Balance of Payments Manual* (BPM), and *Government Finance Statistics Manual* (GFS).

The changes in balance sheet figures from one date to the next necessarily reflect the transactions shown in the flow accounts covering that period. Reproducible tangible capital assets enter the stock of capital through gross capital formation, and leave it through consumption of fixed capital or scrapping, as shown in the capital accumulation account. Non-reproducible tangible assets and intangibles enter the balance sheet when they are the subject of a transaction appearing in the capital accumulation account. Financial assets and liabilities are created and extinguished through actions that appear in the capital finance account.

There are, however, other factors besides those appearing in the flow accounts that lead to changes in balance sheets from one period to the next. The chief of these is revaluation: changes in market prices. In addition, other types of capital gain and loss may occur, and certain other adjustments may be required. All of these gains and losses are accounted for, in SNA, in the reconciliation account. Taken together, the transaction accounts and the reconciliation account provide a complete explanation of the change from one period to the next in the balance sheets of individual transactors, subsectors, sectors, and the nation as a whole.

At the time the Balance Sheet Guidelines were prepared, there was little country experience in the compilation of balance sheets upon which to base them, although there had been experimentation by researchers both in the construction of capital stock figures and in the compilation of partial balance sheets. Country experience has now broadened considerably. Among the statistically more developed countries, capital stock figures are becoming widely available. Balance sheets are still limited, but several countries have had experience in compiling them. It is therefore now possible to approach this topic with somewhat more confidence, both in the utility of the figures and in the feasibility of compiling them. It is also possible to identify certain problem areas, to which attention needs to be given.

Although some of these problem areas are limited to the financial accounts, many of them are the same ones that have already been identified in other contexts. None of the issues raised in this paper is new, and some have been debated from the early years of work on national accounts. But the changing nature of economic problems and policy concerns and the increasing focus on financial questions call into question some of the conventions that have been adopted, and suggest that some reconsideration is now warranted. As the growth of financial analyses outside the national accounting system demonstrates, if the accounting system fails to accommodate the kinds of analyses now of interest to policy-makers and researchers it will simply be by-passed, and the quality of both the traditional uses of the accounts and the newer ones will suffer.

Consistency of the Stock and Flow Accounts

The Balance Sheet Guidelines emphasize that the coverage of the balance sheet accounts must be congruent with that of the transaction accounts. Reproducible tangible assets must have been created by gross capital formation, and stocks of financial assets and liabilities through actions appearing in the capital finance account. Non-reproducible tangible assets, in SNA, in principle, enter the balance sheet only when they have been the object of a market transaction shown in the capital accumulation account, i.e., when they are bought and sold. Some questions have arisen, however, in the application of these principles.

Statistical feasibility

There is, first, a general question of statistical feasibility. It has been suggested that it may sometimes be possible to include items in the balance sheet that cannot be compiled on a flow basis, or vice versa. Statistical feasibility varies, of course, with each country's individual circumstances. In view of the usual methods of compilation, however, it is not readily apparent why coverage of the stock and flow accounts need differ. For reproducible assets, stock figures are most often compiled by perpetual inventory methods, cumulating flows over a period of years. If flows are available, stocks can be compiled. For other assets, the reverse is generally the case: the primary data are for stocks, and flows are obtained as differences. But again, if one is available, the other can be obtained. In conceptual terms, the Guidelines position seems quite justified. Statistical difficulties are inevitable, but they should not be used as a reason for distorting the conceptual framework of the system. Nevertheless, the question needs explicit consideration.

Land and other non-reproducible tangible goods

Land, timber tracts, subsoil deposits and fisheries enter the transaction accounts of SNA when they are bought and sold or improved. While all non-reproducible tangible assets are part of the endowment of a country and yield benefits over an extended period of time, only the streams of benefits from those resources that are used in the commercial production of goods and services are generally priced in the marketplace and included in production. It is usually feasible to value these commercially used assets, and to include them in the balance sheets of their owners. A more debatable question arises in the case of assets of a similar type that have not been sold, but which have owners. It is, for instance, quite unrealistic to omit the value of subsoil assets from the wealth of petroleum-producing countries, just because the assets belong to the government and have never been sold and are not likely to be. Similarly, some countries still have large amounts of unoccupied farm, range, and timber land. Inclusion of such assets does not contravene the principle of congruence of the flow and stock accounts. All accounting systems must begin at a fixed point in time, with an opening balance sheet which would include the value of land at that time. Improvements to it, and increases in its value through discovery of mineral resources, etc., or through price changes, would then enter the accounts in the normal way.

In the absence of a sale, valuation of these assets often presents very difficult problems of both a conceptual and a statistical nature. The problems arise in some cases because long time periods are involved and contracts made in earlier periods may not reflect current conditions. This is true, for instance, of land subject to long leases, or mines whose output is subject to a long-term sales agreement. In other cases, current value depends upon unknown future events — conditions of supply and demand, prices and interest rates — and there is no existing market in the asset itself to provide a guide.

The valuation of subsoil assets is particularly difficult, since large and sudden alterations frequently occur in all of the factors entering into the calculation. Estimates of economically usable physical reserves are highly dependent upon the price of the ultimate product, and that price often swings widely. They are also dependent upon technology, which changes constantly. And finally, new discoveries may be very important. Once the physical quantity of the reserve has been determined, furthermore, valuing it involves predicting prices and rates of return at future exploitation dates and choosing appropriate rates of discount to arrive at present values.

No satisfactory solution to these problems has yet been developed. Attention needs to be devoted to developing an appropriate methodology for the next version of SNA.

Household durable goods

The durable goods of households such as automobiles, refrigerators, washing machines and furniture are excluded from gross fixed capital formation in

SNA. This treatment is somewhat anomalous since the same items are considered to be fixed assets when they are in the possession of producers (such as the providers of rental housing) and they do yield a stream of benefits to households over a number of years. Furthermore, possession of durable goods is an important element in the level of living of households and in their patterns of consumption and financial behavior. However, the benefits households derive from these goods are not, in the present SNA, included in the production or consumption of goods and services, so that the inclusion of such assets in household balance sheets would create serious problems of reconciliation with the transaction accounts. It is on this basis that they are now omitted from the balance sheet, but SNA recommends that a supplementary table be prepared on household holdings of consumer durable goods.

Taken by itself, this treatment of consumer durables may seem reasonable. However, household durable goods are closely related to owner-occupied housing, and as household durable goods (especially automobiles) become more important, it is increasingly difficult to justify treating the two categories as differently as SNA now does. Various suggestions for bringing their treatment into closer harmony have been made. One possibility would be to treat durable goods as housing is now treated, establishing a nominal unincorporated enterprise to own them and furnish their services. This would involve estimating the value of the services of durables, and adding this value to both production and household consumption, while deducting actual expenditures on durables. An alternative possibility would be to treat both consumer durables and owner-occupied housing as assets on the balance sheet of households, and current costs relating to their use (for example, maintenance, interest charges and taxes) as part of household current outlays. As an adjustment in this latter approach, an estimate of both home owners' imputed rental income and the imputed services of durables might be shown as a supplement.

The Structure of the Balance Sheet

To a certain extent, the structure of SNA's balance sheet was determined by earlier decisions taken with respect to other parts of the system. The 1968 SNA dealt mainly with the current transactions accounts, and it did not give much consideration to the impact of decisions taken there upon the balance sheet. The Balance Sheet Guidelines endeavored to maintain compatibility with the current accounts as laid out in 1968, although this did not always prove to be entirely feasible.

Separation of fixed claims and equities
The major division of the balance sheet in the Blue Book is between nonfinancial and financial entries. Nonfinancial entries are those whose changes

appear in the capital accumulation account, and financial entries are those whose changes appear in the capital finance account. That boundary, in turn, is determined by SNA's choice of the concept of net lending as the balancing item in both accounts, and the specific definition given to it. For both of these there are alternatives, which are adopted by some countries. The alternative balancing item is gross saving; the definitional questions relate mainly to intangibles. A different treatment of these questions would lead to a differently structured balance sheet, which might be closer to conventional business and financial accounting practices.

The Balance Sheet Guidelines modify the arrangement adopted in the capital finance account of the Blue Book in one important respect, namely the separation of fixed claims from equity items. The main break, on the liability side, is no longer between liabilities and net worth, but rather between liabilities to 'third parties', on the one hand, and the sum of liabilities to 'second parties' (i.e., owners of the enterprise's equity) and net worth, on the other. On the asset side, capital participations are separated from other financial assets. Thus fixed assets and liabilities are shown separately from equities on both sides of the account. The Guidelines also propose a similar restructuring of the capital finance account, to show changes in capital participations separately from changes in other financial assets and liabilities. This alteration in the structure of the balance sheet and capital finance accounts is clearly an improvement, since corporate and quasi-corporate equities are not liabilities in the usually accepted sense of that term, and this treatment brings the accounts closer to normal business practice. In most business accounts, a similar distinction is also made on the asset side of the balance sheet, separating fixed claim assets from equity securities.

Financial assets and liabilities other than equities

The basic SNA classification of fixed claims is by liquidity, which is of course closely associated with type of instrument. Within this first-level breakdown, two further distinctions are made. A separation is made between accounts payable in national currency and those payable in foreign currencies, and accounts with an original contractual maturity of one year or less are distinguished from those with longer maturities. In only one case does the classification of financial assets and liabilities provided in SNA (Table 7.2) and in the Balance Sheet Guidelines recommend any breakdown by institutional sector beyond the separation of foreign debtors and creditors: it is recommended that short-term bonds and bills be subdivided according to debtor into: resident corporations, central government, state and local government and rest of the world.

Table 24 of SNA does provide for a breakdown of financial transactions by detailed subsectors of debtors and creditors. However, few countries are able to provide data at the level of detail required for this table. Yet the introduction of some institutional sector detail into the main capital finance and balance sheet accounts would be extremely useful. In particular, consideration may be given to the separation of government obligations. It is of considerable importance for financial analysis and the planning of monetary and fiscal policy for the government to know whether the public debt is held by banks and other financial institutions, public or private enterprises, or households. Secondly, a breakdown of long-term loans would be desirable, in order to show debt secured by mortgages on residential and commercial property separately from other types of long-term financing.

The Guidelines argue that fixed claims held as assets should, in principle, be valued in one of two ways, either at nominal face value if they can be realized on demand or at short notice or if they cannot be transferred as assets from one transactor to another, or at market value if they cannot be realized on demand but can be transferred. The application of this principle, tempered by considerations of practicality, results in its proposal that market values should be used to value fixed-claim financial assets in the form of gold and long-term bonds, and that face values be used for all others. However, this raises some problems with respect to the valuation of long-term bonds as liabilities. The general SNA principle is that the same valuation should be used for a given claim whether it is viewed as an asset or as a liability, and this would require that long-term bonds also be valued at market in the accounts of the issuer. The Guidelines offer a number of arguments in favor of this treatment. At the same time, it is recognized that this is not usual business practice, or indeed the practice followed in country financial statistics in many cases. Nor is it the IFS practice. The Guidelines suggest that supplementary tables showing nominal values of long-term bonds should also be compiled. It may be desirable to reconsider this question for the future.

Equities

The Balance Sheet Guidelines note that valuation of the equity of both subsidiaries and quasi-corporate enterprises presents problems, and its recommendations depart from those of the Blue Book. With respect to subsidiaries, where by definition the parent company owns 50 percent or more of the corporate stock, the parent company controls the magnitude of the subsidiaries' net worth since it determines the amount of dividends they pay, and thus fixes the amount of saving they retain. It may therefore be argued that the subsidiaries do not have any independent net worth and that the value of the parents' equity securities in the subsidiaries is equivalent to the total value of the subsidiaries' assets less the total value of the subsidiaries' liabilities, after taking account of any minority interests. A similar argument is made for quasi-corporate enterprises. Quasi-corporate enterprises may be considered to have no independent net worth, since the proprietors determine the amounts they withdraw from or add to the capital of the enterprises and can appropriate all of it. The value of the proprietors' net equity in quasi-corporate enterprises would thus be equivalent to the total value of their assets less the total value of their other liabilities.

With respect to corporate equities as liabilities of the issuing firms, the Guidelines do recommend valuation at market, but point out that a good case can be made for the use of revalued paid-in value. The revalued paid-in value of all the outstanding equity securities, excluding Treasury stock, of an incorporated enterprise is the sum of the actual amounts paid for sold issues of shares and the value of their issue of dividends and bonuses, revalued in terms of the current market prices of the assets of the enterprise. The use of this value for equity securities, together with market values elsewhere in the balance sheet, would result in a concept of net worth which is equivalent to the accumulated retained earnings and capital gains of the enterprise, valued in terms of current market prices of the assets. This definition of net worth is closely related to the concept of accumulated capital that is used in business accounting. It would yield figures of net worth that are indicative of the success of companies and of their dividend policies and the role of internal financing. The relationship between the revalued paid-in values and market values of the equity securities of incorporated enterprises is also of analytical interest.

IFS follows a still different practice. It considers that it is not essential that financial claims be valued identically when they are owned as assets and when they are owed as liabilities, and recommends different valuation of the same item in debtor and creditor balance sheets. The IFS procedure is to value financial assets at the present discounted value of expected future income streams, and to value financial liabilities at face value. For equity securities, 'face value' appears to mean nominal paid-in value, without any revaluation, although IFS does not make this entirely clear.

Recent experience in the analysis of both private financial markets and fiscal policy strongly suggests that the accounting system should provide both valuations based on the discounted future stream of expected earnings and valuations reflecting the actual market value of assets and liabilities owned by enterprises, since the difference between the two is often a determinant of behavior. In terms of financial markets, where a firm's discounted stream of future earnings valuation is lower than the market value of its net assets, it may be the target of a takeover aimed at liquidating its assets. In fiscal policy terms, the two valuations are required to compute Q-ratios, which reflect the extent to which enterprises will spend for new capital formation or will attempt to gain new capacity by merging with existing enterprises.

Intangibles
Various questions may also be raised about the treatment of intangibles. As the

controversy surrounding the treatment of financial leasing makes apparent, such intangible assets as leases share many of the characteristics of financial assets, and it might be useful to combine them with other fixed-claim assets. This is not true, however, of all types of intangibles. Such intellectual property as patents and copyrights (and, increasingly, such things as computer software) are much more akin to tangibles. They do not entail an offsetting liability, and so should enter into national wealth.

Leases of machinery and equipment The treatment of financial leasing is being reconsidered in the review of SNA. Leases for the rental of machinery and equipment are not now considered in SNA to be intangible assets. Rental payments for machinery and equipment are treated as payments for purchased services in the production accounts of both lessor and lessee, and the lease itself is treated like any other long-term contract: it does not specifically enter into the balance sheet. In cases where the lessee controls the choice of equipment and retains the equipment after the expiration of the lease, however, it is argued that what is really going on is a financial transaction: the lessor is lending to the lessee the sum necessary to purchase the equipment. Ownership should therefore reside with the lessee, not the lessor, and the lease should be considered a long-term loan. There is substantial agreement in principle with this position, but numerous problems have arisen in working out the specific provisions.

Leases of land, buildings, etc. The Balance Sheet Guidelines note that an argument very similar to that made with regard to financial leasing of equipment can be made with respect to leases of land and buildings, concessions to exploit mineral deposits etc. Rather than including such leases and concessions in intangible nonfinancial assets, the lump-sum payment might instead be considered to be an advance of the discounted value of the stream of expected rents and royalties over the life of the lease or concession, and therefore might be shown as a financial asset of the payer and a liability of the receiver that is written off year by year over the life of the lease. This procedure would solve the problem of the disposition of expired leases and concessions that arises in the present SNA. It would also handle more neatly the problem that arises when contractual payments depart from market rentals. When this happens, the concomitant increase (or decrease) in the market value of the asset during the life of the lease accrues to the lessee, not the owner, and under the present treatment it is necessary to create a financial asset, amortized over the remaining life of the lease, to record this. If the transaction is treated as a financial one in the first place, and it is valued over its life at current market value, this separate entry is not needed.

Patents, trademarks, and copyrights While a similar argument could be made regarding the intellectual property represented by patents, copyrights and trademarks, it is much less persuasive in this case. The purchaser and seller normally do regard the transaction as an actual sale, even when payments are spread out over a period of time. A study of country practices seems to suggest, however, that in the few instances where estimates of intangibles are made, the payments involved are treated as royalties, not sales. The situation is akin to that of development and exploration expenditures that are embodied in tangibles, suggesting that they might be treated in the same way, as part of gross capital formation. That, in turn, would open up the question of the treatment of research and development expenditures in general. SNA excludes such expenditures from gross capital formation (and, therefore, from the balance sheet) even though they are frequently capitalized on the accounts of business firms, on the ground that they may not yield concrete benefits and are usually not embodied in tangible assets. However, outlays on improving land and developing or extending mining sites, timber tracts, etc. are considered to be capital formation, up to the point when they become productive; thereafter, they are classed as intermediate consumption. The logic of this entire convention has been questioned, and it should perhaps receive further attention.

The Reconciliation Account Entries

The 1968 SNA envisaged a complete accounting for the change in balance sheets from one period to the next through accounts covering transactions and a revaluation account to accommodate changes in prices. However, the Balance Sheet Guidelines issued in 1977 encountered various problems with the scheme as originally formulated. Some entries were needed that could not be considered revaluations, but for which no place had been provided in the transactions accounts. In order to avoid the necessity of altering the transactions accounts as laid out in the Blue Book, the scope of the revaluation account was expanded in the Guidelines to include all of these omitted items, and its name was changed from revaluation account to reconciliation account. This was, however, not intended as a permanent solution. The Guidelines point out that the boundary between the transactions accounts and the reconciliation account needs further study, and that this is one of the reasons why they were called 'provisional'.

The capital accumulation account covers the birth (through gross capital formation) and death (through capital consumption) of most tangible assets. However, there are some exceptions. Gross capital formation includes the birth of certain assets for which estimation of capital consumption is not recommended, such as improvements to land, the development and extension of plantations, and the construction of certain government assets such as roads and bridges. If these assets pass out of existence, their death is not provided for in the transactions accounts. Plantations, timber tracts, etc. may increase in value through natural growth, and this is not reflected in the capital accumulation account. Losses of tangible assets through natural catastrophes or unanticipated accidental damage, or their premature retirement due to unforeseen obsolescence, do not appear in the capital accumulation account. Finally, the birth, through sale, of nonfinancial intangible assets is covered in the capital accumulation account, but their death is not. All of these omitted changes now appear in the reconciliation account.

The capital finance account covers the birth and death of financial assets and liabilities resulting from the foundation, liquidation, and most acquisitions and sales of enterprises. It does not, however, cover the disappearance or appearance of certain financial assets and liabilities because of expansion or contraction of the coverage of statistical units. A parent may actually acquire or divest subsidiaries, or the change may result simply from a redefinition of the statistical unit. Reclassification of statistical units among sectors or kind-of-activity classes may also result in changes not covered in the capital finance accounts of individual sectors, though the account of the nation as a whole will not be affected. All these omissions, again, are presently included in the reconciliation account.

The entries that now appear in the reconciliation account may be divided into those reflecting changes in prices and those reflecting changes in quantities. These are quite different in nature, and they are discussed separately below.

Evaluations due to price change

This category covers the types of change originally envisaged in the 1968 SNA. It includes both realized and unrealized capital gains and losses arising from changes in market price or replacement cost of balance sheet items (depending on the method of valuation used), or in cases where value has been estimated by capitalizing an income stream, changes in the capitalization factor or rate of discount used in making the estimates. Where assets or liabilities are denominated in foreign currencies, changes in exchange rates may also enter here. Although the entries appearing here are often difficult to estimate, they do not usually present boundary problems: they are unambiguously revaluations, and as such belong here and not in the transactions accounts.

Special Drawing Rights

Special Drawing Rights were instituted by the International Monetary Fund after the publication of the 1968 SNA. SDRs are international reserve assets created by the IMF, representing the holder's unconditional right to obtain other reserve assets, usually foreign exchange. They are held exclusively by official holders, which are normally central banks. The process through which SDRs are created (referred to by IMF as allocations of SDRs) and may be extinguished (cancellation of SDRs) resembles an unrequited transfer, in that a resident (the official holder) acquires or gives up a financial asset but does not exchange for it anything of economic value. Increases or decreases in net allocations are accounted for in the Guidelines in the reconciliation account. This treatment is largely a consequence of historical accident; as the Guidelines note, net allocations could with equal or superior logic be accounted for in the transactions accounts, along with other capital transfers.

Changes in the quantity of nonfinancial assets
This group includes both tangible are intangible nonfinancial assets. Changes in these assets that are not accounted for in the transactions accounts fall into two general categories. One consists of items that were not discussed in the 1968 SNA, perhaps through oversight, but which can logically be fitted into the existing structure of the transactions accounts. The second category is of a rather different nature. It consists of capital gains or losses arising from changes in the physical quantity of tangible and nonfinancial intangible assets rather than from changes in their price. Where such changes result from production activities, they are included in the capital accumulation account. But where they result from activities or events not now defined as production-related, they are omitted from the capital accumulation account and shown in the reconciliation account. This in a sense is also a form of oversight — the 1968 SNA did not contemplate the existence of such changes in physical quantities. A good argument can be made that this category should be accommodated in the capital accumulation account, so that this account will reflect the full scope of physical capital accumulation. To accomplish this, however, a new type of entry in the capital accumulation account would be needed. The individual items in question are discussed below.

Unforeseen obsolescence and accidental damage Consumption of fixed capital in principle includes an allowance for obsolescence, which enters into the fixing of an asset's expected useful economic life. There is no place in the transactions accounts, however, for changes in the physical quantity of tangible assets arising from departure of actual experience from that normally expected — actual retirements of tangible assets earlier than, or later than, that postulated in the assumptions about useful life. These are not revaluations; they have nothing to do with price change. Putting them into the same account with price change will tend to obscure the analysis of inflation, whereas omitting them from the capital accumulation account will obscure analysis of changes in the capital stock. An alternative treatment would be to add an entry covering such unforeseen changes in the physical quantity of tangible assets to the capital accumulation account, so that it would account more completely for the accumulation (and decumulation) of the physical stock of tangible assets.

A further question may be raised about the concept of 'normal' accidental damage. Consumption of fixed capital also includes an allowance for 'normal' accidental damage to fixed capital, defined as that which can be expected to occur, for all producers grouped together, regularly every year. The concept derives from the experience of groups of producing units — industries, or the economy as a whole, and depends upon the level of aggregation to which the accounts refer. From the point of view of the individual producing unit, 'normal' accidental damage would be very much smaller than its pro rata share of the industry or national average, being confined to such items as losses of small tools and definitely not including such major items as total destruction of a plant by fire. The latter would be considered by the individual producer to be capital losses, not normal production events. As with unforeseen obsolescence, it would be appropriate to show such capital losses in the capital accumulation account rather than as capital consumption in the production account. Furthermore, the insurance reimbursement for such losses, where they are insured, would also be considered a capital transaction, appropriately shown in the capital finance account rather than the income and outlay account. Inclusion of both accidental damage and its insurance reimbursement in the current transactions accounts reflects, in large part, the incomplete nature of the 1968 SNA; in several instances, entries were included in the current accounts so that they would not be omitted from the system, since the capital accounts were not fully worked out. The next version of SNA may be expected to be more complete, and consideration needs to be given to the proper allocation of these entries.

Uncompensated seizure of assets When governments take possession of the assets of individuals or companies without compensation for reasons other than the payment of taxes, fines or similar levies, or when the compensation falls substantially short of market value, the Balance Sheet Guidelines suggest that an adjustment item be entered in the reconciliation account. The Guidelines note, however, that such seizures of assets could equally well be entered as capital transfers in the capital accumulation account, and there does not seem to be any compelling reason not to do this. They do not differ in any essential characteristic from other capital transfers, which are often accomplished through the transfer of physical assets.

Natural growth and new finds Although the initial outlays on acquiring livestock as fixed assets and on developing and expanding timber tracts, fisheries and plantations, orchards and vineyards are included in gross fixed capital formation, the natural growth in these assets and their depletion through use are not covered in the transactions accounts. Similarly, expenditures on exploration for and development of subsoil assets are counted as gross capital formation, but neither the value of new finds nor depletion is covered in the transactions accounts. The Balance Sheet Guidelines therefore recommend that both of these types of change in the physical quantity of assets be included in the reconciliation account. It is apparent that interest in these questions has risen substantially since the Guidelines — and even more so the 1968 SNA — were prepared. There is a need for a treatment of these topics that is more explicit, more detailed, and above all comprehensive. It is, for instance, not appropriate to introduce an allowance for depletion of subsoil assets without an offsetting estimate of new finds. Here again, inclusion of both new finds (or natural growth, in the case of timber etc.) and depletion in the capital accumulation account would be an appropriate alternative, which would satisfy the needs of industry specialists while at the same time ensuring consideration of these questions in a proper context.

These proposed new entries in the capital accumulation account should not include revaluations of subsoil assets, timber, livestock, etc. for such reasons as a rise in the price of the product or the development of more efficient techniques of exploitation. Changes of this sort are not changes in physical quantity, but rather should be classed as price changes.

Consideration also needs to be given to the relation between the capital accumulation account and the production account. The new entries being suggested here would (like purchases of land and intangibles) enter the capital accumulation account, but not the production account. It has, alternatively, sometimes been proposed that depletion, like depreciation, should be entered on the cost side of the production account. But this adjustment is not reasonable without an offsetting adjustment for new finds, and adding new finds less depletion to value added would significantly alter the concept of production as it is now conceived in SNA.

Natural catastrophes Outlays on improvements of land are treated as gross fixed capital formation in SNA, but losses of land due to natural catastrophes such as earthquakes, volcanic action or storms are not covered in the transactions accounts. The Guidelines show such losses in the reconciliation account. They are, however, quite similar to losses due to accidental damage, and should probably be treated in the same way. The argument presented above would suggest including them in the capital accumulation account. Reductions in the usefulness of land because of slower changes such as erosion, waterlogging and advance of deserts are treated in the Guidelines as a change in market value, however, as is upgrading not due to specific outlays on improvement. The boundary between what is a natural catastrophe resulting in a *quantity* change and what is simply a change in quality is, as always, difficult to draw. Furthermore, the question of whether quality change should be treated as a change in quantity or in price is still an open one. The same considerations apply here as elsewhere in the accounts, but this topic is beyond the scope of this paper.

Assets that are not depreciated SNA specifically recommends that no capital consumption allowances be computed for certain assets, even though their creation is counted as capital formation. These include expenditures on the extension and development of plantations, vineyards and timber tracts, as well as most government construction except for buildings. The logic of this treatment is that with proper maintenance such assets have very long — effectively infinite — lives. Experience shows, however, that maintenance is seldom exactly what would be needed to maintain the asset in 'new' condition. Either it falls below that standard, and the asset deteriorates, or it exceeds that standard, as needs change and upgrading to meet heavier demands is undertaken. Upgrading, in SNA, is a capital expenditure, part of net capital formation. In the absence of a formal depreciation allowance, however, it is difficult to distinguish normal maintenance from capital improvement. The case of undermaintenance also creates problems. Unlike overmaintenance (or capital improvement), there is no provision in SNA for any accounting for undermaintenance. But, undermaintained assets will, by definition, fail to achieve the expected infinite life, and they will at some point be retired. The Guidelines record retirements of these assets in the reconciliation account, in order to arrive at the proper closing stock of tangible assets. But this may not be a satisfactory solution, since the assumption upon which these assets are not depreciated is seldom correct. An old road, for example, does not retain its full value undiminished until the day it is torn up to make way for a new one; it gradually loses its value as it becomes more and more obsolete and inadequate to handle the traffic flow. While it is true that the estimation of capital consumption for assets of these types is difficult, it is not more difficult than estimation of many other entries that are included, and there seems to be no valid conceptual reason for failing to depreciate (or at least amortize) these expenditures.

Nonfinancial intangible assets The creation of nonfinancial intangible assets such as patents, copyrights, and trademarks through purchase is recorded in the capital accumulation account, but their termination is not. The Guidelines put an entry for termination in the reconciliation account. As in the case of the tangible assets mentioned in the preceding paragraph, however, this is not fully satisfactory. It is unrealistic to assume that the value of such an intangible asset is extinguished all at once, at the expiration of the copyright, lease, etc. A more appropriate treatment would amortize the value over the life of the asset — a life that is often known with much more certainty than is true for tangible assets.

Summary

There are two types of capital gains and losses not arising from the economy's current transactions activity that it would be desirable for the accounting system to show. One class arises from changes in prices of capital items, and the other from changes in physical quantities of capital items. Those arising from price changes are true revaluations, and belong in the revaluation account. With respect to those involving quantity changes, however, there is room for a difference of opinion. In view of the increasing importance of many of these gains and losses, it can be argued that they should be brought directly into the capital accumulation and capital finance accounts as new entries. It can equally be argued that they should be left in the reconciliation account, but, because of their increasing importance, that is a satisfactory solution only if the reconciliation account and balance sheet are actually compiled.

There are also a number of 'oversight' items — matters not mentioned in the 1968 SNA — that can logically be accommodated in the transactions accounts. These include uncompensated seizures of assets, terminations of nonfinancial intangible assets, retirement of nondepreciated fixed assets, transfers of life insurance and pension fund reserves to the net equity of households, and certain types of reclassification and restructuring. The Guidelines put these entries in the reconciliation account in order not to require changes in the transactions accounts, but in the next revision of the transactions accounts they can more logically be accommodated there.

2. THE FINANCIAL ACCOUNTS AND INSTITUTIONAL SECTORING

The SNA institutional sectoring conventions differ somewhat both from those of IFS and those generally employed in country financial statistics. This section reviews the main differences with a view to identifying candidates for reconsideration in the next version of SNA, both in order to promote the harmonization of statistical standards and on their own merits.

The IFS sectoring of transactors closely parallels the SNA institutional sectoring, but there are a few important differences. Although in IFS, as in SNA, each institutional reporting unit is usually assigned to a single sector, a few specific exceptions to this rule are made in order to differentiate clearly between the financial system and the nonfinancial public sector. The IFS financial system comprises monetary authorities (rather than SNA's central bank), deposit money banks (rather than SNA's other monetary institutions), and nonmonetary financial institutions (replacing SNA's three remaining subsectors: insurance companies, pension funds, and other financial institutions). IFS further divides its nonmonetary financial institutions sector into two parts; other bank-like institutions and nonbank financial intermediaries.

In addition, unlike SNA, IFS does not regard social security funds as a separate part of government. Rather, social security operations are considered part of the central government or of the other levels of government at which they operate. (In this, IFS differs from the proposed revised version of the IMF'S *Government Finance Statistics*, where the social security funds are separated out.)

Thus the chief differences between the SNA sectoring and that of IFS relate to the boundary between government and the financial system and the way in which the latter is subsectored. But there are also differences, of more importance for SNA than IFS, in the treatment of the nonfinancial part of the economy, i.e., quasi-corporate and unincorporated enterprises, household nonmarket activities, and social security funds. Some of these differences can be reconciled through the provision of more detailed information in one system or the other, but others imply important differences in approach.

Financial Institutions

Central bank/monetary authorities
IFS considers that the international comparability of the data sought for purposes of monetary analysis requires that the monetary authority accounts encompass all monetary authority functions. This functional approach differs from the SNA approach, in which monetary authority functions carried out by bodies other than the central bank are in most instances attributed to the institutional sectors where those bodies are found — usually the government sector. Where governments have retained control over currency issue (either coins or bank notes), the accounts associated with this function are consolidated with the monetary authority accounts in IFS, but not in SNA. Certain functions relating to the maintenance of international reserves are also transferred in IFS, but not in SNA.

SNA recognizes that these central-bank-like functions may be performed outside of the central bank in some cases, but it adopts a different approach to displaying the relationships involved. Because it is concerned with all of the activities of the economic agents whose accounts it presents, not just one particular aspect, such as their role in financial intermediation, SNA considers it important that the institutional integrity of the decision-making transactor units be maintained in the basic accounts. It does recognize, however, that the uses with which IFS is concerned are important to many analysts, and suggests that a supplementary table be drawn up to show central-bank-like functions performed by entities other than the central bank.

Other monetary institutions/deposit money banks
In SNA, the subsector of financial institutions called 'Other monetary institutions' is defined to include all banks except the central bank that have liabilities in the form of deposits payable on demand and transferable by check or otherwise usable in making payments. IFS defines an analogous subsector called 'Deposit money banks', but it is a slightly different group. While banks and similar institutions are usually the main issuers of deposit money, institutional arrangements may permit other financial transactors to incur transferable deposit liabilities that are generally recognized as means of payment. This is particularly true where governmental institutions incur such liabilities through postal giro systems. The IFS regards such financial transactions as taking place in notionally separate financial units which it consolidates with the deposit money bank accounts. Also, when the Treasury or some other governmental unit accepts transferable deposits from the general public, the deposits are classified by IFS, but not SNA, in the deposit money bank account.

Nonmonetary financial institutions
IFS and SNA treat the remaining financial institutions, those not included in the monetary authority and deposit money banks in IFS or in the central bank and other monetary institutions in SNA, in quite different ways.

In the first place, the subsectors that are identified are different. This in itself need not cause any insurmountable problems of comparability, because it can be overcome by adding more detail to both sets of accounts. IFS identifies two subsectors: other bank-like institutions and nonbank financial intermediaries. SNA identifies insurance companies and pension funds and other financial institutions.

Innovations in the field of finance such as credit cards and electronic transfer of funds raise fundamental questions about the measurement of an economy's means of payment, questions that have as yet been addressed by neither IFS nor SNA. Furthermore, some innovations are calling into question the very concept of 'transferable' deposits. In some countries transferable deposits are a declining share of total liabilities of financial institutions, and in others demand deposits are now less important than other deposits even for the deposit money banks. This changing pattern reflects shifts in the preferences of businesses and individuals in favor of interest-earning assets that are readily exchangeable for money, and against actual money holdings, and this is what has led financial analysts to develop $M2$, $M3$ ..., in addition to the $M1$ which SNA is aimed at measuring. IFS regards those nonmonetary financial institutions able to issue money substitutes as a distinct class, which it calls 'bank-like institutions'. This group includes savings banks, credit cooperatives, mortgage banks, government development banks (provided they do not rely exclusively on government sources of funds), and certain 'offshore' units whose main dealings are with nonresidents. In SNA, however, institutions of these types are classified as 'Other financial institutions', together with sales-finance, hire-purchase and other business and personal finance companies, money-lenders, securities brokers, and investment companies, funds, societies and trusts. There would be no conceptual problem, however, in splitting out a subsector in SNA to match the IFS definition. As the proliferation of M measures indicates, different problems require different concepts, and this is one field where showing more detail is probably desirable.

Conversely, SNA distinguishes separately a subsector composed of insurance companies and pension funds. In IFS, these are grouped together with trust and custody accounts, real estate investment schemes, other pooled investment schemes, and compulsory savings schemes in a subsector called 'Nonbank financial intermediaries'. Again, there would be no conceptual problem in showing insurance companies and pension funds separately in IFS. A more serious incompatibility arises, however, in the ways in which the accounts of insurance companies and pension funds are handled in the two systems.

Insurance companies and pension funds
The IFS treatment of insurance companies and pension funds is in most respects the same as that of conventional business accounting. In the IFS view, the primary function of these institutions is the conversion of individual risks into the risks of the entire insured community. Households and businesses regard their transactions with insurance companies and pension funds partly as current expenditures and partly as acquisitions of financial assets, but since the value of the financial assets acquired from these intermediaries depends on future exigencies, their present worth to holders can only be established by imputation. For this reason, IFS does not attempt to measure them. The financial assets of insurance companies and pension funds are clearly definable, however, and data on their holdings of financial instruments are frequently available. Normally, these assets comprise the investments the companies hold to meet required technical reserves. The existence of such technical reserves is, in the IFS view, a necessary condition for classification of insurance companies and pension funds as financial institutions.

The SNA treatment is radically different from this. Casualty insurance is treated quite differently from life insurance and pension funds, but in both cases the entries in the financial accounts and balance sheets are closely related to, and dependent upon, the way these transactions enter the current transactions accounts.

Casualty insurance For casualty insurance companies (fire, theft, health, unemployment etc.), gross premiums received are divided into: a charge for the service of insuring and a payment for risk. The total payment for risk during a given period is taken to be equal to the total claims paid during that period. The charge for the service of insuring is the remainder, namely gross premiums less claims, and this is entered as a sale in the production account of the insurer and a purchase by the insured. The payment for risk enters the income and outlay accounts of both insurer and insured, and the payment of casualty insurance claims is also entered into this account, on the opposite side. Since these last two entries are by definition equal, for the economy as a whole both net casualty insurance premiums and casualty insurance claims drop out.

It follows from this treatment of casualty insurance in the current accounts that there is no place in the system for any casualty insurance technical reserves. Casualty insurance risks are spread over classes of insurance purchasers, but they are not spread over time: the claims of each accounting period are fully paid for in that accounting period. The balance sheet of a casualty insurance company compiled on this basis would contain no indication that it had any future liability to its policyholders. (One consequence of this treatment is that by the IFS definition, casualty insurance companies would not be financial institutions at all, since they would not have any technical reserves.) This conclusion is not only logically indefensible, it is also contrary to the legal requirements of most countries.

Life insurance and pension funds The SNA treatment of life insurance and pension funds is more complex. In addition to payments for the service of insuring and for risk, life insurance premiums are considered to include a substantial element of saving, in the form of accumulated reserves. These reserves are treated as assets of the covered individuals, not as part of the independently held reserves of the insurance companies or pension funds. An entry entitled 'Net equity of households in life insurance and pension funds' is entered as a liability on the balance sheet of the companies or funds, and as an asset on the balance sheet of households. In contrast with the treatment of casualty insurance, life insurance and pension benefits received by individuals do not enter the current transaction accounts of the beneficiaries at all; they appear only as changes in the form of the beneficiaries' assets in the capital finance and balance sheet accounts.

This treatment is a major exception to the general SNA principle of maintaining the integrity of the accounts of institutional transactors. Households do not in fact receive these funds, and, as the IMF notes, it is not possible to make an objective valuation of their worth to the insured. Households do not control the funds, they have no access to them, and often even their claim to ultimate receipt of benefits from them is tenuous. This is particularly true of pension funds, where employees may lose their rights by changing jobs, or through other circumstances over which they have no control, and where the magnitude of the fund often reflects the profitability — or lack of it — of the sponsoring companies, rather than expected benefits. In the case of life insurance, ultimate receipt of benefits depends upon continued payment of premiums over a future interval, and policyholders often fail to maintain the insurance until they can collect on it — a factor that insurance companies rely upon in setting rates. Until the claims become due, the reserve funds are available to the companies for use as earning assets, and the earnings accrue to the companies, not the policyholders. It has therefore been proposed that what should be included in the assets of the policyholder or pension fund participant is only the present cash surrender or loan value of his accumulated rights. In the case of life insurance policies with a substantial element of saving, such as endowment or annuity policies, this may be a substantial fraction of the relevant reserve. But where the insurance element predominates, as in term policies, there may be no cash surrender value at all. For employer-provided pension funds, the cash surrender value is usually negligible until retirement age is reached. The remainder of the reserves, apart from cash surrender value, would be retained as assets of the companies involved. This treatment would, apart from the question of cash surrender value, be compatible with the IFS procedure.

Such a treatment of pension fund and life insurance reserves on the balance sheets of households and financial institutions would, of course, require consistent treatment in their capital finance accounts. It would also have repercussions on their income and outlay accounts, where it would be necessary to alter the treatment of actual benefit receipts to show all benefits (both life insurance and pension) over and above the cash surrender values as current incomes of households at the time they are actually received.

This treatment of life insurance and pension funds would also produce aggregates that would be compatible with the recommendations of the *Guidelines on Statistics of the Distribution of Income, Consumption and Accumulation* (UN, 1977b). These Guidelines, like those on balance sheets, were developed substantially later than the 1968 Blue Book, and, as in the case of the Balance Sheet Guidelines, it was found that difficulties arose from the uncompleted state of the Blue Book system. It was apparent that the Blue Book treatment of pensions and life insurance would produce unacceptable distribution figures, since pensioners and annuity recipients would be shown with zero income. In this case, however, unlike that of the Balance Sheet Guidelines, it was decided that the needs of distribution statistics could not be met using the Blue Book concepts, and new aggregates were developed. The resulting income distribution statistics are therefore compatible with the present aggregate SNA system in only a limited sense; the totals to which the distributions sum can be reconciled, through a series of adjustments, to the SNA aggregates, but these distribution totals appear nowhere in the overall SNA system.

The treatment of insurance and pension funds has been discussed in some detail in another paper (Ruggles and Ruggles, 1983) and a repetition of that discussion is beyond the scope of this paper. The topic is, however, one that needs consideration in the next version of SNA.

The Social Security Sector

The original intent of the framers of SNA in setting up a separate social security funds subsector was to accommodate cases, such as then existed in Sweden, where the administration of the social security system was quite separate from any level of government proper and clearly constituted an independent center of financial decision-making. In such cases, it was considered likely that the central government would not control the level of either contributions or benefits, and that it would not manage the investment of the fund. As time has passed, however, country interpretation of this provision has not followed this principle. A social security funds subsector is often identified even when the social security system is an organ of central government and completely under its control; sometimes, such a subsector is identified even when any fund that exists is inadequate to meet required benefit payments and is regularly supplemented from the ordinary budget. The argument advanced in favor of this treatment is that social security is a large and growing part of the government's total obligations, and it is often considered by both the government and the participants in the system to be separate from other government functions. The growing interest in such concepts as 'social security wealth' — or legal entitlements to future social security benefits — as well as in the potential solvency or insolvency of the fund attest to the importance of providing complete data in this area. But it does not follow from this that provision of a separate subsector is the best way of doing that.

The IMF position on this question is somewhat ambiguous, since there appears to be a difference between the stance taken in IFS that social security systems operating at the national level should be included in central government even if they are separately organized and the recommendations of the revised version of GFS that a separate social security subsector be shown. One possible solution, which may be what the revised GFS intends, would be to show the social security system as a further breakdown within the central government.

Quasi-Corporate and Unincorporated Enterprises

In its production accounts and its capital stock tables, SNA groups all kinds of enterprises together — government, public, private; corporate and non-incorporate; profit-making and nonprofit; and large and small — dividing them up only by kind of activity (industry). IFS apparently extends this unitary enterprise sector to the financial accounts and balance sheets. In SNA's institutional sectoring, however, distinctions are made among types of enterprises. Nonprofit enterprises have a sector of their own. Corporate enterprises are distinguished, and noncorporate enterprises are divided into quasi-corporate and unincorporated. All financial enterprises — down to and including moneylenders — are classed as quasi-corporate and grouped with corporations. For *nonfinancial* enterprises, the basic rule is that quasi-corporate enterprises should have complete financial accounts and balance sheets, separate from those of their owners. In practice SNA recommends that only large enterprises be considered for inclusion in this class. SNA does not define what should be considered to be 'large'. However, the European Community, in its European System of Accounts (ESA), has adopted specific size criteria: more than 100 employees in manufacturing, more than 50 in services, and more than 20 in agriculture. Nonfinancial unincorporated enterprises that do not qualify as quasi-corporate are grouped with households in a combined household and unincorporated enterprise sector.

Country experience does not appear to offer very much support for the SNA position, and even less for the ESA rules. Few have identified a nonprofit sector. Some countries have identified a few public nonfinancial quasi-corporations, but very few have made use of the concept of private non-financial quasi-corporation. As a consequence, the general practice is to leave all private unincorporated enterprises, both financial and nonfinancial and of whatever size, in the household sector.

This does not matter much as long as interest is confined to the production and income and outlay accounts. By definition, any production of the household sector apart from the activities of domestic servants is taking place in an unincorporated enterprise, so that in effect the production account of the household and unincorporated enterprise sector is the production account of unincorporated enterprises alone. Conversely, the income and outlay account of the combined sector is really the income and outlay account of households only, since the income and outlay account of unincorporated enterprises can only contain one pass-through entry (operating surplus) on each side. Much the same is true of the capital accumulation account: all of the entries except for net saving can only pertain to unincorporated enterprises, not to households, and given the treatment of entrepreneurial income, net saving can only pertain to households, not to unincorporated enterprises.

It is only in the capital finance account and balance sheet that any mingling of the unincorporated enterprise and household accounts is conceptually possible. Even here, however, most types of assets and liabilities are clearly separable. In the first place, households, in SNA, cannot own tangible assets; such assets (including owner-occupied dwellings) must all be the property of unincorporated enterprises. Financial assets and liabilities are usually allocable by type. Only unincorporated enterprises, for example, can extend or receive trade credit; only households can have equity in life insurance and pension fund reserves or quasi-corporate enterprises. Consumer loans are made to households; loans secured by productive assets to enterprises. Few unincorporated enterprises will hold corporate equity securities. Even cash and deposits are normally held either in the name of the business or the name of the household. (Where nothing is held in the name of the business, that is in fact a true reflection of the actual situation, and it is not misleading to show it that way.)

This point of view is further reinforced when actual sources of data are considered. Data for the capital finance account and balance sheet are most often obtained primarily from the financial institutions involved, rather than from the business or householder involved. Financial institutions know whether they are dealing with businesses or individuals; they know whether loans are for consumption or production purposes, and whether bank accounts belong to businesses or individuals. What they do not know, and cannot possibly provide information on, is the size of the business: discussions with banking personnel suggest that size criteria such as those of ESA are impossible to apply.

This suggests that some alteration in the SNA recommendation would be desirable. There are several possibilities. Perhaps the most useful would be to set up a combined enterprise sector, divided by legal form of organization into corporate, noncorporate, and nonprofit subsectors. Further subdivisions would also be useful: financial/nonfinancial and public/private, as at present, but also where possible into broad kind of activity groups: farm, mining and manufacturing, trade and service. An alternative would be to subdivide the present household and unincorporated enterprise sector into its two component parts. (This would, however, still leave the question of what to do about quasi-corporations. Leaving them as an unused appendage of corporations has little but inertia in its favor. It would also leave the problem of nonprofits, which is especially important in terms of balance sheets. Common practice now combines nonprofits with households, and this leads to the anomalous result that the only tangible assets allocated to the household sector are hospitals, schools and the like.)

Owner-Occupied Dwellings

SNA includes as production several types of household nonmarket activity, including subsistence farming, small manufactures, and own-account capital formation. None of these create any problems with respect to sectoring; they are all activities of unincorporated enterprises owned by the households engaging in them, and whatever is done with the unincorporated enterprises should also be done with these activities.

There is, however, one type of household nonmarket activity that is of a different nature, and that is the occupation of dwellings by their owners. In most developed countries, this is by far the largest of the imputed household activities. SNA treats it in a way that is different from all other consumption activities. The owner-occupier, in his capacity as owner, is considered to be renting the dwelling to himself in his capacity as occupier, and a notional unincorporated enterprise is set up to accommodate the provision of this service. The unincorporated enterprise is classified in the real estate industry. The household is considered to pay an imputed space rent to the unincorporated enterprise, which in turn owns the house, carries the mortgage, and pays the taxes and the costs of household operation. The unincorporated enterprise then returns any net profit to the household, as imputed rental income. The imputed space rent is in principle set equal to the rental of comparable properties that are rented. In practice, however, it is often the case that no comparable rented property can be found. This is especially likely to be true in rural and suburban areas. In that case, cost is substituted. The costs taken into account include operating costs, maintenance and repair, insurance service charges, property taxes, imputed depreciation and an imputed net return.

This treatment of owner-occupied dwellings in the production and income and outlay accounts, of course, requires consistent treatment in the financial accounts and balance sheets. Owner-occupied dwellings are considered to be the property of unincorporated enterprises in the real estate industry, not of households. Since household durable goods are not considered in SNA to be capital assets, it follows that the household balance sheet (if nonprofit institutions are excluded) can contain no tangible assets at all. This result is an anomalous one when the balance sheet of the sector as a whole is considered, and it becomes entirely unacceptable for the analysis of the distribution of wealth among households. As studies of the distribution of wealth universally show, residential housing is a major share of the total assets of all households except those at the very top and very bottom of the income or wealth distribution. Most home owners consider that what they own is a house or apartment, not net equity in a real estate enterprise. They are very conscious, furthermore, of their outstanding mortgage liability as well as their net equity. While they are often aware that home owning may be cheaper than renting, they do not consider the difference to be an imputed addition to their income, but rather a reduction in their expenditures.

A more realistic treatment would retain owner-occupied dwellings as assets of the household sector, and count the actual costs of owning and operating the house (such as mortgage interest, maintenance, and taxes) as a part of current consumer outlays. This would not preclude gathering all residential housing together in the real estate industry; household-owned dwellings could be included just as government-owned ones now are. Nor would it preclude the estimation of a net imputed return on owner-occupied dwellings if that were considered desirable; but it would make the method of imputation explicit.

3. SUMMARY AND CONCLUSIONS

The issues relating to the financial accounts that need consideration in the review of SNA arise out of the growing uses of these accounts, their sometimes ambiguous role in the SNA structure, and their relation to other international statistical systems. As was noted at the beginning of this paper, the 1968 SNA provided a place in the framework for the financial accounts and balance sheets, but did not develop them in any detail. In the 19 years since the Blue Book was published, the situation has changed significantly. In the first place, policy and analytic interest in questions of financial intermediation and its impact on the operation of the economy have greatly increased, as inflation, high interest rates and debt management have become worldwide problems. In the second place, much work has been done, both on the conceptual development of this part of the system and on the compilation of statistics in many countries. And at the same time, financial statistics outside the SNA system, and the international standards relating to them, have grown rapidly in availability and elaboration. The need for reconciliation is increasingly recognized as of first importance. For all of these reasons, some of the early decisions taken when financial considerations were not the focus of attention need reconsideration, some of the makeshift solutions that have grown up over time are no longer adequate, and some issues that have not been dealt with at all need to be addressed.

The points that have been brought up in this paper fall into two general categories: those dealing with the definition, valuation and arrangement into accounts of financial *transaction flows* and the stock items related to them, and those dealing with the identification and classification into sectors of the transactors of the system. The first group, in this paper, has been called accounting structure, and the second, sectoring.

With respect to accounting structure, there is, first, a group of questions affecting the content of the balance sheet and capital finance account, and the arrangement, classification and valuation of the items they contain. Most important of these, perhaps, is the separation of financial assets and liabilities into two categories, fixed assets and liabilities on the one hand, and equities and net worth on the other. Questions of content include the treatment of land and other natural resources, residential housing and consumer durables; and of pension and life insurance reserves. Questions of classification include the disposition of intangibles and the introduction of institutional sector detail. Questions of valuation arise in connection with the reconciliation of the SNA accounts with IMF and country practices relating to financial liabilities and equities and the treatment of insurance and pension fund reserves.

A second group of questions relates to the reconciliation account and its relation to the capital accumulation account. The most important question here is the separation of capital gains and losses arising from price changes, which properly are accommodated in the revaluation account, from those involving quantity changes, which are forms of capital accumulation or decumulation. Entries involving quantity changes that appear in the reconciliation account because no place was provided for them in the Blue Book can easily be accommodated in the capital accumulation account. Some of them, such as new finds and depletion of subsoil assets, raise important problems of valuation, however. Provision also needs to be made for some items that are now completely omitted, including a more rational treatment of depreciation, depletion and amortization.

Finally, on accounting structure, consideration needs to be given to the impact of changes made in the financial accounts on the current flow accounts. In particular, the treatment of capital consumption, insurance, and expenditures on housing and consumer durables may need attention.

With respect to sectoring, a first group of questions relates to the reconciliation of various international standards. There are differences between SNA and the various IMF standards in the boundary drawn between government and financial institutions, and between households, financial institutions, and non-financial enterprises. There are also differences in the way subsectors are delineated which affect all of the major sectors of SNA. A second group of questions (which overlaps the first) arises out of changing needs and changing institutional forms, including the blurring of the concept of money, the growing importance of pension fund reserves and their domination of financial markets, and the increasing focus on households' distribution of income, saving behavior and holdings of tangibles and financial assets and liabilities.

The SNA framework provides an admirable way to integrate financial information with data on production, income and capital formation. Because of the sequential implementation of the various parts of the system, however, the financial accounts in SNA now have a certain jerry-built character. And because of changing institutional forms and policy problems over the course of the last 19 years, insufficient emphasis is given to problems that are now important and present-day institutional forms are not adequately portrayed. It is to be hoped that the opportunity to rationalize the financial accounts afforded by the ongoing review of SNA will not be allowed to pass by.

REFERENCES

Ruggles, Nancy D. and Richard Ruggles (1983), *The Treatment of Pension and Insurance Transactions in the United Nations System of National Accounts*, Report prepared for the Meeting of National Accounts Experts, OECD, 25–27 May. [A substantially similar paper was published in *Review of Income and Wealth*, **29** (4), 1983.]

United Nations (1968), *A System of National Accounts*, Series F., No. 2, Rev. 3.

———— (1977a), *Provisional International Guidelines on the National and Sectoral Balance-Sheet and Reconciliation Accounts of the System of National Accounts*, Series M, No. 60.

———— (1977b), *Provisional Guidelines on Statistics of the Distribution of Income, Consumption and Accumulation of Households*, Series M, No. 61.

———— (1979), *Guidelines on Statistics of Tangible Assets*, Series M, No. 68.

14. A Note on the Revision of the United Nations System of National Accounts

Richard Ruggles
Yale University

1. THE CURRENT REVISION AND ITS MAJOR CHANGES

The present revision of the United Nations System of National Accounts began in 1975 as an updating, clarification and harmonization of the 1968 SNA with other international statistical systems. The revision process has been more lengthy than expected, and is not scheduled for completion until 1993. Although it is difficult to evaluate something that does not as yet exist, useful proposals have been made for major changes in several areas. However, there is also some evidence that the proposed revision may also perpetuate or even exacerbate some of the more serious inadequacies of the present SNA.

On the positive side, the articulation of full sets of income and outlay accounts, capital finance transactions, revaluations and balance sheets represents a major improvement. Although the framers of the previous SNA system had envisaged such accounts, they were incomplete for some sectors and many of the more detailed questions were not resolved. In particular, the question of consistency with the data collected by other international agencies has been actively pursued by the revisers of the SNA.

Second, the expansion of the definition of capital formation to include research and development, mineral exploration, computer software and possibly other intellectual property is a useful innovation. Such an expansion in capital from purely a 'material product' definition is appropriate now that centrally planned countries are adopting the more utility-oriented concepts of production that recognize services as part of final output.

Finally, there is a proposal to distinguish between consumption and

---

This chapter first appeared in *Review of Income and Wealth*, **36** (4), 1990.

consumption expenditures, and also between individual and collective consumption. The distinction between consumption and consumption expenditures by households is important for analyzing household behavior and for evaluating the welfare of households based on their total consumption. International comparisons of living standards and the assessment of real consumption and poverty within countries require including not only those goods and services individually consumed by households, but also those collective goods and services provided by governments and other organizations.

On the other hand, the SNA revision — or its lack of revision — raises serious questions about its adequacy as an analytic framework. In particular, five problem areas can be distinguished that are not, in my view, adequately treated in the proposed revision. These areas are: sectoring, owner-occupied housing, household capital formation, pensions and insurance, and interest.

2. THE SECTORING OF THE ECONOMY

In the present SNA, the institutional sectoring consists of: corporate and quasi-corporate enterprises, general government, nonprofit institutions serving households, unincorporated enterprises and households and *de facto* the rest of the world. For the revised SNA, it is proposed that nonprofit institutions serving households be eliminated as a major sector and be included as a part of the household sector — thus reducing the number of major sectors by one.

Since, in general, national statistical offices have not implemented the SNA recommendation for treating nonprofit institutions as a separate sector of the economy, it is quite reasonable that such sectoring be abandoned. The preference of many national accountants for including nonprofit institutions in the household sector has been primarily based on the lack of adequate data. The estimates of final consumption for households have usually been derived residually, and often still are. Reliable data on the final consumption of nonprofit institutions have often not been available, so it has been impossible to separate them from household final consumption. Since households were considered as the consumers of the goods and services provided by nonprofit institutions, the most appropriate solution has been not to distinguish separately such goods and services.

However, the current SNA proposal for creating a combined household and nonprofit institution sector needs to be reexamined in light of the other proposed revisions of the SNA and the changed importance of nonprofit institutions themselves. As already noted, the distinction between consumption expenditures by households and their consumption of goods and services is made in the revised SNA. There is also an attempt to provide better integration between the macro- and microdata for households. Both of these changes require a separation of the transactions made by households from those made by nonprofit institutions.

Furthermore, nonprofit institutions in many countries now represent a significant part of the economy. In the United States, nonprofit institutions account for approximately 7 percent of the total employment. They consist of schools, universities, hospitals, and associations, as well as religious and charitable organizations. They cover a broad variety of research, educational, health, recreational and other activities, and exist along with profit-making organizations and public enterprises engaged in the same activities.

Combining households and nonprofit institution transactions within the household sector runs counter to the spirit of the transactor/transaction approach that is being emphasized in the SNA revision. The income and outlay accounts, capital finance accounts, and balance sheets for a combined household/nonprofit sector would have little analytic meaning or use. The combined account could not be partitioned into size distributions or be used as control totals for microdata. Since the revised SNA requires a complete subsectoring of nonprofit institution transactions, a preferable solution is to classify nonprofit institutions with other similar profit-making or public enterprises. Thus, they would be a part of a comprehensive enterprise sector that would cover all private and public enterprises irrespective of their legal form of organization.

The household sector accounts would then represent households, in their role as income recipients and consumers. The enterprise sector would represent all enterprises engaged in either profit or nonprofit activities.

A comprehensive enterprise sector is also needed because the existing SNA distinction between quasi-corporate enterprises included the corporate sector and unincorporated enterprises included in the household sector is difficult to make. The stated criterion is that in order for an enterprise unit to be included with corporate enterprises as a quasi-corporate enterprise, it should have a complete set of accounts. In contrast, it is argued that where the accounts of unincorporated enterprises are not distinguished from household accounts, these enterprises should be relegated to the household sector.

Although, conceptually, this approach appears reasonable, it cannot easily be applied on a case-by-case basis. For farming, for example, it would be more reasonable to treat all farms that sell farm produce as being in the same sector, rather than including some in the enterprise sector and relegating others to the household sector. If distinctions are to be made, farms might be classified by size and type of farm within the enterprise sector rather than relegating different farms to separate major sectors on the basis of subjective accounting criteria.

One of the anomalies in the revision of the SNA sectoring is that, although categories are established for the 'collective and individual consumption' provided by general government and by nonprofit institutions, no such categories exist for enterprises. Certainly, enterprises do provide their employees with health care, day care services and other fringe benefits. If the goods and services in kind that are provided to individuals by enterprises are to be distinguished from consumer expenditures made by individuals, these categories of outlays will need to exist.

3. OWNER-OCCUPIED HOUSING

Both the existing SNA and the proposed revision treat owner-occupied housing differently from other components of consumption expenditures. Households as occupants are considered to be renting their dwellings from themselves as real estate owners. Their activities as owners are considered to be those of unincorporated enterprises. These fictitious unincorporated enterprises own the dwellings and pay all the costs associated with them. To offset these outlays, the unincorporated enterprises receive an imputed space rental from the households as occupiers. The difference between the space rental and the current costs of providing the housing services is returned to households as imputed rental income.

The SNA household income and outlay account thus includes: on the outlay side, imputed space rental as a part of consumption expenditure and, on the income side, imputed rental income on owner-occupied housing as a part of total rental income. The actual costs of owner-occupancy, including maintenance expenditures, property taxes, insurance, mortgage interest, imputed interest on the owner's equity and capital consumption, appear in the SNA as outlays and gross saving by the fictitious unincorporated enterprise.

Although this method of imputation does include the services of owner-occupied housing in both output and final consumption, it does so by distorting the accounts of both households and unincorporated enterprises. In fact, it is households that pay property taxes, interest on the mortgage debt and expenses of repair and upkeep, not unincorporated businesses in the real estate industry, and it is households that do the gross saving reflected in depreciation charges.

For both measuring the total housing consumption of individual households and to provide comparability between owned and rented housing, it is recognized that some type of imputation for the use of owner-occupied housing would be desirable. Such an imputation can, however, be made in the household account as both income and consumption without the necessity of running all the related transactions through a fictitious unincorporated enterprise. By following the transactor/transaction approach, the current costs of owner-occupied housing would be listed as actual expenditures by households. A separate imputation could then be made for the difference between such costs and the space rental value of the owner-occupied housing.

4. HOUSEHOLD CAPITAL FORMATION

Although the framers of the revised SNA are very much concerned with expanding the definition of enterprise and government capital formation to include research and development, computer software and even intellectual property, they are strangely silent about household capital formation. Since owner-occupied housing is treated as being owned and operated by unincorporated enterprises, it is included in capital formation, but other purchases of durable goods by households are treated purely as a category of current expenditures.

It is somewhat paradoxical that if the purchase prices of new houses include the cost of the major kitchen and other appliances, these will automatically be included in capital formation. However, if these appliances are bought separately by households, they are treated as current expenditures. Similarly, automobiles, if bought by enterprises, are classified as capital formation, but when bought by households, are considered to be current expenditures.

Much of the consumer credit extended to households relates to the purchase of automobiles and other consumer durables. Both households and financial institutions recognize that such purchases do not represent merely consumption in the current period, but that the good purchased continues to have value and provide services over a period of years. It is time that consumer durables are recognized in the SNA as capital formation, and, as in owner-occupied housing appropriate imputations for the services that they provide should be introduced into the accounts so that total consumption can be more accurately measured.

5. PENSIONS AND INSURANCE

Although the revisers of the SNA propose reform in the treatment of casualty insurance to bring it in line with the European System of Accounts, there has been no mention of altering the treatment of pensions and other insurance. The present SNA treats employers' contributions to life insurance, private pension and welfare funds as part of current compensation received by employees, and therefore as part of household income. Only that portion of the contribution which represents the costs of operating the insurance companies and pension funds — called the service charge — is treated as personal consumption expenditures.

The full increase in the reserves held by insurance companies and pension funds, therefore, is attributed to personal saving. Households are, thus, considered to own the reserves of the insurance companies and pension funds. The net equity of these funds appears on the household sector balance sheet, and interest earned on the reserves is attributed as current income to households, although of course they do not receive it.

As a corollary to this treatment in the SNA, pension benefits and life insurance annuities actually paid to households do not appear as part of household income because such treatment would involve double counting. It would be included as income initially when the employers' contribution is paid to the insurance company or pension fund and subsequently when the benefit is paid to the household. As a consequence, the receipt of such benefits is considered to represent only a change in the form of the assets held by the household, from net equity in life insurance and pension funds to cash.

Compilers of household survey microdata usually reverse this treatment. Pension and annuity benefit payments received by households are included in household income and employer's payments of contributions to pension funds and insurance are not. Interest on pension and insurance reserves is not attributed to the household, and the household balance sheet does not include equity in employer-financed pension and insurance reserves.

In the United Nations guidelines on income distribution statistics, the household survey treatment of pensions and insurance is recommended rather than that of the SNA. (See United Nations Statistical Office, Series M, No. 61, *Provisional Guidelines on Statistics of the Distribution of Income, Consumption, and Accumulation of Households*, 1977.) Where the focus is on the distribution on income, it is clearly undesirable to treat pensioners as having zero income — that would not contribute much to an understanding of the position of the aged in the economy. Conversely, entitlement of younger persons to benefits that will become available only on retirement or death are substantively different from cash income received in the present period. Furthermore, employers' contributions for insurance and pensions are a poor and unstable measure even of the present value of those future rights.

By modifying the current SNA treatment of pensions and insurance, it is possible to adhere more closely to the transactor/transaction principle and provide better integration with microdata concepts. Employers' contributions to pension and insurance funds should be treated as funds held in escrow for future payment. Pension benefits should be considered as income when they are paid out to individuals.

6. INTEREST

The present SNA treats interest not as a payment for a service, but rather as a transfer of factor income. This exclusion of interest received by financial institutions for services rendered has had an unfortunate impact upon their value added. Computed in the ordinary way as the difference between operating receipts and intermediate costs, value added of financial institutions would be very low or negative. Operating receipts would consist only of actual service charges imposed on depositors and other users of banking services and would not include the receipts of interest that are the major source of banking income.

It is argued, however, that service charges do not cover all of the services provided by these institutions. There is also an implicit exchange between the banks and their customers in which the banks provide services in return for the use of the customers' money to earn interest. The value attributed to the services provided is set equal to the difference between the interest received and the interest paid out, and this attributed amount is added to actual service charges to obtain total banking service charges.

Such a treatment has been particularly unsatisfactory for those countries which have large international payments and receipts of interest. As a consequence, the revised SNA will change the imputed service charge for financial intermediation (previously bank output) to distinguish between those services which constitute intermediate consumption and those that constitute final demand. The exact methodology by which import charges for services of financial intermediaries will be calculated has yet to be agreed, as indeed has the process of dividing the charges within the domestic economy.

Many different alternatives have been proposed for the treatment of interest, but the simplest and most straightforward approach would be to treat interest not as a transfer, but rather as a purchase of a financial service. This would accord more closely with the view of commercial borrowers who regard interest on funds that they borrow for business purposes as part of their costs. It would also accord with the view of individual households who consider the interest costs of installment and other consumer credit as part of the purchase price of such items as automobiles and consumer durables.

7. THE OVERALL DESIGN OF THE REVISED SNA

Finally, in evaluating the overall design of the revised SNA, two questions need to be examined. First, does the proposed revision of the SNA provide a simple and understandable overview of the economic system? Secondly, is the revised SNA a suitable framework for integrating the data required for the wide spectrum of policy and analytic uses that can be anticipated in the next decade?

The proposed revision of the SNA presents an elaborate and complex set of interlinked cascading accounts that have been developed for each institutional sector showing: (1) production, (2) generation of income, (3) appropriation of primary income, (4) entrepreneurial income, (5) appropriation of other primary income, (6) secondary distribution of income, (7) redistribution of income in kind, (8) use of disposable income account, (9) use of adjusted disposable income, (10) capital transactions, (11) financial transactions, (12) other changes in assets, (13) revaluations, (14) neutral revaluations, (15) real holding gains/losses, (16) opening balance sheet, (17) changes in balance sheet and (18) closing balance sheet. As noted in the proposed revision, these set of accounts are designed to answer 'Who does What by means of What for what purpose with Whom in exchange for What with What Changes in stocks?'

Given this level of complexity, there is a distinct danger that when the revised SNA is actually put in place, it, like the Hubble telescope, may not be successful in bringing into focus a clear view of what it was designed to examine. Only professional national accountants will be able to fathom the national accounts. Furthermore, the establishment of such an elaborate system as the standard to be adopted by national and international statistical offices may result in the SNA becoming a statistical behemoth independent of its creators and with an illogic of its own — not unlike a Frankenstein monster. One of the major virtues of national accounting systems used by many countries is that they do provide a relatively simple macroeconomic overview of the economic system. There is a considerable danger that in elaborating the SNA this important function will be lost. Serious reconsideration should be given to implementing the proposal made by the Netherlands Statistical Office for a simpler set of 'core' accounts. These accounts would record the actual transactions of the major transactors in the economy that underlie the larger and more elaborate set of SNA accounts.

With respect to the question whether the SNA will provide an adequate framework for the wide spectrum of analytic uses for data about the economy, it should be recognized that the SNA is both conceptually and statistically a set of aggregate accounts designed to be presented as tabulations. In a sense the SNA is a prisoner of the printed page and punch card mentality: it reflects both data needs and data technology characteristic of the past 50 years. The SNA proposed revision has not been designed to take advantage of the recent developments and anticipated future changes in both data needs and data technology.

Considering the present analytic needs for detailed information about the economic system and the capabilities of modern computers, the national accounts should be constructed in a manner capable of integrating and accessing microdata bases derived from administrative sources and large samples. If the national accounts cannot provide efficient access to such detailed data, both business and governments will increasingly come to depend on private proprietary data bases, and the advantages of an overall integrated system will be lost.

However, if a set of core accounts is used to record the transactions of enterprises, governments and households in the national accounts, these accounts could be directly related to a wide variety of microdata bases referring to such entities and their transactions. Harmonization of concepts used for the national accounts and microdata sources would be required, and the familiar problems of data reconciliation would need to be resolved. However, it is absurd to believe that these problems are insurmountable in a world where computers put through telephone calls almost instantaneously, airline reservations can be made in a few seconds, and credit cards are checked in a matter of minutes.

The revised SNA should be built around the task of integrating macro-aggregates with the underlying microdata. From an analytic point of view such integration is essential if computational techniques such as microsimulation modeling utilizing longitudinal data are to be related to macroeconomic analysis.

15. Statistical Measurements for Economic Systems in Transition: Strategy for Implementing the UN System of National Accounts (SNA)

Richard Ruggles
Yale University

1. INTRODUCTION: THE UNITED NATIONS SYSTEM OF NATIONAL ACCOUNTS

In developing statistical measurements for economies in transition, it has been proposed that the United Nations System of National Accounts (SNA) should be implemented for the Soviet Union. Not only would the UN System of National Accounts be more appropriate than the Material Product System for analyzing and evaluating the behavior of a market-oriented economy, it could also serve as a framework for integrating other types of statistical measures relating to the economy, and provide greater comparability with the statistics of other western countries and international statistical agencies.

If the implementation of the United Nations System of National Accounts involved merely the construction of estimates for a few macro aggregates such as gross national product and gross domestic product, such a task might be accomplished relatively easily. However, the development of a complete national accounting system suitable for understanding the behavior of the Soviet economy in its transition to a market-oriented transactions system is far more complex and involves strategic decisions about the kinds of information that would be required. The United Nations System of National Accounts consists of a logically consistent framework for economic accounts based on

---

This chapter first appeared in Petr O. Aven (ed.) with the assistance of Christoph M. Schneider, *Economies in Transition: Statistical Measures Now and in the Future*, Proceedings of the Sochi International Forum, October 1990.

internationally agreed concepts, definitions, conventions, classifications and accounting rules.

Prior to examining just what strategy might be adopted by the Soviet Union for implementing the United Nations System of National Accounts, it will be useful, as background, to examine briefly the nature and content of the UN System of National Accounts in terms of its origins and development, its revision in 1968 and the background of its current review.

The Origins and Development of the SNA

Although national income measurement has had a long and honorable history that has been chronicled by Paul Studenski and others, national accounting is a relatively recent development. In 1940, Ragnar Frisch in Norway wrote about constructing national accounts for the purposes of macroeconomic analysis, and in the Netherlands, Jan Tinbergen had used national accounting concepts in his development of econometric models. In England, Richard Stone and James Meade, under the guidance of Keynes, developed for the UK Treasury an analysis of national income and expenditure that put into operational form the concepts laid out in Keynes's *General Theory*; this was published in a White Paper in April 1941.

It was clear that national accounting was an idea whose time had come. The ideas presented in the British White Papers were also being developed in the United States. As early as 1942, the two sides of a national income and expenditure account were developed and considerable use was made of this account in analyzing the inflationary gap resulting from the financing of war expenditures.

In the fall of 1945, Richard Stone prepared a report for the League of Nations on *The Measurement of National Income and the Construction of Social Accounts*. In this report, he advocated setting up a system of accounts to record the money flows and related bookkeeping transactions between different sectors in the economy. Although by now these basic principles of national accounting are well recognized, in 1945 they were a major innovation and were not easily accepted. Kuznets, for example, viewed national accounting as 'a dubious addition to the theoretical equipment by aid of which we define national income and reckon its distribution'.

Nevertheless, immediately after World War II, the US Economic Cooperation Administration and the Organization for European Economic Cooperation agreed that national income accounts should be used as the framework for planning and monitoring European economic recovery. Richard Stone was called on to set up a national accounts research unit, and to develop a 'Standardized System of National Accounts'. The resulting six-account system, which appeared in 1952, was far simpler that the system outlined in the 1947

League of Nations report, and bears a striking resemblance to the present national income accounting system used by the United States. It consisted of the following accounts: (1) national product and expenditure account, (2) national income account, (3) general government appropriation account, (4) household and nonprofit institution appropriation account, (5) consolidated capital transactions account and (6) rest-of-world transactions account.

The United States national accounts combine the national product and expenditure account and the national income account into a single national income and product account, but the other accounts are essentially similar to those of the 1952 SNA.

During this period, Stone also chaired an Expert Group that was drawing up a System of National Accounts for the United Nations. Understandably, the UN SNA, which appeared in 1953, was quite similar to the OEEC 'Standardized System'. The major differences were that rudimentary capital reconciliation accounts were shown for households, government and the rest of the world. The latter were intended to show the impact of saving and investment on assets and liabilities, but they were very consolidated and summary in nature.

An additional feature of the first UN SNA was that standard tables were appended to the accounts that gave alternative or more detailed breakdowns of the data in the accounts and provided standard classifications. With this first SNA as a basis, the United Nations Statistical Office developed a National Accounts Questionnaire which it sent out to countries to collect national accounting data. In the late 1950s the United Nations began publication of the *Yearbook of National Account Statistics*.

The 1968 Revision of the SNA

At the same time as the national income accounts were being developed, there were developments in related fields of economic accounting. Wassily Leontief had been working on input–output analysis since the 1930s. By analyzing inter-industry requirements and the destination of industry outputs, Leontief was able to show how the industrial structure of the economic system could be expected to change with changes in the final demand for goods and services. In the period after World War II, many countries undertook the construction of input–output tables, and in some countries, including Norway, Denmark and the Netherlands, input–output tables were integrated with their national accounts.

Over these years, work was also being carried out on monetary and financial statistics. In the US, Morris Copeland developed sources and uses of funds accounts for recording a comprehensive system of money flows. At this same time, Raymond Goldsmith was estimating national wealth and national balance sheets using a perpetual inventory method. This involved cumulating the capital formation data in the national income accounts over long periods to obtain estimates of the stocks of tangible assets. These were then combined with financial transactions data in the flow of funds to obtain balance sheets.

It gradually became apparent that all of these economic accounting systems should be integrated into a single framework, and that the 1952 SNA was not sufficiently comprehensive in its scope to serve as such a framework. In the early 1960s, as a consequence, Stone was again called on to head an effort to create such an integrated system. Although the development of the revised SNA involved the cooperation of statisticians from many national statistical offices, the basic SNA Blue Book (UN, 1968) was primarily the product of Richard Stone working with Abraham Aidenoff, the Director of the United Nations National Accounts Office.

The revised SNA was completed in 1968 and, as intended, it provided a comprehensive and detailed framework for recording the stocks and flows in the economy. It brought together in an articulated coherent system data ranging in degree of aggregation from the consolidated accounts of the old SNA to detailed input–output and flow of funds tables.

The revised SNA, like the old SNA, was designed to provide international guidance to national statistical offices wanting to improve, elaborate and extend their national accounts and their system of basic statistics. It was recognized that many countries would not be able to compile all the data in the full system, but it was felt that the new SNA would establish goals for advancing national accounting and systems of basic statistics for the foreseeable future.

Paradoxically, although the well-known SNA Blue Book was recognized as the basic document describing the SNA, there was no agreement about what actually constituted the SNA. It was not unlike the three blind men describing an elephant. The SNA theorists cited the Blue Book's presentation of the extended matrix as the embodiment of the SNA, but SNA practitioners were quick to point out that the extended matrix was merely used to illustrate the general nature of a complete system that was never intended to be implemented. Instead, SNA practitioners argued that the heart of the SNA was contained in Chapter VIII of the Blue Book where examples of standard accounts and tables were presented.

But even the standard accounts and tables were of an illustrative nature and never were fully implemented by any country. As a consequence, users of SNA statistics held the view that the SNA consisted of the data published in the United Nations National Accounts *Yearbook*, which in turn was based on the United Nations National Accounts Questionnaire. Although the National Accounts Questionnaire was conceptually related to the standard accounts and tables contained in the Blue Book, it omitted many accounts and tables and differed from others in important respects. In 1979, there was a major revision and extension of the UN National Accounts Questionnaire that broke new ground and introduced new kinds of information not contemplated by the Blue Book.

The Background of the Current Review of the SNA

In the early 1970s, before countries had an opportunity to implement the revised SNA, the values implicit in the traditional measures of economic progress began to be questioned. Specifically, it was argued that national income accounting measures did not adequately reflect the deterioration of the environment, the using up of resources and the disamenities of modern society. Some viewed GNP as standing for gross national pollution, and urged that small was beautiful, and that happiness was learning to do without. Even those who did not take such extreme positions were forced to recognize that the data reported in the national accounts did not adequately measure the quality of life. Furthermore there was an increasing concern with the distribution of well-being: it was argued that an increase in aggregate output might be accompanied by a worsening in the distribution of that output.

In the United States, the government programs of the 'Great Society' were intended to address these concerns, and the statistical information required for their planning administration and evaluation was very different from that envisaged by the SNA. What was needed was information about the demographic, social and economic characteristics of the population, so that programs could be designed to help those who needed help. Although the revised SNA recognized the topic of income distribution, preliminary guidelines on this subject were not published until almost a decade later — and these guidelines were in direct conflict with the SNA as presented in the Blue Book. Little attention was devoted to cost/benefit analysis or measurement of the effects of government programs on the distribution of total consumption of the population.

Perhaps the greatest blow to the use of national income accounting as a basis for analyzing the behavior of the economy came from the stagflation which developed in the 1970s. Keynesian economists held the view that inflation and recession could not occur simultaneously. With the fuel crisis of 1973 and subsequent double-digit inflation and recession, this view was largely discredited. Those advocating supply-side or monetarist economic policies felt that income determination models based on the national accounts were largely irrelevant.

The inflationary process of the 1970s, of course, involved changes in relative prices, and revaluations of assets and liabilities that produced both capital gains and capital losses. Although the revised SNA did in principle make provision for balance sheets and even proposed revaluation accounts, these were not implemented in detail in the 1968 Blue Book. As in the case of income distribution statistics, provisional guidelines for balance sheets and reconciliation accounts were not published until almost a decade later.

The concerns of the 1970s and the dissatisfaction with the existing national accounting framework led in a variety of directions. Some investigators undertook to adjust the existing national account aggregates in order to obtain better measurements of economic welfare. Others sought to introduce additional imputations in order to increase the comprehensiveness of the national accounts and improve their usefulness for a wider range of economic analysis. Still others focused on the social demographic and other information which lay outside the framework of national accounts, and sought ways in which to link this information with the accounts.

National accounting aggregates have always contained some imputations. Traditionally, imputations have been made for nonmarket agricultural production, the services of owner-occupied housing, and services provided by financial intermediaries. Many economists have argued that the national accounts should be extended to embrace all nonmarket activity, and that it should include intangible and human capital as well as tangible capital.

National statistical offices looked outside of the national accounts for social indicators which could be used to monitor social conditions, formulate goals for social policy, and evaluate the social change taking place. In this context, Richard Stone developed for the United Nations a System of Social and Demographic Statistics (SSDS). This system set up social and demographic accounts that could be linked to the national accounts.

For development planning, a number of investigators constructed Social Accounting Matrices that introduced social and demographic breakdowns into the SNA national accounting matrix presentation. In France 'Satellite Accounts' were developed to augment the national accounts by providing more detailed or more comprehensive information relating to specific activities in the national accounts. Finally, with computerization and the increased availability of microdata, many investigators were pursuing the analysis of microdata or developing microanalytic modeling quite independently of the national accounts.

In the late 1970s, a review of the 1968 SNA was proposed. The initial reaction of the representatives of the national statistical offices and the international statistical agencies was that since the 1968 revision was in the process of being absorbed and was still unimplemented by most countries, any significant revision would merely confuse matters further. By 1982, however, it was agreed that there should be an SNA review that should clarify and simplify the SNA concepts, harmonize them with other related systems of statistics, and update the system to fit new circumstances.

Despite the general consensus that the SNA should not be altered significantly, the SNA Review has turned into a thoroughgoing and detailed examination of the SNA. From 1982 through 1985, the basic issues to be reviewed were identified and studies on these issues were prepared by international organizations and national statistical offices. These studies were then circulated to experts and to regional meetings where national statistical offices were represented. During the period from 1986 to 1988 expert groups were convened to discuss specific topics such as the structure of the accounts, the public sector accounts, external transactions, the household sector, price and quantity measures, production accounts and input–output tables, and financial flows of the system.

Since 1988, Peter Hill, under the direction of the United Nations Statistical Office, has been engaged in drafting *A Revised System of National Accounts* that incorporates the revisions resulting from the review of the SNA. The OECD, EUROSTAT, the International Monetary Fund, the World Bank, United Nations Regional Commissions and other international organizations have actively participated in contributing to and reviewing preliminary drafts of this manuscript. A final draft of the proposed revision is expected to be submitted to the United Nations Statistical Commission in 1992.

2. STRATEGY FOR IMPLEMENTING THE UN SYSTEM OF NATIONAL ACCOUNTS (SNA)

In developing a strategy for implementing the United Nations System of National Accounts for the Soviet Union, two questions need to be considered: which version of the SNA should be implemented — the 1968 version or the present revision that is expected in 1992? And what is involved in deciding to implement either the 1968 SNA or the current revision?

First, with respect to the choice between the 1968 SNA and the proposed revision, it should be noted the SNA revision is not as yet available in its final form and it may not be available for several years. On the other hand, many of the changes anticipated in the proposed revision consist of incorporating material already included in UN manuals that have been issued since the 1968 Blue Book was published. Similarly, there has been an attempt to harmonize the 1968 SNA with the statistics published by other major international organizations. It would seem most reasonable to adopt those changes that are clear improvements or bring the SNA more in line with other international statistics. Other changes which are primarily extensions of the SNA into new areas of statistics might be postponed until such time as the basic SNA system has been implemented.

Second, the question as to what is involved in implementing the SNA needs clarification. It was already noted in the discussion of the 1968 SNA that there has been considerable confusion as to just what actually constitutes the SNA — the SNA matrix, the standard accounts and tables shown in Chapter VIII of the Blue Book or the UN National Accounts Questionnaire? Recently, the United Nations Statistical Office (1990a), in its discussion paper for the 1990 Regional Commission meetings on the SNA, has clarified this question with respect to the current revision of the SNA with the following statement:

> It should be emphasized that the revised system is foremost a theoretical construct which has been elaborated in all of its detail in order to give guidance to countries with different types of economies and provide a basis for different types of specialized analysis. This implies that the system should not be looked at from the point of view of immediate and/or comprehensive implementation, but from a broader viewpoint of its applicability to a wide range of countries in the long run. A further consequence of this is that the tables, matrices and accounts included in the system are designed to explain the features of the SNA and not for compilation of data at a national or international level.

Given these considerations, it becomes important for Soviet statisticians to examine the central features of both the present SNA and its proposed revision with reference to their appropriateness for monitoring the Soviet economy and analyzing its transition to a market-oriented transactions system. The central features required for constructing an appropriate system of national accounts can be classified into four categories. *First*, an appropriate sectoring will be required to show the interaction of different parts of the economic system. *Second*, an accounting structure will need to be erected to provide a framework for showing the transactions that take place between sectors of the economy. *Third*, specific imputations or attributions will need to be made in order to supplement the transactions information contained in the sector accounts. *Fourth*, economic constructs will need to be built up from the sector core transaction accounts and imputation modules.

Sectoring the Economy

In the present SNA, the institutional sectoring of the economy consists of: corporate and quasi-corporate enterprises, general government, nonprofit institutions serving households, unincorporated enterprises and households, and (*de facto*) rest of the world.

For the revised SNA, it is proposed that nonprofit institutions serving households be eliminated as a major sector and included as part of the household sector, thus reducing the number of major sectors by one. Since, in general, national statistical offices have not implemented the SNA recommendation of treating nonprofit institutions as a separate sector of the economy, it is quite reasonable that such sectoring be abandoned.

The preference of many national accounts for including nonprofit institutions in the household sector has been primarily based on the lack of adequate data. The estimates for final consumption for households have usually been derived residually — and often still are. Reliable data on the final consumption of nonprofit institutions are usually not available, so it has not been possible to separate them from household final consumption. Since households were considered to be the consumers of the goods and services provided by nonprofit institutions, the most appropriate solution has been not to distinguish separately such goods and services.

In reality, the current SNA proposal for creating a combined household and nonprofit institution sector is confirmation of the present macrostatistical approach of treating the household sector as a residual. It is doubtful whether many countries will attempt to produce the more detailed separation of the sector into subsectors of nonprofit institutions and type of households.

Nonprofit institutions in many countries now represent a significant part of the economy, and may become more important in the foreseeable future. They consist of schools, universities, hospitals and associations as well as religious and charitable organizations. They cover a broad variety of research, educational, health, recreational and other activities — and they exist along-side profit making organizations and public enterprises engaged in the same activities.

Combining households and nonprofit institution transactions with the same sector runs counter to the spirit of both the transactor/transaction approach and the integration of macro- and microdata that are being emphasized in the SNA revision. The transactions for the combined account would have little analytic meaning or use; they could not be partitioned into size distributions of income or used as control total for household microdata.

Since the revised SNA requires a complete subsectoring of nonprofit institutions, a preferable solution is to classify nonprofit institutions with other similar profit making or public enterprises. Thus they would be part of a comprehensive enterprise sector that would cover all private and public enterprises irrespective of their legal form of organization or whether or not they are of a profit-making nature. The argument is made that putting nonprofit institutions into the enterprise sector would destroy its homogeneity — and hence its analytic usefulness. This argument neglects the obvious point that the SNA enterprise sector is already extremely heterogeneous. It embraces public nonprofit enterprises, private nonprofit organizations serving business, mutual organizations and cooperatives as well as private profit-making enterprises. For economies in transition, it would be particularly important to subsector the enterprise sector in a manner such that it would be possible to monitor the behavior of market-oriented enterprises.

Both the existing and revised SNA distinguish between quasi-corporate enterprises that are included in the corporate sector and unincorporated enterprises that are included in the household sector. The stated criterion is that in order for an enterprise unit to be included with corporate enterprises as a quasi-corporate enterprise, it should have a complete set of accounts. In contrast, it is argued. where the accounts of unincorporated enterprises are not distinguished from household accounts, these enterprises should be relegated to the household sector.

Although, conceptually, this approach might appear reasonable, it is not easily applied on a case-by-case basis and does not conform to normal reporting unit information. For farming, for example, it is more reasonable to treat all farms that sell farm products as being in the same sector, rather than including some in the enterprise sector and relegating others to the household sector. If distinctions are to be made, farms might be classified by size and type of farm within the enterprise sector rather than relegating different farms to separate sectors on the basis of subjective accounting criteria.

Thus the classification of the economy into major sectors would be as follows: (1) enterprises (public, private, profit and nonprofit), (2) government and governmental units, (3) households and (4) rest of the world.

The Accounting Structure

The 1968 SNA Blue Book presents a relatively simple accounting structure consisting of accounts for: (1) production, (2) consumption expenditure, (3) income and outlays, (4) capital formation and (5) capital finance.

However, this accounting structure was not to be applied to all sectors. Accounts 1, 2 and 4 (production, consumption expenditures and capital formation) were to be drawn up for those industries and sectors directly involved in production or consumption. These accounts were to serve the basis for the make and use matrices underlying input–output tables.

Accounts 3 and 5 (income and outlays and capital finance) were to be implemented for institutional sectors. The omission of production and capital formation accounts for institutional sectors has made it difficult to analyze the relation of saving, capital finance and capital formation in the economy. Although the SNA matrix recognized the existence of balance sheets, these accounts were not specifically included in the accounting structure shown in Chapter VIII of the UN Blue Book.

United Nations manuals on balance sheets and on tangible assets did not appear until 1977 and 1979 respectively (1977a, 1979). The 1980 revision of the SNA (1980) National Accounts Questionnaire did make provision for a full set of accounts, including balance sheets for all institutional sectors, and the current proposed SNA revision has not only incorporated a full set of accounts for institutional sectors; it has gone considerably further and presents an elaborate and complex set of interlinked cascading accounts for each institutional sector showing: (1) production, (2) generation of income, (3) appropriation of primary income, (4) entrepreneurial income, (5) appropriation of other primary income, (6) secondary distribution of income, (7) redistribution of income in kind, (8) use of disposable income account, (9) use of adjusted disposable income, (10) capital transactions, (11) financial transactions, (12) other changes in assets, (13) revaluations, (14) neutral revaluations, (15) real holding gains/losses, (16) opening balance sheet, (17) changes in balance sheet and (18) closing balance sheet

As the proposed revision notes, these sets of accounts are designed to answer 'Who does What by means of What for what purpose with Whom in exchange for What with What Changes in stocks?' (UN, 1990b).

One of the major virtues of the national accounting systems used by most countries is that they do provide a relatively simple macroeconomic overview of the economic system. There is considerable danger that in elaborating the SNA this important function will be lost. Serious reconsideration should be given to implementing the proposal made by the Netherlands Statistical Office for a simpler set of 'core' accounts (Van Bochove and Van Tuinen, 1986).

Considering the present analytic needs for detailed information about the economic system and the capabilities of modern computers, the national accounts should be constructed so that they are capable of integrating and accessing microdata bases derived from administrative sources and large samples. The SNA accounting structure was not designed to meet these needs. It has been and still is conceptually and statistically a set of aggregate accounts designed to be presented as tabulations. The proposed revision of the SNA has not been designed to take advantage of recent developments and anticipated future changes in both data needs and data technology.

The basic accounting structure underlying the revised SNA needs to be built around the task of integrating the macrosector accounts and aggregates with the underlying microdata. From an analytic point of view, such integration is essential if mesodata consistent with the national accounts are to be developed from existing microdata and if microsimulation modeling is to be successfully related to macroeconomic analysis. For these purposes, it is recommended that the following core accounts be established for each of the major sectors of the economy: current receipts and outlays, capital transactions and balance sheets.

These core accounts would be on a consolidated basis and would provide the framework for recording all the actual transactions taking place between enterprises, governments, households and the rest of the world. They represent the basic accounts used for business purposes by enterprises and for budgeting by governments and households. Harmonization of the concepts used for national accounts and related microdata sources would be required, and the familiar problems of data reconciliation would need to be resolved, but the core accounts would provide the framework for both recording all of the transactions contained in the United Nations System of National Accounts, and making it possible to relate them to microdata.

It is recognized that core balance sheet accounts pose many problems and are difficult to implement. There are questions of how assets and liabilities are to be valued and revalued. Few national statistical offices will be capable of providing complete balance sheet accounts within the immediate future. However, for some sectors and for some types of assets and liabilities data on the stock held may be available, and it will be useful if the information on current receipts and outlays and on capital transactions can be related to the information of the existing stock of specific assets and liabilities.

Imputations and Rerouting of Transactions

The national accounts have always taken account of certain nonmarket activities. As already noted, imputations have been made for the food and fuel produced and consumed on farms, the rental value of owner-occupied housing and the provision of financial services by banks. The valuation of imputations is often difficult and in some cases quite arbitrary. Imputed values do not have the same significance as actual transactions. Despite such considerations both the current SNA and its proposed revision combine market transactions and imputations for nonmarket activity in the same account.

Food and fuel consumed on farms
In the case of food and fuel consumed on farms, the problem of imputation is relatively simple. By providing a separate module in the national accounts for imputations, it is possible to distinguish clearly between the actual market transactions taking place in the economy and the imputations for nonmarket activity. In the case of countries where subsistence agriculture is particularly important, this separation would be very useful for monitoring the shift from a subsistence to a market economy.

Owner-occupied housing
The treatment of owner-occupied housing is somewhat more complex: in order to record the services of owner-occupied housing the SNA not only introduces imputations, but it reroutes existing transactions related to owner-occupied housing. Households owning their homes are considered to be renting their dwellings from themselves as real estate owners. Their activities as owners are considered to be those of unincorporated enterprises. These fictitious unincorporated enterprises own the dwellings and pay all the costs associated with them. To offset these outlays, the unincorporated enterprises receive an imputed space rental from the households as occupiers. The difference between

the space rental and the current costs of providing the housing services is returned to households as imputed rental income.

The actual costs of owner-occupancy, including maintenance expenditures, property taxes, insurance, mortgage interest, imputed interest on the owner's equity and capital consumption appear in the SNA as outlays and gross saving by the fictitious unincorporated enterprise.

Although this method of imputation does get the services of owner-occupied housing in both output and final consumption, it does so by distorting the accounts of both households and unincorporated enterprises. In fact, it is households that pay property taxes, interest on mortgage debt, and expenses of repair and upkeep, not unincorporated businesses in the real estate industry, and it is households that do the gross saving reflected in depreciation charges.

For both measuring the total housing consumption of individual households and to provide comparability between owned and rented housing, it is recognized that some type of imputation for the use of owner-occupied housing would be desirable. Such an imputation can, however, be made separately from the household core transactions account both as an income and consumption without the necessity of rerouting all the related transactions through a fictitious unincorporated enterprise. By following the transactor/ transaction approach, the current costs of owner-occupied housing would be recorded in the core account as actual outlays by households. A separate imputation could then be made in the imputation module for the difference between such costs and the imputed space rental value of the owner-occupied housing.

Financial services
The imputation for the provision of financial services arises from the treatment of interest in the national accounts as a transfer rather than as a payment for a financial service. Nevertheless, it is also true that depositors in a financial institution often accept a rate of interest on their deposits that is below the market rate in exchange for receiving financial services — this suggests that they are receiving an imputed return on their funds in the form of financial services. One of the further consequences of treating interest as a transfer is that consumer interest on installment debt for durables such as automobiles is not considered to be part of the cost of purchase or use of automobiles, and therefore is not included as a consumer expenditure. In any case, it would be possible to show imputations for financial services separately from the core accounts in the imputation module.

Services of consumer durables
One of the more obvious omissions in both the present SNA and the proposed revision is the failure to impute the nonmarket services provided by household durable goods. Although the SNA revision is very much concerned with

expanding the definition of enterprise and government capital formation to include research and development, computer software and even intellectual property, it does not recognize household capital formation. Since owner-occupied housing is treated as being owned and operated by unincorporated enterprises, it does get included in capital formation, but other purchases of durable goods by households are considered to be current expenditures.

Much of the consumer credit extended to households relates to the purchase of automobiles and other consumer durables. Both households and financial institutions recognize that such purchases do not represent merely consumption in the current period, but that the good purchased continues to have value and provide services over a period of years. It is appropriate that the national accounts should also recognize consumer durables as capital formation. As is done for owner-occupied housing, an imputation needs to be made for the services of consumer durables so that total consumption and its change over time can be more accurately measured.

Household nonmarket activity

Most national accountants have been reluctant to extend imputations to such household market activities as household services, education and leisure activities. They argue that such imputations are so large that it is very difficult to impute an economically meaningful figure for them. Including imputations of this magnitude would tilt the balance of the system away from monetary transaction and greatly reduce its usefulness for the analysis of markets and for purposes of policy-making.

Insofar as imputations are combined in the national accounts with actual transactions, the argument against introducing imputations for household non-market activity is quite valid. On the other hand, if core accounts contain the actual transactions taking place between the major sectors, and separate modules exist for presenting imputations, it may be found useful to expand the range of imputations beyond what is currently anticipated. Imputations for household nonmarket activity based on time use studies of households have the advantage that they can reveal the substitution taking place between household market activity and nonmarket activity, and show how households allocate their total resources.

Benefits in kind

In the present SNA, benefits in kind received by households from the government are treated as part of household income and household final consumption expenditures. Under the proposed SNA revision transfers in kind by the government will not be included in either household primary income or in household consumption expenditures. Instead, a redistribution of income-in-kind account will show those social benefits in kind, benefits for which the household is reimbursed by the government, and the value of individualized nonmarket services provided by the government, like education, not included in social benefits in kind. This separation of final consumption expenditures from benefits in kind is quite appropriate for analyzing consumer behavior on the one hand and the total consumption of households on the other. Although the introduction of a redistribution-in-kind account can accomplish this separation, the use of a module for imputations accomplishes the same purpose without increasing the complexity of the accounting structure.

With respect to benefits in kind provided by employers to employees — such as medical services and day care services provided by employers — both the present SNA and the proposed SNA revision either omit such benefits entirely by considering them to be part of producers' intermediate costs or include such benefits as part of the compensation received by employees and as imputed household expenditures. Both of these treatments are clearly inconsistent with the proposed treatment accorded to benefits in kind provided by government.

Employers' pensions and insurance

Another major rerouting of actual transactions relates to the handling of employers' payments to life insurance, private pension and welfare funds on behalf of their employees. Both the present SNA and the proposed revision attribute such payments as part of the current compensation received by employees, and therefore as part of household income. Income earned by the pension and insurance funds is also attributed to households as part of their current income. The portion of the contribution which represents the costs of operating the insurance companies and pension funds — called the service charge — is treated as personal consumption expenditures.

As a consequence of these attributions, the full increase in the reserves held by insurance companies and pension funds, therefore, is attributed to personal saving. Households are thus considered to own the reserves of the insurance companies and pension funds. The net equity of these funds appears on the household sector balance sheet, and interest earned on the reserves is attributed as current income to households, although of course they do not receive it.

As a corollary to this treatment in the SNA, pension benefits and life insurance annuities actually paid to households do not appear as part of household income because such treatment would involve double counting. It would be included as income initially when the employers' contribution is paid to the insurance company or pension fund and subsequently when the benefit is paid to the household. As a consequence, the receipt of such benefits is considered to represent only a change in the form of the assets held by the household, from net equity in life insurance and pension funds to cash.

Household survey microdata usually reverse this treatment. Pension and annuity benefit payments received by households are included in household income and employers' payments of contributions to pension funds and insurance are not. Interest on pension and insurance reserves is not attributed to the household, and the household balance sheet does not include equity in employer-financed pension and insurance reserves.

In the United Nations *Guidelines* on income distribution statistics, the household survey treatment of pensions and insurance is recommended rather than that of the SNA (1977b). Where the focus is on the distribution of income, it is clearly undesirable to treat pensioners as having zero income — that would not contribute much to an understanding of the position of the aged in the economy. Conversely, entitlement of younger persons to benefits that will become available only on retirement or death are substantively different from cash income received in the present period. Furthermore, employers' contributions for insurance and pensions and earnings of insurance and pension funds are a poor and unstable measure even of the present value of those future rights.

By modifying the current SNA treatment of pensions and insurance, it is possible to adhere more closely to the transactor/transaction principle and provide better integration with microdata concepts. Employers' contributions to pension and insurance funds would be treated as funds held in escrow for future payment to employees. Pension benefits would be considered as income when they are actually paid out to individuals. Such an approach would also be more in accord with the treatment of public social security pensions and unfunded private pension systems.

3. IMPLEMENTATION OF CORE ACCOUNTS, IMPUTATIONS AND ECONOMIC CONSTRUCTS

In order to provide a better understanding of the strategy of developing core accounts and imputation modules for a system of national accounts, it will be useful to demonstrate how actual core accounts and imputation modules can be created for the United States. These core accounts and modules can then be used to create the major economic constructs and accounts of the United Nations System of National Accounts.

Although the present United States National Accounts do not provide the elaborate structure of either the 1968 United Nations SNA or its current proposed revision, it does resemble the UN 1952 SNA and by adding sector accounts for enterprises it can be converted quite easily to the more recent versions of the UN SNA. Furthermore, unlike the UN SNA, the United States provides separate information on the specific imputations that have been included in the accounts, thus making it possible to construct sector core accounts of the actual transactions taking place in the economy.

A form of such sector core accounts have been drawn up and published in an issue of the *Survey of Current Business* published by the Bureau of Economic Analysis of the Department of Commerce (Ruggles and Ruggles, 1982). The implementation of the core accounts in the following sections draws on the material in that study using a software system PRTAB2 developed by Prospect Research Corporation for the handling of national accounting systems on personal computers.

Sector Core Accounts

Sector core accounts delineate the actual transactions taking place between the major sectors of the economy. In this presentation, core accounts will be developed for enterprises, households, government and gross saving and capital formation. The accounting system is articulated in the sense that each transaction flow appearing in a sector account is matched by a corresponding transaction flow in another sector account. Thus the receipt of one sector is matched by the outlay of another sector. The gross saving and capital formation accounts contain the residual saving entry in each of the sector accounts and their capital transactions. These sector core accounts are as follows:

Table 15.1: ENTCUR (Enterprise Current Receipts and Outlay Account)
Table 15.2: HHCUR (Household Current Market Income and Outlay Account)
Table 15.3: GOVCUR (Government Current Receipts and Outlay Account)
Table 15.4: ROWCUR (Rest-of-World Current Account)
Table 15.5: SICAP (Gross Saving and Capital Formation Account)

The enterprise core account — Table 15.1
The enterprise sector is defined as embracing not only corporate and unincorporated businesses, but also public enterprises, nonprofit organizations and self-employed, including domestic servants. It thus covers all market-oriented production. The enterprise core account shown in Table 15.1 is on a consolidated basis; this means that the current receipts and current outlays of enterprises for goods and services used in intermediate production are consolidated out of the account. At the most detailed level of entries in the account, the name of the sector account and the line number are given where the corresponding entry can be found.

The major source of enterprise receipts is its sales of goods and services. These are shown as: sales to enterprises (line 2), sales to households (line 9), sales to government (line 15) and net sales to rest of world (line 18).

In addition enterprises receive funds in the form of: interest (line 21), income from rest of the world (line 24), transfers received (line 28) and receipts from withheld employer pension contributions (line 32).

Table 15.1 ENTCUR, Enterprise Current Receipts and Outlay Account
($bn, current year prices)

Line		Account	Line	1980
1	TOTAL Enterprise Current Receipts	Sum L(2,9,15,18,21,24,28,32)		2,563.4
2	*Sales to enterprises*	L3+L6		435.4
3	Current purchases (net)	L4+L5		104.6
4	Employee benefits in kind	ENTCUR	L41	55.8
5	Nonprofit benefits in kind	ENTCUR	L62	48.8
6	Capital purchases	SICAP	L9	330.8
7	Structures and durables	SICAP	L10	335.6
8	Change in stocks	SICAP	L11	–4.8
9	*Sales to households*	L10+L11		1,348.8
10	Current consumption expenditures	HHCUR	L18	1,036.8
11	Capital purchases	SICAP	L15	312.0
12	Owner-occupied housing	SICAP	L16	85.2
13	Consumer durables	SICAP	L17	211.9
14	Change in stocks	SICAP	L18	14.9
15	*Sales to government*	L16+L17		318.3
16	Current purchases (net)	GOVCUR	L21	272.3
17	Capital purchases	SICAP	L13	46.0
18	*Sales to rest of the world (net)*	L19+L20		–4.4
19	Exports	ROWCUR	L18	247.0
20	Less: Imports	ROWCUR	L3	251.4
21	*Interest received*	L22+L23		199.7
22	From households	HHCUR	L20	125.6
23	From government	GOVCUR	L40	74.1
24	*Income received from rest of world*	L25+L26+L27		81.0
25	Interest	ROWCUR	L23	42.7
26	Dividends	ROWCUR	L25	22.5
27	Retained corporate profits	ROWCUR	L26	15.8
28	*Transfers received*	L29+L30+L31		57.8
29	Household contribution to nonprofits	HHCUR	L28	39.9
30	Government grants to nonprofits	GOVCUR	L36	10.9
31	Subsidies	GOVCUR	L37	7.0
32	*Employer pension fund reserves*	L33+L34+L35		126.8
33	Enterprise withheld pension contributions	ENTCUR	L40	76.3
34	Government withheld pension contributions	GOVCUR	L28	6.0
35	Interest on pension fund reserves	ENTCUR	L49	44.5

The outlay and gross saving side of the account shows how the enterprise sector distributed the funds it has received and how much has been retained in enterprises on a gross basis. Unlike the United States National Accounts and the United Nations SNA, the compensation of employees (line 37) is not treated as all being paid to households. The enterprise core account recognizes that employer social security taxes (line 39) are paid to the government, employer contributions to pension funds and employee benefits in kind (lines 40 and 41) are withheld, and only actual wage and salary payments (line 38) are disbursed to households. On the other hand, the payment of employee

Line	Account		Line	1980
36 TOTAL Enterprise Current Outlays and Gross Saving	Sum L(37,43..45,50,54,55, 58,59,62,63)			2,563.4
37 *Compensation of employees*	Sum L38..L42			1,327.8
38 Wage and salary payments to households	HHCUR		L3	1,116.4
39 Employer social security taxes	GOVCUR		L3	78.8
40 Withheld pension fund contributions	ENTCUR		L32	76.3
41 Employee benefits in kind	ENTCUR		L4	55.8
42 Wage and salary payments to rest of world	ROWCUR		L7	0.5
43 *Entrepreneurial and self-employed income*	HHCUR		L6	124.3
44 *Rental income*	HHCUR		L7	19.8
45 *Interest paid*	Sum L46..L49			289.4
46 To households	HHCUR		L8	165.5
47 To government	GOVCUR		L6	50.3
48 To rest of the world	ROWCUR		L8	29.1
49 To pension reserve funds	ENTCUR		L34	44.5
50 *Dividends paid*	L51+L52+L53			57.3
51 To households	HHCUR		L9	51.8
52 To government	GOVCUR		L7	1.6
53 To rest of the world	ROWCUR		L9	3.9
54 Retained corporate profits by rest of the world	ROWCUR		L10	3.2
55 *Taxes paid*	L56+L57			268.0
56 Indirect taxes	GOVCUR		L4	185.7
57 Corporate profits taxes	GOVCUR		L5	82.3
58 *Surplus of government enterprises*	GOVCUR		L8	6.4
59 *Transfer payments to households*	HHCUR		L10	58.3
60 Employee pension payments	HHCUR		L11	49.4
61 Nonprofit and other transfer payments	HHCUR		L12	8.9
62 *Nonprofit benefits in kind*	ENTCUR		L5	48.8
63 *Gross enterprise saving*	SICAP		L2	360.1
64 Gross retained earnings by enterprises	SICAP		L3	283.4
65 Net income retained by employee pension funds	SICAP		L4	77.4
66 Statistical discrepancy	SICAP		L5	−0.7

pensions (line 60) and the net income retained by employee pension funds (line 65) are shown explicitly.

The household core account — Table 15.2

The household core account corresponds conceptually to a microdata household survey view of household transactions. On the income side, wage and salaries (line 2) and actual money transfer payments — including employee pension payments — (lines 10 and 11) are shown as income received, but withheld compensation and benefits in kind provided by government and employers

Table 15.2 HHCUR, Household Current Market Income and Outlay Account ($bn, current year prices)

Line		Account	Line	1980
1	TOTAL Household Current Market Income	Sum L(2,6..10,13)		1,999.0
2	*Wages and salaries received*	L3+L4+L5		1,337.6
3	From enterprises	ENTCUR	L38	1,116.4
4	From government	GOVCUR	L26	220.8
5	From the rest of the world	ROWCUR	L21	0.4
6	*Entrepreneurial and self-employed income*	ENTCUR	L43	124.3
7	*Rental income*	ENTCUR	L44	19.8
8	*Interest income*	ENTCUR	L46	165.5
9	*Dividends*	ENTCUR	L51	51.8
10	*Transfers received from enterprises*	ENTCUR	L59	58.3
11	Employee pension payments received	ENTCUR	L60	49.4
12	Nonprofit and other transfers received	ENTCUR	L61	8.9
13	*Transfers received from government*	GOVCUR	L32	241.7
14	Social security payments	GOVCUR	L33	118.7
15	Other transfer payments	GOVCUR	L34	123.0
16	TOTAL Household Current Outlays and Gross Saving	Sum L(17,20,21,27,30)		1,999.0
17	*Current consumption expenditures*	L18+L19		1,052.7
18	Paid to enterprises	ENTCUR	L10	1,036.8
19	Paid to rest of the world	ROWCUR	L5	15.9
20	*Interest payments*	ENTCUR	L22	125.6
21	*Tax payments*	Sum L22..L26		453.1
22	Employee social security taxes	GOVCUR	L10	87.9
23	Personal income taxes	GOVCUR	L11	296.0
24	Estate and gift taxes	GOVCUR	L12	8.8
25	Property taxes	GOVCUR	L13	27.8
26	Other taxes and nontaxes	GOVCUR	L14	32.6
27	*Transfers paid*	L28+L29		41.1
28	Contributions to nonprofits	ENTCUR	L29	39.9
29	Remittances to rest of the world (net)	ROWCUR	L14	1.2
30	*Household gross saving*	SICAP	L7	326.5

are excluded. On the outlay side, consumer expenditures on durables and imputed expenditure on owner-occupied housing are excluded from current consumption expenditures (line 17).

The government core account — Table 15.3
The government core account shows on the receipts side the payments to government by enterprises (line 2), by households (line 9) and by governmental units for social insurance taxes and benefits in kind withheld from the compensation of government employees (line 15). On the outlay side, the current consumption expenditure by government is constructed from a number of different transaction flows. Specifically, the government net current expenditures from enterprises and rest of the world (lines 21 and 22) must be added to the compensation of government employees (line 25) less that portion that is considered to constitute government capital formation (line 30).

Table 15.3 GOVCUR, Government Current Receipts and Outlay Account ($bn, current year prices)

Line		Account	Line	1980
1	TOTAL GOVERNMENT CURRENT RECEIPTS	Sum L(2,9,15,18)		903.6
2	*Payments by enterprises*	Sum L3..L8		405.1
3	Employer social security tax	ENTCUR	L39	78.8
4	Indirect taxes	ENTCUR	L56	185.7
5	Corporate profits taxes	ENTCUR	L57	82.3
6	Interest	ENTCUR	L47	50.3
7	Dividends	ENTCUR	L52	1.6
8	Surplus of government enterprises	ENTCUR	L58	6.4
9	*Payments by households*	Sum L10..L14		453.1
10	Employee social security taxes	HHCUR	L22	87.9
11	Personal income taxes	HHCUR	L23	296.0
12	Estate and gift taxes	HHCUR	L24	8.8
13	Property taxes	HHCUR	L25	27.8
14	Other taxes and nontaxes	HHCUR	L26	32.6
15	*Payments by government*	L16+L17		42.6
16	Employer social insurance taxes	GOVCUR	L27	37.0
17	Employee benefits in kind	GOVCUR	L29	5.6
18	*Interest payments by rest of the world*	ROWCUR	L24	2.8
19	TOTAL GOVERNMENT OUTLAYS AND GROSS SAVING	Sum L(20,31,39,42)		903.6
20	*Current consumption expenditures*	L(21+22+25..30)		506.5
21	Current net purchases from enterprises	ENTCUR	L16	272.3
22	Current net purchases from rest of world	L23..L24		3.8
23	Government purchases from rest of world	ROWCUR	L4	12.5
24	Less: Government sales to rest of world	ROWCUR	L19	8.7
25	Compensation of government employees	Sum L26..L29		269.4
26	Wage and salary payments	HHCUR	L4	220.8
27	Employer social security taxes	GOVCUR	L16	37.0
28	Employer pension contributions	ENTCUR	L34	6.0
29	Employee benefits in kind	GOVCUR	L17	5.6
30	Less: Compensation of government employees engaged in capital formation	SICAP	L14	39.0
31	*Transfer payments*	L32+L35+L38		264.5
32	Payments to households	HHCUR	L13	241.7
33	Social security payments	HHCUR	L14	118.7
34	Other transfer payments to households	HHCUR	L15	123.0
35	Payments to enterprises	L36+L37		17.9
36	Grants to nonprofits	ENTCUR	L30	10.9
37	Subsidies	ENTCUR	L31	7.0
38	Payments to rest of world (net)	ROWCUR	L13	4.9
39	*Interest paid*	L40+L41		86.6
40	To enterprises	ENTCUR	L23	74.1
41	To rest of world	ROWCUR	L11	12.5
42	*Gross government saving*	SICAP	L6	46.0

The rest-of-world core account — Table 15.4

The rest-of-world core account quite simply shows the receipts and payments by the rest of the world. In this account, however, the balancing item is considered to be net foreign investment (line 15) rather than foreign saving. The rationale of this treatment is that if the gross saving of domestic sectors is related to their gross capital formation, it would seem appropriate that any excess of saving should be considered to be net foreign investment.

Table 15.4 ROWCUR, Rest-of-World Current Account ($bn, current year prices)

Line		Account	Line	1980
1	CURRENT RECEIPTS BY REST OF THE WORLD	Sum L(2,6,11,12,15)		339.9
2	Imports	L3+L4+L5		279.8
3	By enterprises	ENTCUR	L20	251.4
4	By government	GOVCUR	L23	12.5
5	By households	HHCUR	L19	15.9
6	*Income paid to rest of the world by enterprises*	Sum L7..L10		36.7
7	Wages and salaries paid	ENTCUR	L42	0.5
8	Interest	ENTCUR	L48	29.1
9	Dividends	ENTCUR	L53	3.9
10	Retained corporate profits by the rest of world	ENTCUR	L54	3.2
11	*Interest paid to rest of the world by government*	GOVCUR	L41	12.5
12	*Transfers paid to rest of the world*	L13+L14		6.1
13	By government (net)	GOVCUR	L38	4.9
14	By households (net)	HHCUR	L29	1.2
15	*Net foreign investment*	SICAP	L19	4.8
16	CURRENT PAYMENTS BY REST OF THE WORLD	Sum L(17,20)		339.9
17	*Exports*	L18+L19		255.7
18	By enterprises	ENTCUR	L19	247.0
19	By government	GOVCUR	L24	8.7
20	*Income received from rest of the world*	Sum L(21,22,25,26)		84.2
21	Wages and salaries received	HHCUR	L5	0.4
22	Interest received	L23+L24		45.5
23	By enterprises	ENTCUR	L25	42.7
24	By government	GOVCUR	L18	2.8
25	Dividends received	ENTCUR	L26	22.5
26	Retained rest of the world corporate profits	ENTCUR	L27	15.8

The gross saving and capital formation account — Table 15.5

The gross saving and capital formation account draws together the gross saving appearing on the outlay side of the enterprise, household and government sector accounts and the capital formation carried out by these sectors. As already indicated, the difference between the gross saving of these sectors and their capital formation is equal to the net foreign investment (line 19).

Sector financial accounts — Table 15.6

Finally, it is possible to present, in the same sector framework, financial accounts showing the financial transactions taking place in the economy. These accounts show the changes in the assets and liabilities held by the various sectors. For many countries, these financial transaction data are provided by

Table 15.5 SICAP, Gross Saving and Capital Formation Account ($bn, current year prices)

Line		Account	Line	1980
1	GROSS SAVING	Sum L(2,6,7)		732.6
2	Enterprise gross saving	ENTCUR	L63	360.1
3	Gross retained earnings by enterprises	ENTCUR	L64	283.4
4	Retained income by pension funds	ENTCUR	L65	77.4
5	Statistical discrepancy	ENTCUR	L66	−0.7
6	Government gross saving	GOVCUR	L42	46.0
7	Household gross saving	HHCUR	L30	326.5
8	GROSS CAPITAL FORMATION	Sum L(9,12,15,19)		732.6
9	Enterprise gross capital formation	L10+L11		330.8
10	Gross fixed capital formation	ENTCUR	L7	335.6
11	Change in stocks	ENTCUR	L8	−4.8
12	Government gross capital formation	L13+L14		85.0
13	Capital purchases from enterprises	ENTCUR	L17	46.0
14	Compensation of government employees engaged in capital formation	GOVCUR	L30	39.0
15	Household gross capital formation	L16+L17+L18		312.0
16	Owner-occupied housing	ENTCUR	L12	85.2
17	Consumer durables	ENTCUR	L13	211.9
18	Change in stocks	ENTCUR	L14	14.9
19	Net foreign investment	ROWCUR	L15	4.8

banking and monetary authorities rather than by the national accounting or statistical offices. In the United States, for example, these data are published in the flow of funds statistics issued by the Federal Reserve Board rather than by the National Accounts Division of the Department of Commerce. Nevertheless, both the 1968 SNA and the current SNA revision quite appropriately integrate such financial data with national income accounting data. Such data can, furthermore, serve as the basis for developing sector and national balance sheets using perpetual inventory methods of cumulating assets, liabilities and their revaluations.

It should be recognized that for financial analysis, the enterprise sector needs to be disaggregated into subsectors along the lines recommended in the proposed revision of the SNA. The primary splitting of the enterprise sector for the purposes of financial accounts would consist of a nonfinancial subsector and a financial subsector. Further subsectoring of the financial subsector would also be needed in order to differentiate among the varieties of financial institutions such as the central bank, other banking, other financial intermediaries, and pension and insurance funds.

Financial accounts, unlike the sector transaction accounts are not articulated in the sense that the transactions taking place between each sector and subsector are shown explicitly. Instead, each type of financial asset held by all sectors should be equal to the corresponding type of liability for all sectors.

Table 15.6 *FINACCT, Sector Financial Accounts, United States, 1980 ($bn, current year prices)*

Line		1 Enter- prises	2 Govern- ment	3 House- holds	4 Rest of world	5 Total
1	TOTAL ASSETS	901.1	142.1	497.8	30.1	1,571.1
2	*Gross capital formation*	330.8	85.0	312.0	4.8	732.6
3	Structures and durables	335.6	78.3	297.1	0.0	711.0
4	Change in stocks	−4.8	6.7	14.9	0.0	16.8
5	*Land*	(NA)	(NA)	(NA)	(NA)	
6	*Gold and SDRs*	0.0	−1.1	0.0	0.0	−1.1
7	*Financial assets*	570.3	58.2	185.8	25.3	839.6
8	Currency and deposits	23.8	−6.1	175.0	1.9	194.6
9	Securities other than shares	147.1	14.4	19.0	−4.5	176.0
10	Loans	215.1	20.7	4.3	1.3	241.4
11	Shares and other equities	44.2	11.1	−19.6	16.2	51.9
12	Insurance technical reserves	77.4	0.0	0.0	0.0	77.4
13	Other accounts receivable	62.7	18.1	7.1	10.4	98.3
14	TOTAL LIABILITIES AND GROSS CURRENT SAVING	901.1	142.1	497.8	30.1	1,571.1
15	*Liabilities*	569.1	109.0	109.3	30.1	817.5
16	Currency and deposits	194.7	1.3	0.0	0.0	196.0
17	Securities other than shares	73.1	103.7	0.0	0.8	177.6
18	Loans	118.1	0.8	105.8	22.3	247.0
19	Shares and other equities	51.9	0.0	0.0	0.0	51.9
20	Insurance technical reserves	77.4	0.0	0.0	0.0	77.4
21	Other accounts receivable	53.9	3.2	3.5	7.0	67.6
22	*Statistical discrepancy*	−28.1	−12.9	62.0	0.0	21.0
23	GROSS CURRENT SAVING	360.1	46.0	326.5	0.0	732.6

Imputation Modules

The imputation modules present information on nonmarket activity that is considered to be useful in the construction of national accounts. There is, however, no clear agreement as to what activities are to be covered or how these activities are to be valued. The current revision of the UN System of National Accounts is attempting to clarify these issues, and although some guidelines are being developed, many problems remain. The imputation module shown in Table 15.7 has been drawn up for the major kinds of imputation that are conventionally included in the national accounts. For the most part, the valuations represent the estimates reported in the United States National Accounts.

Farm income in kind — Line 1: Farm income in kind is relatively unimportant for the United States. This is in part due to the small percentage of the population engaged in farming, and the extent to which farming is a commercial enterprise rather than one involving subsistence farming. One cannot

Table 15.7 IMPUTE, Imputation Module for United States, 1981 ($bn)

Line		Enterprise sector 1	Government sector 2	Household sector 3
1	*Farm income in kind*	0.2	0.0	0.2
2	*Residential housing income in kind*	11.5	5.0	152.2
3	Capital consumption allowances	6.5	4.0	45.9
4	Book value	0.5	0.1	19.0
5	Revaluation	1.5	0.3	26.9
6	Imputed interest	5.0	1.0	106.3
7	*Nonresidential structures in kind*	8.0	89.0	0.0
8	Capital consumption allowances	2.8	31.9	0.0
9	Book value	1.0	11.4	0.0
10	Revaluation	1.8	20.5	0.0
11	Imputed interest	5.2	57.1	0.0
12	*Equipment and durables in kind*	5.9	44.0	233.2
13	Capital consumption allowances	4.0	30.0	180.8
14	Book value	2.5	18.6	140.2
15	Revaluation	1.5	11.4	40.6
16	Imputed interest	1.9	14.0	52.4
17	*Financial services in kind*	18.2	68.6	260.4
18	TOTAL IMPUTED INCOME IN KIND	43.6	206.6	645.8
19	*Total capital consumption*	243.1	65.9	226.7
20	Book value	152.7	31.0	159.2
21	Revaluation	90.4	34.9	67.5

help but speculate, however, whether this imputation might not have been larger if food provided by household gardens had been included.

Residential housing income in kind — Line 2: Residential housing for the household sector refers to owner-occupied housing. Instead of imputing space rental value which would include actual transactions relating to maintenance, property taxes etc., the approach here has been to impute the use of owner-occupied housing in terms of capital consumption allowances and imputed interest. The estimates for the book value of capital consumption allowances are based on the depreciation of historical costs and the revaluation estimates take into account the change in the housing prices. The imputed interest is based on the current market value of owner-occupied housing.

In the case of enterprises and government, residential housing consist of nonprofit and government housing used for students, low-income groups and others. The same method of estimating imputed income in kind is used as that used for owner-occupied housing.

Nonresidential structures in kind — Line 7: Nonresidential structures primarily represent office buildings. Imputations for the services of such buildings are not currently included in the United States National Accounts, but are recommended for inclusion in the UN SNA.

Equipment and durables in kind — Line 12: Consumer durables in both the

United States National Accounts and in the UN SNA are treated as current expenditures, but in the core accounts they have been considered to be capital formation. It is, therefore, necessary to impute the services provided by consumer durables if the conventions of the core accounts are to be followed. The estimates for the services of consumer durables follows the method described for owner-occupied housing.

Equipment and durables income in kind for nonprofit institutions, government and households estimated on the same basis as other durables.

Financial services in kind — Line 17: Imputation for financial services in kind is the consequence of the decision to treat interest as a transfer rather than as the provision of a service. The estimates of financial services in kind shown in Table 15.7 are those provided by the Bureau of Economic Analysis of the Department of Commerce. In this connection it is interesting to note that enterprises received an equivalent of $286.9 billion in interest from pension funds, government, households and the rest of the world. This compares with an imputed interest of $260.4 billion shown in Table 15.7.

Capital consumption — Line 19: Capital consumption allowances do not represent actual transactions. Rather they are important internal bookkeeping entries that play a key role in determining the measurement of profit for tax reporting and other purposes. Depreciation rates used in calculating capital consumption do not necessarily reflect actual depreciation taking place, but may be in accord with what is permitted by the taxing authorities. Furthermore, with changing prices in the economy, measures of capital consumption based on original book value costs may not be relevant. The revaluation of capital consumption estimates may, therefore, be desirable to correct the depreciation rates used and to revalue them for price changes taking place in the economy.

The Development of Economic Constructs

As has been indicated, the sector core accounts and the imputation module are basic to the construction of more comprehensive systems of national accounts and economic constructs. The separation of market transactions from imputations for nonmarket activity makes it possible to analyze more clearly what is taking place in the market sector of the economy. On the other hand, by including the imputations shown in the imputation module more comprehensive measures of income and consumption can be constructed that take into account nonmarket activity.

Gross national income and product account (market transactions) — Table 15.8

The major function of a gross national income and product account is to show how the total production of the nation is divided between consumption and gross capital formation and how economic activity has generated flows of income for different sectors of the economy. Focusing on the actual market transactions that take place in the economy provides a clear understanding of how the different sectors of the economy are involved in these processes.

Table 15.8 GNP–M, Gross National Income and Product Account: Market Transactions ($bn, current year prices)

Line		Account	Line	1980
1	*Total consumption (market transactions)*	L2+L3+L6		1,663.8
2	Household current expenditures	HHCUR	L17	1,052.7
3	Benefits in kind provided by enterprises	ENTCUR	L41	104.6
4	Employee benefits	ENTCUR	L4	55.8
5	Nonprofit benefits	ENTCUR	L5	48.8
6	Government current expenditures	GOVCUR	L20	506.5
7	*Gross capital formation*	L8+L11+L15		727.8
8	Enterprise gross capital formation	SICAP	L9	330.8
9	Structures and durables	SICAP	L10	335.6
10	Change in stocks	SICAP	L11	−4.8
11	Household gross capital formation	SICAP	L15	312.0
12	Owner-occupied housing	SICAP	L16	85.2
13	Consumer durables	SICAP	L17	211.9
14	Changes in stocks	SICAP	L18	14.9
15	Government gross capital formation	SICAP	L12	85.0
16	Capital purchases from enterprises	SICAP	L13	46.0
17	Own force capital formation	SICAP	L14	39.0
18	*Sales to rest of the world (net)*	L19–L22		−24.1
19	Exports	L20+L21		255.7
20	Enterprises	ENTCUR	L19	247.0
21	Government	GOVCUR	L24	8.7
22	Less: Imports	L23+L24+L25		279.8
23	Enterprises	ENTCUR	L20	251.4
24	Households	HHCUR	L18	15.9
25	Government	GOVCUR	L23	12.5
26	GROSS DOMESTIC PRODUCT (market transactions)	L1+L7+L18		2,367.5
27	Income received from rest of world	ROWCUR	L20	84.2
28	Less: Income paid to rest of world	ROWCUR	L6	36.7
29	GROSS NATIONAL PRODUCT (market transactions)	L26+L27−L28		2,415.0
30	GROSS INCOME ORIGINATING IN ENTERPRISES	Sum L31..L42		2,098.1
31	Compensation of employees	ENTCUR	L37	1,327.8
32	Entrepreneurial and self-employed income	ENTCUR	L43	124.3
33	Rental income	ENTCUR	L44	19.8
34	Interest	ENTCUR	L45	289.4
35	Dividends	ENTCUR	L50	57.3
36	Retained corporate profits by rest of world	ENTCUR	L54	3.2
37	Taxes paid	ENTCUR	L55	268.0
38	Surplus of government enterprises	ENTCUR	L58	6.4
39	Transfer payments to households	ENTCUR	L59	58.3
40	Gross enterprise saving	ENTCUR	L62	48.8
41	Compensation of employees	ENTCUR	L64	360.1
42	Less: Adjustments for income received	Sum L43..L46		465.3

(cont)

Table 15.8 (cont)

Line		Account	Line	1980
43	Transfers received by enterprises	ENTCUR	L28	57.8
44	Interest received by enterprises	ENTCUR	L21	199.7
45	Income received from rest of world	ENTCUR	L24	81.0
46	Receipts of employer pension funds	ENTCUR	L32	126.8
47	INCOME ORIGINATING IN GOVERNMENT	L48		269.4
48	Compensation of government employees	GOVCUR	L25	269.4
49	GROSS DOMESTIC INCOME (market transactions)	L30+L47		2,367.5
50	INCOME ORIGINATING IN REST OF WORLD	L51–L52		47.5
51	Income received from rest of world	ROWCUR	L20	84.2
52	Less: Income paid to rest of world	ROWCUR	L6	36.7
53	GROSS NATIONAL INCOME	L49+L50		2,415.0

In those instances where national income and product accounts reflect primarily aggregate estimates of consumption capital formation and income flows, the role that is played by the different sectors of the economy is obscured. It is often difficult to disaggregate the aggregate estimates of consumption or capital formation into their appropriate sector detail. One of the advantages of creating a national income and product account from sector core accounts is that consumption and capital formation and the generation of income are easily delineated in sector terms. The gross national income and product account shown in Table 15.8 is built up from the sector core accounts and is fully articulated with them.

On the product side of the account the transaction flows relating to consumption, gross capital formation and international trade are shown. On the income side, the income originating in each sector of the economy is shown. In the case of the enterprise sector, it has been necessary to deduct, from the payments enterprises make to other sectors, the receipts that do not constitute the sale of goods and services. Thus, when an enterprise receives a subsidy, that subsidy provides funds which augment the amount that can be distributed in the form of production costs and profits.

Gross national income and product account (market and nonmarket) — Table 15.9

Imputations for nonmarket activity can easily be added to the market transactions accounts in order to provide more comprehensive measures of both consumption and gross income originating in specific sectors. Since no imputations were made for nonmarket activity related to capital formation, the capital formation data will not be affected. For households, imputations have been included for consumer durable services, owner-occupied housing services and financial services. For nonprofit enterprises and governmen, imputations have been included for services of buildings, services of durables and financial services.

Table 15.9 *GNP–T, Gross National Income and Product Account: Total Market and Nonmarket ($bn, current year prices)*

Line			Account	Line	1980
1	*Total consumption*		L2+L7+L10		2,559.8
2	Household consumption		L3+L4+L5+L6		1,698.5
3		Household current expenditures	HHCUR	L17	1,052.7
4		Services of consumer durables	IMPUTE	L12C3	233.2
5		Services of owner-occupied housing	IMPUTE	L2C3	152.2
6		Financial services	IMPUTE	L17C3	260.4
7	Enterprise consumption		L8+L9		148.2
8		Enterprise expenditures on benefits in kind	ENTCUR	L3	104.6
9		In-kind services received by nonprofits	IMPUTE	L18C1	43.6
10	Government consumption		L11+L12		713.1
11		Government current expenditures	GOVCUR	L20	506.5
12		In-kind services received by government	IMPUTE	L18C2	206.6
13	*Government capital formation*		L14+L17+L21		727.8
14	Enterprise gross capital formation		SICAP	L9	330.8
15		Structures and durables	SICAP	L10	335.6
16		Change in stocks	SICAP	L11	–4.8
17	Household gross capital formation		SICAP	L15	312.0
18		Owner-occupied housing	SICAP	L16	85.2
19		Consumer durables	SICAP	L17	211.9
20		Change in stocks	SICAP	L18	14.9
21	Government gross capital formation		SICAP	L12	85.0
22		Capital purchases from enterprises	SICAP	L13	46.0
23		Own force capital formation	SICAP	L14	39.0
24	*Sales to rest of world (net)*		L25–L28		–24.1
25	Exports		L26+L27		255.7
26		Enterprises	ENTCUR	L19	247.0
27		Government	GOVCUR	L24	8.7
28	Less: Imports		L29+L30+L31		279.8
29		Enterprises	ENTCUR	L20	251.4
30		Households	HHCUR	L18	15.9
31		Government	GOVCUR	L23	12.5
32	GROSS DOMESTIC PRODUCT (market transactions)		L1+L13+L24		3,263.5
33	Income received from rest of world		ROWCUR	L20	84.2
34	Less: Income paid to rest of world		ROWCUR	L6	36.7
35	GROSS NATIONAL PRODUCT (market transactions)		L32+L33–L34		3,311.0
36	GROSS INCOME ORIGINATING IN ENTERPRISES		(Sum L37..L48)–L49		2,141.7
37	Compensation of employees		ENTCUR	L37	1,327.8
38	Entrepreneurial and self-employed income		ENTCUR	L43	124.3
39	Rental income		ENTCUR	L44	19.8
40	Interest		ENTCUR	L45	289.4
41	Dividends		ENTCUR	L50	57.3
42	Retained corporate profits by rest of world		ENTCUR	L54	3.2
43	Taxes paid		ENTCUR	L55	268.0
44	Surplus of government enterprises		ENTCUR	L58	6.4
45	Transfer payments to households		ENTCUR	L59	58.3
46	Nonprofits benefits in kind		ENTCUR	L62	48.8
47	Gross imputed income of nonprofits		ENTCUR	L18	43.6
48	Gross enterprise saving		ENTCUR	L63	360.1

(cont)

Table 15.9 (cont)

Line		Account	Line	1980
49	Less: Adjustments for income received	Sum L50..L53		465.3
50	Transfers received by enterprises	ENTCUR	L28	57.8
51	Interest received by enterprises	ENTCUR	L21	199.7
52	Income received from rest of world	ENTCUR	L24	81.0
53	Receipts of employer pension funds	ENTCUR	L32	126.8
54	GROSS INCOME ORIGINATING IN HOUSEHOLDS	L55+L56+L57		645.8
55	Gross income from consumer durables	IMPUTE	L12C3	233.2
56	Gross income from owner-occupied housing	IMPUTE	L2C3	152.2
57	Imputed financial services income	IMPUTE	L17C3	260.4
58	GROSS INCOME ORIGINATING IN GOVERNMENT	L59+L60		476.0
59	Compensation of government employees	GOVCUR	L25	269.4
60	Gross imputed income of government	IMPUTE	L18C2	206.6
61	GROSS DOMESTIC INCOME (market and nonmarket)			3,263.5
62	INCOME ORIGINATING IN REST OF WORLD	L63–L64		47.5
63	Income received from rest of world	ROWCUR	L20	84.2
64	Less: Income paid to rest of world	ROWCUR	L6	36.7
65	GROSS NATIONAL INCOME (market and nonmarket)	L61+L62		3,311.0

The imputations increase total consumption in the United States economy for the year 1980 from $1,663.8 to $2,559.8 billion — an increase of 53.8 percent. It may be argued that the magnitude of these imputations is due, in part, to the treatment of consumer durables as capital goods rather than as current consumption, but the imputed services for consumer durables account for only $233.2 million (25 percent) of the total imputations. If the expenditure on consumer durables for 1980 had been used instead of the imputation, it would have added $211.9 million to consumption expenditures.

For analyzing the composition of total consumption it will be useful to classify expenditures and imputations by type of good or service as well as by sector. Thus it is interesting how much medical care is paid for by households, how much is provided by employers to their employees, and how much is provided or paid for by the government.

Net economic constructs — Table 15.10

By applying the imputed estimates for capital consumption it is possible to derive net measures of capital formation, net national product and national income. These economic constructs are shown in Table 15.10. With respect to net capital formation, it can be seen that the capital consumption allowances are quite large relative to gross capital formation, and thus net capital formation is relatively small.

The concept of capital consumption poses a number of problems. In the case of structures, the decline in their value over time depends to a major degree on their repair and maintenance. Although repair and maintenance are not considered to be part of gross capital formation, they can result in

Table 15.10 NNP–T, Net National Income and Product: Total Market and Nonmarket ($bn, current year prices)

Line		Account	Line	1980
1	*Total consumption*	L2+L3+L4		2,559.8
2	Household consumption	GNP–T	L2	1,698.5
3	Enterprise consumption	GNP–T	L7	148.2
4	Government consumption	GNP–T	L10	713.1
6	*Net capital formation*	L7+L12+L17		192.1
7	Enterprise net capital formation	L8–L9		87.7
8	Enterprise gross capital formation	GNP–T	L14	330.8
9	Less: Capital consumption	IMPUTE	L19C1	243.1
10	Book value	IMPUTE	L20C1	152.7
11	Revaluation	IMPUTE	L21C1	90.4
12	Household net capital formation	L13–L14		85.3
13	Household gross capital formation	GNP–T	L17	312.0
14	Less: Capital consumption	IMPUTE	L19C3	226.7
15	Book value	IMPUTE	L20C3	159.2
16	Revaluation	IMPUTE	L21C3	67.5
17	Government net capital formation	L18–L19		19.1
18	Government gross capital formation	GNP–T	L21	85.0
19	Less: Capital consumption	IMPUTE	L19C2	65.9
20	Book value	IMPUTE	L20C2	31.0
21	Revaluation	IMPUTE	L21C2	34.9
22	*Sales to rest of world (net)*	GNP–T	L24	–24.1
23	NET DOMESTIC PRODUCT (market and nonmarket)	L1+L6+L22		2,727.8
24	Income received from rest of world	GNP–T	L33	84.2
25	Less: Income paid to rest of world	GNP–T	L34	36.7
26	NET NATIONAL PRODUCT (market and nonmarket)	L23+L24–L25		2,775.3
27	NET INCOME ORIGINATING IN ENTERPRISES	L28–L29		1,898.6
28	Gross income originating in enterprises	GNP–T	L36	2,141.7
29	Less: Capital consumption	IMPUTE	L19C1	243.1
30	Book value	IMPUTE	L20C1	152.7
31	Revaluation	IMPUTE	L21C1	90.4
32	NET INCOME ORIGINATING IN HOUSEHOLDS	L33–L34		419.1
33	Gross income originating in households	GNP–T	L54	645.8
34	Less: Capital consumption	IMPUTE	L19C3	226.7
35	Book value	IMPUTE	L20C3	159.2
36	Revaluation	IMPUTE	L21C3	67.5
37	NET INCOME ORIGINATING IN GOVERNMENT	L38–L39		410.1
38	Gross income originating in government	GNP–T	L58	476.0
39	Less: Capital consumption	IMPUTE	L19C2	65.9
40	Book value	IMPUTE	L20C2	31.0
41	Revaluation	IMPUTE	L21C2	34.9
42	NET DOMESTIC INCOME (market and nonmarket)	L27+L32+L37		2,727.8
43	INCOME ORIGINATING IN REST OF WORLD	GNP–T	L62	47.5
44	NET NATIONAL INCOME (market and nonmarket)	L42+L43		2,775.3

preventing a decline in the value of a building and can even improve it over time. For some types of equipment that actually wear out, such as motor vehicles, it is possible to determine their physical life, and in these cases, capital consumption measures are meaningful. In other cases where obsolescence is the major factor determining economic life, the use of capital consumption is more questionable.

From a micro point of view, the allocation of durable equipment over its useful economic life is appropriate for calculating profit and for computing the value of an asset at a given moment of time. However, from a macro point of view, obsolescence may arise from rapid technological change reflecting the increased productivity of new equipment over older equipment. A faster rate of technical change in an economy will result in faster obsolescence, but it would not be appropriate to reduce the real output of the economy by deducting the resulting increase in capital consumption.

For these reasons, economists primarily concerned with the behavior of the economic system prefer gross measures of production and capital formation. However, economists attempting to study real measures of output and economic welfare will find it necessary to adjust the gross measures of output and capital formation for the using up of capital.

4. SUMMARY AND CONCLUSIONS

Summary

The United Nations System of National Accounts consists of a logically consistent and integrated set of macroeconomic accounts which conform to a set of internationally agreed concepts, definitions, classifications and accounting rules. Although the system contains certain aggregates such as gross domestic product that are considered to be important, these aggregates are not the major reason for compiling national accounts. The national accounts provide a comprehensive framework for integrating data required for a wide variety of different analytic and policy purposes. As such a framework it is directly relevant to the problem of monitoring the transition of the Soviet system to a market economy.

Despite the acknowledged desirability of adopting many of the definitions, classifications and concepts developed by the United Nations System of National Accounts, implementation of a formal system of accounts poses many problems. On the one hand, implementation of the 1968 version would present the problem of integrating various alternative parts of the 1968 Blue Book with over 50 manuals and guides published by the United Nations on the SNA since 1968 and with the United Nations National Accounts Questionnaire. On the other hand, with respect to the current revision of the SNA which is in progress, it is recognized that the tables, matrices and accounts that are included in the system are designed to explain the features of the SNA and are not intended for the compilation of data at a national or international level. Countries are urged to draw selectively upon the SNA principles, concepts and accounts to provide a system that will meet their analytic and policy needs.

The SNA as outlined in both the 1968 Blue Book and the current draft of the *Review of the SNA* is large and complex. This has caused some statistical offices to seek a simpler approach. It has been proposed that 'core' accounts that would record the actual market transactions for the major sectors of the economy be implemented. These core accounts, together with modules containing the imputations for nonmarket activity and rerouting of transactions, could furnish the basis for developing the more complex and elaborate SNA accounts and economic constructs. It is argued that such a core account system would be simpler and more flexible than alternative approaches and, even more importantly, it can provide for better integration between macro- and microdata.

Before such sector core accounts can be implemented, however, a number of issues relating to the sectoring of the economy, the general accounting structure and the nature of imputations need to be evaluated. The evaluation in this paper has concluded that some changes would be required in the SNA definition of major sectors, accounting structure and treatment of certain imputations and rerouting.

After determining the requirements for sector core accounts, these have been implemented for the United States economy for the year 1980. The basic data source for these core accounts and imputations module is the official United States National Income Accounts. Sector financial accounts were also constructed using United States flow of funds data. The core accounts were then used to construct national income and product accounts that reflected market transactions. By introducing imputations, a more comprehensive national income and product account and a net national income and product account were constructed.

It is argued that this system of core accounts and imputations not only introduces simplicity and flexibility, but also provides information that is analytically more useful and is more capable of being integrated with microdata.

Additional Information Requirements

For developing input–output tables both make-and-use matrices of products made and used by establishments classified by industry are needed. This requires data at the enterprise–establishment level on materials used and products produced by industry. Price indexes are needed to deflate the current price data in both the input–output tables and the national income accounts in order to develop real output and consumption data. Employment data that are matched with production data are needed for measuring changes in labor productivity.

If national balance sheets are to be constructed, information will be required on the holdings of assets and liabilities by different sectors of the economy and the revaluation of these over time.

Disaggregation of the various sectors and aggregate transaction flows will also be needed. The breakdown of the enterprise sector into industries for the measurement of output, and into nonfinancial and financial subsectors for financial analysis has already be mentioned. However, for the Soviet Union, regional breakdowns may also be of central importance. Government needs to be subsectored by level of government, and a functional breakdown of government outlays is needed. For the household sector a breakdown of consumer expenditures is important and a subsectoring of households by size of income would be useful.

Sources and Methods

In any country, the sources for constructing statistical systems consist of administrative data, complete censuses and sample surveys. On a current basis, most countries are coming to rely to a large extent on administrative data supplemented by sample surveys. Complete censuses are primarily useful for developing more exhaustive and reliable benchmark estimates for specific periods, providing sampling frames and evaluating the completeness of administrative sources.

Among administrative sources, data files relating to employment and taxes are often the most comprehensive and, if computerized, are capable of being classified into categories relevant to statistical analysis. In instances where these files are too large to be easily utilized, sampling may be appropriate. To a considerable extent the classifications systems used for statistical data may need to be adapted to the form in which the data are available.

In some instances, the administrative sources can be used to establish the main control totals in the system, and sample surveys can be used to provide the desired detail, breakdowns, or supplementary data. For these reasons, it is important that the link between microdata and the macroconcepts used in aggregate data be preserved as much as possible. Registers of enterprises, governmental units and other types of reporting units and demographic sampling frames are needed not only for the collection of data but also for the evaluation of the completeness and representativeness of specific sets of data.

In developing microdata files that underlie the macrostatistical data, it will often be found that it is necessary to introduce adjustments for missing data. These adjustments may be required because certain respondents were missing from the microdata set or because specific information was not reported or was incorrectly reported by existing respondents. In both of these instances, adjustments will need to be made to bring the macrodata up to the appropriate level. It is of central importance that the adjustments be made at the level of the microunit so that when the microdata are aggregated they will yield consistent macro aggregates. It is only by following this procedure that the microdata sets can successfully be used to generate consistent alternative disaggregations of the macrodata.

Finally, although the United Nations System of National Accounts does not use longitudinal data, it will be found that linking of observations at the microdata level on a longitudinal basis will be analytically very useful. The United States Bureau of the Census currently maintains the *Census of Manufactures* and the *Annual Survey of Manufactures* on a longitudinal basis. The household sample *Survey of Income and Program Participation* is also designed to yield longitudinal data. These types of data make it possible to analyze behavior at the level of the microreporting unit; if the macronational accounts are designed to be compatible with such microdata improved understanding of the processes of aggregate structural change and the behavior of individual units in the economy will be possible.

REFERENCES

Ruggles, Ruggles and Nancy D. Ruggles (1982), 'Integrated economic accounts for the United States, 1947–80', *Survey of Current Business*, **62** (5).

United Nations Statistical Office (1968), *A System of National Accounts*, Series F, No. 2, New York.

_____ (1977a), *Provisional International Guidelines on the National and Sectoral Balance-Sheet and Reconciliation Accounts of the SNA*, Series M, No. 60, New York.

_____ (1977b), *Provisional Guidelines on Statistics of the Distribution of Income, Consumption, and Accumulation of Households*, Series M, No. 61, New York.

_____ (1979), *Guidelines on Statistics of Tangible Assets*, Series M, No. 68, New York.

_____ (1990a), *System of National Accounts (SNA) Review Issues*, Future ST/ESA/ SER.F/2/Rev.4, February.

_____ (1990b), *Revised System of National Accounts: Preliminary Draft Chapters — Chapter II, An Overview of the System*, Future ST/ESA/ STAT/SER.F/2Rev.4, February, p. 11.

_____ and OECD Department of Economic and Statistics (1980), *Instructions and Definitions for the National Accounts Questionnaire*, New York and Paris.

Van Bochove, C.A. and H.K. Van Tuinen (1986), 'Flexibility in the next SNA: The case for an institutional core', *Review of Income and Wealth*, **32** (2), 127–54.

16. Issues Relating to the UN System of National Accounts and Developing Countries

Richard Ruggles
Yale University

1. THE UNITED NATIONS SYSTEM OF NATIONAL ACCOUNTS

The United Nations System of National Accounts (SNA) was first published in 1953. It presented a set of six accounts for recording the main flows in the economy relating to production, consumption, accumulation and external trade. The main purpose of the system was to provide a uniform basis for reporting national income statistics.

The revision of the SNA published in 1968 presented a much more comprehensive and detailed framework for the systematic and integrated recording of flows and stocks in the economy. It brought together the national income accounts, input–output and flow of funds tables and balance sheets into an articulated and coherent system. A dual system of sectoring the accounts was introduced. The production accounts were disaggregated into industries and commodities, and the income and outlay accounts, financial transactions, and balance sheets were disaggregated into institutional sectors and subsectors.

The 1968 SNA was constructed in terms of the economic systems of the developed countries, but, with appropriate modifications, it was also intended to apply to the developing countries as well. Chapter IX of the Blue Book was devoted to the 'Adaptation of the Full System to the Developing Countries'. This chapter acknowledged the importance for the developing countries of explicitly recognizing the 'dualism' of the modern and traditional parts of the economy. Developing countries were, therefore, urged to subclassify industries further in terms of modern and traditional modes of production. Emphasis was

---

This chapter first appeared in *Journal of Development Economics*, **38**, 1994.

also placed on distinguishing private and public activity and on the role of external trade. Finally, it was recognized that for some developing countries it would be useful to compile special national accounting data in respect of selected rural and urban areas. In terms of priorities, the highest priority was given to the consolidated accounts for the nation, the deconsolidated production accounts, the activities of the government, the financial transactions of the monetary system and data on external transactions.

In the decade from 1970 to 1980, the United Nations System of National Accounts continued to develop. A variety of handbooks, manuals and guides was published by the UN Statistical Office in an effort to explain the system and assist countries in implementing it. Some of these publications such as those relating to the balance sheets went beyond what was published in the Blue Book. In 1980, a new National Accounts Questionnaire was issued that, in contrast to the Blue Book, contained full sets of accounts for the institutional sectors and subsectors of the economy.

At the same time as the United Nations and the OECD were collecting national accounting data, other international agencies were collecting a variety of other economic data. In particular, the International Monetary Fund published data for different countries on banking and finance, balance of payments, and government finances. Attempts were made to reconcile these data with the related data in the United Nations National Accounts, and elaborate bridge tables were constructed to provide an account of the conceptual and statistical differences involved.

Although by 1980 almost no countries had succeeded in completing the full SNA system, the UN Statistical Commission convened Expert Group meetings in 1980 and 1982 to review the SNA. These Expert Groups expressed general satisfaction with the basic structure of the SNA but concluded that clarification, harmonization and updating of the 1968 Blue Book should be undertaken. Over the past decade, such a review of the SNA has taken place, and a preliminary version of the proposed revision of the SNA is now available.

2. THE REGIONAL EXPERT MEETINGS AND THE PROPOSED REVISION OF THE SNA

During 1990, a series of regional expert meetings in the developing countries on the revision of the SNA were held in Addis Ababa, Bangkok, Suva, Tunis and Rio de Janeiro. At these meetings the preliminary draft of the SNA revision was discussed in detail. In general, there was consensus that the SNA accounting structure should be extended to provide full sets of accounts for the institutional sectors. There was also strong support for harmonization of the SNA with the Government Financial Statistics and the Balance of Payments.

The reaction to SNA's proposal for imputing rent on government buildings was mixed. Some participants strongly opposed such an imputation, whereas others approved and still others indicated that it would be difficult to make such estimates. The proposed distinction between consumption expenditures and final consumption was universally supported.

There was specific agreement that the revised SNA should apply to developing countries and that there should be no special provisions such as those contained in Chapter IX of the 1968 Blue Book. However, probing questions were also raised as to how the proposed SNA would relate to developing countries with reference to the classification of formal and informal production activities, the definition of market and nonmarket production, and the subsectoring of the household sector. All three of these topics were considered as particularly central for the analysis of developing economies.

Despite the SNA proposal for distinguishing between formal and informal productive activities in the national accounts, no criteria were offered, but it was assumed that all corporate and quasi-corporate enterprises would be in the formal sector and that all informal enterprises would be classified in the household sector. All the Regional Expert Groups emphasized the importance of the formal/informal classification for the developing countries, but they were reluctant to accept the view that corporate and quasi-corporate enterprises solely constituted the formal sector of the economy and that all unincorporated enterprises should be classified in the informal sector of the economy. None of the Expert Groups could come up with a satisfactory solution to this problem.

The SNA criterion for distinguishing between market and nonmarket production was based on whether or not the market receipts of the producer in question were equal to 50 percent or more of his production costs. The Regional Expert Groups concluded that this definition was too rigid and inflexible, and would result in the misclassification of many public enterprises, private corporations, and public utilities operating at a loss. In the most recent recommendations of the Inter-Secretariat Working Group on National Accounts (ISWGNA), it has been suggested that market output should be defined more flexibly as output that is sold at 'economically significant prices'. Nonmarket output would consist of both subsistence output and services provided by government and nonprofit institutions. Several of the Regional Expert Groups pointed out that it would be useful to distinguish between these two types of nonmarket output. The Inter-Secretariat Working Group is, therefore, now recommending that three categories of output: market output, nonmarket output for own use, and other nonmarket output, be recognized.

The proposed revision of the SNA recommends dividing the household sector into four subsectors based on the International Classification of the Status in Employment (ICSE) of the reference person in the household. The four household subsectors would be: employers, own-account workers, employees, and recipients of property or transfer income. The Regional Expert Groups were almost universal in emphasizing the analytic importance of subsectoring the household sector. There was, however, no consensus as to what appropriate subsectoring might be. A number of experts thought that the SNA classifications would not meet the analytic needs of developing countries. Some Expert Groups proposed a rural/urban subsectoring others suggested education, type of employment, or distribution of income. Questions were also raised as to how the distinctions between formal and informal activities and market and nonmarket production could be applied systematically to all household subsectors. Some experts pointed out that social accounting matrices (SAMs) or satellite accounts could be used for subsectoring the household sector. In the most recent Expert Group meeting in Aguascalientes, Mexico, it was concluded that 'households could be categorized and subsectored in alternative ways, for example, using educational characteristics or occupation of a reference person to serve analytic needs, thus, emphasizing the flexibility in the revised SNA'. However, what is considered to be 'flexibility' in the SNA may, in reality, be a reflection of the SNA's inability to provide developing countries with an adequate framework for their economic analysis.

3. THE ANALYSIS OF SAVING AND INVESTMENT AND THE PROPOSED SNA REVISION

In addition to the questions raised by the Regional Expert Groups, there is the more central question as to whether the proposed SNA revision provides an adequate framework for the analysis of saving and capital formation. As Srinivasan points out in his paper, a central problem of economic development is understanding the process by which a country which has had a low level of saving and capital formation converts itself into an economy with rapid capital accumulation. Presumably one of the main purposes in constructing national accounts is to provide evidence on the saving and capital formation taking place in an economy and to decompose it into its sectoral components. Although many of the difficulties in obtaining clear understanding of the saving and capital formation process stem from the lack of reliable data, it is also apparent that an appropriate national accounting framework is basic to the provision of relevant data on saving and capital formation.

One of the main features of the proposed revision of the SNA has been its introduction of full sets of accounts (production, income and outlay, capital finance and balance sheets) for the institutional sectors of the economy. Such full sets of accounts are needed to derive the saving originating in a given sector, and the capital formation undertaken by that sector. The difference between a sector's saving and its capital formation is equal to the amount of its net lending or borrowing.

For analyzing enterprise saving and capital formation, it is important to be able to differentiate among enterprises engaged in different kinds of industrial activities such as agriculture, mining, manufacturing, public utilities, and trade and services, since enterprises in these different activities differ with respect to their saving and capital formation behavior. Unfortunately, the institutional sectoring in the proposed revision of the SNA does not provide such data. Enterprises are not subclassified by their industrial activity.

The measurement of household saving in the proposed revision of the SNA also leaves much to be desired. One of the major problems relates to the treatment of owner-occupied housing. In order to impute the value of services of owner-occupied housing both as a part of nonmarket output and as household consumption, the SNA sets up an account for a fictional unincorporated enterprise that rents the house to the owner-occupant at an imputed space rental value and pays all the costs associated with the house, such as taxes, repairs, mortgage interest and depreciation. The balance between the imputed space rental value and the costs (including depreciation) of owner-occupied housing is returned to the household as net imputed rental income. In the United States in recent years, the net imputed rental income shown in the national accounts has been negative since the imputed space rental value has been less than the costs (including depreciation) of operating the owner-occupied house. This treatment of owner-occupied housing seriously distorts the actual income, expenditures and saving of households. In particular, the depreciation expense charged by the fictional unincorporated enterprise is, in reality, not an expense, but rather represents gross saving of the owner-occupied household. In terms of magnitude this element of household saving in many countries exceeds all other components. In analytic terms, this depreciation of owner-occupied housing may never, in fact, take place. If the owners of owner-occupied housing maintain their houses, these may appreciate rather than depreciate over time.

With respect to capital formation, the proposed revision of the SNA does not recognize household capital formation as such. Purchases of owner-occupied housing are considered to be capital formation by the fictional unincorporated enterprise set up to own such housing. Household purchases of consumer durables are considered to be current expenditures. The stock of consumer durables owned by a household is not considered to be tangible assets on household balance sheets, but rather is carried as a memorandum item.

This treatment of household durables raises serious questions about the consistency of treatment of different items. For example, household appliances that are incorporated in the purchase of a new house are included as part of owner-occupied capital formation, but if these same appliances are purchased separately, they are considered to be current outlays. Similarly, if a household purchases a motor vehicle it is a current expenditure unless it is used to some extent in business; then it becomes part of unincorporated business capital formation. Finally, in the household balance sheet, the measurement of net worth is distorted since the consumer debt relating to consumer durables is treated as a liability, but the consumer durables themselves are not considered to be assets.

It is difficult to judge just what impact the procedures recommend in the proposed revision of SNA would have on the measurement of household saving and capital formation in developing countries. However, for a developed country such as United States, the measurement of household gross saving and capital formation indicates that over the past 45 years, the gross saving of the household sector has been barely sufficient to cover its own capital formation. Indeed, in periods of prosperity, the household sector has been a net borrower, and it is only in recession when household capital formation drops more sharply than household gross saving that households become net lenders. In developing countries with rapid growth, it is also possible that when properly measured, household gross capital formation may exceed household gross saving, making the household sector a net borrower in the economy.

4. THE INTEGRATION OF NATIONAL ACCOUNTS AND HOUSEHOLD SURVEYS

The estimation of gross domestic product in both developed and developing countries is generally based on the estimates of value added originating in different industries in the economy. These production estimates, combined with government receipts and expenditures and custom reports on exports and imports, are used in a 'commodity flow' approach to yield final expenditures on gross domestic product. Household sector accounts, in these circumstances, are generally derived residually. The income of households consists of wages and salaries, interest, property income and transfer payments made to households by enterprises and government. Household consumption expenditures are derived as that part of the GDP not represented by capital formation, government consumption or net exports. In view of this close relation between the estimation of the GDP and the derivation of the household sector in the national accounts, it is not surprising that the resulting concepts and classifications used for both household income and expenditures in the national accounts for the household sector should be quite different from those used in household surveys.

To some degree, sample surveys of household income and expenditures have been used by almost all countries for developing their consumer price indexes. In the Expert Group meeting in Mexico, the need for harmonization of the concepts used in the consumer price indexes (CPI) and the SNA was stressed. Such harmonization is now more feasible, since the proposed revision of the SNA distinguishes between the actual consumer expenditures by households and the imputed consumption in kind by households.

Over the last decade, there has been a substantial increase in the use of household surveys by the developing countries for the collection of demographic, social and economic data. Both the Household Survey Capability Programme (NHSCP) of the United Nations and the Living Standards Measurement Study (LSMS) supported by the World Bank have as their objective the establishment of data collection systems based on a set of integrated household surveys. Unfortunately, in this context there has been little indication that those concerned with designing the integrated household surveys take into account the related concepts in the revised SNA. Similarly, it does not appear that the revised SNA is concerned with the desirability of harmonizing the concepts and classifications used in the national accounts with those used in household surveys.

There is, however, a great deal to be gained by developing a close conceptual relationship between the national accounts and household surveys. The national accounts data should be used to provide the control totals for the major economic aggregates such as household income, expenditures, tax payments, etc. These aggregates must be consistent with the related data contained in the other sector accounts. Household survey data can further check the internal consistency of such estimates within the household sector, and provide information on their distribution among different types of households. Thus size distributions of income and living standards can be provided. Household surveys that are conceptually integrated with the national accounts can provide the basis for drawing the social accounting matrices and satellite accounts recommended in the proposed revision of the SNA. Increasingly, household surveys are being used as microdata bases for the analysis of social and economic policy. In part, this has been made feasible by the rapid spread of microcomputer facilities.

5. SUMMARY AND CONCLUSION

The proposed revision of the United Nations System of National Accounts (SNA) has been primarily concerned with the clarification, updating and harmonization of the 1968 version of the SNA. From the point of view of developing countries the proposed revision was welcomed. In particular, the harmonization of the SNA with the data published by the International

Monetary Fund on the balance of payments, international financial statistics, and government finances was strongly supported. However, the Regional Expert Groups reviewing the proposed revision indicated that a number of important issues directly relating to the developing countries were not fully resolved. Specifically, it was agreed that for developing countries it was important to distinguish (1) the formal and informal sectors, (2) market and nonmarket production and (3) subsectors of the household sector. In each of these instances, it was felt that, although the SNA provided flexibility for the developing countries to handicraft their own solutions, the SNA itself did not provide the needed guidelines.

In addition to the specific questions raised by the developing countries, there is also the more general question as to whether the revised SNA provides an adequate basis for understanding the process of sector saving and capital formation. It was pointed out that the proposed institutional subsectoring of the income and capital accounts is quite inadequate for analyzing the saving and capital formation of enterprises in different industries such as agriculture, mining, manufacturing, public utilities, trade and services. Furthermore, the proposed SNA treatment of actual and imputed transactions in the household sector prevents a clear understanding of household saving and capital formation. The method used to impute owner-occupied housing seriously distorts the measurement of household gross saving, and household capital formation is not taken into account. As a consequence the actual role of household sector saving and capital formation in the economic system is distorted.

Finally, the need for harmonizing the household sector of the national accounts with household surveys was examined. Although household surveys are becoming increasingly important as data bases, their concepts are not integrated with those of the household sector in the national accounts. As in the case of the harmonization of the SNA with the balance of payments, international financial statistics and government finances, it will be necessary to get the various Expert Groups concerned to focus on what conceptual adjustments may be required in both the national accounts and in household surveys. Such harmonization would strengthen both the national accounts and household surveys. On the one hand, if household microdata bases consistent with the household sector of the national accounts were available, the flexibility recommended by the SNA would be feasible and both social accounting matrices and satellite accounts could be constructed with relative ease. On the other hand, the more comprehensive framework provided by the household sector accounts would constitute a common frame of reference for household surveys and show how they related to the economy as a whole.

REFERENCES

Srinivasan, T.N. (1992), 'Data base for development analysis: An overview', Conference on DataBase for Development Analysis, Yale University, 15–16 May.

United Nations (1958), 'A system of national accounts', Studies in Methods, Series F, No. 2, Rev. 3.

―――― (1991a), 'Progress in implementation and co-ordination of the national household survey capability programme', Statistical Commission, 4–13 February, E/CN.3/1991/26.

―――― (1991b), 'Final report of the regional seminar on national accounts convened by the Economic Commission for Latin America and the Caribbean', Statistical Commission, 4–13 February, E/CN.3/1991/9.

―――― (1991c), 'Report of the expert meeting on the revision of the system of national accounts in the Arab World', Statistical Commission, 4–13 February, E/CN.3/1991/10.

―――― (1991d), 'Report of the Economic and Social Commission for Asia and the Pacific Meetings on the Revision of the System of National Accounts (SNA)', Statistical Commission, 4–13 February, E/CN.3/1991/8.

―――― (1991e), 'World Bank initiatives in the design of permanent integrated household surveys', Statistical Commission, February, E/CN.3/1991/27.

―――― (1991f), 'Report of the Economic Commission for Africa Meeting on the System of National Accounts', Statistical Commission, 4–13 February, E/CN.3/1991/7.

―――― (1992). 'Report of the Interregional Seminar on the Revision of the System of National Accounts', Aguascalientes, Mexico, 5–9 October, ESA/STAT/AC.43/8.

―――― (1993), 'Revision of the International Classification of Status in Employment (ICSE)', Statistical Commission, 22 February–3 March, E/CN.3/1993.

17. The United Nations System of National Accounts (SNA) and the Integration of Macro- and Microdata

Richard Ruggles
Yale University

The United Nations System of National Accounts (SNA) has been an evolutionary development over a period of 50 years. It was born in the world of macroeconomics, but statistically its roots have been in the data relating to individual decision-making units of the economy. Since its inception, both the complexity of the economic system and the concern with social problems have increased. Currently, governments are faced with the need to evaluate both the macro- and microaspects of their policies relating to old age entitlements, health care, education, the environment and poverty. The national accounts alone are not sufficient for this task. Both the need and the technical feasibility of linking the macroframework with microdata have increased. The following discussion attempts to trace the evolution of the system with respect to the macro/micro linkage, and to indicate how the macroaccounts and microdata bases can be integrated.

1. THE UN SNA VIEW OF MICRODATA

National Income Concepts and Measurement Prior to the UN SNA

Before World War II, national income concepts consisted of various macroconstructs relating to national output, final sales and income payments. The split between macro- and microtheory was reflected in empirical terms by the macroestimates of national income concepts and the detailed microdata

---

This chapter first appeared in John Kendrick (ed.), *Socio-Economic Accounts*, Kluwer, 1995.

collected from enterprises, households and government by statistical and administrative agencies.

The technology used for data processing prior to World War II precluded any significant use of microdata in the estimation of national income. Punch cards were used to reduce the large masses of detailed microdata into more manageable sets of summary cross-tabulations. Those estimating national income prided themselves on their ability to piece together diverse and often fragmentary sets of information to derive their estimates of aggregates. A wide variety of statistical sources was used to provide the basic estimates. For example, tabulations by statistical and regulatory agencies of the value of product or sales for various industries provided the basis for estimating output. Social security and labor force tabulations were used for estimating wages and salaries originating in various industries, and tabulations of financial data and tax returns provided information for estimating interest and property income.

The 1947 UN Proposal and the 1952 SNA

In 1947, Richard Stone on behalf of the UN proposed a radically different approach to national income measurement (UN, 1947, p. 23):

> It has come to be realized that for different purposes certain related but distinct aggregates are useful and that beyond a given point it is only possible to specify a unique set of operations to define the content of one of these aggregates by adopting certain conventions.
>
> This view based upon experience is reinforced since the ideas can be expounded and presented more lucidly if the elementary transactions rather than the final aggregates are made the starting point of the enquiry. Transactions, whether actual or imputed, take place between accounting entities such as business enterprises and individuals, and the accounts of these entities are much easier to grasp than the consolidated accounts of the whole system. Thus by studying the different classes of accounting entity in an economy and the different types of transaction in which they engage, we shall at once obtain a clearer picture of how the national totals are built up and at the same time exhibit the relationship between the constituent transactions and the implications of setting up the accounts in one way rather than another. This approach will also ensure consistency in the treatment of different transactions and will show the implications in other parts of the system of any treatment proposed.

This 1947 UN presentation clearly viewed macroeconomic accounts as the systematic aggregation of the accounts of individual transactors. As an example of his proposal, Stone presented a set of fully articulated accounts for the institutional sectors of the economy — including business enterprises, financial intermediaries, persons, government, and the rest of the world. But as Bos (1993, p. 6) points out, although the 1947 UN National Accounts proposal was explicit about the importance of the transactor/ transaction principle, it was also viewed as a flexible instrument for achieving more comprehensive and comparable national account figures. Therefore provision was explicitly made for including imputations for such things as the services of owner-occupied housing, income in kind and imputed banking charges.

At about this same time, however, the Economic Cooperation Administration (ECA) decided to utilize national income accounting as a framework for distributing Marshall Plan aid and monitoring European economic recovery. For this purpose, it developed a five account system consisting of (1) national income and product account, (2) personal income and expenditure account, (3) government current receipts and outlay account, (4) a rest of the world account and (5) a consolidated gross saving and investment account (Ruggles, 1949).

The ECA national accounts were functional, rather than institutional, in their nature. The national income and product account included all productive activities in the economy irrespective of their institutional characteristics, and the personal income account was essentially a residual account showing the private income and consumption in the economy. This functional approach to the national accounts was due to lack of institutional information on the one hand, and the need for international comparability in the national accounting data for countries with different institutional characteristics, on the other.

At the request of the Economic Cooperation Administration, Richard Stone was asked to set up a 'National Accounts Research Unit' in Cambridge, to train statisticians from the participating countries in the development of their national accounts and to establish for the OEEC a standardized national accounting system. As a result of this Stone developed *A Simplified System of National Accounts* (SSNA) (OEEC, 1950). The OEEC SSNA was quite similar to the ECA system of accounts except that, like Stone's 1947 proposal, it had an additional account for the transactions of the enterprise sector.

The UN 1952 SNA — also designed by Stone — was, understandably, very similar the OEEC national accounting system. However, the 1952 SNA accounts, like the ECA system, did not have an enterprise sector, and were functional rather than institutional in their nature. These were (1) domestic product, (2) national income, (3) domestic capital formation, (4) households and nonprofit institutions, (5) general government and (6) rest of the world. To some extent, the set of supplementary tables that were appended to the accounts went in the direction of relating institutional data to the economic constructs presented in the macroaccounts. But in 1952 and the following decade, national accountants were still incapable of utilizing microdata sets. Thus the transactor/transaction accounting approach proposed by Stone in 1947 was not a part of the national accounts. The cut, adjust and paste method used for the estimation of macroeconomic constructs continued to be used.

The 1968 UN SNA

The 1968 revision of the United Nations System of National Accounts was a major step forward (UN, 1968). The revised system not only expanded the national income accounts into a much more comprehensive and detailed system, but it integrated within the national accounting framework input–output tables, financial transactions and balance sheets. Richard Stone was the main architect of the 1968 revision and he emphasized the importance of the transactor/transaction accounting principle as contained in the 1947 UN proposal, but the 1968 SNA accounting framework was more comprehensive and complex. In effect a dual sectoring system was introduced that was designed to provide production, consumption and capital formation accounts for industrial activities and types of commodities and income and outlay and finance accounts for institutional sectors — nonfinancial enterprises, financial institutions, general government, private nonprofit institutions and households.

In order to make the aggregates of production and consumption more comprehensive and comparable from country to country, the 1968 SNA included imputations for nonmarket production, bank service charges, and owner-occupied housing, and rerouted to household income and consumption government expenditures for transfers in kind and enterprise expenditures for employee compensation in kind. This inclusion of imputations and reroutings in the macroaggregates, together with the increased complexity of the accounts precluded any attempt to develop microdata sets that would underlie and replicate the aggregates in the macroaccounts.

The 1993 UN SNA Statement on Micro–Macro Links

The 1993 version of the UN SNA (UN, 1993b, p. 12) states, explicitly, its position concerning the relation of the macroaccounts to microdata:

Micro–macro links

The sequence of accounts and balance sheets of the System could, in principle, be compiled at any level of aggregation, even that of an individual institutional unit. It might therefore appear desirable if the macroeconomic accounts for sectors or the total economy could be obtained directly by aggregating corresponding data for individual units. There would be considerable analytical advantages in having micro-databases that are fully compatible with the corresponding macroeconomic accounts for sectors or the total economy. Data in the form of aggregates, or averages, often conceal a great deal of useful information about changes occurring within the populations to which they relate. For example, economic theory indicates that changes in the size of distribution of income may be expected to have an impact on aggregate consumption over and above that due to changes in the aggregate level of income. Information relating to individual units may be needed not only to obtain a better understanding of the working of the economy but also to monitor the impact of government policies, or other events, on selected types of units about which there may be special concern, such as households with very low incomes. Micro-data sets also make it possible to follow the behavior of individual units over time. Given the continuing improvements in computers and communications, the management and analysis of very large micro-databases is becoming progressively easier. Data can be derived from a variety of different sources, such as administrative and business records, as well as specially conducted censuses and surveys.

In practice, however, macroeconomic accounts can seldom be built up by simply aggregating the relevant micro-data. Even when individual institutional units keep accounts or records the concepts that are needed or appropriate at a micro level may not be suitable at a macro level. Individual units may be obliged to use concepts designed for other purposes, such as taxation. The accounting conventions and valuation methods used at a micro level typically differ from those required by the System. For example, as already noted, the widespread use of historic cost accounting means that the accounts of individual enterprises may differ significantly from those used in the System. Depreciation as calculated for tax purposes may be quite arbitrary and unacceptable from an economic viewpoint. . . .

Most households are unlikely to keep accounts of the kind needed by the System. Micro-data for households are typically derived from sample surveys that may be subject to significant response and reporting errors. It may be particularly difficult to obtain reliable and meaningful data about the activities of small unincorporated enterprises owned by households. Aggregates based on household surveys have to be adjusted for certain typical biases, such as the under-reporting of certain types of expenditure (on tobacco, alcoholic drink, gambling, etc.) and also to make them consistent with macro-data from other sources, such as imports. The systematic exploitation of micro-data may also be restricted by the increasing concerns about confidentiality and possible misuse of such databases.

It may be concluded therefore that, for various reasons, it may be difficult, if not impossible, to achieve micro-databases and macroeconomic accounts that are fully compatible with each other in practice. Nevertheless, as a general objective, the concepts, definitions and classifications used in economic accounting should, so far as possible, be the same at both a micro and macro level to facilitate the interface between the two kinds of data.

As a consequence of the 1993 SNA's final conclusion that it may be difficult, if not impossible, to achieve full compatibility between microdata bases and macroeconomic accounts, the SNA recommends two alternative approaches: social accounting matrices (SAMS) and satellite accounts.

Social accounting matrices (UN, 1993a, Ch. XX) are defined as the presentation of *SNA* accounts in matrix form. The 1968 SNA provided an example of the national accounts in a matrix form, and the matrix form is widely used for input–output analysis. For some countries, SAMs have been constructed to show the relationship between structural features of the economy and the distribution of income and expenditures among household groups. The design and construction of SAMs are not standardized; rather, they are developed as disaggregations of the SNA accounts for specific analytic purposes. SAMs draw upon a wide variety of census, survey and administrative data, and utilize them for disaggregating the aggregates in the sector accounts.

Satellite accounts (UN, 1993a, Ch. XXI) are intended to expand the analytic capacity of the national accounts for selected areas of social concern in a flexible manner without disrupting the central system. Typically, satellite accounts allow for (a) additional information of a functional or cross-sector nature, (b) use of alternative classifications, (c) extended coverage of costs and benefits,(d) further presentations of indicators and aggregates and (e) linkage of physical data to the monetary accounting data. Although satellite accounts, unlike SAMs, are not viewed primarily as disaggregations of the macro-accounts, they do provide alternative classification systems, additional detail or supplementary data for the formal SNA accounts. As is true in the case of SAMs, there is no standardized form for satellite accounts; their only requirement is that they be statistically or conceptually related to the SNA accounts.

2. THE PROPOSAL FOR CORE MACROECONOMIC ACCOUNTS

The Problem of Conflicting Demands for National Accounting Data

In the discussions leading to the 1993 revision of the SNA, a number of Netherlands national accountants proposed introducing greater flexibility in the SNA (Van Eck, Gorter, and Von Tuinen, 1983; Van Bochove and Von Tuinen, 1986). They argued that the SNA serves a wide range of different and often conflicting demands and purposes. For example, the definition of the production boundary of the economy depends on the needs of different users. Monetarists prefer a national product concept confined to output related to market transactions. Environmentalists would like the degradation of the environment reflected in the accounts. Development economists want to take into account nonmarket production, and those economists concerned with the measurement of welfare need even more comprehensive measures of production and consumption. For those economists wishing to analyze the effects of fiscal policy, a strict accounting of government receipts and expenditures may be desired, but, for purposes of international comparability a more functional classification of government activities may be more useful.

Much of the conflict in the alternative approaches centers around the question of whether the national accounts are constructed on an institutional or a functional basis. In this context, 'institutional' refers to defining the transactors of the system by their legal form of organization (i.e., enterprises, government and households) and using the sector accounts to record their actual transactions. In contrast, the term 'functional' looks behind and beyond the institutional sector accounts to focus on measuring certain activities (i.e., production, consumption, saving, and capital formation) that are felt to be analytically important. The SNA is basically a system of institutionally defined sector accounts which is made more functional by introducing imputations and by rerouting actual transactions. Because the imputations and rerouting of transactions impair the usefulness of the accounts as a framework for monetary and fiscal data, there has been an effort to limit the extent of these imputations. Such limitations have the effect, however, of reducing the analytic usefulness of the SNA for other purposes.

The Concept of Core Accounts

In order to resolve this dilemma, the Netherlands national accountants proposed that the core of the SNA should consist of a set of institutionally defined sector accounts restricted to the recording of actual market transactions. Wherever possible the conceptions and perceptions of the transactors would be accepted as they are and the transactions described as they appeared. Such a core would represent the economic statisticians, exercise in restraint; the temptation of superimposing the economic statisticians, own views would be resisted. This system of core accounts bears a striking resemblance to the 1947 national accounts proposed by Richard Stone.

It was recognized, however, that in order to develop more comprehensive measures of production and consumption and to achieve greater comparability between countries where there were marked institutional differences, it would be desirable to introduce imputations for nonmarket activity and to reroute some transactions among the various institutional sectors. For this purpose, it was proposed that special modules should be introduced that could serve as the building blocks for developing more functional and more internationally comparable measures (for example, the imputation of the services of owner-occupied housing). This separation of imputations and reroutings from market transactions makes the integration of microdata and the macroaccounts theoretically possible and statistically feasible (Ruggles and Ruggles, 1970–1992).

The core account approach would achieve conceptual comparability between the central macroeconomic accounts and the actual accounts of the individual transactors. Therefore, microdata sets that accurately and fully represented the transactions of institutionally defined sectors of the economy, would aggregate to the totals shown in the core macroeconomic accounts.

3. THE DEVELOPMENT OF MICRODATA BASES

The 1993 SNA View of Data Processing for the National Accounts

The 1993 SNA explicitly recognizes the analytical advantages of having microdata bases that are fully compatible with the corresponding macroeconomic accounts for sectors of the total economy. It is argued, however, that it cannot be expected that the aggregation of data in microdata sets will add up to the totals estimated for the macroeconomic accounts. Conceptual differences, missing data, underreporting, and missing cases will result in the aggregated microdata differing from the macrototals. The estimates in the macroaccounts are considered to be more comprehensive since they are adjusted to reflect data from different sources.

On this basis, the 1993 SNA (UN, 1993a, p. 12) concludes:

> ... it is impractical to try to adjust the individual accounts of thousands of enterprises before aggregating them. It may be much easier to adjust the data after they have been aggregated to some extent. Of course, the data do not have to be aggregated to the level of the total economy, or even complete sectors or industries, before being adjusted and it is likely to be more efficient to make the adjustments for smaller and more homogenous groups of units. This may involve compiling so-called intermediate systems of accounts. At whatever level of aggregation the adjustments are made, the inevitable consequence is to make the resulting macro-data no longer equivalent to simple aggregations of the micro-data from which they are derived. When the micro-data are not derived from business accounts or administrative records but from censuses or surveys designed for statistical purposes, the concepts used should be closer to those required, but the results may still require adjustment at a macro level because of incomplete coverage (the surveys being confined to enterprises above a certain size, for example) and bias from response errors.

This view accurately reflects the past practices and even the current practices of most statistical offices engaged in constructing national account statistics. Prior to the development of the computer, advanced sampling techniques and the development of registers, national accountants have had to rely on tabulations of censuses, fragmentary sample surveys and various kinds of administrative data. Most of these sources were not exhaustive and national accountants generally did not have access to the original microdata. Even where access to microdata was possible, the programming and processing costs made their use for estimating national accounts impractical.

Current Methods of Data Collection, Processing and Utilization

In the past several decades, fundamental changes have occurred in the nature of the basic microdata available and the technology of using them. For households, sampling frames and sample surveys have become much more sophisticated, and the variety and availability of surveys have greatly increased. For enterprises, complete registers have been built up so that the coverage of both sample surveys and administrative records can be ascertained. The records in different microdata sets can be matched with each other. In the more statistically advanced countries both sample survey data and administrative microdata can easily be accessed by statistical offices for their use in national accounts estimation. Computer processing has advanced to the stage where the individual analyst can access and process major bodies of microdata easily and cheaply without requiring special computer programming.

For the most part, however, the 1993 SNA does not view the macro–micro linkage in the context of the existing realities. Rather the SNA accounts have been designed in terms of the data collection and processing capabilities of a half-century ago. In the coming decades, even the developing countries will find it more efficient to use modern computer methods to maintain and process their statistical and administrative information.

Just as the development of national accounts is the function of a central statistical office, so is the creation of microdata bases that are compatible with the macrodata in the national accounts. Contrary to the SNA assumption that editing should be done at intermediate levels of aggregation, experience indicates that it needs to be carried out at the microlevel. Most statistical agencies use computer editing of microdata to correct inconsistencies, impute missing values and to introduce estimates for missing cases. To the extent that there are significant differences between the aggregated data for a specific microdata set and the corresponding estimates in the macroaccounts, the statistical basis of the macroestimates needs to be examined to determine the reasons for the discrepancies. Only by understanding the reasons for data incompleteness or incomparability will it be possible to improve data. In many cases, it will be possible to use other microdata sets and exact or statistical matching to provide the missing values, adjustments or alignment that is required.

Microdata Bases and the Problem of Privacy

The question of whether or not the use of microdata bases by statistical offices should be restricted in the interest of privacy does not relate to the development and use of microdata by a central statistical office, but rather it relates to the release of microdata to the users of the national accounts. In effect, a central statistical office, by being responsible for censuses and sample surveys, and by having legitimate access to administrative and regulatory data, does have access to all microdata collected by the government. To deny them such access would mean that they could not collect or process censuses or sample surveys, or use, for statistical purposes, the records that are maintained and utilized by other government agencies.

However, it is very appropriate to question what microdata bases should be released to the public. Many governments currently release household sample surveys where there is no significant problem of disclosure. Some other microdata sets of a public nature, such as the data collected by the Securities and Exchange Commission (SEC) and the accounts of governmental units, are also released. However, in the case of censuses, tax returns and other administrative data where individual respondents are identified, the microdata are not generally released. In these cases, only those tabulations or aggregated data that do not reveal the identity of individual respondents are provided. From the point of view of statistical offices, however, there are considerable advantages in developing microdata bases even when these cannot be released for general use. For any given microdata base a large variety of different tabulations can easily be generated that will be consistent with each other and with the aggregates in the macroaccounts.

4. THE INTEGRATION OF HOUSEHOLD SECTOR MACROACCOUNTS AND MICRODATA BASES

The Definition of the Household Sector and its Transactions

The household sector in the 1993 SNA is defined as including not only households but also unincorporated enterprises, owner-occupied housing and persons living in institutions. The treatment of unincorporated enterprises primarily relates to their production accounts, and this aspect will be examined in the context of the discussion relating to the enterprise sector. However, with respect to the household income and outlay accounts the SNA treatment of owner-occupied housing, and the inclusion of the institutional population in the SNA household sector need to be considered.

In the SNA, households which own the houses they live in are considered to be renting their houses from themselves as unincorporated real estate enterprises. These fictitious unincorporated enterprises not only own the dwellings and pay all of the costs associated with them, but they also receive an imputed space rent from the households as occupiers. The difference between the imputed space rent and the current costs of providing the housing services is returned by the fictitious unincorporated enterprises to households, as net imputed rental income.

As a consequence of this treatment, what appears in the SNA household income and outlay account is (1) on the outlay side, the imputed space rent (effectively the shadow price) as a part of the household's consumption expenditure and (2) on the income side, net imputed rental income on owner-occupied housing, as a part of household income. The actual costs of owner-occupancy, including maintenance expenditures, property taxes, insurance, mortgage interest and imputed capital consumption, appear in the SNA accounts as costs paid by unincorporated enterprises. In the United States in recent years the costs of owner-occupied housing have exceeded the imputed space rent — hence the net imputed rental income of owner-occupied housing has been negative. This approach does not take into account that in the United States home owners can deduct their mortgage interest payments and their property taxes from the taxes they owe the government whereas renters have no such deductions. Therefore, contrary to imputed space rental approach, the home owners' actual costs may not exceed what they would have to pay in rent.

Although this SNA method of imputation gets the imputed services of owner-occupied housing into output and household consumption, it does so at the cost of distorting the accounts of both households and enterprises. In fact, it is households that pay the property taxes, the interest on the mortgage debt, and the expenses of repair and upkeep, not unincorporated enterprises, and it is households, not enterprises, that do the gross saving reflected by the imputed capital consumption. The distortion may be particularly evident in an inflationary period, when the shadow price which is imputed for space rental may rise much more than the home owner's actual costs. The home owner in such a situation is more comparable to a renter who benefits from rent control. In the case of rent control, the SNA would report the actual rent paid, not its shadow market price, and it would seem logical to do the same for the expenses of owner-occupied housing.

Household survey data usually adopt an approach that is quite different from that of the macroaccounts. Costs of owner-occupancy are considered to be household outlays like any others. Neither space rent nor income from owner-occupancy is imputed. Capital consumption is not usually asked for directly, but information from which it could be estimated is often collected.

The inclusion in the household sector of those individuals residing in institutions violates the transactor/transaction principle. The SNA notes that the individuals in the institutional setting have 'little or no autonomy of action or decisions in economic matters' (UN, 1993a, p. 105). Some of the institutions which are included are prisons run by the government, and hospitals or religious institutions run by nonprofit organizations. A preferable treatment of these populations would be to include their consumption as part of the final consumption services provided by government and nonprofit institutions rather than as outlays by the households. The sampling frames for household surveys rarely include the institutionalized population.

The Development of Household Microdata Bases

Many different sources are available for developing household microdata bases. Although no single microdata set contains in full detail all the data needed for the household macroaccounts, taken together, they can provide highly detailed microdata bases that directly correspond to the household macroaccounts.

As already indicated in the discussion of data processing, the editing of data for inconsistencies, missing data, and missing cases currently takes place at the microlevel. In creating a comprehensive microdata base, therefore, the edited microdata will be in alignment with the national accounting macrodata. In fact, in many instances, it is the macroestimates that will be based upon the more carefully edited sources of basic microdata.

In the United States there are a large number of microdata sets that relate to individuals and households. One of the most comprehensive sets of data relating to households is the Census of Population. From edited versions of the population census, microdata Public Use Samples (PUS) comprising both 1 percent and 5 percent samples of households are generated. Public Use Samples of household microdata have now been developed for almost every Census of Population going back to 1850. On a monthly basis, the Current Population Survey (CPS) sample of approximately 60,000 cases provides the basis for measuring employment and unemployment in the economy.

In addition, there is a large variety of specialized sample surveys and administrative data files that provide an abundance of data on households and individuals. The Survey of Income and Program Participation (SIPP) gives detailed information on household income and the participation of household in government programs. Wages and salaries in this sample survey cover approximately 99 percent of the wages and salaries reported in the national accounts. The social security files also give detailed data on wages and salaries and have been used to construct a 1 percent sample of Longitudinal Employer–Employee Data (LEED). This microdata set provides longitudinal information on the work history and earnings of specific individuals over extended periods of time (Ruggles and Ruggles, 1977a,b). The income tax files have been used to provide samples of personal income tax returns, and these have been supplemented by representative samples for low-income individuals and households. Surveys of Consumer Finances provide data on the financial transactions, assets and liabilities of households, and the Consumer Expenditure Surveys give detailed information on consumer expenditures. The Annual Housing Survey contains longitudinal information on both owner-occupied and rental housing. Because the United States has a large number of statistical agencies unrelated to the national accounts, many of these microdata sets have not been edited and aligned so that they correspond to the macrodata in the published national accounts, but given the abundance of information available and current computer processing methods, such editing and alignment is quite feasible.

A prototype micro–macro link for the Canadian household sector has been constructed by Hans Adler and Michael Wolfson (1988), using a household microsimulation data base of the kind pioneered by Orcutt (1973), and Pechman and Okner (1974). In this instance, the microdata consisted of the Social Policy Simulation Database (SPSD) that had been based on the 1984 Survey of Consumer Finances (SCF). Approximately 40,000 households were included in this sample (about 100,000 individuals). Adjustments and re-weighing of the original sample were undertaken to include the institutionalized population and to be consistent with the data drawn from a sample of 400,000 income tax returns. Information on expenditure patterns were imputed from a Family Expenditure Survey (FAMEX) of 10,000 households containing detailed data on annual expenditure patterns. Finally, the SPSD also included 30,000 synthetically matched cases from unemployment insurance records. Overall, the correspondence between the aggregated microdata and the corresponding household data in the national accounts was quite close. Total household receipts in the SPSD were 91 percent of the national accounts household receipts. The greatest discrepancy on the income side was the reporting of interest and dividends where the aggregated microdata totaled approximately 50 percent of that shown in the national accounts. It does not follow, however, that this difference was due to underreporting in the microdata. The national accounts data include in the household sector the interest and dividends received by nonprofit institutions and by estates and trusts aimed at sequestering funds for households not yet in existence.

A more recent study of the consistency between the macro- and microdata for the Japanese household sector was undertaken by Atsushi Maki and Shigeru Nishiyama (1993). A comparison was made between the SNA household sector consumption macrodata (adjusted for imputations) and the aggregated microdata generated from the Family Income and Expenditure Surveys (FIES — annual samples of 8,000 cases) supplemented by National Survey of Family Income and Expenditures (NSFIE — 54,000 sample every five years). The results were comparable to those achieved by similar experiments for other countries — the microdata for consumption totaled about 80 percent of the SNA household sector macrodata.

In 1979, the United Nations Statistical Office established the 'National Household Survey Capability Program' (NHSCP) that has had as its major objective to assist developing countries in the collection, processing, analysis and dissemination of household survey data (UN, 1993b). Over 50 countries participate in this program, and a variety of different household surveys is undertaken. The World Bank has given substantial support to the Living

Standards Measurement Study (LSMS) which attempts to monitor malnutrition, poverty levels, inequality of income and the characteristics of the poor. Other household surveys have included the saving behavior of households and their willingness to pay for education and health care. It is indeed regrettable that the UN Statistical Office did not take the opportunity to harmonize the 1993 revision of the SNA with its own Household Survey Capability Program. As a consequence of this lack of integration, household income, consumption and saving as measured by household surveys in a given country will differ radically from that shown in the household sector account of the national accounts.

The Imputation and Rerouting of Household Transactions

In most cases, the imputation and rerouting of transactions for analytic purposes can be carried out more accurately and more meaningfully if they are based on edited and aligned microdata bases. For example, the imputation of the services of owner-occupied housing over and above the actual outlays can more easily be made at the microlevel where factors such as the characteristics of the housing, its location, its estimated value and the rental value of similar properties can be taken into account. In a similar manner, imputations for government services in kind to households, such as education and health services, can be allocated on the basis of microdata relating to a household's characteristics or their known participation in specific government programs. The imputation of the services of financial intermediaries to individuals can be based on information relating to the income, expenditures and financial transactions of households.

There may be instances, however, where there is little or no basis for attributing specific imputations to individual households. In such situations the validity of attributing such SNA imputations to the household sector as a whole needs to be questioned. For example, the SNA recommends that pension fund reserves be attributed to households as part of their net equity. These reserves may represent substantial overfunding or underfunding of the actual discounted value of future pension obligations — the individuals concerned may be totally unaware of such valuations and the actual pension fund reserves may not be directly relevant to their own specific future benefits. In such cases, the validity of attributing these pension fund reserves to households needs to be reexamined. A more logical approach would be to use some other method for valuing pension entitlements to households and to treat the reserves held by pension funds as undistributed pension fund reserves much in the same manner as the SNA treats the undistributed profits of corporations. Undistributed profits are not included as a part of household equity; instead it is the market value of the corporate stock that is used as the basis for valuing the equity of stockholders.

In some other cases, such as social security schemes, it may be analytically useful to introduce into individual household accounts imputations for the value of public entitlements. It seems unreasonable, from a household's point of view, that private pension schemes should be considered to be of value, whereas public funded social security pensions should be considered to have no value. Of course, it would be possible to carry the imputation of future government benefits and taxes even further — economists concerned with 'rational expectations' or politicians wishing to emphasize the burden of the government debt might wish to attribute to the grandchildren in households their share of the federal debt — as well as their future inheritance of government bonds.

5. THE INTEGRATION OF ENTERPRISE SECTOR MACROACCOUNTS AND MICRODATA BASES

The Definition of Enterprises and Establishments

The 1993 SNA defines enterprises as those institutional units that engage in production. Thus, corporations, quasi-corporations, unincorporated enterprises and nonprofit institutions all are included as enterprises. A single enterprise such as a corporation, however, may simultaneously engage in a number of different kinds of economic activity and be active in various locations. Thus, for analyzing production or regional activity it is necessary to partition some of the institutional units into smaller and more homogeneous units which the SNA defines as establishments. Furthermore, in the SNA system the production accounts and generation of income accounts for establishments are then compiled into industries, as well as into the institutional sectors. From the point of view of the integration of microdata and macroaccounts, therefore, both enterprise and establishment data need to be considered.

The Development of Enterprise and Establishment Microdata Bases

To a major extent the operation of the economic system depends upon the recordkeeping of enterprises and establishments. Such records are not only needed for the operation of business, but they are also needed for tax returns and in the case of publicly held corporations as statements for the stockholders. In addition, the government conducts periodic censuses and surveys of enterprises and their establishments, and specialized agencies such as the Social Security Administration, the Bureau of Labor Statistics and regulatory commissions require periodic reports.

In the United States, the Bureau of the Census maintains a register, the

Standard Statistical Establishment List (SSEL) that identifies each enterprise and its related establishments. Similarly, the Internal Revenue Service identifies each corporation, partnership, nonprofit institution and unincorporated business. Every employer is assigned an Employer Identification Number (EIN) which is used as the basis of the social security system. Even small family enterprises that have no employees must report their receipts, costs and income on Schedule C of the Personal Income Tax Forms. Thus the government maintains complete and comprehensive registers and data on all enterprises and their establishments in the economy.

Tabulations of the tax records of enterprises have served as the basis for much of the national accounting estimates. In fact, the official US national accounts publish reconciliation tables showing the detailed adjustments made to the IRS tabulations of the tax files for deriving the national accounts estimates of capital consumption, proprietor income, interest taxes, dividends and corporate profits. Almost all of the adjustments made to the aggregate tabulations of the tax files could be implemented at the level of the microdata.

The Security Exchange Commission (SEC) requires that every publicly held corporation provide standardized quarterly financial reports. Until recently, the computerized microdata sets of these SEC reports were primarily used by large financial and commercial institutions, but currently, with the support of the NSF these microdata are being released on Internet free to users.

The specific problems involved in creation of microdata bases are well illustrated by the Longitudinal Establishment Data (LED) project. In the mid-1950s when the Bureau of the Census obtained its first large computer and had put the Census of Manufactures and the Annual Survey of Manufactures on computer tape, a joint project was developed in conjunction with the Social Science Research Council to create a longitudinal file of manufacturing establishments. The task of this project was to match the records of individual establishments for different years so that changes could be observed at the microlevel of the establishment. Thousands of computer tapes were involved and the project lasted for more than five years. At the end of that time, the project was abandoned for three reasons. First, the aggregates of the individual records for each year did not add up to the published data, since the tabulated data had been adjusted at an aggregate level for missing data, missing cases and incorrect data. Second, the percentage of establishments that could be successfully matched from year to year was not as large as desired since the identification of plants, their mergers and industry changes were not systematically maintained. Finally, the matched file of establishments was so large that it was not economically feasible to analyze it on the computers available at that time.

However, 25 years later, in the early 1980s, the handling of the Manufactures Census and the Annual Survey of Manufactures had changed — thanks, in large degree, to Shirley Kalleck who was in charge of the Census of

Manufactures. The Bureau of the Census had developed the Standard Statistical Establishment List that was a complete register of all enterprises and their establishments. Every manufacturing establishment was assigned a permanent plant identification. The editing and imputation of missing data was carried out at the level of the microdata. Finally, computers had advanced to the stage where they could handle large data sets economically. As a consequence, with the support of the National Science Foundation, a second attempt was made to create an LED file. This time the attempt was successful and the Bureau of the Census now maintains on a current basis a longitudinal file for all manufacturing establishments. Special arrangements are made at the Census Bureau to give researchers access to this data base within the restrictions of confidentiality.

Another example relates to the microdata base developed by the Small Business Administration in the 1980s. This agency was charged by Congress with the task of creating a microdata base for small business (including names and addresses), much in the same manner as the Department of Agriculture maintains a microdata file of individual farms. Because of the confidentiality of both Internal Revenue tax records and data on enterprises and establishments collected by the Bureau of the Census, the Small Business Administration was forced to use records from the private sector. By using the data in the credit files of Dun and Bradstreet, supplemented by telephone listings in the Yellow Pages, the Small Business Administration was able to piece together a file of large and small businesses that matched in its comprehensiveness the Standard Statistical Establishment List maintained by the Bureau of the Census.

In an article on macroeconomic accounting and microbusiness accounting, Postner (1986) explores the limits to consistency between macro- and microdata, and urges that national accountants preserve as much as possible the initial sets of data that go into the construction of the published accounts. He argues, quite reasonably, that the pre-adjusted data provide valuable insight into the nature and extent of the inconsistencies and their implications for the specification of the macroeconomic identities.

In a more recent article, Postner (1988, p. 239) points out that much of this problem lies in the nature of microdata themselves:

> ... there is considerable evidence that two or more parties involved in a common market transaction may have inconsistent views and knowledge of the same transaction. The views and knowledge of individual transactors are reflected in their respective accounting records and inevitably affect their respective economic behavior. So inconsistency embodies an important aspect of the real economic world. If such strands of inconsistency are preserved in our national accounting procedures, then it is more likely that accounting relations will furnish information that could be used to eventually 'explain' economic behavior and thus also be of value for purposes of economic policy.

This points up some of the reasons for the imbalances and inconsistencies observed at the macrolevel. For example, within the flow of funds accounts of the Federal Reserve Board, the total amount of financial assets held in the economy is not equal to the amount of financial liabilities outstanding, and in part this results from the creditors and debtors placing different values on their financial assets and claims.

The Imputation and Rerouting of Enterprise Transactions

In the discussion of micro–macro links, the 1993 SNA indicates that one of the difficulties involved in linkage is that concepts such as depreciation as used for tax purposes may be quite arbitrary and quite unacceptable from an economic point of view. This, however, is not a barrier to the integration of macroaggregates and microdata. Nothing prevents the national accountant from imputing his concept of economic depreciation at the microlevel. In fact, this imputation probably could be made more logically and accurately at the microlevel, where relevant information is available to support such an alternative measure of depreciation. In this context, however, Postner's argument is also quite appropriate. The depreciation charges for tax purposes are relevant to the behavior of the individual microunit — in this case the depreciation charges affect the tax payments the enterprise has to make in the current period, and will also affect future tax payments. This information is relevant to understanding the operation of the enterprise and it needs to be preserved in the accounts rather than flushed down the drain. By excluding actual depreciation charged, and showing only imputed 'economic depreciation', the SNA precludes the analysis of the effect of such tax policies as 'accelerated depreciation' upon the economy.

Another area where both imputations and reroutings of transactions are carried out by the national accountant is in the financial intermediation services indirectly measured (FISIM). Since a number of different alternatives are permitted in the SNA, explicit imputations and rerouting at the microlevel would increase an understanding of the implications of the various approaches.

The 1993 SNA takes the position that enterprises and nonprofit institutions serving households cannot have expenditures on consumption. In the case of enterprises, all consumption expenditures are attributed to employees as part of their compensation — this assumption may violate the transactor/transaction principle or treat as an intermediate cost of production consumption goods that are actually provided by enterprises. Some goods or services made available by enterprises may be of a collective nature or, at least, not easily assignable to specific individuals. For example, enterprises may provide services to the community, environmental benefits, or even food and entertainment for customers and suppliers, as well as employees. It is interesting to note, however, that the SNA does recognize that, in principle, the recognition of enterprise consumption is appropriate in certain situations (UN, 1933a, p. 425): 'Under a planned economy enterprises frequently provided health, education and recreational services for their employees (and sometimes the general population) not primarily to attract employees but as an extension of a government policy of providing these services through out the economy.'

In the case of nonprofit institutions serving households, the SNA also considers all of their final expenditures to be transfers of consumption in kind to households. However, in those instances where the nonprofit institution is concerned with broader expenditures such as improvement in the environment, preservation of wild life, or scientific and medical research, it would seem more appropriate to treat these as collective consumption in the same manner as when such goods are provided by general government.

6. THE INTEGRATION OF GOVERNMENT SECTOR MACROACCOUNTS AND MICRODATA BASES

The Definition of the Government Sector and its Transactions

In many respects, the task of integrating the macroaccounts of the government sector and the microdata of different governmental bodies and units is simpler and more straightforward than for other sectors. This is due to the fact that governmental units are required by law to provide detailed accounting of their receipts and expenditures and such accounts are available for public use. The government sector consists not only of central, state and local governments with their related departments, agencies and commissions, but in addition there is a wide variety of semi-independent bodies such as school districts, water districts or other specialized authorities. The 1993 SNA provides consolidated accounts for central, state and local governments, but for many types of analysis, it is important to be able to access the more detailed and deconsolidated data that are available for individual governmental units.

In publishing the United States National Accounts, the Bureau of Economic Analysis provides special tables that show the reconciliation between: the data as given in the federal government budget documents and federal sector in the national accounts and the tabulations of the Census of Government and the State and Local Government Sector in the national accounts. The adjustments contained in these reconciliation tables could, of course, be carried out at the level of the microdata for these governmental units.

The Development of Government Microdata Bases

In the mid-1970s a research project, 'The Measurement of Economic and Social Performance', was undertaken with the support of the National Science Foundation (NSF, 1978). This project had as one of its major objectives the development of microdata bases for enterprises, households and governments. The microdata sets for enterprises and households were limited by the publicly available microdata files at that time (Compustat for enterprises, and Census Public Use and IRS Income Tax samples for households), and the ability of mainframe computers to handle large files. In the case of government, however, the 1972 Census of Government computer tapes provided information on 78,000 governmental units. By adjusting the data in the Census of Government microaccounts to reflect accrual accounting rather than cash accounting, recognizing intergovernmental transfers and distinguishing purchases of goods from the compensation of employees and payments of transfers and subsidies, it was possible to develop data at the level of the individual governmental units that accorded quite closely with the macrodata in the government sector of the national accounts. One of the other objectives of this project was to provide a spatial distribution of public sector activity. For this purpose, the federal, state and local receipts and expenditures were disaggregated to the county level, and data provided on their activities for 3,000 county and standard metropolitan statistical areas (Quigley, 1977). No attempt was made, in this project, to construct longitudinal microdata sets for governmental units.

A more recent and comprehensive account of establishing a link between the microdata on government accounts and the government sector in the national accounts has been provided for the Netherlands (Bloem, 1988). Over an extended period of time, the Netherlands Statistical Office has been involved in the development of two connectable data sets of government statistics — one from the administrative point of view and one fitting in the national accounts. Many of the same problems, such as the conversion from cash to accrual accounting and the reclassification of transactions to correspond with the national accounting classifications, encountered in the NSF project were required. Transformation tables provided a relatively simple and concise connection between the microdata sets relevant from the accounting point of view and the government sector in the national accounts. With respect to the national accounts, however, the link was still somewhat incomplete since a more disaggregated sectoring was needed in the national accounts to fit with the administrative data. This problem, however, was remedied in the course of the revision of the Netherlands national accounts.

The Imputation and Rerouting of Government Transactions

The major imputation in the government sector macroaccount is related to the consumption of fixed capital. The 1993 SNA requires that the consumption of fixed capital be charged for a wide variety of fixed assets owned by the government. It is explicitly stated (UN, 1993a, p. 228) that:

> All buildings and other structures are assumed to have finite service lives, even when properly maintained, so that consumption of fixed capital is calculated for all such fixed assets, including railways, roads, bridges, tunnels, airports, harbors, pipelines, dams, etc. Service lives are not determined purely by physical durability, and many buildings and structures are eventually scrapped because they have become obsolete. However, the service lives for some structures such as certain roads, bridges, dams, etc., may be very long — perhaps a century or more.

Increasingly, governmental units are instituting capital budgets and renewal accounting, or are amortizing their capital costs over extended periods (Postner, 1992). Although such accounting information is important and relevant for many purposes, including the measurement of government surpluses and deficits from the point of view of public policy, it would not necessarily meet all the needs of the macroaccounts. In order to conform to SNA macroconcepts it would be necessary to develop, in addition, imputations based on a perpetual inventory method of keeping track of fixed capital, applying appropriate economic service lives, and computing in current market values the amount of capital consumption taking place. Most governmental units would not maintain their accounts on such a basis, but the data provided by the detailed governmental unit accounts on fixed capital formation could be utilized to make such imputations.

7. SUMMARY AND CONCLUSIONS

The 1993 SNA is a major accomplishment. It represents a further development of the 1969 SNA, embracing within a single integrated system all the major forms of national economic accounting — input–output, national income accounting, financial accounts and balance sheets. Richard Stone would have been pleased at the successful harmonization within the SNA of the macroeconomic data requirements by the major international statistical organizations.

In commenting on the proposed revision of the SNA in 1986, however, Stone stressed four other issues that he felt deserved attention even if they were not ready for international standardization. First, Stone attached importance to the integration of macro- and microdata and argued for more country experience in this area. Second, he urged that more recognition should be given to the statistical procedures for estimating and adjusting entries in the national accounts by least squares or other methods. Third, he felt that the efforts to form links between the SNA and MPS should be continued. Fourth, he hoped that the UN Statistical Office would see what could be done in formulating economic, socio-demographic and environmental statistics in a related manner (Stone, 1986).

The 1993 SNA has only partially followed Stone's recommendations. First, although the SNA explicitly recognizes the theoretical desirability of integrating macro- and microdata, no provision is made for it, and actual integration is considered to be impractical. Second, there is no discussion within the SNA concerning statistical procedures for the estimation or adjustment of entries in the accounts. Third, although some attention is given to the special problems of transition economies, the linkage between the SNA and MPS has become moot. Finally, formulations of economic, socio-demographic and environmental statistics have been relegated to *ad hoc* social accounting matrices and satellite accounts that lie outside the main framework of the SNA.

Macroaccounts and microdata are highly symbiotic, and their integration is basic to both statistical measurement and the analysis of economic, socio-demographic and environmental data. National accountants, however, have not been accustomed to using microdata. In the past, data processing by both statistical and administrative agencies has primarily consisted of data reduction — i.e., aggregating microrecords to produce summary tabulations. It is such sets of tabulations that have constituted the data bases with which national accountants have worked. To the extent that different tabulations have been found to be inconsistent with each other or incomplete, adjustments have been carried out at the level of the aggregate tabulations. In turn, the national accountants have provided users with a consistent macrodata set of national accounting tables that gives a general overview of the economy, but does not provide the distributional, regional, social, and demographic data needed for analyzing most problems of economic and social policy.

In the past several decades, the major advances in the technology of data processing and data storage have altered the way data are developed, maintained and analyzed. It has now become practical to edit and adjust data explicitly at the microlevel. For individual respondents, corrected data can be introduced for inconsistencies or extreme values, and estimates derived from similar respondents can be made for missing data. Sampling frames or registers covering the complete universe of all existing respondents can be used to determine the completeness of data, and imputations based on past information or on data from similar cases can be added at the level of the microdata. In this manner, a given microdata set can be made internally consistent and aligned with other sources of data. In light of this development, to an increasing extent, statistical and administrative agencies are creating, using and providing to users a large variety of microdata bases.

It is simplistic to suppose that the integration of macroeconomic accounts and microdata bases requires that all the variables in a macrosector account be contained within a single microdata base. Rather what is required is: that the reporting units included in the macrosector directly correspond to the reporting units represented in the microdata base, and that for any variables appearing in both the macroaccounts and the microdata base, the totals should match. There are, potentially, for every sector, a large number of different microdata bases that contain important and valuable data. Thus, a microdata base of social security data can provide wage and salary information with considerable geographic and industry detail for all enterprises, whereas another microdata base of corporate tax returns could give more complete data relating to the income accounts and balance sheets of corporations.

It should also be recognized that in some instances it will not be possible to provide microdata sets that are related to the estimates of specific aggregates in the national accounts. For example, the preliminary estimate of GDP on a quarterly basis may be extrapolated by applying an estimated percentage change to the previous quarterly GDP. This percentage change estimate, furthermore, may be based on a variety of 'economic indicators' such as changes in payrolls, retail sales or purchase orders. In such cases, there may be no meaningful microdata that relate to the estimate, and it is only with time that such information will become available and the estimates of GDP can be revised.

The integration of macroaccounts and microdata refers primarily to benchmark periods. In the past, the benchmark periods for estimating the macroaccounts have coincided with years when there were complete censuses or when the basic tabulations provided by administrative agencies, such as the taxing authorities, became available. This has often meant that benchmark periods occurred only once in every five or ten years. With more comprehensive sampling methods and faster processing of administrative records, it should be feasible to provide for the integration of macroaccounts and microdata on a more frequent and up-to-date basis.

National accountants can not only utilize a large variety of different microdata bases for constructing the market transactions of the household, enterprise and government sectors, but they will also find microdata bases useful for making imputations and rerouting transactions. For example, a household or labor force data base that showed the age, sex, occupation and residence of the population would be useful in constructing estimates of nonmarket activity — a household expenditure data base or a housing data base would provide the necessary information for estimating the services of owner-occupied housing. Finally, a microdata base such as the Survey of Income and Program

Participation could assist in estimating benefits in kind received by households from the government. Many of the extensions suggested by Kendrick (1976, 1979) and Eisner (1994) for nonmarket activity of the household or for introducing alternative definitions of capital formation and depreciation can best be estimated by using microdata bases of households and enterprises. SAMs and Satellite accounts would thus, be aggregations of the basic microdata estimates.

The macroeconomic accounts not only benefit from their integration with microdata bases, but, at the same time, the statistical system also benefits. By extending the SNA to microdata, it can serve as the vehicle for integrating economic, social, demographic and regional data. One of the major difficulties in using microdata in the past has been that different microdata sets purporting to cover similar reporting units come out with very different results. As a consequence, analyses of microdata have become suspect — it is felt that by selecting appropriate microdata sets, analysts can arrive at any conclusion they so desire. By developing microdata bases that match the control totals in the macroaccounts, those using microdata will have greater assurance that the data they are using are representative, complete and unbiased.

From an analytic point of view, the integration of macroaccounts and microdata has become increasingly important for problems related to public policy. Thus, for example, in developing equitable tax laws, it becomes necessary to know how different provisions of the tax system affect both the distribution of the tax burden and the generation of tax revenue. Microdata sets of tax returns for individuals and enterprises can provide such information. Social welfare, health care, and pension programs require microdata relating to the social, demographic and economic characteristics of households in order to assess their distributional impact and to develop the total cost of financing such programs. In analyzing the level and character of unemployment in the economy and its relation to the macroperformance of the economy, microdata are needed relating to the social, demographic, occupational and regional characteristics of the unemployed. Many environmental questions require data of a regional nature, and are concerned with the cost–benefit effects on individual households. If there is not integration between the macroaccounts and the basic microdata sets used for such analysis, it will not be possible to evaluate in a consistent manner both the overall economic effects and the distributional effects.

It is the contention of this paper that the 1993 SNA needs to provide explicitly for the integration of microdata. This can be accomplished by developing core transactor/transaction accounts for the institutional sectors with separate modules for introducing imputations and rerouting of transactions. Microdata bases are important both for constructing national accounting aggregates and for providing users with detailed integrated economic, social and demographic information. The cut and paste methods using tabulations of aggregated data are becoming obsolete. The complex social and political problems of the twenty-first century will require both the broad macroeconomic constructs and the underlying microdata relating to enterprises, governments and households. The technology exists — the much-heralded information superhighway has arrived and the modern computer provides the individual analyst with the ability to access, manage and analyze large data sets of macro- and microdata. It is the responsibility of the national accountant to develop such data bases in a coherent manner.

REFERENCES

Adler, Hans and Michael Wolfson (1988), 'A prototype macro–micro link for the Canadian household sector', *Review of Income and Wealth*, **34** (4).

Bloem, Adrian M. (1988), 'Micro–macro link for government', *Review of Income and Wealth*, **34**.

Bos, Frits (1989), 'A systems view on concepts of income in the national accounts', *National Accounts*, Occasional Paper No. NA-033, Netherlands Central Bureau of Statistics.

———— (1992), 'The history of national accounting', *National Accounts*, Occasional Paper No. NA-048.

———— (1993), 'Standard national accounting concepts, economic theory, and data compilation issues', *National Accounts*, NA-061.

Eisner, Robert (1994), 'Expansion of boundaries and satellite accounts', in John Kendrick (ed.), *Socio Economic Accounts: Developments, Issues, Prospects*, New York: Columbia University Press for NBER.

Kendrick, John W. (1976), *The Formation and Stocks of Total Capital*, New York: Columbia University Press for NBER.

———— (1979), 'Expanding imputed values in the national income and product accounts', *Review of Income and Wealth*, **25** (4).

Maki, Atsushi and Shigeru Nishiyama (1993), 'Consistency between macro- and micro-data sets in the Japanese household sector', *Review of Income and Wealth*, **39** (2).

National Science Foundation (1978), 'The measurement of economic and social performance', Report on Project, SOC74-21391, Yale University, January.

Orcutt, Guy H. (1973), *Microanalytic Simulation: A Tool for Policy Analysis*, Washington, DC: The Urban Institute.

Organization for European Economic Cooperation (1950), *A Simplified System of National Accounts*, Cambridge: National Accounts Research Unit.

Pechman, J.A. and B.A. Okner (1974), *Who Bears the Tax Burden?*, Washington, DC: The Brookings Institution.

Postner, Harry H. (1986), 'Micro business accounting and macroeconomic accounting: The limits to consistency', *Review of Income and Wealth*, **32** (3).

———— (1988), 'Linkages between macro and micro business accounts: implications for economic measurement', *Review of Income and Wealth*, **34** (3).

_____ (1992), 'A capital budget, renewals accounting and public accountability', Paper prepared for Government and Competitiveness Reference, February.

Quigley, John (1977), 'The spatial distribution of public-sector activity: A preliminary report,' *Proceedings of the 1976 General Conference of the Society of Government Economists*, Washington, DC: SGE.

_____ with Gail Trask and James Trask (1977), 'Income and product accounts for the local public sector', Institution for Social and Policy Studies, Working Paper 795, Yale University.

_____ with Thanos Catsambas (1977), 'Spatial redistribution through general government activity', Paper presented at the 15th General Conference of the International Association for Research in Income and Wealth, York, England, August Cambridge, Mass., Ballinger.

Ruggles, Richard (1949), *National Income Accounting and Its Relation to Economic Policy*, Paris: Economic Cooperation Administration, Office of the Special Representative.

_____ and Nancy D. Ruggles (1970), 'Macro accounts and micro data sets', *Proceedings of the Business and Economic Statistics Section*, American Statistical Association.

_____ (1975), 'The role of micro data in the national economic accounts', *Review of Income and Wealth*, **21** (2).

_____ (1977a), 'The anatomy of earnings behavior' (Analysis of the social security LEED micro data file), *The Distribution of Economic Well-Being*, NBER Studies in Income and Wealth, Vol. 47, Cambridge, Mass., Ballinger.

_____ with Edward Wolff (1977b), 'Merging micro data, rationale, practice and testing', *Annals of Economic and Social Measurement*, **6** (4).

_____ (1982), 'Integrated economic accounts for the United States, 1947–80', *Survey of Current Business*, **62** (5).

_____ (1983), 'The treatment of pensions and insurance in national accounts', *Review of Income and Wealth*, **29** (4).

_____ (1984), 'The analysis of longitudinal establishment data', Paper presented at the Conference on the Longitudinal Establishment Data Files and Diversification Study, Alexandria, Va., October.

_____ (1986), 'The integration of macro and micro data for the household sector', *Review of Income and Wealth*, **32** (3).

_____ (1992), 'Household and enterprise saving and capital formation in the United States: A market transactions view', *Review of Income and Wealth*, **38** (2).

Stone, Richard (1986), 'Comments on the overall program,' *Review of Income and Wealth* (Special Issue on the Review of the United Nations System of National Accounts, **32** (2).

United Nations (1947), *Measurement of National Income and the Construction of Social Accounts*, Studies and Reports on Statistical Methods, No. 7, Geneva: United Nations.

_____ (1953), *A System of National Accounts and Supporting Tables*, Studies in Methods, Series F, No. 2, New York: United Nations.

_____ (1968), *A System of National Accounts*, Studies in Methods, Series F, No. 2, Rev. 3, New York: United Nations.

_____ (1993a), 'Technical Cooperation: National Household Survey Capability Programme (NHSCP)', Social Dimensions of Adjustment (SDA) and the Living Standards Measurement Study (LSMS), Joint Report of the Secretary General and the World Bank E/CN.3/1993/18, January.

_____ (1993b), *System of National Accounts, 1993*, ST/ESA/STAT/SER.f/ 2/REV.4, New York: United Nations.

Van Bochove, C.A. and H.K. Van Tuinen (1986), 'Flexibility in the next SNA: The case for an institutional core', *Review of Income and Wealth*, **32** (2).

Van Eck, R., C.N. Gorter and H.K. Van Tuinen (1983), 'Flexibility in the system of national accounts', Occasional Paper, NA-001, Netherlands Central Bureau of Statistics, May.

Bibliography

Nancy D. Ruggles and Richard Ruggles

Key to articles included:
P = *Pricing Systems, Indexes, and Price Behavior*
N = *National Accounting and Economic Policy*
M = *Macro- and Microdata Analyses and their Integration*

'Recent Applications of the A-S Reaction Study', Richard Ruggles with Gordon W. Allport, *Journal of Abnormal and Social Psychology*, **34** (4), October 1939.

P11 'The Relative Movements of Real and Money Wage Rates', Richard Ruggles, *Quarterly Journal of Economics*, **55** (1), November 1940.

'The Concept of Linear Total Cost–Output Regressions', Richard Ruggles, *American Economic Review*, **1** (2), June 1941.

M6 'An Empirical Approach to Economic Intelligence in World War II', Richard Ruggles and Henry Brodie, *Journal of the American Statistical Association*, **42**, March 1947.

P3 'Discriminatory and Competitive Pricing', Nancy D. Ruggles, unpublished Ph.D. dissertation, Radcliff College,1949.

An Introduction to National Income and Income Analysis, Richard Ruggles, McGraw-Hill, 1949.

N1 *National Income Accounting and Its Relation to Economic Policy*, Richard Ruggles, Office of the Special Representative in Europe, Economic Cooperation Administration, Paris, 1949.

P2 'Recent Developments in the Theory of Marginal Cost Pricing', Nancy D. Ruggles, *Review of Economic Studies*, 1949.

P1 'The Welfare Basis the Marginal Cost Pricing Principle', Nancy D. Ruggles, *Review of Economic Studies*, 1949.

La Contabilidad del Ingreso Nacional y su Relacion con la Politica Economica, Richard Ruggles, Pan American Union, 1951.

European National Accounts, Richard Ruggles and Nancy D. Ruggles, Economic Cooperation Administration, 1951.

'The French Investment Program and Its Relation to Resource Allocation', Richard Ruggles, in *Modern France, Problems of the Third and Fourth Republics*, Princeton University Press, 1951.

National Accounts Data Book, Richard Ruggles and Nancy D. Ruggles, Economic Cooperation Administration, 1951.

'Concepts, Sources, and Methods of U.S. National Income Statistics', Richard Ruggles, *Econometrica*, July 1952.

Volkseinkommen und Volkswirtschaftliche Gesamtrechnungen, Richard Ruggles, Humboldt-Verlag, Wien–Stuttgart, 1952.

M11 'Methodological Developments', Richard Ruggles, in B.F. Haley (ed.), *Survey of Contemporary Economics*, Vol. II, Richard D. Irwin, Inc., 1952.

'Economies of Europe Prior to and During World War II', Richard Ruggles, paper presented March 18, 1953 at Industrial College of the Armed Forces, Washington DC (published with discussion).

National Income Accounts and Income Analysis, 2nd edition, Richard Ruggles, translated into Chinese by Mr Leon S. Geoffery, Agency for International Development, United States Aid Mission to China, McGraw-Hill, 1953.

P4 'The Value of Value Theory', Richard Ruggles, *American Economic Review*, May 1954.

P12 'The Nature of Price Flexibility and the Determinants of Relative Price Changes in the Economy', Richard Ruggles, in *Business Concentration and Price Policy*, National Bureau of Economic Research, 1955.

Primary responsibility for the following sections of the United Nations *World Economic Surveys*, Nancy D. Ruggles:

'The Balance of Payments Experience of Industrial Countries: The Impact of Structural Change', 1956.

'Inflation in the Nineteen Fifties: The Character of Recent Price Inflation', 1957.

'Recent Trends in Industrial Countries: Developments in Foreign Trade and Payments', 1958.

Graduate Training in Economics, Richard Ruggles, Yale University Press, 1956.

National Income Accounting and Income Analysis, Richard Ruggles and Nancy D. Ruggles, revised edition, McGraw-Hill, 1956.

'Tendencias Recientes en la Contabilidad del Ingreso Nacional', Richard Ruggles, *Boletin del Banco Central de Venezuela*, **16**, 1956.

'Government Budgets and their Relation to National Accounts', Richard Ruggles and Nancy D. Ruggles, paper prepared for the Subcommittee on Fiscal Policy of the Joint Economic Committee and Statement November 18–27, 1957.

'The Nation's Income and Product Accounts', Richard Ruggles, The Executive Program in Business Administration, Columbia University, 1958.

'Objectives of National Economic Accounts and Their Implications for the General Form of the Accounts', Richard Ruggles, Chapter V of *The National Economic Accounts of the United States*, Report of the National Accounts Review Committee, published in Hearings, Subcommittee on Economic Statistics, Joint Economic Committee; also reprinted by the National Bureau of Economic Research, General Series, No. 64, 1958.

'Prices, Costs, Demand and Output in the United States, 1946–1957', Richard Ruggles and Nancy D. Ruggles, Paper prepared for the Joint Economic Committee and Statement, May 15, 1958.

'Recent Price Increases and their Relation to Administered Prices', Richard Ruggles, Hearings, Subcommittee on Antitrust and Monopoly, Committee on the Judiciary, US Senate, July 9–16, 1957; reprinted in part in Richard Mooney and Edwin L. Dale Jr (ed), *Inflation and Recession*, Doubleday and Co., 1958.

'Prices, Costs, and Profits in the United States Economy, 1947–1957', Richard Ruggles and Nancy D. Ruggles, in Hearings before the Joint Economic Committee, US Congress, September, 1959.

'Public Sector Accounts and National Economic Accounts', Richard Ruggles, Paper for United Nations Workshop on Classification of Government Accounts, Santiago, Chile, published by the United Nations, 1960.

M7 'Study of Differential Fertility Based on Census Data', Richard Ruggles and Nancy D. Ruggles, in *Demographic and Economic Change in Developed Countries*, National Bureau of Economic Research, 1960.

N2 'Concepts of Real Capital Stock and Services', Richard Ruggles and Nancy D. Ruggles, in *Output, Input, and Productivity Measurement*, National Bureau of Economic Research, 1961.

P6 'Measuring the Cost of Quality', Richard Ruggles, *Challenge*, November 1961.

'Regional Breakdowns of National Economic Accounts', Richard Ruggles and Nancy D. Ruggles, in W. Hochwald (ed.), *Design of Regional Accounts*, Johns Hopkins Press, 1961.

P5 'The Wholesale Price Index', Richard Ruggles, Chapter V of *The Price Statistics of the Federal Government*, Report of the Price Statistics Review Committee, published in Hearings, Subcommittee on Economic Statistics of the Joint Economic Committee, 1961.

Comparison of National Accounts Data for the United States Classified According to the Concepts of the United Nations System of National Accounts and the Material Product System, Richard Ruggles and Nancy D. Ruggles, a study prepared for the Office of Statistical Standards, US Bureau of the Budget, and submitted to the Conference of European Statisticians of the United Nations, February 1962.

Contabilidada Nacional e Análise Macroeconómica, Richard Ruggles and Nancy D. Ruggles, Livraria Sá da Costa, Lda., Lisboa, 1962, copyright 1956 by McGraw-Hill Book Company, Inc.

P13 'Price Stability and Economic Growth in the United States', Richard Ruggles and Nancy D. Ruggles, published in German in *Konjunkturpolitik*, **8** (3), 1962, also published in Spanish in *Economia*, **20** (71), 1962.

'Relation of the Undergraduate Major to Graduate Economics', Richard Ruggles, *American Economic Review*, Proceedings, May 1962.

'Contabilidad Economica Nacional y Contabilidad del Sector Publico', Richard Ruggles and Nancy D. Ruggles, in M. Balboa (ed.), *El Ingreso y la Riqueza*, Mexico: Fondo de Cultural Economica, 1963.

Evaluation of the Venezuelan Plan, Richard Ruggles, Report of the Committee of Nine of the Organization of American States, 1963.

'Summary of the Conference on Inflation and Growth in Latin America', Richard Ruggles, in W. Baer and I. Kerstenetszky (eds), *Inflation and Growth in Latin America*, Richard D. Irwin, Inc., 1964.

A System of National Accounts and Historical Data, Richard Ruggles and Nancy D. Ruggles, Yale University Press, 1964.

An Economic Data Reporting System for the Agency for International Development, Richard Ruggles and Nancy D. Ruggles with W. Abraham, Yale University Press, 1965.

A Generalized Economic Information Retrieval System, Richard Ruggles and Nancy D. Ruggles, Economic Growth Center, Yale University Press, 1965.

P7 'Domestic Price Statistics: Their Reliability as History and Their Usefulness for Economic Policy', Richard Ruggles, Statement before the Subcommittee on Economic Statistics of the Joint Economic Committee, May 26, 1966.

'Economic Data and the Invasion of Privacy', Richard Ruggles, Hearings, Subcommittee of the Committee on Government Operations, House of Representatives, 89th Congress, 2nd Session, July 26–28, 1966, *The Computer and the Invasion of Privacy*.

P8 'Redundancy in Price Indexes for International Comparisons: A Stepwise Regression Analysis', Nancy D. Ruggles, Progress Report for the Agency of International Development and the Yale Growth Center, November 15, 1966.

Report of the Committee on the Preservation and Use of Economic Data to the Social Science Research Council, Richard Ruggles, April 1965, published in Hearings, Subcommittee of the Committee on Government Operations, House of Representatives, 89th Congress, Second Session, July 26–28, 1966, *The Computer and the Invasion of Privacy*.

'The Co-ordination and Integration of Government Statistical Programs', Richard Ruggles, Hearings, Subcommittee on Economic Statistics of the Joint Economic Committee, May 15–17, 1967.

'Data Files for a Generalized Economic Information System', Richard Ruggles and Nancy D. Ruggles, *Social Sciences Information*, **6**, August 1967.

'The Federal Government and Federalism: Past and Future', Richard Ruggles, in *Revenue Sharing and the City*, Committee on Urban Economics of Resources for the Future, Inc., Johns Hopkins Press, 1967.

'History and Development of Economic Data', Richard Ruggles, in *International Encyclopedia of the Social Sciences*, 1967.

'The Role of a National Data Center in Economic Statistics', Richard Ruggles, Federal Statistical Users' Conference, October 14, 1966, Washington, DC.

'Economic Data', Richard Ruggles, *Encyclopedia of the Social Sciences*, 1968.

'Ethical Problems of Privacy and Information Needs in Modern Society', Richard Ruggles, Paper presented at University of Minnesota, 1968.

N3 'The Evolution and Present State of National Economic Accounting', Richard Ruggles and Nancy D. Ruggles, Center for International Education and Research in Accounting, University of Illinois, 1968.

'How Will It Work?', Richard Ruggles, Statement for Joint Economic Committee, October 29, 1968

'On the Needs and Values of Data Banks', *Symposium: Computers, Data Banks and Individual Privacy*, Richard Ruggles, University of Minnesota, May 2, 1968.

P9 'Price Indexes and International Price Comparisons', Richard Ruggles, in W. Fellner (ed.), *Ten Economic Studies in the Tradition of Irving Fisher*, John Wiley and Sons, 1968.

'The Adequacy of the National Data Base for Economic and Social Research and the Design and Evaluation of Public Policy', Richard Ruggles, 1969

'How a Data Bank Might Operate', Richard Ruggles, *Think*, May 1969.

'The National Data Bank: Privacy and Freedom', Richard Ruggles, *Science and Society Seminar,* Brown University, February 19, 1969.

'The Preservation and Use of Machine Readable Records', Richard Ruggles, National Archives, 1969.

The Design of Economic Accounts, Richard Ruggles and Nancy D. Ruggles, National Bureau of Economic Research, 1970.

Economics: The Behavioral and Social Sciences Survey, Nancy D. Ruggles (ed.), Report of the Economics Panel of the Behavioral and Social Sciences Survey of the National Academy of Sciences and the Social Science Research Council, Englewood Cliffs, NJ: Prentice-Hall, 1970.

'Income Distribution Theory', Richard Ruggles, *Review of Income and Wealth*, **16** (3), September 1970.

M12 'Macro Accounts and Micro Data Sets', Richard Ruggles and Nancy D. Ruggles, *Proceedings of the Business and Economic Statistics Section*, American Statistical Association, 1970.

'National Income Accounting', Richard Ruggles, *Encyclopedia Britannica*, 1970.

N8 'The Evolution of National Accounts and the National Data Base', Richard Ruggles and Nancy D. Ruggles, *Survey of Current Business*, Part II, July 1971.

M13 'The Relation of Methodology to the Technology of Economic Research', Richard Ruggles and Nancy D. Ruggles, American Statistical Association and Biometric Society Meetings, Montreal, Canada, August 15, 1972.

'Communication in Economics: The Media and Technology', Richard Ruggles and Nancy D. Ruggles, *Annals of Economic and Social Measurement*, **1** (2), April 1972.

'A Proposal for a System of Economic and Social Accounts', Richard Ruggles and Nancy D. Ruggles, in Milton Moss (ed.), *The Measurement of Economic and Social Performance*, National Bureau of Economic Research, 1973.

The Role of the Computer in Economic and Social Research in Latin America, Nancy D. Ruggles (ed.), proceedings of a conference held in Cuernavaca, Mexico, National Bureau of Economic Research, 1974.

'The Role of the Computer in Economic and Social Research in Latin America: Summary of the Conference', Richard Ruggles in Nancy D. Ruggles (eds), *The Role of the Computer in Economic and Social Research in Latin America*, National Bureau of Economic Research, 1974.

M15 'Social Indicators and a Framework for Social and Economic Accounts', Richard Ruggles and Nancy D. Ruggles, *Proceedings of the Social Statistics Section*, American Statistical Association, 1974.

M8 'A Strategy for Merging and Matching Microdata Sets', Richard Ruggles and Nancy D. Ruggles, *Annals of Economic and Social Measurement*, **3** (2), April 1974.

M16 'The Measurement of Economic and Social Performance: A Progress Report on a National Bureau of Economic Research Project', Richard Ruggles and Nancy D. Ruggles, paper presented at the 14th General Conference of the International Association for Research in Income and Wealth, Aulanko, Finland, August 1975.

M1 'Recession and Recovery in the United States, 1929–1974, and Sectoral Saving and Investment Accounts', Richard Ruggles, in *Nasjonalregnskap Modeller og Analyse* (*National Accounts Models and Analysis*), Oslo, Norway, 1975.

M14 'The Role of Microdata in National Economic Accounts', Richard Ruggles and Nancy D. Ruggles, *Review of Income and Wealth*, **21** (2), June 1975 (also published as 'El Papel de los Microdatos en las Cuentas Nacionales Economicas y Sociales', *Estadistica*, **113**, December 1975).

M2 'Economic Growth in the Short Run: Its Behavior and Measurement', Richard Ruggles in *U.S. Economic Growth from 1976 to 1986: Prospects, Problems and Patterns*, Vol. 2, *The Factors and Processes Shaping Long Run Economic Growth*, Studies for the Joint Economic Committee, 94th Congress, 2nd Session, November 10, 1976.

P14 'Chronic Inflation in the United States, 1950–73', published as 'La Inflacion Cronica en los Estados Unidos, 1950–1973', Richard Ruggles and Nancy D. Ruggles, in Carlos Diaz-Alejandro, S. Teitel and V.E. Tokman (eds), *Politica Economica en Centro y Periferia*, Mexico: Fondo de Cultura Economica, 1976.

P15 'The Anatomy of Earnings Behavior', Richard Ruggles and Nancy D. Ruggles, presented at the Conference on Research in Income and Wealth, Ann Arbor, May 1974 and published in *The Distribution of Economic Well-Being*, Studies in Income and Wealth, Vol. 41, National Bureau of Economic Research, 1977.

Distributive Impacts of the Budget and Economic Policies', Richard Ruggles, statement and testimony before the House Committee on the Budget, September 29, 1977.

Guidelines on Principles of a System of Price and Quantity Statistics, Nancy D. Ruggles, United Nations Publication, Series M, No. 59, New York, 1977.

M9 'Merging Microdata: Rationale, Practice and Testing', Richard Ruggles and Nancy D. Ruggles with Edward N. Wolff, *Annals of Economic and Social Measurement*, **6** (4), October 1977.

P10 'The Wholesale Price Index: Review and Evaluation', published as *Review and Evaluation of the Wholesale Price Index*, Richard Ruggles, Report for the Council on Wage and Price Stability, Washington, DC, 1977. (Also published in Joint Economic Committee Hearings, 1977.)

'Review of the Implementation of the Revised System of National Accounts', Nancy D. Ruggles, United Nations document (mimeo), E/CN.3/507, 1978.

M17 *The Development of Integrated Data Bases for Social, Economic and Demographic Statistics*, Nancy D. Ruggles, United Nations Publication, Series F, No. 27, New York, 1979.

Employment and Unemployment Indexes as Measures of Economic Activity and Capacity Utilization, Richard Ruggles, Background Paper No. 28, National Commission on Employment and Unemployment Statistics, April 1979.

P16 'The Measurement of the Supply and Use of Labor', Richard Ruggles, Background paper for the National Commission on Employment Statistics, 1979.

Studies in the Integration of Social Statistics, Nancy D. Ruggles, Part 2, 'Strategy for Further Work on the Framework for the Integration of Social and Demographic Statistics', United Nations publication, Series F, No. 24, New York, 1979.

'Future Directions for Work on the System of National Accounts', Nancy D. Ruggles, United Nations (mimeo), E/CN.3/541, 1980.

'The Role of Macro and Micro Data Structures in the Integration of Demographic, Social and Economic Statistics', Nancy D. Ruggles, United Nations document (mimeo), E/CN.3/552, 1980.

Instructions and Definitions for the National Accounts Questionnaire, Nancy D. Ruggles, United Nations and Organization for Economic Co-operation and Development, 1980.

'The Conceptual and Empirical Strengths and Limitations of Demographic and Time Based Accounts', Richard Ruggles, in F.T. Juster and K.C. Land (eds), *Social Accounting Systems: Essays on the State of the Art*, Academic Press, 1981.

N10 'Integrated Economic Accounts for the United States 1947–1980', Richard Ruggles and Nancy D. Ruggles, *Survey of Current Business*, **62** (5), May 1982.

N11 'Integrated Economic Accounts: Reply', Richard Ruggles and Nancy D. Ruggles, *Survey of Current Business*, **62** (11), November 1982.

'The National Accounts', Richard Ruggles, *Aspects of Italian Official Statistics: Review and Proposals*, Report of the International Statistical Commission, February 1982.

'Price Indexes and Statistics', Nancy D. Ruggles, *Aspects of Italian Statistics: Review and Proposals*, Report of the International Statistical Commission, February 1982.

N12 *The System of National Accounts: Review of Major Issue and Prospects for Future Work and Short Term Changes*, Richard Ruggles, Expert Paper for the United Nations Statistical Office, ESA/STAT/AC.15/2, April 15, 1982.

'Guide to the Yearbook of National Accounts Statistics', Nancy D. Ruggles, *Handbook of National Accounting*, Vol. 1, United Nations Statistical Office, 1983.

'Gross Domestic Product', Nancy D. Ruggles, *Handbook of National Accounting*, Vol. 2, United Nations Statistical Office, 1983.

'Public Sector Accounts', Nancy D. Ruggles, *Handbook of National Accounting*, Vol. 4, United Nations Statistical Office, 1983.

Reference Documentation for Longitudinal Establishment Data (LED), Richard Ruggles and Nancy D. Ruggles with Catherine Viscoli, prepared for the Bureau of the Census, December 1983.

Review and Development of the System of National Accounts (SNA), Richard Ruggles, Report for the Statistical Commission of the United Nations, E/CN.3/1983/5, July 21, 1982, for the 22nd Session 7–16 March 1983.

'The Treatment of Pension and Insurance Transactions in the United Nations System of National Accounts (SNA)', Nancy D. Ruggles and Richard Ruggles, report prepared for OECD Meeting on National Accounts, Paris, May 1983.

N5 'The Treatment of Pensions and Insurance in National Accounts', Nancy D. Ruggles and Richard Ruggles, *Review of Income and Wealth*, **29** (4), December 1983.

N9   'The United States National Income Accounts, 1947–1977: Their Conceptual Basis and Evolution', Richard Ruggles, in Murray Foss (ed), *The U.S. National Income and Product Accounts: Selected Topics*, Chicago: University of Chicago Press for NBER, 1983. (Paper presented at Conference on Income and Wealth, Washington, 1979.)

M10 'The Analysis of Longitudinal Establishment Data', Richard Ruggles and Nancy D. Ruggles, Presentation at the Bureau of the Census and NSF Conference on Longitudinal Establishment Data File and Diversification Study, Alexandria, Virginia, October 17–18, 1984.

'The Current Review of International Standards for National Accounting', Nancy D. Ruggles, Presentation to Statistics Canada, Ottawa, Canada, April 30, 1984.

'Financial Accounts and Balance Sheets: Issues for the Revision of SNA', Nancy D. Ruggles, Study prepared for the United Nations Statistical Office, January 1984.

'Possible Future Directions for National Accounting', Richard Ruggles, Presentation to Statistics Canada, Ottawa, Canada, April 30, 1984.

'Recent Developments in International Standards for National Accounting', Nancy D. Ruggles, Presentation to Statistics Canada, Ottawa, Canada, November 15, 1984.

N4   'The Role of the National Accounts in the Statistical System', Richard Ruggles, Presentation to Statistics Canada, Ottawa, Canada, November 15, 1984.

'The System of National Accounts: Review of Major Issues', Richard Ruggles, *Statistical Journal of the United Nations ECE*, **2**, 1984.

'The Treatment of Noncash Benefits in Measuring Poverty and Income', Richard Ruggles and Nancy D. Ruggles, Presentation at the First Annual Research Conference, Bureau of the Census, Reston, Virginia, March 22, 1985.

M18 'The Integration of Macro and Micro Data for the Household Sector', Richard Ruggles and Nancy D. Ruggles, *Review of Income and Wealth*, **32** (3), September 1986.

'Social Accounting', Nancy D. Ruggles and Richard Ruggles, *The New Palgrave: A Dictionary of Economic Theory and Doctrine*, Macmillan, 1986.

N13 'Financial Accounts and Balance Sheets: Issues for the Revision of SNA', Nancy D. Ruggles, *Review of Income and Wealth*, **33** (1), 1987.

'Saving and Capital Formation of Enterprise Sectors: A Market Transactions View', Nancy D. Ruggles and Richard Ruggles presented at Conference of Income and Wealth, Baltimore MD, March 29, 1987 (not published in conference volume).

M3 'Theoretical Concepts and Empirical Measurement of Saving and Investment', Richard Ruggles, Paper Presented at AEA Meetings, December 30, 1987

N14 'A Note on the Revision of the United Nations System of National Accounts', Richard Ruggles, *Review of Income and Wealth*, **36** (4), December 1990.

'Review of *The Total Incomes System of Accounts*, by Robert Eisner', Richard Ruggles, *Review of Income and Wealth*, **37** (4), December 1991.

N15 'Statistical Measurements for Economic Systems in Transition: Strategy for Implementing the UN System of National Accounts (SNA)', Richard Ruggles, *Economies in Transition Statistical Measures Now and in the Future*, Proceeding of the Sochi International Forum, October 1990, Editor Petr O. Aven with the assistance of Christoph M. Schneider, CP-91-4, September 1991.

M4 'Household and Enterprise Saving and Capital Formation in the United States: A Market Transactions View', Nancy D. Ruggles and Richard Ruggles, *Review of Income and Wealth,* **38** (2), June 1992.

M5 'Accounting for Saving and Capital Formation in the United States, 1947–1991', Richard Ruggles, presented at the ASSA meetings Anaheim, California, January 6, 1993; published in *Journal of Economic Perspectives*, **7** (2), Spring 1993 and in Philip D. Oliver and Fred W. Peel (eds), *Tax Policy*, The Foundation Press, 1996.

N6 'National Income Accounting Concepts and Measurement: Economic Theory and Practice', Richard Ruggles, *Economic Notes*, by Pashi di Siena, **22** (2), 1993.

N16 'Issues Relating to the UN System of National Accounts and Developing Countries', Richard Ruggles, *Journal of Development Economics*, **38**, 1994.

'The United Nations System of National Accounts (SNA): Its Implementation for Developing Countries', Richard Ruggles, *Journal of Development Economics,* **44,** 77–85, 1994.

N17 'The United Nations System of National Accounts (SNA), and the Integration of Macro and Micro Data', Richard Ruggles, in John Kendrick (ed), *Socio-Economic Accounts*, Klower, 1995.

N7 'The Value Added of National Accounting', Richard Ruggles and Patricia Ruggles, *Review of Income and Wealth,* **41** (2), 1995.

'Factor Cost', Richard Ruggles, articles for *The Encyclopedia Americana*, Grolier, 1998. Also available on CD-ROM.

'The Middle Ages of the International Association for Research in Income and Wealth', Richard Ruggles, Paper presented at the IARIW 50th Anniversary Conference, Cambridge, England, August 1998.

'National Income', Richard Ruggles, articles for *The Encyclopedia Americana*, Grolier, 1998. Also available on CD-ROM.

'Saving and Capital Formation', Richard Ruggles, articles for *The Encyclopedia Americana*, Grolier, 1998. Also available on CD-ROM.

'The International Association for Research in Income and Wealth: Its First 50 Years', Richard Ruggles, *Review of Income and Wealth*, forthcoming, 1999.

Index

accidental damage 425-6
Adler, Hans J. xvi, 305, 307, 308, 309, 310, 313, 314, 318, 331, 336, 507
advertising 364
affiliated enterprises, transfers between 407
aggregation (consolidation) problem 11, 67-9, 81
agricultural sector 21, 24
  animal livestock 409
  in early concepts of production 72, 129-30
  natural growth 426-7
  nonmarket activity 34, 325, 365, 462
  recording of transactions 323, 325
  saving in 149, 153
Aidenoff, Abraham xvii
Altimir, Oscar 400
Alvaro, P. 134
animal livestock 409
annuities *see* life insurance and annuities
arbitrage transactions 406
Atcherley, P.N. 393, 394, 396, 405
Aukrust, O. 85

Bakker, G.P. den 163
balance of payments 18, 394
banks
  bank-like institutions 431-2
  central 430-1
  deposit banks 431
benefits in kind 326, 363-4, 464-5
Bentzel, Ragnar 70
Bloem, A.M. 165, 166, 514
Boisguillebert, Pierre le Pesant 130
Bos, Frits 496
Boschan, Charlotte xvi
budgets, national 35

Canada
  national income accounting in 336
  computerization 85
  development 73
  social information 83
capacity measurement, capital and 53-4
capital 39, 62-6, 130-1, 141
  capacity measurement and 53-4
  capital account
    basic 279-80
    integration of capital and current accounts 255-8, 260-86
    sectoral 281-6
  consumption of 132, 220
  financial flows and integrated economic accounting 54
  formation (production) 50-3, 132, 141, 259, 472
    consumer durable goods 64-5, 141, 148, 178, 227, 368, 417-18, 463-4
    corporate sector 149-54, 288-90
    extension of UN SNA to developing countries and 489-91
    government/state sector 51, 132, 177-8, 256, 257, 289, 290
    household sector 64-5, 144-9, 256-7, 289, 290, 291-6, 323, 446
    intangible 177
    own account 408-9
    recording of transactions 323, 332-3
    saving and 144-54, 288-91, 332-3
  measurement of
    rationale of 42-7
    real services of capital 49-50
    use of capital stock measures 47-9
  productivity and 40-2, 43

transfers 373-6, 397-8
see also interest
Carson, Carol S. xvi, 166, 187, 244, 305, 306, 308, 309, 310, 312, 313, 314, 317, 318, 320, 322, 324, 326
casualty insurance 91-2, 112-13, 232-4, 297-8
   fire insurance 232-4, 297-8, 329-30
   health insurance 113-15, 226, 234-6, 298-9, 330, 363-4
   income replacement insurance 115
   property damage insurance 118-19
   recording of transactions 329-30
   term life insurance 115-18
   in UN System of National Accounts 91-2, 112-28, 375, 433
catastrophes, natural 427-8
central banks 430-1
Coats, R.H. 73
commuting expenses 82
computerization 68, 84-7, 155-6, 167-8, 179
Conference on Research in Income and Wealth 57
consignment, goods shipped on 406
consolidation problems 11, 67-9, 81
construction, uncompleted 408
consumer durable goods 64-5, 141, 148, 178, 227, 368, 417-18, 463-4
consumption 15-17, 62
   corporate sector 178-9, 267-71, 363-5
   individual consumption paid for by government 358-60
   measurement of 358-69
   nonmarket imputations 365-9
   subsidies to consumption 362-3
   total consumption 360-2
Copeland, Morris 58, 78, 138, 453
copyright 373, 423, 428-9
corporate sector 181, 218, 467-9
   capital formation 149-54, 288-90
   consumption by 178-9, 267-71, 363-5
   current account 267-71
   establishment-firm dichotomy 309-11
   fire and casualty insurance purchase 232-3, 297-8
   health insurance purchases 234-5, 298-9, 363-4
   interest payments 239-41, 301-2
   microdata 253, 319-20, 509-13
   quasi-corporations 379-81, 420-1, 435-7
   saving 149-54
   statistical consistency 318
   transfers between affiliated enterprises 407
   in USA 181, 218, 267-71, 319-20
   see also nonprofit organizations
Creamer, Daniel 48, 49

damage, accidental 425-6
Deane, Phyllis 163
debt problems 36-7
defence expenditures 408
Dell, Sidney xvii
demographic information *see* social and demographic information
Denison, Edward F. xvi, 42-6, 49, 53, 305, 306, 307, 312, 313, 314, 315, 316, 317, 322, 324, 327, 328, 331, 333-4
Denmark, national income accounting in, development 78, 138, 453
depreciation 323, 324, 428
Depression 6, 56-7, 73-4, 172-3
Derksen, Johannes B.D. 163
developing countries 58, 365-7
   UN System of National Accounts and 486-93
direct investment enterprises 406
disasters, natural 427-8
distribution of income 80, 361, 399-402
dividends 248
Domar, Evsey 47, 53
domestic service 314-15
domestic territory, definition of 407
Duisenberg, W.F. 166
durable goods 64-5, 141, 148, 178, 227, 368, 417-18, 463-4

economic analysis, national income accounting and 25-6
economic constructs in national income accounting 62-6, 476-82
   effects of change in 66
economic depreciation 323, 324, 428
economic development, economic

policy and 4
economic planning 4
economic policy
 availability of resources 34–5
 economic development and 4
 formulation of 3–8, 33
 increasing necessity for 4
 information problems 5
 national income accounting and 3–8, 33–8
 operation of the economy 35–8
 quantitative effect of 38
education and training, expenditure on 63, 141, 177
Eisner, Robert 82, 83, 134, 518
enterprises *see* corporate sector
environmental problems 80, 164, 250
equities 420–1
establishment-firm dichotomy 309–11
European Community 211, 277
 social security in 96
 value added tax 409–10
excise duties 28
external transactions *see* 'rest of world' transactions

Fellegi, Ivan 85
final sales approach 131, 132
financial assets 418–20
 equities 420–1
financial deregulation 141
financial flows and integrated economic accounting 54
financial institutions 154, 248, 296–7, 326, 365, 430–5, 472–4
financial leasing 376–7, 406, 422
fire insurance 232–4, 297–8, 329–30
firms *see* corporate sector
Fisher, Irving 78, 130–1
foreign investment 290–1
France
 national income accounting in development 71–2, 129–30
 satellite accounts 84
 social information 83
Franchet, Y. 166
Frisch, Ragnar 57, 75, 136, 452

Gainsbrugh, Martin 89
Galiani, Ferdinando 130

Gilbert, Milton xiii, 57, 75, 136
gold 406
Goldsmith, Raymond 58, 78, 138, 453
Gorman, John A. xvi, 305, 327, 328, 329, 330, 331
Gorter, C.N. 500
government and the state 17–18, 60, 61, 65–6, 133–4, 249, 470–1
 capital formation 51, 132, 177–8, 256, 257, 289, 290
 current account 273–7
 expenditure 4, 82, 141, 408
 individual consumption paid for by 358–60
 interest payments 241–2, 303, 331–2
 microdata 253, 320, 513–15
 public debt problems 36–7
 seizure of assets by 426
 United Nations System of National Accounts 380, 382–6, 397–8, 408, 410
 in USA 181, 271–7, 320
 see also social security; taxation
Grootaert, Christiaan 400
gross national product (GNP) 11, 27, 30, 247, 261–7, 476–80

Hanssen, Orin xvi
health insurance 113–15, 226, 234–6, 298–9, 330, 363–4
Hemenway, Harrison xiv
Hibbert, Jack 370, 371
Hicks, J.R. 131
Hill, Peter 457
Hoover, Herbert 74
household sector 60, 61, 64–5, 134, 140, 141–2, 155, 183, 249, 252–3, 316–18, 320–1, 469–70, 491–2
 balance sheets 92–6, 292–6
 capital formation 64–5, 144–9, 256–7, 289, 290, 291–6, 323, 446
 consumer durable goods 64–5, 141, 148, 178, 227, 368, 417–18, 463–4
 current account 271–2
 definition of 'dwelling' 409
 domestic service 314–15
 fire and casualty insurance purchase 233–4, 298

health insurance purchases 236, 299, 330
interest payments 239, 302-3
microdata 155, 183, 252-3, 316-18, 320-1, 491-2, 504-9
net worth 291-2
nonmarket activities 464
owner-occupiers 64, 134, 140, 145, 148, 249, 256-7, 292-6, 314, 365, 367-8
  in UN System of National Accounts 437-9, 445, 462-3
saving 144-9, 291-2
USA 145, 148, 180-1, 217-18, 223-8, 230-2, 271-3, 291-6, 314, 320-1

illegal transactions 407
income
  distribution of 80, 361, 399-402
  early measures of 71-2
  income replacement insurance 115, 116-17
  income statements 9-10, 11
  measurement of
    effects of inflation on 369-71
    financial leasing 376-7
    intangible assets 371-3
    land/subsoil 371-3
    pensions, insurance and capital transfers 373-6
    terms of trade 377-8
  permanent income hypothesis 144, 148
  taxation on property income 407
  see also national income accounting
industrial sector 21-3
  resource allocation 31-3
  saving in 153
  sources of production 30-1
  see also corporate sector
inflation 37, 80-1, 164, 455
  effects on measurement of income 369-71
informal sector 164
information problems 137, 163-4
  economic policy 5
input-output analysis 57, 59, 72, 78, 138, 309-11, 402-4, 453
insurance see casualty insurance; life insurance and annuities; pensions; social security
intangible assets 371-3, 421-3, 425-9
intangible capital formation 177
intellectual property rights 373, 423, 428-9
interest 135, 227, 237, 248, 300-1
  consumer interest payments 239, 302-3
  corporate interest payments 239-41, 301-2
  government interest payments 241-2, 303, 331-2
  net interest approach 237-8, 300, 330
  recording of transactions 330-2
  UN approach 238-9, 447-9
International Monetary Fund, Special Drawing Rights 424-5
international transactions see 'rest of world' transactions
investment 18-20, 143-4, 178
  direct investment enterprises 406
  extension of UN SNA to developing countries and 489-91
  foreign investment 290-1
  integration of national income accounts 287-96
Italy, national income accounting in 130

Jain, Shalil 400
Jaszi, George xiii, xv, xvi, 57, 195-6, 197, 213, 219, 221, 228, 305, 306, 308, 309, 310, 312, 313, 314, 317, 318, 320, 322, 324, 326
Jorgenson, Dale 134
Juster, F. Thomas 65

Kallek, Shirley 86, 510
Katz, Arnold J. 256
Kendrick, John W. xviii, 46, 82-3, 134, 518
Keuning, S. J. 166
Keynes, John Maynard 57, 74, 75, 135-6, 452
Keynesian economics 57, 80, 455
kind, benefits in 326, 363-4, 464-5
King, Willford I. 56
King, Gregory 71, 130
Knauth, Oswald W. 56
Kravis, Irving B. 360

Kuznets, Simon xiii, 57, 73-4, 76, 133, 137, 149, 187

labor 32-3, 35
  early concepts of production and 72-3, 130
  labor theory of value 73
land/subsoil 371-3, 416-17
  leases of 422
Lavoisier, Antoine 72
League of Nations 57-8, 75-7, 136-7, 138, 142, 188, 346, 452
leasing 376-7, 406, 422
leisure activity 82
Leontief, Wassily 57, 78, 138, 453
Leuchtenberg, Phyllis xiv
life cycle hypothesis of saving 144, 149
life insurance and annuities 91, 93, 107, 236-7, 248
  balance sheet 109
  insurance companies 432-5
  measurement of income 373-6
  proposals 109-12, 119-28
  recording of transactions 326-30
  term life insurance 115-18
  treatment of benefits 108-9
  treatment of contributions 107-8, 299-300
  in UN System of National Accounts 91, 93, 107-12, 119-28, 373-6, 433-5, 446-7, 465-6
livestock 409

Macaulay, Frederick R. 56
maintenance 52, 428
Maki, Atsushi 507
Malthus, Thomas 73, 130
Marimont, Martin L. xvi, 305, 307, 321, 322, 332
market imputations 322, 323-4
Marshall, Alfred 73, 130
Marshall Plan 8, 77, 497
Marx, Karl 63, 73, 130, 232
Mayer, Jacques 415
Meade, James E. 57, 75, 136, 452
Mercantilism 72, 129
merchanting transactions 407
microdata
  availability of 318-21
  core macroeconomic accounts and 500-1
  corporate sector 253, 319-20, 509-13
  development of data sets
    corporate sector 509-12
    data collection and processing 502-3
    existing sets 183
    government sector 514
    household sector 506-8
    matrix presentation 182
    new synthetic data sets 183-4
    privacy and 503-4
    reporting units 182
    UN SNA and 184, 502-4
  government sector 253, 320, 513-15
  household sector 155, 183, 252-3, 316-18, 320-1, 491-2, 504-9
  integration with national income accounts 83, 154-6, 167, 184, 252-4, 308-9, 315-21, 391-3, 491-2, 495-519
  statistical consistency 254, 318
  in UN System of National Accounts 184, 391-3, 491-2, 495-519
military expenditures 408
Mill, John Stuart 73, 130
mineral resources 371-3, 416-17
Mitchell, Wesley C. 56, 73
modeling
  economic 164-5, 179-80
  US economy 174-6
monetarist economics 80
monetary institutions 430-1
monetary statistics 398-9
monetary system 4
Moser, Claus xvii
Mozack, Jacob xvii
Musgrave, John xvi

national budgets 35
national income accounting
  casualty insurance in 91-2, 112-28, 232-4, 297-8, 375, 433
  consuming sector *see* consumption; household sector
  development of 6-8, 56-69
    computerization 68, 84-7, 155-6, 167-8, 179
    early concepts of production 72-3
    early measures of income of

nations 71-2, 129-31, 163
future 79-90, 215-32
League of Nations study 57-8,
    75-7, 136-7, 138, 142, 188,
    346, 452
modern 57-60, 75-9, 136-43, 163
modifications and amplifications
    81-4
prior to World War II 73-5, 131-5,
    187
problems of 1970s 79-81, 158,
    162, 455-6
United Nations and 59-60, 77-9,
    138-42, 143, 204-11, 346-7,
    452-3, 495-7
in USA 56-8, 59-60, 73-5, 136,
    138, 171-84, 185-215
wartime economy and 75, 135-6,
    173, 187-8
economic constructs in 62-6, 476-82
    effects of change in 66
economic policy and 3-8, 33-8
government sector *see* government
    and the state
information problems in 137, 163-4
integration of 243-4, 305, 337-41
    conceptual issues 244-58
    current and capital accounts 255-8,
        260-86
    microdata 83, 154-6, 167, 184,
        252-4, 308-9, 315-21, 391-3,
        491-2, 495-519
    nature of integration 306-7
    network of transactions flows
        254-5, 260
    recording of transactions 321-37
    role of national accounts in 306-11
    sectoring of economy and 311-21
    social/demographic information
        68-9, 83-4, 154-6, 167,
        182-4, 252-4
    US 67-9, 228-9, 243-303
international transactions *see* 'rest of
    world' transactions
life insurance and annuities in 91, 93,
    107, 237-8, 248
    balance sheet 109
    proposals 109-12, 119-28
    treatment of benefits 108-9
    treatment of contributions 107-8,
        299-300
    in UN System of National
        Accounts 91, 93, 107-12,
        119-28, 373-6, 433-5, 446-7,
        465-6
nature of 8-25
pensions in 91-3, 99-100, 140,
    236-7, 248
    balance sheet 103
    proposals 103, 104-6, 119-28, 141
    treatment of benefits 100, 102-3,
        145, 226, 227
    treatment of contributions 99,
        100-2, 145
    in UN System of National
        Accounts 91-3, 99-106,
        119-28, 140, 141, 373-6,
        433-5, 446-7, 465-6
producing sector *see* production
    sector
savings and investment 18-20
social security in 91, 93-4, 145
    balance sheet 96-7
    proposals for 97, 98, 119-28
    treatment of benefits 93-4, 95-6,
        145
    treatment of contributions 93, 95,
        145
    in UN System of National
        Accounts 91, 93-8, 119-28,
        435
in statistical system 70-90
structure of 60-2, 76-7
use of 25
    availability of resources 34-5
    economic analysis 25-6
    formulation of economic policy
        3-8, 33
    general level of production 26-30
    operation of economy 35-8
    quantitative effect of economic
        policy 38
    resource allocation 31-3
    sources of production 30-1
    utilization of production 33
natural catastrophes 427-8
natural growth 426-7
natural resources 371-3, 416-17
net income approach 131
net interest approach 237-8, 300

net national product 28–30, 480–2
net product approach 131
Netherlands
  national income accounting in 162–8
  development 57, 75, 78, 136, 138, 163, 452, 453
Nishiyama, Shigeru 507
nonmarket activities 61, 82–3, 134–5
  agricultural sector 34, 325, 365, 462
  consumption 365–9
  household 464
  recording of transactions 322, 325
  USA 134, 219–22, 251, 259–60
nonprofit organizations
  in UN System of National Accounts 386–8, 437
  USA 60–1, 119, 217, 223, 226, 249, 312, 313–14
Nordbatten, Sven xvii, 85
Nordhaus, William 81–2, 134
Norway
  national income accounting in
    computerization 85
    development 57, 75, 78, 136, 138, 452, 453

obsolescence 46, 425–6
Okner, B.A. 85, 507
Oomens, Peter C. 163
Orcutt, Guy H. 167, 507
Organization for Economic Cooperation and Development (OECD) 352, 370, 376–7
Organization for European Economic Cooperation (OEEC) 58, 77, 137–8, 204, 346, 452, 497

Palmieri, Giuseppe 130
patents 373, 423, 428–9
Paukert, Felix 400
Pechman, J.A. 85, 507
pensions 91–3, 99–100, 140, 236–7, 248
  balance sheet 103
  funded 99, 100–1, 102, 103
  measurement of income 373–6
  pension funds 432–5
  proposals 103, 104–6, 119–28, 141
  recording of transactions 326–30
  treatment of benefits 100, 102–3, 145, 226, 227
  treatment of contributions 99, 100–2, 145
  in UN System of National Accounts 91–3, 99–106, 119–28, 140, 141, 373–6, 433–5, 446–7, 465–6
  unfunded 99, 100, 101–2, 103
permanent income hypothesis 144, 148
Peskin, Janice 256
Petre, Jean 358–60, 361–2
Petty, William 56, 71, 130
Physiocrats 72, 129
Postner, Harry H. 149, 511, 512, 515
price
  capital goods 43
  constant prices estimates 286–7
  evaluation due to price changes 424
  indexes 26
  see also inflation
production sector 9, 26–31, 60–4, 245–51
  capital see capital
  early concepts of production 72–3, 129–30
  general level of production 26–30
  income statement and activity of individual producers 9–10
  measurement of production 245–6
  production statement for the economy 10–15, 246–7
  resources
    allocation of 31–3
    availability of 34–5
  sources of production 30–1
  utilization of production 33
  see also corporate sector
productivity 35, 39
  capital and 40–2, 43
  slowdown of 81
property damage insurance 118–19
property income, taxation on 407
public sector see government and the state

quarterly accounts 388–90
quasi-corporations 379–81, 420–1, 435–7
Quesnay, François 72, 129
Quigley, John 320, 514

recording of transactions
  benefits in kind 326
  capital formation and saving 323,
    332–3
  form of accounts 333–4
    IEAs and FOF accounts 334–6
    matrix presentation 336
    need for alternative forms 336–7
  imports/exports 405–6
  imputations 322–3
    agricultural sector 323, 325
    economic depreciation 323, 324
    market 322, 323–4
    nonmarket 322, 325
  interest 330–2
  pensions and insurance 326–30
  transactor approach 321–2
regional accounts 390
Reich, Utz-Peter 131, 166
reinvestment by direct investment
  enterprises 406
rent 372–3
repair costs 52, 428
research and development, expenditure
  on 51–2, 63, 141, 166, 177
resources
  allocation of 31–3
  availability of 34–5
  natural 371–3, 416–17
'rest of world' transactions 249, 277–8,
  471–2
  balance of payments 18, 394
  foreign investment 290–1
  international trade 18
    terms of 377–8
    timing of recording
      imports/exports 405–6
  United Nations System of National
    Accounts 393–7, 405–7
Ricardo, David 63, 73, 130, 232
Robinson, Joan 41, 42
Roosevelt, Franklin D. 74
Ruggles, Nancy D. vii–xi, xiii–xviii,
  137, 319, 435, 467, 501
Ruggles, Richard vii–xi, xiii–xviii, 137,
  319, 435, 467, 501

Salter, Jean xvi
satellite accounts 84, 154, 219, 308
saving 18–20, 143–54, 178, 472
  capital formation and 288–91
  corporate sector 149–54
  enterprise 149–54
  extension of UN SNA to developing
    countries and 489–91
  household 144–9, 291–2
  integration of national income
    accounts 287–96
  Keynesian analysis of 143–4
  recording of transactions 332–3
Sawyer, Malcolm 400
Schulz, James 68
seizure of assets 426
service sector 248–9, 250
  domestic service 314–15
  saving in 153–4
services of capital, measurement of
  49–50
Shubik, Martin xv
Smith, Adam 63, 72–3, 130, 132, 232,
  239
social and demographic information 68–
  9, 83–4, 154–6, 167
  integration of national accounts and
    308–9, 318
  in UN System of National Accounts
    154, 390–3
  USA 83, 182–4, 252–4, 308–9
social security 91, 93–4, 145
  balance sheet 96–7
  contributions 28, 93, 95
  proposals for 97, 98, 119–28
  treatment of benefits 93–4, 95–6, 145
  treatment of contributions 93, 95, 145
  in UN System of National Accounts
    91, 93–8, 119–28, 435
socialist countries
  national income accounting in 58–9,
    63, 73, 130, 177
  UN System of National Accounts and
    transition to market economies
    451, 457–85
Solow, R.M. 41, 42
Soviet Union, UN System of National
  Accounts and 451, 457–85
Special Drawing Rights 424–5
stagflation 80–1, 162
state *see* government and the state
statistical system, role of national
  income accounting in 70–90

statistics, economic policy 5
Stigler, George 63
Stone, Richard vii, xiv, xvii, 57, 70, 75, 76, 77, 78, 83-4, 136, 137, 138, 142-3, 180, 182, 188, 204, 346, 347, 452-3, 456, 496, 497, 515-16
Studenski, Paul 130, 452
subsidiary enterprises, transfers between 407
subsidies 248
  to consumption 362-3
Sunga, Preetom S. xvi, 135, 305, 307, 308, 309, 310, 313, 314, 318, 331, 336
supply-side economics 80

taxation 28, 133-4, 166
  progressive 37
  on property income 407
  social security contributions 93, 95
  value added tax 409-10
Taylor, Stephen xvi, 305, 307, 314, 327, 328-9, 332, 335, 337
technology 35
term life insurance 115-18
terms of trade 377-8
Tice, Helen S. xvi, 305, 312, 314, 332, 333, 334, 335, 336
time allocation 166
Tinbergen, Jan 75, 136, 163, 167, 452
Tobin, James xvi, 81-2, 134, 305, 312, 321, 324, 327, 333, 336
trademarks 423, 428-9
training and education, expenditure on 63, 141, 177
Trask, James 320
traveling expenses 82

uncompensated seizure of assets 426
uncompleted construction 408
unemployment insurance 95, 115
unincorporated enterprises 435-7
United Kingdom
  national income accounting in development 56, 57, 71, 75, 130, 136, 188, 452
  social information 83
United Nations System of National Accounts 345-6, 451-2, 482-5
  1968 revision 78-9, 138-40, 143, 184, 204-11, 347-9, 453-5, 498
  casualty insurance in 91-2, 112-28, 375, 433
  current (1975 onwards) revision 442-3, 455-7
    household capital formation 446
    interest 447-9
    overall design 448-50
    owner-occupied housing 445
    pensions and insurance 446-7
    sectoring 443-5
  developing countries and 486-93
  development 59-60, 77-9, 138-42, 143, 204-11, 346-7, 452-3, 495-7
  economic constructs 62-6, 476-82
  external transactions 393-7, 405-7
  financial accounts in 414-16, 429, 439-40
    balance sheet structure 418-23
    consistency of stock and flow accounts 416-18
    institutional sectoring and 429-39
    reconciliation account entries 423-9
  future work 353-5
    extension to developing countries 486-93
    extension to socialist countries in transition 457-82
    implementation 349-50, 355-6, 457-82
    organizing and scheduling 356-7
  government/public sector 380, 382-6, 397-8, 408, 410
  harmonization
    activity classifications and input-output 402-4
    external transactions 393-7
    income distribution statistics 399-402
    monetary statistics and flow of funds 398-9
    public sector statistics 397-8
  implementation 349-50, 355-6, 466-82
    strategy for 457-66
  imputations and rerouting of transactions 462-6
  integration of national economic

accounts 67, 210, 306
interest in 238-9, 447-9
life insurance and annuities in 91, 93, 107-12, 119-28, 373-6, 433-5, 446-7, 465-6
microdata in 184, 391-3, 491-2, 495-519
National Accounts Questionnaire 352-3
pensions in 91-3, 99-106, 119-28, 140, 141, 373-6, 433-5, 446-7, 465-6
proposals 87-90, 140-2, 156-9
recording of transactions 324, 326
sectoring 379-88, 429-30, 458-60
   current (1975 onwards) revision 443-5
   financial institutions 430-5, 463
   government/public sector 380, 382-6, 397-8, 408, 410
   nonprofit organizations 386-8, 437
   owner-occupied dwellings 437-9, 445, 462-3
   quasi-corporate and unincorporated enterprises 435-7
   social security sector 435
short-term action proposals 405
   external sector 405-7
   other proposals 407-10
social and demographic information 154, 390-3
social security arrangements in 91, 93-8, 119-28, 435
structure of accounts 60-1, 378-9, 460-2
   implementation of 466-82
updating 357-8
   accounting structure 378-9
   extensions of accounts 388-93
   measurement of consumption 358-69
   measurement of income 369-78
   sectoring 379-88
United States of America
   model of economy 174-6
   national income accounting in 13-15, 17-24, 29-30
   1947 system 173, 188-93, 311, 321
   1951/1954 system 174, 193-5

1955 Conference on Income and Wealth 195-7, 219-20, 228
1957 Report of NARC 197-8, 228
1958/1965 revisions 174, 198-203, 228, 311
1971 Conference on Income and Wealth 211-12, 213, 220, 228
1975 revision 214
capital accounts 279-86
capital formation 132, 144-54, 177-8, 259, 288-91
computerization 85-7
consumption 178-9
corporate sector 181, 218, 267-71, 319-20
development 56-8, 59-60, 73-5, 136, 138, 171-84, 185-215, 452, 453
economic constructs 62-6
future 215-32
government sector 181, 271-7, 320
household sector 145, 148, 180-1, 217-18, 223-8, 230-2, 271-3, 291-6, 314, 320-1
insurance in 94, 95, 107-8, 119-21, 124-5, 232-7, 297-300
integration of 67-9, 228-9, 243-303, 305-41
interest in 237-42, 300-3
nonmarket activity 134, 219-22, 251, 259-60
nonprofit organizations 60-1, 119, 217, 223, 226, 249, 312, 313-14
pensions in 94, 99, 102, 119-21, 124-5, 226, 227, 236-7
problems of 1970s 80-1, 162
recording of transactions 222-3
'rest of world' transactions 277-8
saving/investment in 145, 148, 149, 178, 287-96
sectoring 145, 148, 180-1, 216-19, 251-2, 258-9, 311-15
social information 83, 182-4, 252-4
social security in 94, 119-21, 124-5, 145
structure of accounts 60-1
UN system and 211, 216

urbanization, disamenities of 82
utility 130, 132
utilization of production 33

value, labor theory of 73
value added, measurement of 12-13, 246-7
value added tax 409-10
Van Bochove, C.A. 156, 461
Van Eck, R. 500
van Eijk, C.J. 164
van Ginneken, Wouter 400
van Kleef, Ed 57, 163
Van Tuinen, H.K. 156, 163-4, 165, 461, 500
van Zanden, J.L. 163
Vauban, Marshal 71-2, 130

Verbruggen, J.P. 164, 165
Verri, Pietro 130
Visaria, P. 400
Viscoli, Catherine xvi

Waite, Preston J. 319
wartime economics 6-8, 75, 135-6, 173, 187-8
welfare, economic 82, 164, 175, 309
Wolff, Edward 149
Wolfson, Michael 507
workmen's compensation insurance 115, 116-17
World Bank 84

Zalm, G. 164, 165